GLOBAL SHIFT

PETER DICKEN

WITHDRAWN

6TH EDITION

GLOBAL SHIFT

MAPPING THE CHANGING CONTOURS
OF THE WORLD ECONOMY

PETER DICKEN

Los Angeles | London | New Delhi
Singapore | Washington DC

© Peter Dicken 2011

First edition published by Paul Chapman
First SAGE edition (second) published 1992
Third edition published 1989
Fourth edition published 2003, reprinted in 2004, 2005 and 2006
Fifth edition published 2007, reprinted 2007, 2008 and 2009

SAGE Publications Ltd
1 Oliver's Yard
55 City Road
London EC1Y 1SP

SAGE Publications Inc.
2455 Teller Road
Thousand Oaks, California 91320

SAGE Publications India Pvt Ltd
B 1/I 1 Mohan Cooperative Industrial Area
Mathura Road, Post Bag 7
New Delhi 110 044

SAGE Publications Asia-Pacific Pte Ltd
33 Pekin Street #02-01
Far East Square
Singapore 048763

Library of Congress Control Number: 2010924373

British Library Cataloguing in Publication data

A catalogue record for this book is available from
the British Library

ISBN 978-1-84920-766-9
ISBN 978-1-84920-767-6 (pbk)

Typeset by C&M Digitals (P) Ltd, Chennai, India
Printed and bound in Great Britain by TJ International Ltd, Padstow, Cornwall
Printed on paper from sustainable resources

For Lesley and Roger

Praise for Global Shift

SIXTH EDITION

"A magnificent achievement. Since the publication of the first edition of *Global Shift* in 1986 Peter Dicken has constructed in successive editions a phenomenal record of the changing geography of capital accumulation on a world scale. This wholly new sixth edition of 2011, is an essential companion for anyone concerned to understand the rapid geographical shifts occurring in the world's economic power relations in these stressful and troubled times."

—David Harvey, Distinguished Professor, CUNY Graduate Center, New York

"A masterful new edition of a masterful text. Once again, Peter Dicken is at the cutting edge of the analysis of economic globalization and global trends. *Global Shift* is the authoritative text on these issues."

—David Held, Co-Director, Centre for the Study of Global Governance, LSE

"*Global Shift*, sixth edition, continues to deconstruct globalization to show that distance (economic geography) still matters, Dicken uses insights from international business research to demonstrate that world business activity is more regional than global. Multinational enterprises are at the hub of global production networks and service delivery; they interact with governments and generally act as agents of economic development. In short economic geography and international business are closely aligned in their approach to globalization."

—Alan Rugman, Henley Business School, University of Reading

FIFTH EDITION

"A comprehensive, balanced, thorough, interdisciplinary review of one of the critical issues of our time. A 'must' for anyone interested in globalization."

—Stephen J. Kobrin, The Wharton School, University of Pennsylvania

"Impressive in the extent of empirical research, *Global Shift* successfully captures the historical continuities and basic changes marking the world economy. Peter Dicken's new edition is a vividly written guide to globalizing processes."

—James H. Mittelman, School of International Service, American University

"*Global Shift, Fifth Edition*, remains the benchmark for studies of the geography of globalization. In accessible prose, Dicken presents tightly argued propositions about the emerging economic landscape. The fields of international business, economic geography, international relations, and economic sociology can profitably use the book to communicate the fundamentals of globalization. Clear, effective, and engaging case studies are ideal for classroom use. There is no other text with such a broad reach or appeal for anyone interested in understanding the contemporary international economy."

—Amy K. Glasmeier, Department of Geography,
The Pennsylvania State University

"*Global Shift* just keeps on getting better. There is no other source that gives you the full story on globalization in such a fluent and authoritative way. This book is not just recommended, but essential."

—Nigel Thrift, Vice-Chancellor, University of Warwick, UK

"With this edition of *Global Shift*, Dicken confirms his mastery as one of the preeminent authorities in the study of globalization. This careful and penetrating analysis of the complexities of a unifying world should prove a seminal text for students, scholars, and policymakers. If you wish to explore beyond 'flatland,' I can't recommend a better source."

—William E. Halal, Department of Management Science,
George Washington University

"The fifth edition of *Global Shift* remains at the top of the ever more crowded field of globalization texts. Peter Dicken is a master of weaving together new theoretical arguments, visually compelling charts and graphs, and insightful industry case studies. If you had to use just one book to convey globalization's promise and perils, this is the book I would recommend."

—Gary Gereffi, Department of Sociology and Center on Globalization,
Governance and Competitiveness, Duke University

FOURTH EDITION

"Dicken identifies states and transnational corporations as the two key actors in the multiple processes of restructuring and institutionalization that we usually call the global economy. In so doing, he has written a political economy of globalization and produced a far more comprehensive account than is typically the case in books about the global economy, most of which tend to confine the analysis to firms and markets."

—Saskia Sassen, Ralph Lewis Professor of Sociology,
The University of Chicago

"In these uncertain times, it is reassuring to have Peter Dicken as our guide to the world economy. No other commentator has his eye equally attuned to both the big picture of global corporations and capital flows, and the fascinating stories of local places, people, and industries. In this new edition of *Global Shift*, Dicken shows us once again why he has become one of the most respected social scientists studying the world of global business and economy."

—Meric Gertler, Department of Geography, University of Toronto, Canada

"...the book presents not only a thorough and balanced description and analysis of globalization, but also a nuanced explanation of the globalization–antiglobalization debates and provocative examination of the distributional consequences of globalization. I will certainly continue to use *Global Shift* in my graduate seminar. In fact, I am contemplating using it in my introductory economic geography course as well."

—Robin Leichenko in *Economic Geography*

"...a solid 640-page text on the phenomena of globalization in the modern age.... provides detailed case studies of crucial global industries, more than 200 updated figures and tables, and well serves to broaden and illustrate the critical points toward understanding the world's economic future. This is an ideal text for classroom instruction and recommended to the attention of non-specialist general readers with an interest in understanding the complexities of global economics."

—Library Bookwatch

"One of human geography's miniscule number of ambassadorial texts. The social sciences, the humanities, and international business studies, will be much poorer when *Global Shift* ceases emerging as regularly as a Tissot watch keeps time."

— Kris Olds, *Progress in Human Geography*

THIRD EDITION

"Global Shift has become a landmark and a classic. It remains a popular text whose strength lies in its clear presentation and analysis of empirical data and in its focus on the production chain. This alone makes it a welcome corrective for the many speculative works on globalization based, as Dicken says, more 'on rhetoric and hype than on reality'."

—Paula Cerni in *Review of Radical Political Economics*

"By far the best and most readable account of the past three decades of economic globalization. Replete with maps, graphs, and tables, the book offers the clearest and most complete exposition of the scale and depth of the transformation currently affecting all societies."

—John O'Loughlin in *Lingua Franca*

"A first-rate and eminently readable work, with a unique blend of empirical and conceptual material and an analytical depth rarely achieved in textbooks. The third edition of *Global Shift* continues to be one of the most useful, interesting, and readable texts in the field of economic geography. I thoroughly recommend it both to students of geography and to readers in other disciplines who are interested in seeing what contemporary economic geography is really all about."

—John Holmes, Department of Geography, Queen's University, Kingston, Ontario, Canada

Contents

List of Abbreviations

ABS	Advanced business services
AFTA	ASEAN Free Trade Agreement
APEC	Asia–Pacific Economic Cooperation Forum
ASEAN	Association of South East Asian Nations
B2B	Business-to-business
B2C	Business-to-consumer
BRIC	Brazil, Russia, India, China
CAFTA	Central American Free Trade Agreement
CAP	Common Agricultural Policy (EU)
CME	Coordinated market economy
CSO	Civil society organization
CSR	Corporate social responsibility
CUSFTA	Canada–US Free Trade Agreement
ECB	European Central Bank
ECE	Eastern and Central Europe
EDB	Economic Development Board (Singapore)
EMU	European Monetary Union
EOI	Export-oriented industrialization
EPB	Economic Planning Board (South Korea)
EPZ	Export processing zone
ETDZ	Economic and Technological Development Zones (China)
EU	European Union
FCCC	Framework Convention on Climate Change
FDI	Foreign direct investment
FTAA	Free Trade Area of the Americas
GATS	General Agreement on Trade in Services
GATT	General Agreement on Tariffs and Trade
GCC	Global commodity chain
GCSO	Global civil society organization
GDP	Gross domestic product
GHG	Greenhouse gas
GM	Genetic modification

GNH	Gross national happiness
GNI	Gross national income
GNP	Gross national product
GPN	Global production network
GSP	Generalized system of preferences
GVC	Global value chain
HVF	High-value foods
ICT	Information and communications technology
ILO	International Labour Organization
IMF	International Monetary Fund
IPCC	Intergovernmental Panel on Climate Change
ISI	Import-substituting industrialization
IT	Information technology
JIT	Just-in-time
LAFTA	Latin American Free Trade Area
LAIA	Latin American Intregation Association
LDC	Less developed country
LME	Liberal Market economy
MAI	Multinational Agreement on Investment
METI	Ministry for Economy, Trade and Industry (Japan)
MFA	Multi-Fibre Arrangement
MFN	Most-favoured nation
MITI	Ministry of International Trade and Industry (Japan)
MNC	Multinational corporation
MSW	Municipal solid waste
NAC	Newly Agriculturalizing Country
NAFTA	North American Free Trade Agreement
NGO	Non-governmental organization
NIE	Newly Industrializing Economy
NTB	Non-tariff barrier
OECD	Organization for Economic Cooperation and Development
OFC	Offshore financial centre
OPEC	Organization of the Petroleum Exporting Countries
OPT	Outward Processing Trade
PLC	Product life cycle
PRC	People's Republic of China
PTA	Preferential trading arrangement
R&D	Research and development
RIA	Regional integration agreement
RTA	Regional trade agreement
SEZ	Special Economic Zones (China)
SOE	State-owned enterprise
SUV	Sports utility vehicle

SWF	Sovereign wealth fund
TCC	Transnational capitalist class
TEU	Treaty on European Union
TNC	Transnational corporation
TNI	Transnationality index
TRIMS	Trade-related investment measures
TRIPS	Trade-related intellectual property rights
UNCTAD	United Nations Conference on Trade and Development
WTO	World Trade Organization

Preface to the Sixth Edition

As this sixth edition is published in 2011, it is exactly 25 years since the publication of the first edition in 1986. That, in itself, is a very sobering thought, for all kinds of reasons. What began, in the early 1980s, as a faltering, and very naïve, one-off attempt to make sense of the changing geographies of the world economy has developed into an evolving longitudinal project. Each subsequent edition, in effect, constitutes a temporal marker of the empirical changes in the configuration of the global economy and of changing interpretations of, and attitudes towards, 'globalization'.

We tend to think of our world as one that is continuously changing. That, of course, is a truism. Underlying the surface of change there is a great deal of longer-term continuity. Indeed, one lesson I have learned from monitoring developments in the global economy over these past 25 years is the danger of making hasty judgements about immediate events and extrapolating them into the future. Two current examples, one 'macro' and one 'micro', illustrate my point. Example one: will the G20 really come to constitute a new global power structure, thus ending the hegemony of the US-led Western institutions that have dominated since 1945? Example two: will the huge safety scandal that is currently engulfing Toyota result in permanent damage to its position as the world's biggest automobile manufacturer and change the competitive playing field in that industry? In both cases, as in all others, only time will tell.

However, our collective predictive track record is not especially good. In the late 1990s, for example, many were predicting the demise of East Asia in the light of the region's 1997 financial crisis. How wrong that prediction was. At the same time, however, the nature of East Asia did change, primarily, although not entirely, because of the (re-)emergence of China. It is important to keep this methodological problem in mind when we are in the midst of a global financial crisis of epic proportions. Of course, a great deal of attention is devoted throughout the book to the current global financial crisis. The world will not be the same as it was (we hope it will be better) but we cannot clearly see what it will actually be like. It will depend upon the choices society makes. It is this interplay between the short and the long term that makes a project like *Global Shift* so challenging. The exhortation to 'watch this space' can never have been more apt.

With these principles in mind, the basic aim of this sixth edition, as of its five predecessors, is to provide a clear path through the dense thickets of what are large, often conflicting, often confusing, debates and arguments about globalization: to show how the global economy works and what its effects are. It tries to separate the reality from the hype: to provide a balanced, grounded – but emphatically not an uncritical – perspective on a topic often richer in rhetoric than reality. It focuses on the longer-term, underlying processes of global economic change within which 'events of the moment' can be better understood.

What is new about the sixth edition? It is emphatically not a mere cosmetic exercise. As in the previous editions, I set out to produce the most up-to-date and comprehensive account of economic-geographic globalization. Hence, all the empirical data have been fully updated using the latest available sources as of early 2010. Because maps and charts are so important to this book, there are even more in this edition. Although the established four-part structure of the book remains, I make greater use of the concept of the global production network (GPN) as a major organizing principle throughout the book in order to demonstrate the fundamentally relational nature of the processes involved and to emphasize the power-laden dynamics of the interactions between transnational corporations, states, consumers, labour and civil society organizations. Every chapter has been completely revised and extensively rewritten not only to take into account new empirical developments but also to incorporate new ideas on the shaping and reshaping of production, distribution and consumption in the global economy. Two entirely new chapters have been written: one on the extractive industries (Chapter 8), the other on the environmental impacts of GPNs (Chapter 15). Part Four, in particular, has been completely redesigned to produce a much tighter argument about the impacts of globalizing processes on people, places and the environment.

The book is organized into four closely related, but distinct, parts.

Part One focuses on the *shifting contours of the global economic map*: the 'global shifts' that are continuously reshaping the global economy.

Part Two explores the complex and multifarious ways in which *the actors, institutions and processes* that make up the global economy interact to produce global production networks: the 'gales of creative destruction' set in motion by new technologies; the increasingly complex and extensive production networks created and controlled by transnational corporations; the actions of states in their roles as containers of distinctive institutions and practices, as competitors, and as collaborators with other states; the uneasy relationships between TNCs and states, as each tries to exercise bargaining power over the other.

Part Three presents six *sectoral case studies* to illustrate the diverse ways in which these processes actually operate. Precisely how such networks are configured and operate, precisely how TNCs, states, labour, consumers and CSOs are involved, precisely how they are subject to technological pressures, vary enormously between different kinds of economic activity. The six cases have been carefully chosen to range across the entire spectrum of economic activities, from the basic/primary industries of mineral extraction and agro-food production, through such key global manufacturing industries as clothing and automobiles, to the advanced business, financial, logistical and distribution services that provide much of the 'lubrication' of the global economy.

Part Four is concerned with *'winning' and 'losing'* in the global economy: the problems for national and local economies of capturing value in global production networks; the destruction of value through environmental degradation; the staggeringly uneven contours of development; and, finally, the questions of how the world might be made a better place for all.

Global Shift is both a *cross-disciplinary* and a *multilevel* book. It deliberately spans, and draws from, a wide range of academic disciplines, including business and management, development studies, economics, economic geography, political science and sociology, amongst others. At the same time the book is designed for use at different levels. On the one hand, my aim has been to make the book accessible to readers without prior specialist knowledge by ensuring that all key terms are clearly defined, by avoiding excessive jargon, and by making extensive use of graphics. On the other hand, for the specialist reader, each chapter contains end-of-chapter notes that connect to the extremely extensive and up-to-date research bibliography. Through such means, the book should be useful to graduate students and researchers, as well as to policy makers and to people in business. Certainly my experience of the reception of previous editions suggests that this is the case.

★★★

With each successive edition, my debt to friends, colleagues and users of the book widens and deepens. Indeed, without a rich network of friends and colleagues from all round the world, a book like this simply could not exist. To all of them, I offer my sincere thanks and I hope they will forgive me for not mentioning them all by name. However, several people deserve special mention.

Roger Lee (despite the handicap of being a Manchester United supporter) has provided the most remarkable support and inspiration over many years and, above all, with Lesley, friendship and sharing of mutual interests and pleasures. I hope they are not too embarrassed by the book's dedication. Nick Scarle, Senior Cartographer at the University of Manchester, has produced all the illustrations for every edition in a truly creative manner. Always superb, they have simply got better and better. Everybody who uses this book praises the graphics and I only wish I could take the credit for them.

I am very fortunate to remain part of the community of geographers at the University of Manchester and I much appreciate the friendship of colleagues there, especially Gavin Bridge, Noel Castree, Neil Coe, Martin Hess and Kevin Ward. Gavin, Neil and Martin deserve specific thanks. Gavin provided invaluable advice and guidance on the extractive industries, without which I could not have produced Chapter 8 (of course, he bears no responsibility for any weak parts of that chapter). Neil and Martin have been superb collaborators over a number of years, most notably, along with Henry Yeung, in developing the global production network (GPN) framework for which Manchester has something of a reputation. Neil specifically provided the data for Figure 9.10.

I particularly want to thank Henry Yeung for so many things, both professional and personal, since he first burst into my office in 1992. My life was never the same after that! I am immensely grateful to Liu Weidong, for introducing me to China, providing help with Chinese materials and translating an earlier edition into Chinese; and Anders Malmberg, for involving me in the vibrant academic community at Uppsala and for suggesting the subtitle (or was it Anna?), as well as many other ways of improving the book over the years. Kris Olds and Ray Hudson made detailed evaluations of the various editions that made me think about some ways forward. None of these, of course, bears any responsibility for all the weaknesses that remain, but they can certainly claim credit for any strengths and I am enormously grateful to all of them.

I am extremely grateful to the team at Sage Publications in London. Sage is a publisher for whom I am proud to write. In particular, Robert Rojek is the most caring, encouraging and stimulating publisher and friend. He has been truly supportive in every way. He is also great to go to galleries with. Katie Metzler has done brilliant work in helping to develop this edition in so many ways. Katherine Haw has lavished great skill and care on creating a visually stimulating book. Fiona Moore of Royal Holloway, University of London has done an excellent job with the support materials for business and management users of the book. Thanks, too, to Seymour Weingarten and the staff at The Guilford Press in New York.

As always, of course, it all ultimately comes back to the people who matter to me most of all: my (now dispersed) family. Sadly, they continue to treat me with the disrespect I don't deserve. But they are all – Christopher and Annika in Germany; Michael, Sally, Jack and Harry in Switzerland – such stimulating people and such great fun to be with. And then there is my wife, Valerie, who makes everything worthwhile and who (still) does so with so much love, humour and tolerance, despite threatening to leave me every time I start a new edition. But she's still here. And finally there are JSB, LvB, GM, WAM, HO, DDKB, MCO, WB and so many, many more.

Peter Dicken
Manchester, 2010

About the Companion Website

Be sure to visit the companion website accompanying the sixth edition at www.sagepub.co.uk/Dicken6 to find a range of teaching and learning materials for lecturers and students. The website has been expanded to offer tailored resources for lecturers and students in Geography, International Business, Sociology and Politics. Online readings from SAGE journals have been provided for each discipline, in addition to the resources designed for all of *Global Shift's* diverse users.

FOR LECTURERS:

Powerpoint Slides for each chapter containing all of the tables and figures from the book are available to be used in class.

Lecturers' Notes, **Case Studies** and additional pedagogical **PowerPoint Slides** are available to download from the website for International Business lecturers. The slides can be edited by instructors to suit their needs and teaching styles.

FOR STUDENTS:

Full text **Online Readings** compiled from key journals in the field by academics in Geography, International Business, Sociology and Politics. The full text journal articles are linked to the discussion within the book and provide additional coverage of key topics in each chapter.

A **Glossary** to check your understanding of key terms.

Annotated web links which take you to useful websites where you can find further empirical data, reports and statistics.

Study Skills material to help you study effectively and efficiently. A bank of free downloadable chapters from existing SAGE books are provided, packed with ideas and advice to help you succeed in your course.

Homepage
About the Book
Description
Author Details
Table of Contents
Resources

RESOURCES *for* ALL USERS

Lecturer resources
PowerPoint Slides
Student resources
Glossary
Annotated Web Links
Study Skills Material
Other Resources

RESOURCES *for* GEOGRAPHY

Student resources
Online Readings

RESOURCES *for* INTERNATIONAL BUSINESS

Student resources
Online Readings
Lecturer Resources
Lecturer's Notes
Case Studies and Questions
PowerPoint Slides

RESOURCES *for* SOCIOLOGY

Student resources
Online Readings

RESOURCES *for* POLITICS

Student resources
Online Readings
Book Details

Peter Dicken

Welcome to the Companion Website for the sixth edition of Dicken, *Global Shift*.

Global Shift, sixth edition, continues to deconstruct globalization to show that distance (economic geography) still matters, Dicken uses insights from international business research to demonstrate that world business activity is more regional than global. Multinational enterprises are at the hub of global production networks and service delivery; they interact with governments and generally act as agents of economic development. In short economic geography and international business are closely aligned in their approach to globalization.
Alan Rugman, Henley Business School, University of Reading

A masterful new edition of a masterful text. Once again, Peter Dicken is at the cutting edge of the analysis of economic globalization and global trends. ***Global Shift*** is the authoritative text on these issues.
David Held, Co-Director, Centre for the Study of Global Governance, LSE

The website for the sixth edition has been expanded to offer tailored resources for lecturers and students in Geography, International Business, Sociology and Politics. Online readings from SAGE Journals have been provided for each discipline, in addition to the resources designed for all of *Global Shift*'s users.

Many thanks to Paul James, Fiona Moore and Matthew Caygill for their contributions to the website material for the sixth edition.

About the Book
This section contains details about the new edition and its author.

Resources
Along the left hand side of this page, you will see tabs linking you to lecturer and student resources for all users. Brand new additional resources for Geography, International Business, Sociology and Politics have also been developed with this edition. Click on a tab to take you to resources tailored to your discipline, but also feel free to browse through the resources for other disciplines, as these may be helpful for you too.

Author
Peter Dicken
Pub Date: 11/2010
Pages: 632
Click here for more information.

One

INTRODUCTION: QUESTIONING 'GLOBALIZATION'

What in the world is going on?

The end of the world?

On 15 September 2008, the fourth largest US investment bank, Lehman Brothers, collapsed. It was an unprecedented event in the midst of what was developing into the biggest global economic crisis since the late 1920s. Although the sudden demise of Lehman was only one of many casualties in the financial system in 2008, its collapse was highly symbolic. Lehman was one of those institutions that epitomized the neo-liberal, free market ideology (sometimes known as the 'Washington Consensus') that had dominated the global economy for the past half century. This was the ideology of free and efficient markets: that the market knew best and all hindrances to its efficient operation were undesirable. But in 2008, all this was suddenly thrown into question. As one financial institution after another foundered, as governments took on the role of fire-fighters, and as several banks became in effect nationalized, the entire market-driven capitalist system seemed to be falling apart.

Question: does the economic turmoil that began in 2008 herald 'the end of globalization'? Well, it all depends on what we mean by 'globalization'. It helps if we distinguish between two broad meanings of globalization.[1] One refers to the actual *structural* changes that are occurring in the way the global economy is organized and integrated. The other meaning refers to the neo-liberal, free-market *ideology* of the 'globalization project'. Of course, the two are not separate. As a result, confusion reigns. It is too early to say whether the free-market ideology has been irrevocably changed by the global financial crisis. Many think it has. Others believe that, once the dust settles, it will be business as usual. That may, or may not, be the case. But globalization, as we shall see, has never been the simple all-embracing phenomenon promulgated by the free-market ideologists. We need to take a much more critical and analytical view of what is actually going on over the longer term; to move beyond the rhetoric, to seek the reality. That is one of the primary purposes of this book.

Confusion and uncertainty

Globalization is a concept (though not a term) whose roots go back at least to the nineteenth century, notably in the ideas of Karl Marx. But it has only been in the last 30 years or so that globalization has entered the popular imagination in a really big way. Now it seems to be everywhere. A Google search reveals millions of entries. Hardly a day goes by without its being invoked by politicians, by academics, by business and trade union leaders, by journalists, by commentators on radio and TV, by consumer and environmental groups, as well as by 'ordinary' individuals. Unfortunately, it has become not only one of the most used, but also one of the most *mis*used and one of the most *con*fused, terms around today. As Susan Strange argued, it is, too often,

> a term ... used by a lot of woolly thinkers who lump together all sorts of super-ficially converging trends ... and call it globalization without trying to distinguish what is important from what is trivial, either in causes or in consequences.[2]

The current explosion of interest in globalization reflects a pervasive feeling that something fundamental is happening in the world; that there are lots of 'big issues' that are somehow interconnected under the broad umbrella term 'globalization'. In the words of one contemporary commentator,

> We live in an era in which everything has changed and most things are still changing. The ice has melted on the familiar landscape of the second half of the 20th century. Power in all its forms is shifting rapidly and unpredictably. You might even say that we are at the beginning of history.[3]

Such feelings of uncertainty are intensified by an increased awareness that what is happening in one part of the world is deeply – and often very immediately – affected by events happening in other parts of the world. A crisis in an obscure financial market (the US subprime housing market) spreads almost instantaneously to far distant places. Part of this is simply the result of the revolution in electronic communications that has transformed the speed with which information spreads. Nowadays, we hear about events on the other side of the world virtually as they happen – in 'real time'. But part of it is also to do with the fact that many of the things we use in our daily lives are derived from an increasingly complex geography of production, distribution and consumption, whose scale has become, if not totally global, at least vastly more extensive, and whose choreography has become increasingly intricate. Many products, indeed, have such a complex geography – with parts being made in different countries and then assembled somewhere else – that labels of origin no longer have meaning.

To the individual citizen the most obvious indicators of change are those which impinge most directly on her/his daily activities: making a living, acquiring the necessities of life, providing for their children to sustain their future. In the industrialized countries, there is fear – very much intensified by the current financial crisis - that the dual (and connected) forces of technological change and global shifts in the location of economic activities are adversely transforming employment prospects. The current waves of concern about the outsourcing and offshoring of jobs in the IT service industries (notably, though not exclusively, to India), or the more general fear that manufacturing jobs are being sucked into a newly emergent China or into other emerging economies, suddenly growing at breakneck speed, are only the most recent examples of such fears. At the same time, the spectres of global climate change and energy uncertainties raise even bigger questions over the future.

But the problems of the industrialized countries pale into insignificance when set against those of the poorest countries in what used to be called the 'Third World'. Although there are indeed losers in the developed and affluent countries, their magnitude is totally dwarfed by the poverty and deprivation of much of Africa and of many parts of South Asia and of Latin America. The development gap continues to widen, the disparity between rich and poor continues to grow. It is, of course, totally naïve to explain all such problems in terms of a single causal mechanism called 'globalization':

> Establishing a link between globalization and inequality is fraught with difficulty, not only because of how globalization is defined and how inequality is measured, but also because the entanglements between globalization forces and 'domestic' trends are not that easy to separate out.[4]

Despite, or perhaps because of, its 'woolliness', globalization generates heated and polarized argument across the entire political and ideological spectrum. Most dramatic of all, since the turn of the millennium, has been the proliferation of global protest movements: the explosion of street demonstrations at major international political meetings, notably of the WTO, the G8 and, most recently, the G20. These have involved a remarkable *mélange* of pressure groups, ranging from long-established civil society organizations (CSOs) to totally new groups with either very specific, or very general, foci for their protest, together with anarchist and revolutionary elements with a broad anti-capitalist agenda.

But beyond these 'organized' movements, there is growing evidence in world-wide opinion polls of wide divergences of opinion on whether globalization is good or bad, whether it is proceeding too quickly or proceeding too slowly. A poll of 34,500 people in 34 countries, commissioned by the BBC World Service in 2008, concluded that

> in 22 out of 34 countries around the world, the weight of opinion is that 'eco-nomic globalization, including trade and investment' is growing too quickly … Related to this unease is an even stronger view that the benefits and burdens of 'the economic developments of the last few years' have not been shared fairly … In developed countries, those who have this view of unfairness are more likely to say that globalization is growing too quickly … In contrast, in some developing countries, those who perceive such unfairness are more likely to say globalization is proceeding too slowly.[5]

There is, in fact, a highly differentiated geography of the awareness of, and attitudes towards, globalization.[6]

Conflicting perspectives on 'globalization'

The primary focus of this book is the global *economy*. There are, of course, other forms of globalization - political, cultural and social – and these are often difficult to separate. Indeed, the 'economy' itself is not some kind of isolated entity. Not only is it deeply embedded in social, cultural and political processes and institutions but also these are, themselves, often substantially imbued with economic values. Not surprisingly, therefore, this is a highly contested topic. In this section, we identify two of the major positions within the 'globalization' debate.[7]

'Hyper-globalists' to the right and to the left

Probably the largest body of opinion – and one that spans the entire politico-ideological spectrum – consists of what might be called the *hyper-globalists*, who argue that we live in a borderless world in which the 'national' is no longer relevant. In such a world, globalization is the new economic (as well as political and cultural) order. It is a world where nation-states are no longer significant actors or meaning-ful economic units and in which consumer tastes and cultures are homogenized and satisfied through the provision of standardized global products created by global corporations with no allegiance to place or community. Thus, the 'global' is claimed to be the *natural* order, an inevitable state of affairs, in which time–space has been compressed, the 'end of geography' has arrived and everywhere is becoming the

Figure 1.1   Globalization as inevitable trajectory: the hyper-globalist view

same. In Friedman's terms, 'the world is flat'.[8] Such a hyper-globalist view is shown in Figure 1.1 as an inexorable process of increasing geographical spread and increasing functional integration between economic activities.

This hyper-globalist view of the world is a myth. It does not – and is unlikely ever to – exist. Nevertheless, its rhetoric retains a powerful influence on politicians, business leaders and many other interest groups. It is a world-view shared by many on both the political right and the political left. Where they differ is in their evaluation of the situation and in their policy positions.

- To the neo-liberals on the right – the *pro*-globalizers - globalization is an ideological project, one that, it is asserted, will bring the greatest benefit for the greatest number. Simply let free markets (whether in trade or finance) rule and all will be well. The 'rising tide' of globalization will 'lift all boats'; human material well-being will be enhanced. Although the neo-liberal pro-globalizers recognize that such a state of perfection hasn't yet been achieved, the major problem, in their view, is that there is too little, rather than too much, globalization.[9] Globalization is the *solution* to the world's economic problems and inequalities. This, then, is the global manifestation of the 'Washington Consensus' referred to earlier: the ideology of free and efficient markets regardless of national boundaries.
- To the hyper-globalizers of the left – the *anti*-globalizers – globalization is the *problem*, not the solution.[10] The very operation of those market forces claimed to be beneficent by the right are regarded as the crux of the problem: they are

a malign and destructive force. Free markets, it is argued, inevitably create inequalities. By extension, the globalization of markets increases the scale and extent of such inequalities. Unregulated markets inevitably lead to a reduction in well-being for all but a small minority in the world, as well as creating massive environmental problems. Markets, therefore, *must* be regulated in the wider interest. To some anti-globalists, in fact, the only logical solution is a complete rejection of globalization processes and a return to the 'local'.

'Sceptical internationalists'

Although the notion of a global*ized* economic world has become widely accepted, some adopt a more *sceptical* position, arguing that the 'newness' of the current situation has been grossly exaggerated. The world economy, it is claimed, was actually more open and more integrated in the half century prior to the First World War (1870–1913) than it is today.[11] The empirical evidence used to justify this position is *quantitative* and *aggregative*, based on national states as statistical units. Such data reveal a world in which trade, investment and, especially, population migration flowed in increasingly large volumes between countries. Indeed, such levels of international trade and investment were not reached again (after the world depression of the 1930s and the Second World War) until the later decades of the twentieth century. Indeed, international population migration has not returned to those earlier levels, at least in terms of the proportion of the world population involved in cross-border movement. On the basis of such quantitative evidence Hirst and Thompson assert that 'we do not have a fully globalized economy, we do have an international economy'.[12]

Grounding 'globalization': geography really does matter

Such national-level quantitative data need to be taken seriously. But they are only part of the story. They do not tell us what kinds of *qualitative* changes have been occurring in the global economy. Most important have been the transformations in the *where* and the *how* of the material production, distribution and consumption of goods and services (including, in particular, finance). Old geographies of production, distribution and consumption are continuously being disrupted; new geographies of production, distribution and consumption are continuously being created. There has been a huge transformation in the *nature* and the *degree* of interconnection in the world economy and, especially, in the *speed* with which such connectivity occurs, involving both a *stretching* and an *intensification* of economic relationships. Without doubt, the world economy is a qualitatively different place from that of only 60 or 70 years ago, although it is not so much more open as *increasingly interconnected in rather different ways.*

International economic integration before 1914 – and even until only about four or five decades ago – was essentially *shallow integration*, manifested largely through arm's-length trade in goods and services between independent firms and through international movements of portfolio capital and relatively simple direct investment. Today, we live in a world in which *deep integration*, organized primarily within and between geographically extensive and complex *global production networks*, and through a variety of mechanisms, is increasingly the norm.

Such qualitative changes are simply not captured in aggregative trade and investment data of the kind used by the sceptics. For example, in the case of international trade, what matters are not so much changes in volume – although these are certainly important – as changes in *composition*. There has been a huge increase in both *intra-industry* and *intra-firm* trade, both of which are clear indicators of more functionally fragmented and geographically dispersed production processes.[13] Above all, there have been dramatic changes in the operation of financial markets, with money moving electronically round the world at unprecedented speeds, generating enormous repercussions for national and local economies.

The crucial diagnostic characteristic of a 'global economy', therefore, is *the qualitative transformation of economic relationships across geographical space* and not their mere quantitative geographical spread. This involves 'not a single, unified phenomenon, but a *syndrome* of processes and activities'.[14] There is not a single 'driver' of such transformative processes – certainly not the technological determinism so central in much of the popular globalization literature. In other words,

> globalization is a ... supercomplex series of multicentric, multiscalar, multi-temporal, multiform and multicausal processes.[15]

Globalizing processes are reflected in, and influenced by, multiple geographies, rather than a single global geography: the 'local and the global intermesh, running into one another in all manner of ways'.[16] Although there are undoubtedly global*izing* forces at work, we do not have a fully global*ized* world. In fact, as Figure 1.2 shows, several tendencies can be identified, reflecting different combinations of geographical spread and functional integration or interconnection rather than the unidirectional trajectory shown in Figure 1.1:

- *localizing* processes: geographically concentrated economic activities with varying degrees of functional integration
- *internationalizing* processes: simple geographical spread of economic activities across national boundaries with low levels of functional integration
- *globalizing* processes: both extensive geographical spread and also a high degree of functional integration
- *regionalizing* processes: the operation of 'globalizing' processes at a more geographically limited (but supranational) scale, ranging from the highly integrated and expanding European Union to much smaller regional economic agreements.

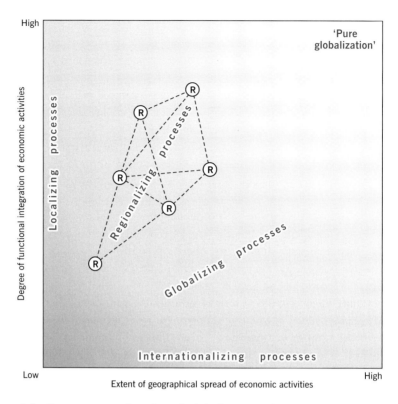

Figure 1.2 Processes and scales of global economic transformation

Globalization, therefore, is not an inevitable end-state but, rather, a complex, indeterminate set of *processes* operating very unevenly in both time and space. As a result of these processes, the nature and the degree of interconnection between different parts of the world is continuously in flux. A major task, therefore, is to challenge some of the more egregious *globalization myths*:

- The world is *not* flat (*contra* Friedman).
- The world is *not* borderless (*contra* Ohmae).
- Global corporations do *not* rule the world (*contra* Korten).
- Globalization is *not* always good (*contra* the neo-liberal hyper-globalizers).
- Globalization is *not* always bad (*contra* the anti-globalizers).

In questioning globalization, therefore, we need to get real: to develop a firmly grounded understanding of both the processes involved and their impacts on people's lives. Of course, there will always be differences of diagnosis, prognosis and recommended treatment. But at least these should be based on sound conceptual and empirical analysis. This book represents an attempt to do this.

NOTES

1　Chase-Dunn et al. (2000).
2　Strange (1995: 293).
3　Stephens (2005). The reference to the 'beginning of history' seems to be a deliberate contrast to Fukuyama's (1992) prediction of the 'end of history' following the collapse of the Soviet system.
4　Amin (2004: 218).
5　BBC World Service (2008).
6　ILO (2004b: 12–23).
7　Held and McGrew (2007: Chapter 1) provide a useful discussion of some of the major strands in the globalization debates. See also Cameron and Palan (2004).
8　Friedman (2005).
9　For an example of this position, see Friedman (1999; 2005). More nuanced writers within this general framework include Bhagwati (2004) and Wolf (2004).
10　See, for example, Greider (1997).
11　Hirst and Thompson (1992), Hirst et al. (2009).
12　Hirst and Thompson (1992: 394).
13　See Feenstra (1998), Gereffi (2005).
14　Mittelman (2000: 4).
15　Jessop (2002: 113–14).
16　Thrift (1990: 181).

PART ONE

THE SHIFTING CONTOURS OF THE GLOBAL ECONOMY

Two

GLOBAL SHIFT: CHANGING GEOGRAPHIES OF THE GLOBAL ECONOMY

What's new? The imprint of past geographies

The global economic map is always in a state of 'becoming'; it is always, in one sense, 'new'. But it is never finished. Old geographies of production, distribution and consumption are continuously being disrupted and new geographies are continuously being created. The new does not totally obliterate the old. On the contrary, there are complex processes of path dependency at work; what already exists constitutes the preconditions on which the new develops. Today's global economic map, therefore, is the outcome of a long period of evolution during which the structures and relationships of previous historical periods help to shape the structures and relationships of subsequent periods. In that sense, we cannot fully understand the present without at least some understanding of the past. Indeed, traces of earlier economic maps – earlier patterns of geographical specialization or divisions of labour – continue to influence what is happening today, although there are debates amongst economic historians over when we can first identify a 'world' or a 'global' economy. To some, this appeared during what has been called the 'long sixteenth century' (1450 to 1640)[1] or with the 'eighteenth century transition to an industrial world'.[2] To others, the key period was the second half of the nineteenth century.[3] Whatever,

> by 1914, there was hardly a village or town anywhere on the globe whose prices were not influenced by distant foreign markets, whose infrastructure was not financed by foreign capital, whose engineering, manufacturing, and even business skills were not imported from abroad, or whose labour markets were not influenced by the absence of those who had emigrated or by the presence of strangers who had immigrated. The economic connections were intimate.[4]

Over a period of 300 years or so, therefore, a *global division of labour* developed, and intensified with industrialization, in which the newly industrialized economies of the West (led by the 'Atlantic' economies, notably Britain, some Western European countries, and later the US) became increasingly dominant in a *core–periphery* configuration (Figure 2.1). Of course, over time, this structure became more complex in detail, and also changed in its geographical composition. Some core economies experienced a progressive decline to semi-peripheral status during the eighteenth century and new economies emerged, especially in the late nineteenth and early twentieth centuries. Figure 2.2 shows some of these dramatic changes, notably the steep decline of Asia and the emergence to unrivalled dominance of the US, measured in terms of shares of global gross domestic product (GDP).

The broad contours of this core–periphery global economic map persisted until the outbreak of the Second World War in 1939. Manufacturing production remained strongly concentrated in the core: 71 per cent of world manufacturing production was concentrated in just four countries and almost 90 per cent in only 11 countries. Japan produced only 3.5 per cent of the world total. The group

Figure 2.1   A simple geographical division of labour: core and periphery
in the global economy

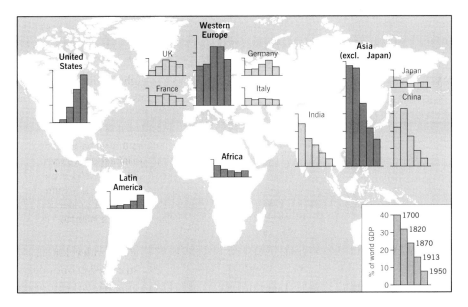

Figure 2.2   Global shifts in GDP, 1700–1950

Source: calculated from Maddison, 2001: Table B-20

of core industrial countries sold two-thirds of its manufactured exports to the
periphery and absorbed four-fifths of the periphery's primary products.[5]

This long-established global division of labour was shattered by the Second
World War. Most of the world's industrial capacity (outside North America) was
destroyed. At the same time, new technologies were created and many existing
industrial technologies were refined and improved. The world economic system
that emerged after 1945 reflected the new geopolitical realities of the post-war
period – particularly the sharp division between East and West – as well as the

harsh economic and social experiences of the 1930s. The major geopolitical division of the world after 1945 was that between the capitalist West (the US and its allies) and the communist East (the Soviet Union and its allies). Outside these two major power blocs was the so-called 'Third' World, a highly heterogeneous – but generally impoverished – group of nations, many of them still at that time under colonial domination. Both major powers made strenuous efforts to extend their spheres of influence into the Third World.

The Soviet bloc drew clear boundaries around itself and its Eastern European satellites and created its own economic system quite separate, at least initially, from the capitalist market economies of the West. In the West the economic order built after 1945 reflected the domination of the US. Alone of all the major industrial nations, the US had emerged from the war strengthened, rather than weakened. It had both the economic and technological capacity and the political power to lead the way in building a new order. As Figure 2.2 shows, by 1950 the US accounted for no less than 27 per cent of global GDP.

It is from this historical baseline, therefore, that recent global shifts in economic activity will be examined in this chapter. Today's world is far more complex than it was even a few decades ago. Since 1950, two highly significant political events have occurred: the emergence of China into the global market economy, although still under Communist Party control, starting in 1979; and the collapse of the prevailing political systems in the Soviet Union and its Eastern European satellites in 1989.

More broadly – and most significantly – we are seeing the *re*-emergence of Asia as the world's most dynamic economic region.[6] In 1700, Asia dominated; its share of global GDP was 62 per cent compared with the West's 23 per cent. But by 1950 those positions had been almost exactly reversed: the combined share of global GDP of Western economies was almost 60 per cent; that of Asia (including Japan) was a mere 19 per cent. Much of this was due to the relative economic decline of China and India. In 1700, their combined share of global GDP was almost 50 per cent; by 1950, it had plummeted to less than 10 per cent. They had become totally peripheral. Today, the picture is very different. East Asia is back.

Roller-coasters and interconnections

Two particularly important features have characterized the global economy since 1950: the increased volatility of aggregate economic growth; and the growing interconnectedness between different parts of the world.

Aggregate trends in global economic activity

The path of economic growth certainly does not run smooth. It's a roller-coaster. Sometimes the ride is gentle, with just minor ups and downs; at other times, the

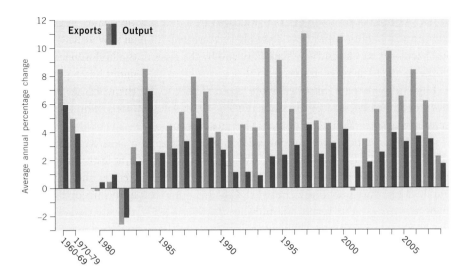

Figure 2.3   The roller-coaster of world merchandise production and
trade, 1960–2008

Source: calculated from GATT/WTO *International Trade Statistics*, various issues

ride is truly stomach-wrenching, with steep upward surges separated by vertiginous
descents to what seem like bottomless depths. Booms and slumps are endemic:

> Between 1870 and 2006, there were no fewer than 255 recessions in a sample
> of 17 western economies … [However] two-thirds of the downturns were over
> within a year, and only 33 lasted longer than two years. Apart from the reces-
> sions associated with the world wars and the Great Depression, there was a
> tendency for economies to show resilience and bounce back quickly.[7]

Figure 2.3 depicts this roller-coaster pattern for the period since 1960. The years
immediately following the Second World War were ones of basic reconstruction of
war-damaged economies. Rates of economic growth reached unprecedented levels;
the period between the early 1950s and the early 1970s became known as the
'golden age'. In fact, it was only partly golden: it was more golden in some places
than others, and for some people than others.[8] But then, in the early 1970s, the sky
fell in. The long boom suddenly went bust; the 'golden age' became tarnished.

Rates of growth again became extremely variable, ranging from the negative
growth rates of 1982 through to two years (1984 and 1988) when growth of world
merchandise trade reached the levels of the 1960s once again. But then, in the early
1990s, recession returned. In 1994 and 1995, strong export growth reappeared. A
similarly volatile pattern characterized the final years of the twentieth century. There
was spectacular growth in world trade in 1997, followed by far slower growth in
1998 and 1999 (partly related to the East Asian financial crisis and to its contagious
effects on other parts of the world). Then, once again, there was spectacular

acceleration in world trade in 2000, followed by an equally spectacular bursting of the growth bubble, a problem certainly exacerbated (though not caused) by the 9/11 terrorist attacks on New York City and by the crisis in the IT (dotcom) sector of the so-called 'new' economy.

High growth rates returned once again. Then, in 2008, seemingly without warning, the deepest recession since the late 1920s suddenly occurred. The roller-coaster was back with a vengeance. The most recent golden age of the 2000s (as it seemed at the time) was short-lived. However, we are too close to events to be able to predict what happens next. On the one hand, in early 2009, it appeared that 'global trade was in freefall'[9] and that 'the global economy was shrinking much faster than previously thought'. On the other hand, by mid 2009 global trade was rising 'at its fastest rate in more than five years'.[10] By the time you read this book, things will have changed again. Whatever the precise situation, however, there is little doubt that the 2008 recession will have long-lasting, though very uneven, effects. In the words of the OECD Secretary-General,

> it's not just a case of saying [the world] will recover its growth in 2010 and then live happily ever after – there are wounds and there is scar tissue.[11]

Growing interconnectedness within the global economy

One major characteristic of global economic growth, therefore, is its inherent volatility. A second is the increasing interconnectedness of the global economy. Such interconnectedness has three major dimensions: trade has grown faster than output; foreign direct investment has grown faster than trade; and serious structural imbalances in the world economy have emerged. Let's look at each of these.

Trade has grown faster than output

Figure 2.3 shows that exports have grown much faster than output in virtually every year since 1960. In the second half of the twentieth century, world merchandise trade increased almost twentyfold while world merchandise production increased just over sixfold. More and more production is being traded across national boundaries. Countries are becoming more tightly interconnected through trade flows. This is reflected in the ratio of trade to GDP. The higher the figure, the greater is the dependence on external trade. There is huge variation between countries in such trade integration. For example, international trade is bound to be more important for geographically small countries than for large ones, the result of a simple size effect (contrast, say, the US with Singapore). However, in virtually all cases the importance of trade to national GDP has increased significantly, as Table 2.1 shows.

Figure 2.4 maps the network of world merchandise trade. It shows the strong tendency for countries to trade most with their neighbours.

Table 2.1   The increasing importance of trade for national economies, 1960–2007
(exports + imports as % GDP)

	1960	1970	1985	1995	2007
By income group					
High income	23.7	27.1	37.3	39.8	49.1
Middle income	..	..	..	55.9	55.9
Upper-middle income	34.3	36.4	41.8	51.4	52.0
Lower-middle income	..	..	..	58.7	59.6
Low income	..	34.6	41.8	60.5	62.6
By region					
East Asia and Pacific	20.1	18.6	35.7	58.3	75.3
China	9.3	5.2	24.0	40.4	67.8
India	12.5	8.2	15.0	27.7	30.8
Latin America and Caribbean	25.8	23.4	30.8	35.6	41.2
Sub-Saharan Africa	47.4	44.3	51.0	56.1	59.7
World	24.5	27.1	37.1	42.5	51.0

Source: based on Kaplinsky, 2004: Table 1; World Bank, 2009a: Table 6.1

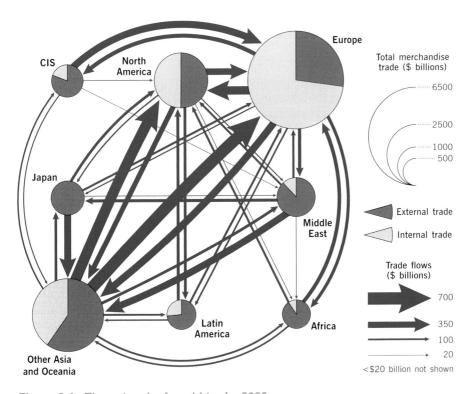

Figure 2.4   The network of world trade, 2008

Source: calculated from WTO, 2009: Table A2

- Europe is the world's major trading region. However, almost three-quarters of that trade is intra-regional, that is between European countries themselves. Around 7 per cent of Europe's exports go to North America and 7 per cent to Asia (including Japan).
- Asia is the second most significant trade region, with a little under one-half of its trade conducted internally. Just under one-fifth of Asia's external trade goes to North America and a further 18 per cent to Europe.
- North America also conducts around 50 per cent of its trade internally, with an especially large increase in trade involving Mexico. Asia and Europe each account for almost 20 per cent of North America's external trade and Latin America for 8 per cent.

FDI has grown faster than trade

One indicator of growing interconnectedness in the global economy, therefore, is the fact that the growth of trade has outpaced the growth of output. A second indicator is that the growth of foreign direct investment (FDI) has outpaced the growth of trade. 'Direct' investment is an investment by one firm in another, with the intention of gaining a degree of control over that firm's operations. 'Foreign' direct investment, therefore, is direct investment across national boundaries to buy a controlling investment in a domestic firm or to set up an affiliate. It differs from 'portfolio' investment, the situation in which firms purchase stocks/shares in other companies purely for financial reasons. Unlike direct investment, portfolio invest-ments are not made to gain control.

Although FDI grew very rapidly during the first half of the twentieth century, this was nothing compared with its spectacular acceleration and spread after the end of the Second World War.[12] Figure 2.5 shows that during the 1970s and into the first half of the 1980s the trend lines of both FDI and exports ran more or less in parallel. Then from 1985 the rate of growth of FDI and of exports diverged rapidly. With some exceptions, FDI grew faster than trade. This divergence in growth trends between FDI and trade is extremely significant. It suggests that the primary mechanism of interconnectedness within the global economy has shifted from trade to FDI. Of course, these trends in the growth of FDI and trade are not independent of one another.

The common element is the transnational corporation (TNC). The number of TNCs has grown exponentially over the past three decades. In 2009, according to UNCTAD, there were around 82,000 parent company TNCs controlling around 810,000 foreign affiliates.[13] TNCs account for around two-thirds of world exports of goods and services, of which a significant share is intra-firm trade. In other words, it is trade within the boundaries of the firm – although across national boundaries – as transactions between different parts of the same firm. The 'ballpark' estimate is that approximately one-third of total world trade is intra-firm, although that is probably an underestimate. One calculation is that

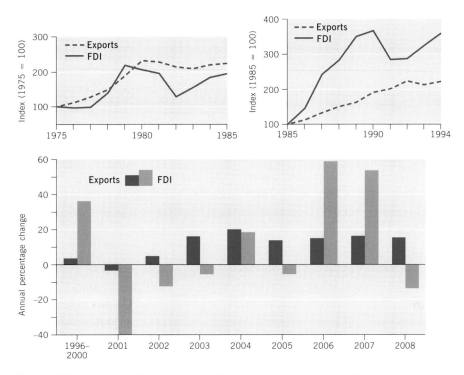

Figure 2.5 Growth of foreign direct investment compared with exports, 1975–2008

Source: calculated from UNCTAD *World Investment Report*, various issues

> 90 per cent of US exports and imports flow through a US [T]NC, with roughly 50 per cent of US trade flows occurring between affiliates of the same [T]NC.[14]

Unlike the kind of trade assumed in international trade theory, intra-firm trade does not take place on an 'arm's-length' basis. It is subject not to external market prices but to the internal decisions of TNCs. Such trade has become especially important as the production networks of TNCs have become more complex and, in particular, as production circuits have become more fragmented. Such 'disintegration of production itself leads to more trade, as intermediate inputs cross borders several times during the manufacturing process'.[15] These are processes we will examine in some detail in Chapter 5.

A further measure of global integration, therefore, is the relative importance of inward and outward FDI to a country's economy, measured by its GDP. Again, we might expect there to be some correlation with country size, although other factors are significant – not least, in the case of inward FDI, differing national policies (see Chapter 6). The relative importance of FDI to national economies has increased virtually across the board, a clear indication of increased inter-connectedness within the global economy. But, as in the case of trade, the relative

Table 2.2   Inward foreign direct investment as a share of gross domestic product, 1990 and 2008 (% share of GDP)

	1990	2008		1990	2008
Japan	0.3	4.1	China	5.8	8.7
Italy	5.4	14.9	Korea	2.1	9.8
Germany	6.6	19.2	India	0.5	9.9
US	6.9	16.0	Taiwan	6.1	11.6
Australia	23.7	27.4	Philippines	7.4	12.7
Canada	19.6	27.5	Indonesia	7.7	13.1
Poland	0.2	30.7	Brazil	8.0	18.3
France	7.1	34.7	Argentina	6.2	23.0
UK	20.6	36.9	Mexico	8.5	27.1
Spain	12.8	39.6	Malaysia	23.4	33.0
Hungary	1.7	41.4	Thailand	9.7	38.4
Denmark	6.9	44.1	Vietnam	25.5	53.6
Czech Republic	3.9	52.7	Chile	33.2	59.6
Sweden	5.3	52.9	Singapore	83.1	179.3
Ireland	88.9	63.7			
Switzerland	15.0	76.1			
Netherlands	23.3	74.0			
Belgium	…	102.9			

Source: based on data in UNCTAD, 2001; 2009

importance of FDI to national economies is highly variable. Table 2.2 shows this for a sample of countries. In virtually all cases, inward FDI has increased greatly in relative importance.

Structural imbalances in the world economy

The flexing and fluxing global economic map is the outcome of the major global shifts that have occurred over the past four decades or so. It is made up of complex interconnections, most notably those constituted through networks of trade and FDI. But such flows have created huge structural imbalances within the global economy. Figures 2.6 to 2.8 show the pattern of trade balances in manufacturing, services and agriculture. The accumulated result of these three sets of trade balances creates a huge dilemma for the global economy: the potential instability created by the fact that some countries have huge trade and current account surpluses whilst others have enormous deficits.

> Countries with trade surpluses accumulated capital beyond their capacity to absorb it. Many ran large current account surpluses and accumulated record reserves. Countries with trade deficits financed their current account by increased borrowing abroad … China's current account surplus rose from 2 per cent of GDP in 2000 to an average of 10 per cent during 2005–07 … The largest deficits were in high-income countries, with the US accounting for

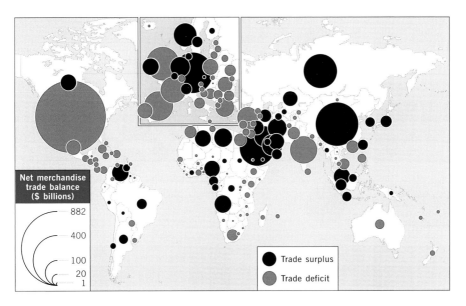

Figure 2.6 The pattern of merchandise trade surpluses and deficits, 2008

Source: calculated from WTO, 2009: Tables A6, A7

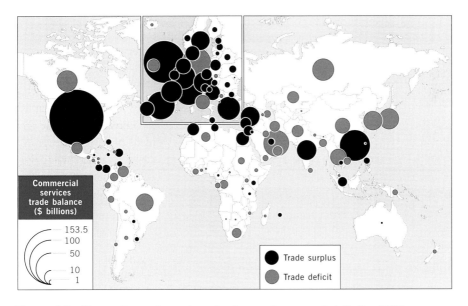

Figure 2.7 The pattern of services trade surpluses and deficits, 2008

Source: calculated from WTO, 2009: Tables A8, A9

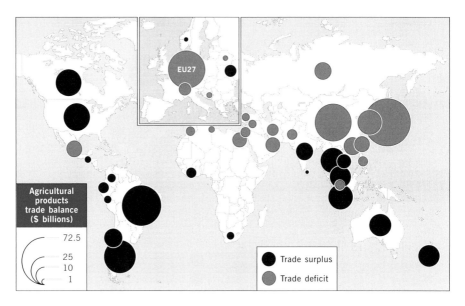

Figure 2.8   The pattern of agricultural trade surpluses and deficits, 2008

Source: calculated from WTO, 2009: Tables II.16, II.17

more than half the world's current account deficits. The US current account deficit increased from 4.3 per cent of GDP in 2000 to an average of 6 per cent in 2005–07 … As the global imbalances between savings and investment grew, countries with large deficits borrowed from countries with surpluses, while fast-growing exporters depended on expanding markets in deficit countries. China and other surplus economies accumulated record reserves … and sent capital overseas. The US and other deficit countries consumed more and financed their deficits by issuing more debt and equity.[16]

The changing contours of the global economic map: global shifts in production, trade and FDI

So far, we have been concerned with broad trends in economic activity, emphasizing the volatility and increasing interconnectedness of the global economy. In this section, we look specifically at the changing configuration of the global economic map itself, focusing on production, trade and FDI. This is illustrated in the series of figures collected together later in this section (pp. 36–43):

- *Shifting geographies of production* in manufacturing, services and agriculture are illustrated in Figures 2.10 to 2.12.
- *Changing patterns of trade* in the same sectors are shown in Figures 2.13 to 2.15.
- *Changing patterns of foreign direct investment* are shown in Figures 2.16 to 2.18.

The figures are largely self-explanatory and do not need individual discussion, although they do merit close attention. In what follows I will simply summarize some of the recent trends, focusing on the major geographical components of the global economy. The scale of analysis is, primarily, the nation-state, simply because this is the only geographical scale for which comprehensive trade, production and direct investment data are collected and published.

Continuing geographical concentration within the global economy: the old and the new

Substantial geographical shifts have undoubtedly occurred in the global economic map in the last few decades. Although the established developed economies continue to dominate, their position has undoubtedly changed. At the broadest level, for example, the developing countries' share of GDP, exports and inward FDI has increased significantly, as Table 2.3 shows. A small number of developing countries, primarily in East Asia, together with the Russian Federation and some of the Eastern European economies, have emerged through rapid growth.

Table 2.3   Developing countries' share of world production, trade and foreign direct investment, 1990 and 2007

	1990	2007
Share of world GDP	18.4	26.0
Share of world exports	19.0	30.3
Share of world inward FDI stocks	20.6	28.7

Source: calculated from World Bank and UNCTAD data

Nevertheless, the geographies of production, trade and FDI remain highly uneven and strongly concentrated. Around three-quarters of global manufacturing and services production, and almost four-fifths of world agricultural production, are concentrated in just 15 countries (Figures 2.10–2.12). Around one-fifth of world trade in goods, services and agriculture is accounted for by the leading two countries in each sector (Figures 2.13–2.15). The picture is similar in the case of FDI. More than 80 per cent of outward FDI stock originates from 15 countries; the leading two source countries – the US and the UK – account for almost 30 per cent of the world total (Figure 2.17). Half of all the inward FDI in developing countries is concentrated in just five host countries; almost 30 per cent is concentrated in China and Hong Kong alone (Figure 2.18).

The newly *industrializing* economies (NIEs), that have become so important in global manufacturing, have their agro-food counterparts: the newly *agriculturalizing* countries (NACs). As in the case of manufacturing, a small number of developing countries account for a disproportionate share of high-value food production and exports (Figure 2.11). For example,

> Brazil is to agriculture what India is to business offshoring and China to manufacturing: a powerhouse whose size and efficiency few competitors can match … the country is the world's largest or second largest exporter of sugar, soybeans, orange juice, coffee, tobacco and beef and is rapidly building a strong position in products such as cotton, chicken and pork. Brazil has the largest agricultural trade surplus in the world.[17]

The BRICs: a new phenomenon – or a chaotic category?

Acronyms are seductive; people are always on the lookout for a catchy label. The term 'BRICs' (Brazil, Russia, India, China) was invented in 2001 by the chief economist of the US investment bank Goldman Sachs, with the claim that these would become the major players in a future world economy. Maybe they will. Certainly they are big and have experienced rapid rates of economic growth in recent years. But apart from this, it is difficult to make a case for seeing them as a coherent grouping (other than in the minds of investment bankers). Their differences far outweigh their similarities.

> Russia and Brazil are big commodity exporters, whereas China is a big commodity importer; China is a proponent of the Doha trade round, India a sceptic; India and China vie for influence in the Indian Ocean, Russia and China compete in Central Asia.[18]

China is substantially more important on every measure shown in Table 2.4. So, these four – potentially very important – countries will be dealt with separately in this chapter in their geographical context, rather than as an artificial grouping.

Table 2.4   The BRICs: some vital statistics

	% world GDP	Av. annual % growth 2000–7	Share of world production			Share of world exports		
			Mfg	Serv.	Agr.	Mfg	Serv.	Agr.
Brazil	2.3	3.3	2.4	2.3	4.8	1.2	0.8	4.6
Russia	2.1	6.6	2.5	2.0	3.9	2.9	1.3	1.9
India	2.2	7.8	1.9	1.6	12.9	1.1	2.7	1.6
China	8.8	10.2	10.4	3.4	21.5	8.9	3.9	3.2
Total	15.4		17.2	9.3	43.1	14.1	8.7	11.3

Source: calculated from World Bank data

The US still dominates the global economy – though less so

The US has been the pre-eminent force in the global economy for almost 100 years, having displaced the original industrial leader, the UK, early in the twentieth century. The US accounts for one-fifth of the world's manufacturing production, 28 per cent of services production, and 8 per cent of agricultural production. It is also the world's biggest foreign direct investor, the largest exporter of commercial services and agricultural products, and the third largest exporter of manufactured goods.

But, although still the world's leading economic power, its dominance has been much reduced as other competitors have emerged. Between 1980–1990 and 1990–2003, US GDP grew at an annual average rate of 3.6 and 3.3 per cent respectively, slightly above the world growth rate of 3.3 and 2.8 per cent. Between 2000 and 2007, its average annual rate of growth was 2.7 per cent, below the world average of 3.2 per cent. The 2008 recession hit the US especially hard: 'the worst downturn in post-war history'.[19] Over the longer run, the deterioration in the US position is most apparent in the trade data, although trade is a smaller proportion of GDP in the US than in all its major competitors, apart from Japan. Nevertheless, the US share of world merchandise exports has fallen from 17 per cent in 1963 to less than 10 per cent. At the same time, its share of merchandise imports has surged from less than 9 per cent to 13 per cent. Although US merchandise exports have grown at around 5 per cent a year, imports have grown at between 8 and 9 per cent a year. As a result, as we have seen, the US has an enormous trade deficit. In effect, it has become the 'importer of last resort' for the global economy. More pointedly, China has become, in effect, America's banker through its huge holdings of US Treasury bonds.

There have been very substantial changes in the US position as a source of, and destination for, FDI. In 1960, the US generated almost 50 per cent of all the world's FDI, compared with less than 20 per cent today. The biggest change, however, has been in the country's position as a host for FDI. Although the US has attracted FDI for many decades, such inward investment was always a tiny fraction of the country's outward FDI. However, the US has become significantly more important as an FDI destination. Inward and outward FDI are now much more equal than in the past.

Europe is still a major player – but its performance is uneven

Europe, as a region, is the world's biggest trading area and the primary focus of global FDI. However, despite being the most politically integrated region in the world (see Chapter 6), the European economy is actually very diverse, experiencing uneven rates of economic growth over the past two decades, as well as uneven rates of decline in the 2008 recession. Between 2000 and 2007, the average annual rate of GDP growth in the core European countries (the EU15) was only 2.3 per cent, significantly lower than the world average of 3.2 per cent and way behind the rates in East Asia and, indeed, in Eastern Europe. In general, prior to 2008, the fastest-growing Western European countries were the more 'peripheral' economies of Finland, Norway, Greece, Ireland and Spain. However, the last three, together with Portugal, were heavily affected by the 2008 recession and experienced severe contraction.

Germany is by far the biggest European economy in global terms: it is the fourth largest manufacturing producer (after the US, China and Japan), the largest manufacturing exporter (just, but to be overtaken by China), the third largest commercial services exporter, and the third most important source of FDI. But its growth in GDP has been below the world average for a long period (only 1.1 per cent between 2000 and 2007), and it still faces difficult problems in integrating the former East Germany into the economy as a whole.

Europe's second biggest economy, the UK, has experienced the greatest long-term relative decline in so far as it once dominated the world. However, it is still the world's second biggest source of FDI and second biggest exporter of commercial services. Indeed, its GDP growth rate has been very close to the world average over the past 20 years, significantly better than either Germany or France, Europe's third largest economy. Between 2000 and 2007, the UK economy grew by 2.6 per cent per year. However, the UK was hit harder by the 2008 recession largely because, like the US, its property bubble burst, and it is also more highly exposed to the collapse in the financial sector than most other European countries.

There are considerable differences in trade performance between individual European countries. Whereas France, the UK, Spain and Italy have merchandise trade deficits, Germany, the Netherlands and Sweden have surpluses. In contrast, in commercial services the UK has a big trade surplus, France and Spain modest surpluses, while Germany has a substantial deficit. Europe remains a major magnet for inward investment as well as the leading source of outward FDI. For all the major European countries (excluding the UK), more than half of their FDI outflows are to other European countries. In most cases, this regional orientation has actually increased.

Emergence of the 'transitional economies' of Eastern Europe and the Russian Federation

On 9 November 1989, the Berlin Wall came down, making possible the reunification of West and East Germany. But this unforeseen event was of much broader significance. It represented both a concrete and a symbolic indicator of enormous geopolitical (and geoeconomic) change. The political collapse of the Soviet-led group of countries, and, indeed, of the Soviet Union itself, produced a group of so-called 'transitional economies': former command economies that transformed themselves into capitalist market economies. The process of transition, from a centrally planned economic system, with a heavy emphasis on basic manufacturing industries, to a capitalist market system, was painful in many cases. The kinds of industries favoured in the centrally planned system were less viable in the context of a highly competitive global economy, as were the kinds of industrial organization themselves. In 1985, for example, the Soviet Union accounted for almost 10 per cent of world manufacturing output; by the mid 1990s, the share of the Russian Federation was around 1 per cent. Despite considerable progress since then, its share in 2008 was only 2.5 per cent. Nevertheless, as we saw earlier in discussing the BRICs, Russia has become an increasingly significant presence in the global economy, especially in terms of its wealth of extractive resources, including oil and gas.

There are big differences within the group of economies, both in terms of their scale and in terms of their potential for growth within a market, as opposed to a centrally planned, system. The four most significant economies are the Russian Federation, Poland, the Czech Republic and Hungary, although their combined share of global GDP is a mere 4 per cent. Together, these four account for most of the manufacturing production and exports. The latter three became members of the European Union in 2005 and this undoubtedly changed their prospects for economic development.

These economies achieved impressive export performances during the 1990s. Poland, Hungary and the Czech Republic each had double-digit export growth while the Russian Federation and Slovenia grew at around 7–8 per cent per year. Much of this growth was underpinned by inward FDI, which grew substantially from the early 1990s, especially in the Czech Republic, Hungary, Poland, Slovakia and the Russian Federation. Between 2000 and 2007, the annual average growth rate of the leading Eastern European countries was 5.2 per cent. Russia grew at an annual rate of 6.6 per cent between 2000 and 2007, on a par with, or even better than, some of the East Asian economies. However, the 2008 crisis created huge problems for these rather fragile economies and a real fear that Eastern Europe could experience the kind of economic collapse that occurred in East Asia in 1997.

'Back to the future' – four tigers, a dragon, and the resurgence of Asia

Without any doubt, the most significant global shift in the geography of the world economy during the past 50 years has been the resurgence of Asia – especially East Asia. As noted earlier, this is, in fact, a real 'back to the future' event, although a complex one that is too often overhyped and oversimplified in the media. Observers in the early 1980s began to write about the twenty-first century being 'the Pacific Century', and of the future belonging to Asia, rather than to the North Atlantic economies, as had been the case for 200 years. But commentators are fickle. The unexpected East Asian financial crisis of 1997 brought out the doom-sayers. More than 10 years on, the position looks more like it did before 1997: the

Asia boosters are out again in force, although now their focus is rather different. The future, it seems, is China – and, possibly, India.

Empirically, the resurgence of Asia can be seen as consisting of four major processes:

- The rise of Japan after the Second World War.
- The rapid growth of what came to be called the 'four tigers': the newly industrializing economies of Hong Kong, Korea, Singapore and Taiwan. This was followed by the emergence of a second tier of East Asian developing economies, primarily Indonesia, Malaysia and Thailand.
- The (re-) emergence of China – the 'dragon' - as a major participant in the global market economy.
- The potential economic dynamism of India.

Japan's rising sun

We have become so obsessed with China that we tend to forget just how spectacular Japan's post-war economic growth really was. It is worth restating because it transformed the global economy and laid the foundations for the subsequent development of other parts of East Asia. In the early 1960s Japan ranked fifth in the world economy; by 1980 it had risen to second place. During the 1960s, Japan's rate of manufacturing growth averaged 13.6 per cent per year: two-and-a-half times greater than the US and four times greater than the UK. The Japanese economy continued to grow at very high rates throughout the 1970s and most of the 1980s. Japan's share of world FDI grew from less than 1 per cent in 1960 to almost 12 per cent in 1990. As a result, 'Japan Inc.' came to be seen as the biggest threat facing both the US and Europe, as a deluge of polemical, protectionist literature (especially in the US) at the time demonstrated.

In the late 1980s, however, Japan's rapid growth rate fell as dramatically as it had increased in the 1960s, with the collapse of the so-called 'bubble economy'. Between 1990 and 2003, Japanese GDP grew at an annual average rate of only 1.2 per cent and its manufacturing sector by a mere 0.7 per cent. Merchandise exports, which had grown at almost 9 per cent a year between 1980 and 1990, grew at less than 3 per cent a year between 1990 and 2003. Growth was even lower between 2000 and 2007 (a mere 1.7 per cent). The US fear of the Japanese threat receded; the 'bash Japan' literature virtually disappeared. Nevertheless, Japan remains the world's second largest economy after the US and Japan's decline has been much exaggerated, even though it faces substantial problems. The 2008 crisis, with its impact on trade, hit Japan hard. Its trade deficit soared in early 2009 to its biggest since 1979.

The four tigers

At the same time as Japan was surging up the ranks of industrialized countries, a small group of East Asian developing countries also appeared on the scene as foci of manufacturing growth, especially in labour-intensive industries. The 'pioneers' were the so-called four 'tiger' economies of Hong Kong, Korea, Singapore and Taiwan. In terms of manufacturing production, for example:

- Korea's manufacturing sector grew at annual average rates of 18 per cent during the 1960s, 16 per cent during the 1970s, 13 per cent during the 1980s, and 7 per cent during the 1990s (to 2003).
- Taiwan's manufacturing sector grew at rates of 16 per cent, 14 per cent, 8 per cent and 6 per cent respectively during the same periods.

Subsequently, Malaysia, Thailand and Indonesia also displayed extremely high rates of manufacturing growth.

The relative importance of these East Asian economies is especially marked in the sphere of exports. Indeed, in the global reorganization of manufacturing production and trade the increased importance of East Asia as an exporter of manufactures is unique in its magnitude. Seven East Asian NIEs (Korea, Hong Kong, Singapore, Taiwan, Indonesia, Malaysia, Thailand) increased their collective share of total world manufactured exports from a mere 1.5 per cent in 1963 to almost 20 per cent in 1999 (and remember that this period includes the East Asian financial crisis of 1997–8, which had a devastating effect on most of the East Asian economies). By 2008, this share had declined to 12 per cent, largely as a result of the growth of China.

So, it is especially in their role as exporters that the East Asian economies are most significant. In some cases the transformation has been nothing short of spectacular. For example, in 1980, less than 20 per cent of Malaysia's exports were of manufactures; by 1998 the figure was 79 per cent. In 1980 a mere 2 per cent of Indonesia's exports were of manufactures; in 1998 almost half was in that category. Others show a similar transformation. But they now face a very different competitive environment. Between 2000 and 2007, these economies grew at an annual average rate of 5.2 per cent – significantly above the world average but far lower than in their 'golden age'.

Rebirth of the dragon

The most recent – and the biggest – development within East Asia is, without question, the (re-) emergence of China. As a consequence, 'China bashing' is replacing the 'Japan bashing' of an earlier period. China has rather suddenly become a hugely significant presence in the global economy.

> The entry of China's massive labour force into the global economy may prove to be the most profound change for 50, and perhaps even for 100 years … China's growth rate is not exceptional compared with previous or current emerging economies in Asia, but China is having a more dramatic effect on the world economy because of two factors: not only does it have a huge, cheap workforce, but its economy is also unusually open to trade. As a result,

> China's development is not just a powerful driver of global growth; its impact on other economies is also far more pervasive ... China's growing influence stretches much deeper than its exports of cheap goods: it is revolutionising the relative prices of labour, capital, goods and assets in a way that has never happened so quickly before.[20]

Between 1980 and 2003, China's growth rate (of GDP as a whole and of manufacturing) was the highest in the world: annual average rates were around 10 per cent. This remarkably high rate continued through to 2007. The 2008 global crisis inevitably had an effect and growth slackened but it was still of the order of 8 per cent and, by 2009, it was even higher. Its average annual rate of growth of merchandise exports was 13 per cent in the 1980s and 14 per cent between 1990 and 2003. Exports as a share of China's GDP increased from 38 per cent in 2002 to 67 per cent in 2007. As a result, China is now the world's second largest manufacturing producer, the largest agricultural producer, the second largest exporter of merchandise (about to be the first) and the world's third largest importer.

Figure 2.9 shows China's global trade networks in manufactures and fuels and mining products. The contrast between the two is striking. In the case of manufactures, exports dominate: China's main markets for its manufactures are other parts of Asia (40 per cent), the EU (21 per cent) and the US (18 per cent). In the case of fuels and mining products, imports dominate: China's main sources for these commodities are the Middle East (24 per cent), other parts of Asia (34 per cent), Africa (16 per cent) and South and Central America (13 per cent).

Overall, then, China's impact on the global economy is manifested in the following ways:[21]

- *Resource-intensive growth.* 'By 2006, China already consumed 32 per cent of the world's steel, 25 per cent of the world's aluminium, 23 per cent of the world's copper, 30 per cent of the world's zinc and 18 per cent of the world's nickel ... China accounted for 31 per cent of the global incremental demand for oil between 2000 and 2006.'
- *Prices of manufactures and commodities.* The initial impact of China's entry into the global economy was to reduce the price of manufactured goods, especially labour-intensive goods which China could produce so cheaply and in such large quantities. On the other hand, its voracious appetite for resources has helped to increase world prices of commodities.
- *Exports of capital.* Not only is China now a massive exporter of goods, it is also an increasingly significant exporter of capital. 'China's current account surplus has exploded upwards in recent years, from ... 3.6 per cent of GDP as recently as 2004, to a recent forecast of ... 11.9 per cent of GDP. This year [2007] its current account surplus will be much the biggest in the world and as big as the surpluses of Germany and Japan together. As a share of GDP, China's surplus is more than double the largest surplus Japan has ever generated ... China's [foreign currency] reserves are now more than $500bn bigger than those of Japan.'

(a) **Manufactures**

(b) **Fuels and mining products**

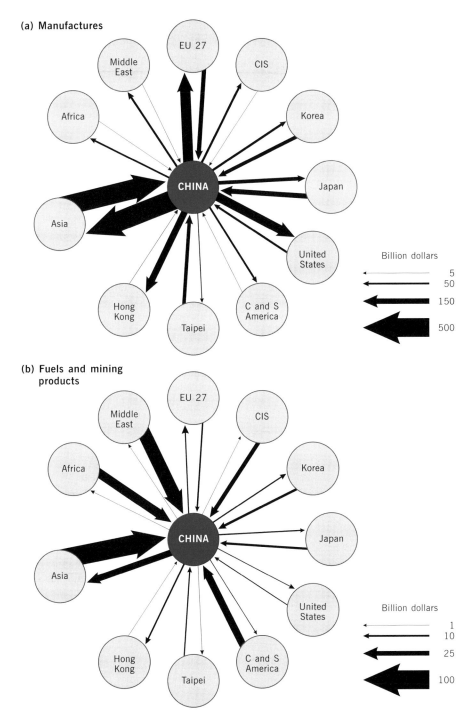

Figure 2.9   China's global trade network, 2008

Source: calculated from WTO, 2009: Table A22

Indian summer?

Although most of the focus remains on China, recently attention has been drawn to the other very large Asian country (in population terms): India. Indeed, some commentators envisage a world economy that will increasingly be dominated by 'Chindia', defined by one writer as 'where the world's workshop meets its office',[22] an allusion to China's growth as a manufacturer and to India's growth in IT services. But beware the hype.

India has recently shown spectacular growth in one specific type of economic activity: the outsourcing of IT services (software, data processing, call centres and the like). As such it has attracted huge publicity and a growing view that India could be 'the next China', given the size of its population and other advantages. That may be so. But, at present, the evidence is slender. India's GDP growth rate between 1980 and 2003, though well above the world average at between 5 and 6 per cent, was half that of China during the same period. Between 2000 and 2007, this difference lessened: India grew at almost 8 per cent per year, compared with China's 10.2 per cent.

India is the world's 14th largest manufacturing economy; China is the fourth largest. India is not in the top 15 merchandise exporters; China is the second largest. Of course, it might be argued that India's strength lies in services rather than in manufacturing. Certainly it is true that the share of services in India's GDP is much higher than China's: 52 per cent compared with 40 per cent. Conversely, India has only 16 per cent of its GDP in manufacturing, compared with China's 32 per cent. Despite this, China generated 40 per cent more commercial services exports than India in 2008. Unlike all the other fast-growing East Asian NIEs, India does not have a strong export base in manufactures. China's merchandise exports are eight times larger than India's. Indeed, if India were ranked along with the nine leading NIEs of East Asia in terms of merchandise exports, it would be next to last, just ahead of Indonesia.

None of this is to suggest that India does not have the *potential* to become a really major economic power but, at present, the evidence is rather thin.

> The rates of change [between China and India] are indeed getting closer, but the level has remained consistently higher for China, implying that in terms of *absolute* levels of achievement, there is little likelihood of India catching up, or overtaking China, except hypothetically in the Keynesian long term, that is when we are all dead. India is projected to have a per capita income in 2050 that is still only 55 per cent that for China, although Indian GDP per capita growth rates are projected to exceed Chinese rates by 2020–25.[23]

Latin America – unfulfilled potential

> The Latin American and Caribbean region is once again facing a crisis of development. In 2005–6, growth rates lagged behind those of emerging economies in Africa, Asia and Eastern Europe and, except in certain pockets, indicators of social and human development were uninspiring and levels of inequality remained the highest in the world.[24]

Latin American countries are among the most resource-rich in the world. Several also have a long history of industrialization. Some, like Brazil and Mexico are, in

population terms, very large indeed. And yet, most of the Latin American economies have not figured very prominently in the redrawing of the global economic
map. Certainly, their modest economic performance contrasts markedly with that
of East Asia, although annual average growth in GDP between 2000 and 2007 in
most Latin American countries was a little above the world average. Within Latin
America itself, there is a clear contrast between relatively faster-growing economies, like Chile and Mexico (until recently), on the one hand, and relatively
slower-growing economies like Argentina and Brazil, on the other. None of these
countries 'punches its weight' as exporters; over the past 20 years, their average
export growth has been significantly lower than that of the East Asian economies.

During the 1990s, the major exception was Mexico (which does not really regard
itself as 'Latin American' anyway). Mexico's export growth rate of over 14 per cent
undoubtedly reflected its increasing integration with the US through the North
American Free Trade Agreement (NAFTA: see Chapter 6). However, Mexico's
recent economic performance has been weak. Its GDP growth between 2000 and
2007 was the lowest among the region's major economies (2.6 per cent, well below
the world average as well). More worrying for the Mexican economy is its failure
to take advantage of its preferential access (including its geographical proximity) to
the US. In particular, Mexico is being out-competed in the US market by China.

> Over half of Mexico's non-oil exports are under partial or direct threat from
> their Chinese counterparts. This 'threat' comprises all but a handful of
> Mexico's top 15 exports. What is more, recent changes indicate that Mexico's
> loss of export competitiveness to China may also be threatening the techno-
> logical sophistication of its exports. Since 1994, Mexico has gained ground on
> China only in primary products … Thus, Mexico is losing out in sectors abun-
> dant in unskilled labor where value-to-transport costs are cheap, but holding
> steady in assembly sectors where transport costs are more significant, and
> NAFTA's rules of origin serve as local content rules mandating that production
> stay in North America, such as lorries and autos.[25]

Today, as we saw earlier, the money is on Brazil, as one of the BRICs. But as Table 2.4
shows, Brazil's GDP growth rate between 2000 and 2007 was by far the lowest of the
four BRICs: half that of Russia, one-third that of China and less than half that of India.
Despite a long history of industrialization, and some undoubted successes (in automobiles, for example: see Chapter 11), Brazil's involvement in the world economy is
mainly in primary commodities (agriculture, mining products). As such, it is highly
vulnerable to the fluctuations in commodity prices (see Chapter 8). When commodity
prices are very high – as they were in the febrile 'gold rush' conditions of the early to
mid 2000s – then all is well. But in 2007, commodity prices collapsed. Like India, Brazil
has enormous economic potential but such potential is far from being realized.

The persistent peripheries

Alongside the areas of strong, though differential, economic growth in the global
economy – the peaks as it were – are those parts of the world whose economic
growth remains very limited. These are the 'persistent peripheries'. All of the maps

shown in Figures 2.10–2.18 tell more or less the same story: most of the continent of Africa, parts of Asia and parts of Latin America constitute the 'troughs' of the global economic map. Sub-Saharan Africa, as is so often noted, is the largest single area of 'economic peripherality'. These are the parts of the world enmeshed in the deepest poverty and deprivation and whose existence poses one of the biggest social challenges of the twenty-first century. We will return to this issue in Part Four.

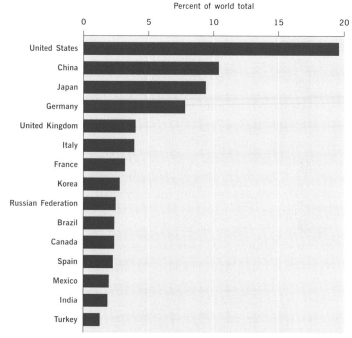

Figure 2.10   The global map of manufacturing production, 2007

Source: calculated from World Bank, 2009a: Table 4.2

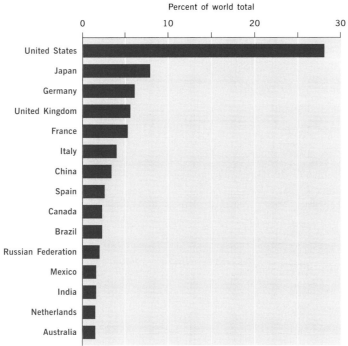

Figure 2.11   The global map of services production, 2007

Source: calculated from World Bank, 2009a: Table 4.2

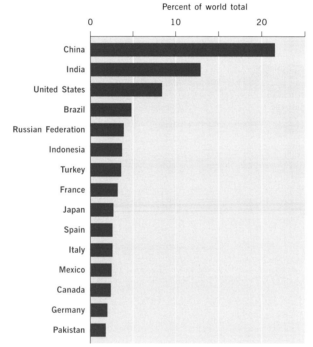

Figure 2.12   The global map of agricultural production, 2007

Source: calculated from World Bank, 2009a: Table 4.2

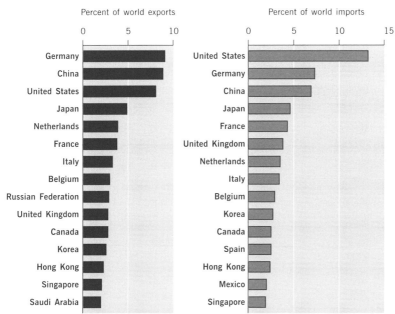

Figure 2.13   The global map of merchandise trade, 2008

Source: calculated from WTO, 2009: Tables A6, A7

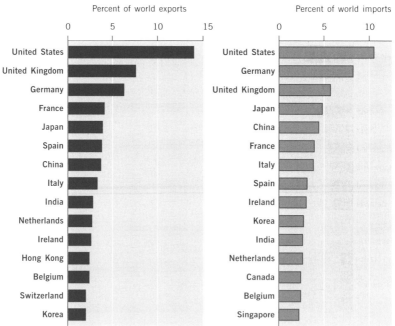

Figure 2.14 The global map of services trade, 2008

Source: calculated from WTO, 2009: Tables A8, A9

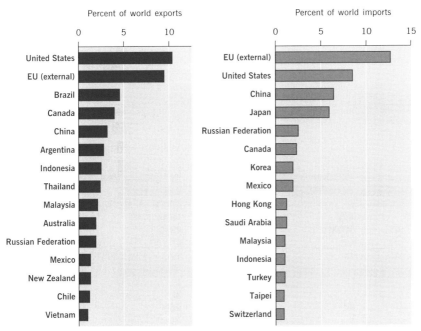

Figure 2.15 The global map of agricultural trade, 2008

Source: calculated from WTO, 2009: Tables II.16, II.17

Figure 2.16   The global map of inward and outward foreign direct investment, 2008

Source: calculated from UNCTAD, 2009: Annex Table B2

Figure 2.17   Changing shares of leading source countries in outward foreign direct investment, 1960–2008

Source: calculated from UNCTAD *World Investment Report*, various issues

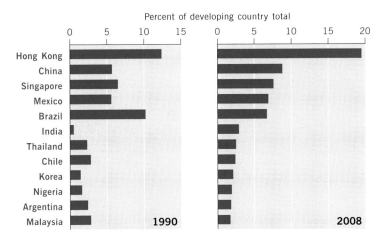

Figure 2.18   Concentration of inward foreign direct investment in
developing countries, 1990–2008

Source: calculated from UNCTAD *World Investment Report*, various issues

The micro-scale: cities as foci of economic activity

If we could observe the earth from a very high altitude we certainly would not
see the kinds of national economic boxes we have had to use as the basis of
our analysis of the global economic map. Particularly if we were making the
observation at night, what we would see are distinctive clusters, picked out by
the lights of localized agglomerations of activity. This is the image used on the
cover of this book. To use a different metaphor, 'the world is spiky'.[26]
Unfortunately, data disaggregated in this way, showing details of production,
trade and investment, are simply not available. We have to resort to surrogate
measures or individual case studies. But it is vital to stress this most fundamental
fact of economic life: the place-specific and clustered nature of most economic
activity (see Chapter 3). The most widely available micro-scale indicator of the
localized clustering of economic activity is the map of the world's cities (Figure
2.19). Virtually all manufacturing and business service activity is located in
urban places.

It is these cities, and their associated local regions, which generate a country's
economic activity, not some national statistical box. Within any individual country,
there is considerable diversity between cities and local regions, not only in terms
of their particular economic specializations but also in terms of their growth rates.
In most cases, this reflects their specific historical trajectory. In others, however,
such differentials may be the outcome of very specific political decisions to
develop one particular part of a country rather than another. In some countries,
just one, or perhaps two, major cities dominate; in other countries there is a 'flatter'
urban hierarchy and a wider spread of activity among more evenly sized cities.

Figure 2.19   The world's major cities by size of population

Source: http://www.citypopulation.de/world/Agglomerations.html

Increasingly, however, it is necessary to think of cities as being involved in networks that transcend national boundaries. In one sense, therefore, 'the city is embedded in a global economy … All cities today are world cities.'[27]

Cities differ in importance not only in terms of their population size (Figure 2.19) but also – and more importantly – in terms of the functions they perform and the influence they exert. In particular, observers of world cities emphasize the role of high-level service functions (financial and business services, corporate control and coordination functions) and their uneven concentration in certain cities, creating a global hierarchical network (see Chapters 5 and 12). But it is extraordinarily difficult to produce a single map of the world city network.[28] One illustrative example is shown in Figure 2.20, based upon Taylor's analysis of business advertisements in *The Economist*. It shows the clear dominance of a relatively small number of cities. Although different criteria would yield a rather different map in detail, the dominant cities in the network recur again and again. The inset table within Figure 2.20 shows the top 10 cities ranked in terms of their global network connectivity.

The meso-scale: transborder clusters and corridors

Cutting across both nationally bounded economic spaces and the highly localized concentrations of economic activity in cities lies a meso-scale of economic-geographic

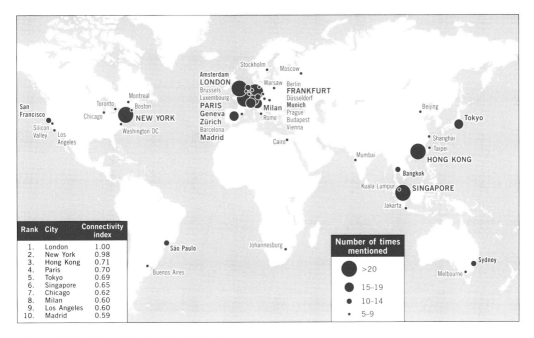

Figure 2.20   Key cities in the global economy

Source: based on Taylor, 2001: Figure 2; Taylor, 2004: Table 3.5

organization, which crosses, or sometimes aligns with, national boundaries. In some cases, this scale of organization is actually defined and created by the existence of the political boundary itself. In others it develops in spite of such boundaries and simply extends across them. Two examples illustrate this particular kind of spatial economic organization.

- *Europe's major economic growth axis.* Within Europe, the pattern of economic activity is extremely uneven, both within and between individual countries. But as Figure 2.21 shows, we can also identify a distinctive 'growth axis' running north-west to south-east across the core area and cutting across national boundaries.

  > The most advanced areas of Europe and most of Europe's major international cities lie on or near an axis extending from the north-west of London through Germany to Northern Italy ... Along this axis lie two major foci: in the north-west are found the historic capitals of Europe's major colonial powers (Paris, London and Randstad-Holland) ... in the south-east are cities and regions whose faster recent economic growth has pulled the axis' centre of gravity to the south-east.[29]

- *The US–Mexico Border Zone.* The second example is one where the form of economic and urban development is actually defined and created by the

Figure 2.21 Europe's major growth axis

Source: based on Dunford, 2007: Figure 1

existence of a border between countries. Where there is a very marked differential between two adjacent countries – for example, in taxation rates or production costs – there is often a strong incentive for development to occur on one side of the border to take advantages of benefits on the other side. One of the best examples of this is the US–Mexico border, the sharpest geographical interface between an extremely wealthy economy and a much poorer developing economy. Far from being just a line on the map, the US–Mexican border is defined in the starkest of physical terms by a whole string of towns and concentrations of manufacturing activity along its entire length (Figure 2.22). These simply would not exist, at least in their present scale and form, were it not for the border and the special legislation that created the *maquiladora*.

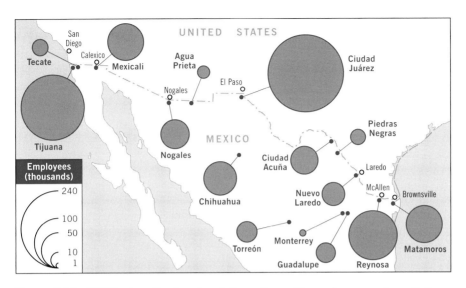

Figure 2.22   US/Mexico: the border defines the pattern of economic activity

Source: calculated from data in Instituto Nacional de Estadística, Geografía e Informática, 2007, *Industria Maquiladora de Exportación*

The dynamic global economic map

Today's global economic map is vastly more complicated than that of only a few decades ago. Although there are clear elements of continuity, dramatic changes have indeed occurred. The overall trajectory of world economic growth has become increasingly volatile: short-lived surges in economic growth are punctuated by periods of downturn or even deep recession.

Within this uneven trajectory there has been major geographical reconfiguration. Although a handful of older core economies still dominates (although less so than in the past), the most important single global shift of recent times has been the emergence of East Asia – including the truly potential giant, China – as the dynamic growth region. This, together with the political events of 1989 in Eastern Europe and the former Soviet Union, represents the most significant influence on the changing geography of the global economy.

However, the fact remains that the actual extent of global shifts in economic activity is rather limited. Only a small number of developing countries have experienced substantial economic growth; a good many are in deep financial difficulty, whilst others are at, or even beyond, the margins of survival. Thus, although we can indeed think in terms of a new global division of labour, its extent is far more limited than is sometimes claimed. A relatively simple global geographical division of labour has been replaced by a far more complex, multiscalar, structure: 'a mosaic of unevenness in a continuous state of flux'.[30]

NOTES

1   Wallerstein (1979).
2   Kozul-Wright (1995: 137).
3   See Bayly (2004), O'Rourke and Williamson (1999)
4   O'Rourke and Williamson (1999: 2).
5   League of Nations (1945).
6   Frank (1998).
7   Paul Ormerod, cited in *The Guardian* (15 December 2008).
8   Webber and Rigby (1996: 6).
9   OECD figures cited in *The Guardian* (1 April 2009).
10 *Financial Times* (26 September 2009).
11 Cited in the *Financial Times* (25 June 2009).
12 Historical trends in FDI are discussed by Dunning and Lundan (2008), Kozul-Wright (1995).
13 UNCTAD (2009: 17).
14 Blonigen (2006: 1).
15 Feenstra (1998: 34).
16 World Bank (2009a: 3).
17 Beattie (2005: 17).
18 *The Economist* (18 June 2009).
19 *Financial Times* (1 March 2009).
20 *The Economist* (20 July 2005).
21 Wolf (2008a).
22 Ramesh (2005).
23 Saith (2008: 748).
24 Phillips (2009: 231).
25 Gallagher et al. (2008: 1376).
26 Florida (2005: 48).
27 King (1983: 7, 15).
28 Taylor (2004) provides a huge variety of mappings of world city networks based on different criteria.
29 Dunford and Kafkalas (1992: 25, 27).
30 Storper and Walker (1984: 37).

PART TWO

PROCESSES OF GLOBAL SHIFT

Three
TANGLED WEBS: UNRAVELLING COMPLEXITY IN THE GLOBAL ECONOMY

An analytical point of entry

In the previous chapter, we explored the changing contours of the global economic map, noting its immense geographical unevenness and temporal volatility. We now turn, in the chapters of Part Two, to the *processes* of globalization; to an explanation of how these global shifts are brought about. But this is far easier said than done. Notwithstanding the hype of much of the globalization literature referred to in Chapter 1, there are, emphatically, no simple explanations of what are extremely complex and interrelated processes. So how do we start? What is a suitable analytical point of entry?

The conventional unit of analysis of the global economy is the individual country. It's not difficult to see why this should be so. Virtually all the statistical data on production, trade, FDI and the like are aggregated into national 'boxes'. Indeed, the word 'statistics' itself originally denoted facts collected about the 'state' ('state-istics'). However, such a level of statistical aggregation is less and less useful in light of the changes occurring in the organization of economic activity. Unfortunately, as in Chapter 2, we have to rely heavily on national-level data to explore the changing maps of production, trade and FDI. But, because national boundaries no longer 'contain' production processes in the way they once did, we need to find ways of getting below the national scale – to break out of the constraints of the 'national boxes' – in order to understand what is really going on in the world.

The clue to how we might proceed lies in the notion of *connectivity*. As we saw in Chapter 1, a diagnostic characteristic of contemporary globalization is that the component parts of the world economy are increasingly interconnected in qualitatively different ways from the past. Another way of saying this is that the world economy consists of *tangled webs of production circuits and networks* that cut through, and across, all geographical scales, including the bounded territory of the state. It is through an analysis of such networks – their participants, their interconnections, their power relationships – that we can begin to understand what is going on.

> The critical point about networks is that they involve relational thinking. What links people together across time and space? How are things and people connected and embedded economically, politically, and culturally? In what ways do goods and information and capital flow and why are they channelled down particular vertices and nodes? ... Thinking in terms of networks forces us to theorize socioeconomic processes as intertwined and mutually constitutive.[1]

Figure 3.1 is based on such a network perspective. We need to bear in mind that it is an *idealized* representation of a world that is, in reality, infinitely more complex. Its purpose is to provide both a structural perspective on globalization processes and outcomes and also a sense of how the key 'actors' behave. In particular, it emphasizes the complex ways in which they are interconnected and governed through highly unequal *power* relationships. Of course, such a simplified diagram attempts the impossible: to capture and represent the multidimensionality of the global economy in just two dimensions. Inevitably, it both grossly oversimplifies, and also distorts, relationships and causalities. In particular, it is difficult not to

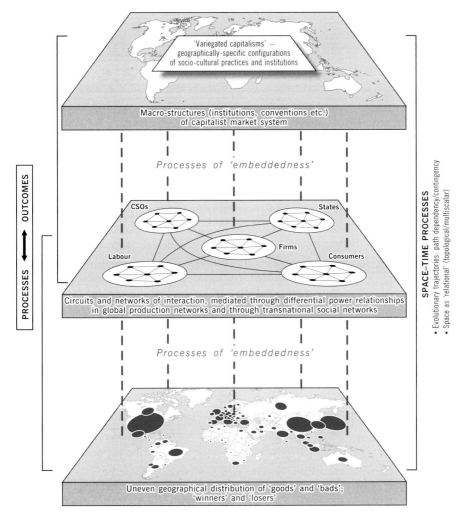

Figure 3.1 A simplified analytical framework of the global economy

Source: based on Dicken, 2004: Figure 2

imply a top–down set of processes whereas, in fact, we are dealing with a world of very complex, dynamically interconnected and simultaneous processes. So, the three layers in Figure 3.1 are not hierarchical, 'top–down' levels but, rather, should be seen as three mutually interconnected 'slices'. Chapter 2 was concerned with the bottom slice: it mapped some of the *outcomes* of globalizing processes. Others will be examined in Parts Three and Four.

We can choose to cut into the highly interconnected system of Figure 3.1 at many different points, according to our specific interest. But that necessitates understanding the relationships between the chosen 'slice' and the others. For example, the networks in the central slice of Figure 3.1 do not exist in isolation. They are simultaneously both deeply embedded in the broader institutional macro-structures of the global economy (the upper slice) and grounded in the prevailing geographical structures of the material world (the lower slice). Both history and geography matter. Previous structures and trajectories exert a powerful influence on present and future patterns and processes. As we saw in Chapter 2, the precise geographical configuration of the global economy at any one point in time constrains (though does not necessarily determine) subsequent developments. It constitutes the context within which subsequent processes operate. The whole process is circuitous and highly path dependent.

In a similar vein, we must think of geographical scale in rather more nuanced ways than the conventional 'global–local' dichotomy allows. Figure 1.2 hinted at this. However, although terms like 'global', 'local', 'national' or 'regional' may be helpful, a network perspective forces us to think of scale as a *continuum*, rather than as a series of discrete 'boxes'. Instead of being thought of solely in *territorial* terms, scale can also be conceived in topological, that is, *relational* terms.[2] Networks, therefore, may be seen as being 'more or less long and more or less connected'.[3] But this sharp distinction between a territorial and a topological view of geographical scale should not be pushed too far. A topological perspective is not, in itself, in conflict with the fact that, in terms of jurisdictional and regulatory practices, territorial scales of governance remain fundamental to the organization and operation of the global political economy and its constituent parts. Bounded political spaces matter. Some, like the nation-state, matter more than others (Chapter 6). In this sense, therefore, we have a very complex situation in which topologically defined networks (for example, of TNCs: see Chapter 5) both 'interrupt' – and are interrupted by – political-territorial boundaries. What matters, however, is to think of territories not simply as 'bounded' spaces but, more importantly, as *interrelated* with a whole variety of other socially constructed scales of activity. Globalizing processes, therefore, can be thought of as an increasing *multiplication of scales* – local, national, regional, global – that overlap and interpenetrate in increasingly complex ways as the *relationships* between such scales change.[4]

Institutional macro-structures of the global economy

In this book, I choose to focus primarily (though not exclusively) on the 'central slice' of Figure 3.1: the *major actors* in the global economy and the webs of *networked relationships* between them. However, adopting such an actor-centred approach runs the risk of underestimating (even ignoring) the broader social, cultural, political and economic macro-structures in which such network processes

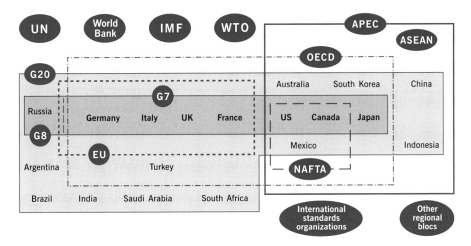

Figure 3.2 Major governance institutions in the global economy

Source: based in part on Cable, 1999: Figure 3.1

operate. There is a real danger of focusing only on atomistic decision-making, rather than understanding such decisions as being 'socially and institutionally situated … enmeshed in wider structures of social, economic, and political rules, procedures and conventions'.[5] Institutions broadly defined, therefore, play a vital role in how network actors behave, whether or not they are aware of this:

> Such institutional influences are subtle but pervasive: indeed, often so subtle that firms and individuals are not even conscious of the impact they exert over their own choices, practices, attitudes, values and expectations.[6]

The macro-structures of the global economy are essentially the institutions, conventions and rules of the capitalist market system. These are not naturally given but socially constructed – in their present form predominantly as a neo-liberal political-economic ideology. Virtually the entire world economy has become a market economy. Figure 3.2 maps the 'thickening web of multilateral agreements, global and regional institutions and regimes, and transgovernmental policy networks and summits'[7] that has developed during the past half-century or so. The International Monetary Fund (IMF), the World Trade Organization (WTO) and the World Bank, together with the various 'G' meetings (such as the G7 and, more recently, the G20) and the many international standard-setting organizations, are the most obvious manifestations of such global institutions, whose activities will be addressed at various points throughout the following chapters.

These global governance institutions are, themselves, only a part of the broader socio-cultural matrix of practices, rules and conventions that shape how the capitalist market economy works. The rules and conventions relate to, for example, private property, profit-making, resource allocation on the basis of market signals, and the consequent commodification of production inputs (including labour). Such institutions and conventions continue to be manifested in *specific configurations* in specific places (notably within national states, but not only at that scale). In other words, they are *territorially embedded*. The geography of capitalism in the global economy, therefore, is highly *variegated*.[8] It is emphatically not the same everywhere, as we shall see.

Global production networks

The production, distribution and consumption of commodities, goods and services are set within this geographically differentiated macro-structural framework and occur through complex webs of production circuits and networks. Although such circuits and networks operate at all geographical scales, we will focus on *global* production networks (GPNs).[9] The term 'global' does not necessarily imply that such networks actually span the entire world; rather, it suggests that they are highly geographically extensive and functionally integrated across national boundaries.

The 'core' of a GPN: transforming 'inputs' into 'outputs'

The core of a GPN is the *circuit* of interconnected functions, operations and transactions through which a specific commodity, good or service is produced, distributed and consumed. (Note that 'services', like any other item of consumption, have to be 'produced'.) Figure 3.3 identifies the major elements of a GPN: the four basic operations, connected by a series of transactions between one element and the next. Inputs are transformed into products that are distributed and consumed. But note that the processes are two-way. It is a *circuit*, rather than a chain, in which

- materials, semi-finished goods and final products flow in one direction
- information (the demands of customers – tastes, preferences etc.) and money (payments for goods and services) flow in the other direction.

But there is much more to it than this, as Figure 3.3 shows. Each individual element in the production circuit depends upon:

- technology inputs
- energy inputs
- service inputs

- logistical (movement) systems
- financial systems
- regulation, coordination and control systems.

(a)

(b)

(c)

➤ Flows of materials and products

⬅ Flows of information (including customer orders)

Figure 3.3   The basic components of a production circuit

The key role of services

Each of the individual elements in a production circuit depends upon many other kinds of input, both those directly related to production and also those related to circulation. In particular, what are often called advanced business services (ABS) have become especially important.

> Service functions are assuming a more pivotal role in the production process. At one level, this is a reflection of a continuing escalation in the complexity of the division of labour ... At another, profitability increasingly depends not just on the manufacturing part of the production process, but on the knowledge aspects and service functions within which products are embedded: R&D, design, brand creation, advertising, finance packages, service package or upgrade packages are now the sources of profitability.[10]

> Service activities not only provide linkages between the segments of production within a [production circuit] and linkages between overlapping [production circuits], but they also bind together the spheres of production and circulation. Services have come to play a critical role ... because they not only provide geographical and transactional connections, but they *integrate* and *coordinate* the atomized and globalized production process.[11]

Chapters 12 and 13 examine these advanced business services in some detail. At this point, however, we need to emphasize the dominant position of *finance* in contemporary economies.

Financialization

Of all the advanced business services, financial systems play *the* central role. The decisions of financiers exert an extraordinarily powerful influence, not only in 'lubricating' production circuits but also in shaping them through their evaluative decisions on what (and where) to invest in order to gain the highest (and sometimes the quickest) return. But there is more to finance than this.

One of the most significant developments of recent years has been the pervasive *financialization* of virtually all aspects of production, distribution and consumption.[12] Financialization can be defined as

> the increasing role of financial motives, financial markets, financial actors and financial institutions in the operation of the domestic and international economies.[13]

Financialization, therefore, consists of much more than just the increased importance of financial services firms. More and more non-financial (e.g. manufacturing) firms are now driven by motives of financialization and this connects closely into the growing incidence of geographically dispersed, tightly integrated GPNs controlled and coordinated by lead firms, primarily TNCs.

> [T]he shareholder value revolution ... beginning in the 1980s shifted power in corporate governance from managers to shareholders ... This resulted in a change in corporate strategy from the ... concern with firm growth, through retaining profits and reinvesting them, to an emphasis on shareholder value and short-run return on investment through downsizing the firm and distributing a greater share of profits back to shareholders ... traditionally non-financial firms became more like financial holding companies, with a spectrum of financial services and financial investments swamping production in terms of their contribution to company revenues.
>
> Largely coincidental with financialization in the 1980s was a growing tendency by firms to break up the process of producing goods and services and locate different parts in different locations depending on costs, markets, logistics or politics ...
>
> Financialization has encouraged a restructuring of production ... And the rising ability of firms to disintegrate production vertically and internationally has allowed these firms to maintain cost mark-ups – and thus profits and shareholder value – even in a context of slower economic growth ... global production strategies have helped to sustain financialization.[14]

In other words, financialization is an all-pervasive system of values based on the overriding prioritization of an equity culture, in which 'shareholder value' and profitability have become central to *all* aspects of economic activity to the virtual exclusion of all other interests. It is a free-market ideology in which regulation of financial markets is regarded with suspicion because it is seen to reduce market efficiency. It is the market that is regarded as the most appropriate allocator of resources. The 2008 global financial crisis made nonsense of this claim. But what kind of future system will (or should) emerge is still unclear; this is an issue we will address in the final chapter.

GPNs as arenas of contested relationships

Individual production circuits are, themselves, enmeshed in broader *production networks* of inter- and intra-firm relationships. Such networks are, in reality, extremely complex structures with intricate links – horizontal, vertical, diagonal – forming multidimensional, multilayered lattices of economic activity. They vary considerably both within, and between, different economic sectors, as we shall see in the case study chapters of Part Three.

In particular, GPNs are not simply technical-economic mechanisms through which the production, distribution and consumption of commodities, goods and services occur. They are

> simultaneously economic and political phenomena ... organizational fields in which actors struggle over the construction of economic relationships, governance structures, institutional rules and norms and discursive frames ... GPNs thus exist within the 'transnational space' that is constituted and structured by transnational elites, institutions, ideologies.[15]

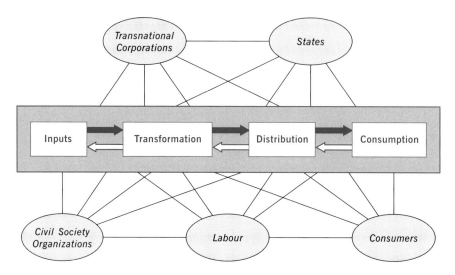

Figure 3.4   Major actor-centred networks in the global economy

In fact, it is primarily the actions of, and the interactions between, the five actor-centred networks shown in Figure 3.4 – transnational corporations, states, labour, consumers, civil society organizations – that shape the changing geographical configuration of the global economy through their differential involvement in production circuits and networks. Let us look briefly at each of these five actors. Much more will be said about each of them in subsequent chapters.

Transnational corporations

In capitalist market economies, production networks are coordinated and regulated primarily by *business firms*, through the multifarious forms of intra- and inter-organizational relationships that constitute an economic system. As Figure 3.5 shows, economies are made up of many different types of business organization – transnational and domestic, large and small, public and private – in varying combinations and interrelationships. The firms in each of the segments shown in Figure 3.5 operate over widely varying geographical ranges and perform rather different roles in the economic system.

A major theme of this book, however, is that it is the *transnational corporation* (TNC) that plays the key role in coordinating *global* production networks and, therefore, in shaping the geoeconomy.

> **Transnational corporations (TNCs) are firms that have the power to coordinate and control operations in more than one country, even if they do not own them.**

In fact, TNCs generally do own such assets but they are also, as we will see in Chapter 5, typically involved in intricate and multiple spiders' webs of collaborative relationships with other legally independent firms across the globe.

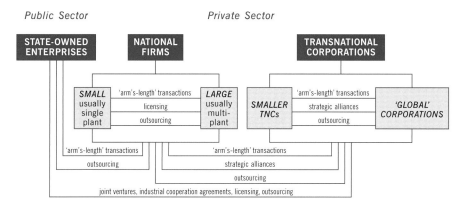

Public Sector *Private Sector*

Figure 3.5 Types of firms in an economy

The significance of the TNC lies in three basic characteristics:

- its ability to coordinate and control various processes and transactions within transnational production networks, both within and between different countries
- its potential ability to take advantage of geographical differences in the distribution of factors of production (for example, natural resources, capital, labour) and in state policies (for example, taxes, trade barriers, subsidies)
- its potential geographical flexibility – an ability to switch and to reswitch its resources and operations between locations at an international, or even a global, scale.

Hence, much of the changing geography of the global economy is shaped by the TNC through its decisions to invest, or not to invest, in particular geographical locations. It is shaped, too, by the resulting flows – of materials, components, finished products, technological and organizational expertise, finance – between its geographically dispersed operations. Although the relative importance of TNCs varies considerably – from sector to sector, from country to country, and between different parts of the same country – there are now very few parts of the world in which TNC influence, whether direct or indirect, is not important. In some cases, indeed, TNC influence on an area's economic fortunes can be overwhelming.

The nature of the coordination process within a TNC's production network depends, in part, on where the firm draws the boundary between those functions it *internalizes* (i.e. performs 'in-house') and those it *externalizes* (i.e. outsources to other firms). Theoretically, at one extreme, the whole TNC production network may be internalized within the firm as a *vertically integrated* system crossing national boundaries. In this case, the links consist of a series of *internalized transactions*, organized 'hierarchically' through the firm's internal organizational structure. At the other extreme, each function may be performed by separate firms. In this case, the links consist of a series of *externalized transactions*, organized either through 'the market' or in collaboration with other firms in a kind of 'virtual' network.

This dichotomy – between externalized, market-governed transactions and internalized, hierarchically governed transactions – grossly simplifies the richness and diversity of the governance mechanisms in the contemporary economy. In fact, there is a *spectrum* of different forms of coordination, consisting of networks of interrelationships within and between firms. Such networks increasingly consist of a mix of intra-firm and inter-firm structures. These networks are dynamic and in a continuous state of flux; the boundary between internalization and externalization is continually shifting. They are also affected by the shifting *power relationships* between firms within a GPN. In some cases, one dominant actor calls all the shots; in other cases, power may be more widely dispersed with a greater degree of collaboration involved.

Territorial embeddedness of production networks: states as regulators in GPNs

Capital, it is often argued, has become 'hyper-mobile', freed from the 'tyranny of distance' and no longer tied to 'place'. In other words, economic activity is becoming 'deterritorialized' or 'disembedded'. The sociologist Manuel Castells argues that the forces of globalization, especially those driven by the new information technologies, are replacing this 'space of places' with a 'space of flows'.[16] Anything can be located anywhere and, if that does not work out, can be moved somewhere else with ease. But such seductive ideas are highly misleading. The world is *both* a 'space of places' *and* a 'space of flows'. GPNs don't just float freely in a spaceless/placeless world. Although transportation and communications technologies have, indeed, been revolutionized (see Chapter 4), both geographical distance and, especially, place are fundamental.

Every component in a GPN – every firm, every economic function – is, quite literally, 'grounded' in specific locations. Such grounding is both physical (in the form of the built environment) and also less tangible (in the form of localized social relationships and in distinctive institutions and cultural practices). Hence, the precise nature and articulation of firm-centred production networks are deeply influenced by the concrete socio-political, institutional and cultural contexts within which they are embedded, produced and reproduced.[17]

The *national state* continues to be the most important bounded territorial form in which production networks are embedded (Chapter 6). *All* the elements in a GPN are regulated within some kind of political structure, whose basic unit is the national state, but which also includes such supranational institutions as the IMF and the WTO, regional economic groupings such as the EU or the NAFTA, and 'local' states at the subnational scale. The international institutions themselves exist only because they are sanctioned by national states; subnational institutions are commonly subservient to the national level, although the situation is more complex in federal political systems. As we shall see, the number of national states has grown markedly in the past 20 years.

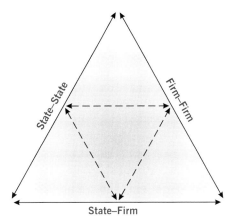

Figure 3.6 The triangular nexus of relationships between firms and states

Source: based on Stopford and Strange, 1991: Figure 1.6

All *global* production networks, by definition, have to operate within *multiscalar* regulatory systems. They are, therefore, subject to a multiplicity of geographically variable political, social and cultural influences. On the one hand, TNCs attempt to take advantage of national differences in regulatory regimes whilst, on the other hand, states attempt to minimize such 'regulatory arbitrage'. The result is a very complex situation in which firms and states are engaged in various kinds of power play (Chapter 7): a triangular nexus of interactions comprising firm–firm, state–state, and firm–state relationships (Figure 3.6).[18] In other words, the geoeconomy is essentially being structured and restructured not by the actions of either firms or states alone but by complex, dynamic interactions between the two sets of institutions.

Of course, TNCs and states are not the only actors involved in the operation of GPNs. As Figure 3.1 suggests, TNCs and states are continuously engaged in relationships with other major actors – labour, consumers, civil society organizations – some of which also have strong territorial bases.

Labour

In most economic analyses, labour tends to be treated as a commodity – as a mere 'factor of production'. But such a dehumanized view overlooks the many and varied ways in which labour (whether organized in labour unions or acting as individuals) influences how production networks operate.[19] Indeed, labour is absolutely *central* to production networks because it embodies the knowledge and skills necessary for production to be carried out. *All* production of goods and services needs labour, either directly in the form of workers, or indirectly in the labour that is embodied in machinery and equipment. However, there are significant asymmetries in the relative power of labour and capital and these asymmetries have profound implications for how global production networks operate.

One of the most fundamental differences between labour and, especially, transnational capital (in the form of TNCs) is that, on balance, labour is more *place-bound* and generally far less geographically mobile than capital. Of course, the strength of labour's tie to place varies a great deal between different types of labour. On average, male workers are more mobile than female workers; skilled workers are more mobile than unskilled workers; professional white-collar workers are more mobile than blue-collar workers. Clearly, there are exceptions to such generalizations, as shown by the substantial waves of labour migration at different periods of history. Such flows do not, however, contradict the basic point that labour is strongly differentiated spatially and deeply embedded in local communities in distinctive ways. As Harvey has observed, 'unlike other commodities, labour power has to go home every night'.[20]

This spatial asymmetry between capital and labour, though not the only issue, is fundamental in the context of *global* production networks. The dispersed nature of TNC operations and the tendency towards remoteness in corporate decision-making have made it very difficult for labour unions (which tend to be nationally based) to organize effectively to counter such issues as plant closure or retrenchment. In order to counteract the geographically extensive operations of TNCs, therefore, labour has to find ways of organizing across national boundaries. Although there have been some successful international labour union initiatives, their impact has been relatively limited.[21] Indeed, the proportion of the labour force organized into labour unions has been falling for a long time. For example, in the US, the unionization rate fell from 20 per cent of the labour force in 1983 to 12 per cent in 2006; in the EU, there was a reduction in union membership of 15 per cent between 1993 and 2003. At the same time, the effective global labour supply quadrupled between 1980 and 2005 as countries like China, in particular, became more integrated into the global economy.

Consumers

Production networks involve more than just 'production'; they are driven, ultimately, by the necessity, the willingness and the ability of customers to acquire and consume the products themselves, and to continue doing so (see Figure 3.3). Each of the case study chapters of Part Three shows how the nature of consumption varies according to the specific sector involved. Here, we need simply to emphasize some basic aspects of consumption processes.

First, we need to distinguish between the consumption of 'producer' goods or services (sometimes called intermediate products because they are purchased by firms within a production circuit for further transformation) and 'consumer' goods ('final demand' goods: those purchased by individuals and households). In fact, the boundary between these two types of consumption is often blurred. Second, consumption is very much more than merely the economic process of 'demand'. Obviously, it is greatly influenced by levels of income. But it is also a complex set of *social and cultural* processes, in which all kinds of personal motivations are involved. People buy (or aspire to buy) particular goods for a bewildering variety of reasons, ranging from the satisfaction of basic *needs* to ensure survival (food, shelter, clothing) through to ever more sophisticated *wants* (discretionary goods, such as fashionable clothing, particular kinds of car, exotic or organic foods, and the like).

Consumption, therefore, may be driven by the desire to acquire particular kinds of products (even specific varieties or brands) either because they are regarded as desirable in themselves or because they send out social messages signifying the particular lifestyles, attitudes, social positions or self-evaluations of the consumer. 'Positional' goods have become increasingly important. However, they lose their value as more and more people have access to them. New positional goods have to be sought.[22]

> 'The material object being sold is never enough' ... Commodities meet both the functional and symbolic needs of consumers. Even commodities providing for the most mundane necessities of daily life must be imbued with symbolic qualities and culturally endowed meanings.[23]

It is, of course, precisely these *symbolic* qualities of consumption that the advertising, retailing and media industries attempt to manipulate. How far consumption is, or can be, manipulated in such ways is open to question. Some argue that consumption (and consumers) is becoming increasingly more important in the global economy than production (and producers). In Miller's view, the consumer has become the 'global dictator' and he describes consumption as the 'vanguard of history'.[24]

The bewildering proliferation of choice within many product areas is a direct reflection of producers' perceived need to meet the increasingly fragmented demands of consumers. The days when Henry Ford could dictate to his potential customers by telling them that they could have any colour Model T, as long as it was black, are long gone. Of course, in many cases the variety on offer is more apparent than real (heavily advertised 'newness' often being little more than superficial modification). But, in some cases, there is no doubt that consumer demands directly drive production circuits. It is also clear that the emergence of the Internet (Chapter 4) is transforming the abilities of consumers to make informed choices:

> Consumers select what they want from a far greater variety of sources – especially with a few clicks of a computer mouse. Thanks to the internet, the consumer is finally seizing power ... consumer power has profound implications for companies, because it is changing the way the world shops ... Today, window-shopping takes place online. People can compare products, prices and reputations.[25]

Hence, the idea that consumers are becoming more alike, that local tastes and preferences are being replaced by global consumer brands, needs to be treated with caution. The 'globalization of markets' identified by Levitt some 25 years ago is not as clear as he claimed.[26] Other than in a superficial sense, Levitt has been proved wrong. Consumer diversity is the norm almost everywhere. Although there are some, mostly generation-related, mass markets, geographical variation in consumption patterns persists. Indeed, the experiences of many leading consumer-product TNCs, especially American, show that failure to be sensitive to local variations in tastes and preferences can be almost fatal.

Global civil society organizations

In so far as both labour and consumers are often (though not always) relatively powerless compared with the TNCs that dominate GPNs, they need to *organize* to be effective. The problem is that such organization needs to be *transnational* to operate on the same playing field as TNCs. Within the past 25 years, as Figures 3.7 and 3.8 show, there has been phenomenal growth in the number and diversity of global civil society organizations (GCSOs), ranging from the pre-1970 'old' social movements through the 'new' social movements of the 1970s/1980s, the NGOs and the transnational civic networks of the late 1980s and 1990s, the 'new'

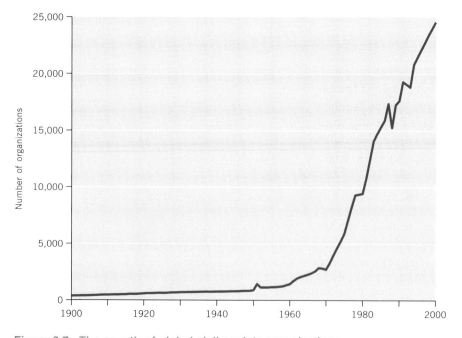

Figure 3.7 The growth of global civil society organizations

Source: based on Glasius et al., 2002: Figure 8.1

	'Old' social movements pre-1970	'New' social movements c. 1970s and 1980s	NGOs, think-tanks, commissions c. late 1980s and 1990s	Transnational civic networks c. late 1980s and 1990s	'New' nationalist and fundamentalist movements 1990s	'New' anti-capitalist movement c. late 1990s and 2000s
Issues	Redistribution, employment and welfare; self-determination and anti-colonialism	Human rights; peace; women; environment; third world solidarity	Human rights; development and poverty reduction; humanitarianism; conflict resolution	Women; dams; land mines; international criminal court; global climate change	Identity politics	Solidarity with victims of globalization; abolition or reform of global institutions
Forms of organization	Vertical, hierarchical	Loose, horizontal coalitions	Ranges from bureaucratic and corporate to small-scale and informal	Networks of NGOs, social movements and grass roots groups	Vertical and horizontal, charismatic leadership	Networks of NGOs, social movements and grass roots groups
Forms of action	Petition, demonstration, strike, lobbying	Use of media, direct action	Service provision; advocacy; expert knowledge; use of media	Parallel summits; use of media; use of local and expert knowledge; advocacy	Media, mass rallies, violence	Parallel summits; direct action; use of media; mobilization through Internet
Relation to power	Capturing state power	Changing state/society relations	Influencing civil society, the state and international institutions	Pressure on states and international institutions	Capturing state power	Confrontation with states, international institutions and transnational corporations

Figure 3.8 The diversity of global civil society organizations

Source: based on Kaldor, 2003: Table 4.1

nationalist movements of the 1990s, and the 'new' anti-capitalist movements of the late 1990s and 2000s.

They include the long-established NGO pressure groups such as Oxfam, Greenpeace and Friends of the Earth; more recent ones like Jubilee 2000; organized labour unions like the AFL-CIO or the TUC; labour support organizations like Women Working Worldwide or the Maquila Solidarity Network; organizations focused primarily on TNCs and big corporations (like Corporate Watch or Global Exchange); right-wing nationalist/populist groups (exemplified by such figures as Pat Buchanan in the US or Jean-Marie Le Pen's extreme right party in France); anti-capitalist groups (like ATTAC or the Socialist Workers Party); and various anarchist groups. Widespread awareness of such groups dates primarily from the street protests at the Seattle WTO meeting in December 1999. Since then, similar protests (both peaceful and violent) have occurred at virtually every international meeting of government leaders and of bodies such as the IMF, the WTO, the World Bank, the G8 and, more recently, the Copenhagen global environmental summit.

Although the influence of GCSOs varies enormously, there is no doubt that, as important actors in the global system, they have to be taken into account in any analysis of global production networks. In some GPNs, as we shall see in the case studies in Part Three and in Chapter 17, they are particularly prominent and have a significant influence on corporate behaviour.

The unevenness of power relations within GPNs

As we observed earlier, GPNs are contested fields. Each of the actors and institutions involved has their own agendas. The extent to which these can be realized depends on the relative power configuration in specific situations. Significant variables in determining relative power are, first, control over key assets (such as capital, technology, knowledge, labour skills, natural resources, consumer markets) and, second, the spatial and territorial range and flexibility of each of the actors. The two are not unconnected. Ability to control access to specific assets is a major bargaining strength. Where such assets are available virtually everywhere, then the power gradient is shallow or even non-existent. But where assets are 'localized', whether geographically, organizationally or even personally, then the power gradient may be very steep. However, actors able to tap into localized assets across geographical space have a significant advantage over those without such spatial flexibility. Power relationships within GPNs are highly *asymmetrical*.

But there is a further dimension. Each of the major actors in GPNs is involved in *both* cooperation and collaboration on the one hand *and* conflict and competition on the other. Such apparently paradoxical behaviour warns us against assuming that relationships between certain actors are always of one kind: for example, that those between TNCs, or between TNCs and states, or between TNCs and labour, or between TNCs and CSOs, are always conflictual or competitive. Or, conversely, that relationships between groups of workers or labour organizations are always cooperative (in the name of class solidarity). Not so. These various actor networks are imbued with an ever-changing mixture of both conflict and collaboration. Thus, although power relationships within GPNs are asymmetrical, they are not fixed.

So, for example, TNCs in the same industry are fierce competitors but also, invariably, enmeshed in a complex web of collaborative relationships (see Chapter 5). States compete in cut-throat fashion with other states to entice internationally mobile investment by TNCs (see Chapter 7) or to find ways to keep out certain types of imports whilst, at the same time, increasingly engaging in preferential trading arrangements, including bilateral and multilateral agreements, often within broader regional groupings (see Chapter 6). Labour unions in one country engage in competition with labour unions in other countries in the scramble for new jobs or to protect existing jobs whilst, at the same time, unions strive to create international alliances with unions in other countries, especially those involved in the geographically dispersed operations of major TNCs. They also increasingly attempt to negotiate international framework agreements with TNCs to protect workers' rights. CSOs, likewise, are not immune from these conflicting actions. In the context of the anti-globalization protests, for example, CSOs have developed collaborations across national boundaries but, at the same time, the goals and values of individual CSOs are not always compatible, to say the least.

Even in a globalizing world, economic activities are geographically localized

The view of the 'hyper-globalizers' (see Chapter 1) is that increasing *geographical dispersal* at a global scale is now the norm. But, as we saw in Chapter 2, as soon as we break free of the national statistical boxes in which most economic data are packaged, *geographical concentrations* of economic activity not only still exist but are, indeed, the normal state of affairs. Such concentrations occur at different geographical scales, though the most prominent is, of course, the city. One of the most striking features of the global economic map, therefore, is the degree to which cities and localized clusters at smaller geographical scales dominate. Why do such 'sticky places' continue to exist in 'slippery space'? [27]

The bases of geographical clusters

Figure 3.9 identifies two types of geographical cluster: *generalized* and *specialized*. Both are based on the notion of *externalities*, the positive 'spillovers' created when activities in a particular place are connected with one another, either directly (through specific transactions) or indirectly. Both are based on the idea that the 'whole' (the cluster) is greater than the sum of the parts because of the benefits that spatial proximity provides.

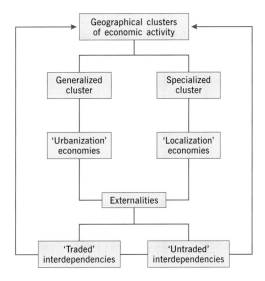

Figure 3.9   The bases of geographical clusters

- *Generalized clusters* simply reflect the fact that human activities tend to agglomerate to form urban areas. Hence, such benefits have traditionally been labelled *urbanization economies*. General clustering of activities creates the basis for sharing the costs of a whole range of services. Larger aggregate demand in, say, a large city encourages the emergence and growth of a variety of infrastructural, economic, social and cultural facilities that cannot be provided where their customers are geographically dispersed. The larger the city, quite obviously, the greater the variety of available facilities and vice versa.
- *Specialized clusters*, on the other hand, reflect the tendency for firms in the same, or closely related, industries to locate in the same places to form what are sometimes termed 'industrial districts' or 'industrial spaces'. Such benefits have been called *localization economies*. The bases of specialized clusters arise from the geographical proximity of firms performing different – but *linked* – functions in particular production networks.

Clusters generate two types of interdependency:

- *Traded interdependencies* are direct transactions between firms in the cluster (e.g. the supply of specialized inputs of intermediate products and services). In such circumstances, spatial proximity is a means of reducing transaction costs either through minimizing transportation costs or by reducing some of the uncertainties of customer–supplier relationships.
- *Untraded interdependencies* are the less tangible benefits, ranging from the development of an appropriate pool of labour, to particular kinds of institutions (such as universities, business associations, government institutions and the like) to broader socio-cultural phenomena. In particular, geographical agglomeration or clustering facilitates three important processes: face-to-face contact; social and cultural interaction; and enhancement of knowledge and innovation.

Above all, it is the potential for *face-to-face contact* that is the single most important 'glue' in the localized clustering of activities. We will see this, especially, in Chapter 4 in the context of innovation and technology, and in Chapter 12 in the context of advanced business services, including finance. But it underlies the geographical concentration of *all* human activities. It is a key element of the human condition.

Why do clusters develop in the first place?

But why do clusters form in the first place? Why do they arise in one place rather than another? And how do they develop over time? These are difficult questions to answer. The reasons for the origins of specific geographical clusters are highly contingent and often shrouded in the mists of history.

> Within broad limits the power of attraction today of a center has its origin mainly in the historical accident that something once started there, and not in a number of other places where it could equally well or better have started, and that the start met with success.[28]

Once established, a cluster tends to grow through a process of *cumulative, self-reinforcing development* involving:

* attraction of linked activities
* stimulation of entrepreneurship and innovation
* deepening and widening of the local labour market
* economic diversification
* enrichment of the 'industrial atmosphere'
* 'thickening' of local institutions
* intensification of the socio-cultural milieu
* enhanced physical infrastructures.

The cumulative nature of these processes of localized economic development suggests that the process is *path dependent*. In other words, an economy becomes 'locked into' a pattern that is strongly influenced by its particular history. This may be either a source of continued strength or, if it embodies too much organizational or technological rigidity, a source of weakness. However, even for 'successful' clusters, such path dependency does not imply the absolute inevitability of continued success. Rigidity of local practices may reduce the capacity to adapt to external changes. Cities rise and fall – and some rise again if a new virtuous circle of development can be initiated. Decline, like growth, can become locked in.

Networks of networks

We can think of the global economy as the linking together of two sets of networks:

* the *organizational* (in the form of production circuits and networks)
* the *geographical* (in the form of localized clusters of economic activity).

The major advantage of adopting such a grounded network approach to understanding the global economy is that it helps us to appreciate the interconnectedness of economic activities across different geographical scales and within and across territorially bounded spaces. The production of any commodity, whether it is a manufactured product or a service, involves an intricate articulation of individual activities and transactions across space and time. Such production networks – the nexus of interconnected functions and operations through which goods and services are produced and distributed – have become both organizationally and geographically more complex.

Global production networks not only integrate firms (and parts of firms) into structures which blur traditional organizational boundaries (for example, through the development of diverse forms of equity and non-equity relationships) but also integrate national and local economies (or parts of such economies) in ways which have enormous implications for their economic development and well-being. At the same time, the specific characteristics of national and local economies influence and 'refract' the operation and form of larger-scale processes. In that sense, 'geography matters' a lot.

The process is especially complex because, while states and local economies are essentially territorially specific, production networks themselves are not.[29] Production networks 'slice through' boundaries in highly differentiated ways, influenced in part by regulatory and non-regulatory barriers and in part by local socio-cultural conditions, to create structures that are 'discontinuously territorial'. This has major implications for the relative bargaining powers of the actors involved, including labour, consumers and CSOs. The geoeconomy, therefore, can be pictured as a geographically uneven, highly complex and dynamic web of production networks, economic spaces and places connected together through threads of flows.

Figure 3.10 captures the major dimensions of these relationships. Individual production networks can be regarded as vertically organized structures configured

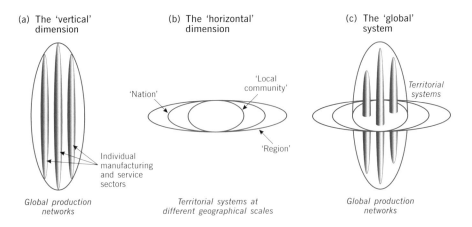

Figure 3.10   Interconnecting dimensions in a globalizing economy

Source: based in part on Humbert, 1994: Figure 1

across increasingly extensive geographical scales. Cutting across these vertical structures are the territorially defined political-economic systems which, again, are manifested at different geographical scales. It is at the points of intersection of these dimensions in 'real' geographical space where specific outcomes occur, where the problems of existing within a globalizing economy – whether as a business firm, a government, a local community or an individual – have to be resolved.

NOTES

1   Mitchell (2000: 392).
2   Amin (2002).
3   Latour quoted in Thrift (1996: 5).
4   See Swyngedouw (2000).
5   Martin (2000: 79). See also Berndt and Boeckler (2009), Lee (2006; 2009).
6   Gertler (2003: 93).
7   Held and McGrew (2007: 137).
8   Peck and Theodore (2007).
9   The GPN concept is explored in detail in a theme issue of *Journal of Economic Geography* (vol. 8, 2008). See, in particular, Coe et al. (2008a), Henderson et al. (2002). The GPN perspective is closely related to, but broader than, that of global commodity chains (GCCs), initially pioneered by Gary Gereffi (1994; 2005), and global value chains (GVCs), developed by Gereffi et al. (2005). See also Neilson and Pritchard (2009).
10   Daniels and Bryson (2002: 978).
11   Rabach and Kim (1994: 123).
12   Dore (2008), Epstein (2005), Lee et al. (2009), Milberg (2008).
13   Epstein (2005: 3).
14   Milberg (2008: 423, 424, 445).
15   Levy (2008: 948).
16   Castells (1996).
17   Granovetter (1985) pioneered the concept of 'embeddedness' within the field of economic sociology. It has become a ubiquitous (though contested) term since then. See Hess (2004) for a recent discussion of the concept in a spatial/territorial context. Neilson and Pritchard (2009) stress the need to reinsert place and institutions in these analyses.
18   Stopford and Strange (1991).
19   See, for example, Castree et al. (2004), Cumbers et al. (2008), Herod (2001), Hudson (2001), Jones (2008), Peck (1996).
20   Cited in Peck (2000: 141).
21   Some examples are provided by Cumbers et al. (2008), Herod (2001), Wills (1998; 2002).
22   Hirsch (1977).

23   Hudson (2005: 65).

24   Miller (1995: 1).

25   *The Economist* (2 April 2005: 9).

26   Levitt (1983).

27   Markusen (1996). 'Clustering' has become a hot topic in policy debates in virtually all parts of the world (Martin and Sunley, 2003; Porter 1990; 1998; 2000). However, the concept itself, as opposed to its policy connotations, has a very long history. See, for example, Amin and Thrift (1992), Bathelt et al. (2004), Dicken and Lloyd (1990), Krugman (1998), Malmberg (1999), Scott (1998; 2008), Storper (1995; 1997), Storper and Venables (2004).

28   Myrdal (1958: 26).

29   Dicken and Malmberg (2001).

Four

TECHNOLOGICAL CHANGE: 'GALES OF CREATIVE DESTRUCTION'

Technology and economic transformation

> The fundamental impulse that sets and keeps the capitalist engine in motion comes from the new consumers' goods, the new methods of production or transportation, the new markets, the new forces of industrial organization that capitalist enterprise creates.[1]

In writing these words, Joseph Schumpeter set technological change, specifically *innovation* – the creation and diffusion of new ways of doing things – at the very heart of the processes of economic growth and development.[2] Technological change is, without any doubt, 'a fundamental force in shaping the patterns of transformation of the economy'.[3] Self-evidently, therefore, it is one of the most important processes underlying the globalization of economic activity. However, we must not see technology as being deterministic: as 'causing' a specific set of changes, making particular structures and arrangements 'inevitable', or creating a linear and predictable path of technological change. Innovation is an 'unruly phenomenon'.[4] Two important points need to be made.

First, technology does not have a life of its own.

> Specific choices within the frontier of technological possibilities are not the product of technological change; they are, rather, the product of those who make the choices within the frontier of possibilities. Technology does not drive choice; choice drives technology.[5]

Technological change, therefore, is a *socially and institutionally embedded process*. The ways in which technologies are used – even their very creation – are conditioned by their social and their economic context. In the contemporary world this means primarily the values and motivations of capitalist business enterprises, operating within an intensely competitive system. Choices and uses of technologies are influenced by the drive for profit, capital accumulation and investment, increased market share, and so on.

Second, technology should be seen as, essentially, an *enabling* or a *facilitating* agent. It makes possible new structures, new organizational and geographical arrangements of economic activities, new products and new processes, while not making particular outcomes inevitable. It is emphatically not deterministic. On the other hand, in a highly competitive environment, once a particular technology is in use by one firm, then its adoption by others may become virtually essential to ensure competitive survival.

In this chapter we focus primarily on those aspects of technological change that specifically influence the globalization of economic activity.

Processes of technological change: an evolutionary perspective

Technological change is a form of *learning* – by observing, by doing, by using – of how to solve specific problems in a highly differentiated and volatile environment.

However, it is much more than a narrowly 'technical' process. It is also about much more than just 'the new'; older technologies persist and often remain useful.[6] Technological change not only involves the invention of new things, or new ways of doing things, but also – more importantly – depends upon the transformation of inventions into usable *innovations*, and the subsequent adoption and diffusion or spread of such innovations. In the economic sphere, this is essentially an *entrepreneurial* process.[7]

Types of technological change

There are four broad types of technological change,[8] each of which is progressively more significant and far-reaching in its impact:

- *Incremental innovations*: small-scale, progressive modifications of existing products and processes, created through 'learning by doing' and 'learning by using'. Although individually small – and, therefore, often unnoticed – they accumulate, often over a very long period of time, to create highly significant changes.
- *Radical innovations*: discontinuous events that drastically change existing products or processes. A single radical innovation will not, on its own, have a widespread effect on the economic system; what is needed is a 'cluster' of such innovations.
- *Changes of technology system*: extensive changes in technology that impact upon several existing parts of the economy, as well as creating entirely new sectors. These are based on a combination of radical and incremental technological innovations, along with appropriate organizational innovations. Changes of technology system tend to be associated with the emergence of key generic technologies (for example, information technology, biotechnology, materials technology, energy technology, space technology, nanotechnology).
- *Changes in the techno-economic paradigm*: truly large-scale revolutionary changes, embodied in new technology systems. These

> have such pervasive effects on the economy as a whole that they change the 'style' of production and management throughout the system. The introduction of electric power or steam power or the electronic computer are examples of such deep-going transformations. A change of this kind carries with it many clusters of radical and incremental innovations, and may eventually embody several new technology systems. Not only does this fourth type of technological change lead to the emergence of a new range of products, services, systems and industries in its own right – it also affects directly or indirectly almost every other branch of the economy ... the changes involved go beyond specific product or process technologies and affect the input cost structure and conditions of production and distribution throughout the system.[9]

Long waves

The notion that economic growth occurs in a series of cycles or 'waves' goes back almost 100 years. One particular type of wave – usually known as a Kondratiev wave (K-wave) – is a long wave of more or less 50 years' duration.[10] In Figure 4.1, four complete K-waves are identified; we are now in the early stages of a fifth. Each wave may be divided into four phases: prosperity, recession, depression and recovery. Each wave tends to be associated with particularly significant techno-logical changes around which other innovations – in production, distribution and organization – swarm or cluster and ultimately spread through the economy.

   Although such diffusion of technology stimulates economic growth and employment, demographic, social, industrial, financial and demand conditions also have to be appropriate. In other words, it's the 'total package' that counts. At some point, however, growth slackens: demand may become saturated or firms' profits become squeezed through intensified competition. As a result, the level of new investment falls, firms strive to rationalize and restructure their operations and unemployment rises. Eventually the trough of the wave will be reached and eco-nomic activity will turn up again. A new sequence will be initiated on the basis of key technologies – some of which may be based on innovations that emerged during recession itself – and of new investment opportunities. Although there is disagreement over the precise mechanisms and timing involved, each of the waves is generally associated with changes in the techno-economic paradigm, as one set of techno-economic practices is displaced by a new set. This is not a sudden pro-cess but one that occurs gradually and involves the ultimate 'crystallization' of a new paradigm.

   As Figure 4.1 shows, the process of change involves more than just technical change. Each phase is also associated with characteristic forms of economic orga-nization, cooperation and competition. Organizational change has followed a path from an early focus on individual entrepreneurs in K1, through small firms (but of larger average size) in K2, to the monopolistic, oligopolistic and cartel structures of K3, the centralized, hierarchical TNCs of K4 and, it is argued, the 'network' and alliance organizational forms of K5. (These are issues we will explore in Chapter 5.) Each successive K-wave also has a *specific geography* as technological leadership shifts over time, both in terms of lead nations (as the bottom row of Figure 4.1 makes clear) and also at the micro-geographical scale. In effect, 'the locus of the leading-edge innovative industries has switched from region to region, from city to city',[11] a clear reflection of the clustering processes introduced in Chapter 3.

Information and communications technologies (ICTs): entering a digital world

The fifth Kondratiev cycle is associated primarily with *information and communica-tions technologies* (ICTs) and, especially, with *digital* technologies.

For the first time in history, information generation, processing and transmission have become the main commodities and sources of productivity and power and not only a means of achieving better ways of doing things in the production process. New information technologies are not simply tools to be applied but processes to be developed.[12]

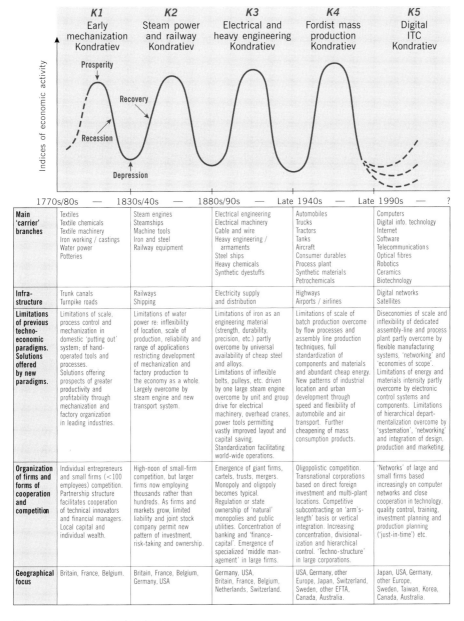

	K1 Early mechanization Kondratiev	**K2** Steam power and railway Kondratiev	**K3** Electrical and heavy engineering Kondratiev	**K4** Fordist mass production Kondratiev	**K5** Digital ITC Kondratiev
	1770s/80s —	1830s/40s —	1880s/90s —	Late 1940s —	Late 1990s — ?
Main 'carrier' branches	Textiles Textile chemicals Textile machinery Iron working / castings Water power Potteries	Steam engines Steamships Machine tools Iron and steel Railway equipment	Electrical engineering Electrical machinery Cable and wire Heavy engineering / armaments Steel ships Heavy chemicals Synthetic dyestuffs	Automobiles Trucks Tractors Tanks Aircraft Consumer durables Process plant Synthetic materials Petrochemicals	Computers Digital info. technology Internet Software Telecommunications Optical fibres Robotics Ceramics Biotechnology
Infrastructure	Trunk canals Turnpike roads	Railways Shipping	Electricity supply and distribution	Highways Airports / airlines	Digital networks Satellites
Limitations of previous techno-economic paradigms. Solutions offered by new paradigms.	Limitations of scale, process control and mechanization in domestic 'putting out' system; of hand-operated tools and processes. Solutions offering prospects of greater productivity and profitability through mechanization and factory organization in leading industries.	Limitations of water power re: inflexibility of location, scale of production, reliability and range of applications restricting development of mechanization and factory production to the economy as a whole. Largely overcome by steam engine and new transport system.	Limitations of iron as an engineering material (strength, durability, precision, etc.) partly overcome by universal availability of cheap steel and alloys. Limitations of inflexible belts, pulleys, etc. driven by one large steam engine overcome by unit and group drive for electrical machinery, overhead cranes, power tools permitting vastly improved layout and capital saving. Standardization facilitating world-wide operations.	Limitations of scale of batch production overcome by flow processes and assembly line production techniques, full standardization of components and materials and abundant cheap energy. New patterns of industrial location and urban development through speed and flexibility of automobile and air transport. Further cheapening of mass consumption products.	Diseconomies of scale and inflexibility of dedicated assembly-line and process plant partly overcome by flexible manufacturing systems, 'networking' and 'economies of scope'. Limitations of energy and materials intensity partly overcome by electronic control systems and components. Limitations of hierarchical depart-mentalization overcome by 'systemation', 'networking' and integration of design, production and marketing.
Organization of firms and forms of cooperation and competition	Individual entrepreneurs and small firms (<100 employees) competition. Partnership structure facilitates cooperation of technical innovators and financial managers. Local capital and individual wealth.	High-noon of small-firm competition, but larger firms now employing thousands rather than hundreds. As firms and markets grow, limited liability and joint stock company permit new pattern of investment, risk-taking and ownership.	Emergence of giant firms, cartels, trusts, mergers. Monopoly and oligopoly becomes typical. Regulation or state ownership of 'natural' monopolies and public utilities. Concentration of banking and 'finance-capital'. Emergence of specialized 'middle man-agement' in large firms.	Oligopolistic competition. Transnational corporations based on direct foreign investment and multi-plant locations. Competitive subcontracting on 'arm's-length' basis or vertical integration. Increasing concentration, divisional-ization and hierarchical control. 'Techno-structure' in large corporations.	'Networks' of large and small firms based increasingly on computer networks and close cooperation in technology, quality control, training, investment planning and production planning ('just-in-time') etc.
Geographical focus	Britain, France, Belgium.	Britain, France, Belgium, Germany, USA	Germany, USA, Britain, France, Belgium, Netherlands, Switzerland.	USA, Germany, other Europe, Japan, Switzerland, Sweden, other EFTA, Canada, Australia.	Japan, USA, Germany, other Europe, Sweden, Taiwan, Korea, Canada, Australia.

Figure 4.1 Kondratiev long waves

Source: based in part on Freeman and Perez, 1988: Table 3.1

Information technologies, in themselves, are nothing new.[13] But the current generation of information technologies has one very special characteristic, as Figure 4.2 shows. It is based upon the *convergence* of two initially distinct technologies: *communications technologies* (concerned with the transmission of information) and *computer technologies* (concerned with the processing of information). Both are now based on digital, rather than analogue, technologies. Digitization is, without doubt, the most pervasive and influential technological development of recent years. All kinds of information can now be stored in numerical (binary) form as electronic 'digits'. This means they can then be processed, manipulated and stored by computers and transmitted anywhere in the world almost instantly. In particular, the remarkable, and very recent, growth of the Internet and of mobile telephony, together with big changes in the electronic mass media, are generating major global effects at all levels, including individuals, households, local communities, nation-states and, of course, business organizations, especially transnational corporations.

As the power and sophistication of computer technology have increased, and as it has become increasingly widely available through networked systems, it is

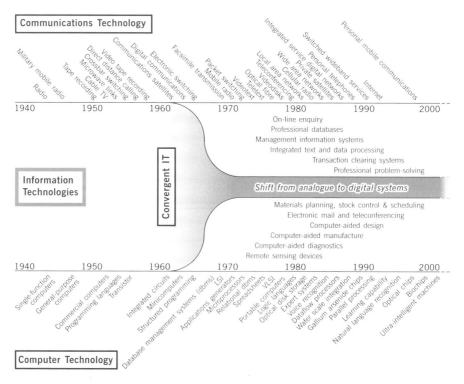

Figure 4.2   Information technologies: the convergence of communications technologies and computer technologies

Source: based on Freeman, 1987: Figure 2

taking on the characteristics of a utility. Computing is becoming analogous to the electricity generating industry of the nineteenth century.[14] Just as businesses abandoned their own individual electricity generators to take advantage of the new electric grid system so, increasingly, today they are beginning to move away from individual computer systems to networked systems provided through the Internet. An example of such new computers-as-utility systems is Google's global network of 'server farms'.

> Designed to house tens of thousands of PCs, all wired together to work as a single supercomputer [these are] ... the information-processing equivalent of a nuclear power station, able to pump data and software into millions of homes and businesses ... No corporate computing system, not even those operated by big companies, can match the efficiency, speed and flexibility of plants such as Google's. One analyst estimates that Google can carry out a computing task for one-tenth of what it costs a typical company ... Cheap and plentiful electricity shaped the world we live in today ... The transformation in the supply of computing promises to have equally sweeping consequences.[15]

This development is sometimes called 'cloud computing': clusters of servers 'in the sky', as it were.

Time–space shrinking technologies

As Figure 3.3 shows, *processes of circulation* are fundamental to the operation of production circuits and networks: indeed, to the operation of society as a whole. Circulation technologies – transportation and communications technologies – overcome the frictions of space and time.[16] Although these cannot be regarded as the cause of globalization, without them, today's complex global economic system simply could not exist. Transportation and communications technologies perform two distinct, though closely related and complementary, roles.

- *Transportation systems* are the means by which materials, products and other tangible entities (including people) are transferred from place to place.
- *Communications systems* are the means by which information is transmitted from place to place in the form of ideas, instructions, images and so on.

For most of human history, transportation and communications were effectively one and the same. Prior to the invention of electric technology in the nineteenth century, information could move only at the same speed, and over the same distance, as the prevailing transportation system allowed. Electric technology broke that link, making it increasingly necessary to treat transportation and communication as distinct, though intimately related, technologies. Such developments have transformed societies in all kinds of ways. From a specifically economic and business perspective, two points are especially important.

> [First] technologies of communications and transport shape and reshape systems of market access across *and* within geographical space ... [Second] communications revolutions are, in effect *control* revolutions. They change the environment of profit opportunities by providing firms with different and more intensified types of control over space and time in economic activity. Such control in turn enables firms to create new routes to efficiency in the form of more innovative routines. As firms discover these routes to more efficient routines, they are compelled to assume new and different capabilities in order to capture the profit ... from doing things differently. In recasting business practices and assuming new capabilities, the innovative firm reorganizes the structure of its enterprise and in the process reshapes the territory in which it assumes control over newly crafted routines.[17]

Through their influence on how – and where – business organizations are able to operate, therefore, these technologies have helped progressively to transform the economic-geographical landscape, at increasing geographical scales and over shorter periods of time. Figure 4.3 summarizes this process. We will focus on how such transformations in firms' activities and their geographies are actually being worked out later in this chapter and in Chapter 5. Before that, we need to identify some of the major innovations in transportation and communications, which have been so important in helping to transform the economic landscape.

Accelerating geographical mobility: innovations in transportation technologies

A shrinking world

In terms of the time it takes to get from one part of the world to another there is no doubt that the world has 'shrunk' dramatically (Figure 4.4). Throughout most of human history, the speed and efficiency of transportation were staggeringly low and the costs of overcoming the friction of distance prohibitively high. Movement over land was especially slow and difficult before the development of the railways. Indeed, even as late as the early nineteenth century, the means of transportation were not really very different from those prevailing 2000 years ago.

The major breakthrough came with two closely associated innovations: steam power as a means of propulsion and the use of iron and steel for trains, railway tracks and ocean-going vessels. These, coupled with the linking together of over-land and oceanic transportation (for example, with the cutting of the canals at Suez and Panama), greatly telescoped geographical distance at a global scale. The railway and the steamship introduced a new, and much enlarged, scale of human activity. The decline in global transportation cost was truly amazing.[18] For example,

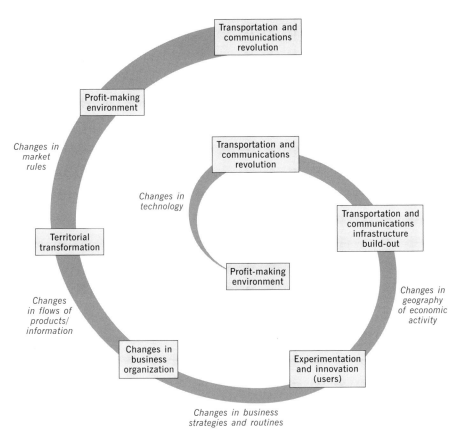

Figure 4.3 Transportation/communications revolutions and economic transformation

Source: based on Fields, 2004: Figure 2.1

the trade costs for grain, the main internationally traded good, fell by 40 per cent between 1880 and 1914 within Europe and between the US and Europe.[19]

Flows of materials and products were enormously enhanced and the possibilities for geographical specialization greatly stimulated. Such innovations were a major factor in the massive expansion in the global economic system during the nineteenth century.

The past few decades have seen an acceleration of this process of global shrinkage. For example, transportation costs fell 'from an average of 8 per cent of total import costs in 1970 to about 3 per cent in 2002'.[20] Two developments have been particularly important, both of them appearing for the first time during the 1950s.

1960s

Jet passenger aircraft, 500–600 m.p.h.

1940s

Propeller aircraft, 200–300 m.p.h.

1850–1930

Steam locomotives averaged 65 m.p.h.
Steam ships averaged 36 m.p.h.

1500–1840

Best average speed of horse-drawn coaches and sailing ships was 10 m.p.h.

Figure 4.4   Global shrinkage: the effects of transportation innovations on 'real' distance

Source: based on McHale, 1969: Figure 1

Take-off: the introduction of jet aircraft

One was the introduction of *commercial jet aircraft*. This had two major effects. First, it enabled unprecedentedly rapid individual travel over vast distances, allowing face-to-face meetings at times and in places hitherto unrealistic. For TNCs, in particular, jet transport made possible the coordination and control of geographically dispersed operations. Direct control at a distance became a reality. It is no coincidence that the take-off of TNC growth and the (more literal) take-off of commercial jets both occurred during the 1950s. One estimate is that '320 million people meet annually at professional and corporate events after travelling by air'.[21]

The second significant effect of jet transport was in the movement of certain kinds of freight. Most heavy and bulky freight moves by sea but, for certain kinds of good and certain kinds of activity, air transport is crucial.

> Between 1950 and 2004, air freight prices fell from $3.87 per ton-kilometer to less than $0.30, in 2000 US dollars … Of the world's $12 trillion of merchandise trade, 35 per cent by value was shipped by air in 2006 … [for example] air transport fills an important niche in just-in-time production systems. While shipments by sea are routine, firms use air cargo to fine-tune intermediate input flows and to ship goods with high value-to-weight ratios … [air transport] also enabl[es] exports of perishable goods over long distances.[22]

Moving in bulk: containerization

The other major development was the introduction of *containerization* for the movement of heavy and bulky ocean and land freight, an innovation that vastly simplified transhipment of freight from one mode of transportation to another, increased the security of shipments, and greatly reduced the cost and time involved in moving freight over long distances.[23] The first container ship, launched in 1956 to move goods from Newark, New Jersey to Houston, Texas, through the Gulf of Mexico, was merely a conventional oil tanker strengthened to take 58 boxes each 9 metres long. Today, around 90 per cent of all non-bulk cargo is moved in containers.

> Container shipping certainly is the great hidden wonder of the world, a vastly underrated business … It has shrunk the planet and brought about a revolution because the cost of shipping boxes is so cheap. People talk about the contribution made by the likes of Microsoft. But container shipping has got to be among the 10 most influential industries over the past 30 years … Before container shipping, seaborne trade was slow and unreliable. In the early Sixties, unloading a ship at, say, Liverpool docks could take weeks, even months. And during that time a substantial proportion of the goods could fall prey to thieves, or the weather. Today, the goods are protected in a container, during passage and in port. With cranes specially built to lift the containers, a ship can be in and out of a port in 10 hours, saving thousands in port charges and speeding trade.[24]

However, the very success of containerization, in a world in which trade has grown very rapidly, especially on certain routes like those from China to North America and to Europe, has created immense problems, especially in port bottlenecks. In 2004, a new generation of container ships, more than 300 metres long, more than 40 metres wide, and capable of carrying 8000 containers each 6 metres long, entered service, with even larger ones expected in the near future.[25] Relatively few ports have the capacity to take such huge vessels and this will, inevitably, enhance their dominance over smaller ports. In any case, there are already massive problems of delays at most major world ports because of the sheer volume of freight traffic and the physical and human problems of handling it quickly. However, the shrinkage of world trade created by the 2008 financial crisis has, at least for now, created huge over-capacity in the container shipping industry.

The unevenness of time–space convergence

Although the world has indeed shrunk in relative terms, we need to be aware that such shrinkage has been, and continues to be, highly uneven. This is contrary to the impression given by Figure 4.4. In fact, technological developments in transportation have a very strong tendency to be geographically concentrated. The big investments needed to build transportation infrastructures tend to go where demand is greatest and financial returns are highest. Consequently, *time–space convergence* affects some places more than others. While the world's leading national economies and the world's major cities are being pulled closer together in relative time or cost terms, others – less industrialized countries or smaller towns and rural areas – are, in effect, being left behind. The time–space surface is highly plastic; some parts shrink whilst other parts become, in effect, extended. By no means everywhere benefits from technological innovations in transportation.

'Everywhere is at the same place': innovations in communications technologies

> We know that telecommunication tends to push the meaning of space towards zero, nevertheless, the earth still has simultaneous night and day, and depending on one's location an inconsiderate phone call can still get people out of bed.[26]

Both the time and the relative cost of transporting materials, products and people have fallen dramatically as the result of technological innovations in the transportation media. However, such developments would have been impossible without parallel developments in communications technologies – *the* key technologies transforming relationships at the global scale.

> The new telecommunications technologies are the electronic highways of the informational age, equivalent to the role played by railway systems in the process of industrialization.[27]

As Figure 4.2 shows, global communications systems have been transformed radically during the past 20 or 30 years through a whole cluster of significant innovations in information technologies. In terms of communications infrastructure – the transmission channels through which information flows – two innovations have been especially significant: satellite communications and optical fibre technologies.

Transmission channels: satellites and optical fibre cables

Satellite technology began to revolutionize global communications from the mid 1960s when the Early Bird or Intelsat I satellite was launched.[28] This was capable of carrying 240 telephone conversations or two television channels simultaneously. Since then, the carrying capacity of communications satellites has grown exponentially. Satellite technology made possible remarkable levels of global communication of both conventional messages and the transmission of data. A message could be transmitted in one location and received in another on the other side of the world almost simultaneously. Today, there are more than 100 geostationary satellites in orbit.

> Satellites appear in a variety of sizes and capacities. Large satellites, capable of handling international traffic, sit 35,700 km (22,300 miles) high in geostationary orbits ... A broad-beam geostationary satellite can transmit to (i.e. leave a 'footprint' over) roughly 40 per cent of the earth's surface, so that only three or four are sufficient to provide global coverage. Because the cost of satellite transmission is not related to distance, the technology is commercially competitive in rural or low density areas (e.g. remote islands), where high marginal costs dissuade other types of providers such as fibre optics.[29]

However, for most parts of the world, satellite communications have been increasingly challenged by *optical fibre* technology carried within submarine cables.

> Satellites were ideal for broadcasting ... as well as providing a larger number of telephone circuits than the combined capacity of all submarine cables. The life of satellites, however, is much shorter than that of cables and the number of 'parking spots' available in geosynchronous orbit is limited ... Satellites also forced a shift from analogue to digital transmission and digital signals are optimally carried by fibre-optic cables, which appeared in the 1980s, making both old telephone cables and even most satellites themselves obsolete.[30]

The first commercially viable optical fibre system was developed in the US in the early 1970s. Since then, the speed, carrying capacity and cost of optical fibre transmission cables have changed dramatically. Optical fibre systems have a huge carrying capacity, and transmit information at very high speed and, most importantly, with a high signal strength. By the end of the 1990s, for example,

> a single pair of optical fibres, each the thickness of a human hair ... [could] carry North America's entire long-distance communications traffic. Gemini, a transatlantic undersea cable ... completed ... [in 1998] ha[d] more capacity than all existing transatlantic cables combined.[31]

Since then, technological developments in optical fibres have continued to accelerate, vastly increasing the speed and capacity of communications networks. At the same time, the geographical spread of optical fibre systems has increased.

Only 35 countries were connected by submarine cables in 1979, with a total bandwidth of 321.4 megabits per second – less than that connecting a mid-size US city today. The most connected country, the USA, accounted for 19.6% of total world bandwidth ... By 1989, the first fibre-optic cables were being installed within Europe ... During the 1990s, 209 new submarine cables were installed, tripling the world total in 1989. The new cables provided cable links to a total of 92 countries and increased total submarine bandwidth 100-fold ... Cables installed during the 1990s focused on the North Atlantic market ... The newest cables, installed between 2000 and 2005, linked 28 countries previously unconnected by cable ... Perhaps the most important shift is the most recent one: despite a 'fibre glut' in developed countries ... new cables have continued to be installed in Asia and the Middle East.[32]

Figure 4.5 shows the enormous increase in the carrying capacity of submarine oceanic cable systems created by developments in optical fibre technologies.

As a consequence, more than 90 per cent of all international telecommunications is now transmitted using optical fibre cables. Figure 4.6 maps the world's submarine cable system. The system continues to expand as a response to rapidly increasing demands, especially from the growth of Internet traffic. In particular, video and data

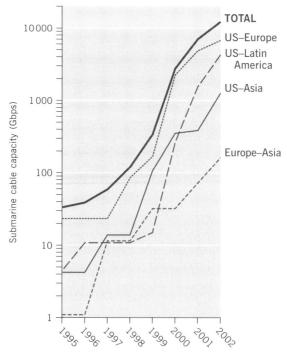

Figure 4.5 **The growth in the information carrying capacity of submarine cable systems**

Source: based on material in the *Financial Times*, 15 November 2000

Figure 4.6   The world's submarine cable system

Source: based on material in *The Guardian*, 1 February 2008: 18 August 2008

Cable capacity
(gigabytes/second)

> 500

50–500

10–50

Estimated international
bandwidth usage
by country
(gigabytes/second)

> 1000

200–999

50–199

1–49

< 1

transmissions require much higher bandwidth than speech. There is also a need to build in extra capacity to cope with cable failure (as happened in mid 2008 when three submarine cables serving the Middle East and South Asia were damaged).

The Internet: the 'skeleton of cyberspace'

> The Internet has revolutionized the way the world communicates. In less than a decade … it [was] transformed from a relatively obscure computer network into a global system of hundreds of millions of networked computers (hosts) and tens of millions of formal sites for interaction and commerce (domains).[33]

The phenomenally rapid spread of the Internet has been one of the most remarkable developments of recent decades.[34] Its origins go back to the early 1970s and are to be found within the US Department of Defense. It spread initially through the linking of more specialized academic computer networks and, for some time, it seemed that it would remain a niche technology. Not so. As Figure 4.7 shows, the growth of the Internet has been dramatic. Most important of all have been the development of the World Wide Web (invented by Tim Berners-Lee in the mid 1990s) and the rapid increase in access to broadband and wireless transmission.

Internet communication has replaced (in whole or in part) a huge swathe of conventional communications methods. A large proportion of business communication (both within and between firms) is now through the Internet. Similarly for

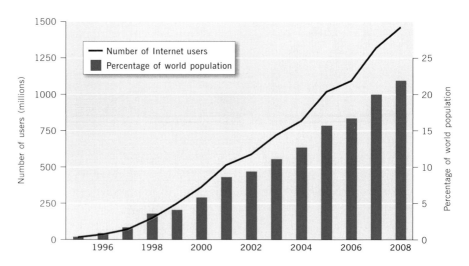

Figure 4.7 Exponential growth of the Internet, 1995–2008

Source: based on material in www.worldinternetstats.com

millions of individuals, e-mail has become the preferred means of communication. At the same time, the Internet gives access to a phenomenal amount of information on virtually everything under the sun through the World Wide Web. A few years ago, hardly anybody was familiar with the term 'dotcom'; it's now part of most people's vocabulary. Without doubt, the Internet – for those with access to it – has changed the world and promises to do so even further as mobile access increases and as more and more physical objects are connected to it.

The electronic mass media

The development of electronic media (radio, TV) during the twentieth century provided one of the major ways in which people living in one part of the world learned about what is happening in other parts of the world. Such media are especially powerful and influential not only because of their apparent immediacy but also because they do not require the high level of literacy of books or newspapers. The electronic media, therefore, are particularly important in making people aware of the wider world. This is, of course, very important politically but it is also very important commercially. Large business firms require large markets to sustain them; global firms aspire to global markets. The existence of such markets obviously depends on income levels, but it depends, too, on potential customers becoming *aware* of a firm's offerings and being persuaded to purchase them. Even where consumer incomes are low, the ground may be prepared for possible future ability to purchase by creating an aspirational image. The electronic mass media are particularly powerful means both of spreading information and of persuasion; hence their vital importance to the advertising industry and, in particular, to branded products.

Today, TV is the mass medium that has the most dramatic impact on people's awareness and perception of worlds beyond their own direct experience. Although the electronic media transmit messages of all kinds, a very large proportion of these messages are *commercial* messages aimed at the consumer. Because commercial advertising is a feature of most mass media networks throughout the world, the communications media open the doors of national markets to the heavily advertised, branded products of the transnational producers.

During the past three decades there has been a major 'phase shift' in the mass media with the appearance of cable and satellite broadcasting and a widespread deregulation of the media. As a result, the number of TV channels has grown dramatically, from a small number in each country to, potentially, hundreds of channels accessible through cable or satellite. This has had major effects on the ways in which TV is used. Prior to the media diversification wave of the 1980s, there was a high level of standardization in the kinds of TV programme available. It was this kind of 'mutual experience' that led Marshall McLuhan to coin the metaphor of the *global village* in which certain images are shared and in which events take on the immediacy of participation. Although in one sense the world may not have shrunk for the rural peasant or the urban slum dweller, with no adequate means of personal transportation, it had undoubtedly shrunk in an indirect sense. It was now possible to be aware of distant places, of lifestyles, of consumer goods through the vicarious experience of the electronic media.

But the increasing segmentation of TV messages means that the global village idea is no longer an accurate picture of reality:

> the fact that not everybody watches the same thing at the same time, and that each culture and social group has a specific relationship to the media system, does make a fundamental difference *vis-à-vis* the old system of standardized mass media ... While the media have become indeed globally interconnected, and programs and messages circulate in the global network, we are not living in a global village, but in customized cottages globally produced and locally distributed.[35]

Communications on the move: towards a wireless world

Communications, of course, depend on a massive physical infrastructure. But within that infrastructure, one of the most significant developments of recent years has been the phenomenal growth of *mobile* communications, especially the mobile phone. One of the first patents for a 'radio-telephone' system linked to base stations was taken out by Motorola in 1973. But development was slow. In the early 1980s, what was then still a relatively rare, and very prestigious, instrument – the mobile phone – was the size of a brick, weighed around 800 grams and cost almost $4000. Today, the weight is down to 90 grams and the typical cost of a basic handset is less than $100. At the same time, the geographical range and sophistication of mobile phones and their operating systems have increased dramatically. As a consequence, there has been an explosion in ownership throughout the world. In the early 1990s, there were only a few hundred thousand subscribers to mobile systems; now there are around 4 billion.[36]

> There has been a clear shift from fixed to mobile cellular telephony, especially since the turn of the century. By the end of 2008, there were over three times more mobile cellular subscriptions than fixed telephone lines.[37]

Not surprisingly, the rate of innovation in mobile phone technology has accelerated. The '3G' system was introduced early in the 2000s to

> function as a phone, a computer, a television, a pager, a videoconferencing centre, a newspaper, a diary and even a credit card ... it will support not only voice communication but also real-time video and full-scale multimedia.[38]

The next generation 'after-3G' or '4G' system aims to enhance and further to extend all of these qualities at higher levels of coverage and access. In particular,

4G will enable a huge growth in the speed and quality of mobile Internet services of the kind increasingly demanded by businesses. The introduction of 'smartphones', like the iPhone, is transforming the mobile phone to a multipurpose, integrated communications device which can do almost anything.

Underlying these developments is a broader trend towards an increasingly 'wireless world' in which the kinds of technological *convergence* between computing and communications shown in Figure 4.2 have entered a new phase.

> The computing revolution was about information – digitizing documents, photographs and records so that they could more easily be manipulated. The wireless-communications revolution is about making digital information about anything available anywhere at almost no cost. No longer tied down by wires and cables.[39]

Such developments have the potential to generate enormous social and economic changes as they free users (whether they be businesses or individuals) from the physical tie to fixed communications infrastructure.

> Ancient nomads went from place to place – and they had to take a lot of stuff with them (including their livelihoods and families). The emerging class of digital nomads also wander, but they take virtually nothing with them; wherever they go, they can easily reach people and information.[40]

Digital divides: an uneven world of communications

Although technological developments in transportation and communications have transformed space–time relationships between virtually all parts of the world, the outcomes are immensely uneven. Not all places are equally connected. The time–space surface is highly plastic; some parts shrink whilst other parts become, in effect, extended in relative though not, of course, in absolute terms. By no means everywhere benefits from technological innovations in communications. The places that tend to benefit most are the already 'important' places. New investments in technology are market related; they go to where the returns are likely to be high. The cumulative effect is both to reinforce certain communications routes at the global scale and to enhance the significance of the nodes (cities/ countries) on those routes.

For example, when we look at the map of the Internet we find a very uneven geography.[41] Figure 4.8 shows that two-thirds of all the registered domain names are in just three countries (the US, Germany, the UK). The US alone has one-third of the world total, although this is less than in the past.[42] These very strong geographical concentrations are further reflected in the pattern of Internet capacity between world regions (Figure 4.9).

So, the Internet is far from being the placeless/spaceless phenomenon so often envisaged. In particular, as far as provision of its basic infrastructure is concerned, it is overwhelmingly an urban – especially a big city – phenomenon:

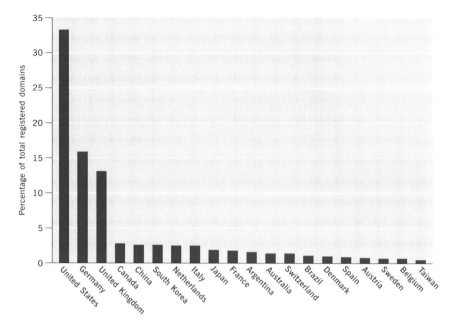

Figure 4.8   The uneven geography of the Internet

Source: based on Zook, 2005: Table 2.1

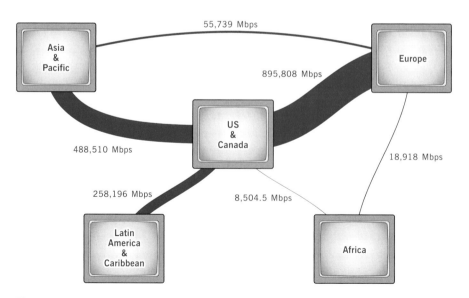

Figure 4.9   Inter-regional Internet bandwidth

Source: based on material in *Telegeography*, 2007

> This is partly an historical accident … the Internet's fibre-optic cables often piggyback on old infrastructure where a right-of-way has already been established: they are laid alongside railways and roads or inside sewers … Building the Internet on top of existing infrastructure in this way merely reinforces real-world geography. Just as cities are often railway and shipping hubs, they are also the logical places to put network hubs and servers, the powerful computers that store and distribute data. This has led to the rise of 'server farms', also known as data centres or web hotels – vast warehouses that provide floorspace, power and networks connectivity for large numbers of computers and which are located predominantly in urban areas.[43]

Indeed, the network of Google server farms, referred to earlier, is located as close as possible to the largest concentrations of potential customers because

> as fast as electrons travel, physical distance still affects [online] response speed … Reducing [it] by even a fraction of a second mattered to users as Google discovered when it ran experiments to see if users noticed a difference between [a wait of] 0.9 seconds [and one of] 0.4 seconds … Users were conspicuously more likely to grow bored and leave the Google site after waiting that interminable 0.9 seconds.[44]

To a considerable extent, therefore, the map of the Internet mirrors the network of global cities, although the match is not perfect:

> [Although] the evolving infrastructure of the Internet is reinforcing old patterns of agglomeration … At the same time, new technologies cause new 'disturbances' … The prominence of Amsterdam and Stockholm in Europe and of Salt Lake City and Atlanta in the US suggests that new clusters can emerge.[45]

The persistent geographical unevenness in the provision of communications infrastructure is a major problem at the global scale. There is a real, and serious, *digital divide* between those places and people with access to communications technologies and those without.[46] Because such access is the key to so much information and knowledge, this poses severe developmental problems. Figure 4.10 summarizes some of these global inequalities in access to the communications media.

The most promising new development for helping to bridge the digital divide is, without doubt, the mobile phone and the spread of wireless capabilities. One of the biggest obstacles to communications growth and access in poor countries is the lack of fixed line infrastructures and the immense cost of providing them in poor and, especially, in rural areas. Wireless communications have the potential to overcome this.

> Mobile phones do not rely on a permanent electricity supply and can be used by people who cannot read or write. Phones are widely shared and rented out by the call, for example by the 'telephone ladies' found in Bangladeshi villages. Farmers and fishermen use mobile phones to call several markets and work out where they can get the best price for their produce. Mobile phones

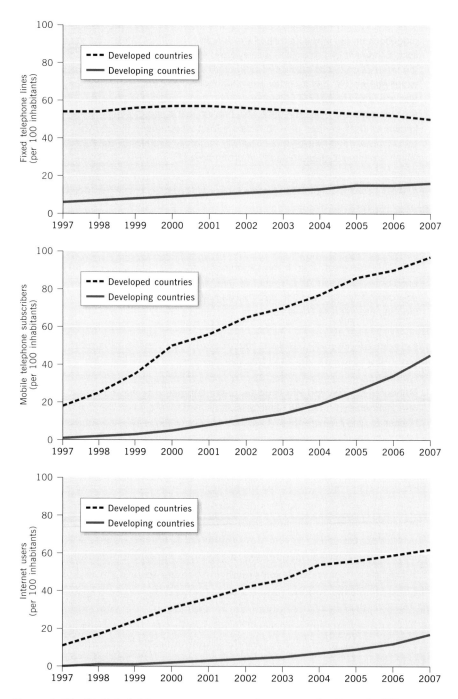

Figure 4.10   Digital divides: uneven access to communications facilities, 1997–2007

Source: based on material in www.itu.int/ITU-D/ict/statistics

are used to make cashless payments in Zambia and several other African countries. Even though the number of phones per 100 people in poor countries is much lower than in the developed world, they can have a dramatic impact ... The digital divide that really matters, then, is between those with access to a mobile network and those without.[47]

In fact, there have been

great strides towards connecting the previously unconnected, with growth most significant in developing regions, where, by the end of 2007, mobile cellular penetration has reached close to 40 per cent ... By the end of 2007, 64 per cent of the world's mobile subscriptions were from developing countries. Five years earlier ... they represented only 44 per cent ... Amongst the developing regions, Africa continues to have the highest mobile growth rate ... Since growth rates continue to be strongest in those regions where penetration is relatively low, the mobile cellular divide is expected to be reduced further over time.[48]

The digital divide between the 'global North' and the 'global South' is reflected in many ways, not least in the immense unevenness in geographical coverage in Wikipedia, as an analysis of geotagged articles has shown.

There is clearly a highly uneven geography of information in Wikipedia. The US has the most articles about places or events (almost 100,000), while some smaller countries such as Tonga have few than 10 ... But it's not just size that is correlated with extremely low levels of wiki representation. Almost the entire continent of Africa is geographically poorly represented in Wikipedia. Remarkably, there are more Wikipedia articles written about Antarctica than all but one of the 53 countries in Africa.[49]

Technological innovations in products and processes

Product and process innovation

A firm's profitability can be enhanced through increased penetration of existing markets or expansion into new geographical markets. However, there are limits. In an intensely competitive environment the introduction of a continuous stream of new products becomes essential to a firm's profitability and, indeed, its very survival. However, all products have a limited life span: what is generally referred to as the *product life cycle* (PLC).[50] Figure 4.11 shows the major characteristics of an idealized PLC: the growth of sales follows a systematic path from initial innovation through a series of stages.

This kind of development path has very important implications for the growth of firms and for their profit levels. Of course, the rate at which the cycle proceeds

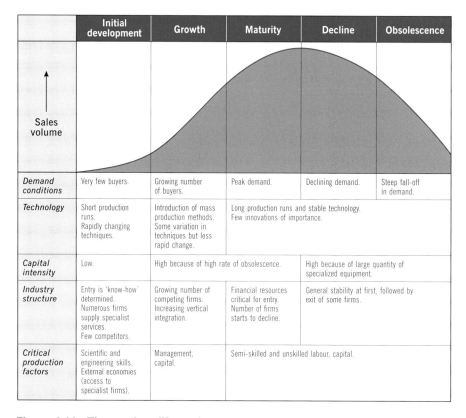

	Initial development	Growth	Maturity	Decline	Obsolescence
Demand conditions	Very few buyers.	Growing number of buyers.	Peak demand.	Declining demand.	Steep fall-off in demand.
Technology	Short production runs. Rapidly changing techniques.	Introduction of mass production methods. Some variation in techniques but less rapid change.	Long production runs and stable technology. Few innovations of importance.		
Capital intensity	Low.	High because of high rate of obsolescence.		High because of large quantity of specialized equipment.	
Industry structure	Entry is 'know-how' determined. Numerous firms supply specialist services. Few competitors.	Growing number of competing firms. Increasing vertical integration.	Financial resources critical for entry. Number of firms starts to decline.	General stability at first, followed by exit of some firms.	
Critical production factors	Scientific and engineering skills. External economies (access to specialist firms).	Management, capital.	Semi-skilled and unskilled labour, capital.		

Figure 4.11   The product life cycle

will vary from one product to another. In some highly ephemeral products the cycle may run its course within a single year or even less. In others the cycle may be very long. However, in general, product cycles have been becoming shorter, increasing the pressure on firms to develop new products or to acquire them from other firms. There are three major ways in which a product's sales may be maintained or increased:

- to introduce a new product as the existing one becomes obsolete so that 'overlapping' cycles occur
- to extend the cycle for the existing product, either by making minor modifications in the product itself to 'update' it or by finding new uses
- to make changes to the production technology itself to make the product more competitive.

However, product innovation alone is inadequate as a basis for a firm's survival and profitability. Firms must strive to produce their products as efficiently as possible. Recent developments in *process* technology – and, especially, in ICT – are having profound effects upon production processes in all economic sectors. There is a close relationship between the progress of a product through its life cycle and the way it is made, as Figure 4.11 shows. Each stage has particular production characteristics. In general, as the cycle proceeds, the emphasis shifts from product-related technologies to process technologies and, in particular, to ways of minimizing production costs. In this respect, the relative importance of labour costs – especially of semi-skilled and unskilled labour – increases. More generally, different types of geographical location are relevant to different stages of the product cycle.

This view of systematic changes in the production process as a product matures is appealing and has some validity. There undoubtedly are important differences in the nature of the production process between a product in its very early stages of development and the same product in its maturity. But this linear, sequential notion of change is overly simplistic and deterministic. At any stage, the production process may be 'rejuvenated' by technological innovation. There may not necessarily be a simple sequence leading from small-scale production to standardized mass production.

Changes in production systems: towards greater flexibility and leanness

Most technological developments in production processes are, as we observed earlier, gradual and incremental: the result of 'learning by doing' and 'learning by using'. But periods of radical transformation of the production process have occurred throughout history. Over the long time-scale of industrialization, the production process has developed through a series of stages, each of which represents increasing efforts to mechanize and to control more closely the nature and speed of work.

Five stages are generally identified:

- *Manufacture*: the collecting together of labour into workshops and the division of the labour process into specific tasks.
- *Machinofacture*: the application of mechanical processes and power through machinery in factories together with further division of labour.
- *Scientific management* ('Taylorism'): the subjection of the work process to scientific study in the late nineteenth century. This enhanced the fineness of the division of labour into specific tasks together with increased control and supervision.
- *'Fordism'*: the development of assembly-line processes that controlled the pace of production and permitted the mass production of large volumes of standardized products.
- *Flexible and lean production*: the development of new production systems based upon the deep application of information and communication technologies.

These stages map fairly closely on to the long-wave sequence shown earlier in Figure 4.1. The first Kondratiev wave was associated with the transition from manufacture to machinofacture. The application of scientific management principles to the production process emerged in the late phase of K2 and developed more fully in K3. The bases of Fordist production were established during K3, but reached their fullest development during K4. The Fordist system was epitomized by very large-scale production units, using assembly-line manufacturing techniques and producing large volumes of standardized products for mass market consumption. It was a type of production especially characteristic of particular industrial sectors, notably automobiles (see Chapter 11). Not all sectors, or all production processes, lent themselves to such a system, but it was seen to be the main characteristic of the K4 phase.

The key to production flexibility today lies in the deep and extensive use of ICT, which provides more sophisticated control over production. Two particularly important processes are those of *flexible specialization* and *flexible mass production*. The potential of such flexible technologies is immense, and their implications are enormous. They involve three major tendencies:[51]

- A trend towards information intensity, rather than energy or materials intensity, in production.
- A much enhanced flexibility of production that challenges the old best-practice concept of mass production in three central respects:
  - A high volume of output is no longer necessary for high productivity; this can be achieved through a diversified set of low-volume products.
  - Because rapid technological change becomes less costly and risky, the 'minimum change' strategy in product development is less necessary for cost effectiveness.
  - The new technologies allow a profitable focus on segmented rather than mass markets; products can be tailored to specific local conditions and needs.
- A major change in labour requirements in terms of both volume and type of labour. This involves a shift towards multitasking rather than narrow labour specialization; a greater emphasis on team-working; and individualized payments systems.

The current position, therefore, is that of a *diversity* of production systems (Figure 4.12), but where the relative importance of specific processes is changing. In fact, no single production system is ever completely dominant. Even during the heyday of Fordist mass production there were firms and sectors in which smaller-scale, more craft-based production persisted. Today, when all the emphasis is on flexible production, there is still a good deal of mass production and, indeed, of craft production. Figure 4.13 summarizes some of the contrasts between the three systems of production.

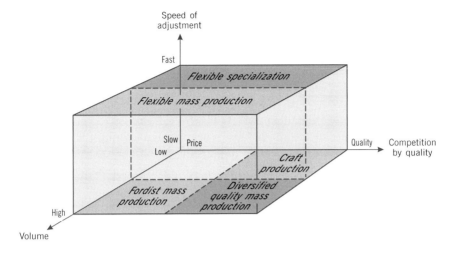

Figure 4.12   Ideal-types of production system

Source: based on Hollingsworth and Boyer, 1997: Figure 1.3

Characteristic	Craft production	Mass production	Flexible/lean production
Technology	Simple but flexible tools and equipment using non-standardized components.	Complex but rigid single-purpose machinery using standardized components. Heavy time and cost penalties in switching to new products.	Highly flexible production methods using modular component systems. Relatively easy to switch to new products.
Labour force	Highly skilled in most aspects of professional production.	Very narrowly skilled workers design products but production itself performed by unskilled/semi-skilled 'interchangeable' workers. Each performs a relatively simple task repetitively and in predefined time sequence.	Multi-skilled, polyvalent workers operate in teams. Responsible for several manufacturing operations plus simple maintenance and repair.
Supplier relationships	Very close contact between customer and supplier. Most suppliers located within single city.	Distant relationships with suppliers, both functionally and geographically. Large inventories held at assembly plant 'just in case' of supply disruption.	Very close relationships with functionally-tiered system of suppliers. Use of 'just-in-time' delivery systems encourages geographical proximity between customers and suppliers.
Production volume	Relatively low.	Extremely high.	Extremely high.
Product variety	Extremely wide: each product customized to specific requirements.	Narrow range of standardized designs with only minor product modifications.	Increasingly wide range of differentiated products.

Figure 4.13   The major characteristics of craft production, Fordist mass production, and flexible/lean production

Source: based in part on material in Womack et al., 1990

Thus, we can see a trend towards:

- *increasingly fine degrees of specialization* in many production processes, enabling their fragmentation into a number of individual operations
- *increasing standardization and routinization* of these individual operations, enabling the use of semi-skilled and unskilled labour; this is especially apparent during the mature stage of a product's life cycle
- *increasing flexibility* in the production process that is altering the relationship between the scale and the cost of production, permitting smaller production runs, increasing product variety, and changing the way production and the labour process are organized
- *increasing modularity* of production – what Berger calls the 'Lego' model of production – involving networks of firms (as we will see in Chapter 5).[52]

Geographies of innovation

Innovation – the heart of technological change – is fundamentally a *learning* process. Such learning – by doing, by using, by observing and sharing with others – depends upon the accumulation and development of relevant knowledge. These processes have a very distinctive geography. Despite the fact that the development of highly sophisticated communications systems has facilitated the diffusion of knowledge at unparalleled speed and over unprecedented distances, 'conditions of knowledge accumulation are highly localized'.[53] Knowledge is *produced in specific places* and often used, and enhanced most intensively, in those same places. Hence,

> to understand technological change, it is crucial to identify the economic, social, political and geographical context in which innovation is generated and disseminated. This space may be local, national or global. Or, more likely, it will involve a complex and evolving integration, at different levels, of local, national and global factors.[54]

National innovation systems

The idea underlying the notion of national innovation systems is that the specific combination of social, cultural, political, legal, educational and economic institutions and practices varies systematically between national contexts.[55] Such nationally differentiated characteristics help to influence the kind of technology system that develops there. These underlying forces help to explain the gradual shifts in national technological leadership evident in successive K-waves (see Figure 4.1). Despite the claims of the hyper-globalists that national distinctiveness is declining, the evidence strongly suggests that national variations in technology systems – and therefore in technological competence – persist. Certainly there is a lot of evidence to show that the volume and characteristics of technological innovation vary greatly by country.

One indicator is the number of patents granted by country. Patents are the mechanism by which an individual or a company can protect an invention for a period of years. As Figure 4.14 shows, the patent map is highly uneven.

> Patent grants are concentrated in a small number of countries. Applicants from Japan, the United States of America, the Republic of Korea and Germany received 73% of total patent grants worldwide. Between 2000 and 2006, the number of patents granted to applicants from China and the Republic of Korea grew by 26.5% and 23.2% a year, respectively (average annual growth rate).[56]

The rapid growth of Chinese patents is matched by the 'awe-inspiring expansion of Chinese science' and its emergence as 'the second largest producer of scientific knowledge' as revealed by an analysis of 10,500 scientific journals worldwide for the period 1981–2008.[57]

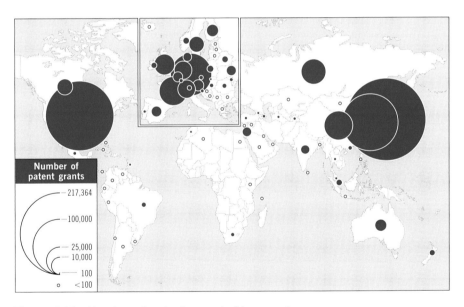

Figure 4.14   Number of patents granted by country

Source: based on data in WIPO, 2008: Table A1

Localized knowledge clusters

National systems of innovation are not homogeneous entities. They consist of aggregations of *localized* knowledge clusters.[58] One reason for the significance of 'localness' in the creation and diffusion of knowledge lies in a basic distinction in the nature of knowledge itself, which is broadly of two kinds:[59]

- *codified (or explicit) knowledge*: the kinds of knowledge that can be expressed formally in documents, blueprints, software, hardware etc.
- *tacit knowledge*: the deeply personalized knowledge possessed by individuals that is virtually impossible to make explicit and to communicate to others through formal mechanisms.

This distinction is fundamental to understanding the role of space and place in technological diffusion. Codified knowledge can be transmitted relatively easily across distance. It is through such means that, throughout history, political, religious and economic organizations, for example, have been able to 'act at a distance' – to exert control over geographically dispersed activities.[60] Developments in transportation and communications technologies have enabled such 'acting' or 'controlling' to take place over greater and greater distances. Tacit knowledge, on the other hand, has a very steep 'distance-decay' curve. It requires direct experience and interaction; it depends to a considerable extent – though not completely by any means – on geographical proximity. It is much more 'sticky'. However, it is a mistake to take the 'tacit = local, codified = global' contrast too far because 'both tacit and codified knowledge can be exchanged locally and globally'.[61]

   The specific socio-technological context within which innovative activity is embedded – what is sometimes called the *innovative milieu* – is a key factor in knowledge creation. This context consists of a mixture of both tangible and intangible elements:

- the economic, social and political institutions
- the knowledge and know-how which evolve over time in a specific context (the 'something in the air' notion identified many decades ago by Alfred Marshall)
- the 'conventions, which are taken-for-granted rules and routines between the partners in different kinds of relations defined by uncertainty'.[62]

The basis of localized knowledge clusters, therefore, lies in several characteristics of the innovation process that are highly sensitive to geographical distance and proximity:[63]

- *Localized patterns of communication*: geographical distance greatly influences the likelihood of individuals within and between organizations sharing knowledge and information links.
- *Localized innovation search and scanning patterns*: geographical proximity influences the nature of a firm's search process for technological inputs or possible collaborators. Small firms, in particular, often have a geographically narrower 'scanning field' than larger firms.

- *Localized invention and learning patterns*: innovation often occurs in response to specific local problems. Processes of 'learning by doing' and 'learning by using' tend to be closely related to physical proximity in the production process.
- *Localized knowledge sharing*: because the acquisition and communication of tacit knowledge are strongly localized geographically, there is a tendency for localized 'knowledge pools' to develop around specific activities.
- *Localized patterns of innovation capabilities and performance*: geographical proximity, in enriching the depth of particular knowledge and its use, can reduce the risk and uncertainty of innovation.

Local innovative milieux, therefore, consist primarily of a *nexus of untraded interdependencies* set within a temporal context of *path-dependent* processes of technological change. We outlined the major elements of such processes in general terms in Chapter 3. The point of emphasizing the 'untraded' nature of the interdependencies within such milieux is to distinguish the social 'cement' (especially face-to-face contact) which binds this kind of localized agglomeration from that which may be associated with the minimization of transaction costs (for example, of materials and components transfers) through geographical proximity. The 'buzz' derived from 'being there' is at the heart of these social processes.[64]

But that is not the entire story. Localized knowledge clusters cannot be sustained and developed entirely through such incestuous relationships. A key additional process involves the connections between some of the actors in a given locality with outsiders (for example, firms with suppliers, customers, or sources of specific information and knowledge). In other words, as well as 'local

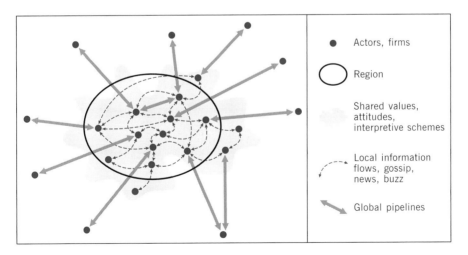

Figure 4.15   Localized knowledge clusters in a wider context: local buzz and global pipelines

Source: based on Bathelt et al., 2004: Figure 1

buzz' there also have to be 'pipelines': channels of communication to other actors in other places. The processes of knowledge creation and innovation, therefore, consist of a complex set of networks and processes operating *within and across* various spatial scales, from the global, through the national and the regional, to the local.

Figure 4.15 provides an idealized picture of this very complex process. It is based on the argument that

> the existence of local buzz of high quality and relevance leads to a more dynamic cluster ... These actors and their buzz are, however, of little relevance if firms are not 'tuned in' ... It is likely that a milieu, where many actors with related yet complementary and heterogeneous knowledge, skill and information reside, provides a great potential for dynamic interaction ...
>
> A well-developed system of pipelines connecting the local cluster to the rest of the world is beneficial for the cluster in two ways. First, each individual firm can benefit from establishing knowledge-enhancing relations to actors outside the local cluster. Even world-class clusters cannot be permanently self-sufficient in terms of state-of-the-art knowledge creation. New and valuable knowledge will always be created in other parts of the world and firms who can build pipelines to such sites of global excellence gain competitive advantage. Second, it seems reasonable to assume that the information that one cluster firm can acquire through its pipelines will spill over to other firms in the cluster through local buzz ... That is why a firm will learn more if its neighbouring firms in the cluster are globally well connected rather than being more inward-looking and insular in their orientation.[65]

NOTES

1   Schumpeter (1943: 83).
2   The term 'creative gales of destruction' is borrowed from Schumpeter (1943).
3   Freeman (1988: 2).
4   Mattsson (2007: 42).
5   Borrus, quoted in Cohen and Zysman (1987: 183, emphasis added).
6   Edgerton (2007).
7   This approach is, essentially 'neo-Schumpeterian'. See Dosi et al. (1988), Fields (2004), Freeman (1982; 1987), Metcalfe and Dilisio (1996), Perez (1985; 2010).
8   Freeman and Perez (1988), Perez (2010).
9   Freeman (1987: 130).
10 See Freeman et al. (1982), Freeman and Perez (1988), Hall and Preston (1988), Rennstich (2002).
11 Hall and Preston (1988: 6).
12 Rennstich (2002: 174).
13 Hall and Preston (1988).
14 Carr (2008b).
15 Carr (2008a: 2).

16 For broad-ranging discussions of these technologies see Brunn and Leinbach (1991), Castells (1996), Graham and Marvin (1996), Hall and Preston (1988), World Bank (2009b: Chapter 6).

17 Fields (2004: 14, 15).

18 See O'Rourke and Williamson (1999: Chapter 3) for a detailed discussion of these developments.

19 World Bank (2009b: 174).

20 Dean and Sebastia-Barriel (2004: 314).

21 World Bank (2009b: 177).

22 World Bank (2009b: 177).

23 Levinson (2006) provides a comprehensive and highly readable account of the development of containerization.

24 *The Independent* (30 August 2000).

25 *The Economist* (3 March 2007: 74).

26 Luhmann (1998: 85). Thanks to Roger Lee for this.

27 Henderson and Castells (1987: 6).

28 Malecki and Hu (2006), Warf (2006; 2007) provide recent analyses of satellite and cable systems.

29 Warf (2007: 386).

30 Malecki and Hu (2006: 7).

31 *Financial Times* (28 July 1998).

32 Malecki and Hu (2006: 14, 15).

33 Zook (2005: 1).

34 Zook (2005) provides an excellent analysis of the development of the Internet. See also Castells (1996), Dodge and Kitchin (2001), Malecki (2002).

35 Castells (1996: 341).

36 International Telecommunication Union statistics. For a detailed account of the global spread of mobile phones see Comer and Wikle (2008). Castells et al. (2007) explore the social implications of mobile communications.

37 International Telecommunication Union (2009: 3).

38 International Telecommunication Union (2000), cited in *The Economist* (4 September 2004).

39 *The Economist* (28 April 2007: 12).

40 *The Economist* (12 April 2008: 16).

41 Dodge and Kitchin (2001), Malecki (2002), Zook (2001; 2005).

42 Malecki (2002: 405), Zook (2001: Table 1).

43 *The Economist* (11 August 2001: 18).

44 Stross (2008) quoted in *The Guardian* (1 November 2008).

45 Malecki (2002: 419).

46 See International Telecommunication Union (2009).

47 *The Economist* (12 March 2005: 9).

48 International Telecommunication Union (2009: 3, 4).

49 Graham (2009: 3).

50 O'Shaughnessy (1995) explores this concept in a marketing context. Vernon (1966; 1979) pioneered its application to international production and international trade.

51 Perez (1985).

52   Berger (2005: 57). See also Sturgeon (2002).

53   Metcalfe and Dilisio (1996: 58).

54   Archibugi and Michie (1997: 2).

55   See Archibugi and Michie (1997), Archibugi et al. (1999), Freeman (1997), Lundvall (2007), Lundvall and Maskell (2000), Patel and Pavitt (1998).

56   WIPO (2008: 7).

57   *Financial Times* (26 January 2010).

58   There is a vast literature on this topic. See, for example, Bathelt et al. (2004), Bunnell and Coe (2001), Gertler (1995; 2003), Gertler et al. (2000), Mattsson (2007), Morgan (2004), Sonn and Storper (2008), Storper (1997), Storper and Venables (2004).

59   Gertler (2003).

60   Fields (2004), Law (1986).

61   Bathelt et al. (2004: 32).

62   Storper (1995: 208).

63   Howells (2000: 58–9).

64   Bathelt et al. (2004), Gertler (1995), Storper and Venables (2004), Sturgeon (2003).

65   Bathelt et al. (2004: 45–6).

Five

TRANSNATIONAL CORPORATIONS: THE PRIMARY 'MOVERS AND SHAPERS' OF THE GLOBAL ECONOMY

A transnational corporation is a firm that has the power to coordinate and control operations in more than one country, even if it does not own them.

Why firms transnationalize

Most TNCs are capitalist enterprises. As such, they must behave according to the basic 'rules' of capitalism, the most fundamental of which is the drive for profit. Of course, business firms may well have a variety of motives other than profit, such as increasing their share of a market, becoming the industry leader, or simply making the firm bigger. But, in the long run, none of these is more important than the pursuit of profit itself. A firm's profitability is the key barometer to its business 'health'; any firm that fails to make a profit at all over a period of time is likely to go out of business (unless rescued by government or acquired by another firm). At best, therefore, firms must attempt to increase their profits; at worst, they must defend them.

Of course, a capitalist market economy is an intensely *competitive* economy. One firm's profit may be another firm's loss unless the whole system is growing sufficiently strongly to permit all firms to make a profit. Even so, some will make a larger profit than others. Two key features of today's world are: first, competition is increasingly global in its extent and, second, such competition is extremely volatile. 'This creates an environment of hyper-competition – an environment in which advantages are rapidly created and eroded.'[1] Firms are no longer competing largely with national rivals but with firms from across the world. Given these circumstances, therefore, one way of explaining TNCs is simply as a reflection of the 'normal' expansionary tendencies of the different *circuits of capital*.[2] In these terms, the question of 'Why transnationalize?' might almost be better put as 'Why *not* transnationalize?'

Although a firm's motivation for engaging in transnational operations may be highly individual, we can classify them into two broad categories (although the boundary between them is by no means as sharp as this dichotomy suggests):

- market orientation
- asset orientation.

Market orientation

Most foreign direct investment, whether it is in production of goods or services or in marketing and sales, is designed to serve a specific geographical market by locating inside that market. The good or service produced abroad may be virtually identical to that being produced in the firm's home country, although there may well be modifications to suit the specific tastes or requirements of the local market. In effect, such specifically market-oriented investment is a form of horizontal expansion across national boundaries. Three attributes of markets are especially important:

- The most obvious attraction of a specific market is its *size*, measured, for example, in terms of per capita income. Figure 5.1 shows the enormous variation in income levels per capita on a global scale. The largest geographical markets in terms of incomes, although not in terms of population, are obviously the US and Western Europe. Such variations in per capita income provide a crude indication of how the *level* of demand will vary from place to place across the world.
- Countries with different income levels will tend to have a different *structure* of demand. As incomes rise, so does the aggregate demand for goods and services. But such increased demand does not affect all products equally. Populations in countries with low income levels tend to spend a larger proportion of their income on basic necessities while, conversely, people in countries with high income levels tend to spend a higher proportion of their income on 'higher-order' manufactured goods and services.
- Markets vary in their *accessibility*. In the past, a major barrier was the cost of transportation. Today, this is far less significant, although not totally unimportant, especially for some products. However, political constraints in the form of various kinds of trade barrier remain highly significant (see Chapter 5).

Asset orientation

Most of the various assets needed by a firm to produce and sell its specific products and services are unevenly distributed geographically. This is most obviously the case in the natural resource industries, where firms must, of necessity, locate their extractive activities at the sources of supply. Often, such investments form the first element in an organizational sequence of vertically integrated operations whose later stages (processing) may be located quite separately from the source of

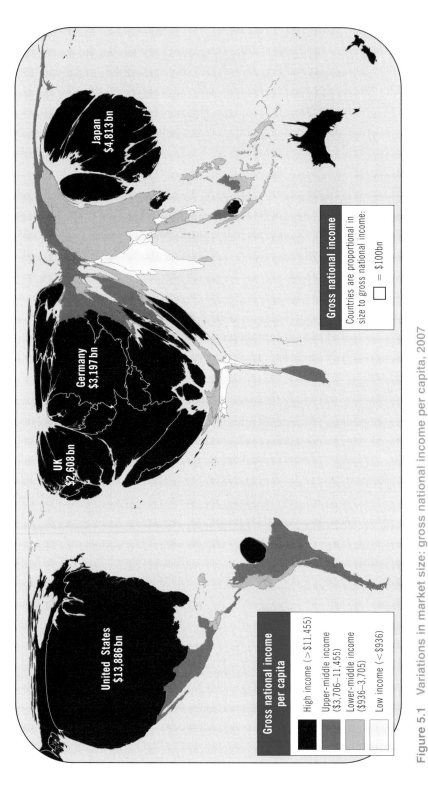

Figure 5.1 Variations in market size: gross national income per capita, 2007

Source: based on World Bank, 2009b: Table 1; projection supplied by Danny Dorling (SASI Group, University of Sheffield) supply itself. In many cases, final processing of natural resources occurs close to the final market. Natural-resource-oriented foreign investments have a very long history and remain highly significant in the global economy (see Chapter 8).

However, there are other asset-oriented foreign investments closely related to the developments in product and process technologies discussed in Chapter 4. Technological changes in production processes and in transportation have evened out the significance of location for some of the traditionally important factors of production (for example, natural resources). Many now hold the view that, at least at the global scale, the two most important location-specific factors are:

- access to *knowledge*
- access to *labour*.

The strong tendency for knowledge and technological innovation processes to appear in *geographical clusters* (see Chapter 4) creates a major incentive for firms to locate their relevant operations in such locations. Particularly in those activities in which technological change, whether in product or process development, is especially rapid and unpredictable, the incentive to locate 'where the knowledge and the action are' becomes very powerful. Such knowledge may be based in specific kinds of institution (such as universities, research institutes, industry associations). However, much of the attraction exerted by such knowledge clusters derives from the skills and knowledge embodied in *labour*.

From a TNC's perspective, the locational significance of labour as a 'production factor' is reflected in a number of ways although, of course, workers are much more than 'crude abstractions in which ... [they are] ... reduced to the categories of wages, skill levels, location, gender, union membership and the like'.[3] Such characteristics vary, of course, in their significance according to the specific kind of labour being sought, as the cases in Part Three demonstrate. For some activities, it is cheap, unskilled, non-unionized labour that is being sought; for others, it is highly skilled and educated 'knowledge workers' that are the attraction. In general terms, however, four especially important attributes of labour show large geographical variations.

- *Knowledge and skills*. Knowledge and skills depend on such conditions as the breadth and depth of education and the particular history of an area's development. As a result, there are wide geographical variations in the availability of different types of labour. One very approximate indicator at the global scale is the variation in educational levels (for example, extent of literacy, enrolment in various stages of education, public expenditure on education etc.). Figure 5.2 maps one such indicator: the proportion of the relevant population in tertiary education. As might be expected, there is a very high correlation between these measures and the distribution of per capita income shown in Figure 5.1.

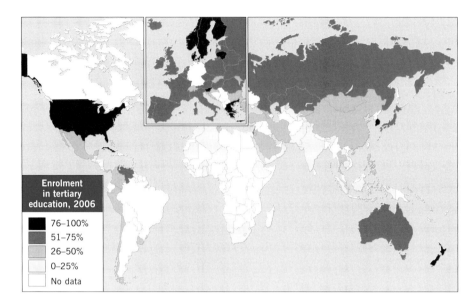

Figure 5.2   Enrolment in tertiary education

Source: based on data in USAID, 2008, *Global Education Database*

- *Wage costs*. International differences in wage levels can be staggeringly wide, as Figure 5.3 shows. These figures should be treated with some caution; they are averages across the whole of manufacturing industry and are therefore affected by the specific industry mix. Some industries have much higher wage levels than others. Even so, the contrasts are striking.
- *Labour productivity*. Spatial variations in wage costs are only a partial indication of the geographical importance of labour as a production factor. What matters from a firm perspective is the scale of output per worker for a given wage or salary. The 'performance capacity' of labour varies enormously from place to place, a reflection of a number of influences including education, training, skill and motivation, as well as the kind of machinery and equipment in use. Simply chasing low wage costs, without taking into account differences in productivity, is not a good strategy (though one that is often pursued).
- *Labour 'controllability'*. Largely because of historical circumstances, there are considerable geographical differences in the degree of labour 'militancy' and in the extent to which labour is organized through labour unions. The proportion of the workers who are members of labour unions has declined markedly in some countries, as we noted in Chapter 3. The fact that most firms are very wary of 'highly organized' labour regions is demonstrated by their tendency to relocate from such regions or to make new investments in places where labour is regarded as being more malleable.

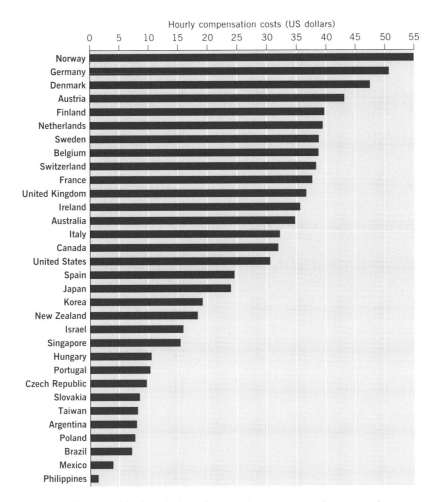

Figure 5.3 Geographical variations in hourly compensation costs in manufacturing, 2008

Source: based on US Bureau of Labor statistics, 2009

Global variations in production costs are a highly significant element in the trans-national investment-location decision. This is obviously the case for asset-oriented investments but it is also a critical consideration for market-oriented investments. In that case there is always a trade-off to be made between the benefits of market proximity on the one hand and geographical variations in production costs on the other. But the problem is not merely one of variations in production costs at a single moment in time or even the obvious point that such costs change over time. A particularly important consideration is the *uncertainty* of the level of future pro-duction costs in different locations. One way of dealing with such uncertainty is for the TNC to locate similar plants in a variety of different locations and then to adopt a flexible system of production allocation between plants. However, this strategy is further complicated by the volatility of currency exchange rates between different countries. What appears to be a least-cost source with one set of exchange rates may look very different if there is a major change in these rates. At the present time, currency exchange rates are highly volatile.

How firms transnationalize

Is there an identifiable *evolutionary sequence* of TNC development? Does the transition from a firm producing goods or services entirely for its domestic market to one engaged in foreign production of those goods and services follow a systematic development path?

The traditional view of a sequential development trajectory

The conventional view in the international business literature has been that there is a clear sequential trajectory to a firm's development from being domestically oriented to becoming a TNC. A vast literature beginning with Hymer's pioneering work in the 1960s,[4] and developed most notably by Dunning in his self-styled 'eclectic' theory,[5] emphasized that a prerequisite for a firm to operate beyond its domestic borders (other than through trade) was the possession of some firm-specific assets, developed to a high degree in its domestic market, which could then be transferred – across borders geographically but inside the firm organizationally – to foreign locations. Such assets are primarily those of: firm size and economies of scale; market power and marketing skills (for example, brand names, advertising strength); technological expertise (product, process or both); or access to cheaper sources of finance. The implicit assumption is that only a firm that has reached a substantial size will have the resources to begin to operate transnationally. The TNC, therefore, became associated unequivocally with bigness.

This notion of beginning with a strong domestic position and then expanding geographically was also captured in the concept of the product life cycle, already encountered in Chapter 4. The PLC was specifically adopted and adapted as an explanation of the evolution of international production by Raymond Vernon in 1966.[6] Vernon's major contribution was to introduce an explicitly *locational* dimension into the product cycle. Figure 5.4 shows Vernon's PLC model, based upon the experience of US TNCs, especially during the 1960s (it should be read in conjunction with Figure 4.11).

Vernon assumed that firms are more likely to be aware of the possibility of introducing new products in their home market than producers located elsewhere.

Phase I	*Phase II*	*Phase III*	*Phase IV*	*Phase V*
All production in US US exports to many countries	Production started in Europe US exports mostly to LDCs	Europe exports to LDCs US exports to LDCs displaced	Europe exports to US	LDCs exports to US

Figure 5.4   The product life cycle as an evolutionary sequence of US TNCs' development

Source: based on Wells, 1972: Figure 15

The kinds of new products introduced, therefore, would reflect the specific characteristics of the domestic market. In the US case, high average-income levels together with high labour costs encouraged the development of new products that catered to high-income consumers and were labour saving (for both consumer and producer goods).

In this first phase of the locational product life cycle, as Figure 5.4 shows, all production would be located in the US and overseas demand would be served by exports. But this situation would be unlikely to last indefinitely. The domestic market might reach saturation and continued profitability would necessitate expansion into new markets. Hence, US firms would eventually set up production facilities in the overseas market, either because they saw an opportunity to reduce production and distribution costs or because of a threat to their market position. Such a threat might come from local competitors or from government attempts to reduce imports through tariff and other trade barriers.

It follows from the nature of the product cycle model that the first overseas production of the product would occur in other high-income markets. The newly established foreign plants would come to serve these former export markets and thus displace exports from the US. These would be redirected to other areas where production had not yet begun (phase II in Figure 5.4). Eventually, the production cost advantages of the newer overseas plants would lead the firm to export from them to other, third-country, markets (phase III) and even back to the US itself (phase IV). Finally, as the product became completely standardized, production would be shifted to low-cost locations in developing countries (phase V). It is interesting to note that when Vernon first suggested this possibility he regarded it as a 'bold projection'. At that time (the mid 1960s) there was still little evidence of developing country export platforms in East Asia serving European and US markets. How times have changed!

Is the product life cycle still valid as an explanation of the geographical evolution of TNCs?[7] There is no doubt that a good deal of the *initial* overseas investment by US firms did fit the product cycle sequence quite well. But it can no longer explain the increased diversity of transnational investment by TNCs. As these firms have become more complex globally it is unrealistic to assume a simple evolutionary sequence from the home country outwards. Even within strongly innovative TNCs, the initial source of the innovation and of its production may be from any point in the firm's global network. In addition, as we saw in Chapter 2, much of the world's FDI is reciprocal, or cross, investment between the industrialized countries. Such investment cannot easily be explained in product cycle terms.

Diverse trajectories and 'born globals'

The traditional developmental sequence is shown in the centre of Figure 5.5. It is a PLC-type view, which begins with the assumption that, initially, the firm is purely a domestic firm in terms both of production and of markets. It is generally assumed that overseas expansion is done initially through exports, using the services of overseas sales agents. Such agents are independent of the exporting firm. However, the potential benefits of exerting greater control may eventually stimulate the firm to set up overseas sales outlets of its own. This may be achieved in one of two ways: by setting up an entirely new facility or by acquiring, or merging with,

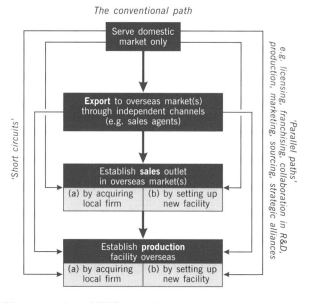

Figure 5.5   Diverse paths of TNC evolution

a local firm (possibly the previously used sales agency itself). Actual production of goods and services overseas may eventually follow.

There is a good deal of anecdotal material to support such a sequence of development among firms that actually became TNCs. Apart from Vernon's US evidence, Japanese firms investing in Europe showed a similar path. Actual manufacturing operations came rather late following a long period of development of Japanese service investments in the form of the general trading companies, banks and other financial institutions and the sales and distribution functions of the manufacturing firms themselves.[8]

However, there is nothing inevitable about the progression through each of the stages. Our broad definition of the TNC allows for other possibilities. Figure 5.5 shows several possible developmental paths. A firm may bypass the intermediate stages and set up overseas production facilities without using intermediaries. This has been especially common among firms from small countries, such as the Netherlands, Switzerland or Sweden.

> Switzerland is a small country. Within five months of its creation, Nestlé was already manufacturing abroad. The mentality here was never to export from the home market but to produce locally.[9]

Increasingly, firms engage in a bewildering variety of collaborative arrangements with other firms and these provide further diverse paths of TNC development. For example, a firm may tap into existing TNC networks as suppliers of specific products, functions and services. Alternatively, a firm may take on various kinds of transnational networking roles and yet remain relatively small.

One important pathway is through the acquisition of another domestic firm that already has foreign operations. Thus, a firm may become transnational almost incidentally. More generally, merger and acquisition is one of the most common methods of entry both to new product markets and to new geographical markets. It offers the attraction of an already functioning business compared with the more difficult, and possibly more risky, method of starting from scratch in an unfamiliar environment. Virtually all TNCs have grown, at least partially, through acquisition and merger, although it tends to be a path favoured by TNCs from some countries more than others. Certainly it is the way in which a new generation of TNCs from developing countries, like China and India, are becoming major global players. For example, the Chinese computer firm Lenovo acquired IBM's PC business in 2004, while the Indian Tata Group acquired the luxury car company Jaguar from Ford in 2008.

Although these examples illustrate increasing diversity in TNC development, they still imply a more or less lengthy temporal sequence. However, there is growing evidence of new entrepreneurial ventures actually starting out as transnational operations from the very beginning. In other words, they are what have been called 'born globals'.[10] Such firms

> started and operate from day one in global markets as global players, servicing their customers wherever they are to be found ... they are all characterized by their accelerated internationalization ... and they are thereby changing the dynamics of international competition ... The new species of [TNC] are different from traditional multinationals in that they are created by internationally experienced individuals and global in their outlook already from inception, seizing the opportunities offered by an increasingly integrated and interconnected global economy ... firms identified as born globals or international new ventures have been found to target and penetrate international markets from very early on, and in some cases from the outset organize operations around internationally dispersed knowledge and resources.[11]

Two examples can be used to illustrate this new form of TNC. First, Proteome Systems Ltd (PSL) was established by academics at Macquarie University in Australia as a biotech company. The firm

> sought to develop its customer base internationally from inception. Its pattern of market expansion was rapid and opportunistic, and focused on gaining access to resources wherever they might be available. In the US it expanded by acquisition of the pieces left after a biotech firm in Boston went out of business. In Japan it entered into a strategic alliance with an established trading house, Itochu ... In Malaysia it entered the market through the services of an agent. In other words, there was a heterogeneous entrepreneurial process of market entry and resource deployments as and when circumstances and opportunities presented themselves, but always with a view to sustaining a global market presence from the outset.[12]

Second, Momenta Corporation of Mountain View Colorado was a

> 'start-up' in the emerging pen-based computer market. Its founders were from Cuba, Iran, Tanzania, and the US. From its beginning in 1989, the founders wanted the venture to be global in its acquisition of inputs and in its target market ... Thus, software design was conducted in the US, hardware design in Germany, manufacturing in the Pacific Rim, and funding was received from Taiwan, Singapore, Europe, and the US.[13]

Such 'born global' TNCs are very different from traditional TNCs. Not only do they inject much greater diversity into the TNC population but also they emphasize the importance of social networks and networked knowledge. Many of these new-style firms are in sectors where technology is changing very rapidly – where it is vital to get new products or processes to market very quickly. The ability to tap into geographically dispersed networks of firms and individuals, as well as into knowledge networks using the Internet, is vital. Clearly, therefore, it is no longer valid to equate transnationality with firm size. Although many TNCs are, indeed, very large, many others are not. Size does not always matter. TNCs come in all shapes and sizes.

TNCs as 'networks within networks'

Although TNCs come in 'all shapes and sizes', two basic characteristics apply to all of them, whether they are involved in manufacturing, services, agriculture or resource exploitation. First, TNCs are *networks within networks*, structured through a myriad of complex relationships, transactions, exchanges and interactions within their own internal corporate network and between that network and those of the other key actors with whom TNCs must interact (see Figures 3.1 and 3.4). Second, the fact that a TNC's networks are spread across, and embedded within, different national jurisdictions and contexts means that coordinating and controlling its internal and external networked activities are vastly more complex than is the case for a purely domestic firm.

Such a relational network view of a TNC raises the question of where its organizational boundaries begin and end.[14] In a legal sense, of course, the boundary of a firm is clear; companies have to be registered in the jurisdictions in which they operate. But for firms that operate across national boundaries, there is no international legal framework. Nevertheless, at a TNC's core is a set of formally organized rules and conventions, regulated and institutionalized through the firm's own internal mechanisms. But in a functional sense – especially when we see them as networks within networks – a TNC's boundaries are much less clear. The distinction between what goes on inside and what goes on outside is not only very fuzzy but also continuously in a state of flux. In the following sections, we explore these complex internal and external relationships of TNCs in order to show how – and where – their operations are coordinated, controlled and configured.

Figure 5.6 sets out the basic framework for this analysis. It shows that different parts of a TNC have network relationships both inside and outside the firm's boundaries. The important point to note is that a subsidiary is not solely embedded within a rigid hierarchical corporate structure but may have networked business relationships outside that structure that are specific to its operations.

> The configuration of a business network is specific to each individual subsidiary. First, some subsidiaries may be embedded in relationships that are both external and internal *vis-à-vis* the [TNC], as in the case of subsidiary A, while other subsidiaries like subsidiary B have external business relationships only. Thus we can distinguish between external and corporate embeddedness. Second, individual business relationships can range from arm's-length exchange to a high degree of mutual adaptation of resources and activities, that is to a high degree of embeddedness. A subsidiary may be dominated by highly embedded relationships – external, internal or both. Other subsidiaries, in contrast, may have only relationships consisting of arm's-length exchanges – external, internal or both. Since every relationship has its own specific characteristics and history, we would expect to find a high degree of variation as regards embeddedness both within the individual subsidiary and between the different subsidiaries in [a TNC].[15]

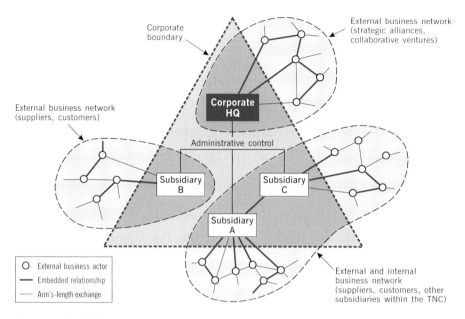

Figure 5.6   TNCs as networks within networks

Source: based in part on Forsgren et al., 2005: Figure 7.3

The precise manner, therefore, in which TNCs organize and configure their networks arises from a number of interrelated influences,[16] notably:

- the nature and complexity of the *industry environment(s)* in which the firm operates, including the nature of competition, technology, regulatory structures etc.
- the *firm's specific history and geography*, including

  o its *culture and administrative heritage* in the form of accepted practices built up over a period of time, producing a particular 'strategic predisposition'[17]
  o characteristics derived from its *home-country embeddedness*.

The geographical embeddedness of TNCs

Home-country influences

This latter influence merits more attention because it is too often assumed that TNCs are all much the same, regardless of their geographical origin. This is emphatically not the case.[18] TNCs are 'produced' through an intricate process of embedding, in which the cognitive, cultural, social, political and economic characteristics of the national home base continue to play a dominant part. This is not to claim that TNCs from a particular national origin are identical. This is self-evidently not the case. Within any national situation there will be distinctive corporate cultures, arising from the firm's own specific corporate history, which predispose it to behave strategically in particular ways. But, in general, the similarities between TNCs from one country will be greater than the differences between them.

> For example, a detailed study of US, German and Japanese firms found little blurring or convergence at the cores of firms based in Germany, Japan, or the US ... Durable national institutions and distinctive ideological traditions still seem to shape and channel crucial corporate decisions ... the domestic structures within which a firm initially develops leave a permanent imprint on its strategic behavior ... our findings underline, for example, the durability of German financial control systems, the historical drive behind Japanese technology development through tight corporate networks, and the very different time horizons that lie behind American, German, and Japanese corporate planning.[19]

One reason for continuing national distinctiveness is the extent to which TNCs continue to recruit their senior executives from their home country. This is especially apparent amongst US firms in which, in addition, senior executives tend to have far less international experience than, say, those in UK companies.[20] Within Europe, too, distinct differences continue to exist between TNCs from different European countries, despite the high level of economic integration within the EU. For example, an analysis of the national diversity of executive positions in large European companies showed that the overwhelming majority were from the TNC's home country.

> The recruitment dynamics on the executive board level in the EU are still strongly determined by characteristics of national government regimes and, as a result, their managerial labour markets seem highly segmented along national borders.[21]

Similarly, although there are some similarities between firms from East Asia, there are also distinct differences between them.[22] The major similarities are:

- formation of intra- and inter-firm business relationships
- reliance on personal relationships
- strong relationships between business and the state.

However, it is a mistake to think in terms of *one* East Asian business model because, in fact, there is considerable *diversity* between firms from different East Asian countries.

Japanese companies tend to be characterized by highly structured and formal relationships between firms within groups known as *keiretsu* (Figure 5.7).[23] Five diagnostic characteristics of these groups can be identified:[24]

- Transactions are conducted through alliances of *affiliated* companies. This creates a form of organization intermediate between vertically integrated firms and arm's-length markets.

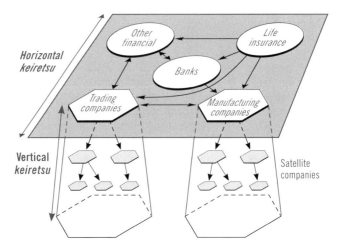

Figure 5.7   Basic elements of the Japanese *keiretsu*

Source: based in part on Gerlach, 1992: Figure 1.1

- Inter-firm relationships tend to be *long term* and stable, based upon mutual obligations.
- These inter-firm relationships are *multiplex* in form, expressed through cross-shareholdings and personal relationships as well as through financial and commercial transactions.
- Bilateral relationships between firms are embedded within a broader 'family' of *related companies*.
- Inter-corporate relationships are imbued with *symbolic significance* which helps to sustain links even where there are no formal contracts.

Firms from other East Asian countries, notably South Korea and Taiwan, also have strong and distinctive relational structures. Yet, despite sharing a common heritage of Confucian-based familism, they have developed different corporate systems. In South Korea, the dominant type of business group is the *chaebol*, modelled on the pre-Second World War Japanese *zaibatsu*, the giant family-owned firms which had been so important in the development of the Japanese economy. The *chaebol*

> are highly centralized, most being owned and controlled by the founding patri-arch and his heirs through a central holding company. A single person in a single position at the top exercises authority through all the firms in the group. Different groups tend to specialize in a vertically integrated set of economic activities.[25]

As a result, the South Korean economy became highly concentrated and oligopo-listic, with a relatively underdeveloped small- and medium-firm sector. Not only this, but many of these smaller firms are tightly tied into the production networks of the *chaebol*, which have developed into some of the most highly vertically integrated business networks in the world:

> the firms in the *chaebol* are the principal upstream suppliers for the big down-stream *chaebol* assembly firms ... in Samsung electronics, most of the main component parts for the consumer electronics division are manufactured and assembled in the same compound by Samsung firms.[26]

Taiwanese business networks, in contrast, have low levels of vertical integration. The more horizontal Taiwanese networks consist of two main types: 'family enter-prise' networks and 'satellite assembly' networks (independently owned firms that come together to manufacture specific products primarily for export).

These contrasts between the South Korean and Taiwanese business groups – despite the strong similarities between the two countries – have been explained as arising from

> differences in social structures growing out of the transmission and control of family property. In South Korea, the kinship system supports a clearly demar-cated, hierarchically ranked class structure in which core segments of lin-eages acquire elite rankings and privileges. These are the 'great families' ... In Taiwan, however, the Confucian family was situated in a very different social order ... Unlike Korea the Chinese practiced partible inheritance, in which all sons equally split the father's estate ... This set of practices pre-served the household and made it the key unit of action, rather than the lin-eage itself ... In summary, although based on similar kinship principles, the Korean and the Chinese kinship systems operate in very different ways.[27]

Such differences in socio-cultural practices largely explain the contrasts between the ways that business firms are organized in the two neighbouring countries.

Convergence or differentiation?

Our argument is that TNCs retain distinctive characteristics derived from their country of origin. But this does not imply that nationally embedded TNCs are unchanging. On the contrary, the very interconnectedness of the contemporary global economy means that influences are rapidly transmitted across boundaries. Corporations are *learning* organizations: they strive to tap into appropriate practices wherever they occur. This will, inevitably, affect the way business organizations are configured and behave. There 'is essentially a process of co-evolution through which different business systems may converge in certain dimensions and diverge in other attributes'.[28] The very fact that TNCs are *trans*national – that they operate in a diver-sity of economic, social, cultural and political environments – means that they will, inevitably, take on some of the characteristics of their host environments.

Non-local firms invariably have to adapt some of their domestic practices to local conditions. It is virtually impossible to transfer the whole package of firm advantages and practices to a different national environment. For example, Japanese overseas manufacturing plants tend to be 'hybrid' forms rather than the pure organizations found in Japan itself.[29] The same argument applies to US firms operating abroad. Even in the UK, where the apparent 'cultural distance' between the US and the UK is less than in many other cases, there is a very long history of American firms having to adapt some of their business practices to local conditions.

We can find plenty of evidence of change within TNCs in response to these various forces. For example, the *keiretsu* have been at the centre of Japanese economic development during the post–Second World War period. But the financial crisis in Japan that has persisted since the bursting of the 'bubble economy' at the end of the 1980s has put them under considerable pressure to change at least some of their practices. In particular, the recent influx of foreign capital to acquire significant, sometimes controlling, shares in some of these companies has had a catalytic effect. The most notable example was the acquisition by the French automobile company, Renault, of 44 per cent of the equity of Nissan (see Chapter 11). There are strong pressures, particularly from Western (notably US) finance capital, for Japanese business groups to open up to outsiders, to reduce or eliminate the intricate cross-shareholding arrangements, and to become more like Western (that is, US) firms with their emphasis on 'shareholder value' rather than the broader socially based 'stakeholder' interests intrinsic to Japanese companies. However, the 2008 financial crisis has greatly reduced the 'attractiveness' of the US model.

While, without doubt, some changes are occurring it would be a mistake to assume that Japanese firms will suddenly be transformed into US clones. The Japanese have a very long history of adapting to external influences by building structures and practices that remain distinctively Japanese. Similarly, Korean and other East Asian firms have come under enormous pressure to change some of their business practices in the aftermath of the region's financial crisis of the late 1990s. In Korea, the *chaebol* are being drastically restructured and the relationships with the state diluted. Among Chinese businesses, the strong basis in family ownership and control is being challenged by both internal and external forces. Greater involvement in the global economy is forcing these firms to modify some of their practices.[30] Similar observations apply to firms from other home countries. In the case of Germany, for example, while some of the established characteristics of German business are under threat, the evidence suggests that many of the core elements remain in place.[31]

It would be extremely surprising if the distinctive nature of nationally based TNCs were to be replaced by a universal form. Continued differentiation would appear to be the most likely scenario, although undoubtedly containing elements of change and some degree of convergence. A recent comparison of Japanese and American TNCs in the Asia–Pacific, for example, showed precisely that.

> The results point to a certain degree of inertia among American and Japanese TNCs regarding organizational change in international environments. While selection and mimetic convergence may not have been completely absent ... the reproduction of structures from the home country would seem also to have contributed to persistent differentiation ... pressures for convergence appear to have been mediated by some degree of contingency that suggests that TNCs will likely continue to exhibit national characteristics in international environments.[32]

In other words,

> the empirical evidence ... suggests that distinctive national histories have left legacies that continue to affect the behavior of leading [TNCs] ... The scope for corporate interdependencies across national markets has unquestionably expanded in recent decades. But history and culture continue to shape both the internal structures of [TNCs] ... and the core strategies articulated through them.[33]

So, where are we heading? Are TNCs converging towards a more or less universal form or are we likely to see continued differentiation? In my view, the answer is emphatically the latter.

These observations on the continuing geographical distinctiveness of TNCs need to be kept in mind during the remainder of this chapter as we outline some of the broad characteristics of TNC networks.

Configuring the TNCs' internal networks

Coping with complexity: a diversity of organizational architectures

One of the basic 'laws' of growth of any organism or organization is that as growth occurs its internal structure has to change. In particular, the *functional role* of its component parts tends to become more *specialized* and the links between the parts become more *complex*. In other words, its 'organizational architecture' has to change. As the size, organizational complexity and geographical spread of TNCs have increased, the internal interrelationships between their geographically separated parts have become a highly significant element in the global economy.

The traditional approach to changing a TNC's organizational architecture – based primarily on the hierarchical Western (that is, US) model – depicts it as a sequential process, whereby firms transform their organizational structures from a *functional* form, in which the firm is subdivided into major functional units (production, marketing, finance etc.), into a *divisional* form (usually product based). In such a divisional structure, each product division is responsible for its own functions, particularly of production and marketing, although some functions

Figure 5.8   Types of transnational organizational architecture

(especially finance) tend to be performed centrally for the entire corporation. Each product division also usually acts as a separate profit centre. The main advantage of the divisional structure is its greater ability to cope with product diversity.

Adoption of a divisional structure gave firms greater control over their increasingly diverse product environment. However, operating across national boundaries, rather than within a single country, poses additional problems of coordination and control. Largely through trial and error, TNCs have groped their way towards more appropriate organizational structures. Figure 5.8 shows four commonly used structures. Which one is actually adopted depends upon a number of factors, including the age and experience of the enterprise, the nature of its operations and its degree of product and geographical diversity.

The form most commonly adopted in the early stages of TNC development is simply to add on an *international division* to the existing divisional structure (Figure 5.8a). This tends to be a short-lived solution to the organizational problem if the firm continues to expand its international operations because problems of coordination and tension inevitably arise between the parts of the organization operated on product lines (the firm's domestic activities) and those organized on an area basis (the international operations).

There are two obvious possible solutions. One is to organize the firm on a *global product* basis: that is, to apply the product-division form throughout the world and to remove the international division (Figure 5.8b). The other possibility is to organize the firm's activities on a *worldwide geographical* basis (Figure 5.8c). But neither of these structures resolves the basic tension between product- and area-based systems. For such reasons some of the largest TNCs have adopted sophisticated *global grid* or *global matrix* structures (Figure 5.8d), containing elements of both product and area structures and involving dual reporting links.

Although there is plenty of evidence to support such a sequence, there is also plenty of evidence to demonstrate far greater organizational diversity. In this regard, Bartlett and Ghoshal's typology, though far from perfect, is very useful.[34] Table 5.1 summarizes the major features of each ideal-type.

Table 5.1   Some ideal-types of TNC organization: basic characteristics

Characteristics	Multinational	International	Global	Integrated network
Structural configuration	Decentralized federation. Many key assets, responsibilities, decisions decentralized	Coordinated federation. Many assets, responsibilities, resources, decisions decentralized but controlled by HQ	Centralized hub. Most strategic assets, resources, responsibilities and decisions centralized	Distributed network of specialized resources and capabilities
Administrative control	Informal HQ–subsidiary relationship; simple financial control	Formal management planning and control systems allow tighter HQ–subsidiary linkage	Tight central control of decisions, resources and information	Complex process of coordination and cooperation in an environment of shared decision-making
Management attitude towards overseas operations	Overseas operations seen as portfolio of independent businesses	Overseas operations seen as appendages to a central domestic corporation	Overseas operations treated as 'delivery pipelines' to a unified global market	Overseas operations seen an integral part of complex network of flows of components, products, resources, people, information amongst interdependent units
Role of overseas operations	Sensing and exploiting local opportunities	Adapting and leveraging parent company competencies	Implementing parent company strategies	Differentiated contributions by national units to integrated worldwide operations
Development and diffusion of knowledge	Knowledge developed and retained within each unit	Knowledge developed at the centre and transferred to overseas units	Knowledge developed and retained at the centre	Knowledge developed jointly and shared worldwide

Source: based on material in Bartlett and Ghoshal, 1998

Figure 5.9 'Multinational organization' model

Source: based on Bartlett and Ghoshal, 1998: Figure 3.1

The *'multinational organization'* model emerged particularly during the 1930s. A combination of economic, political and social factors forced firms to decentralize their operations in response to national market differences. The result was a decentralized federation of overseas units and simple financial control systems, overlain on informal personal coordination (Figure 5.9). The company's worldwide operations are organized as a portfolio of national businesses. This was the kind of transnational organizational form used extensively by expanding European companies. Each of the firm's national units has a very considerable degree of autonomy and a predominantly 'local' orientation. It is able, therefore, to respond to local needs, but its fragmented structure lessens scale efficiencies and reduces the internal flow of knowledge.

The *'international organization'* model came to prominence in the 1950s and 1960s as large US corporations expanded overseas to capitalize on their firm-specific assets of technological leadership or marketing power. This ideal-type involves far more formal coordination and control by the corporate headquarters over the overseas subsidiaries (Figure 5.10). Whereas 'multinational' organizations are, in effect, portfolios of quasi-independent businesses, 'international' organizations see their overseas operations as appendages to the controlling domestic corporation. Thus, the international subsidiaries are more dependent on the centre for the transfer of knowledge and the parent company makes greater use of formal systems of control. The 'international' TNC is better equipped to leverage the knowledge and capabilities of its parent company but its particular configuration and operating systems tend to make it less responsive than the 'multinational' model. It is also rather less efficient than the next ideal-type.

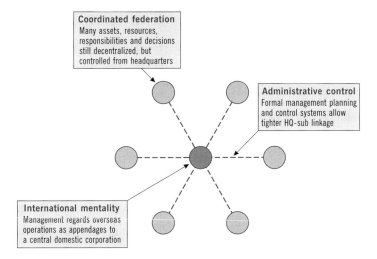

Figure 5.10 'International organization' model

Source: based on Bartlett and Ghoshal, 1998: Figure 3.2

The '*global organization' model* was one of the earliest forms of international business (used, for example, by Ford and by Rockefeller in the early 1900s, as well as by Japanese firms in their much later internationalization drive of the 1970s and 1980s). It is based upon a tight centralization of assets and responsibilities in which the role of the local units is to assemble and sell products and to implement plans and policies developed at the centre (Figure 5.11). Overseas subsidiaries have far less freedom to create new products or strategies or to modify existing ones. Thus, the 'global' TNC capitalizes on scale economies and on centralized knowledge and expertise. But this implies that local market conditions tend to be ignored and the possibility of local learning is precluded.

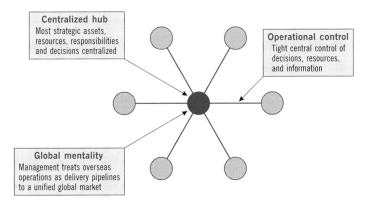

Figure 5.11 'Global organization' model

Source: based on Bartlett and Ghoshal, 1998: Figure 3.3

Although each of these three organizational types developed initially during specific historical periods, one did not simply replace the other. Because each has its strengths (as well as weaknesses), each has tended to persist, in either a pure or a hybrid form, helping to produce today's diverse TNC population.[35] There is some correlation between organizational type and nationality of parent company but it is by no means perfect; it is better to regard firms of different national origins as having a predisposition to one or other form of organization.[36]

The dilemma facing TNCs is that they need the best features of each organizational form: to be globally efficient, geographically flexible, and capable of capturing the benefits of worldwide learning – all at the same time. Hence, it is argued, we are now seeing the emergence of a fourth ideal-type TNC: the '*integrated network organization*' *model*, characterized by a distributed network configuration and a capacity to develop flexible coordinating processes (Figure 5.12). Such capabilities apply both inside the firm, displacing hierarchical governance relationships with

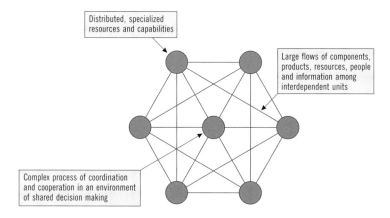

Figure 5.12 'Integrated network organization' model

Source: based on Bartlett and Ghoshal, 1998: Figure 5.1

what Hedlund terms a *heterarchical* structure,[37] and also outside the firm through a complex network of inter-firm relationships. We will explore this issue further later in the broader context of networks of externalized relationships.

The point to emphasize is the continuing diversity of organizational architectures: TNCs come in all shapes, sizes and forms of governance. Their internal architecture reflects not only the external constraints and opportunities they have to face – including the structures made possible by new communications technologies[38] – but also a strong element of path dependency. Firms organized on hierarchical principles not only still exist but also may still be in a majority. The newer, 'flatter', organizational forms tend to be confined to a limited number of firms in certain sectors.

Headquarters–subsidiary relationships

The various TNC architectures discussed in the preceding section, and especially those shown in Figures 5.9 to 5.11, assume a clear distinction between a TNC's organizational centre – its headquarters – and its subsidiary operations. In a pure hierarchical model, the relationship is assumed to be top-down. In reality, headquarters–subsidiary relationships tend to be highly contested, even in a hierarchical organization. In a *heterarchical* organization (Figure 5.12) the position is far more complex.[39] The roles played by a subsidiary, therefore, vary between different organizational structures and in terms of a TNC's specific strategy. Within all of this, the roles – and the powers – of subsidiary managers are in a continuous state of flux.

Three broad types of subsidiary role can be identified:[40]

- *The local implementer*: limited geographical scope and functions. Its primary purpose is to adapt the TNC's products for the local market.
- *The specialized contributor*: specific expertise tightly integrated into the activities of other subsidiaries in the TNC. Narrow range of functions and a high level of interdependence with other parts of the firm.
- *The world mandate*: worldwide (or possibly regional) responsibility for a particular product or type of business.

These different subsidiary roles have important implications for the impact of TNC activities on national and local economies (see Chapter 14). How these roles develop and possibly change – for example from local implementer to world mandate – depends upon the nature of the bargaining relationships within the TNC. Relationships within firms reflect internal power structures and bargaining relationships. In a similar way, the individual affiliates of a firm (its subsidiaries, branches etc.) are continuously engaged in competition to improve their relative position within the organization by, for example, winning additional investment or autonomy from the corporate centre. At the same time, the performance of each affiliate is continuously monitored against the relevant others (internal benchmarking) and this is used as an integral part of the internal bargaining processes within the firm.

In fact, the actual *geography* of a TNC influences these internal bargaining processes as well:

> Different 'places' within the firm, organizationally and geographically, develop their own identities, ways of doing things and ways of thinking over time … The firm's dominant culture, created by and expressed through the activities and understandings of top management at headquarters, necessarily contains multiple subcultures. Some of these may revolve around functions and cut across places (engineers versus sales people, for example), but some will have real geographical locations – they will have grown up in specific plants in particular places.[41]

'Grounding' the TNC: mapping the firm's internal geographies

> Every business is a package of functions and within limits these functions can be separated out and located at different places.[42]

Given their chosen organizational architecture, how do TNCs choose to locate their productive assets and capabilities? This is a fundamental issue for all TNCs, regardless of the kind of business they are in: whether they produce manufactured goods or business services; whether their product is 'hard', like cars or semiconductors or food, or 'soft', like information or money (another kind of information) or retailing. It is important to make this point because we are concerned in this book with all kinds of 'production', not only manufacturing.

Different business functions have different locational needs and, because these needs can be satisfied in various types of geographical location, each part tends to develop rather distinctive spatial patterns. Some functions tend to be geographically dispersed; others are geographically concentrated and co-located with other parts of the firm. In the following sections, we look at the geographical orientations of four of the major business functions:

- control and coordination
- research and development
- marketing and sales
- production.

Centres of strategic control and coordination

The *corporate headquarters* is the locus of overall control of the entire TNC.[43] It is the strategic centre responsible for all the major strategic investment and disinvestment decisions that shape and direct the enterprise: which products and markets to enter or to leave, whether to expand or contract particular parts of the enterprise, whether to acquire other firms or to sell off existing parts.

> The headquarters has to prevent subsidiaries from pursuing strategic initiatives that diverge from the [TNC's] strategy. In addition, the headquarters assesses the value of strategic resources distributed across the [TNC] network and coherently affects their mobility so as to assure that resources are made available where they are actually necessary.[44]

The headquarters is also the legal core of the TNC, responsible for complying with all the legal, financial and regulatory functions required of the firm by the jurisdictions in which it is located. One of its key roles is *financial*. The corporate headquarters holds the purse strings and decides on the allocation of the corporate budget between its component units. Headquarters offices are, above all, handlers, processors and transmitters of *information* to and from other parts of the enterprise and also between similarly high-level organizations outside. The most important of these are the major business services on which the corporation depends (financial, legal, advertising) and also, very often, major departments of government, both foreign and domestic. There is evidence that the size and complexity of corporate headquarters varies substantially between firms from different home countries.[45]

Regional headquarters offices constitute an intermediate level in the corporate organizational structure, having a geographical sphere of influence encompassing several countries. Regional headquarters perform several distinctive roles.[46] Most commonly, their primary responsibility is to *integrate* the parent company's activities within a region, that is, to coordinate and control the activities of the firm's affiliates (manufacturing units, sales offices etc.) and to act as the intermediary between the corporate headquarters and its affiliates within its particular region. Regional headquarters, therefore, are both coordinating mechanisms within the TNC and also an important part of the TNC's 'intelligence-gathering' system. A regional headquarters may also have an *entrepreneurial* role: to act as a base to initiate new regional ventures or to demonstrate to governments that the company has a commitment to the region. In either case, regional headquarters act as 'strategic windows' on regional developments and opportunities.[47] In some cases, regional headquarters are located close to the firm's major production facilities in a particular country or region. But that is not always the case.

These characteristic functions of corporate and regional headquarters define their particular *locational* requirements.

- Both require a *strategic location* on the global transportation and communications network in order to keep in close contact with other, geographically dispersed, parts of the organization.
- Both require access to *high-quality external services* and a particular range of *labour market skills*, especially people skilled in information processing.
- Since much corporate headquarters activity involves interaction with the head offices of other organizations, there are *strong agglomerative forces* involved. Face-to-face contacts with the top executives of other high-level organizations are facilitated by close geographical proximity. Such high-powered executives invariably prefer a location that is rich in social and cultural amenities.

Such locational criteria are met in only a small number of major cities in the world. For example, not only are the headquarters of the world's 500 largest TNCs located in only 125 cities but also four cities – New York, Tokyo, London and Paris – stand head and shoulders above all the others.[48] For such reasons, these four *global cities* are sometimes described as the geographical 'control points' of the global economy.[49] Below them is a tier of other key headquarters cities in each of the three major economic regions of the world: Europe (e.g. Amsterdam, Brussels, Düsseldorf, Frankfurt); North America (e.g. Atlanta, Chicago, Houston, Los

Angeles, Montreal, San Francisco, Toronto); Asia (e.g. Beijing, Hong Kong, Osaka, Seoul, Singapore, Taipei).

One of the most striking features of the geography of corporate headquarters (as opposed to regional headquarters) is their *geographical inertia*. Very few, if any, major TNCs have moved their ultimate decision-making operations outside their home country. An analysis of headquarters relocations of the *Fortune* Global 500, covering the period 1994–2002,[50] found only one! And this was the result of the (ultimately failed) merger between Daimler of Germany and Chrysler of the US. Such geographical fixedness is a further strong indicator of the continuing significance of the home base for corporate behaviour. On the other hand, TNCs are more willing to shift regional headquarters to meet changing circumstances. In East Asia, for example, there is an identifiable shift northwards as some firms move their regional HQs from Singapore to Shanghai (although Singapore remains a major regional focus).[51]

Within individual countries, on the other hand, the locational pattern of both corporate – and especially regional – headquarters is far from static, with substantial geographical decentralization of corporate headquarters out of the city centres of New York and London. In the case of London, most of these shifts are a short distance to the less congested outer reaches of the metropolitan area. In the US, on the other hand, there appears to be a much higher degree of locational change in headquarters functions. Nevertheless, corporate headquarters tend not to be spread very widely within any particular country. In the UK, for example, there are very few corporate headquarters of major firms or regional headquarters of foreign TNCs outside London and the south-east; in France few locate outside Paris. In Italy the most important centre is Milan, in the highly industrialized north, which is more important than Rome as a location for foreign TNCs.

Apart from corporate and regional headquarters, there are other key coordination functions that may be separated out geographically. For example, although a TNC's supply chain management is normally located at or near the corporate headquarters, or at one or more of the regional headquarters sites, there are cases where this function has been located beyond this part of the network. The Anglo-Dutch consumer products company, Unilever, has concentrated all its European supply chain coordination and management at a completely new site at Schaffhausen in Switzerland. IBM has moved its global procurement headquarters from New York to Shenzhen, China.

Corporate R&D facilities

The process of research and development (R&D) is a complex sequence of operations (Figure 5.13) consisting of three major phases, each of which tends to have rather different locational requirements although, in each case, the TNC has to reconcile several factors.[52] One of these is the advantage of gaining scale economies from concentrating R&D in one or a few large establishments. Another is the possible benefit of locating R&D close to corporate headquarters

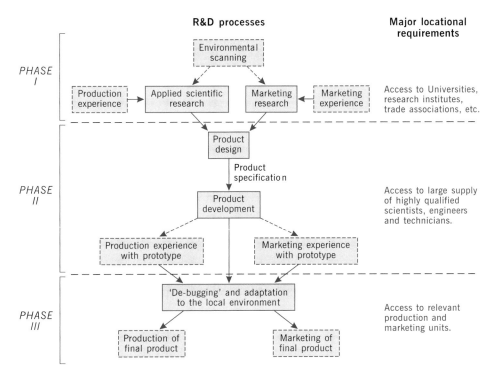

Figure 5.13   Corporate R&D processes

Source: based in part on Buckley and Casson, 1976: Figure 2.7

or, alternatively, close to production units to enhance communications and the sharing of ideas. Yet another possible locational pull is to markets, in order to benefit from closeness to customer needs, tastes and preferences.

The type of R&D undertaken by TNCs within their own transnational network can be classified into three major categories. The lowest level is the *support laboratory*, whose primary purpose is to adapt parent company technology to the local market and to provide technical back-up. It is by far the most common form of overseas R&D facility. The *locally integrated R&D laboratory* is a much more substantial unit, in which product innovation and development are carried out for the market in which it is located. The *international interdependent R&D laboratory* is of a quite different order. Its orientation is to the integrated global enterprise as a whole rather than to any individual national or regional market. Indeed, there may be few, if any, direct links with the firm's other affiliates in the same country. Only a small number of technologically intensive global corporations operate international interdependent laboratories.

Of course, these categories are not fixed and unchanging. In particular, the development of so-called 'open innovation' is changing the nature and relationships of corporate R&D units.

> Open innovation … means the end of the traditional R&D centre where scientists worked on confidential corporate projects in relative isolation from the outside world. Instead, companies are working with growing networks of external partners to commercialize their internal innovations and find other people's inventions to exploit.[53]

There is considerable disagreement over the extent to which TNCs are dispersing their R&D geographically. On the one hand, they continue to show a very strong preference for keeping their high-level R&D at home. Why should such home-country bias persist? The answer lies in the importance of the kinds of *untraded interdependencies* and of knowledge clusters discussed earlier (see Chapters 3 and 4):

> Two key features related to the launching of major innovations may help explain the advantages of geographic concentration: the involvement of inputs of knowledge and information that are essentially 'person-embodied', and a high degree of uncertainty surrounding outputs. Both of these are best handled through geographic concentration. Thus it may be most efficient for firms to concentrate the core of their technological activities in the home base with international 'listening posts' and small foreign laboratories for adaptive R&D.[54]

On the other hand, there is some evidence of increasing geographical dispersal of R&D activities within TNC networks. For example, by the late 1990s, there was 'an increasing share of company-financed R&D performed abroad by US firms *as compared to domestically financed* industrial R&D … US firms' investment in overseas R&D increased three times faster than did company-financed R&D performed domestically.'[55] In this regard, Asia is playing an increasingly important role as a location for certain kinds of R&D, especially in product development.[56] There are two major reasons for Asia's increasing significance.

> Asia's greatest overall advantage is its huge supply of scientists and engineers, particularly in China and India, at a time when students in the west are turning away from science and engineering. Companies in the US and Europe … can exploit Asia's trained workforce by building research and development centres there or collaborating with Asian companies and universities.[57]

The other advantage of an Asian location for some kinds of R&D is cost:

> The relative costs of doing research in Asia vary enormously according to circumstances … [However] the pay of newly graduated researchers in India and China is around one-quarter of US levels. For more senior staff, it is usually at least half the US level and in exceptional circumstances may even exceed it.[58]

Support laboratories tend to be the most widely spread geographically, in so far as they generally locate close to production units. But the larger-scale, and more complex, R&D activities tend to be confined to particular kinds of location. The need for a large supply of highly trained scientists, engineers and technicians, together with proximity to universities and other research institutions, confines such facilities to large urban complexes. These are often also the location of the firm's corporate headquarters. A secondary locational influence is that of 'quality of living' for the highly educated and highly paid research staff: an amenity-rich setting, including a good climate and potential for leisure activities as well as a stimulating intellectual environment.

Spatial patterns of corporate R&D in both the US and the UK illustrate both of these locational influences. In the US, corporate R&D is still predominantly a big-city activity despite recent growth in smaller urban areas. The pull of the amenity-rich environment is illustrated by the considerable concentration of R&D activities in locations such as Los Angeles, San Francisco and San Diego in California, Denver–Boulder in Colorado and the 'Research Triangle' in North Carolina. In the UK corporate R&D, like corporate headquarters and regional offices, is disproportionately concentrated in south-east England. Almost two-thirds (61 per cent) of the research undertaken by foreign affiliates in the UK is located in the south-east region of the country (compared with only 40 per cent of domestic firms' research).[59]

Marketing and sales units

Of all the various functions within a TNC, it is the marketing, and especially the sales, units that are likely to be the most geographically dispersed. The reason is obvious. These functions need to be as close as possible to the markets served by the firm. They must be sensitive to local conditions in order to be able to feed back relevant information. They must be in a position to help to tailor the firm's products to local tastes. Not least, they must be in a position to prevent the firm from making costly, and often embarrassing, mistakes in misreading the various consumer cultures in which the firms are operating. The marketing literature is full of examples of insensitive, sometimes culturally insulting branding or packaging decisions made by foreign TNCs, which have not fully understood local conditions. It is for such reasons that firms such as the Swiss company Nestlé have developed a strategy in which

> the consumer is paramount. Every decision has to be made as close to the consumer as possible. It makes no sense for us in Vevey to decide on the taste of a soup to be sold in Chile.[60]

Apart from the obvious tendency to locate marketing and/or sales units in the firm's most important geographical markets, there is a good deal of flexibility in the precise geographical articulation of such activities. Marketing functions, in particular, are often concentrated either at corporate headquarters or, increasingly, within regional headquarters where they are responsible for all the marketing decisions in the specific region. In some cases, they are located close to some of the firm's R&D activities, especially those at the development end of the spectrum, in order to create positive synergy between product development and market needs. Of course, with sophisticated internal communications systems, virtual geographical proximity may replace physical proximity. Sales units, on the other hand, tend to be smaller and very widely dispersed.

Production facilities

There are clearly some identifiable geographical regularities in the patterns of
TNC headquarters, R&D and marketing and sales activities. This is because their
locational needs are broadly similar for all firms, regardless of the particular activities
– 'hard' or 'soft' – in which they are involved. This is not so for production units, whose
locational requirements vary considerably according to the specific organizational and
technological role they perform within the enterprise and the geographical distribution of the relevant location-specific resources they need. It is certainly true that,
compared with corporate headquarters and R&D facilities, production units of TNCs
have become more and more dispersed geographically. But there is no single and
simple pattern of dispersal, whether at the global scale or within individual nations.
The pattern varies greatly from one industry to another. Figure 5.14 illustrates four
types of geographical orientation that a TNC might adopt for its production units.

(a) Globally concentrated production

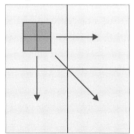

All production occurs at a single location.
Products are exported to world markets.

(b) Host-market production

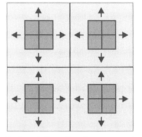

Each production unit produces a range of
products and serves the national market
in which it is located. No sales across
national boundaries. Individual plant size
limited by the size of the national market.

(c) Product specialization for a global or regional market

Each production unit produces only one
product for sale throughout a regional
market of several countries. Individual
plant size very large because of scale
economies offered by the large regional
market.

(d) Transnational vertical integration

Each production unit performs a separate
part of a production sequence. Units are
linked across national boundaries in a
'chain-like' sequence – the output of
one plant is the input of the next plant.

Each production unit performs a separate
operation in a production process and
ships its output to a final assembly plant
in another country.

**Figure 5.14   Alternative ways of organizing the geography of transnational
production**

Figure 5.14a presents the simplest case. All production is concentrated at a single geographical location (or, at least, within a single country) and exported to world markets through the TNC's marketing and sales networks. This is a procedure consistent with the classic global strategy shown in Table 5.1 and Figure 5.11. In contrast, in Figure 5.14b, production is located in, and oriented directly towards, a specific host market. Where that market is similar to the firm's home market the product is likely to be virtually identical to that produced at home. The specific locational criteria for the setting up of host-market units are:

- size and sophistication of the market
- structure of demand and consumer tastes
- cost-related advantages of locating directly in the market
- government-imposed barriers to market entry.

In effect, this kind of production is import substituting. Although the need to establish a production unit in a specific geographical market has become less necessary in purely cost terms (this may be changing as energy costs rise), there are two main reasons for the continued development of host-market production:

- the need to be sensitive to variations in customer demands, tastes and preferences, or to be able to provide a rapid after-sales service
- the existence of tariff and, particularly, non-tariff barriers to trade.

During the past four decades or so a radically different form of production organization has become increasingly prominent. Figure 5.14c shows production being organized geographically as part of a rationalized product or process strategy to serve a global, or a large regional, market (such as the European Union, North America or East Asia). The existence of a huge geographical market, together with differences in locationally specific characteristics between countries within a region, facilitates the establishment of very large, specialized units of TNCs to serve the entire regional market rather than single national markets. The key locational consideration, therefore, involves the trade-off between

- economies of large-scale production at one or a small number of large plants
- additional transportation costs involved in assembling the necessary inputs and in shipping the final product to a geographically extensive regional market.

This trade-off is once again becoming increasingly problematic as rising energy prices feed through to increased transportation costs. Firms that have been moving towards a network of fewer but very large production units are having to rethink this strategy.

A rather different kind of transnational production strategy involves geographical specialization by process or by semi-finished product, in which different parts of the firm's production system are located in different parts of the world. Figure 5.14d shows two ways in which such transnational process specialization might be organized as part of a vertically integrated set of operations across national boundaries. Materials, semi-finished products, components and finished products are transported between geographically dispersed production units in a highly complex web of flows. In such circumstances, the traditional geographical connection between production and market is broken. The output of a plant in one country may become the input for a plant belonging to the same firm located in another country. Alternatively, the finished product may be exported to a third-country market or to the home market of the parent firm. In such cases, the host country performs the role of an 'export platform'. Its role is to act as international sourcing point for the TNC as a whole.

Such offshore sourcing and the development of vertically integrated production networks at a global scale were virtually unknown before the early 1960s. The pioneers were US electronics firms that set up offshore assembly operations in East Asia as well as in Mexico. Since then, the growth of such transnational production networks has been extremely rapid in most sectors. Indeed, there has been a veritable avalanche of firms in the older industrialized countries of the West shifting some of their manufacturing or lower-level service operations (like call centres or basic information processing) to cheaper developing country locations.

The choice of location for a production unit at the global scale is by no means as simple as it is often made out to be. It is not just a matter of looking at differences in labour costs between one country and another or at the subsidies, grants or tax incentives offered by governments to attract investment (see Chapter 7). Despite the enormous shrinkage of geographical distance that has occurred, the relative geographical location of parent company and overseas production unit may still be significant. The sheer organizational convenience of geographical proximity may encourage TNCs to site offshore production in locations close to their home country even when labour costs there are higher than elsewhere.

Of course, just as geographical proximity may override differentials in labour costs, so too may other locational influences dominate in any particular case. For the largest TNCs the world is indeed their oyster. Their production units are spread globally, often as part of a strategy of *dual or multiple sourcing* of components or products. This is one way of avoiding the risk of over-reliance on a single source whose operations may be disrupted for a whole variety of reasons. In a vertically integrated production sequence, in which individual production units are tightly interconnected, an interruption in supply can seriously affect the other units, perhaps those located at the other side of the world. In an extreme case, a whole segment of the TNC's operations may be halted.

Nevertheless, major TNCs have developed highly complex and geographically extensive networks of control, R&D, sales and marketing and production facilities. Figure 5.15 provides just one example: the electronics firm Solectron.

> Solectron was concentrated in a single campus in Silicon Valley until 1991, when its key customers, Sun Microsystems, Hewlett Packard and IBM, began to demand global manufacturing and process engineering support. Within ten years, the company's footprint had expanded to nearly 50 facilities worldwide … Today, Solectron operates a set of global and regional headquarters, high and low mix manufacturing facilities, purchasing and materials management centers, new product introduction centers, after-sales repair service centers for products manufactured by Solectron and others, and technology centers to develop advanced process and component packaging technologies.[61]

Solectron was taken over by Flextronics in 2008 and a process of rationalization will inevitably change the shape of the production network shown in Figure 5.15.

Figure 5.15 Solectron's global network

Source: based on Sturgeon, 2002: Table 2

However, there are dangers in simply shifting production offshore.

> Many companies that tried to set up manufacturing networks across several parts of the world have produced a 'haphazard collection of plants which typically lacks global coherence'. And the costs are much higher than expected.[62]

> Moving production abroad remains, by far, the dominant trend. But … for a wide variety of reasons, ranging from poor decision-making and preparation and rising transport and labour costs, some European companies [are] moving production back closer to home.[63]

> More manufacturers in the US and western Europe are putting their investments closer to domestic operations, as part of an effort to simplify supply structures … This trend towards so-called 'near-shoring' … highlights difficulties facing US companies, in particular in managing their production operations in China. In the past few years, US companies have been more willing than they were at the end of the 1990s to invest in production operations in Mexico. Many see it as a low-cost region that is easier to operate in than China … [in Europe] more companies … are finding it more attractive to put production investments in low-wage areas in eastern Europe, as opposed to grappling with the problems of bringing in parts and finished goods over much longer distances.[64]

Of course, this should not be interpreted as heralding a complete reversal of long-distance networks. On the contrary. But what are sometimes presented as inexorable trends in one particular direction are, in fact, far less determinate. Reality consists of exceedingly complex cross-cutting tendencies both in time and over geographical space.

TNCs within networks of externalized relationships

In the previous section, the focus was on how TNCs organize and geographically configure their internalized networks. However, TNCs are also locked into *external* networks of relationships with a myriad of other firms: transnational and domestic, large and small, public and private (see Figure 3.5). As we saw earlier, the *boundary* between what is inside and what is outside the firm has become far more blurred.

Outsourcing relationships

No firm is completely self-sufficient. Overall, between 50 and 70 per cent of manufacturing costs are to purchase inputs. Indeed, a very strong general trend among both manufacturing and service firms in recent years has been for a greater proportion of activities to be *outsourced* to supplier firms.[65]

> The increasing implementation of outsourcing strategies is one of the most remarkable changes that has characterized firm behavior in the last decades. This strategy allows firms to concentrate their capabilities and resources in their respective core businesses, giving up those activities where firms do not have any competitive advantage.[66]

As a consequence, specialist 'outsourcing firms' have emerged, particularly in the case of those business services whose function is to arrange and facilitate outsourcing (see Chapter 13).

Outsourcing, especially through longer-term relationships, is a kind of halfway house between complete internalization of procurement on the one hand and arm's-length transactions through the open market on the other. It is a *multitiered* process, as Figure 5.16 suggests, in which firms in each tier may themselves outsource some of their activities. There are, broadly, two major types of outsourcing, both based on a supplier firm producing a good or service to a principal firm's specifications:

- '*Commercial*' *outsourcing*: the manufacture of a finished product. The supplier plays no part in marketing the product, which is generally sold under the principal's brand name and through its distribution channels. The principal firm may be either a producer firm, that is, one that is also involved in manufacturing, or a retailing or wholesaling firm whose sole business is distribution.

- '*Industrial*' *outsourcing*:
  - *Speciality* outsourcing involves the carrying out, often on a long-term basis, of specialized functions which the principal chooses not to perform for itself but for which the supplier has special skills and equipment.
  - *Cost-saving* outsourcing is based upon differentials in production costs between principal and supplier for specific processes or products.
  - *Complementary or intermittent* outsourcing is a means adopted by principal firms to cope with occasional surges in demand without expanding their own production capacity. In effect, the supplier is used as extra capacity, often for a limited period or for a single operation.

Figure 5.17 summarizes some of the major features of the outsourcing relationship.

Outsourcing obviously has profound geographical implications. Initially, it depended on close proximity between firms and suppliers and was a major factor underlying the development and persistence of traditional 'industrial districts' – agglomerations of

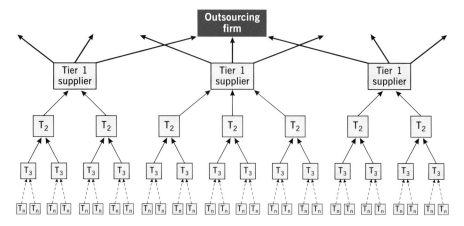

Figure 5.16   Outsourcing as a multitiered process

Figure 5.17   Outsourcing relationships

linked firms. However, innovations in transportation and communications have greatly increased the geographical extensiveness of outsourcing networks. Much of the increase in long-distance sourcing was driven by the desire to take advantage of the wide differentials in labour costs between different parts of the world. As the distance between customers and suppliers increased, however, problems inevitably arose in terms of the reliability of supplies. Many firms had to establish sophisticated – and very costly – systems of stock/inventory holding to insure against interruptions in the supply of finished goods or components. This is the kind of 'just-in-case' system shown on the left-hand side of Table 5.2.

Table 5.2 'Just-in-case' and 'just-in-time' systems of supplier relationships

'Just-in-case' system	'Just-in-time' system
Characteristics	
Components delivered in large, but infrequent, batches	Components delivered in small, very frequent, batches
Very large 'buffer' stocks held to protect against disruption in supply or discovery of faulty batches	Minimal stocks held – only sufficient to meet the immediate need
Quality control based on sample check after supplies received	Quality control 'built in' at all stages
Large warehousing spaces and staff required to hold and administer the stocks	Minimal warehousing space and staff required
Use of large number of suppliers primarily on the basis of price	Use of small number of preferred selected suppliers within a tiered supply system
Remote relationships between customer and suppliers	Very close relationships between customer and suppliers
No incentive for suppliers to locate close to customers	Strong incentive for suppliers to locate close to customers
Disadvantages	
Lack of flexibility – difficult to balance flows and usage of different components	Must be applied throughout the entire supply chain
Very high cost of holding large stocks	Reliance on small number of preferred suppliers increases risk of interruption in supply
Remote relationships with suppliers prevents sharing of developmental tasks	
Requires a deep vertical hierarchy of control to coordinate different tasks	

Source: based on material in Sayer, 1986

However, as we saw in Chapter 4, production processes have changed dramatically. The emphasis is increasingly on rapid product turnover, speed to market, responsiveness to customer needs: on what, in the context of the automobile industry, has come to be called 'lean' production (see Chapter 11). In such a production system, holding large stocks of inventory in warehouses is anathema. Supplies must be delivered precisely when (and where) they are needed, that is, *just-in-time* (JIT). The major features of a JIT system are shown on the right-hand side of Table 5.2. When JIT first came to prominence, largely within Japanese automobile and electronics firms in the 1970s, it was widely predicted that the result would be a large-scale geographical reconcentration of suppliers near to their customers. In other words, there would be a return to the old-style industrial clusters. In fact, although there have undoubtedly been some geographical shifts towards closer links between customers and suppliers, there has not been universal reconcentration. Rather, a wide variety of geographical scales is involved, depending on firm- and industry-specific circumstances.

It is tempting to regard suppliers as always being in a subservient position – merely small cogs in a much larger structure over which they have no influence. Often that is the case, although much depends on the position they occupy within a production network and also the kind of network involved (see the next section). However, Andersen and Christensen argue that some subcontractors act as important 'connective nodes in supply networks.[67] They identify five such 'bridging roles':

- *Local integrator*: firms able to provide access to additional production capacity through their relationships with other firms in the same locality. 'Local integrators may take on a host of different roles in the supply network, depending on fluctuations in the demand situation … [they] may even take over commercial contracting, functioning as end producers – e.g. act as private label producers for a trading firm or look for market opportunities in a broad range of industrial branches' (1266).
- *Export base*: such firms act as 'the gate of access to a local technological district … These subcontractors provide … superior knowledge regarding the competences of local suppliers … This bridging role is most likely found in speciality subcontracting or systems supplies, through which the subcontractor adds knowledge to the products of the customer … Export base subcontractors utilize their relations with customers to marshal relations with other subcontractors in their local area. Often, they take on the complex task of coordinating a local network of suppliers' (1266, 1267).
- *Import base*: these firms represent 'the gateway to international resources or skills for customers in the local or national area, as the international customer–supplier relations of the import base suppliers are used as generators of foreign market and product knowledge … compared to the local integrator, this firm depends heavily on representing a specific international range of technologies to local customers … the important task of the subcontractor is to foresee demand fluctuations and buffer them accordingly, either via extended information exchange with subcontractors or by keeping an extended inventory' (1268).
- *International spanner*: often, such firms have evolved from being an export or import base subcontractor as their supply sources and buyers have internationalized. 'The position of the international spanner is a precarious one. There are pressures at both end of the supply chain, which seek to attract the subcontractor further into the supply source or further to the logistical basis of the buyer … international spanners sometimes base their business potential on information asymmetries between subcontractors and buyers … The ability to orchestrate these activities globally is the required coordinative capability of these firms' (1269).
- *Global integrator*: 'A hybrid form of subcontractor … responsible for all bridging activities of the international supply chain … connecting internationally

dispersed buyers and subcontractors and supplying the necessary logistical infrastructure for carrying out exchange. The primary strategic asset … is its developed infrastructure and its ability to often manage quite different streams of manufactured goods … Compared to the roles taken by the other subcontractors in the typology, the global integrator has a strong bargaining position towards buyers as well as subcontractors' (1270).

Benefits and costs of outsourcing

For the outsourcing firm the process is widely seen as a way of enabling it to focus on its 'core competences' and to shed activities that do not fit. The logic is that costs will be reduced and profits enhanced through such concentration on core activities. This may well be the case. But there are also risks in outsourcing, as a number of well-publicized cases have shown. In 2005, for example, British Airways became mired in a very messy dispute with the firm supplying all its airline food, Gate Gourmet. Originally, BA had produced all its catering needs in-house and what became Gate Gourmet was the result of a sell-off of these activities to a US venture capital firm. Should BA have retained the catering function as one of its core activities? The company said no; others were less sure.

A more recent example of the potential problems of outsourcing to cheap labour locations occurred in 2007 when toys produced under outsourcing arrangements by Wal-Mart were found to contain lead. The case clearly illustrates the problems of controlling geographically and organizationally extended production networks.

> Wal-Mart squeezes Mattel [the toy maker], Mattel squeezes its supplier, that supplier squeezes its supplier, and at the end of the chain you have a remote business far out in the countryside that takes a different approach. They don't put lead in paint because they are wicked, it's just what works for them. China is so large, and industrialization has been so rapid, that maintaining any control over multiple sites is extremely difficult.[68]

For supplier firms, on the other hand, one of the major benefits of the increasing trend for firms to outsource some of their major functions is that it provides opportunities to fill the gap. This has certainly been a major reason for the rapid industrialization of a number of developing countries, especially in East Asia but also elsewhere, as well as in Eastern Europe.

In fact, however, the trend towards outsourcing, though very strong at present, is not inevitable or irreversible. There are many examples of activities that have been outsourced being brought back in later as the firm reassesses its priorities. The unpredictability of supply and the changing impact of volatile currency exchange rates have encouraged a good many firms to switch to supplier firms closer to home or even to take the process back in-house. In other words, the boundary between externalization and internalization and between sourcing abroad and at home is continuously shifting, and not always in predictable directions.

Different ways of coordinating transnational production networks

In Chapter 3 we noted that production networks can be coordinated in a variety of different ways, involving a mix of intra-firm and inter-firm structures. It is now time to examine this more closely.[69] Figure 5.18 shows one way of categorizing types of network coordination. In this discussion I will concentrate on three of the five coordination types shown in Figure 5.18: captive, relational and modular production networks. In all three networks, what we are interested in are the changing relationships between 'lead' firms and suppliers. We will encounter examples of these different types of network in the case studies of Part Three.

Captive production networks

These are networks in which a lead firm is dominant and effectively controls – although it does not own – all the major components in the network.

Coordination mechanism	Complexity of transactions	Ability to codify transactions	Capabilities of potential suppliers	Degree of explicit coordination and power asymmetry
Hierarchy Vertical integration within a firm with governance of subsidiaries and affiliates based on head-quarters' managerial control.	HIGH	LOW	LOW	HIGH
Captive Small suppliers transactionally dependent on larger buyers. Suppliers face significant switching costs.	HIGH	HIGH	LOW	
Relational Complex interactions between buyers and sellers often creating mutual dependence and high levels of asset specificity.	HIGH	LOW	HIGH	
Modular Production to customer's specification.	HIGH	HIGH	HIGH	
Market May involve repeat transactions but switching costs low for both parties.	LOW	HIGH	HIGH	LOW

Figure 5.18   Different ways of coordinating transnational production networks

Source: based on material in Gereffi et al., 2005

> Lead firms seek to lock-in suppliers in order to exclude others from reaping the benefits of their efforts. Therefore, the suppliers face significant switching costs and are 'captive'. Captive suppliers are frequently confined to a narrow range of tasks – for example, mainly engaged in simple assembly – and are dependent on the lead firm for complementary activities, such as design, logistics, component purchasing, and process technology upgrading.[70]

In such networks, the instructions to suppliers are highly codifiable while power is highly asymmetrical and lies unequivocally with the lead firm.

The hierarchically organized networks of major Japanese and Korean companies, discussed earlier, are captive networks. An especially graphic (although not necessarily a typical) example is provided by the US sports footwear company, Nike. Nike does not wholly own any production facilities but consists entirely of a complex tiered and tightly coordinated network of subcontractors that perform specialist roles controlled from the corporate headquarters in Beaverton, Oregon, where most of the firm's R&D is also carried out (Figure 5.19).

Nike employs indirectly more than 800,000 workers in its 'contract supply chain' in a vast number of factories (Figure 5.20). In terms of its geographical extensiveness it is certainly global. However, there is a strong bias towards East Asia, which contains almost 60 per cent of total suppliers. Of these, the majority are located in China, followed by Thailand. Indonesia, Vietnam and Malaysia are also significant elements in the network. Only around 8 per cent of the total suppliers are in South Asia (mostly in Sri Lanka and India); 10 per cent are in Central/Latin America (mostly in Mexico and Brazil); and 12 per cent are in Europe (primarily Portugal and Turkey).

Relational production networks

> Relational production networks are governed less by the authority of lead firms, and more by social relationships between network actors, especially those based on trust and reputation.[71]

Relational production networks, therefore, have more symmetrical power relationships than captive production networks. They are the kinds of network that exist among overseas Chinese businesses and some other ethnic/social groups. The 'technical' transnational communities that have developed in the US electronics industries around Taiwanese, Chinese and Indian immigrants have facilitated rapid and extensive growth of global production networks based on relational processes.[72] In many cases, these individuals have created relational production networks in their home countries that are integrated into global networks. Many of these are the kinds of 'born global' enterprises discussed earlier.

Within Europe, examples of relational networks have been identified in Germany (the complex contracting relationships between small and medium firms) and in Italy. In both cases, as well as in other parts of the world, it has been

Figure 5.19   Organization of the Nike production network

Source: based on Donaghu and Barff, 1990: Figure 4; 542–4.

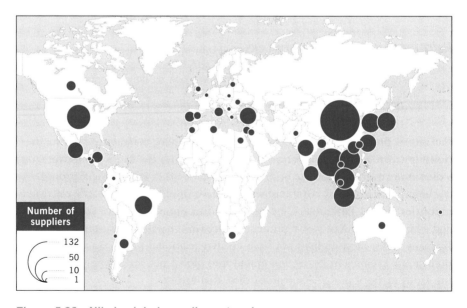

Figure 5.20   Nike's global supplier network

Source: based on data in Nike Inc., 2009, *Nike Contract Disclosure List* argued that it is the close *spatial proximity* between firms and other social institutions that provides the 'relational cement' for the networks to exist. During the 1980s, in particular, it became extremely popular to eulogize such 'industrial districts' as the way forward from the old rigidities of Fordist mass production systems. However, important as close spatial proximity may be in facilitating the development of relational production networks, on its own it is not sufficient, as we saw in discussing localized knowledge clusters in Chapter 4.

One view of relational networks is that they may point the way towards the emergence of the *virtual firm* or the *cellular network* organization (Figure 5.21).[73] Organizationally, the entire network structure is relatively 'flat' and non-hierarchical. Its essence is that the participants are all separate firms with no common ownership. They are cooperative, *relational*, structures between independent and quasi-independent firms that are based upon a high degree of trust, something that takes time to develop. However, this does not mean that there are not *power* differentials within the network. There certainly are. Network forms of this broad type are gradually emerging in such 'knowledge businesses' as advanced electronics, computer software design, biotechnology, design and engineering services, healthcare and the like.

Modular production networks

For many industries, the changes of the past twenty years mean that organizing production has become more like playing with a set of Legos than building a model airplane or a car. In other words, it's now possible to create many

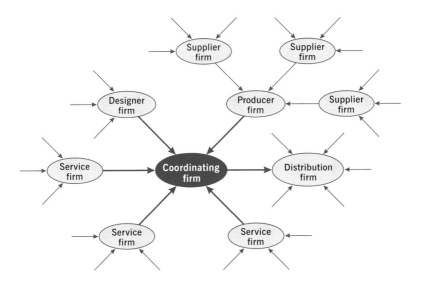

Figure 5.21   A 'pure' relational network

Source: based in part on Miles and Snow, 1986: Figure 1

> different models using the same pieces. New components can be added on to old foundations; elements from old structures can be reused in new configurations; parts can be shared by many players with different construction plans in mind ... the myriad possibilities of organizing a company have grown out of new digital technologies that create countless opportunities for using resources, organizations, and customers all over the world to build businesses that did not even exist ten years ago.[74]

The development of modular production networks[75] depends largely on the fact that some modern production circuits have 'natural' breakpoints, where there is a transition from dependence on tacit knowledge to one where information can be codified through standard, agreed protocols. This has led, in an increasing number of industries, to a situation in which lead firms concentrate primarily on product development, marketing and distribution, while what are termed *turnkey suppliers* concentrate on producing those functions outsourced by lead firms and to sell them, in effect, as services to a wide range of customers. To achieve this, turnkey suppliers develop three types of cross-cutting specialization:[76]

- '*base process*, one which is used to manufacture products sold in a wide range of end-markets (e.g. pharmaceutical manufacture, semiconductor wafer fabrication, plastic injection molding, electronics assembly, apparel assembly, brewing, telecommunications backbone switching)'
- '*base component*, one that can be used in a wide variety of end-products (e.g. semiconductor memory, automotive braking systems, engine controls)'
- '*base service*, one that is needed by a wide variety of end-users (e.g. accounting, data processing, logistics), rather than on processes or services that are idiosyncratic or highly customer-specific'.

> Turn-key suppliers, then, tend to develop *generic* manufacturing capacity and services that allow product variation to be very large as long as their specifications fall within the parameters of the base process. In the manufacturing sectors mentioned above, most turn-key suppliers use highly automated production systems (apparel assembly is a major exception) that can be programmed and re-programmed on short notice to produce a wide variety of products.[77]

Figure 5.22 shows how such modular production networks differ from that of a traditional vertically integrated hierarchical firm.

The development of contract manufacturing in the electronics industry provides a clear example of the development of modular production networks.[78] The increasing scale and complexity of outsourcing by US electronics firms in the 1980s and 1990s created a demand for suppliers to develop large capabilities at a global scale in order to serve the increasingly transnationalized lead electronics firms. The result was the emergence of a small number of very large electronics contract manufacturers from North America – Solectron, Flextronics, Sanmina/SCI, Celestica, Jabil

(a) Vertical integration

(b) Modularity

Figure 5.22   From vertical integration to modular production networks

Source: based on Sturgeon, 2002: Figure 1

Circuit – which now operate a global network of establishments serving the leading brand-name electronics manufacturers (see Figure 5.15).

These different types of production network – hierarchical, captive, relational and modular – coexist in varying combinations in different industries and in different parts of the world. There is some evidence to suggest that firms from particular national origins tend to adopt particular types of production network. For example, the modular network form has developed most clearly in the US and reflects a relative openness of procedures and a desire to reduce the degree of mutual dependence. Key to this system is the extensive and intensive use of 'IT suppliers that provide widely applicable "base processes" and widely accepted standards that enable the codifiable transfer of specification across the inter-firm link. These preconditions lead to generic (not product-specific) capacity at suppliers that has the potential to be shared by the industry as a whole'.[79] The extent to which such a system will be adopted more widely and lead to convergence of practice is an open question and relates to the comments made about the persistence of nationally grounded variations in TNC structures and practices discussed earlier in this chapter.

Transnational strategic alliances

Related to the development of relational and modular production networks is one of the most significant developments in the global economy in recent years: the growth and spread of transnational *strategic alliances* between firms.[80] Collaborative ventures between firms across national boundaries are nothing new. What is new is their current scale, their proliferation, and the fact that they have become *central* to the global strategies of many firms rather than peripheral to them. Most strikingly, the overwhelming majority of strategic alliances are *between competitors*. In other words, they reflect a new form of business relationship, a 'new rivalry … in the way collaboration and competition interact'.[81] Many companies are forming not just single alliances but *networks of alliances*, in which relationships are increasingly multilateral rather than bilateral, polygamous rather than monogamous. In effect, they create new *constellations* of economic power. As a result, a new component – 'collective competition' – has been added to the economic landscape.

Strategic alliances are formal agreements between firms to pursue a *specific* strategic objective; to enable firms to achieve a specific goal that they cannot achieve on their own. It involves the sharing of risks as well as rewards through joint decision-making responsibility for a specific venture. Strategic alliances are not the same as mergers, in which the identities of the merging companies are completely subsumed. In a strategic alliance only *some* of the participants' business activities are involved; in every other respect the firms remain not only separate but also usually competitors.

Three major modes of collaboration are involved in strategic alliances (Figure 5.23): research oriented, technology oriented and market oriented. Alliances offer the following (potential) kinds of advantage to the participants:

- overcoming problems of access to markets
- facilitating entry into new/unfamiliar markets
- sharing the increasing costs, uncertainties and risks of R&D and of new product development
- gaining access to technologies
- achieving economies of synergy, for example by pooling resources and capabilities and by rationalizing production.

Very often, the motivations for strategic alliances are highly specific. In the case of R&D ventures, for example, cooperation is limited to research into new products and technologies while manufacturing and marketing usually remain the responsibility of the individual partners. Cross-distribution agreements offer firms ways of widening their product range by marketing another firm's products in a specific market area. Cross-licensing agreements are rather similar but they also offer the possibility of establishing a global standard for a particular technology. Joint manufacturing agreements are used both to attain economies of scale and also to cope with excess or deficient production capacity. Joint bidding consortia are especially important in very large-scale projects in industries such as aerospace or telecommunications, where the sheer scale of the venture or, perhaps, the specific regulatory requirements of national governments put the projects out of reach of individual companies.

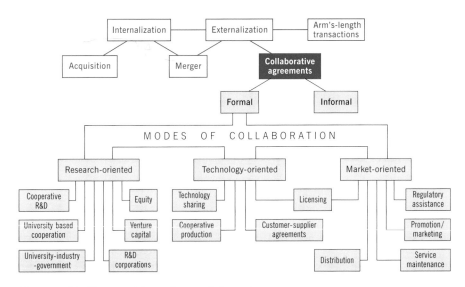

Figure 5.23 Types of inter-firm collaboration

Source: based on Anderson, 1995: Figure 1

The majority of strategic alliances, therefore, are in sectors with high entry costs, scale economies, rapidly changing technologies and/or substantial operating risks.

> Pharmaceuticals, chemicals, electronic equipment, computers, telecommuni-cations, and financial and business services are examples of industries char-acterized by a large number of strategic alliances ... Although a large number of alliances are still formed in manufacturing industries, more and more stra-tegic alliances are taking place in the services ... As the world economy becomes more service-based, strategic alliances are playing a more impor-tant role in cross-border restructuring in service sectors.[82]

Advocates of strategic alliances claim that by cooperating, companies can combine their capabilities in ways that will benefit each partner. But not everybody shares this rosy view. Many fear that entering into such alliances will result in the loss of key technologies or expertise by one or other of the partners. More broadly, strategic alliances are clearly more difficult to manage and coordinate than single ventures; the potential for misunderstanding and disagreement, particularly between partners from different cultures, is great. Certainly many such alliances have relatively short lives. For example, the global network alliances in the global telecommunications industry (Global One, Concert, AT&T World Partners) all failed and were dismantled.[83] Nevertheless, the obvious attractions of international strategic alliances in today's volatile and competitive global economy are likely to guarantee their continued growth as a major organizational form.

Perpetual change: reshaping TNCs' internal and external networks

Transnational corporate networks – both internal and external – are always in a state of flux. At any one time, some parts may be growing rapidly, others may be stagnating, yet others may be in steep decline. The functions performed by the component parts and the relationships between them may alter. Change itself may be the result of a planned strategy of adjustment to changing internal and external circumstances or the 'kneejerk' response to a sudden crisis.

Forces underlying reorganization and restructuring

Corporate reorganization and restructuring are driven by two, often overlapping, forces:

- *External conditions*: these may be negative pressures, such as declining demand, increased competition in domestic or foreign markets, changes in the cost or availability of production inputs, militancy and resistance of labour forces in particular places, the pressure of national governments to modify their activities or even to cede control. Conversely, changes in external conditions may be positive, for example the growth of new geographical markets or the availability of new production opportunities. A good illustration is the formation of regional economic groupings, where the creation of a large regional market provided an unprecedented opportunity for TNCs to restructure their production activities to serve the regional market. Investments that had made sense in the context of an individual national context are no longer necessarily rational in the wider context (see Figure 5.14).
- *Internal pressures*: these may relate to the enterprise as a whole or to one or other individual parts: for example, sales may be too low in relation to the firm's target, production costs may be too high. In a TNC the performance of individual plants in widely separate locations can be continuously monitored and compared to assess their efficiency. A key influence is often the 'new broom factor': a new chief executive who undertakes a sweeping evaluation of the enterprise's activities and makes changes that stamp his/her authority on the firm.

In reality, external and internal pressures may be so closely interrelated that it is often difficult to disentangle one from the other. More than this, precisely how firms both identify and respond to changes in their circumstances is very much conditioned by the firm's culture.[84]

Complex corporate restructuring occurs at all geographical scales, from the global to the local, as strategic decisions are made about the organizational coordination and geographical configuration of the TNC's production network. Decisions to outsource or internalize particular functions, to centralize or to decentralize decision-making powers, or to cluster or disperse some or all of the firm's functions in particular ways are, however, contested decisions. They are the outcome of power struggles within firms, both within their headquarters and between headquarters and affiliates. How they are resolved depends very much on the nature and the location of the dominant coalition.

The 'global–local' question: an oversimplified view of the TNC's dilemma

Such processes also have to be seen within the context of an apparently funda-mental tension facing TNCs: whether to globalize fully or to respond to local differentiation. In broad terms, the intensification of global competition in a world that retains a high degree of local differentiation creates, for all TNCs, an internal tension between globalizing forces on the one hand and localizing forces on the other. As Figure 5.24 shows, there are considerable potential advantages for a firm pursuing a globally integrated strategy. But there are also substantial disadvantages. Figure 5.25 captures this basic tension within a 'global integration, local responsiveness' framework. The vertical axis shows the major pressures on firms to strive for global strategic coordination of their activities; the horizontal axis shows the countervailing pressures on firms to develop locally responsive strategies.

Advantages	Costs and risks
✓ The firm's oligopoly power is increased through the exploitation of scale and experience effects beyond the size of individual national markets.	✗ The TNC may be vulnerable to disruption of its entire operations (or part of them) because of labour unrest or government policy changes affecting a particular unit.
✓ The TNC is placed in a better position to exploit the growing discrepancy between a relatively efficient market for goods (created by freer trade) and very inefficient markets for production factors.	✗ Fluctuations in currency exchange rates may disrupt integration strategies, drastically altering the economies of intrafirm transactions of intermediate or final goods.
✓ The possibility of exploiting differences in tax rates and structures between countries is increased and so, therefore, is the possibility of engaging in transfer pricing.	✗ Governments may impose performance require-ments or other restrictions which impede the optimal operation of the firm's integrated production chain.
✓ The specialized and integrated function of indi-vidual country operations makes hostile govern-ment action less rewarding and less likely.	✗ The task of managing a globally integrated oper-ation is more complex and demanding than that of managing separate national subsidiaries.

Figure 5.24   The advantages and disadvantages of a globally integrated strategy

Source: based on material in Doz, 1986b

Figure 5.25   A global integration, local responsiveness framework

Source: based on material in Prahalad and Doz, 1987: Figure 2.2; 18–21

In reality, firms engaged in transnational production face far more complex and multidimensional decisions about the geographical configuration and organizational coordination of their operations than the simple global/local dichotomy suggests. Production circuits and production networks are immensely complex structures, made up of many different functions and activities. From a TNC's perspective, operating in many different economic, political, social and cultural environments, very difficult decisions have to be made about every one of them:

- Which functions are to be performed internally (in-house) and which are to be outsourced to other firms?
- Where should each of the firm's own internalized functions be located? Which functions need to be located close to each other? Which ones can be separated out and located elsewhere to enhance efficiency? What should the balance be between domestic production and producing offshore?
- Where should suppliers be located? Should they be close to the firm's home base or should they be in other countries (i.e. offshore)? Do suppliers need to be located nearby or can they be geographically dispersed to take advantage of lower costs or other locationally specific attributes?
- How is control over geographically dispersed activities – both internal and external – to be exercised?

As if these were not sufficiently complicated decisions, there is the fundamental problem that, of course, TNCs are not dealing with a 'clean surface': their geographically dispersed assemblage of functions, offices, factories and the like have evolved over time rather than having been planned. Some will have been located in particular places for reasons that may have been valid at the time the decisions were made but which, in the light of changed circumstances, may no longer be optimal for the firm's current needs. Because so much TNC growth and expansion have been through acquisition and merger, virtually all TNCs consist of elements originally put in place by quite different firms (often of different nationalities and ways of doing things). In many cases, these have been only partially integrated into the new corporate entity, often creating a veritable 'dog's breakfast' of bits and pieces. This is one reason why so many mergers and acquisitions are far less successful than their advocates predict.

Not only is the entire system in flux because of the dynamics of competition or the uncertainties inherent in operating in uncertain, and sometimes volatile, political environments, but also each of the individual elements is continuously faced with uncertainty. One of the diagnostic characteristics of TNCs is that they continuously monitor the performance of each of their individual operations and benchmark them against some best-practice metric. Hence, transnational corporate networks are almost always in a state of rationalization and restructuring, either in whole or in part. Precisely because TNC operations are located in different countries, such adjustments – perhaps involving the closure, downsizing or functional status of individual establishments – have very sensitive political implications.

The geography of reorganization and restructuring

Whether corporate reorganization is the result of a consciously planned strategy for 'rational' change or simply a reaction to a crisis (internal or external), its geographical outcome may take several different forms (Figure 5.26). The very large global corporations are developing into *global scanners*. They use their immense resources to evaluate potential production locations in all parts of the world. The performance of existing corporate units and external suppliers is monitored and evaluated against competitors, against the rest of the corporate network, and also against potential alternative locations. Those existing plants or suppliers that fall short of expectations created by such *benchmarking* procedures[85] may be disposed of. As plants become obsolete in one location they are closed down; whether or not new investment occurs in the same locality depends upon its suitability for the TNC's prevailing strategy. The chances are, in many cases, that the new investment will be made at a different location – quite possibly in a different country altogether.

However, we should beware of over-exaggerating the speed and ease with which TNCs can, and do, radically restructure their operations. There are 'barriers to exit'. Production units represent huge capital investments – sunk costs – which 'once undertaken, cannot be fully recovered through their transfer or sale'.[86] Political pressures may also inhibit firms from closing plants, especially in areas of

Figure 5.26   Reorganization, restructuring and geographical change

economic and social stress. On the other hand, TNCs do have a highly tuned capacity to *switch* and *reswitch* operations within their existing corporate network. They also have the resources to alter the shape of their geographical network through locational shifts.

Hence, the processes of reorganization and restructuring are complex, dynamic and far from predictable. Overall, however, four continuing general tendencies are especially apparent:

- redefining core activities by stripping away activities that no longer 'fit' the firm's strategy
- placing greater emphasis on downstream, service functions
- geographically reconfiguring production networks transnationally to redefine the roles and functions of individual corporate units
- redefining the boundary between internalized and externalized transactions.

The myth of the 'global' corporation

One of the central claims of the hyper-globalists is that transnational firms are abandoning their ties to their country of origin and converging towards a universal *global* organizational form. Technological and regulatory developments in the world economy, it is argued, have created a 'global surface' on which a dominant organizational form is developing and wiping out less efficient competitors no longer protected by national or local barriers. Such an organization is, it is argued, 'placeless' and 'boundaryless'. Throughout this book we challenge this view.

How 'global' are the world's leading TNCs?

If the 'global corporation' hypothesis were valid then we would expect to find that at least the majority of the world's largest TNCs would have the overwhelming majority of their operations outside their home country. One measure of such geographical spread is the *transnationality index* (TNI) of each of the leading 100 TNCs.[87] The TNI is a weighted average of three indicators: foreign sales as a percentage of total sales; foreign assets as a percentage of total assets; and foreign employment as a percentage of total employment. The higher the value, the greater the extent of a firm's transnationality; the lower the value, the more a firm is domestically oriented.

Figure 5.27 compares TNIs for firms from individual countries over a 15-year period. It shows that the degree of transnationality among the leading 100 TNCs has increased progressively. In 1993 the average TNI was 51.6; in 2007 it was 62.7. Nevertheless, this still means that around 40 per cent of their activities are based in their home countries. Of course, the composition of the top 100 did not remain constant because of entries and exits into the list over the period. However, the degree of transnationality continues to vary substantially between firms from different geographical origins. Part of this is explained by country size: the smaller the country, in general, the more transnational its companies tend to be. But that is not the entire story. Japanese firms continue to have the lowest average TNI of the major home countries, though it increased substantially between 1993 and 2007. Although the US average increased from 36.7 to 57.2, the overall extent of transnationality of US firms remains significantly lower than that of other major countries. Thus, despite many decades of international operations,

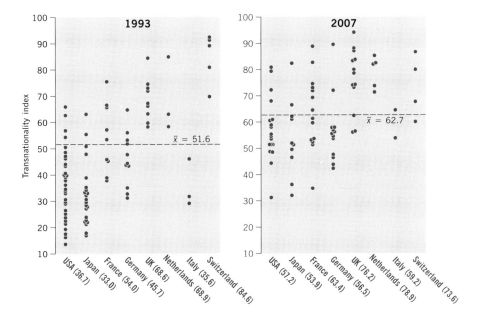

Figure 5.27 Transnationality indices by country of origin

Source: calculated from UNCTAD *World Investment Report*, various issues

TNCs – at least in quantitative terms – remain strongly connected with their home base.

The TNI, in fact, goes only a very small way towards answering the question of how global the world's leading TNCs are. It tells us something about the relative *geographical extent* of TNC activities outside the home country but it only distinguishes between home and foreign. A firm might have a TNI of, say, 80 (meaning that 80 per cent of its activities were outside its home country) but all of those activities might be located in just one foreign country. An example would be the large number of US firms that operate only in Canada. Neither does it help us to establish whether or not TNCs of different national origins are becoming similar in their modes of operation. It is at least possible that TNCs may retain more of their assets and employment in their home country but still be converging organizationally and behaviourally towards a universal, global form.

Regionalizing transnational production networks

A growing body of research suggests that rather than being globally organized, most of the largest TNCs have a very strong propensity to organize their production networks *regionally* (that is, at the multinational scale of groups of contiguous states).[88] For example, 'for Western core companies, regionalism has become the institutional framework of choice within which the struggle for preservation of their core positions is played out ... *the acceleration in the rate of internationalization after 1995 was an intra-regional phenomenon*'.[89] In 2004, four-fifths of the 500 largest TNCs in the world had almost 80 per cent of both their sales and their assets concentrated in their home region.[90] 'Global' this is certainly not.

The basis for such a regional orientation is evident in Figure 5.14c. In effect,

> a regional strategy offers many of the efficiency advantages of globalization while more effectively responding to the organizational barriers it entails ... From the perspective of a TNC, a regional strategy may represent an ideal solution to the competing pressures for organizational responsiveness and global integration.[91]

In particular:[92]

- Regional-scale manufacturing facilities may represent the limits of potential economies of scale.
- Regionalization allows for faster delivery, greater customization and smaller inventories than would be possible under globalization.
- Regionalization accommodates organizational concerns and exploits subsidiary strengths.

The tendency we noted earlier for firms to draw back somewhat from all-out 'global' sourcing (whether intra- or inter-firm) is strongly reflected at the regional scale, as a recent report suggested.

> Manufacturers are abandoning global supply chains for regional ones in a big shift brought about by the financial crisis and climate change concerns … Companies are increasingly looking closer to home for their components, meaning that for their US or European operations they are more likely to use Mexico and Eastern Europe than China, as previously. 'A future where energy is more expensive and less plentifully available will lead to more regional supply chains', Gerard Kleisterlee, chief executive of Philips, one of Europe's biggest companies.[93]

In some instances, TNC regionalization is reinforced by regional political structures – as in the cases of the EU or the NAFTA – although this is not necessarily the case. Simple geographical proximity is, itself, a very powerful stimulus for integrating operations.

Transnational production networks organized at the regional scale are evident in most parts of the world but most especially in the three major regions of Europe, North America and East Asia, as we shall see in several of the case study chapters in Part Three. In North America, the establishment of the NAFTA has led to a reconfiguration of corporate activities (especially in Mexico) to meet the opportunities and constraints of the new regional system.[94] In Europe, the increasing integration and enlargement of the European Union is leading to substantial reorganization of existing corporate networks and the establishment of pan-EU systems by existing and new TNCs. 'The EU can be seen as a gigantic international production complex made up of the networks of TNCs which straddle across national boundaries and form trade networks in their own right.'[95]

There is abundant evidence of US and Japanese TNCs – as well as many European firms themselves – creating regional networks within the EU. Some Japanese companies, for example, have adopted

> a three-tier European operation, partly centralised and partly decentralised. A number of them have set up small, new, pan-European head offices, with a purely strategic role: financial control, overall direction, high-level brand management … The real work is done, however, by the next two tiers of the business: the operational centres (production, distribution, logistics) organised on a pan-European basis and sited where convenient. For distribution, this means in the heartland of western Europe, with easy access to France and Germany; for production it will increasingly mean in eastern and central Europe, where costs are lower. Sales and tactical marketing are handled at a national level. Perhaps where two or three countries have very similar characteristics, such as the Nordic region, they can be aggregated together. But, in general, national markets are sufficiently distinctive to require their own local sales operations.[96]

The process is complicated. On the one hand, supply-side forces are stimulating a pan-EU structure of operations to take advantage of scale efficiencies. On the other hand, demand-side forces are still articulated primarily at the country-specific level, where linguistic and cultural differences play a major role in the demands for goods and services. In effect, the strategic tensions between global integration and local responsiveness, discussed at the beginning of this chapter, are played out at the EU regional level.

Although East Asia does not have the same kind of regional political framework as the EU or NAFTA, there is very strong evidence of the existence of regional production networks organized primarily by Japanese firms, although non-Asian as well as some other Asian firms (from Korea, Hong Kong, Singapore, and Taiwan, for example) also tend to organize their production networks regionally.[97] Within East Asia, a clear intra-regional division of labour has developed consisting of four tiers of countries: (1) Japan; (2) Hong Kong, Korea, Singapore and Taiwan; (3) China; and (4) Malaysia, Thailand, Indonesia, the Philippines and Vietnam. Of course, the rapid emergence of China both as a huge potential market and as a production location is transforming intra-regional networks in East Asia.

NOTES

1   D'Aveni (1994: 2).
2   See Palloix (1975; 1977).
3   Herod (1997: 2).
4   Hymer (1976).
5   Dunning (1992; 2000).
6   Vernon (1966; 1979), Wells (1972).
7   Cantwell (1997).
8   Dicken and Miyamachi (1998), Mason (1994).
9   Peter Brabeck, CEO of Nestlé, quoted in the *Financial Times* (22 February 2005).
10   Gabrielsson and Kirpalani (2004), Mathews and Zander (2007), Melén and Nordman (2009), Oviatt and McDougall (2005), Sasi and Arenius (2008).
11   Mathews and Zander (2007: 390).
12   Mathews and Zander (2007: 388).
13   Oviatt and McDougall (2005: 38).
14   See Badaracco (1991), Blois (2006), Cerrato (2006), Dicken and Malmberg (2001), Forsgren et al. (2005), Markusen (1999).
15   Forsgren et al. (2005: 97–8).
16   Bartlett and Ghoshal (1998), Faulconbridge (2008), Forsgren et al. (2005), Hedlund (1986), Heenan and Perlmutter (1979), Morgan et al. (2004), Schoenberger (1997), Whitley (2004).
17   Heenan and Perlmutter (1979).
18   Dicken (2000; 2003b).
19   Pauly and Reich (1997: 1, 4, 5, 24).
20   *Financial Times* (4 December 2007).

21 Van Veen and Marsman (2008: 196).

22 Yeung (2000: 408).

23 Fruin (1992), Gerlach (1992).

24 Gerlach (1992: 4).

25 Wade (2004a: 324).

26 Hamilton and Feenstra (1998: 128–9).

27 Hamilton and Feenstra (1998: 134, 135).

28 Yeung (2000: 425). See also Yeung (2004).

29 Abo (1994; 1996). See also Beechler and Bird (1999).

30 Yeung (2004).

31 See, for example, Bathelt and Gertler (2005), Buck and Shahrim (2005).

32 Poon and Thompson (2004: 123).

33 Doremus et al. (1998: 3, 9).

34 Bartlett and Ghoshal (1998).

35 Harzing (2000), Malnight (1996).

36 Heenan and Perlmutter (1979).

37 Hedlund (1986: 218–30).

38 Fields (2004), Roche and Blaine (2000).

39 Birkinshaw (2001), Birkinshaw and Morrison (1995), Cerrato (2006), Phelps and Fuller (2000).

40 Birkinshaw and Morrison (1995: 732–5).

41 Schoenberger (1999: 210–11).

42 Haig (1926: 426).

43 See Baaij et al. (2004), Cerrato (2006), Collis et al. (2007), Young et al. (2000).

44 Cerrato (2006: 261).

45 Collis et al. (2007), Young et al. (2000).

46 Lasserre (1996).

47 Yeung et al. (2001: 165).

48 Alderson and Beckfield (2004). See also Carroll (2007).

49 Friedmann (1986), Sassen (2001), Taylor (2004).

50 Baaij et al. (2004: 143).

51 *Financial Times* (19 March 2007).

52 See Blanc and Sierra (1999), Cantwell (1997), Hotz-Hart (2000), Patel (1995), Zanfei (2000).

53 *Financial Times* (30 October 2006).

54 Patel (1995: 152).

55 Blanc and Sierra (1999: 188).

56 *Financial Times* (23 June 2005).

57 *Financial Times* (9 June 2005).

58 *Financial Times* (9 June 2005).

59 Cantwell and Iammarino (2000: 322).

60 CEO of Nestlé, cited in the *Financial Times* (22 February 2005).

61 Sturgeon (2002: 461–2).

62 Institute for Manufacturing, Cambridge University, quoted in the *Financial Times* (17 December 2007).

63 *Financial Times* (5 June 2008).

64 *Financial Times* (10 June 2005).

65   Mol et al. (2005), Berggren and Bengtsson (2004).

66   Merino and Rodriguez (2007: 1147).

67   Andersen and Christensen (2004: 1261). Numbers in parentheses in the following paragraphs refer to pages in this study.

68   Teagarden, quoted in the *Financial Times* (4 September 2007).

69   This section draws, in part, on Gereffi et al. (2005), Sturgeon (2002; 2003).

70   Gereffi et al. (2005: 87).

71   Sturgeon (2003: 482).

72   Saxenian (2002: 186).

73   Miles et al. (1999).

74   Berger (2005: 61).

75   This section draws heavily on Sturgeon (2002; 2003). See also Berger (2005).

76   Sturgeon (2002: 466–7); quotations are from that work.

77   Sturgeon (2002: 467).

78   Sturgeon (2002; 2003), Lüthje (2002).

79   Sturgeon (2002: 486).

80   See Anderson (1995), Gomes-Casseres (1996), Kang and Sakai (2000), Mockler (2000).

81   Gomes-Casseres (1996: 2).

82   Kang and Sakai (2000: 20).

83   Ulset (2008).

84   Schoenberger (1997: 204).

85   See Sklair (2001: Chapter 5).

86   Barham and Coomes (2005: 162). See also Schoenberger (1997: 88).

87   The data are derived from the annual UNCTAD *World Investment Report*.

88   Elango (2004), Kozul-Wright and Rowthorn (1998), Morrison and Roth (1992), Muller (2004), Rugman and Brain (2003), Rugman and Verbeke (2004; 2008).

89   Muller (2004: ix, 219, original emphasis).

90   Rugman and Verbeke (2008: Tables 1 and 2).

91   Morrison and Roth (1992: 45, 46).

92   Morrison and Roth (1992: 46–7).

93   *Financial Times* (10 August 2009).

94   Eden and Monteils (2002), Holmes (2000).

95   Amin (2000: 675).

96   *Financial Times* (8 November 2001).

97   Abo (2000), Borrus et al. (2000), Coe (2003a), Dicken and Yeung (1999), Yeung (2001), Yeung et al. (2001).

Six

THE STATE *REALLY DOES* MATTER

'The state is dead' – oh no it isn't!

That was then; this is now

> The nation state is just about through as an economic unit.[1]

Such a sentiment has formed a central claim of the 'hyper-globalizers' over the past 40 years: that we live in a borderless world where states no longer matter. A combination of the revolutionary technologies of transportation and communications (see Chapter 4) and the increasing power of TNCs (see Chapter 5) has, it was argued, shifted economic power out of the control of nation-states to 'the market'. 'Market fundamentalism' – a neo-liberal agenda that urged the reduction of state involvement in the economy, the privatization of state economic and social assets, lower direct taxation, unfettered trade and financial movements, a reduction in the state's social welfare role – became the mantra, especially in the US and the UK. 'Government', argued US President Ronald Reagan in the early 1980s, 'was not a solution to our problem, government is the problem'. A similar sentiment was echoed by the UK government of Margaret Thatcher. Such a free market ideology formed the basis of what came to be called the 'Washington Consensus', a set of views that exerted immense influence on both developed and, especially, developing countries.

That was then.

This is now – and how the world has changed! The cataclysmic events that stunned the global economy in 2008 saw a dramatic reversal in the apparently unchallenged dominance of the free market and a revival of the view that 'states really do matter'. The change was most apparent in the financial sector (see Chapter 12), where the 'Masters of the Universe'[2] had to go on bended knee to the state to be rescued, but also in such industries as automobiles (see Chapter 11). Governments poured billions of dollars, pounds and euros into propping up the financial sector. In some cases, notably in the US and the UK, this amounted to little short of nationalization, a bête noire of the market fundamentalists. Quite how this will play out over the next few years is not yet clear. However, there is a generally held view that things will never be quite the same again.

> Something big is happening. What started out as a series of pragmatic ad hoc responses by governments and central banks is moving the boundary between state and market. Politicians are now overlaying expediency with ideology. Government is no longer a term of abuse ... The consequences of the crash of 2008 will be felt well beyond the eventual recovery ... What is certain is that things cannot be as they were.[3]

The state is back.

In fact, the state never really went away. The notion that the power of the state had been totally emasculated by globalizing forces was always a highly misleading view. While some of the state's capabilities were reduced, and there may well have been a process of 'hollowing out',[4] the process was not a simple one of uniform decline on all fronts.[5]

> While smaller or less influential states might have experienced a decline in power … other states (such as the USA) experience no diminution, and perhaps even an enhancement of geopolitical and geoeconomic power … *Much of the 'end of the state' or 'reasserting the state' literature focuses on western notions of statehood and experiences* … Implicit is a common experience of the emergence of the state in the nineteenth century and its zenith in the postwar Fordist regime of accumulation … *In many parts of the world, however, experiences of statehood have followed a quite different trajectory and are, in a postcolonial context, still being actively constructed, strengthened and extended rather than weakened.*[6]

The state, therefore, has remained a most significant force in shaping the world economy, despite the hyper-globalist rhetoric. It has always played a fundamental role in the economic development of *all* countries and, indeed, in the process of globalization itself. After all, an increased facility to transcend geographical distance made possible by transportation and communication technologies is of little use if there are political barriers to such movement. An important enabling factor underlying globalization, therefore, has been the progressive reduction in political barriers to flows of commodities, goods, finance and other services.

In fact, the more powerful states have actually used globalization as a means of increasing their power:

> States actively construct globalization and use it as soft geo-politics and to acquire *greater* power over, and autonomy from, their national economies and societies respectively … [for example] The US and the G-7's other dominant members design and establish the international trade agreements, organizations, and legislation that support and govern the trans-border investments, production networks, and market-penetration constitutive of contemporary economic globalization. Advanced capitalist states, particularly, use these political instruments to shape international economic decision-making and policy in their interests.[7]

Governments have also used the rhetoric of the supposedly unstoppable forces of globalization to justify particular kinds of domestic policy (including not taking certain kinds of action) on the argument that 'there is no alternative'.

States, nations, nation-states

We need to be clear about what we mean by the terms 'state', 'nation' and 'nation-state:[8]

- A *state* is a portion of geographical space within which the resident population is organized (i.e. governed) by an authority structure. States have externally recognized sovereignty over their territory.
- A *nation* is a 'reasonably large group of people with a common culture, sharing one or more cultural traits, such as religion, language, political institutions, values, and historical experience. They tend to identify with one another, feel closer to one another than to outsiders, and to believe that they belong together. They are clearly distinguishable from others who do not share their culture.' A nation is an *imagined community*. Note that whereas a state has a recognized and defined territory, a nation may not.
- A *nation-state* is the condition where 'state' and 'nation' are coterminous. 'A nation-state is a nation with a state wrapped around it. That is, it is a nation with its own state, a state in which there is no significant group that is not part of the nation.'

Although it is often regarded as a natural institution (for all of us it has always been there), the nation-state is actually a relatively recent phenomenon. It emerged from the particular configuration of power relationships in Europe following the Treaty of Westphalia that ended the Thirty Years War in 1648. Since then, the map of nation-states has been redrawn continuously, sometimes peacefully and incrementally, often violently through revolution. During the second half of the twentieth century, two particular events had a profound effect on the map of nation-states. First, the waves of decolonization that swept through Africa and Asia in the 1960s created a whole new set of nation-states. Second, the collapse of the former Soviet Union, after 1989, resulted in the creation not only of a new Russian Federation but also of a number of newly independent states throughout Eastern Europe. As a result, the number of nation-states has grown dramatically (Figure 6.1).

But that isn't all. An important feature of the contemporary world is the tension that exists between the triad of nation, state and nationalism. Increasingly, it seems, there are more and more 'nations without states', manifested in separatist movements engaged in conflict with the state in which they are (wrongly in their view) embedded (obvious examples include the Basques in Spain and France, the indigenous groups in Chiapas, Mexico, the East Timoreans in Indonesia, the Palestinians in Israel).

States as *containers*

The term 'container' should not be taken too literally. It is used as a fairly loose metaphor to capture the idea that nation-states are *one* of the major ways in which distinctive cultures, practices and institutions are 'bundled together'.[9] Of course, such containers are not (except in very rare cases) hermetically sealed off from the outside world. The container is permeable or leaky to varying degrees. Most

Figure 6.1   A world of nation-states

obviously, a major impact of modern communications systems, especially the Internet, is to make national containers even more permeable. But that does not mean that the container no longer exists at all. Indeed, there is a good deal of compelling evidence to show the persistence of national distinctiveness – although not necessarily uniqueness – in structures and practices which help to shape local, national and global patterns of economic activity.

Cultural dimensions

All economic activity is embedded in broader cultural structures and practices,[10] although 'culture' is an extremely slippery concept to define. Here it is taken to be

> a learned, shared, compelling, interrelated set of symbols whose meanings provide a set of orientations for members of a society. These orientations, taken together, provide solutions to problems that all societies must solve if they are to remain viable.[11]

From an economic perspective, there are relatively few comprehensive and robust analyses of how cultures vary between countries. The most widely known is Hofstede's classic study of more than 100,000 workers employed by the American company IBM in 50 different countries.[12] Hofstede claimed that, by focusing on a controlled population within a common organizational environment, he was able to isolate *nationality* as a variable. He identified four distinct cultural dimensions:

- *Individualism versus collectivism*: societies vary between those in which people, in general, are motivated to look after their own individual interests – where ties between individuals are very loose – and those in which ties are very close and the collectivity (family, community etc.) is the important consideration.
- *Large or small power distance*: societies vary in how they deal with inequalities (for example, in power and wealth) between people. This is reflected in the extent to which authority is centralized and in the degree of autocratic leadership within society.
- *Strong or weak uncertainty avoidance*: in some societies, the inherent uncertainty of the future is accepted; each day is taken as it comes, that is, the level of uncertainty avoidance is weak. In other societies, there is a strong drive to try to 'beat the future'. Efforts (and institutions) are made to try to create security and to avoid risk. These are strong uncertainty avoidance societies.
- *Masculinity versus femininity*: societies can be classified according to how sharply the social division between males and females is drawn. Societies with a strong emphasis on traditional masculinity allocate the more assertive and dominant roles to men. They differ substantially from societies where the social gender role division is small and where such values are less evident.

Group	1. Anglo		2. Germanic		3. Nordic		4. More developed Asian
Characteristics	Low power distance Low to medium uncertainty avoidance High individualism High masculinity		Low power distance High uncertainty avoidance Medium individualism High masculinity		Low power distance Low to medium uncertainty avoidance Medium individualism Low masculinity		Medium power distance High uncertainty avoidance Medium individualism High masculinity
Countries	Australia Britain Canada	Ireland New Zealand USA	Austria Germany Israel	Italy South Africa Switzerland	Denmark Finland Netherlands	Norway Sweden	Japan
Group	**5. Less developed Asian**		**6. Near Eastern**		**7. More developed Latin**		**8. Less developed Latin**
Characteristics	High power distance Low uncertainty avoidance Low individualism Medium masculinity		High power distance High uncertainty avoidance Low individualism Medium masculinity		High power distance High uncertainty avoidance High individualism Medium masculinity		High power distance High uncertainty avoidance Low individualism Whole range on masculinity
Countries	India Pakistan Philippines	Singapore Taiwan Thailand	Greece Iran Turkey		Argentina Belgium Brazil	France Spain	Chile Colombia Mexico	Peru Portugal Venezuela

Figure 6.2   National variations in cultural characteristics

Source: based on Hofstede, 1980: 336

Hofstede went on to show how different countries could be characterized in terms of their positions on varying combinations of these four dimensions (Figure 6.2).

Although Hofstede's work has stood the test of time remarkably well,[13] it is not without its critics. For example, Schwartz[14] argued that not enough countries were included fully to capture national cultural variation and that the respondents were too narrowly drawn to be truly representative of the entire population. Using rather different methods, Schwartz identified the following seven distinctive cultural dimensions:

- *Conservatism*: places an emphasis on preserving the status quo and on restricting behaviour likely to disrupt the traditional order.
- *Intellectual autonomy*: the extent to which people are free to pursue their own intellectual ideas.
- *Affective autonomy*: the extent to which people are free to pursue their own personal and emotional desires.
- *Hierarchy*: the extent to which an uneven allocation of power and resources is legitimized.
- *Egalitarian commitment*: the extent to which individuals are prepared to subjugate self-interest for the greater communal good.
- *Mastery*: the extent to which individual self-assertiveness is legitimized as a means to achieve specific goals.
- *Harmony*: the importance placed on fitting harmoniously into the environment.

Although there is obviously some overlap between these two schemes, what matters for our purposes is not so much the detail as the fact that there *are* identifiable cultural attributes that do appear to vary across countries and that this, in turn, affects both how the major actors we identified in Chapter 3 are likely to behave and also the kinds of institutions within which such behaviour is organized and regulated. Although it is always rather dangerous to classify phenomena into statistical boxes, the categories shown in Figure 6.2 seem intuitively reasonable. Most of us would be able to recognize our own national contexts, whilst also realizing the danger of using simple stereotypes without due care.

East Asia's emergence as the most dynamic growth region in recent decades has sometimes been attributed to its having a very distinctive set of value systems: specifically, an emphasis on collective responsibility rather than individualism and on the roles and responsibilities of the state, which is seen as essentially paternalistic. Figure 6.3 sets out the major components of this concept of 'Asian values' which, in effect, 'recast "Asia" as a moral opposite of the West. Thus … the Asian penchant for hard work, frugality and love of the family are unproblematically figured as things the West lacks or has lost.'[15] Whether such opinions reflect the situation across all of East Asia (let alone across Asia as a whole) is doubtful. This is, after all, a region of immense social, cultural and religious diversity. But in so far as they reflect at least some of the social and political characteristics of some successful East Asian economies, they form a considerable contrast with the situation in other parts of the world and help to explain some of the differences between East Asia's and, say, Latin America's economic development trajectories.

Figure 6.3   Asian values?

Source: based on material in Koh, 1993

Variegated capitalisms

The specific cultural and institutional forms that have evolved over time in different national contexts have resulted in distinctive modes of economic organization, even within the apparently universal ideology of capitalism. Capitalism, in other words, is *variegated*, not uniform.[16] The traditional 'varieties of capital' literature focuses on just two broad categories of 'national' capitalism: the *liberal market economy* (LME), generally associated with the US and, to a lesser extent, the UK; and the *coordinated market economy* (CME), most commonly associated with such countries as Germany, Sweden and Japan. However, this is not a very satisfactory classification, for a whole variety of reasons.[17] In particular, the CME category encompasses enormous diversity and needs to be further unpacked. Here we identify four variants of capitalist organization, based on differing conceptions of the 'proper' role of government in regulating the economy.

- *Neo-liberal market capitalism.* Market mechanisms are used to regulate all, or most, aspects of the economy. Individualism is a dominant characteristic; short-term business goals tend to predominate. The state does not overtly attempt to plan the economy strategically. Capital markets are decentralized, open and fluid. The dominant philosophy is 'shareholder value' – facilitating maximum returns to the owners of capital. Exemplified by the US and, to a large extent, the UK.
- *Social-market capitalism.* In contrast to neo-liberal market capitalism, a higher premium is placed upon collaboration between different actors in the economy with a broader identification of 'stakeholders' beyond that of owners of capital. The concept of 'social partnership' is more prominent. Capital markets tend to be bank centred. Exemplified by Germany, Scandinavia and many other European countries.
- *Developmental capitalism.* The state plays a much more central role (although not usually in terms of public ownership of productive assets). The state sets substantive social and economic goals within an explicit industrial strategy. Capital markets tend to be bank centred. There is a strong emphasis on tight business networks. Exemplified by Japan, South Korea, Taiwan, Singapore and most other East Asian countries.
- *Authoritarian capitalism.* Here, a highly centralized political system is combined with an increasingly open capitalist market system. The prime example is China but there are others, notably Russia. In the case of China, the process of liberalizing the economy (in a highly controlled way) began in 1979. Nevertheless, the Chinese Communist Party retains tight political control. In the case of Russia, the system is rather more messy. Both political and economic structures were liberalized after 1991 but the Russian state still exerts strong control (though less effectively than in China).

A key question is the extent to which such variegated capitalism will continue to exist. One view is that

> there are inherent obstacles to convergence among social systems of produc-
> tion of different societies, for where a system is at any one point in time is
> influenced by its initial state … Existing institutional arrangements block cer-
> tain institutional innovations and facilitate others … There are critical turning
> points in the history of highly industrialized societies, but the choices are
> limited by the existing institutional terrain. Being path dependent, a social
> system of production continues along a particular logic until or unless a fun-
> damental societal crisis intervenes.[18]

An alternative view is that the pressures exerted by globalizing forces will inevitably produce a convergence of economic governance systems towards a 'best practice' form. Many argued that the neo-liberal model, based on the 'success' of its leading advocate, the US, would come to replace national systems. In other words,

> even though the unique kinds of state capacities found in Japan and Germany
> have deep-rooted political preconditions, these face the prospect of 'perma-
> nent dismantling' by way of gradual 'liberal erosion.[19]

But, as we have seen, the 'pure gold' of the neo-liberal model is now looking distinctly tarnished and it is difficult to imagine that it will retain its attractiveness. If this is so, then variegated capitalism will continue to be the norm although in a dynamic, not static, form. As we have seen, 'the state is back', although its precise presence will vary widely. According to one commentator,

> Neo-authoritarian states may indeed offer an alternative political model to
> other developing countries … But they do not offer a credible alternative to
> liberal democracy as a form of government for countries with sophisticated
> high-income economies. Is there an alternative economic model on offer? The
> answer is 'no' if one means there is a viable alternative to the market economy.
> The answer is 'yes' if one means viable variants of the market economy.
>   The wide divergences among high-income countries over the size of the
> state, the generosity of welfare systems, the structure of corporate gover-
> nance and the pervasiveness of financial markets all demonstrate the possible
> divergences.[20]

States as *regulators*

Recognizing that countries continue to differ as 'containers' of distinctive structures and practices is important in emphasizing that we do not live in a homogenized world. In this section, we focus specifically on some of the ways states
regulate how their economies operate as they attempt to control what happens
within, and across, their boundaries.

Managing national economies

> The institutions of the state … are not simply involved in regulating economy and society, for *state activity is necessarily involved in constituting economy and society* and the ways in which they are structured and territorially organized.[21]

In other words, states do not merely 'intervene' in markets; they underpin and help to constitute their very existence. Although a high level of contingency may well be involved in how states strive to manage their economy (no two states behave in exactly the same way), certain themes can be identified. These will reflect the kinds of cultural, social and political structures, institutions and practices in which the state is embedded – the kind of 'capitalism' the state practises (see above). However, the precise policy mix adopted by a state will also be influenced by:

- the *size* of the national economy, especially that of the domestic market
- its *resource endowment*, both physical and human
- its *relative position* in the world economy, including its level of economic development and degree of industrialization.

Two basic types of macroeconomic policy are used by the state to manage its national economy:

- *Fiscal policies* to raise or lower taxes on companies and/or individual citizens and to determine appropriate levels and recipients of government expenditure. Raising taxes dampens down domestic demand; lowering taxes stimulates demand (although, as the Japanese experience during the 1990s showed, such automatic responses to changes in fiscal policy do not always occur). Similarly, raising or lowering public expenditure – or targeting specific types of expenditure – can influence the level of economic activity in the economy.
- *Monetary policies* aimed at influencing the size of the money supply within the country and at either speeding up, or slowing down, its rate of circulation (its velocity). The main mechanism employed is manipulation of the interest rate on borrowing. Lowering interest rates should stimulate economic activity through increased investment or private expenditure while, conversely, raising interest rates should dampen down activity. Again, however, rapid and automatic adjustment does not always occur. In the international context, exchange rates also have to be taken into account because their level (and volatility) affect the costs of exports and imports.

Such policies are also underpinned by the state's regulation of financial services (see Chapter 12).

At a more tangible and material level, governments generally provide – or at least secure the provision of – those 'conditions of production that are not and cannot be obtained through the laws of the market'.[22] One example is the *physical infrastructure* of national economies – roads, railways, airports, seaports, telecommunications systems – without which private sector enterprises, whether domestic or transnational, could not operate. They are the providers, too, of the *human infrastructure*: in particular of an educated labour force as well as of sets of laws and regulations within which enterprises must operate.

For several decades after the end of the Second World War in 1945, the role of the state in the developed economies expanded considerably, notably through the provision of welfare benefits for particular segments of the population and the development of a considerable (though varied) degree of public ownership of productive assets. The majority of economies, outside the command economies of the state-socialist world, became *mixed economies*. In many countries certain economic sectors, such as telecommunications, railways, energy, steel and the like, became state owned or controlled. As a result, government spending as a percentage of GDP rose very substantially. In the OECD countries, such spending increased from less than 20 per cent of GDP in the early 1960s to 35 per cent in the early 1990s. In the developing countries, the average growth was from around 15 per cent to 27 per cent. Of course, the pattern varied a lot between countries.

Starting in the mid 1980s, many states reduced their direct involvement in their economies, most notably through a systematic process of *marketization*, that is, extending the principles of market transactions into more and more aspects of public life. This was apparent not only in the older industrialized countries but also in many developing countries and, most dramatically of course, in the former state-socialist countries of Eastern Europe, in the former Soviet Union, and in China. Such *market liberalization* consisted of two related processes.

The first was *deregulation*. To varying degrees, virtually all industrialized countries jumped aboard the deregulation bandwagon. However, the issues are far less simple than the 'deregulationists' claim. Because no activity can exist without some form of regulation (otherwise anarchy ensues), 'deregulation cannot take place without the creation of new regulations to replace the old'.[23] In effect, what is often termed *de*-regulation is really *re*-regulation. Processes of deregulation spread to most economic sectors, most notably in financial services (see Chapter 12), telecommunications and utilities (such as energy and water). The *labour market* also became a particularly significant focus of deregulation.

The second – related – process was that of *privatization*. The state pulled out of a whole variety of activities in which it was formerly centrally involved and transferred them to the private sector. The selling of state-owned assets, and the greater participation of the private sector in the provision of both 'private' goods (the denationalization of state-owned economic activities) and 'public' goods (such as healthcare or education), have demonstrated a pervasive, though uneven, movement. However, this has not reduced government expenditure as much as might have been expected; the rhetoric has often been stronger than the reality, as Figure 6.4 shows. The average GDP share of government spending in the 26 countries shown was 43.6 per cent.

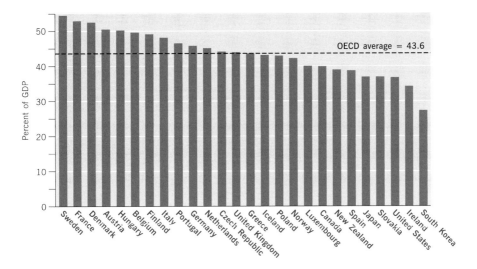

Figure 6.4   Central government spending as a share of GDP (2004–7 average)

Source: OECD data

In response to the deep economic crisis that began in 2008, however, these figures will have to be revised upwards very extensively as all governments have intervened in a massive way in an attempt to re-stimulate their economies. The figures are astronomical.[24] The combined stimulus expenditure of the G20 countries for 2009 was $692 billion, the equivalent of 1.4 per cent of their GDP. The US accounted for almost 40 per cent of this. In 2010, the US share of the total stimulus package will be even higher, at 60 per cent. Its total over the 2009–10 period will be $841 billion. The other countries with very large stimulus packages are China ($204 billion), Germany ($130 billion) and Japan ($104 billion).

Such large-scale intervention during a period of economic recession reflects the influence of John Maynard Keynes, whose analysis of the Great Depression of the 1930s demonstrated that markets do not necessarily correct themselves.[25] Under certain circumstances, they have to be stimulated by government actions – possibly in a very large-scale way – through, for example, reducing interest rates, providing financial assistance to specific firms and sectors, and investing heavily in infrastructure.

Regulating trade and industry

National governments possess an extensive kit of regulatory tools with which to control and to stimulate economic activity and investment within their own boundaries and to shape the composition and flow of trade and investment at the international scale. They may be employed as part of a deliberate, cohesive, all-embracing national economic strategy; alternatively, individual policy measures may be implemented in an *ad hoc* fashion with little attempt at strategic coordination.

Trade strategies

Of all the measures used by nation-states to regulate their international economic position, policies towards trade have the longest history. The shape of the emerging world economy of the seventeenth and eighteenth centuries was greatly influenced by the mercantilist policies of the leading European nations. Figure 6.5 summarizes the major types of trade policy pursued by national governments. In general, policies towards imports are restrictive whereas policies towards exports, with one or two exceptions, are stimulatory.

Policies towards imports	Policies towards exports
1. Tariffs	Financial and fiscal incentives to export producers
2. Non-tariff barriers Import quotas (e.g. 'voluntary export restraint', 'orderly marketing agreements') Import licences Import deposit schemes Import surcharges Rules of origin Anti-dumping measures Special labelling and packaging regulations Health and safety regulations Customs procedures and documentation requirements Subsidies to domestic producers of import-competing goods Countervailing duties on subsidized imports Local content requirements Government contracts awarded only to domestic producers Exchange rate manipulation	Export credits and guarantees Setting of export targets Operation of overseas export promotion agencies Establishment of export processing zones and/or free trade zones 'Voluntary export restraint' Embargo on strategic exports Exchange rate manipulation

Figure 6.5   Major types of trade policy

Policies on *imports* fall into two distinct categories:

- *Tariffs* are taxes levied on the value of imports that increase the price to the domestic consumer and make imported goods less competitive (in price terms) than otherwise they would be. In general, the tariff level tends to rise with the stage of processing, being lowest on basic raw materials and highest on finished goods. The purpose of such 'tariff escalation' is to protect domestic manufacturing industry whilst allowing for the import of industrial raw materials. Thus, although tariffs may be regarded simply as one means of raising revenue, their major use has been to *protect* domestic industries: either 'infant' industries in their early delicate stages of development or 'geriatric' industries struggling to survive in the face of external competition.
- *Non-tariff barriers (NTBs)*. While tariffs are based on the value of imported products, non-tariff barriers are more varied: some are quantitative, some are technical.

Although, in general, tariffs have continued to decline, the period since the mid 1970s witnessed a marked increase in the use of non-tariff barriers. Indeed, today NTBs are more important than tariffs in influencing the level and composition of trade between nation-states. It has been estimated that NTBs affect more than a quarter of all industrialized country imports and are even more extensively used by developing countries. Certainly much of what has been termed the 'new protectionism' consists of the increased use of NTBs.

National trade policy is unique in that since the late 1940s it has been set within an *international* institutional framework: the GATT/WTO. We will have much more to say about this in Chapter 17. Here we merely need to note the basic features of this regulatory system. The purpose of the GATT was to create a set of *multilateral rules* to facilitate free trade through the reduction of tariff barriers and other types of trade discrimination. The GATT was eventually replaced by the World Trade Organization (WTO) in 1995, an institutional change which greatly broadened the remit of the trade regulator. Today, around 97 per cent of world trade is covered by the WTO framework.

Foreign direct investment strategies

In a world of transnational corporations and of complex flows of investment at the international scale, national governments have a clear vested interest in the effects of FDI, whether positive or negative. From a national viewpoint, such investment is of two types: *outward* investment by domestic enterprises and *inward* investment by foreign enterprises. Few national governments operate a totally closed policy towards FDI, although the degree of openness varies considerably.

Figure 6.6 summarizes the major types of national FDI policy. Most are concerned with inward investment, although governments may well place restrictions on the export of capital for investment (for example, through the operation of exchange control regulations) or insist that proposed overseas investments be approved before they can take place. Historically, there have been very large differences in the policy positions adopted by countries towards inward FDI. At the broadest level, developed countries tended to adopt a more liberal attitude towards inward investment than developing countries,[26] although there were exceptions within each broad group. For example, among developed countries France had a much more restrictive stance than most other European countries. Among developing countries, Singapore had a particularly open policy, far more so than most other Asian countries. In the past two decades, however, national FDI policies have tended to converge in the direction of liberalization. Attempts to regulate at the international scale have not been successful (see Chapter 7).

Although national differences still exist, therefore, they are now rather less stark than in the past. Figure 6.7 summarizes the major regulatory changes towards FDI between 1991 and 2008. The proportion of regulatory changes that are more favourable to FDI continues to far outweigh those that are unfavourable. However,

Policies relating to inward investment by foreign firms

Entry
Government screening of investment proposals.
Exclusion of foreign firms from certain sectors or restriction on the extent of foreign involvement permitted.
Restriction on the degree of foreign ownership of domestic enterprises.
Compliance with national codes of business conduct (including information disclosure).

Operations
Insistence on involvement of local personnel in managerial positions.
Insistence on a certain level of local content in the firm's activities.
Insistence on a minimum level of exports.
Requirements relating to the transfer of technology.
Locational restrictions on foreign investment.

Finance
Restrictions on the remittance of profits and/or capital abroad.
Level and methods of taxing profits of foreign firms.

Incentives
Direct encouragement of foreign investment: competitive bidding via overseas promotional agencies and investment incentives.

Policies relating to outward investment by domestic firms

Restrictions on the export of capital (e.g. exchange control regulations).
Necessity for government approval of overseas investment projects.

Figure 6.6   Major types of FDI policy

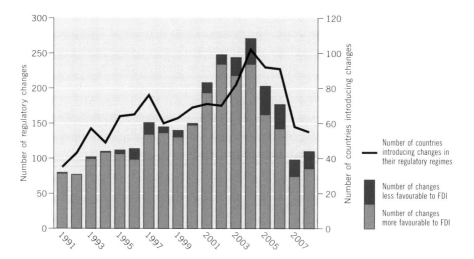

Figure 6.7   Changes in national regulation of FDI, 1991–2008

Source: based on UNCTAD, 2009: Table I.14

scepticism about foreign direct investment (FDI) now appears to be spreading among the rich nations. A succession of developed countries has recently tightened up their laws and declared high profile assets off-limits to foreign investors ... Usually about 90 per cent of the new laws governing FDI passed around the world made it easier for foreigners to invest … But in the last three years, 30 or 40 per cent of the laws have gone in the direction of being less welcome to investment.[27]

The US will not let foreigners buy airlines, television networks or – increasingly – any business remotely connected with security. France protects 11 sectors from foreign takeovers, including casinos and defence subcontractors … But companies bent on acquiring a British business need have few concerns about interference – even if they come from countries that practise such protectionism.[28]

Industry strategies

National policies towards trade or FDI are explicitly concerned with cross-border issues. But there is a third policy area – industry policy – that, although essentially concerned with internal issues, also has broader international implications. Indeed, the boundaries between trade, FDI and industry policies are extremely blurred. Figure 6.8 sets out the major types of regulatory industry policies that may be used by national governments.

The various stimulatory and regulatory policies may be applied *generally* across the whole of a nation's industries or they may be applied *selectively*. Such selectivity may take a number of forms: particular sectors of industry, particular types of

Figure 6.8   Major types of industry policy

firms (including, for example, the efforts to attract foreign firms), particular geographical locations. In particular, there has been a deluge of interest, in most countries, in trying to encourage the development of *growth clusters*: an attempt to capture the virtuous circle of growth that has come to be associated with the kinds of clusters described in Chapter 4.

Labour market strategies

States, especially in the older industrialized economies, have become increasingly involved in labour market policies, especially in terms of attempting to make labour markets more *flexible*. A new conventional wisdom has emerged whose essence is that of removing what are seen to be *rigidities* in the labour markets of the older industrialized countries: to make their labour markets more in tune with what are seen to be the dominant characteristics of a globalizing world economy. The 'flexibilization' of labour markets through deregulation involves greatly increased pressures and restrictions on labour organizations, the drastic cutting back of welfare provisions, and the move away from welfare towards *workfare*.[29]

The process has gone furthest in the US. Its apparent success in continuing to create large numbers of jobs (albeit with the widening of income gaps) has 'been the most persuasive argument for neo-liberal policies'.[30] It certainly stimulated the UK government to move along the same path. As yet, the countries of continental Europe have not moved as far, or as fast, down the flexibilization route. Most European governments are concerned that the social costs of reducing unemployment using the US model may be politically unacceptable in a system in which the social dimension of the labour market is very strongly entrenched. But there are clear signs of change as governments become increasingly concerned about the financial costs of sustaining existing practices and the continuing loss of competitive edge.

As a result, a variety of labour market measures, employed in various combinations in different European countries, has emerged. These include:

- the use of more temporary and fixed-term contracts
- the introduction of different forms of flexible working time
- moves to encourage greater wage flexibility by getting the long-term unemployed and the young to take low-paid jobs
- increased vocational training to provide more transferable skills
- reforms in state employment services
- incentives to employers to take on workers
- measures to encourage workers to leave the labour market
- reductions in the non-wage labour cost burdens on employers
- specific schemes to target the long-term unemployed.

Economic strategies in the older industrialized economies

As we saw earlier, the continental European countries on the one hand, and the US on the other, represent distinctively different types of capitalism. Historically, a major difference has been the centrality of some kind of industrial policy, together with a greater degree of social accountability of business in Europe, and the absence of such policy and accountability in the US.[31] The UK occupies an intermediate position between the virtually pure market capitalism of the US and the kinds of social market capitalism practised in continental Europe, but with a tendency in some areas (notably labour market policy) to be closer to the US.

The policy stance of the *United States* reflects both the sheer scale and wealth of its domestic economy and also a basic philosophy of non-intervention by the federal government in the private economic sector (until the 2008 crisis, when this stance was overturned, at least for the time being). As far as industry is concerned the role of the federal government has generally been *regulatory*: to ensure the continuation of competition. Action at the federal level has been based primarily on macroeconomic policies of a fiscal and monetary kind. The aim has been to create an appropriate investment climate in which private sector institutions could flourish. This has not, however, prevented the federal government from rescuing specific firms – especially very large ones – from disaster. At the other end of the size spectrum, the Small Business Administration has provided aid to stimulate new and small firms. Federal procurement policies are generally non-discriminatory but the sheer size of federal government purchases, particularly in the defence and aerospace industries, has exerted an enormous influence on US industry. Entire economic sectors, regions and communities are heavily dependent on the work created by federal defence and other procurement contracts and on subsidies in such sectors as agriculture (see Chapter 9).

US policy towards international trade during most of the post-Second World War period has been one of urging liberalization and the reduction of tariffs in *multilateral* negotiations through the GATT/WTO. However, since the 1980s there has been an increasing willingness to develop bilateral trading arrangements with other countries. US trade policy is complicated by the structure and composition of the US Congress and the ways that new trade policies have to be negotiated with domestic interest groups.[32] As the world's strongest economy the US, like Britain in the nineteenth century, has been the leading advocate of free trade. Even so, the federal government has intervened with the use of tariff and non-tariff barriers to protect particular interests. A 'Buy American' initiative was part of the Obama administration's stimulus measures introduced in 2009.

In the eyes of many parts of the world, the US is seen as having a strong *unilateralist* tendency, very much at odds with its traditional multilateral trading stance. The US has become increasingly embroiled in a whole series of trade disputes, particularly with East Asian countries (increasingly this means China) and with the European Union. There is also concern that the US has a tendency to introduce *extra-territorial* trade legislation to achieve its broader political objectives. One example was the Helms–Burton law that penalized foreign companies from doing business with Cuba.

Within *Europe*, despite the existence of the EU (see below), an ideological divide continues to exist between the so-called 'market' and 'social' models of how the economy should be organized, that is, between the UK's more 'neo-liberal' position and that of France and Germany, where the principle of the 'social market' remains strongly entrenched. However, the lines are not always quite as clear as is often claimed. Although the *United Kingdom*'s policy position does contrast in a number of ways with that of the continental European countries, and is closer to that of the US, the UK remains more interventionist than the US. Nevertheless, the UK has strongly adopted economic policies of privatization and deregulation. Its labour market policies, in particular, are far closer to the US model than to the EU model.

There are considerable differences in policy emphasis between continental European member states. Of the leading EU states, *France* maintains the most 'nationalistic' economic position, having long had the most explicit state industrial policy, a reflection of a tradition of strong state involvement dating back to the seventeenth century. A major component of French industrial policy has been the promotion of 'national champions' in key industrial sectors, often through state ownership of large-scale enterprises. France's current policy position retains many of these traditional qualities (and an especially strong antagonism to the Anglo-American neo-liberal economic model). Despite considerable privatization the French state retains a very considerable direct involvement in the economy.

The major exception among the continental European nations to a centralized approach to industrial policy has been *Germany*. In part, at least, this reflects its federalist political structure, with power divided between the federal government and the provinces (*Länder*). But although often described as 'light', the federal government's role has been far from insubstantial. It has pursued policies of active intervention in industrial matters, including a substantial programme of financial subsidy. Such involvement has to be seen within the German model of a social market economy.[33] The German economy is characterized both by a considerable degree of competition between domestic firms and also by a high level of consensus between various interest groups, including labour unions, the major banks and industry. The major challenge facing Germany since 1990, of course, has been to cope with the fundamental transformation of the economy brought about by reunification. Putting together the strongest economy in Europe (the former West Germany) with one that, for half a century, had existed in a completely different ideological system, has been an immense undertaking. It has put enormous strains on the federal budget because of the huge problems of rebuilding infrastructure and dealing with the unemployment brought about by restructuring.[34]

Japan can be regarded as the archetypal *developmental capitalist state* in which the government's economic role has been very different from that in most Western countries.[35] There has long been a high level of consensus between the major interest groups in Japan on the need to create a dynamic national economy. This consensus is often regarded as a cultural characteristic of Japanese society, with its deep roots in familism. But it also reflected the poor physical endowment of Japan and the limited number of options facing the country when, in the 1860s, it suddenly emerged from its feudal isolation. In other words, consensus was also a pragmatic stance built up over more than 100 years. Given virtually no natural resources and a poor agricultural base, Japan's only hope of economic growth lay in building a strong manufacturing base, both domestically and internationally through trade. In this process, the state played a central role not through direct state ownership but rather by *guiding* the operation of a highly competitive domestic market economy. Indeed, there has been relatively little state-owned enterprise in Japan and a generally much smaller public sector than in most Western economies.

For more than 50 years after the end of the Second World War, the key government institution concerned with both industry policy and trade policy was the Ministry of International Trade and Industry (MITI), renamed the Ministry for Economy, Trade and Industry (METI) in 2001. After its establishment in 1949, MITI became the real 'guiding hand' in Japan's economic resurgence, although its role has often been misunderstood and exaggerated in the West. Until the 1960s Japan operated a strongly protected economy and it was not until 1980 that full internationalization of the Japanese economy was reached. During the 1950s and early 1960s MITI, together with the Ministry of Finance, exerted very stringent controls on all foreign exchange, foreign investment and the import of technology.

Initially, MITI focused its energies on the basic industries of steel, electric power, shipbuilding and chemical fertilizers but then progressively encouraged the development of petrochemicals, synthetic textiles, plastics, automobiles and electronics. Japan was transformed from a low-value, low-skill economy to a high-value, capital-intensive economy. The foundation of this transformation was the clearly targeted, selective nature of Japanese industry policy together with a strongly protected domestic economy.

A key element in Japanese economic policy was the specific treatment of inward FDI which, for much of the post-war period, was extremely tightly regulated. The technological rebuilding of the Japanese economy was based on the purchase and licensing of foreign technology and *not* on the entry of foreign branches or subsidiaries. However, the inward investment laws have been liberalized and foreign firms do indeed operate within Japan in increasing numbers and, in some cases, in highly significant ways.

Since the early 1990s, Japanese policy has been especially exercised by the problem of a high-value currency, with contentious trading relationships with the US and Europe, and especially with the deep domestic recession which accompanied the collapse of the so-called 'bubble economy' at the end of the 1980s. Currently, there is much debate about whether Japan can recover its economic dynamism and what kind of role the government should play. Certainly attempts throughout the 1990s by successive Japanese governments to stimulate the domestic economy through fiscal mechanisms were not successful. Questions over the kind of capitalism that might develop in Japan abound. Changes are certainly occurring but the core characteristics of the Japanese economy are unlikely to disappear.

Jump-starting economic development

Ever since Britain emerged as the world's first fully industrialized nation in the late eighteenth and early nineteenth centuries, most other countries have tried to go down the same path. Underlying all of these attempts have been explicit state policies, notably those based, initially, on the ideas of the nineteenth-century German economist Friedrich List.[36] List heavily criticized Britain for advocating free trade policies only after it had attained a position of global industrial leadership. In fact, all the 'newly industrializing economies' of the nineteenth century – in particular the US, Germany, France and other European nations, as well as Japan – adopted a set of policies that were strongly protectionist in order to nurture their infant industries, before relaxing some of the trade barriers when those industries were seen to be strong enough to face external competition. A similar strategy was subsequently followed by the next wave of newly industrializing economies of East Asia and Latin America in the second half of the twentieth century. In other words,

> every successful industrial power at some point in its history has carried out an activist industrial policy.[37]

From import substitution to export orientation

The essence of most policies aimed at 'jump-starting' the process has been one of an initial emphasis on import-substituting industrialization (ISI): the manufacture of products that would otherwise be imported, based upon protection against such imports. The aim is to protect a nation's infant industries so that the overall industrial structure can be developed and diversified and dependence on foreign technology and capital reduced. To this end, many of the policies listed in Figures 6.5, 6.6 and 6.8 have been employed.

The ISI strategy, in theory, is a long-term *sequential* process involving the progressive domestic development of industrial sectors through a combination of protection and incentives. The realization that an import-substituting strategy cannot, on its own, lead to the desired level of industrialization began to dawn in a growing number of countries; some during the 1950s, rather more during the 1960s. Generally it was the smaller industrializing countries that first began to shift towards a greater emphasis on *export orientation* because of the constraints imposed upon such a policy by their small domestic market. Increasingly, an export-oriented industrialization (EOI) strategy became the conventional wisdom among such international agencies as the Asian Development Bank and the World Bank.

A shift towards export-based industrialization was made possible by:

- the rapid liberalization and growth of world trade during the 1960s
- the 'shrinkage' of geographical distance through the enabling technologies of transportation and communications
- the global spread of transnational corporations and their increasing interest in seeking out low-cost production locations for their export platform activities.

Such export orientation was invariably based upon a high level of government involvement in the economy. The usual starting point was a major devaluation of the country's currency to make its exports more competitive in world markets. The whole battery of export trade policy measures shown in Figure 6.5 was invariably employed by the newly industrializing economies. In effect, these amounted to a subsidy on exports that greatly increased their price competitiveness. Of course, the major domestic resource on which this export-oriented industrialization rests has been that of the labour supply – not only its relative cheapness but also its adaptability and, very often, its relative docility. Indeed, in many cases, the activities of labour unions have been very closely regulated and often suppressed, sometimes violently.

In fact, the 'paths of industrialization' followed by individual NIEs have been rather more complex than is often suggested. Figure 6.9 sets out a five-phase sequence of industrialization based upon the experiences of the Latin American and East Asian NIEs. A number of important points can be made:[38]

- The distinction commonly drawn between inward-oriented Latin American industrialization strategies and outward-oriented East Asian industrialization strategies is misleading.
- The initial stages of industrialization were common to NIEs in both regions; 'the subsequent divergence in the regional sequences stems from the ways in which each country responded to the basic problems associated with the continuation of primary ISI'.[39]
- 'The duration and timing of these development patterns varied by region. Primary ISI began earlier, lasted longer, and was more populist in Latin America than in East Asia ... The East Asian NICs began their accelerated export of manufactured products during a period of extraordinary dynamism in the world economy ... [after 1973] the developing countries began to encounter stiffer protectionist measures in the industrialized markets. These new trends were among the factors that led the East Asian NIEs to modify their EOI approach in the 1970s.'[40]

Figure 6.9   Paths of industrialization in Latin America and East Asia: common and divergent features

Source: based on material in Gereffi, 1990: Figure 1.1; 17

- Some degree of convergence in the strategies of the Latin American and East Asian NIEs began to occur in the 1970s and 1980s. Each 'coupled their previous strategies from the 1960s (secondary ISI and primary EOI respectively) with elements of the alternate strategy in order to enhance the synergistic benefits of simultaneously pursuing inward- and outward-oriented approaches.'[41]

The attraction of FDI has been an integral part of both import–substituting and export–oriented industrialization in many developing countries, although the extent to which particular countries have pursued this strategy varies considerably. In general, the Latin American NIEs have been more restrictive in their attitudes to FDI than the Asian NIEs, although there have been recent shifts towards more liberal investment policies in Latin America. In general, ownership requirements in Latin America have tended to be stricter than in most East Asian countries and the number of sectors in which foreign involvement is prohibited rather greater.

Amongst all the measures used by developing countries to stimulate their export industries and to attract foreign investment, one device in particular – the *export processing zone* (EPZ) – has received particular attention.[42] The ILO defines EPZs as

Industrial zones with special incentives set up to attract foreign investors, in which imported materials undergo some degree of processing before being (re-) exported again.[43]

Table 6.1 shows the rapid growth in EPZs, especially during the past 30 years. Some 90 per cent of all EPZs in the developing countries are located in Latin America, the Caribbean, Mexico and Asia. However, in terms of employment, Asia is by far the most important region for EPZs, with 85 per cent of the total. Of these, the biggest concentration is in China, which has 40 million of the world total of 66 million EPZ workers.[44]

Table 6.1   Growth in export processing zones

	1975	1986	1995	1997	2003	2007
No. of countries with EPZs	25	47	73	93	116	130
No. of EPZs	79	176	500	845	3000	3500
Employment (millions):	na	na	na	22.5	43	66
Asia					37	56
Central America and Mexico					2.2	5.3
Middle East					0.7	1.0
North Africa					0.4	0.6
Sub-Saharan Africa					0.4	0.9
North America					0.3	0.3
South America					0.3	0.5
Transition economies					0.3	1.4
Caribbean					0.2	0.6
Indian Ocean					0.1	0.2
Europe					0.05	
Pacific					0.01	

Source: ILO, 2003: Table 1; 2007b: 1–2

EPZs come in a number of different forms: 'free trade zones, special economic zones, bonded warehouses, free ports, and *maquiladoras*'.[45] Within developing countries, EPZs have been located in a variety of environments. Some have been incorporated into airports, seaports or commercial free zones or located next to large cities. Others have been set up in relatively undeveloped areas as part of a regional development strategy. EPZs themselves vary enormously in size, ranging from geographically extensive developments to a few small factories; from employment of more than 30,000 to little more than 100 workers.

EPZs in developing countries share many features in common. The overall pattern of incentives to investors is broadly similar, as is the type of industry most commonly found within the zones. Historically, the production of textiles and clothing and the assembly of electronics – both employing predominantly young female labour – has dominated. However, the position is not static:

Zones have evolved from initial assembly and simple processing activities to include high tech and science zones, logistics centres and even tourist resorts. Their physical form now includes not only enclave-type zones but also single-industry zones (such as the jewellery zone in Thailand or the leather zone in Turkey); single-commodity zones (like coffee in Zimbabwe); and single-factory (such as the export-oriented units in India) or single-company zones (such as in the Dominican Republic).[46]

Variations on a theme

Although the recurring central theme running through the development of all NIEs has been the role of the state, each individual NIE performs a specific variation on that general theme – a reflection of its particular historical, cultural, social, political and economic complexion.[47] In all cases, the state has played a highly interventionist role, although the degree and nature of its involvement, as well as the extent of its success, vary greatly from one NIE to another. In some cases, state ownership of production has been very substantial; in others it has been insignificant. In some cases, the major policy emphasis has been upon attracting foreign direct investment; in others such investment has been tightly regulated and the policy emphasis placed on nurturing domestic firms.

As we noted earlier (Figure 6.9), newly industrializing economies in East Asia and Latin America have followed similar, though distinctive, 'paths to industrialization'. Of the two geographical areas, the East Asian NIEs have been significantly more successful in creating dynamic economies. Three examples can be used to illustrate how the state has been involved.

South Korea (officially the Republic of Korea) came into being in 1948, following the partition of Korea into two. From 1910 to 1945, Korea was a Japanese colony, very tightly integrated into the imperial economy. Between 1948 and 1988, when political liberalization occurred, South Korea was governed by a succession of authoritarian, military-backed and strongly nationalistic governments that operated a strong state-directed economic policy articulated through a series of five-year plans.[48] Two important developments during the 1950s helped to provide the basis for industrialization: the land reform of 1948–50, which removed the old landlord class and created a more equitable class structure; and the redistribution of Japanese-owned and state properties to well-connected individuals which helped to create a new Korean capitalist class.[49]

A powerful economic bureaucracy was created, with a key role played by a new Economic Planning Board (EPB). At the same time, the financial system was placed firmly in the hands of the state. This highly centralized 'state-corporatist' bureaucracy, in effect, 'aggressively orchestrated the activities of "private" firms'.[50] In particular, the state made possible – and actively encouraged – the development of a small number of extremely large and highly diversified firms – the *chaebol* – that continue to dominate the Korean economy.

By controlling the financial system, particularly the availability of credit, the Korean government was able to operate a strongly interventionist economic policy. The *chaebol* were consistently favoured through their access to finance and very strong, long-term relationships were developed between them and the state. From the 1960s Korean policy had a strong sectoral emphasis as the state decided which particular industries should be supported through a battery of measures, including financial subsidy and protection against external competition.

Like Japan at a similar stage in its development, Korea, for the most part, eschewed the use of inward foreign investment to acquire technology. Indeed, Korea adopted the most restrictive policy towards inward foreign investment of all the four leading Asian NIEs. Korean government policy has been to build a very strong domestic sector. As a consequence, the share of FDI in the Korean economy has been relatively modest (Table 2.2).

In the early 1980s the emphasis of Korean economic policy began to shift towards a greater degree of (restricted) liberalization. Indeed, much of Korea's traditional industry policy has been gradually diluted.[51] Major changes were made in policies of financial regulation, exchange rate management and investment coordination. The formerly tightly controlled financial sector was significantly liberalized and the policy of exchange rate management virtually abandoned. The central pillar of South Korean industrial policy for 40 years – the coordination of investment – began to be dismantled.

When the East Asian financial crisis of 1997 hit Korea, the country's problems – as for the other affected East Asian economies – were attributed by the IMF, and by the Western financial community in general, to the existence of an over-regulated, state-dominated economy with excessively close (even corrupt) relationships between government and business. Yet, in the case of Korea, that was no longer entirely the case. It could be argued, in fact, that the Korean government had already gone too far in abandoning the principles on which its spectacular economic growth had been based. Clearly, certain reforms were needed as both the Korean economy itself and the broader global environment were changing. Not least was the need to reform the *chaebol*, which had come to distort the economy and which were, themselves, in great financial difficulty. That battle is still being fought. The *chaebol* argue that the proposed reforms will leave them vulnerable to foreign takeover; the government argues that reform of cross-shareholdings will make them more competitive. The issue of 'foreign takeover' is, however, very sensitive in Korea as a whole.

Singapore demonstrates a very different model of industrialization, albeit one in which the state has played a dominant role.[52] Singapore is by far the smallest of all the East Asian NIEs. Like both Korea and Taiwan, it had a very long history as a colony (within the British system). Unlike the two larger Asian countries, however, it was less tightly integrated into its imperial system, although it played a highly significant role as a commercial *entrepôt*, a reflection of its strategic geographical position. Singapore became fully independent in 1965 when it separated from Malaysia. Since then, although Singapore is a parliamentary democracy, it has been governed by one political party (the People's Action Party). For the first 30 years of its existence, it was led by one powerful individual, Lee Kuan Yew.

From the very beginning, the Singapore government pursued a very aggressive policy of export-oriented, labour-intensive manufacturing development. Concentration on manufacturing – especially labour-intensive manufacturing – was adopted because of the need to reduce a very high unemployment rate in a society that, at the time, had one of the fastest population growth rates in the world. The twin pillars of the policy were those of complementary economic and social planning, the latter being much more overt than in other East Asian NIEs.

The particular ways in which Singapore has operated its export-oriented policy have been substantially different from those of Korea and Taiwan. Most signifi-cantly, the central pillar was a strategy of attracting FDI, as a result of which the Singaporean economy is overwhelmingly dominated by foreign firms (Table 2.2). The most explicit industrialization measures, therefore, were those of incentives to inward investors, using a sectorally selective process. The government agency responsible was the Economic Development Board (EDB), which still plays an extremely influential role in the Singapore economy. With a few exceptions, Singapore operated a free port policy with little use of trade protectionist meas-ures. The second set of direct measures used to promote industrial development was the establishment of a high-quality physical infrastructure.

At the same time, a series of social policy measures was introduced aimed at creating an amenable environment for foreign investment. Most notably, the labour unions were effectively incorporated into the governance system through the establishment of a National Trades Union Council. 'Strikes and other indus-trial action were declared illegal unless approved through secret ballot by a major-ity of a union's members. In essential services, strikes were banned altogether ... These labour market regulations resulted in the creation of a highly disciplined and depoliticised labour force in Singapore.'[53] Thus, through a whole battery of interlocking policies, the Singapore government has created a very high-growth, increasingly affluent, industrialized society in which foreign firms have played the dominant economic role in production but within a highly regulated political and social system.

Singapore sets out to market itself as a global business centre on the basis of the very high quality of its physical and human infrastructure and its strategic geo-graphical location. Government policies are geared towards this goal, which also includes an explicit strategy to 'regionalize' the Singaporean economy by encour-aging domestic firms to set up operations in Asia while Singapore develops as the 'control centre' of a regional division of labour. The government introduced a series of initiatives using government-linked corporations to develop major infra-structural projects in Asia and, more broadly, to develop international networks.[54] At the same time, the emphasis on research and development and technological upgrading continues, with a specific emphasis on biotechnology to enhance its already significant role as a pharmaceuticals centre, and on IT.[55] Two recent policy initiatives have been the greater liberalization of the financial system and a push for greater 'Asian regionalism'. The key question, however, is the extent to which this highly paternalistic state is able to loosen its grip on the country's political and social life without damaging its economic influence.

The *People's Republic of China* (PRC) came into being in 1949 with the replacement of the nationalist government by a communist government led by Mao Zedong. For the next 30 years, China followed a policy of economic self-reliance. This policy was pursued through a series of major – often extreme – initiatives. Initially, the new government followed the example of the Soviet Union in establishing a Five-Year Plan (1953–7). This relatively successful policy was jettisoned in 1958 when Mao announced the 'Great Leap Forward': a total transformation of economic planning, with the emphasis on small-scale and rural development. Although this initiated the notion of rural industrialization, the Great Leap Forward was disastrous in its consequences, with mass famine one of the results. In 1966, policy changed again with the introduction of the 'Cultural Revolution', a phase that lasted for some 10 years with, again, disastrous human and social implications.

The period after Mao's death in 1976 was one of political hiatus that was eventually resolved by the emergence of Deng Xiaoping as leader. It was under Deng's leadership that China began to jettison the self-reliance policy of the previous 30 years and to make links with the world market economies.[56] This has been done, however, without substantial political change. In the words of the new Party Constitution of 1997, it is 'Socialism with Chinese characteristics'.

The pivotal year was 1979, when China began its 'open policy' based upon a carefully controlled trade and inward investment strategy. This was set within the so-called 'Four Modernizations' (concerned with agriculture, industry, education, and science and defence). A central element of the new policy has been the opening up of the Chinese economy to foreign direct investors. As we saw in Chapter 2, FDI has grown very rapidly indeed in China since the early 1980s The organizational form of these investments varies from wholly owned foreign subsidiaries to equity joint ventures with Chinese partners and other partnership arrangements.

The most distinctive feature of the open policy, however, is the explicit use of *geography* in its implementation. Partly in order to control the spread of capitalist market ideas and methods within Chinese society, and partly to make the policy more effective through external visibility and agglomeration economies, FDI was steered to specific locations. Initially, the foci were the four Special Economic Zones (SEZs) established in 1979 at Shenzhen, Zhuhai, Shantou and Xiamen (Figure 6.10). Significantly, each of these was located to maximize their attraction to investors from overseas Chinese, notably in Hong Kong, Macau and Taiwan. The Chinese SEZs offered a package of incentives, including tax concessions, duty-free import arrangements and serviced infrastructure. The original SEZs were located in areas well away from the major urban and industrial areas in order to control the extent of their influence. However, since the mid 1980s there has

Figure 6.10   The geography of China's 'open policy'

been considerable development of Economic and Technological Developments Zones (ETDZs), as Figure 6.10 shows.

Despite massive inflows of foreign capital and technologies, China remains a centrally controlled command economy in which state-owned enterprises (SOEs) predominate, despite more than halving in numbers. Reform of the SOEs is an immense task and one surrounded by massive controversy. A major problem for a country trying economically to 'modernize' is the sheer inefficiency (by Western standards) and high levels of corruption of the SOEs. SOEs are embedded within the Communist Party system and this fact pervades their operations.[57]

The problems posed by the SOEs have been intensified with China's accession to the WTO. Although this greatly enhanced China's economic potential it also imposes severe stresses on the domestic economy and institutions. Not only have tariff levels fallen from their previously high levels, thus exposing Chinese enterprises to intense competition, but also non-tariff barriers, matters relating to intellectual property rights, safety regulations, financial and telecommunications regulations are all affected. It is notable that the Chinese government now actively encourages Chinese businesses to invest overseas and there have been a number of significant Chinese acquisitions of foreign businesses, notably the IBM PC business by Lenovo in 2004. Financially, China continues to be under pressure to revalue the *renminbi*, not least because it has the largest trade surplus in the world.

Overall, it is clear that the institutional structure of the Chinese economy is in a state of flux, with a much increased variety of forms. As in the past, however, the key lies in the internal political power struggles between the 'modernizers', who wish to sustain and develop the open policies of the recent past, and those who wish to retain a degree of isolation. So far, China's reform policies are proving successful. But the key test of the survival of such a policy is its continued success in delivering economic growth and raising incomes for the majority of Chinese, and not just those in the more developed parts of the country. For a country so large and so populous, this is a very tall order indeed.

States as *competitors*

Do states compete? Can we think of nations as being in competition with each other just as firms compete with other firms? Although Krugman argues that the very idea of 'competitive' states is a 'dangerous obsession',[58] the generally accepted view is very different:

> The transformation of the nation-state into a 'competition state' lies at the heart of political globalization.[59]

Engaging in economic competition is another manifestation of the exercise in 'soft power' by states.[60] Books, government reports, newspaper articles, TV programmes in virtually all countries resonate with the language and imagery of the competitive struggle between states for a bigger slice of the global economic pie.

Prior to the East Asian crisis of the late 1990s, much of the concern focused on the perceived loss of economic standing by the US and European countries *vis-à-vis* Japan and the East and South East Asian NIEs. Today, although the focus is different – the big threat is now seen to be China and, to a lesser extent, India and possibly Brazil and Russia (the so-called BRICs) – the rhetoric remains the same. Indeed, the Swiss business school IMD publishes an annual *World Competitiveness Yearbook* with a 'competitiveness scoreboard' (or 'league table') of 49 countries based on no fewer than 286 individual criteria!

States compete to enhance their international trading position in order to capture as large a share as possible of the gains from trade. They compete to attract productive investment to build up their national production base which, in turn, enhances their international competitive position. Indeed, one of the most graphic expressions of competition between states is their intense involvement in what have been called 'locational tournaments': the attempts to entice investment projects into their own national territories. There has been an enormous escalation in the extent

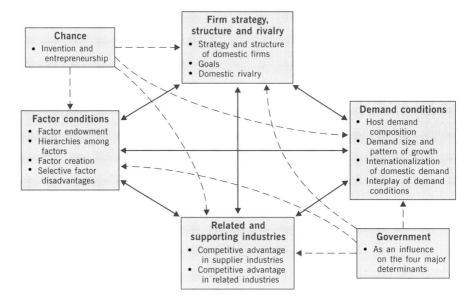

Figure 6.11   National competitive advantage: the Porter 'diamond'

Source: based on material in Porter, 1990: Chapter 3

of *competitive bidding* between states (and between local communities within the same state) to attract the relatively limited amount of geographically mobile investment (see Chapter 7).

Michael Porter argues that national competitive advantages are created through highly localized processes internal to the country. Porter conceives of this set of processes as a 'diamond': an interconnected system of four major determinants (Figure 6.11). Connecting all of the components (other than 'chance') by double-headed arrows emphasizes the fact that the 'diamond' is a mutually reinforcing system.

Each of the four determinants can be broken down into several subcomponents: [61]

- *Factor conditions*. 'The factors most important to competitive advantage in most industries, especially the industries most vital to productivity growth in advanced economies, are not inherited but are *created within a nation, through processes that differ widely across nations and among industries ... Thus, nations will be competitive where they possess unusually high quality institutional mechanisms for specialized factor creation*' (74, 80, emphasis added). The most important include the levels of skills and knowledge of the country's population and the provision of sophisticated physical infrastructure, including transport and communications.
- *Demand conditions*. 'The home market usually has a disproportionate impact on a firm's ability to perceive and interpret buyer needs ... proximity to the right type of buyers ... [is] of decisive importance in national competitive advantage'

(86, 87). However, the extent to which a nation's firms are connected into international markets also increases national competitiveness.

- *Related and supporting industries that are internationally competitive*. 'Perhaps the most important benefit of home-based suppliers ... is in the *process of innovation and upgrading*. Competitive advantage emerges from close working relationships between world-class suppliers and the industry' (103).
- *Firm strategy, structure, and rivalry*. 'The way in which firms are managed and choose to compete is affected by national circumstances ... Some of the most important are attitudes toward authority, norms of interpersonal interaction, attitudes of workers toward management and vice versa, social norms of individualistic or group behaviour, and professional standards. These, in turn, grow out of the education system, social and religious history, family structures, and many other often intangible, but unique, national conditions' (109). Porter lays great emphasis on the importance of intense rivalry between domestic firms, arguing that this creates strong pressures on firms to innovate in both products and processes, to become more efficient and to become high-quality suppliers of goods and services. 'Vigorous local competition not only sharpens advantages at home but pressures domestic firms to sell abroad in order to grow ... Toughened by domestic rivalry, the stronger domestic firms are equipped to succeed abroad. It is rare that a company can meet tough foreign rivals when it has faced no significant competition at home' (119).

In addition to the four primary competitive determinants that, in combination, form his 'diamond', Porter attributes secondary importance to two other components:

- *The role of chance*. For example, the occasionally random occurrence of innovations or the 'historical accidents' that may create new entrepreneurs.
- *The role of government*. Porter explicitly refuses to regard government as a competitive determinant of the same order as the four primary determinants of his 'diamond'. He sees government as merely an 'influence' on his four determinants, a contingent rather than a central factor.

Porter's competitive 'recipes' have been adopted by many governments, both national and local, in their attempts to improve their competitive position. On the other hand, there are considerable criticisms:

- It is highly reductionist in compressing immense complexity into a simple four-pointed 'diamond'. Hence, as a policy prescription, it needs to 'carry a public policy health warning'.[62]
- Its underplaying of the role of the state in pursuit of national competitiveness is a significant omission. As we have seen, all states perform a key role in the ways in which their economies operate, although they differ substantially in the specific measures they employ and in the precise ways in which such measures are combined.

- It neglects the influence of the transnationalization of business activity on national 'diamonds': 'there is ample evidence to suggest that the technological and organizational assets of TNCs may be influenced by the configuration of the diamonds of the foreign countries in which they produce and that this, in turn, may impinge upon the competitiveness of the resources and capabilities in their home countries.'[63]

States as *collaborators*

While there is controversy over whether states do, or should, see themselves as competitive states, there is no doubt that states *collaborate* with other states to achieve specific economic and welfare goals.[64] Such collaborations can take many forms. Here we focus on one dimension: the tendency for states to develop political-economic relationships at the *regional* scale through regional trade agreements (RTAs). Indeed, such regionalism has become one of the dominant features of the contemporary global economy.

The proliferation of regional trade agreements

The basis of regional trade agreements is the preferential trading arrangement (PTA). Technically, PTAs are not necessarily 'regional', that is involving states that are geographically proximate. They simply involve states agreeing to provide preferential access to their markets to other specified states wherever they are located – primarily through tariff reductions, at least initially. However, the WTO uses the term 'regional trade agreement' for all such arrangements. RTAs have a two-sided quality: they liberalize trade between members whilst, at the same time, discriminating against third parties.[65] There has been an especially marked acceleration in RTA formation since the early 1990s, as Figure 6.12 shows. At least one-third of total world trade occurs within RTAs.

Such growth reflects a number of motivations by national governments. Most have a strongly defensive character; they represent an attempt to gain advantages of size in trade by creating large markets for their producers and protecting them, at least in part, from outside competition. There is also an undoubted 'bandwagon' effect: a 'fear of being left out while the rest of the world swept into regionalism, either because this would be actually harmful to excluded countries or just because "if everyone else is doing it, shouldn't we"'.[66]

The classic analysis of the trade effects of regional trade agreements identifies two opposing outcomes:

- *Trade diversion* occurs where, as the result of regional bloc formation, trade with a former trading partner (now outside the bloc) is replaced by trade with a partner inside the bloc.

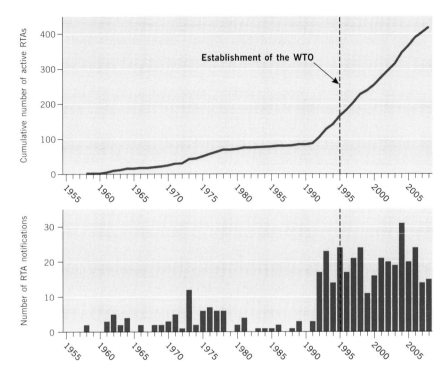

Figure 6.12 The acceleration in regional trade agreements

Source: WTO data

- *Trade creation* occurs where, as the result of regional bloc formation, trade replaces home production or where there is increased trade associated with economic growth in the bloc.

In addition, regional trading blocs also have a major influence on *flows of investment* by TNCs. The effects of regional integration on direct investment, like those on trade, can also be conceptualized in terms of 'creation' and 'diversion'. In the latter case, the removal of internal trade (and other) barriers may lead firms to realign their organizational structures and value-adding activities to reflect a regional rather than a strictly national market (see Figure 5.14). This, by definition, 'diverts' investment from some locations in favour of others.

Despite a widespread view that RTAs are a relatively new phenomenon they have, in fact, been an important feature of the global economic landscape since the middle of the nineteenth century. But their basis and their nature have changed over time. Four 'waves of regionalism' can be identified:[67]

- During the second half of the nineteenth century there were a number of trade agreements in place, especially in Europe: for example, the German *Zollverein*, the customs unions between the Austrian states, and those between several of the Nordic countries. 'As of the first decade of the twentieth century, Great Britain had concluded bilateral arrangements with forty-six states, Germany had done so with thirty countries, and France had done so with more than twenty states' (596).

- After the disruptive effects of the First World War (1914–18) a new wave of regional arrangements occurred, but this time in a more discriminatory form. 'Some were created to consolidate the empires of major powers, including the customs union France formed with members of its empire in 1928 and the Commonwealth system of preferences established by Great Britain in 1932. Most, however, were formed among sovereign states … The Rome Agreement of 1934 led to the establishment of a PTA involving Italy, Austria and Hungary. Belgium, Denmark, Finland, Luxembourg, the Netherlands, Norway and Sweden concluded a series of economic agreements throughout the 1930s … Outside of Europe, the US forged almost two dozen bilateral commercial agreements during the mid-1930s, many of which involved Latin American countries' (597).

- Since the end of the Second World War (1939–45) there have been two distinct waves of regionalism. 'The first took place from the late 1950s through the 1970s and was marked by the establishment of the EEC, EFTA, the CMEA, and a plethora of regional trade blocs formed by developing countries. These arrangements were initiated against the backdrop of the Cold War, the rash of decolonisation following World War II, and a multilateral commercial framework, all of which coloured their economic and political effects' (600).

- A further wave of economic regionalism – from the late 1980s onwards – occurred in the drastically changed geopolitical circumstances of the collapse of the Soviet-led system and the increased uncertainties of a more fragmented political and economic situation. 'Furthermore, the leading actor in the international system (the US) is actively promoting and participating in the process. PTAs also have been used with increasing regularity to help prompt and consolidate economic and political reforms in prospective members, a rarity during prior eras. And unlike the interwar period, the most recent wave of regionalism has been accompanied by high levels of economic interdependence, a willingness by the major economic actors to mediate trade disputes, and a multilateral (that is, the GATT/WTO) framework' (601).

Types of regional economic integration

There are four major types of politically negotiated regional integration agreements, involving increasing degrees of economic and political integration:

- *Free trade area*: trade restrictions between member states are removed by agreement but member states retain their individual trade policies towards non-members.
- *Customs union*: member states both operate a free trade arrangement with each other and also establish a common external trade policy (tariffs and non-tariff barriers) towards non-members.
- *Common market*: not only are trade barriers between member states removed and a common external trade policy adopted but also the free movement of factors of production (capital, labour etc.) between member states is permitted.
- *Economic union*: the highest form of regional economic integration short of full-scale political union, in which not only are internal trade barriers removed, a common external tariff operated and free factor movements permitted but also broader economic policies are harmonized and subject to supranational control.

As Figure 6.13 shows, the progression is cumulative: each successive stage of integration incorporates elements of the previous stage, together with the additional element that defines each particular stage.

The vast majority of regional trade agreements fall into the first two categories shown in Figure 6.13: the free trade area and the customs union. Indeed, around 90 per cent of all RTAs are free trade areas. There is a small number of common market arrangements, but only one group – the European Union – comes close to being a true economic union. In fact, not only is there enormous variation in the scale, nature and effectiveness of these regional trade agreements but also there is, in some cases, a considerable overlap of membership of different groups. Table 6.2 shows the major regional trade agreements currently in force, while Figure 6.14 maps the intricate webs of preferential trading relationships that involve, but also go beyond, the major regional blocs.

Levels of economic integration	Free Trade Area	Customs Union	Common Market	Economic Union
Removal of trade restrictions between member states	✔	✔	✔	✔
Common external trade policy towards non-members		✔	✔	✔
Free movement of factors of production between member states			✔	✔
Harmonization of economic policies under supra-national control				✔

Figure 6.13 Types of regional economic integration

Figure 6.14   The tangled web of major regional trade agreements

Source: based on WTO data; *Financial Times*, 19 November 2003; press reports

Table 6.2   Major regional trade agreements

Regional group	Membership	Date(s)	Type
EU (European Union)	Austria, Belgium, Bulgaria, Cyprus, Czech Republic, Denmark, Estonia, France, Finland, Germany, Greece, Hungary, Ireland, Italy, Latvia, Lithuania, Luxembourg, Malta, Netherlands, Poland, Portugal, Romania, Slovakia, Slovenia, Spain, Sweden, UK	1957 (European Common Market) 1992 (European Union)	Economic union
NAFTA (North American Free Trade Agreement)	Canada, Mexico, US	1994	Free trade area
EFTA (European Free Trade Association)	Iceland, Norway, Lichtenstein, Switzerland	1960	Free trade area
Mercosur (Southern Cone Common Market)	Argentina, Brazil, Paraguay, Uruguay, Venezuela (2006)	1991	Common market
ANCOM (Andean Common Market)	Bolivia, Colombia, Ecuador, Peru, Venezuela	1969 (revived 1990)	Customs union
CARICOM (Caribbean Community)	Antigua & Barbuda, Bahamas, Barbados, Belize, Dominica, Grenada, Guyana, Haiti, Jamaica, Montserrat, St Kitts & Nevis, St Lucia, St Vincent & the Grenadines, Suriname, Trinidad & Tobago	1973	Common market
AFTA (ASEAN Free Trade Agreement)	Brunei Darussalam, Cambodia, Indonesia, Laos, Malaysia, Myanmar, Philippines, Singapore, Thailand, Vietnam	1967 (ASEAN) 1992 (AFTA)	Free trade area
China–ASEAN Free Trade Agreement	China, Brunei Darussalam, Cambodia, Indonesia, Laos, Malaysia, Myanmar, Philippines, Singapore, Thailand, Vietnam	2010	Free trade area

Regional integration within Europe, the Americas, East Asia and the Pacific

In Chapters 2 and 4 we observed a strong tendency for a disproportionate share of global production, trade and FDI to be 'regionalized'. Such concentrations reflect, first and foremost, the basic economic–geographical processes of preference for proximity to markets and suppliers and a general tendency to 'followership' in location decision-making. But there are also rather different kinds of regional integration agreement in each of the three major regions. In this section we briefly explore these different manifestations of regional integration.

The European Union

> The European Union is the duck-billed platypus of the political world: a curi-ous-looking animal that defies simple categorization. Some people think it resembles a bird, others a reptile or a mammal. Similarly, everyone interprets the EU according to their own preconceptions rather than seeing it for the singular institution it is.[68]

The EU is by far the most highly developed and structurally complex of all the world's regional economic blocs. Although initially established as a six-member European *Economic* Community (EEC) in 1957, it was always more than simply an economic institution. Indeed, the initial stimulus was the desire to bring together France and Germany in such a way that their traditional enmities could no longer find their outlet in another round of European wars and also to strengthen Western Europe in the face of the perceived Soviet threat. Figure 6.15 shows how the EU has grown from its original six member states in 1957 to 12 in the 1970s/1980s, 15 in the 1990s, 25 in 2004, and its current 27 member states.

Since the early 1990s, four developments have been especially important for the EU. The first was the drive to complete the *Single European Market* in 1992. Almost 40 years after the Treaty of Rome, individual countries were still resorting to tactics which prevented, or delayed, the import of certain products from other member nations through the use of various kinds of non-tariff barrier. The European Commission argued that the costs of 'non-Europe' amounted to a sig-nificant loss of potential GDP and of jobs as well as a lessened ability to compete with the US and Japan.

The Single European Act aimed at the removal of the remaining physical, tech-nical and fiscal barriers; the liberalization of financial services; the opening of public procurement; and other measures. Such internal liberalization and deregu-lation, it was argued, would create a virtuous circle of growth for the European Community as a whole, for its member states and for those business firms success-fully taking advantage of the changes. It is virtually impossible to measure pre-cisely the actual effects of the Single Market process. However, a review of a range of evaluative studies concluded that

> there is no convincing empirical evidence of European integration having led to either short-term or sustained economic growth effects. The regulatory changes of the Single Market project were part of a global process of eco-nomic restructuring and mainly served to enhance the competitiveness of world-market oriented European countries.[69]

The second major event in the EU since the early 1990s was the *Treaty on European Union* (TEU), signed at Maastricht in 1991. This introduced a far more ambitious political agenda, aimed at creating a fully fledged *economic union*. In particular it

Figure 6.15 The European Union: from six to 27 members (and beyond?)

- strengthened social provisions through (a) the incorporation of the Social Charter; (b) the enlargement of the EC Structural Funds; (c) the creation of a new Cohesion Fund to assist poorer areas of the Union
- set out the mechanisms for the creation of a single European currency and monetary union (EMU).

European Monetary Union came into effect in 1999, when 11 (later 12) of the 15 member states joined the system. The issue of monetary union and the adoption of a single European currency (the *euro*) crystallized some of the most difficult political problems within the EU, notably the sensitive issue of national sovereignty. Within the EMU, national control over monetary policy – notably the setting of interest rates – has been passed upwards to the European Central Bank based in Frankfurt. The ECB, therefore, has an immense influence over the economies of individual member states. Each member state in the EMU has to comply with the Stability and Growth Pact, which sets limits on permissible budget deficits and debts.

The pros and cons of a single European currency remain finely balanced. The major benefits are the reduced costs and uncertainties associated with having to deal with many separate currencies within the Single Market and the overall stability this is intended to produce. Set against this is the fact that an individual state's ability to use monetary mechanisms to deal with periodic economic crises is greatly reduced. Such constraints on national freedom of manoeuvre become especially apparent during major financial crises, as in 2010 with Greece. The crisis in 2010 demonstrated the potential fragility of the Eurozone. At the same time, the fact that some EU members (notably Denmark, Sweden and the UK) remain outside the EMU creates further difficulties in achieving consensus on EU-wide actions.

The third major development has been the dramatic *enlargement of membership* during the mid 2000s to 27 states, with the potential of further enlargement. In this regard, the most contentious applicant is Turkey, over which opinion within the EU is highly polarized. The majority of the new members were previously embedded within the Soviet-dominated system, with very different recent histories and socio-political structures from the existing EU members. Others are smaller countries like Cyprus and Malta. Significantly, the income gap between existing and new members is much wider than in previous rounds of enlargement. The average GDP per head of the 10 new members in 2004 was only 46.5 per cent of the existing EU average. This compares with the average of 95.5 per cent for Denmark, Ireland and the UK when they joined in 1973, and the 103.6 per cent for Austria, Finland and Sweden on their accession in 1995. Such huge income differences pose massive problems for the already stressed EU budget.

Nevertheless, political-economic integration in the EU is unique in its extent and depth. Many – though not all – of the economic policies of individual member states have been 'relocated' to the supranational EU level. For example, there is just one EU trade commissioner representing the EU in the WTO and in all other international trade negotiations. There are EU-wide policies on competition, on subsidies (both industrial and agricultural) and on investment incentives. On the other hand, there are significant areas where policy is set at the national level: for example, in labour markets and taxation.

However, even in areas of 'common' EU policy, the differing ideological positions of individual member states clearly affect the process of reaching consensus. Trade negotiations, for example (including issues relating to the Common Agricultural Policy), have become increasingly contested within the EU, with a sharp divide opening up between states with a more protectionist stance (notably France, but also Poland) and those espousing more open trade policies (notably the UK and some of the northern European states). In the sphere of competition policy, as well, there is much heated argument over the acquisition of domestic firms even by firms from other EU member states.

The greatly increased size and diversity of the EU enlargement makes the process of consensus even more difficult; hence the fourth major development was the implementation of the Lisbon Treaty on 1 December 2009. This had been an immensely tortuous and contested process over several years, with a number of states refusing to ratify the original EU Constitution. The result is a considerably less ambitious structure but one that does, nevertheless, involve some important changes. In particular, the position of the European Parliament is strengthened with greater powers regarding EU legislation, the EU budget and international agreements. National parliaments are to have greater involvement, especially in ensuring that the EU only acts where this will result in better outcomes than would be achieved at the national level (the principle of 'subsidiarity'). The aim is to create 'a more efficient Europe, with simplified working methods and voting rules, streamlined and modern institutions for a EU of 27 members and an improved ability to act in areas of major priority for today's Union.'[70] Significantly, it makes it possible for a member state to leave the EU.

The Americas

Whereas the history of political-economic integration in Europe has been one of progressive deepening and widening – albeit with many interruptions and uncertainties – the history of attempts to create regional trade agreements in the Americas has been far more fragmented and shallow. To a great extent, this reflects the overwhelming dominance of the US in the region; the fact that, until very recently, the US had chosen not to enter into bilateral or regional trading arrangements; and the limited success among Latin American countries in creating robust and lasting regional agreements. The picture in the Americas, therefore, is of a mosaic of regional trade agreements of different type and scope (Figure 6.16).

By far the most important regional trade agreement in the Americas is the *North American Free Trade Agreement* (NAFTA) between the US, Canada and Mexico. By integrating two highly developed countries and one large developing country into a single free trade area it radically changed the economic map of North America. The income gap between the US and Mexico is very much greater than that between the richest and poorest states within the EU. The NAFTA came into force in 1994, but its origins can be traced back into the 1980s.

One important building block, although this was not its intent, was the Canada–US Free Trade Agreement (CUSFTA) signed in 1988 and implemented in 1989. As the CUSFTA was being signed, two other developments were also occurring. President George Bush (Senior) had made freer trade with Mexico a campaign issue in 1988. At the same time, President Carlos Salinas of Mexico made clear his determination to negotiate a free trade area with the US. Within a short time of bilateral talks starting, Canada had joined in an obvious defensive response.

The arguments in favour of creating the NAFTA varied between the three parties. For the US, it formed part of its long-term objective of ensuring stable economic and political development in the western hemisphere and also gave access to Mexican raw materials (especially oil), markets and low-cost labour. It also promised further US leverage in a world of increasing regional integration. The Canadian government was anxious to consolidate the recent CUSFTA. The motives of the Mexican government were primarily to help to lock in the economic reforms of the previous few years, to create a magnet for inward investment,

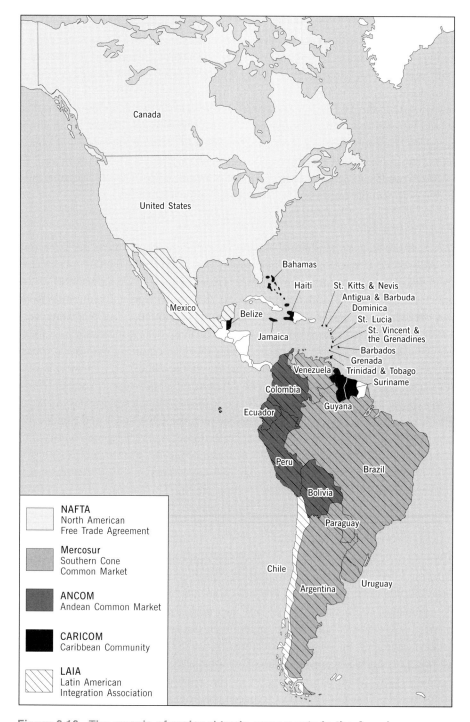

Figure 6.16   The mosaic of regional trade agreements in the Americas

not only from the US but also from Europe and Asia, and to secure access to the US and Canadian markets.

The aims of the NAFTA were gradually to eliminate most trade and investment restrictions between the three countries over a 10- to 15-year period. The possibility of other countries joining the NAFTA was left open to negotiation. The NAFTA is not a customs union; it does not incorporate a common external trade policy. Each member is free to make trade agreements with other states outside the NAFTA. In contrast to the EU, political-economic integration is minimal so that, unlike the EU, there are no social provisions within the NAFTA, although two 'side agreements' (on the environment and on labour standards) were incorporated to meet US and Canadian concerns.

The NAFTA was – and remains – a highly controversial issue in all three member countries. Against the claimed benefits of an enlarged economic space (from both a production and a marketing point of view) is set a number of concerns. In the US, there are particular worries about environmental and labour impacts. In the latter case, a former presidential candidate Ross Perot offered the spectre of a 'giant sucking sound' as jobs left the US for Mexico.[71] A similar fear was expressed in Canada. One politician saw the NAFTA as a 'nightmare of US continentalists come true: Canada's resources, Mexico's labour, and US capital'.[72] In Mexico, the fear was expressed that the country would become even more dominated by the US. The jury is divided.

> Today, most trade economists read the evidence as saying that NAFTA has worked: intra-area trade and foreign investment have expanded greatly. Trade sceptics and anti-globalists look at the same history and feel no less vindicated ... Politically, the skeptics ... can fairly claim victory. NAFTA is unpopular in all three countries. In Mexico ... the agreement is widely regarded as having been useless or worse ... In all three countries, the perceived results of NAFTA seem to have eroded support for further trade liberalization.[73]

Not surprisingly, therefore, attempts to create a *Central American Free Trade Agreement* (CAFTA) between the US and five Central American countries (Costa Rica, El Salvador, Honduras, Nicaragua plus the Dominican Republic) have been far from smooth. Although the legislation was passed in the US in July 2005, the agreement has not been fully implemented. The major opposition has come from US labour organizations and sugar farmers fearing job relocations to the cheap labour economies (and poorer working conditions) of Central America. On the other hand, CAFTA is seen as being a way for Central American producers of sugar and of garments to gain better access to their biggest markets. In fact, unlike the NAFTA, which removed most US barriers to imports from Mexico and Canada, 'CAFTA largely makes permanent the access Central America already has to the US market ... under the Caribbean Basin Initiative ... in exchange for significantly greater access to the Central American market'.[74]

Whereas US interest in regional trade agreements did not emerge until the late 1980s, Latin America has a long history of attempts to create free trade areas and customs unions, dating back to 1960 with the establishment of the *Latin American Free Trade Area* (LAFTA).[75] As Figure 6.16 shows, there has been a complex overlapping of bilateral and multilateral agreements between Latin American countries. Some of these agreements have failed to develop, notably the LAFTA, despite its reinvention as LAIA (Latin American Integration Association) in 1980.

Two Latin American regional trade agreements have had rather more staying power: the Andean Community and Mercosur. Of the two, *Mercosur* is the more widely significant.[76] It was established in 1991 with the intention of liberalizing trade between the four founding member states, establishing a common external tariff, coordinating macroeconomic policy, and adopting sectoral agreements. Economically, Mercosur has certainly increased the degree of internal trade.

In some respects Mercosur has some features in common with the EU. Like the EU, one of its primary motivations was to deal with security relationships between Argentina and Brazil (a parallel with the Franco-German relationship in Europe). It certainly goes some way beyond a simple free trade area (such as the NAFTA). On the other hand, Mercosur does not have any of the supranational institutions that are at the heart of the EU.

> Conflict continues to plague the organization because of a lack of coordinated economic policies and supranational institutions. Deepening of the integration process has slowed because member states have not established common mechanisms for coordinated macro-economic policy nor have they truly committed themselves, despite the rhetoric, to establishing a regional institutional framework … rather, loose regulations and shallow institutionalism have been maintained at a relatively low political cost … Put simply, the member states of Mercosur want the maximum economic and political benefits from integration while forgoing as little sovereignty as possible.[77]

Looming over all attempts to create a more vigorous regional economy in Latin America is the US, which aspires to create a pan-hemispheric Free Trade Area of the Americas (FTAA), encompassing North, Central and South America. So far, the negotiations involving 34 countries have stalled. Partly to subvert an FTAA, there are counter-moves to create a South America Community of Nations, whose core would be a merger, over 15 years, between Mercosur and the Andean Community.

East Asia and the Pacific

Regional trading arrangements in the Asia–Pacific are much looser, less formalized, and more open than the EU and NAFTA.[78] Until 2010 there were two main

Figure 6.17   The China–ASEAN Free Trade Agreement

regional economic collaborations and a host of bilateral agreements. An *ASEAN Free Trade Agreement* (AFTA) was initiated in 1992 among the ASEAN countries. ASEAN itself had been established in 1967 as a group of four, then, six South East Asian countries (Singapore, Malaysia, Thailand, Indonesia, the Philippines, Brunei). ASEAN's membership grew to 10 countries in the 1990s, with the addition of Cambodia, Laos, Myanmar and Vietnam (Figure 6.17).

> ASEAN as an intergovernmental institution established to promote regional cooperation, offers a striking contrast to the Western institutions such as EU and NAFTA … it is … based on a different concept of institutionalization …

> Paying full respect for the sovereignty and independence of each member state is one of the fundamental principles of the Association … most of the decisions have been made by consensus through the 'consultation based on the ASEAN tradition', which means to negotiate and consult thoroughly till achieving an agreement …
>
> [The] mechanism for dispute settlement also reflects ASEAN's preference for an informal approach. This is a striking contrast with the Western approach to dispute settlement in which preference is clearly on the side of judicial settlement based on clear rules and binding decisions.[79]

Such a system has both strengths and weaknesses.[80] One of its strengths is that it has helped what is a very diverse group of countries to maintain positive relationships. One of its weaknesses is that firm and rapid response to problems is often difficult, especially in the light of the principle of non–interference in domestic matters of member states. ASEAN has had only limited success in stimulating economic activity. As a consequence, in 1992, the original six member states agreed to initiate an ASEAN Free Trade Agreement.

Increasing competitive pressures on the ASEAN region from other East Asian countries (notably China) has forced the organization to look towards making agreements with other countries in East Asia. Some ASEAN members, notably Singapore, have negotiated bilateral trade agreements with China, South Korea and Japan, and with the EU, the US, Canada, Mexico and Chile (see Figure 6.14). However, the China–ASEAN agreement (Figure 16.17), which came into being in January 2010, is at a different scale.

> The deal creates the third largest regional trading agreement by value after the European Union and the North American Free Trade Agreement, covering countries with mutual trade flows of $231bn (€161bn) in 2008 and combined gross domestic product of about $6,000bn) … However, the deal remains short of genuine free trade. The trade in goods agreement provides for each country to register hundreds of sensitive goods on which tariffs will continue to apply, in many cases until at least 2020.[81]

At the same time, a free trade agreement has been reached between ASEAN, Australia and New Zealand. An agreement has also been negotiated with India to establish an Indo–ASEAN free trade area by 2012.

The other major regional economic organization in East Asia is the *Asia–Pacific Economic Cooperation* forum (APEC), established in 1989 on the initiative of the Australian government. Figure 6.18 shows the extremely diverse composition of APEC. It includes not only the obvious East and South East Asian states themselves (including China and Taiwan) but also Australia and New Zealand on the one hand and the US, Canada, Mexico and Chile on the other. However, APEC is, so far, little more than a broadly based 'forum' and little real progress has been made in fulfilling its stated goal of 'open regionalism'. Particularly following the Asian financial crisis of 1997, APEC became increasingly criticized by Asian participants.

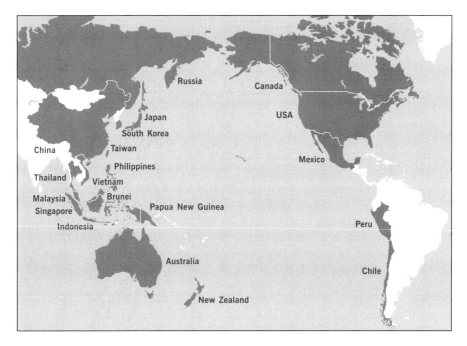

Figure 6.18   The Asia–Pacific Economic Cooperation Forum (APEC)

> APEC's failure to provide any meaningful response to the biggest economic crisis in the Asia–Pacific region since 1945 made it, if not irrelevant, then less important for many Asian members … Increasingly, Asian observers evaluated APEC as a tool of American foreign economic policy. And the resistance of Asian policy makers to a strengthened APEC was caused by their fear of US dominance … APEC has not been successful in creating a joint identity as the basis for further pan-Pacific cooperation and the lack of tangible benefits has been progressively criticized … APEC has failed to provide much-needed political legitimacy for the wider regional liberal economic project.[82]

This failure of APEC has led to various initiatives within East Asia to create a more robust regional economic (and financial) framework. It is suggested that

> We are seeing the emergence of a new regionalism in Asia that exhibits three overlapping and complex trends:
>
> 1   An interest in monetary regionalism arising from the desire … to combat financial volatility.
> 2   An interest in bilateral trade initiatives within the context of the wider multilateral system, largely at the expense of the APEC style open regionalism of the 1990s.
> 3   The emergence of a voice of region beyond that of the sub-regions – Southeast and Northeast Asia – but more restricted than that of the Pacific as a mega-region … the voice of region in the global political economy that is emerging is a new one, an 'East Asian' one.[83]

NOTES

1 Kindleberger (1969: 207).
2 This was the term coined by the novelist Tom Wolfe in *The Bonfire of the Vanities* (1988).
3 Stephens (2008).
4 Jessop (1994).
5 See Gilpin (2001), Gritsch (2005), Hirst et al. (2009), Hudson (2001), Jessop (2002), Wade (1996), Weiss (1998; 2003).
6 Kelly (1999: 389–90, emphasis added).
7 Gritsch (2005: 2–3). Nye (2002) also addresses the question of 'soft power' in the context of the US's current geopolitical position.
8 Glassner (1993: 35–40).
9 Agnew and Corbridge (1995) and Taylor (1994) discuss the general notion of states as 'containers' and the nature and significance of territoriality and space in geopolitics.
10 See Granovetter and Swedberg (1992), Lee (2009), Smelser and Swedberg (2005).
11 Terpstra and David (1991: 6).
12 Hofstede (1980).
13 A study of 700 managers across a large number of countries confirmed the persistence of significant cultural differences (*Financial Times*, 15 October 2004). See also Drogendijk and Slangen (2006).
14 Schwartz (1994), Drogendijk and Slangen (2006).
15 Yao (1997: 238).
16 See Berger and Dore (1996), Brenner et al. (2010), Hall and Soskice (2001), Hollingsworth and Boyer (1997), Peck and Theodore (2007), Whitley (1999; 2004).
17 Peck and Theodore (2007: 750–8).
18 Hollingsworth (1997: 266, 267–8).
19 Peck and Theodore (2007: 756).
20 Wolf (2008b: 1).
21 Hudson (2001: 48–9, emphasis added).
22 Hudson (2001: 76).
23 Cerny (1991: 174).
24 Brookings Institution (2009): www.brookings.edu/articles/2009/03_g20_stimulus_prasad.aspx.
25 Keynes (2007). Most standard economics texts contain a discussion of Keynesianism.
26 Mortimore and Vergara (2004) and Mytelka and Barclay (2004) discuss FDI policies with particular reference to developing countries.
27 *Financial Times* (25 April 2008).
28 *Financial Times* (24 January 2007).
29 Peck (2001: 10).
30 Faux and Mishel (2000: 101).
31 See Gilpin (2001: Chapter 7).
32 See Chorev (2007).
33 Contributors to Vitols (2004) explore the extent to which the 'German model' is sustainable.

34 Gretschmann (1994: 471).

35 Accounts of Japanese economic policy are provided by Dore (1986), Johnson (1985), Porter et al. (2000).

36 List (1928).

37 Gilpin (2001: 201).

38 Gereffi (1990: 18).

39 Gereffi (1990: 21).

40 Gereffi (1990: 21).

41 Gereffi (1990: 22).

42 ILO (2003; 2007a).

43 ILO (2003: 1).

44 ILO (2007a).

45 ILO (2003: 1).

46 ILO (2003: 2).

47 Douglass (1994: 543).

48 Especially useful accounts of Korean industrialization policy are by Amsden (1989), Chang (2007), Koo and Kim (1992), Wade (1990; 2004a).

49 Koo and Kim (1992).

50 Wade (2004a: 320). See also Amsden (1989).

51 See the detailed analysis provided by Chang (1998a).

52 Singapore's developmental policies are discussed by Lall (1994), Ramesh (1995), Rodan (1991), Yeung (1998).

53 Yeung (1998: 392).

54 The 'regionalization' strategy of Singapore is discussed in detail by Yeung (1998; 1999).

55 Coe (2003b).

56 Useful accounts of Chinese economic development policy are provided in Benewick and Wingrove (1995), Crane (1990), Hutton (2007), Nolan (2001), Zheng (2004).

57 Nolan (2001).

58 Krugman (1994).

59 Cerny (1997: 251).

60 Gritsch (2005: 2).

61 Numbers in parentheses in the following list refer to pages in Porter (1990).

62 Martin and Sunley (2003: 5).

63 Dunning (1992: 142).

64 Cable and Henderson (1994), Gamble and Payne (1996), Gibb and Michalak (1994), Hoekman and Kostecki (1995: Chapter 9), Lawrence (1996), Mansfield and Milner (1999), Schiff and Winters (2003).

65 Mansfield and Milner (1999: 592).

66 Schiff and Winters (2003: 9).

67 Mansfield and Milner (1999: 595–602). Numbers in parentheses in the following list refer to pages in this work.

68 Thornhill (2008).

69 Ziltener (2004: 953).

70 www.europa.eu/lisbon_treaty/glance/index_en.html.

71 Lawrence (1996: 72–3).

72 Quoted in McConnell and MacPherson (1994: 179).

73 *The Economist* (3 January 2004).

74 *Financial Times* (23 February 2005).

75 See Grugel (1996), Gwynne (1994), Kaltenthaler and Mora (2002).

76 This discussion of Mercosur is based upon Kaltenthaler and Mora (2002).

77 Kaltenthaler and Mora (2002: 92, 93).

78 Bowles (2002), Dieter and Higgott (2003), Haggard (1995), Hamilton-Hart (2003), Higgott (1999).

79 Liao (1997: 150–1).

80 Narine (2008).

81 *Financial Times* (2 January 2010).

82 Dieter and Higgott (2003: 433).

83 Dieter and Higgott (2003: 446).

Seven

THE UNEASY RELATIONSHIP BETWEEN TNCs AND STATES: DYNAMICS OF CONFLICT AND COLLABORATION

CHAPTER OUTLINE

The ties that bind
Bargaining processes between TNCs and states
    Seducing investors: 'locational tournaments' and competitive bidding
    The problem of transfer pricing
    Relative bargaining powers of TNCs and states
    Attempts at regulating transnational corporations

The ties that bind

In the preceding two chapters we focused on the major characteristics of TNCs and of states as separate actors in shaping the global economy. However, so far, the relationships between TNCs and states have been merely hinted at (see Figure 3.6). In this brief chapter we focus explicitly on these relationships because they are, in many ways, at the very centre of the processes of global shift and of global economic transformation. In the case studies of Part Three we will see how these relationships are played out in different industries, whilst in Chapter 14 we will examine the potential impact of TNCs on home and host economies. Here, the aim is simply to outline the major general features of the relationships between TNCs and states.

There is a widespread view that the major cause of the state's (alleged) demise is the counterpoised growth of the TNC. Indeed, one of the most common arguments is to compare the size of TNCs and national states. The typical argument is as follows.[1]

- 'Of the 100 largest economies in the world, 51 are corporations; only 49 are countries (based on a comparison of corporate sales and country GDPs) ... To put this in perspective, General Motors is now bigger than Denmark; DaimlerChrysler is bigger than Poland; Royal Dutch/Shell is bigger than Pakistan.'
- 'The 1999 sales of each of the top five corporations (General Motors, Wal-Mart, Exxon Mobil, Ford Motor, and DaimlerChrysler) are bigger than the GDPs of 182 countries.'

Of course, the precise numbers and identities of TNCs and states used in such comparisons vary over time (these figures refer to the years 1999 and 2000), but the theme is constant. These are, indeed, very striking comparisons. But are they really meaningful? The answer is that, beyond their value as polemic, they are not. They are superficial and misleading, although they certainly make eye-catching headlines. In fact, the statistics do not measure the same thing quantitatively, and they certainly do not capture the qualitative differences between TNCs and states.

> GDP is a measure of value-added, not sales. If one were to compute total sales in a country one would end up with a number far bigger than GDP. One would also be double-, triple-, or quadruple counting ... if corporations, too, are measured by value added as national economies are ... they tend to shrink by between 70 and 80 per cent ... Properly measured, Denmark's economy is more than three times bigger than GM. Even impoverished Bangladesh has a bigger economy than GM.[2]

Relationships between TNCs and states are, in fact, far more complex and ambiguous than the popular view would have us believe:

> [they are] both cooperative and competing, both supportive and conflictual. They operate in a fully dialectical relationship, locked into unified but contradictory roles and positions, neither the one nor the other partner clearly or completely able to dominate.[3]

This quotation captures the essence of the intricate relationships between TNCs and states: they contain elements of both rivalry and collusion.[4] On the one hand, there is no doubt that the fundamental goals of states and TNCs differ in important respects. In ideal-type terms, whereas the basic goal of business organizations is to maximize profits and 'shareholder value', the basic economic goal of the state is to maximize the material welfare of its society. Figure 7.1 indicates some of the dimensions of these conflicting objectives of TNCs and states.

	TNC objectives	**State objectives**
Performance	Maximize profits and shareholder value. Minimize cost base consistent with customer need.	Maximize growth of GDP. Maximize quantity and quality of employment opportunities.
Technology	Undertake R&D at locations optimal to the needs of the firm as a whole. Gain access to all necessary technology.	Stimulate the development of locally-rooted technology.
High-order functions	Locate headquarters and other high-order functions to fit optimal pattern of the firm's overall operations.	Maintain indigenous headquarters. Attract and retain key operations of TNCs.
Responsiveness	Retain flexibility to move profits in optimal manner. Retain flexibility to modify the geographical configuration of the firm's production network to meet changing conditions. Retain flexibility to use the labour force as required.	Retain power to gain a fair return on local operations of TNCs through taxation policies. Maximize the extent and benefits of local supplier linkages. Prevent the closure/scaling down of local TNC operations. Develop a flexible, high-skill, high-earning labour force.

Figure 7.1   Some conflicting objectives of TNCs and states

Source: based in part on Hood and Young, 2000: Table 1.1

On the other hand, although their relationships may be conflictual in certain circumstances, *states and firms need each other*. Clearly, *states need firms* to generate material wealth and provide jobs for their citizens. They might prefer such firms to be domestically bounded in their allegiance but that is not an option in a capitalist market economy. Indeed, many regard TNCs as important extensions of their state foreign policy. For example, in addition to ensuring control of key natural resources,

> American political leaders have believed that the national interest has also been served by the foreign expansion of US corporations in manufacturing and services. Foreign direct investment has been considered a major instrument through which the US could maintain its relative position in world markets, and the overseas expansion of multinational corporations has been regarded as a means to maintain America's dominant world economic position.[5]

Conversely, *TNCs need states* to provide the infrastructural basis for their continued existence: both physical infrastructure in the form of the built environment and also social infrastructures in the form of legal protection of private property, institutional mechanisms to provide a continuing supply of educated workers, and the like. TNCs, in particular, look to their home-country government to provide it with diplomatic protection in hostile foreign environments.

> In the last resort ... [a TNC's] directors will always heed the wishes and commands of the government which has issued their passports and those of their families.[6]

As we saw in Chapter 6, states are both *containers* of distinctive business practices and cultures – within which firms are embedded – and also *regulators* of business activity. National boundaries, therefore, create significant differentials on the global political-economic surface; they constitute one of the most important ways in which location-specific factors are 'packaged'. They create discontinuities in the flow of economic activities that are extremely important to the ways in which TNCs can operate. In particular, states have the potential to determine two factors of fundamental importance to TNCs:[7]

- the terms on which TNCs may have *access* to markets and/or resources
- the *rules of operation* with which TNCs must comply when operating within a specific national territory.

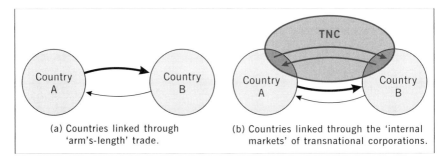

(a) Countries linked through 'arm's-length' trade.

(b) Countries linked through the 'internal markets' of transnational corporations.

Figure 7.2   Territorial interpenetration: the 'incorporation' of parts of a state's territory into a TNC

At the same time the fact that TNCs not only span national boundaries but also, in effect, incorporate *parts* of national economies within their own firm boundaries (Figure 7.2) creates major potential problems for states. There is, in other words, a *territorial asymmetry* between the continuous territories of states and the discontinuous territories of TNCs. The nature and the magnitude of the problem created by such asymmetry vary considerably according to the kinds of strategies pursued by TNCs. Most important is the extent to which TNCs pursue globally integrated strategies within which the roles and functions of individual units are related to that overall global strategy.[8] As we saw in Chapter 5, geographical segmentation and fragmentation of transnational production networks has become increasingly common. States tend to be fearful about the autonomy and stability of those TNC units located within their national territory as well as concerned about the leakage of tax revenues. At the extreme, of course, TNCs have the potential capability to move their operations out of specific countries.

At first sight it seems obvious that TNCs would seek the removal of all regulatory barriers that act as constraints and impede their ability to locate wherever, and to behave however, they wish. Such barriers include: those relating to entry into a national market, whether through imports or a direct presence; freedom to export capital and profits from local operations; freedom to import materials, components and corporate services; freedom to operate unhindered in local labour markets. Certainly, given the existence of differential regulatory structures in the global economy, TNCs will seek to overcome, circumvent or subvert them. Regulatory mechanisms are, indeed, constraints on a TNC's strategic and operational behaviour.

Yet it is not quite as simple as this. TNCs may perceive the very existence of regulatory structures as an *opportunity*, enabling them to take advantage of regulatory differences between states by shifting activities between locations according to differentials in the regulatory surface – that is, to engage in *regulatory arbitrage*. One aspect of this is the ability of TNCs to stimulate competitive bidding for their mobile investments by playing off one state against another as states themselves strive to outbid their rivals to capture or retain a particular TNC activity (see below). More generally, TNCs seem to have a rather ambivalent attitude to state regulatory policies:

> TNCs have favoured minimal international coordination while strongly supporting the national state, since they can take advantage of regulatory differences and loopholes ... While TNCs have pressed for an adequate coordination of national regulation, they have generally resisted any strengthening of international state structures ... Having secured the minimalist principles of national treatment for foreign-owned capital, TNCs have been the staunchest defenders of the *national state*. It is their ability to exploit national differences, both politically and economically, that gives them their competitive advantage.[9]

More specifically, it has been argued that TNCs will tend increasingly to support a strategic trade policy in their home country, with the expectation that this will open up market access in foreign countries and enable them to benefit from large economies of scale and learning curve effects.[10]

Bargaining processes between TNCs and states

It is clear that the relationships between TNCs and states are exceedingly complex. In the final analysis, such relationships revolve around their relative bargaining power: the extent to which each can implement their own preferred strategies. The situation is especially complex when TNCs pursue a strategy of transnational integration – but geographical fragmentation – of their activities, in which individual units in a specific host country form only a part of the firm's overall operations. In such circumstances, governments have a number of legitimate concerns:[11]

- that integrated TNCs might relocate their operations to other countries because of relative differences in factor costs
- that integrated TNCs use their operations to engage in transfer pricing to reduce the taxes they pay
- that integrated TNCs retain their key competencies outside host countries (typically in the firm's home country) and locate only lower-skill, lower-technology operations in host countries
- that national decision centres no longer operate within an integrated TNC, making negotiations difficult between host-country governments and the local affiliate.

Although the degrees of freedom of TNCs to move into and out of territories at will are often exaggerated, the *potential* for such locational mobility is obviously there. In fact, the TNC–state bargaining process is immensely complex and highly variable from one case to another. Despite such contingency, however, we need to try to understand some of the *general* features of the bargaining process. Here, for the sake of simplicity, we assume that a host country can be regarded as a single entity in the bargaining relationship. In fact, of course, many competing interest groups are involved, including domestic business interests, labour organizations and other civil society organizations, each of which will have different attitudes towards TNCs. In other words, it is, in reality, a *multiparty* bargaining situation.[12]

Figure 7.3 is a highly simplified, hypothetical example. The vertical axis of the graph shows the rate of return a TNC may seek for a given level of investment (XA) on the horizontal axis. The bargaining range for this level of TNC investment is shown to vary between

- a lower limit (XY), which is the minimum rate of return that the TNC is prepared to accept for the amount of investment XA
- an upper limit (XZ), which is determined by the cost to the host economy of either developing its own operation, or finding an alternative investor, or managing without the particular advantages provided by the TNC.

XZ is the maximum return the TNC can make for the amount of direct investment (XA) permitted by the host economy. It is in the interests of the TNC to try to raise the upper limit (XZ). Conversely, it is in the interests of the host economy to try to lower that upper limit: 'The higher is the cost to the host economy of losing the proposed [investment], the greater are the possibilities for the TNC of setting the bargain near the maximum point.'[13]

On the other hand, the more possibilities the host economy has of finding alternatives, the greater are its chances of lowering that upper limit. The greater the competition between TNCs for the particular investment opportunity, the greater are the opportunities for the host country to reduce both the upper and

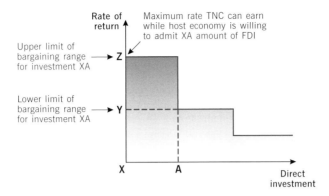

Figure 7.3   A simplified model of the bargaining relationship between a TNC and a host country

Source: based on Nixson, 1988: Figure 1

lower limits: 'In addition, the host economy has an interest in lowering the lower limit, through the creation of an advantageous "investment climate" (political stability, constitutional guarantees against appropriation, etc.) which might persuade the TNC to accept a lower rate of return.'[14]

Seducing investors: 'locational tournaments' and competitive bidding

The greater the competition between potential host countries for a specific investment the weaker will be any one country's bargaining position, because countries will tend to bid against one another to capture the investment. Indeed, one of the most striking developments of the last few decades has been the development of so-called *locational tournaments*. There has been an enormous intensification in *competitive bidding* between states (and between communities within the same state) for the relatively limited amount of internationally mobile investment. It has also become increasingly common for TNCs to try to lever various kinds of state subsidies in order to persuade them to keep a plant in a particular location. Otherwise, it is threatened, the plant will be closed or much reduced in scale.

Such cut-throat bidding undoubtedly allows TNCs to play off one state against another to gain the highest return for their investment. An example from the US illustrates this situation.

> The latest [2008] cheap manufacturing site for European companies is not in Asia or eastern Europe but the US ... The reason is less the value of the dollar ... but rather the large number of incentives that some US states are offering companies to set up factories in their region. Tennessee has disclosed

> that it agreed to give German carmaker Volkswagen $577m in incentives for
> its $1bn plant in Chattanooga. A senior executive of Fiat … said: 'with the
> amount of money US states are willing to throw at you, you would be stupid
> to turn them down at the moment' …
>
> ThyssenKrupp, the German steelmaker and industrial group, is receiving
> more than $811m to build a steel mill in Alabama. It turned down an offer from
> Louisiana, which is reported to have offered as much as $2bn, as well as an
> additional $900m in cheap debt from Alabama …
>
> A VW official suggested that the US had a competitive advantage because
> European Union state aid rules made support for factories complicated. 'It is
> more difficult in Europe.'
>
> The chairman of a large Swiss group said: 'States are willing to pay for new
> roads, re-train workers and offer huge tax breaks – that is a competitive pack-
> age that not many parts of the world can match when you look at how produc-
> tive US workers are and where the dollar is.'[15]

The EU has strong state aid rules to control such competitive subsidization but it
is always a highly sensitive and contested process. For example, the tortuous saga
of the on-off sale of GM's European operations in 2009 raised the issue of countries where the plants are located outbidding each other in subsidies to retain
employment (see Chapter 11). The situation has become especially complex
within the expanded EU. After 1989, but prior to the accession of Eastern
European states into the EU, firms from the West had moved rapidly into the
newly emerging market economies attracted by very generous incentives.

> Generous deals were made across eastern Europe to spur investment in fields
> as diverse as banking, sugar production and agribusiness. Subsidies, tax
> breaks, import quotas and other commercial advantages were granted to
> those willing to invest and help create jobs. But the subsequent need to adhere
> to EU rules has meant an end to the highly lucrative arrangements for the
> companies involved, and that, in turn, has provoked calls for compensation.[16]

At the international scale, the use of relatively lower tax as an incentive to TNCs
is increasingly common. Corporate tax rates indeed vary widely and it has become
a frequent occurrence for TNCs to threaten to leave a particular country because
of perceived high tax rates. Although often the threat is more apparent than real,
states do not necessarily know that. Such a strategy is especially marked in regions
like Europe where, as Figure 7.4 shows, there are very substantial differences in
national rates of corporate tax, offering many possible locational options within
what is a huge regional market and production space. Evidence suggests that tax
competition has increased sharply in Europe, driven not only by the influx of new
member states but also by the aggressive competition for FDI by countries like
Ireland and Switzerland.

> Studies show that location of FDI is becoming more sensitive to taxation,
> and that corporate income tax rates can influence a TNC's decision to
> undertake FDI, especially if competing jurisdictions have similar enabling

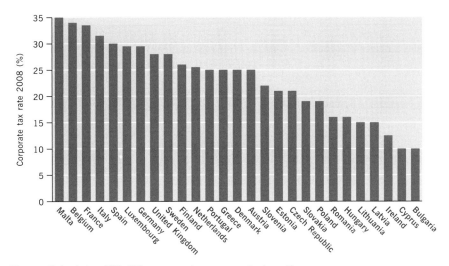

Figure 7.4   Intra-EU differences in corporate taxation

Source: based on material in the *Financial Times*, 8 September 2008

conditions. For instance, EU investors were found to increase their FDI positions in other EU member states by approximately 4% if the latter reduced their corporate income tax rates by one percentage point relative to the European mean.[17]

The threat of increased taxation on companies following the 2008 financial crisis provoked a wave of predictions that TNCs would relocate operations to lower-tax countries. In the UK, for example, a number of TNCs have relocated (or threat-ened to relocate) their headquarters to countries like Ireland or Switzerland to avoid higher taxes. Examples include WPP, the world's largest advertising com-pany, Shire Pharmaceuticals, United Business Media and Henderson Global Investors. However, there is some doubt as to the exact extent that these firms have actually relocated their HQ operations, an issue under investigation by the UK tax authorities.

The problem of transfer pricing

One of the most problematical – yet most opaque – issues in the relationships between TNCs and states is that of how a TNC's internal transactions, and its profits, are actually taxed by the states in which that TNC has a presence. By definition, a TNC moves both tangible materials and products (finished and semi-finished), and also various kinds of corporate services, across international borders to the various parts of its operations. In external markets, prices are charged on an 'arm's-length' basis between independent sellers and buyers. In

Figure 7.5   The incentives for TNCs to engage in transfer pricing

the internal 'market' operated by TNCs, however, transactions are between related parties – units of the same organization. The rules of the external market do not apply. The TNC itself sets the transfer prices of its goods and services within its own organizational boundaries and, therefore, has very considerable flexibility in setting those transfer prices to help achieve its overall goals.

The ability to set its own internal prices – within the limits imposed by the vigilance of the tax authorities – enables the TNC to adjust transfer prices either upwards or downwards and, therefore, to influence the amount of tax or duties payable to national governments. For example, as Figure 7.5 suggests, it would be in a TNC's interest to charge more for the goods and services supplied to its subsidiaries located in countries with high tax levels and vice versa. A similar incentive exists where governments restrict the amount of a subsidiary's profits that can be remitted out of the country.

In general, the greater the geographical differences in levels of corporate taxes, tariffs, duties and exchange rates, the greater will be the incentive for the TNC to manipulate its internal transfer prices. The very large, highly centralized, global TNC has the greatest potential for doing so. But it has proved extremely difficult for governments (and researchers) to gather hard evidence on its actual extent:

> Picture a General Motors plant in Windsor, Ontario, producing hundreds of items for assembly in [autos] … that will be sold in the Canadian market as well as for assembly by its sister plants in Michigan. No independent public market exists for many of the items, since no other firm produces these products. Nor is it obvious what the production cost may be of the items that cross the US–Canadian border – that kind of estimate will depend heavily on how the fixed costs of the Windsor plant are allocated among the many items produced, an allocation that cannot fail to be arbitrary. Without an obvious selling price or an indisputable cost price, all the ingredients exist for a pitched battle over the transfer price. When the item crossing the border is intangible, such as a right bestowed by the parent on a foreign subsidiary to use the trademark of the parent or to draw on its pool of technological know-how, the indeterminateness of a reasonable price becomes even more apparent. How much is the use of the IBM trade name worth to its subsidiary in France? How valuable is the access granted to a team of engineers in an Australian subsidiary to the databank of a parent in Los Angeles?[18]

A US House of Representatives study claimed that more than half of almost 40 foreign companies surveyed had paid virtually no taxes over a 10 year period. The Internal Revenue service estimated that some $53 billion was lost through the transfer pricing mechanism in 2001 alone.[19] In the UK, a study of 210 TNCs showed that 83 per cent had been involved in a transfer pricing dispute.[20] According to a UK House of Commons Report, one in four of the largest companies in the UK paid zero corporation tax in 2006–7.[21] In 2009, both the US and the UK governments began investigations into the tax disclosure practices of TNCs.[22] The UK is arguing that there should be international agreement on country-by-country reporting, so that TNCs would have to reveal the profits they make, and the tax they pay, in each country in which they operate. Even in developed economies, like the US or the UK, it is extremely difficult for government to assess the actual extent of transfer pricing. It is even more difficult for developing countries to do so because they simply do not have the resources. A country-by-country reporting system would undoubtedly help them.

Relative bargaining powers of TNCs and states

In general, TNCs wish to maximize their locational flexibility to take advantage of geographical differences in the availability, quality and cost of production inputs in serving their existing and new markets. Their ideal would be to pursue such goals without any hindrance from the regulatory practices of states. States, on the other hand, strive to capture as much as possible of the value created from production within their territories. In this latter sense, a primary aim of a host state is to try to embed a TNC's activities as strongly as possible in the local/national economy.

One way of thinking about this specific process is to conceive of two ideal-types of embeddedness: *active* embeddedness and *obligated* embeddedness.[23] Active embeddedness is where a TNC seeks out localized assets and incorporates them, as a matter of choice, within its operations. Where such localized assets are widely available in different geographical locations then the power of such choice rests primarily with the TNC. However, the less widely available the assets (or where access to them is controlled by the state) the more likely the state is to have a greater degree of bargaining power over the terms on which the TNC can utilize them.

In such circumstances, obligated embeddedness is likely to occur; that is, the TNC is forced to comply with state criteria in order to gain access to, and use of, the desired asset. Obligated embeddedness, therefore, is most likely to occur where two conditions are satisfied. First, there must be a localized asset that is highly important to a TNC (this may include a natural resource, a human resource and/or a significant market) and to which it needs access in order to achieve its business goals. Second, access to that resource must be controlled by the state within whose territory the asset is located and the state must have the power to exert that control.

The extent to which a state feels the need to offer large incentives to attract a foreign investment or to retain an existing investment, or is able to impose access or performance requirements, will depend on its relative bargaining strength in any specific case. Conversely, the extent to which a TNC is able to obtain such incentives, or to operate as it wishes, will depend on its relative bargaining strength. The outcome will depend on a number of factors.

On the one hand, the price that a host country will ultimately pay is a function of:

- the number of foreign firms independently competing for the investment opportunity
- the recognized measure of uniqueness of the foreign contribution (as against its possible provision by local entrepreneurship, public or private)
- the perceived degree of domestic need for the contribution.

On the other hand, the terms the TNC will accept are a function of:

- the firm's general need for an investment outlet
- the attractiveness of the specific investment opportunity offered by the host country, compared to similar or other opportunities in other countries
- the extent of prior commitment to the country concerned (e.g. an established market position).

Figure 7.6 sets out the major components of the bargaining relationship between TNCs and host countries. Both possess a range of 'power resources' that are their

Figure 7.6　Components of the bargaining relationship between TNCs and host countries

Source: based on material in Kobrin, 1987

major bargaining strengths. Both operate within certain constraints that will restrict the extent to which these power resources can be exercised. The relative bargaining power of TNCs and host countries, therefore, is a function of three related elements:

- the *relative demand* by each of the two participants for resources which the other controls
- the *constraints* on each which affect the translation of potential bargaining power into control over outcomes
- the *negotiating status* of the participants.

Figure 7.6 suggests that, in general, host countries are subject to a greater variety of constraints than are TNCs, a reflection of the latter's greater potential flexibility to switch their operations between alternative locations. Nevertheless, the extent to which a TNC can implement a globally integrated strategy is constrained by nation-state behaviour. Where a company particularly needs access to a given location and where the host country does have leverage, then the bargain that is eventually struck may involve the TNC in making concessions. In general, the scarcer the resource being sought (whether by a TNC or a host country), the greater the relative bargaining power of the controller of access to that resource and vice versa.

For example, states that control access to large, affluent domestic markets have greater relative bargaining power over TNCs pursuing a market-oriented strategy than states whose domestic markets are small (China is the obvious case). It is in this kind of situation that the host country's ability to impose performance requirements – such as local content levels – on foreign firms is greatest. It may also give the host country sufficient leverage to persuade the inward investor to establish higher-level functions such as R&D facilities. On the other hand, the nature of the domestic market may not be a consideration for a TNC pursuing an integrated production strategy. Where, for example, the TNC's need is for access to low-cost labour that is very widely available, then an individual country's bargaining power will be limited. On the whole, cheap labour is not a scarce resource at a global scale.

On the other hand, 'host countries wield the power to limit the extent of, or even to dismantle, the [T]NC integrated manufacturing and trade networks with more regulations and restrictions on foreign investments and market access'.[24] At the extreme, of course, both institutions – TNCs and governments – possess sanctions which one may exercise over the other. The TNC's ultimate sanction is not to invest in a particular location or to pull out of an existing investment:

> The meta-power that global business interests have in relation to nation-states is based on the *exit option* … It is the experience … of actual or threatened *exclusion of states* from the world market that demonstrates and maximizes the power of global business in contrast to isolated individual states.[25]

A nation–state's ultimate sanction against the TNC is to exclude a particular foreign investment or to appropriate an existing investment.

The problem, of course, is that the whole process is *dynamic*. The bargaining relationship changes over time, as the bottom section of Figure 7.6 suggests. In most studies of TNC–state bargaining the conventional wisdom is that of the so-called 'obsolescing bargain' in which

> once invested, fixed capital becomes 'sunk', a hostage and a source of bargaining strength. The high risk associated with exploration and development diminishes when production begins. Technology, once arcane and proprietary, matures over time and becomes available on the open market. Through development and transfers from FDI the host country gains technical and managerial skills that reduce the value of those possessed by the foreigner.[26]

In this view, after the initial investment has been made, the balance of bargaining power shifts from the TNC to the host country; in other words, it moves to the right in Figure 7.6. But although this may well be the case in natural-resource-based industries (see Chapter 8), it is far less certain that this applies in those sectors in which technological change is frequent and/or where global integration of operations is common. In such circumstances, 'the bargain will obsolesce slowly, if at all, and the relative power of [T]NCs may even increase over time'.[27]

Not surprisingly, there are few detailed studies of TNC–state bargaining processes outside the resource extractive sectors (see the example of the Kazakhstan oil industry in Chapter 8). The participants regard them as being far too sensitive (and possibly embarrassing). A rare example is Seidler's study of Ford's strategy to enter the Spanish market in the early 1970s.[28] This case demonstrates just how powerful a large TNC can be in persuading a host-country government to change its existing regulations. The Spanish automobile market in the early 1970s was heavily protected. Not only were tariffs on imports very high (81 per cent on cars, 30 per cent on components) but also cars built in Spain had to have 95 per cent local content. In addition, no foreign company could own more than 50 per cent of a company operating in Spain. Such restrictions were very much in conflict with Ford's own preferences for a Spanish operation. Ford's aim was not only to penetrate the local market but also to create an export platform from which to serve the entire European market. As such, it wanted the lowest possible import tariffs on components and a minimal level of local content so that it could source components from other parts of its transnational network. Ford's preferred policy was also to have complete ownership of its foreign affiliates. On the other hand, the Spanish government was very anxious to build up its automobile industry and especially to increase exports.

Two years of negotiations at the highest political level ensued, a reflection of the 'new' diplomacy in the global economy in which heads of TNCs talk directly to heads of government. And Ford certainly did that across Europe. The eventual agreement showed just how powerful Ford's position was. The fact that virtually all other European governments were trying to entice Ford to locate in their countries gave the company substantial negotiating leverage. On the other hand, Ford regarded a Spanish location as vital to its future European operations, although the Spanish government could not be sure of this. Under the agreement finally signed, virtually all of Ford's demands were met. In particular, for Ford the tariff on imported components was reduced from 30 per cent to 5 per cent; the local content requirement was reduced from 95 per cent to 50 per cent, provided that two-thirds of production was exported (precisely what Ford wanted to do anyway); and Ford was allowed 100 per cent ownership of its Spanish subsidiary. But, of course, the benefits were not all one way. In return, Spain gained a massive boost to its automobile industry, which was subsequently enhanced by the entry of other TNCs, including General Motors. As a result, Spain became one of the world's leading automobile producers (see Chapter 11).

However, states are not always as weak as is often assumed. Or at least in certain circumstances this is the case. A prime example is China and its policy towards automobile firms.[29] The prospect of access to the world's largest and fastest-growing market led many automobile firms to try to enter China. But the Chinese government has complete control over such entry and has adopted a policy of limited access for foreign firms. Here, then, we have the obverse of the usual situation. Whereas in most cases TNCs play off one country against another to achieve the best deal, in the Chinese case it is the state whose unique bargaining position enables it to play off one TNC against another. Of course, China is something of a special case. But although 'some developing countries have few attractive productive assets or locational advantages for which TNCs will compete with each other, and as a result may not be able to play off one TNC against another … equally there are many others who can play this game, as they have at least some "bargaining chips"'.[30]

It is important, therefore, not to fall into the usual trap of assuming that the bargaining advantage always lies with the TNC and that the state is always in a weak position. Neither should we assume that a state's bargaining power remains unchanged. The transitional economies of Eastern Europe illustrate this very clearly.[31] As highly centralized, state-controlled economies (though to differing degrees) before 1989, they were in a position to determine the terms on which TNCs could enter, and operate within, their economies. With political liberalization after 1989 came a headlong rush into neo-liberal, market-driven economic policies. This considerably reduced their relative bargaining power as individual states in relation to TNCs.

Western multinationals enjoyed more favourable terms of entry in Eastern Europe than in other capital-importing regions during earlier phases of FDI. The small size, economic weakness, and geopolitical vulnerability of the East European states prompted local officials to offer foreign investors unusually generous tax holidays and profits repatriation allowances. The international economic conditions prevailing at the time of Eastern Europe's opening further bolstered MNCs' bargaining position. The global ascent of economic liberalism simultaneously lowered national barriers to FDI and intensified bidding for foreign investment among capital-importing countries, allowing Western companies to obtain local-content waivers and other concessions from post-communist governments.[32]

However, the increasing political integration of the Eastern European states into the EU, with its particular regulations on the concessions and incentives that can be granted to TNCs, has enabled those states to retrieve some of their bargaining power. Ford's experience in Hungary is a case in point. 'The dramatic developments of 1989 thwarted the company's plan to use Ford Hungária as a trade-balancing instrument, while Hungary's subsequent convergence toward Western trade norms hindered Ford's attempts to extract concessions from post-communist governments.'[33] But this was only possible because, in effect, the EU acted as a 'strong state'. Left alone, the post-communist Eastern European countries would have been relatively powerless. As it is, their degrees of bargaining freedom should not be over-exaggerated. As experience throughout Europe shows, the intensity of competition between states for mobile investment is extremely high. There are far more substitutable locations within Europe for potential investors to retain considerable bargaining strength.

TNCs and states, therefore, are continuously engaged in intricately choreographed negotiating and bargaining processes. On the one hand, TNCs attempt to take advantage of national differences in regulatory regimes (such as taxation or performance requirements, like local content). On the other hand, states strive to minimize such 'regulatory arbitrage' and to entice mobile investment through competitive bidding against other states. The situation is especially complex because while states are essentially territorially fixed and clearly bounded geographically, a TNC's 'territory' is more fluid and flexible.[34] Transnational production networks slice through national boundaries (although not necessarily as smoothly as some would claim). In the process, parts of different national spaces become incorporated into transnational production networks (and vice versa).

Such territorial asymmetry translates into complex bargaining processes in which, contrary to much conventional wisdom, there is no unambiguous and totally predictable outcome. TNCs do not always possess the power to get their own way, as some writers continue to assert. In the complex relationships between TNCs and states – as well as with other institutions – the outcome of a specific bargaining process is highly contingent. States still have significant power *vis-à-vis* TNCs, for example to control access to their territories and to define rules of operation. In collaboration with other states, that power is increased (the EU is an example of this). So, the claim that states are universally powerless in the face of the supposedly unstoppable juggernaut of the 'global corporation' is nonsense; the question is an empirical one.

Attempts at regulating transnational corporations

In the case of foreign direct investment and transnational corporations there is no international body comparable to the WTO, although the Uruguay Round included a set of *trade-related investment measures* (TRIMS). Within this framework, some of the industrialized countries, led by the US, wish to prohibit or restrict a number of the measures listed in Figure 6.6, notably local content rules, export performance requirements and the like. TRIMS advocates argue that such measures restrict or distort trade. Their opponents see such measures as essential elements of their economic development strategies. They, in turn, wish to see a tightening of the regulations against the restrictive business practices of transnational corporations. Similarly, organized labour groups are generally opposed to measures that they feel will increase the ability of TNCs to affect workers' interests or to switch their operations from country to country.

In fact, there is a lengthy history of attempts to introduce an international framework relating to FDI and TNCs (apart from those agreed bilaterally or within the context of regional trade blocs).[35]

- OECD Guidelines for Multinational Enterprises (first introduced in 1976).
- ILO Tripartite Declaration of Principles Concerning Multinational Enterprises and Social Policy (1977).
- UN Code of Conduct for Transnational Corporations (initiated in 1982, abandoned in 1992).
- OECD Multilateral Agreement on Investment (MAI). The most recent attempt was launched in the mid 1990s. Its main provisions were:

  o Countries were to open up all sectors of the economy to foreign investment or ownership (the ability to exempt key sectors in the national interest was to be removed).
  o Foreign firms were to be treated in exactly the same manner as domestic firms.
  o Performance requirements (for example, local content requirements) were to be removed.
  o Capital movements (including profits) were to be unrestricted.
  o A dispute resolution process would enable foreign firms to be able to sue governments for damages if they felt that local rules violated MAI rules.
  o All states were to comply with the MAI.

Not surprisingly, the MAI generated a huge amount of opposition and was eventually blocked. Opposition was drawn from a very broad spectrum indeed, across both developed and developing countries.

> The choice of the OECD as the venue for the negotiations was a serious mistake because the OECD is a rich-country club and many LDCs were excluded from the discussions; why would LDCs accept an agreement that

> they had no part in formulating and that protected the interests of [T]NCs?
> Even many OECD countries objected to rules that would harm their own
> interests … Labor and environmentalists objected that MAI would give [T]NCs
> license to disregard workers' interests and pollute the environment. Many crit-
> ics charged that no protection was provided against the evils committed by
> [T]NCs. Even official American enthusiasm cooled when people realized that
> the MAI dispute mechanism could be used against the US and its [T]NCs.[36]

The major dilemma in any attempt to establish a global regulatory framework for
FDI and TNCs is the sharp conflict of interest inherent in the process involving
TNCs, states, labour groups and CSOs. Should the focus be on regulating the
conduct of TNCs (the viewpoint of most developing countries, some developed
countries, labour and environmental groups) or should it be concerned with the
protection of TNCs' interests? Both TRIMS and the aborted MAI were stacked in
favour of TNCs.

NOTES

1   Anderson and Cavanagh (2000: 3).
2   Wolf (2002: 9).
3   Gordon (1988: 61).
4   Pitelis (1991).
5   Gilpin (1987: 242). See also Lynn (2005).
6   Stopford and Strange (1991: 233).
7   See Reich (1989).
8   Doz (1986a) provides an extensive discussion of these issues.
9   Picciotto (1991: 43, 46).
10 Yoffie and Milner (1989).
11 Doz (1986a: 231–4).
12 See Levy and Prakash (2003).
13 Nixson (1988: 379).
14 Nixson (1988: 380).
15 *Financial Times* (8 September 2008).
16 *Financial Times* (23 June 2009).
17 UNCTAD (2005: 22–3).
18 Vernon (1998: 40).
19 *Financial Times* (3 February 2005).
20 The study was conducted by Ernst & Young and reported in the *Financial Times*
    (23 November 1995).
21 Cited in the *Financial Times* (21 October 2008).
22 *Financial Times* (6 May 2009), *The Guardian* (16 June 2009).
23 Liu and Dicken (2006).
24 Doz (1986b: 39).
25 Beck (2005: 53).

26   Kobrin (1987: 611–12).
27   Kobrin (1987: 636).
28   Seidler (1976).
29   Chang (1998b), Liu and Dicken (2006).
30   Chang (1998b: 234).
31   Bartlett and Seleny (1998).
32   Bartlett and Seleny (1998: 320).
33   Bartlett and Seleny (1998: 328).
34   Dicken and Malmberg (2001).
35   See Braithwaite and Drahos (2000: Chapter 10), Gilpin (2000: Chapter 6), Kolk and van Tulder (2005).
36   Gilpin (2000: 184–5).

PART THREE

THE PICTURE
IN DIFFERENT
ECONOMIC SECTORS

Eight

'MAKING HOLES IN THE GROUND': THE EXTRACTIVE INDUSTRIES

Beginning at the beginning

> Everything we use to communicate, move, stay warm, stay cool, sit, sleep, cook and refrigerate comes from the … raw material that humans extract from the earth each year.[1]

In a very real sense, the extractive industries represent the 'beginning of the beginning'; the initial stage in the basic production circuit and in the web of global production networks that make up the global economy.[2]

> Minerals … [excluding oil] account for a small share of world production and trade. Nonetheless, their supply is essential for the sustainable development of a modern economy. They are basic, essential and strategic raw materials … No modern economy can function without adequate, affordable and secure access to raw materials.[3]

The basis of the extractive industries is the notion of the *natural resource*: materials created and stored in nature through complex biophysical processes over vast periods of time. However, natural resources are not, in fact, 'naturally' resources. An element or a material occurring in nature is only a 'resource' if it is defined as such by potential users. A resource, therefore, is both a *socio-cultural* and a *political* construction. It is given meaning by its socio-cultural context and given differential priorities through political choices.[4] Basically, there must be an effective demand, an appropriate technology, and some means of ensuring 'property rights' over its use. 'If any of these conditions ceases to hold, resources could "unbecome".'[5] The resources that form the basis of the extractive industries (energy materials like oil, as well as ferrous and non-ferrous minerals like iron ore and copper) are, effectively, *non-renewable*. They are fixed in overall quantity, at least under known technological conditions. The more we use today, the less will be available for tomorrow.

Quite apart from their finiteness, a key characteristic of extractive resources is that they are *locationally specific*. They are where they are. They have to be exploited, at least initially, where they occur, although later stages of refining might well be located elsewhere. In either case, their use involves vast investment and expenditure, not only on exploration, extraction and processing but also on transportation infrastructures.

> The most significant differences about the extractive production network relate, in one way or another, to the 'landed' nature of assets … on the one hand, the nature-based character of extractive enterprises and the influence that the *materiality* of [the resource] exerts on the organization of production; and on the other … the *territoriality* of [the resource] in the sense of its embeddedness in the territorial structures of the nation-state … Resources are closely bound to notions of sovereign territoriality and national identity.[6]

This combination of finite quantities, fixed locations and territorial embededdness creates the specific shape and developmental path of the extractive industries.[7] They help to explain why the extractive industries are so sensitive economically, politically, environmentally and even culturally; why they are the focus of such intense conflict and bargaining between firms, between states, and between firms and states. To a greater extent than most other industries, the extractive industries are made up of a strong mix of private firms (TNCs) and state-owned enterprises (SOEs). They are also dominated by giant firms: no fewer than nine of the 50 largest companies in the *Financial Times* Global 500 are oil or mining companies.[8] They are overwhelmingly *producer-driven* industries.

These industries, then, are at the heart of many of the most pressing and most controversial debates in the global economy. As we saw in Chapter 2, the roller-coaster trajectory of production and trade in the past 50 years has been closely related to sharp fluctuations in the supply – and, therefore, the price – of oil and other natural resources. 'The race for resources' has been a central component of the development of a global economy for centuries.[9] It still is. The extractive industries are also at the centre of the development dilemma facing many resource-rich but deeply impoverished countries, especially in Africa. The paradox of the so-called 'resource curse' will be examined in Chapter 16.

Production circuits in the extractive industries

As Figure 8.1 shows, the extractive industries fall into three broad categories based upon the kind of minerals involved. In this chapter we will focus primarily on two of these industries: oil and copper. (Copper is one of the most important of the metallic metals industries, accounting for a little under one-fifth, by value, of world metallic mineral production.)[10] Both oil and copper are employed in an enormous variety of end uses. In the case of oil, this includes final consumer demands for transportation and heating fuel as well as feedstocks for the chemical and related industries. Copper, on the other hand, like most of the base and ferrous metals, is overwhelmingly a producer commodity.

> Copper is one of the oldest metals ever used … Because of its properties, singularly or in combination, of high ductility, malleability, and thermal and electrical conductivity, and its resistance to corrosion, copper has become a major industrial metal … Electrical uses of copper, including power transmission and generation, building wiring, telecommunication, and electrical and electronic products, account for about three quarters of total copper use.[11]

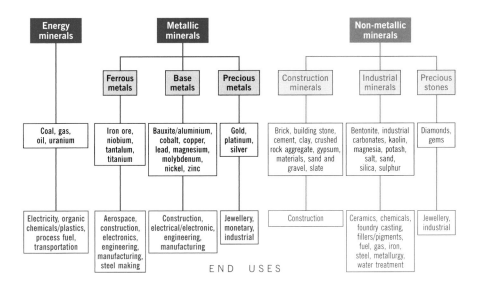

Figure 8.1 Classification of extractive industries

Source: based on UNCTAD, 2007: Box III.1.1

Figure 8.2 outlines the basic production circuit for extractive industries. At the most general level it is a relatively straightforward sequence of stages from exploration through to final consumption, although in fact it is a highly complex and contested process. Something of that complexity is shown in Figure 8.3, which goes beyond the basic production circuit to depict the production of oil as a

> global production network of inter-firm and firm–state relations that link nationalized oil companies, resource-holding states and publicly traded, transnational firms. It reveals a number of lateral/horizontal relations not captured by the linear commodity chain.[12]

Overall, the production circuits in the extractive industries are highly capital and technology intensive, involving primarily large firms (or consortia of firms), both privately and state owned.

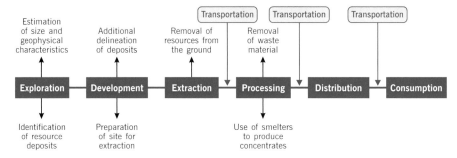

Figure 8.2   **The basic extractive industry production circuit**

Source: based in part on Turner et al., 1994: Box 16.4

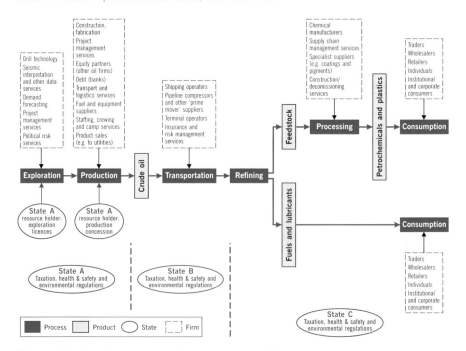

Figure 8.3   **A global production network for oil**

Source: based on Bridge, 2008b: Figure 3

Global shifts in the extractive industries

Oil

Between 1975 and 2007, world oil *production* grew by 46 per cent, from 56 billion to 82 billion barrels. Production of crude oil is quite widely spread geographically, as Figure 8.4 shows. But, in many cases, the quantity produced is relatively small. In 2007, a mere 12 countries accounted for 68 per cent of the world total, of which two – Saudi Arabia and the Russian Federation – produced one-quarter of the total. However, major changes have occurred in the global map of oil production since 1975 (immediately after the 'first oil shock'). Important new producers have emerged, the most significant being the Russian Federation, China, Mexico, Canada, Nigeria, Norway and the UK, together with new production centres in former Soviet states like Kazakhstan and Azerbaijan as well as in some African countries such as Angola. So, although the Middle East still accounts for 31 per cent of world oil production, the world production map is much more complex than it was 30 years ago.

> The geography of global oil production has … undergone a quite radical change. The new emphasis is on supply diversity, security of supply arrangements and, where possible, the development of indigenous or regional availabilities … As a result, the world is now a patchwork of oil producing areas.[13]

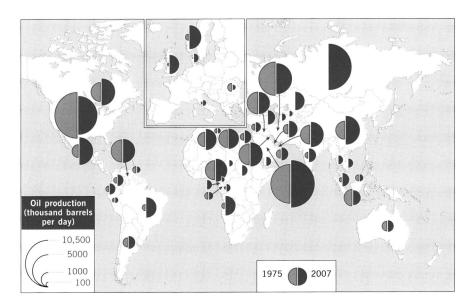

Figure 8.4 The changing geography of global oil production

Source: based on data in *BP Statistical Review of World Energy* 2008

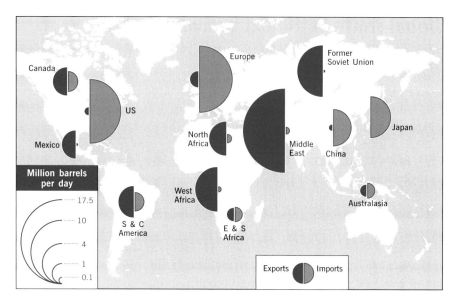

Figure 8.5   Patterns of world trade in oil

Source: based on data in *BP Statistical Review of World Energy* 2008

The pattern of world *trade* in oil is shown in Figure 8.5. More than half of total oil imports go to Europe and the US, with a further one-fifth going to Japan and China. In particular, China's significance as an oil importer has increased enormously as its economy has grown at the dramatic rates discussed in Chapter 2. In the early 1990s, China was the biggest exporter of oil in Asia; today it is the fastest-growing importer of oil in the world. Much of that shift has involved China's sourcing of oil from Africa,[14] as we shall see in later sections. For many of the world's major oil exporters, oil is by far the most important commodity, in some cases constituting virtually the entire basis of the country's export sector (Figure 8.6).

Copper

World copper production has increased even more rapidly than that of oil during the past two decades: by 76 per cent between 1988 and 2007 (from 8.8 million tonnes to 15.5 million tonnes).[15] Such growth reflects the particular qualities of copper in a wide range of end uses (see above) and, again, the growth of China and its seemingly insatiable hunger for raw materials. Figure 8.7 maps the world distribution of both mine production and refined

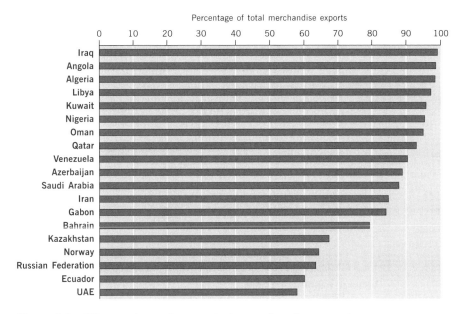

Figure 8.6 Oil as a share of a country's merchandise exports

Source: based on data in WTO, 2009: Table II.26

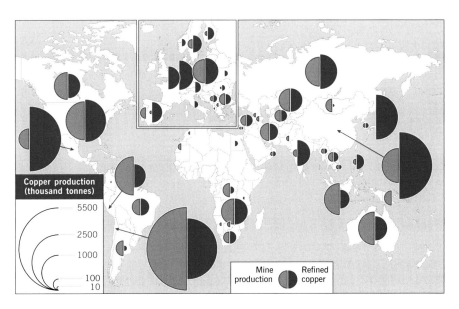

Figure 8.7 The geography of world copper production

Source: based on data in Brown et al., 2009: 28, 30

copper. Ten countries produce more than four-fifths of mined copper. Latin America (including Mexico) dominates, accounting for almost one-half of world production. By far the biggest producer is Chile, with 36 per cent of the world total. Indeed, Chile's share of world production doubled between 1988 and 2007.[16] Copper production in Africa, notably in Zambia and the Democratic Republic of Congo, as well as in China, has also grown significantly. Chile is also the world's second biggest producer of refined copper (with 14 per cent), preceded by China (17 per cent) and followed by Mexico (16 per cent). The pattern of refined copper production reflects the fact that it incorporates about 20 per cent of copper scrap in its production, such scrap being generated by major copper users. This explains, for example, the presence of countries like Japan and Germany as major producers of refined copper only.

Table 8.1   The world's leading exporters and importers of copper, 2005

Exporter	Value of exports ($US000)	Share (%)	Importer	Value of imports ($US000)	Share (%)
Chile	11,590,400	19.3	China	9,328,506	16.0
Germany	5,513,485	9.2	US	7,145,349	12.2
Japan	3,266,764	5.4	Germany	4,185,263	7.2
China	2,623,647	4.4	Italy	4,000,215	6.9
Russian Federation	2,519,643	4.2	France	3,183,164	5.5
US	2,231,375	3.7	Taiwan	3,107,164	5.3
Peru	2,130,080	3.5	Republic of Korea	2,633,385	4.5
France	2,094,293	3.5	Hong Kong, China	1,766,526	3.0
Canada	2,043,340	3.4	UK	1,670,048	2.9
Republic of Korea	1,982,472	3.3	Thailand	1,516,392	2.6

Source: based on *International Trade Centre Statistics* 2009 (www.intracen.org/tradestat/ sitc3-3d/ip682.html)

The major exporters and importers of copper are shown in Table 8.1. In terms of exports, as might be expected from the production figures, Chile dominates with almost one-fifth of world exports, followed a long way behind by Germany. The leading 10 exporters account for 60 per cent of the world total. Copper imports are rather more concentrated: the top 10 account for 66 per cent of world imports. Here, China (16 per cent) and the US (12 per cent) are by far the most important copper importers.

Volatile demand

> Welcome to the new world of runaway energy demand
>
> (*Financial Times,* 14 November 2007)
>
> Global oil demand to collapse
>
> (*Financial Times,* 10 December 2008)

These two headlines, separated by almost exactly one year, capture the extreme volatility of the market for the extractive industries. Periodic boom and bust are the norm. Indeed, the history of the world economy during the twentieth century, as we saw in Chapter 2, was a roller-coaster ride whose vertiginous ups and downs were closely related to the commodity cycle.

Periods of strong economic growth intensify the demand for commodities; periods of economic decline produce the opposite effect so that demand may collapse, at least until the next upturn. This means that the extractive industries are much more sensitive to the general state of the economy than most other sectors, although the speed of adjustment to ups and downs in the cycle may not be immediate and this can cause problems of over- and under-capacity.

Such massive swings in demand are, of course, reflected in massive fluctuations in prices. Figure 8.8 shows how the prices of oil and metallic minerals fluctuated in the six decades since the 1940s in response to changing market conditions.

> 1974 marked the end of the 30-year 'golden period' of strong world economic growth, and high demand for minerals that began after the Second World War ... From the first oil crisis in 1973–1974 until the early 1980s, oil prices began to climb steeply ... Metal prices, on the other hand, began a long-term declining trend ... Crude oil prices also began to decline in real terms in 1985 ... The depressed mineral prices of the 1980s and 1990s had important consequences: instead of being regarded as strategically important to economic development, oil and metals were increasingly treated as simple commodities ... It is only in recent years that the gradual decline in mineral prices has been reversed.[17]

In fact, this reversal, especially in the case of minerals, came with unexpected suddenness. The first half of the 2000s, especially after 2004, saw what were in effect 'gold rush' conditions. This acceleration in demand reflected in general terms the rapid overall growth of the global economy, but it was especially driven by the vast increase in demand for resources from some developing countries, most notably China. Depiction of China as 'a ravenous dragon' became common.[18]

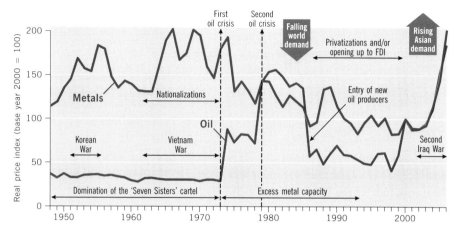

Figure 8.8   Fluctuations in the prices of oil and metallic minerals (base year 2000 = 100)

Source: based on UNCTAD, 2007: Figure III.1

> There is no exaggerating China's hunger for commodities. The country accounts for about a fifth of the world's population, yet it ... has swallowed over four-fifths of the increase in the world's copper supply since 2000.[19]

In light of these new circumstances, the predictions in 2007 were that prices would remain high and even accelerate.

> The economic ascendancy of China, India and other developing countries, along with the resource-intensive stages of their current development phase, could well result in a long-running acceleration of commodity demand growth. *This can be seen as a new stage in international commodity markets, with prices remaining at unprecedentedly high levels ... there are no indications of an impending world recession.*[20]

Of course, this reflects China's increasingly significant role as an export producer of a whole range of metal-intensive (and energy-intensive) manufactured goods.

So much for prediction. One year later, the financial conflagration had resulted in a collapse of commodity prices. The price of oil fell from $150 per barrel in July 2008 to below $40 a few months later. The price of copper fell from more than $8000 per tonne in June 2008 to less than $3000 per tonne in June 2009. And although there has been some recovery in prices, it is clear that the current bonanza is over – at least for now. Of course, if history is the guide, the process will occur again at some time in the future, although we cannot know when, and precisely how, this will happen. It is likely, however, that virtually all the growth in the demand for oil and many other commodities over the next 20 years will come from developing countries. Of course, these shifts in demand reflected in price fluctuations are not only the result of changes in the market for oil or metals. Supply side changes, especially those generated by changes in state policies and corporate strategies, play a highly significant role, as we shall see in subsequent sections.

Technologies of exploring, extracting, refining, distributing

The core of the extractive industries, as Figure 8.2 shows, is the sequence of stages from exploration through development, extraction, processing and distribution to consumption. Each of these stages poses immense technological challenges. The reason lies in the basic characteristics of the resource-based industries alluded to earlier: their finiteness and their locational specificity. In general, highly expensive, sophisticated technologies have to be employed at all stages of the production circuit.

> Building a large base-metals mine can cost over a billion dollars. The magnitude of investments in the oil and gas industry is even greater. Constructing a pipeline, developing an oil deposit or revitalizing an ailing, underinvested mineral industry can run into many billions of dollars.[21]

As a consequence, capital intensity is extremely high while labour intensity is low. These industries employ few workers relative to their size. For example, the biggest non-state oil company in the world, ExxonMobil, employs around 80,000 workers. The biggest metal mining company, BHP Billiton, employs 42,000. In comparison, the retailer Wal-Mart employs 2,100,000 workers while the automobile company Toyota employs more than 300,000. The difference is especially dramatic if we compare sales per worker: ExxonMobil $4.83 million; BHP Billiton $1.43 million; Wal-Mart $180,000; Toyota $730,000.

Firms in the extractive industries face three closely related technological challenges: finding new sources of supply, extracting the highest yield from these sources, and getting them to the market. Of course, such challenges face firms in all industries. But the extractive industries are unique in that they are faced with 'managing a depleting asset'.[22] Unlike the agro-food industry, for example (see Chapter 9), a new crop can't be grown next year. Once an oil well dries up or a copper mine becomes exhausted it cannot be regenerated, although in some cases technological innovation enables some further extraction to occur.

New sources of supply must continuously be sought as existing sources become exhausted and/or too expensive to exploit at prevailing market prices. This is not unlike searching for needles in haystacks. Immensely sophisticated techniques of geochemical, geophysical and satellite remote sensing techniques are involved.

> The exploration period may take up to 10 years, and in many cases such investments turn out to be unsuccessful … Even if the exploration is successful and a new mine is developed and brought into production, the investor still faces various technical risks, market risks (related to demand and price forecasts), political risks (e.g. changes in mining laws, nationalizations), and social and environmental risks.[23]

In addition, the time (and investment) needed to develop a new resource – its gestation period – can be very long indeed. The situation is not unlike that in the pharmaceuticals industry, where vast investments are made over many years in the hope that a drug breakthrough will occur. In fact, of course, the majority fail, and that is also true of the extractive industries.

> [I]n the actual process of extraction, the raw materials tend to get more and more difficult to harvest as time goes on; for example, surface deposits of minerals are used up and people have to dig deeper, the most pure ores are depleted and users must shift to more amalgamated sources, etc. This requires the application of bigger, more powerful equipment, new techniques, etc.[24]

A major problem, therefore, is that most of the easily accessible sources have already been exploited. New resources almost invariably tend to be found in less accessible locations and also often in circumstances making their extraction extremely difficult and, therefore, costly. The deeper the resource below the surface, the greater the problems involved. The purity of a resource is an especially important factor. The lower the degree of purity, the greater the cost involved in extraction and processing, to the point where they become uneconomic. In the case of oil, for example,

> variations in the quality of crude include its density (lighter grades … are more highly valued than heavier grades because they contain a higher gasoline and kerosene fraction), the lack of sulphur compounds (a 'sweet' oil is more highly valued than a 'sour' oil because sulphur compounds require additional 'cleaning' for transportation and refining), the pouring point (related to the wax or bitumen content) and the presence of salt or metal (vanadium, nickel, iron).[25]

There is, inevitably, a connection between such explorative activity and market (i.e. price) conditions. Periods of high prices for oil and minerals stimulate a wave of exploration and the bringing into use of what are, in less favourable market conditions, marginal supplies. Conversely, when prices fall – especially when they fall very steeply and rapidly, as happened in 2008 – investors pull back from such risky ventures. A notable example is the Canadian oil sands project.

> After five years of frenetic building and activity, a race to extract crude from vast tracts of the Canadian oil sands has abruptly stalled, hit by a collapse in the price of a barrel of oil … Until recently, Canada's oil sands were the venue for one of the most spectacular races for profit of modern times. The remote, boggy landscape contains between 1.7tn and 2.5tn barrels of oil, of which an estimated 173bn can be extracted using expensive, hi-tech filtering technology. Canada's reserves are second only to Saudi Arabia's, and a year ago 60 projects were being constructed … But since oil prices began a downward tumble, energy companies … have shelved more than US$90bn worth of oil sands investment.[26]

Boom and bust is the way the extractive world works – and will continue to do so in the future, no doubt.

Both exploration and extraction/processing, therefore, involve very high sunk costs.[27] The same is also true of the distribution stage. Again, all industries face problems in getting their products to market. But the particular characteristics of the extractive industries – especially their bulk and remoteness from markets – generate the need for a massive scale of transportation infrastructure that is virtually unique. The trade-off between increasing the scale of production and being able to transport the outputs is a central problem in these industries. Massive investments in pipelines, supertankers, port facilities and the like are a prerequisite. Not only are they costly but also they have a long gestation period. They represent a very high sunk cost indeed, not least because many of these facilities are highly specialized and not easily transferred to alternative uses.

The effects of such transience are graphically reflected in those places where the 'resource frontier' has moved on, leaving behind the relics of technology.

> Few sights are as impressive as the massive port works, open-pit mines, and 500-mile railways developed to tap the natural resources of frontier regions, or so bittersweet as the relic landscapes left behind in the wake of resource booms. Abandoned mines, idle processing facilities, vacant warehouses, empty ports, disused railroads, boarded-up buildings, and under-employed residents in once vibrant regions speak not only to the capricious nature of resource economies but also to the salience of 'rigidities' in investments in extractive industries.[28]

The centrality of state involvement in the extractive industries

A basic argument of this book is that the state plays a major role in *all* global production networks. However, nowhere is the degree of state involvement as deep or as pervasive as in the extractive industries. In these industries, the state is absolutely central. The reason, of course, lies in the unique *territorial embeddedness* of resources. Access to such resources is controlled, ultimately, by the national state in which they are located.

As Figure 8.3 shows, the state operates within an extractive GPN as both a *regulator* (of access, taxation, and health, safety and environmental issues) and an *operator* (an actual producer). This situation gives states potentially enormous power over how such resources are exploited. How effective that power is and how it is exercised, of course, depend very much on the nature of the state in question, notably its strength (both domestically and internationally) and its political orientation. This, of course, brings the state into sharp confrontation with private companies, especially TNCs, as well as with other states. The history of the resource extractive industries, therefore, is one of continuously shifting power struggles between firms and states, states and states, and firms and firms. Again, although this is true of virtually all industries, it is most evident in the extractive industries. However, its precise form varies between different extractive industries, especially between oil on the one hand and the metal mining industries on the other.

Nationalizing the assets

The central problem facing all resource-rich states is how to exploit their resources to achieve the maximum gain when, as we have seen, the costs of finding, developing, extracting, processing and distributing the product can be astronomically high. Given that such a large proportion of the world's extractive resources are located in poorer countries, this poses immense problems. To what extent can a state develop its own indigenous resources using domestic capital and know-how? How far must it depend on outside investment by foreign TNCs which will, inevitably, result in some loss of control? Over time, these problems have been approached in different ways.

In most cases, the initial development of a country's resource industry has depended on outside investment. Indeed,

> in the early twentieth century, FDI went mostly into these industries, reflecting the international expansion of firms that originated from the colonial powers. The objective of TNCs in the extractive industries was to gain direct control over the mineral resources required as inputs for their growing manufacturing and infrastructure-related industries. During the Great Depression (1929–1933), the international expansion of oil companies continued unabated despite the crisis in other overseas investments.[29]

However, by the 1960s, this situation had changed radically:

> As former colonies gained independence after the Second World War and with the creation of the Organization of the Petroleum Exporting Countries (OPEC), many governments chose to nationalize their extractive industries, resulting in a declining involvement of the TNCs that hitherto had been dominant.[30]

In fact, nationalization in the extractive industries – the complete transfer of ownership from a private firm to the state – has a long history. This is especially true in the case of the oil industry.[31]

> Outright nationalization of oil and gas … first took place in the context of the Russian Revolution in 1917. This was followed by nationalizations in Bolivia (1937, 1969), Mexico (1938), Venezuela (1943), Iran (1951), and Argentina, Burma, Egypt, Indonesia and Peru in the 1960s … In the 1970s, nationalizations occurred in Algeria, Iraq, Kuwait, Libya and Nigeria and there was a gradual increase in Saudi ownership of Aramco … [Such nationalizations] have changed the global landscape of petroleum extraction and contributed to the emergence and subsequent strengthening of State-owned firms.[32]

A clear indication of such a change in the global landscape is provided by the prominent position of state-owned firms among the world's largest oil companies (see Table 8.2).

Controlling prices

The nationalization of oil production makes possible (though far from inevitable) collaboration between oil producing countries to control production levels and, therefore, prices. The clearest example, of course, is that of OPEC: the Organization of the Petroleum Exporting Countries. OPEC was set up in 1960 as a reaction to the cut in the oil price made unilaterally by Standard Oil. Its aim was

> to defend the price of oil – more precisely, to restore it to its [1960] level. From here on, the member countries could insist that the companies consult them on the pricing matters that so centrally affected their national revenues.[33]

The original OPEC membership consisted of five oil producing countries: Iran, Iraq, Kuwait, Saudi Arabia and Venezuela. A further seven countries subsequently joined: Qatar (1961), Libya (1962), United Arab Emirates (1967), Algeria (1969), Nigeria (1971), Ecuador (1973; left and rejoined 2007) and Angola (2007).

OPEC's influence was limited until the outbreak of the 1973 Arab–Israeli War when

> it was the oil weapon, wielded in the form of an embargo – production cutbacks and restrictions on exports – that … altered irrevocably the world as it had grown up in the postwar period … The embargo signalled a new era for world oil … The international order had been turned upside down. OPEC's members were courted, flattered, railed against, and denounced. There was good reason. Oil was at the heart of world commerce, and those who seemed to control oil prices were regarded as the new masters of the global economy.[34]

Today, although OPEC's influence is much lessened in the light of new oil discoveries elsewhere, it remains highly significant and reminds us of the highly politicized nature of the oil industry. In 2007, in fact, OPEC controlled 43 per cent of total world production, compared with a 49 per cent share in 1975.

A (partial) return to privatization

Nationalization has also been a strong trend in the metal mining industries. For example, the number of expropriations of foreign mining enterprises increased from 32 between 1960 and 1969 to 48 between 1970 and 1976.[35] As in the oil industry, this resulted in a squeeze on the private companies.

> For example, the share of the seven largest TNCs in copper mining outside the centrally planned economies fell from 60% in 1960 to 23% in 1981 as a result of nationalizations … By the early 1980s, the participation of TNCs in many developing countries had become limited to minority holdings and non-equity agreements with State-owned enterprises. However, many of the nationalizations undertaken in Africa and Latin America in the metal mining industry turned out to be failures.[36]

As a result of such failures, the emphasis has shifted towards a greater liberalization of the ownership/exploitation laws in many mining countries. Between 1985 and the early 2000s, more than 90 states introduced new laws, or relaxed existing laws, in order to attract foreign investment.[37] Widespread privatization, often as part of a broader neo-liberalization project, became the norm. 'By the early 2000s, the privatization process in the [metal mining] industry worldwide, apart from China, had been more or less completed.'[38]

Power games: states and firms; states and states

As we saw in Chapter 7, the power relationships between states and firms are highly dynamic and contingent. In some cases the balance of power lies one way, in other cases it lies the other way. That balance tends to shift over time. In Chapter 7 we met the term 'obsolescing bargain', which refers to the situation in which, once private capital is 'sunk' in a fixed form, the advantage tends to move away from the investor to the state which controls access to the resource. Although this situation may not generally prevail in many sectors, it certainly applies in the extractive sector. A recent detailed study of the development of the oil industry in Kazakhstan[39] provides evidence of how a state can learn how to renegotiate contracts with a foreign investor; in other words it shows how the balance of power can shift over time.

Kazakhstan achieved independence from being a Soviet republic in 1991. It was rich in oil but lacked the technology to develop its resource. It needed foreign investors. Like many other former Soviet republics and allies, Kazakhstan rushed into the wholesale privatization of its assets, primarily its resource extraction activities. By 2002, around half of the FDI entering Kazakhstan was concentrated in the petroleum industry. One-quarter of the country's oil production originates from the Tengiz oilfield in the west. It is a rich field, but difficult to exploit:

> it is the deepest high pressure deposit in the world, with oil that emerges from the ground scalding hot, at a very high pressure, and laden with poisonous hydrogen sulfide, which must be removed from the oil.[40]

Such a challenging field required very sophisticated technology. The US company Chevron had started negotiations with the Soviet government in 1990. After independence in 1991, the negotiations shifted to Kazakhstan, a state with absolutely no experience in such complex political bargaining. In contrast, Chevron, one of the world's biggest and oldest oil companies, was a very old hand at this game. Ten years after the contract was signed, Kazakhstan attempted to renegotiate the terms, based on the kinds of circumstances implied in the obsolescing bargain concept:

> the agreement had been made, the investments were sunk, the oil was beginning to turn a profit for the corporation, and the state started to feel that the distribution of benefits were too much in favor of the MNC. The country called for renegotiations.[41]

Kazakhstan had already negotiated some improvements over a period of time but without a firm contractual basis. It was this that was now being sought.

> *In such an event*, the renegotiations in question were not a simple affair and likely did not progress as Kazakhstan had predicted. The renegotiations involved the financing arrangements for major gas processing and recycling projects designed to reduce pollution as well as for projects to increase production at the TengizChevroil venture. Looking back … it may seem surprising that Chevron would shut down its operations in protest of the renegotiations. Yet initially it did … the result of Chevron's following through on its threat, and being taken by surprise that Kazakhstan indeed demanded renegotiations. After recalculating its costs, expected value, and strategic play, and given the strategy revealed by the State's move, Chevron reversed its decision after just two months. TengizChevroil's operations were resumed in January of 2003, with Chevron agreeing to some revisions in the contractual terms.[42]

On the basis of this learning experience, Kazakhstan subsequently managed to introduce a series of regulatory measures for its oil industry as a whole: renegotiations with other companies; more stringent rules for foreign investors; a reversal of over-generous VAT exemptions; power to cancel a contract that did not meet its economic expectations; introduction of a new oil export duty; and better environmental provisions, including the banning of all gas flaring. Eventually, in 2002, the state set up its own National Oil Company to ensure a more active role in its extractive sector.

This example is one of state–firm rivalry. But given the strategic importance of extractive resources for all states, these industries are also characterized by a high degree of state–state rivalry. This is especially true of the major users of resources: the established industrialized countries and the newer, fast-growing countries of Asia. For those countries possessing a substantial resource base of their own, like the US, for example, a major aim is to sustain as much of that resource as possible for strategic reasons whilst importing resources to meet their needs. In this latter case, there is a strong incentive to attempt to control access to resources located overseas through either state-owned or private firm investment. In other words, it is in the resource extractive industries that direct state–state competition is most evident.

Currently, the most obvious example concerns the involvement of both the US and China in the 'scramble' for oil and other minerals in Africa, through direct or indirect government participation.

> The US and China are competing to secure access for the oil riches of Africa … Both the American and Chinese governments were important in paving the way for American and Chinese oil interests in expanding in Africa. The US government used diplomatic instruments … economic incentives … and military aid (the largest portion of US military aid to Africa was aimed at Nigeria and Angola). While the US government assisted private US firms in obtaining oil concessions for oil exploration and production, the Chinese government focused instead on securing oil supplies through bilateral agreements. As the most notable example, Sinopec – a Chinese state-owned oil company – acquired oil concessions in [Angola] … on the back of a US$2 billion oil-backed credit from China's Eximbank in 2004 to rebuild the country's railways, government buildings, schools, hospitals, and roads … The Angola example demonstrates how China has adopted an aid-for-oil strategy.[43]

Inter-state rivalry for resources is also apparent in international trade disputes. Again, it is not surprising that the most recent cases involve China. In mid 2009, the US and EU initiated action in the WTO against China for its alleged restrictions on exports of key materials, such as silicon, coke and zinc.

> China imposes restrictions, including minimum export prices and tariffs of up to 70% on a range of raw materials of which it is a major producer. The EU claims these not only break general WTO rules on world trade, but specific promises China made when it joined the organization in 2001, becoming a fully fledged player in global markets.[44]

Corporate strategies in the extractive industries

Consolidation and concentration

The oil industry

The top ten companies shown in Table 8.2 account for around 40 per cent of world oil production. No fewer than four of the top five and 12 of the world's 20

Table 8.2 The world's largest oil companies

Rank 2005	Rank 1995	Company	Home country	State ownership (%)	Total production (million barrels)
1	1	Saudi Aramco	Saudi Arabia	100	4148.8
2	3	Gazprom	Russian Federation	51	3608.5
3	3	NIOC	Iran, Islamic Republic	100	1810.5
4	5	ExxonMobil	US	–	1725.7
5	4	Pemex	Mexico	100	1666.2
6	13	BP	UK	–	1572.6
7	6	Royal Dutch Shell	UK/Netherlands	–	1482.7
8	7	CNPC/PetroChina	China	100	1119.6
9	33	Total	France	–	997.6
10	12	Sonatrach	Algeria	100	911.8
11	8	Petróleos de Venezuela	Venezuela	100	902.6
12	9	Kuwait Petroleum Corp.	Kuwait	100	897.3
13	16	Chevron	US	–	816.9
14	23	Abu DhabiNational Oil Co.	United Arab Emirates	100	794.9
15	11	Lukoil	Russian Federation	–	781.1
16	40	ConocoPhillips	US	–	755.4
17	20	Petrobras	Brazil	56	749.6
18	18	Abu Dhabi Co. Onshore Oil Operator	United Arab Emirates	40	710.9
19	22	Nigerian National Petroleum Co.	Nigeria	100	697.7
20	51	TNK-BP	Russian Federation	–	691.8

Source: based on UNCTAD, 2007: Table IV.8

largest oil producers are fully or majority state owned, the result of the widespread nationalizations discussed in the previous section. This is in stark contrast to the situation that prevailed before the early 1970s.

> Until the 1970s, a few major TNCs from the US and Europe dominated the international oil industry. In 1972, 8 of the top 10 oil producers were privately owned … including the so-called Seven Sisters … These were fully integrated oil companies, active in the extraction and transportation of oil as well as in the production and marketing of petroleum products.[45]

In order to compete on what the private oil companies see as a very uneven playing field, there has been a great deal of consolidation through merger and acquisition, as well as a proliferation of collaborative ventures between private firms and also between private firms and state-owned companies. Today, five mega-companies dominate the private oil sector: ExxonMobil, BP, Royal Dutch Shell, Total and Chevron. The private oil companies, therefore, 'are increasingly being squeezed by the growing power of the national companies and by dwindling reserves and production in accessible and mature basins outside OPEC countries. The super-majors have been struggling to replace their proven reserves and expand production.'[46] At the same time, the capital intensity of production, refining and transportation reinforces the position of the major companies and raises the already high barriers to entry.[47]

The metal mining industries

Historically the metal mining industries have been highly fragmented, but this is changing rapidly as a smaller number of very large companies control an increasing share of world production.

> Worldwide, today there are more than 4,000 metal mining firms, mostly engaged in exploration and extraction … Most of the 149 'majors' are TNCs, the majority of which have production facilities covering mining, smelting as well as refining. These companies account for some 60% of the total value at the mining stage of all non-energy minerals produced … The degree of concentration in the metal mining industries increased significantly between 1995 and 2005.[48]

The top 10 metal mining companies shown in Table 8.3 produce around one-third of total world output. Whereas the oil industry is now dominated by national companies, the degree of state ownership in metal mining is significantly less. Only one of the top 10 mining companies, the Chilean company Codelco, is fully state owned; and only one other, the Brazilian company Vale, has significant state involvement. This is a consequence, as we saw in the previous section, of the widespread adoption of privatization policies by many national resource holders in recent years.

At the same time, there has been a wave of mergers and acquisitions in the metal mining industries. This was undoubtedly stimulated by the surge in commodity prices that occurred in the mid 2000s (see Figure 8.8). In 2006 alone, the value of mergers and acquisitions in these industries was $55 billion. Two of the biggest acquisitions in that year were of Inco (Canada) by the Brazilian company Vale, and of Falconbridge (Canada) by Xstrata, the Swiss mining company. The pace accelerated in 2007 and included Rio Tinto's acquisition of the alumina producer Alcan and the attempted hostile acquisition of Rio Tinto by BHP Billiton. This latter case turned out to be highly contentious and was abandoned in 2008, largely because of the collapse in commodity prices. This situation was made especially complex because the Chinese state-owned company Chinalco attempted to double its equity stake in Rio Tinto in order to stop the BHP Billiton takeover. What would have been China's biggest overseas investment was acrimoniously prevented by Australian pressure. The disagreements were exacerbated by the

Table 8.3 The world's largest metal mining companies

Rank 2007	Rank 1995	Company	Home country	State ownership (%)	% share of world production
1	6	Vale	Brazil	12	5.2
2	4	BHP Billiton Group	Australia	–	4.6
3	1	Anglo American PLC	UK	–	4.3
4	2	Rio Tinto PLC	UK	–	4.0
5	5	Codelco	Chile	100	3.4
6	11	Freeport McMoran	US	–	3.3
7	7	Norislk Nickel	Russian Federation	–	2.7
8	8	Xstrata PLC	Switzerland	–	2.4
9	14	Barrick Gold Corp.	Canada	–	2.3
10	22	Grupo Mexico	Mexico	–	1.6

Source: based on Ericsson, 2008: Table 1; UNCTAD, 2007: Table IV.4

proposal of BHP and Rio Tinto to form an iron ore joint venture. Again, we see the immensely political nature of the extractive industries. Talks also began in 2009 on a possible merger between Xstrata and Anglo American to create a rival to BHP Billiton and Rio Tinto.

Notwithstanding the sharp drop in acquisition and merger activity that began in 2008,

> The fragmented structure of mining is slowly disappearing ... [T]he industry is getting more and more polarised, to the one side there are the large, established mining TNCs controlling a major share of global metal production and on the other side are the junior exploration companies without any production, only 'blue sky' hopes of future production. There is a lack of medium and small sized producers, which can grow organically and become major producers with time. These companies are important in that they concentrate on smaller deposits which often have good grades but which are discarded by the majors.[49]

Organizational and geographical restructuring

The geography of the extractive industries is, of course, basically constrained by the distribution of the territorially embedded resources on which they are based, together with the need to transport outputs at each stage of the production circuit, particularly to the final market. It is also, in the case of the oil industry, strongly influenced by the ownership of the firms involved. In general, most of the state-owned firms have a very restricted geography, mostly limited to their home territory. In contrast, the production spaces of the private companies are globally extensive. However, some state companies have begun to develop more extensive geographies. CNPC, for example, has operations in 14 foreign locations, Kuwait

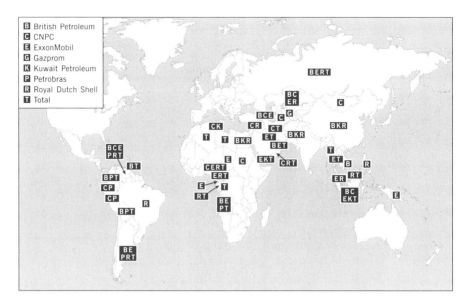

Figure 8.9   Geographies of oil production by some major companies

Source: based on data in UNCTAD, 2007: Table IV.10

Petroleum Corporation and Petrobras in eight. Figure 8.9 maps the geographical distribution of some of the leading oil companies.

Figure 8.10 shows the distribution of some metal mining companies' operations. Their geographical extensiveness varies considerably both by size of firm and by type of operation (exploration, production, refining/smelting).

> In *exploration*, the activities of certain TNCs, such as Anglo American and Xstrata (present in 14 countries each) were widely spread … All but four of the top-25 producers … were involved in exploration activities in at least one foreign country. In terms of *mining production*, Rio Tinto was the company with activities in the largest number (10) of host countries … In *smelting and refining*, Glencore was the most internationalized top metal mining company, with a presence in 13 host countries, followed by BHP Billiton (9) … Leading firms appear to be more internationalized in exploration and mining production than in smelting and refining.[50]

The major extractive companies vary enormously in their degree of *product diversification*. Some focus on one or two specific resources; others operate as highly diversified companies. They also differ in the extent of their *functional integration* along their production circuit. Four broad types can be identified:[51]

- *Vertically integrated companies*: active in all stages of exploration, development, extraction, refining and distribution. In the case of oil companies such vertical integration extends into retailing.

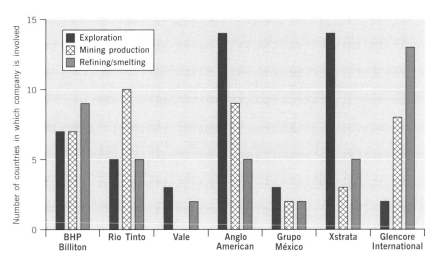

Figure 8.10   Distribution of exploration, production and refining/smelting
projects by leading mining companies

Source: based on data in UNCTAD, 2007: Tables IV.5–IV.7

- *Independent producers*: specialize in upstream activities with very limited downstream activity.
- *Independent transporters, refiners and distributors*: specialize in the middle and/or the downstream segments of the production circuit.
- *Service companies*: provide 'drilling, interpretation and logistical services to producers'.

One of the most significant developments in the organization and operation of the extractive industries has been the huge increase in the influence of specialist services firms. In the case of oil, for example,

> drilling operations are often outsourced to a contract drilling company who may also provide the rig or drill-ship (e.g. Parker Drilling) and who undertakes to crew the rig. Drilling tool supply may be contracted to a specialist tool company (e.g. Baker Hughes), with data logging, data analysis and well maintenance contracted to another firm (e.g. Schlumberger). For many large projects, engineering, design and project management functions may also be outsourced (e.g. AMEC). These specialist upstream oil service companies operate on a global scale, with patterns of inter-firm relations developed in one geographical setting (e.g. Gulf of Mexico) often replicated in other regional contexts (e.g. offshore West Africa or the North Sea) … This … dramatic growth of the oil service market has led several commentators to suggest that the balance of power is shifting away from the majors as a number of oil service providers – Halliburton, Schlumberger, Baker Hughes – assume an increasingly dominant role in the production chain.[52]

A similar trend towards the increasing importance of specialist service suppliers is also evident in the metal mining industries.

> The growing role of such suppliers is being driven by the reorganization of global mining production and technological rejuvenation of the industry, with continued improvements in exploration, mining and mineral processing. Suppliers are focused on specific niches in which they have a globally dominant position … Examples … include large international consulting firms that integrate engineering, project management, procurement and construction activities, such as Kvaerner (Norway), Hatch (Canada), and Bechtel Group (US); medium-sized specialized engineering consulting companies, such as Bateman (South Africa), SRK Consulting (South Africa), and AMC Consultants (Australia); and small- to medium-sized mining and geological software providers, such as Maptek (Australia).[53]

Resources, reserves and futures

The dilemma facing all extractive industry producers, whether state owned or privately owned, is that 'as extractors of non-renewable resources … they *necessarily consume their resource base during production*'.[54] Hence, there is a continuous search for new sources of supply and for new techniques that enable the extraction of materials from less and less pure deposits. The big question, of course, is the extent to which the world is running out of viable resources. On this issue, views are highly polarized.

On the one hand there is the 'Malthusian' view that resource exhaustion is inevitable; the only question is the time-scale over which such exhaustion will occur. On the other hand, there is the view that new technologies of exploration leading to discoveries of new reserves, better means of exploitation leading to more efficient use of the resource (including recycling), and the development of appropriate substitutes will put off the dreadful day. Such polarization of views is reflected clearly in the current arguments about 'peak oil' – the assertion that oil production is about to peak and then move into inexorable decline.[55] The problem is that there are so many variables at work that it is extraordinarily difficult to assess the extent of future reserves of minerals. All the estimates of future reserves are based on *assumptions*. A small change in one of the variables, whether on the demand or the supply side, can drastically change the predictions.

Figure 8.11 provides a framework (known as a McKelvey box) for understanding the complex relationships between reserves and resources.

> The reserves category includes all geologically identified deposits that can be economically recovered and is subdivided into proved, probable and possible reserves on the basis of geological certainty. All other deposits are labelled resources, either because they have not yet been discovered or because their

exploitation is not currently feasible (technical and economic problems are inhibiting their extraction) … Thus, resources are continuously reassessed in the light of new geologic knowledge, scientific and technical progress and changing economic and political conditions. Known resources are therefore classified on the basis of two types of information: geologic or physical/chemical characteristics (grade, quality, tonnage, thickness and depth of material in place); and financial profitability based on costs of extraction and marketing at a given point in time.[56]

Identified Resources those whose location, grade, quality and quantity are known or estimated from specific geologic evidence. This includes economic and subeconomic components and can also be subdivided on geologic certainty grounds into measured (proved), indicated (probable) and inferred (possible).			Undiscovered Resources the existence of which are only postulated, comprising deposits that are separate from identified resources.	
Demonstrated Resources measured plus indicated.		Inferred Resources	Hypothetical Resources	Speculative Resources
Measured Resources size, shape, depth and mineral content of the resource are well established.	Indicated Resources geologic data not as comprehensive as for measured but still probably good enough to estimate the characteristics of the deposits.	assumed continuity of data, estimates not supported by samples or measurements.	undiscovered resources that are similar to known mineral bodies and that may reasonably be expected to exist in the same producing district or region under analogous geologic conditions.	undiscovered resources that may occur either in known types of deposit in favourable geologic settings where mineral discoveries have not been made, or in types of deposit as yet unrecognized for their economic potential.
ECONOMIC RESERVES that part of the reserve base which could be economically extracted or produced at the time of determination.				
SUBECONOMIC			**RESOURCES**	

Increasing degree of economic feasibility (prices, costs, technology) →

Increasing degree of geological assurance (chemical composition, concentration, orientation and extent of deposits, plus constraints) ←

Figure 8.11 McKelvey box framework for resources and reserves

Source: adapted from Turner et al., 1994: Box 16.1

This way of looking at resources and reserves is essentially techno–economic. But there are also environmental, ecological and geographical dimensions[57] that relate to the impact of continued resource exploitation on sustainable development and the effects of resource extraction on the places where it occurs and of transportation between places of extraction/production and consumption. We will return to these issues in Chapters 14 and 15. In a sense overriding all of these considerations, however, is the fact that the 'limits' to resources are, essentially, socially and therefore politically determined. Choices have to be made, for example, as to how much money should be thrown at finding and extracting increasingly difficult resources, or over what is the acceptable degree of environmental and ecological damage. The disastrous oil leakage in the Gulf of Mexico in 2010 demonstrated the potential scale of environmental damage posed by attempts to extract oil from very difficult physical locations. It will surely not be the last example. The future shape of the extractive sectors therefore 'will be determined not by natural limits but by social choice'.[58]

NOTES

1   Emel et al. (2002: 377).
2   Smith (2005) makes this argument in his plea for research on global commodity chains to take the extractive sector more seriously.
3   UNCTAD (2007: 83).
4   See Bridge (2009).
5   Hudson (2001: 301).
6   Bridge (2008b: 413).
7   See, for example, Bunker and Ciccantell (2005), Bridge (2008b), Yergin (1991).
8   The *Financial Times* Global 500 (*Financial Times*, 30 May 2009).
9   Bunker and Ciccantell (2005).
10 UNCTAD (2007: Table III.1).
11 USGS (2009: 1).
12 Bridge (2008b: 400).
13 Odell (1997: 321).
14 Council on Foreign Relations (2008), www.cfr.org/publication/9557; Frynas and Paulo (2006).
15 Brown et al. (2009: 25).
16 Brown et al. (2009: 25).
17 UNCTAD (2007: 88).
18 *The Economist* (15 March 2008).
19 *The Economist* (15 March 2008).
20 UNCTAD (2007: 90–91, emphasis added).
21 UNCTAD (2007: 92).
22 Bridge (2008b: 403).
23 UNCTAD (2007: 92).
24 Smith (2005: 152).
25 Bridge (2008b: 404).
26 *The Guardian* (7 February 2009).
27 Barham and Coomes (2005).
28 Barham and Coomes (2005: 160).
29 UNCTAD (2007: 99).
30 UNCTAD (2007: 99).
31 Yergin (1991).
32 UNCTAD (2007: 115).
33 Yergin (1991: 523).
34 Yergin (1991: 588, 613, 633).
35 UNCTAD (2007: 108).
36 UNCTAD (2007: 107–8).
37 Bridge (2004: 407).

38 UNCTAD (2007: 108).
39 Hosman (2009). The following section draws from this analysis.
40 Hosman (2009: 19).
41 Hosman (2009: 19).
42 Hosman (2009: 20).
43 Frynas and Paulo (2006: 229, 238–9).
44 *The Guardian* (24 June 2009).
45 UNCTAD (2007: 115).
46 International Energy Agency (2009: 10).
47 Bridge (2008b: 408).
48 UNCTAD (2007: 109).
49 Ericsson (2008: 114–15).
50 UNCTAD (2007: 111).
51 Bridge (2008b: 397–8). See also UNCTAD (2007: 113).
52 Bridge (2008b: 400, 408).
53 UNCTAD (2007: Box IV.3, p. 113).
54 Bridge (2004: 407).
55 See, for example, the debate between Strahan (2007) and Clarke (2007).
56 Turner et al. (1994: 222, 224).
57 Emel et al. (2002: 383–8).
58 Gavin Bridge, personal communication.

Nine

'WE ARE WHAT WE EAT': THE AGRO-FOOD INDUSTRIES

Transformation of the food economy: the 'local' becomes 'global'

The production of food is the most basic of all human needs. Like the activities discussed in the previous chapter, it is based upon the *extraction* of materials from the natural environment. In principle, food production is a *renewable* activity, although over-production, soil erosion and water shortages can, in effect, make agriculture impossible under certain conditions. Having changed relatively slowly over long periods of time,[1] the production, distribution and consumption of food have been transformed during the past four decades. They have become increasingly *industrialized*.[2] In addition, although for millions of people basic subsistence is still the norm and starvation is always imminent, for millions of others food has become as much a statement about lifestyle as about survival. 'Abundance amidst scarcity' is a glaring paradox of today's world.[3]

In some respects, therefore, the modern agro-food industries may seem little different from other manufacturing industries. But, despite the industrialization of much food production, this greatly oversimplifies what are highly complex and geographically differentiated activities. The basic fact remains that food production is fundamentally different from other manufacturing industries in one particular way: it is literally *grounded* in biophysical processes.

> The role of biology in plant and animal growth is key ... on a farm – unlike a factory – it is the biological time necessary for plant and animal growth that dictates the work schedule ... In addition, the land-based character of farm production poses severe constraints to industrialization ... because land is a fixed and limited resource, and because land markets are deeply colored by localized social conditions, farmers cannot easily or quickly adjust their investment in land.[4]

Food *production* remains an intensely *local* process, bound to specific climatic, soil and often socio-cultural conditions. At the same time, certain kinds of local production, notably high-value foods, have become increasingly *global* in terms of their *distribution* and *consumption*. For the affluent consumer, with access to the overflowing cornucopias of supermarket shelves, the seasons have been displaced by 'permanent global summertime' (PGST).[5] But such apparently idyllic circumstances for affluent consumers have a dark and contentious side.

Producing food for a global market requires huge capital investment and gives immense power to the transnational food producers and the big retailers. It creates serious problems – as well as opportunities – for food suppliers as they become increasingly locked into (or out of) transnational agro-food production networks. Global food production and distribution create huge environmental disturbances in terms of excessive exploitation of sensitive natural ecosystems, the application of chemical fertilizers and pest controlling agents, the increasing attempts to genetically modify seeds, plants and even animals and to 'patent life', and the transportation of high-value foods (HVFs) over vast geographical distances. These processes make agro-food an intensely sensitive industry, raising the fundamental question of 'who owns nature'.[6] It is at the centre of the continuing acrimonious arguments within the WTO to agree a 'development round' in the Doha trade round (see Chapter 17).

Cutting across trade issues are those relating to food safety and to the ethics of genetic modification (GM) of seeds, plants and animals. In the past few years, for example, there have been several serious food safety scares: BSE ('mad cow disease'), foot (hoof) and mouth disease, avian flu and swine flu. Such outbreaks have a huge impact on agro-food trade and, therefore, on the livelihoods of farmers, growers and distributors. They create massive fluctuations in consumer buying patterns, often out of ignorance. At the same time, there is widespread scepticism – and considerable fear – of genetic modification. Both food safety and GM help to stimulate consumer resistance to the products of the global agro-food industries and to reinforce demands for a return to local sourcing of organically grown products. Without doubt, the agro-food industries have become a battleground with several 'fronts': between producers and producers, between producers and consumers, between producers and governments (not least because agro-food is one of the most heavily regulated industries), and between governments. These contentious issues were greatly exacerbated in 2006–8 when food prices surged and millions more people became 'food insecure'.[7]

Agro-food production circuits

Production circuits in the agro-food industries are immensely varied.[8] In the case of traditional commodities, like grains, the circuit is relatively simple (though more intricate than in the past). In the case of high-value foods, however, which are the primary focus of this chapter, the situation is far more complex. For that reason, we provide several examples here.

Figure 9.1 shows the highly complex structure of the US chicken (broiler) production circuit. This is an industry which has become increasingly domi-nated by very large integrated producers. From a producer's perspective, a major advantage of integrated chicken production is that it facilitates the coor-dination of chicken raising processes which are subject to intrinsic biological lags. It isn't possible to speed up the 'assembly line' as can be done in automo-biles. It is, however, as much a 'just-in-time' system as that in automobile pro-duction. At the same time, integration gives closer control over product quality and food safety.

Figure 9.2 displays the fresh fruit and vegetable production circuit between the producing countries of Kenya and Zimbabwe and the consumer markets of Europe, particularly the UK. Its focus is more on the distribution and marketing functions of these agro-food production circuits and their coordination and gov-ernance. In particular, it sets out the different ways of coordinating transnational production networks discussed in Chapter 5 (Figure 5.18 and associated text). The key point to make about the fruit and vegetable production circuit is that it is driven by the large supermarket chains, rather than by the producers of the crops themselves.

Figures 9.1 and 9.2 both depict conventional agro-food production circuits. However, there are other, 'alternative', circuits which involve the production of organic food and/or the involvement of various kinds of non-economic actors,

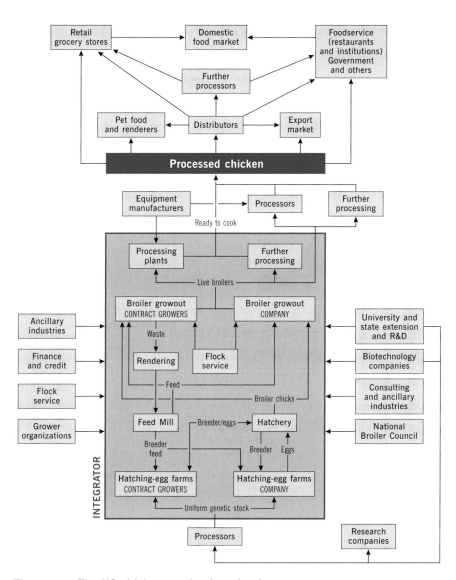

Figure 9.1   The US chicken production circuit

Source: based on Boyd and Watts, 1997: Figure 8.4

notably 'fair trade organizations'.[9] The driving forces underlying the development of some alternative food networks are the increasing concerns with food quality and food safety and concerns for fairer treatment of farmers/growers in developing countries (see later in this chapter). Such networks 'redistribute value through the network against the logic of bulk commodity production ... reconvene "trust" between food producers and consumers ... and ... rearticulate new forms of

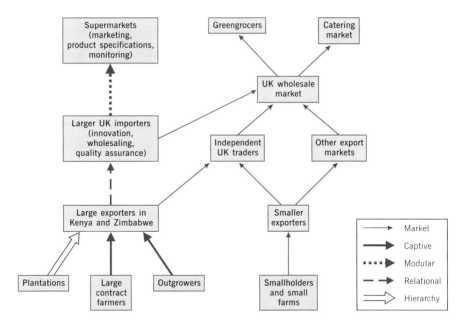

Figure 9.2   The fresh vegetable production circuit

Source: based on Dolan and Humphrey, 2002: Figure 3

political association and market governance'.[10] Figure 9.3 provides one example of an alternative agro-food production circuit: fair trade coffee.[11]

The kind of food circuit shown in Figure 9.3 is just one of a number of alternatives to the tightly controlled, highly integrated, industrially based agro-food circuits that have become so dominant in recent years. Currently, there is also a growing (re-)emergence of explicitly *territorially based* food production networks.

> A key characteristic of the new supply networks is their capacity to re-socialize or re-spatialize food, which comes to be defined by its locale ... by drawing upon an image of the farm or the region as a source of 'quality', alternative food networks 're-localize' food.[12]

Although these developments need to be kept in perspective – the vast bulk of modern food production and distribution is contained within the big producer- and buyer-dominated networks – they do suggest that we need to adopt a more nuanced position. The agro-food industries seem to be bifurcating into two main sets of processes:[13]

- standardized, specialized production processes responding to economic standards of efficiency and competitiveness
- localized, specialized production processes attempting to trade on the basis of environmental, nutritional or health qualities.

(a) A fair trade coffee network

Premium	Relation to market	Certification
Administration by cooperatives of premium to establish medical, agricultural and educational services.	All aware of commodity market prices; but specifically exporting cooperative and UK fair trade organization close contracts; cooperative aims to keep costs within fair trade contract prices.	Either 'Fair Trade Marked' or marked 'Fairly Traded'. May be certified organic.

Producer → Cooperative → Exporting cooperative → UK fair trade organization → Consumer purchase

Buying strategy	Bean	Marketing
Cooperatives buy from producer for contract price which includes fair trade (and organic) premium with differential for quality. Buying high quality.	Organic production encouraged and enhanced.	Marketing explicitly with reference to the social conditions of farmers. May also be organic certified and marketed.

(b) A commercial coffee network

Premium	Relation to market	Certification
May, or may not, pay extra to individual farmers for organically certified product. No premium for social programmes.	Aims to keep cost of physicals down when buying, particularly in relation to fluctuating commodity prices.	May be certified organic.

Producer → Dealers → Commercial company → Consumer purchase

Buying strategy	Bean	Marketing
Buys centrally, or from farm gate if sourcing difficult. Takes variable quality, offers cash in hand.	Growing strategies oriented to crop maximization and direct or indirect encouragement of industrial growing practices.	Brand-related and niche marketing not concerned with social and environmental conditions.

Figure 9.3 'Alternative' agro-food production circuits: fair trade and commercial coffee

Source: based on Whatmore and Thorne, 1997: Figure 11.2

Global shifts in the agro-food industries

In this chapter, our concern is with the *high-value* segments of agricultural production and trade. We will focus, in this section, on three examples: chicken, fresh fruit and vegetables, and coffee.

Chicken production has become an immensely complex, highly integrated agro-food industry (Figure 9.1). At the global scale it is dominated by three countries, the US, China and Brazil, which together account for almost half the world total (Figure 9.4). Until very recently the US was also the world's leading exporter

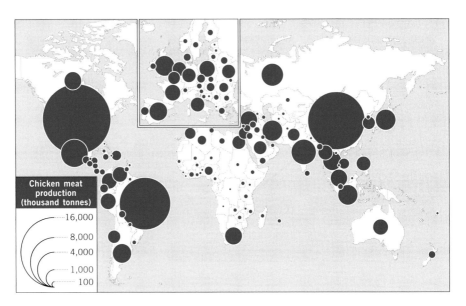

Figure 9.4   Global production of chickens

Source: FAO *Statistical Yearbook*, 2009: Table B11

of chickens, but it has been overtaken by Brazil. 'In 1997, Brazil's chicken exports were less than a third those of the US. But production has taken off since 2000 – growth averaged 230 per cent the past two years – and today Brazil exports to 127 different countries and controls 36 per cent of the world share.'[14]

Fresh fruit and vegetable production is also heavily concentrated at the global scale (Figure 9.5). China (38 per cent of the world total) is by far the world's biggest producer (although much of this production is consumed domestically). India is far behind at 9 per cent, followed by the US (4.5 per cent) and Brazil (3.4 per cent). However, the composition and pattern of trade in fruits and vegetables have changed markedly during the past two decades.[15] Export growth rates of traditional products (e.g. oranges, canned pineapples, canned mushrooms, concentrated orange and apple juices) were very low. Non-traditional products grew fastest: 'Some commodities – mangoes, frozen potatoes, single-strength orange and apple juices, fresh mushrooms, garlic, sweet corn (prepared or preserved), and avocado – achieved, or were close to, double-digit growth rate in their exports.'[16]

The geography of global trade in fruits and vegetables is strongly regionalized. Not only are Europe and North America the leading importers of such products (along with Japan), they are also substantial exporters. Both regions contain a variety of climatic conditions conducive to certain kinds of fruit and vegetable production: the Mediterranean rim in the case of Europe; Mexico and the Caribbean in the case of North America. Figure 9.6 shows the origins of imports

Figure 9.5 Global production of fruits and vegetables

Source: FAO *Statistical Yearbook*, 2009: Tables B6, B7

of fruits and vegetables to the world's 30 leading importers. Quite apart from the intra-regional trade flows to the highest-income countries of North America, Europe and Japan, the role of the Southern Hemisphere countries is especially significant. Unlike the banana producing countries, for which this single product accounts for almost 90 per cent of their fresh fruit exports, the Southern Hemisphere countries produce and export an increasing variety of products for consumption in the affluent markets of the Northern Hemisphere.

(a) Fresh fruits

(b) Fresh vegetables

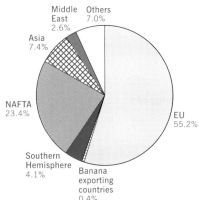

(c) Processed fruits and vegetables

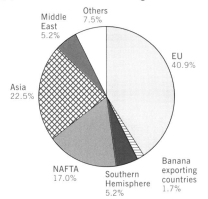

(d) Fruit and vegetable juices

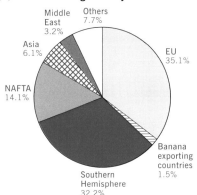

Figure 9.6   Origins of imports of fruits and vegetables to the world's 30 leading importers

Source: based on Huang, 2004: Figure 2.2

These countries have taken advantage of the seasonal differences to expand their exports, particularly for many temperate-climate fruits ... more than half of the fresh fruits exported by the Southern Hemisphere countries were temperate-climate fruits such as grapes, apples, and, to a much lesser extent, pears. About two-thirds of apples exported by the Southern Hemisphere countries came from Chile and New Zealand, while Chile and Argentina were the dominant suppliers for grapes and pears ...

In addition to fresh fruits, the group of Southern Hemisphere countries is a major supplier for fruit juices, accounting for nearly one-third of the import value for juices purchased by the world's top 30 importers ... Brazil accounted for nearly three-fourths of the region's juice exports, while Argentina (shipping mainly apple and grape juices) was the second largest exporter in the region (11 per cent of the exports).[17]

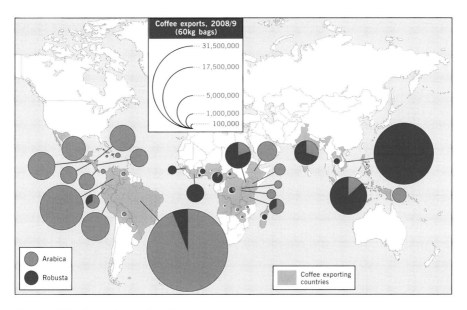

Figure 9.7   Exporters of coffee

Source: International Coffee Organization data, 2009

Finally, Figure 9.7 maps global exports of coffee. As coffee *aficionados* will know, there are two major types of coffee bean: arabica beans, grown at higher altitudes and more difficult to grow, and robusta beans, grown on low lands in the humid tropics. In general, arabica beans are regarded as being of higher quality though, as always, it is not quite as simple as this. Four countries generate 66 per cent of total coffee exports: Brazil (32 per cent, of which 94 per cent is arabica), Vietnam (18 per cent, all robusta), Colombia (10 per cent, all arabica), and Indonesia (7 per cent, 87 per cent robusta).

The pattern of production and trade in high-value foods, therefore, combines elements of global, regional and local scales. Globally, the emergence of Southern Hemisphere producers, basing their advantage on their seasonal complementarity with the temperate markets of the Northern Hemisphere, generates massive flows of long-distance trade. Regionally, the existence of areas of more exotic production within the major regional markets of North America, Europe and East Asia has led to strong intra-regional trade flows of high-value foods. Locally, the increasing interest in alternative food networks, especially those which focus on local (often organic) production, has created much shorter movements of agro-food products.

Consumer choices – and consumer resistances

For most of human history, people have had to struggle to obtain enough food to survive. Only a very tiny proportion of the population could afford to obtain the more exotic foods from distant places. That is, of course, still the case today for millions of people in the poorest countries and for some people in affluent countries. But as incomes have risen for many through economic growth, and with the associated urbanization of the population, demand for food has changed dramatically. In developed economies, consumers now spend only around one-tenth of their income on food, compared with one-third 50 or 60 years ago. However,

> food's unique nature has made it uniquely central to human social life … and therefore a carrier of historically constructed meanings, both intimate and political … These meanings in turn enter into food markets at a variety of levels. Different groups' and societies' ideas of food purity and danger, of the 'proper meal' and the proper treatment of farmland and livestock, of government's responsibility to protect producers and consumers from food risks … [mean] that food is never free of the meanings that make it the subject of bread riots, trade wars, and media scares.[18]

These factors make the relationship between food production and consumption more complex than is often assumed. What we choose to eat has become a far more intricate process: a mix of taste, culture, religion, health concerns, ethical position and lifestyle as well as disposable income. On the one hand, food producers strive to produce and market foods that will attract the largest number of consumers (and enhance profits) whilst, on the other hand, consumers themselves have widely varying 'food agendas'.

In the affluent consumer markets of North America, Europe and parts of East Asia, it is the *changing patterns* of demand and consumption, rather than the overall level of food consumption, that are especially important. Increasing affluence stimulates a desire for greater choice in food products. As a result – but also, of course, driven by the marketing strategies of the transnational food producers – the market for food has become highly segmented.

At one level, this is reflected in the huge diversity of products sold through the major supermarkets and, especially, their provision of all-year-round perishable foods from across the globe. It is reflected in the rapid growth of new food products: for example, the chilled convenience food market. It is reflected in the ever-changing dietary fashions of the affluent in their search for the route to beauty and long life. It is reflected, too, in the development of the specialist 'lifestyle' drinks markets, for example, the 'latte revolution' driven by Starbucks' colonization of much of the world.[19]

At the same time, however, there is increasing *consumer resistance* to many of the food products being sold through the big supermarkets, as well as to the more traditional providers of fast food. In early 2006, for example, McDonalds announced that it was actually going to close a significant number of its outlets in the UK. McDonalds, of course, has long been the focus of much criticism for its allegedly unhealthy products, culminating in the movie *Supersize Me*. In some countries, though not all, there is widespread opposition to GM foods and to the use of non-organic production methods. In the case of GM foods, there is considerable difference in consumer attitudes between the US, where GM crops tend to be more acceptable, and Europe, where there is greater resistance.[20] A European Commission public opinion survey in 2001 found that 80 per cent of those surveyed did not want GM food and 95 per cent wanted the right to choose.[21]

There are also pressures to 'relocalize' food production: both to rely more on local sources and also to stimulate and protect areas of local production of key products. Such resistances derive from a combination of concern over environmental damage and fears about the safety of foods grown using what are increasingly regarded as suspect or ethically unacceptable methods. For example, 'fresh' supermarket food

> is predicated on a new nature-defying order where every conceivable fruit and vegetable grown anywhere is available all the time ... PGST [permanent global summertime] may look good, but in the name of consumer choice and public health the irregularity and diversity that is part of the natural order has been eliminated, not to benefit consumers but to fit the way our big food retailers like to do business. In essence, this means sourcing vast quantities of easy-to-retail, long-shelf-life standard varieties, grown to rigid size and cosmetic specifications, that can be supplied 365 days a year.[22]

There has been significant recent growth in the ethical consumer movement in the agro-food industries.[23] For example, some 7 million farmers and workers in around 60 developing countries are now covered by the 'Fairtrade' charitable scheme, which pays a guaranteed price covering basic costs and a surplus to reinvest in further development. Fairtrade is especially active in such foods as coffee (see Figure 9.3), tea, bananas and chocolate, although the proportion of total world trade in these products covered by Fairtrade agreements remains small: for example, around 5 per cent of the UK banana market.[24] Nevertheless, according to the Fairtrade Foundation, global consumption of Fairtrade products grew by 47 per cent between 2006 and 2007.

Set against these kinds of consumer resistance, we have to recognize that such movements are, at least in part, facilitated by the choices of the affluent consumer. While there is no doubt that demand is growing from consumers for food whose quality and geographical provenance are regarded as being superior to food from the large-scale sources, for most people the overwhelming need is still for enough food to survive. For every 'enlightened' consumer pursuing her organic food, or for the lifestyler drinking his designer coffee, there are many for whom such foods are out of reach. For people working long hours or for the elderly, the availability of convenience foods is a major benefit. The fact that such foods may not be especially healthy is another issue. Clearly, therefore, demand for and consumption of food represent an extremely complex set of processes. As we shall see in subsequent sections of this chapter, this has major implications for the changing technologies of food production, for state regulatory policies, and for the strategies of the transnational food producers.

Transforming technologies in agro-food production

Global cool chains

Traditionally, food production was a relatively simple process. Of course, technological innovations in crop growing and animal husbandry have been significant throughout human history. For example, without the important agricultural innovations of the eighteenth and nineteenth centuries, the Industrial Revolution simply could not have occurred. Equally, without the developments in transportation and communications discussed in Chapter 4, long-distance movement of agricultural products would not have been possible. These, together with innovations in refrigeration and food-freezing technologies – the development of what have been called 'global cool chains' – transformed the availability of a much wider range of agricultural products over vast geographical distances.[25]

One of the most widely quoted indicators of globalization is the distance over which the food in our shopping basket or on our dinner table has travelled. For example, a basket of 20 fresh foods bought from major UK retailers was found to have clocked up a total of 100,943 miles.[26] On the other hand, long-distance movement of agricultural produce also makes possible the continued existence of many traditional producers through their access to a larger market (including that of Fairtrade production). The carbon footprint per pound of food of the biggest container ships is significantly lower than that of much 'local' sourcing.[27] The rapid growth in world trade in fresh foods depends critically on the use of controlled atmosphere (CA) technologies to move fragile and perishable products over long distances without destroying their 'freshness'.[28] Technologies of fresh food preservation are, of course, greatly enhanced by the use of air freight to transport low-weight, high-value exotic foods to distant, affluent markets.

Industrialization of food production and the shift towards biotechnology

The technologies of agro-food production have been transformed by their *industrialization* and, most recently, through the introduction of *biotechnologies*. Such developments are intimately related to the increasing role of very large agro-food corporations in all aspects of food production. We will look specifically at the corporate dimension in a later section of this chapter. Here, our concern is with the increasing importance of biotechnologies in food production.

The application of industrially produced chemicals to agricultural production (fertilizers to stimulate higher crop yields, pesticides to inhibit disease and insect damage) has been common for many decades. The development of newer varieties of crops has also been a continuing process. The so-called 'Green Revolution' of the 1960s and 1970s was the most significant combination of such practices: an attempt to solve the food problems of poor countries through the development of new varieties of basic crops such as wheat, rice and maize, using fertilizers, pesticides and irrigation.

The Green Revolution was, in many ways, a precursor of what has become the most controversial aspect of agro-food production: *genetic modification* (GM). As before, the objective is to improve plants' resistance to disease and to herbicides, to increase yields, and to improve nutritional value. This is done by changing basic genetic structures and producing new varieties of seeds.[29] Such GM techniques are immensely complex and costly. They involve massive levels of capital expenditure on a scale that can only be afforded by the big biotechnology and agro-food companies. Not least, they encourage the patenting of what had hitherto been regarded as 'public' goods: the seeds needed to produce the next generation of crops. This is the patenting of life itself. Traditionally, a farmer would set aside some seeds from one year for use in the following year. GM seeds, on the other hand, 'belong' to the seed company, which produces 'terminator' seeds that cannot be reproduced by the user, who has to purchase the next year's seeds from the seed company.

Whereas the application of biotechnologies is relatively recent, and mainly applied in the early stages of the agro-food production circuit, the use of chemical additives in food products themselves has been common for some time. One of the results of the increasing industrialization of food production was a loss of some of the desirable qualities of taste, texture, colour and so on. To counteract these changes, and to enhance the attractiveness of food products, producers have developed a bewildering variety of food additives: preservatives, antioxidants, emulsifiers, flavourings, colourings. One calculation is that some 4500 different flavouring compounds are available to food manufacturers and that 90 per cent of additives are purely cosmetic.[30]

What about the workers?

The impacts of these technological transformations in how food is produced, and how far and how quickly it can be transported, are immense. In addition to their effect on what people eat – and the potential effects on their health – they also impact greatly on those people who work in agriculture. The proportion of the labour force working on the land has fallen markedly, especially in developed countries. The industrialization of agro-food processes has, in effect, shifted the locus of much of the work from the field to the factory or to the packaging plant. The seasonal rhythms of agricultural work have been displaced for many by the rhythms of the food processing and packaging assembly lines. To that extent, many workers in the agro-food industries are more like workers in automobile or electronics production, engaged in 'lean and flexible production', than farmers.[31]

Because all governments are heavily involved in regulating their food industries for health and safety reasons (see next section), the working conditions in processing and packaging plants are more tightly monitored than is the case in some other industries (such as clothing). The work itself may be mind-numbingly boring and repetitive but so, too, are many other jobs in today's society (and not just in manufacturing: think of telephone call centres). Of course, wide variations in working conditions exist, especially between developed and developing countries, despite the ubiquitous involvement of the big supermarket chains in sourcing from such plants.

But not all jobs in food processing and packaging are permanent or full-time. Agro-food is probably the largest user of casual labour of all modern industries. Indeed, these industries depend fundamentally on a huge floating labour force of workers who are employed only when the producer needs them and who are often organized by subcontractors or 'gangmasters'. Since the supply of such labour invariably exceeds demand, wages are extremely low and working hours very long. The majority of such workers are migrants, with virtually no bargaining power and often very little protection from abuse. The seasonality of agricultural processes creates vast periodic movements of migrant workers within and across borders.[32] In the US, the majority of these workers are Hispanic (especially Mexican); in Europe, they come predominantly from Eastern Europe or from North Africa.

An Oxfam report on American agriculture provides graphic details of what the report terms 'sweatshops in the fields'.

> Farmworkers are among the poorest – if not *the* poorest – laborers in the US ... farm labor is also one of the most dangerous jobs in America. At work, farmworkers suffer higher rates of toxic chemical injuries than workers in any other sector of the US economy, with an estimated 300,000 suffering pesticide poisonings each year. They also suffer extremely high rates of workplace accidents ...
>
> Farmworkers are much more likely to have temporary jobs ... Just 14% of all workers in crop agriculture are employed full time in year-round positions, while fully 83% work on a seasonal basis ... 56% of farmworkers in crop agriculture are migrant workers, travelling more than 75 miles to get a job ...
>
> Thirty percent of migrant workers (or 17% of all crop workers) are characterized as 'follow-the-crop' migrants, moving year-round like those portrayed in John Steinbeck's *The Grapes of Wrath* ...
>
> Farmworkers in general, and immigrant farmworkers in particular, have low levels of education ... Their literacy and communication skills in English are especially limited ...

> Finally, yet perhaps most significantly, these immigrant workers typically lack work authorization … Given the vulnerabilities of their legal status, US farmworkers tend to face widespread workplace and human rights abuses, and are rarely able to take the risk of challenging abuses when they occur.[33]

While some of these characteristics of the agro-food workforce are far from new, there is little doubt that they have intensified as the industry's production circuits have become more tightly controlled by larger and larger producers and buyers.

The role of the state

The state plays an immensely important role in the agro-food industries, which are among the most highly regulated, heavily subsidized, and vigorously protected of all economic activities.

Regulating agro-food industries

A vast array of government agencies and departments operates to oversee various parts of the agro-food industries, for example, the UK Department of Environment, Food and Rural Affairs and the Food Standards Agency; the US Department of Agriculture and its Food and Drug Administration. A primary focus of such regulatory activity is the issue of food safety, a problem greatly exacerbated by the growth of international trade in food. Before the 1970s, as much as 90 per cent of world food production was consumed in the country in which it was produced.[34] That situation has changed dramatically. As a result, national food regulatory measures have become increasingly embedded in international codes, such as the Codex Alimentarius, set within the Food and Agricultural Organization and the World Health Organization. This consists of 'over 200 standards, forty codes and guidelines for food production and processing, maximum levels for about 500 food additives, and 2700 maximum-residue limits for pesticide residues in foods and food crops'.[35]

A striking feature of regulatory policies in these industries is the extent to which they are deeply intertwined with the strategies of the major food producers.

> The biggest funder of the establishment of the Codex Alimentarius Commission was not the US state but the US food industry … Indeed, the Codex has become one of the more industry-dominated international organizations.[36]

In other words, there is a substantial amount of 'private' regulation in the agro-food industries sanctioned by national governments. A major problem facing food safety regulators is the continuing proliferation of new products that cross the boundaries between food and medicine: the development of so-called functional foods or 'nutriceuticals', which claim to improve various aspects of health.[37]

Even within the EU, there are national variations in regulatory practices. This is seen most clearly in the context of the food safety scares that have occurred from time to time and also in the GM food controversy. Such cases invariably create conflict between the state within which the disease originates and its export markets, leading to trade boycotts and disputes over the efficacy of safety measures. The case of GM food is potentially the biggest source of difference between states and one that spills over into trade disputes, especially between the US and the EU. The US position is that GM foods are not only safe but also vital to increasing food supply in poor countries. Driven by consumer resistance (see earlier), the EU has taken a more restrictive position. Although it lifted its six-year moratorium on GM food in 2004 and allowed limited approvals of GM products, several EU states continue to ban them.

There is also a proliferation of nationally specific regulations governing the extent to which foreign food retailers are permitted to operate. For example, it has been quite common for countries to restrict entry of foreign food retailers. Although this practice has declined in recent years, the rules of operation in national retail markets continue to differ substantially. The US has the most lenient regulatory system towards retailing. The Japanese retail market is far more heavily regulated, although Japan has revised the Large-Scale Retail Store Law, which had been a major obstacle to the growth of large retail stores. Certainly the law had discouraged major foreign retailers from trying to enter the Japanese market. India also operates a highly restrictive policy, although it has begun to relax some restrictions on the entry of foreign retailers. In Eastern Europe, although retailing has been opened up, there is considerable opposition to the spread of foreign-owned supermarkets.

Subsidizing and protecting agro-food industries: the *major focus of trade conflict*

For reasons that lie deeply embedded in national emotions, as well as in the need to guarantee a secure food supply for its citizens, most countries have adopted policies to nurture, sustain and, where felt necessary, protect their agro-food industries from external competition. Such policies include the trade measures shown in Figure 6.5, as well as direct financial support (subsidies) for domestic farmers. Figure 9.8 shows that agricultural subsidies are heavily concentrated in particular countries.

> More than 90 per cent of the dollar value of agricultural support in OECD countries is provided by the European Union (which alone provides about half); Japan; the US; and the Republic of Korea.[38]

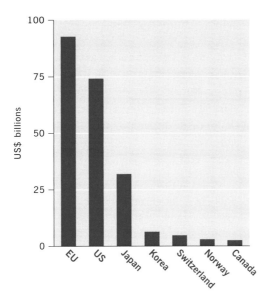

Figure 9.8   Agricultural subsidies

Source: WTO data

For example, both Japan and Korea have adopted highly protectionist policies towards their rice industries, which have deep cultural meanings as well as dietary significance. In Europe the French, in particular, regard the rural economy as sacrosanct. In the US farming remains a national obsession, a reflection of the country's desire for food security as well as the emotional connotations of the development of the national space in the nineteenth century. Subsidies to US farmers began in the 1930s under the New Deal programme.

The EU's Common Agricultural Policy (CAP) has long absorbed the largest single share of the EU's total budget and has, as a result, become a source of dissatisfaction for several member states. The CAP has become increasingly controversial, not only within the EU itself but also in the context of the WTO trade negotiations. The CAP was reformed most recently in 2003, when the level of subsidy to farmers was separated from production, a practice which had led to notorious cases of over-production in the past. Now, subsidy is linked to 'compliance with environmental, food safety, and animal welfare standards' and part of the process of 'transforming the CAP from a sectoral policy of farm community support to an integrated policy for rural development'.[39] In some member states (Austria, Denmark, Finland, the Netherlands, Sweden and the UK) further radical reform of the CAP is regarded as essential.

The issue of agricultural subsidies has become possibly the biggest bone of contention in the current WTO negotiations, especially in the context of the

Doha 'development round'. It is often pointed out, for example, that the average subsidy per cow in the EU is more than the $2 per day on which half the world's population has to live, whilst US farm subsidies allow 'farmers to export wheat at 28 per cent less than it costs to produce, corn at 10 per cent less and rice at more than a quarter less than cost price'.[40] We will discuss the WTO negotiations more fully in Chapter 17. Financial subsidization of some, or all, agricultural production continues to be common in many countries, although there has been some movement within OECD countries:

> The average support to agricultural producers fell from 37 per cent of the gross value of farm receipts in 1986–88 (the beginning of the Uruguay Round) to 30 per cent in 2003–05 … [however] while the 7 percentage point decline in support is progress, the amount of support increased over the same period from $242 billion a year to $273 billion.[41]

But, despite the general reduction in tariffs and subsidies, many agricultural products remain heavily protected, to the detriment, especially, of poor countries.

A new phenomenon: state land grabs

Fears over future food and fuel shortages have led in recent years to the emergence of a new phenomenon: 'land grabbing', that is state-supported actions to acquire agricultural land in foreign countries.[42] A 2009 report estimated that

> an area half the size of Europe's farmland … [was] targeted in the last six months ... at least 30m hectares is being acquired to grow food for countries such as China and the Gulf states who cannot produce enough for their populations … The land grab is being blamed on wealthy countries with concerns about food security.
>   Some of the largest deals include South Korea's acquisition of 700,000 ha in Sudan, and Saudi Arabia's purchase of 500,000 ha in Tanzania.
>   India has lent money to 80 companies to buy 350,000 ha in Africa. At least six countries are known to have bought large landholdings in Sudan, one of the least food-secure countries in the world.
>   Other countries that have acquired land in the last year include the Gulf states, Sweden, China and Libya. Those targeted include not only fertile countries such as Brazil, Russia and Ukraine, but also poor countries like Cameroon, Ethiopia, Madagascar and Zambia.[43]

Corporate strategies in the agro-food industries

The exploitation of agricultural resources across the world by companies based in developed countries has a very long history.

Early examples of TNC involvement in agricultural production include FDI in the nineteenth and twentieth centuries by companies based in Japan, Europe and the US, primarily to produce cash and food crops such as cotton, rubber, sugar and others ... The history of foreign investment in agriculture is actually even older, and goes back to the early colonial era (from the sixteenth century onwards), when foreign expansion by European powers to the developing countries of today was largely motivated by the search for natural resources, combined with cheap labour by indentured workers or slaves.[44]

Concentration and consolidation

The massive transformation of the agro-food industries that has occurred during the past few decades is inexorably bound up with the increasing dominance of very large transnational firms. This is apparent at all stages in the production circuit, from seeds through growing, processing and retailing. What was historically a highly fragmented set of industries – although some parts were always more concentrated than others – has become one in which a relatively small number of giant, transnational firms shapes what food is produced, how it is produced, who produces it, and how it is marketed and distributed to final consumers.

Figure 9.9 lists the 10 leading companies in the world in four agro-food industries: seeds, pesticides, food and beverage manufacture, food retailing. Global seed production is dominated by European (five) and US (three) firms. In fact, US dominance has increased following Monsanto's acquisition of Seminis in 2005 to

Top 10 seed companies		$m sales 2007
1. Monsanto	US	4,964
2. DuPont	US	3,300
3. Syngenta	Switzerland	2,018
4. Groupe Limagrain	France	1,226
5. Land O'Lakes	US	917
6. KWS AG	Germany	702
7. Bayer Crop Science	Germany	524
8. Sakata	Japan	396
9. DLF-Trifolium	Denmark	391
10. Taikii	Japan	347

Top 10 pesticide companies		$m sales 2007
1. Bayer	Germany	7,458
2. Syngenta	Switzerland	7,285
3. BASF	Germany	4,297
4. Dow AgroSciences	US	3,779
5. Monsanto	US	3,599
6. DuPont	US	2,369
7. Makhteshim Agan	Israel	1,895
8. Nufarm	Australia	1,470
9. Sumitomo Chemical	Japan	1,209
10. Arysta Lifescience	Japan	1,035

Top 10 food & beverage companies		$m sales 2007
1. Nestlé	Switzerland	83,600
2. Pepsi Co.	US	39,474
3. Kraft Foods	US	37,241
4. Coca-Cola	US	28,857
5. Unilever	UK/Netherlands	26,985
6. Tyson Foods	US	26,900
7. Cargill	US	26,500
8. Mars	US	25,000
9. ADM Co.	US	24,219
10. Danone	France	19,975

Top 10 food retailers		$m sales 2007
1. Wal-Mart	US	180,621
2. Carrefour	France	104,151
3. Tesco	UK	72,970
4. Schwarz Group	Germany	58,753
5. Aldi	Germany	55,966
6. Kroger	US	52,082
7. Ahold	UK	50,556
8. Rewe Group	Germany	49,651
9. Metro Group	Germany	49,483
10. Edeka	Germany	45,397

Figure 9.9   Dominant firms in the global agro-food industries

Source: based on data in ETC Group, 2008

create the world's largest seed company. US firms also dominate food and beverage production, although the world's biggest food manufacturer, Nestlé, comes from one of the smallest European countries, Switzerland, while the fifth largest is the UK/Netherlands company Unilever. In global food retailing, on the other hand, eight of the top 10 are European, and only two are American, including by far the largest: Wal-Mart.

According to one agro-food industry observer:[45]

- Two-thirds of the world seed market is controlled by the leading 10 companies.
- Almost 90 per cent of the world pesticide market is controlled by the leading 10 firms.
- Twenty-six per cent of the world packaged food market is controlled by the leading 10 firms.
- The leading 100 global food retailers account for 35 per cent of total world grocery sales. The top three produce half of the total revenues of the top 10.

Most of this increased concentration in the agro-food industries is the result of *merger and acquisition*. Indeed, these have been among the most takeover-intensive industries in recent years, as firms have striven not only to acquire a wider portfolio of brands (as well as to drive out competition for their own existing brands) but also to extend their reach into new geographical markets. Much of this activity has been driven by the increased *financialization* of the leading firms: 'the prioritization of objectives to boost "shareholder value" in the strategic management of large corporations'.[46] Virtually all the leading food companies have followed a similar trajectory varying, of course, according to their specific company history.

Among the more important examples in recent years was the US tobacco company Philip Morris, which transformed itself through a whole series of acquisitions. In 1985 Philip Morris acquired General Foods; in 1988 it acquired Kraft Foods; in 1989 these were combined to form Kraft General Foods, the largest food company in the US; in 2000 it acquired Nabisco Holdings of the US and integrated Nabisco brands into Kraft Foods worldwide; in 2007 the entire Kraft Foods business was sold and became the world's third largest food company; and in 2010 Kraft controversially acquired the major UK company Cadbury.

Among the diversified food companies, Unilever acquired Brooke Bond in 1984 to make it the world's leading tea company; in 2000 the company acquired the US food company Bestfoods, as well as Ben & Jerry's ice cream; in 2007 Unilever acquired the Buavita vitality drinks brand in Indonesia, and Inmarko, the leading ice cream business in Russia. The more narrowly specialized food companies have also grown through acquisition as well as through organic growth (no pun intended). Tyson Foods, for example, the world's biggest poultry company, began its 'expand or expire' strategy in 1963 by acquiring the Garrett Poultry Company of Arkansas and then made 19 further acquisitions between 1966 and

1989. In 1995 Tyson purchased Cargill's US broiler operations and has subsequently made acquisitions in other food companies outside poultry. By 2001, Tyson was 'the world's largest processor and marketer of not only chicken but also red meat with the acquisition of beef and pork powerhouse, IBP, Inc.'[47]

Acquisition and merger have also been important factors in the growth of the major transnational food retailers. One of the biggest deals was Wal-Mart's acquisition of the British supermarket chain Asda for almost $11 billion, and its acquisition of the German chain Wertkauf and the Japanese company Seiyu. Because of national regulatory restrictions, the major food retailers have often had to enter foreign markets through joint ventures with local partners. Examples include Tesco's alliance with Samsung in Korea.

Strategies of combining 'global' brands with 'local' products

The agro-food industries are dominated by the drive to introduce, develop and sustain *branded products*. It is through branding that firms strive to convince consumers that there is something special (in terms of quality, reliability, safety and so on) about the foods they are purchasing. The degree of product differentiation through branding is probably greater in the agro-food industries than in most other industries. Each of the leading agro-food companies has a vast portfolio of brands serving different market segments. Nestlé, for example, has around 8000 brands in up to 20,000 variants.[48] Such brand portfolios are excessive; most have evolved through acquisition and merger, as we have seen. One important strategy being pursued by all the leading food companies, therefore, is to rationalize their brand portfolio, usually by selling some of the brands to other firms. By 2001, for example, Unilever had reduced its number of brands from 1600 to 900, and the process continues.

Obviously, the aim has to be to sell each brand to the largest number of consumers. The ideal, from a producer viewpoint, would be brands that sell everywhere without any need for modification. But agro-food markets are not like that, as we have seen. A major problem for the big agro-food producers, therefore, is in creating *global* brands in circumstances where much food consumption is still very strongly influenced by *local* tastes and preferences. A distinction must, of course, be made between the manufacture of a product for a global market (based on large-scale production plants serving geographically extensive markets) and the way that product is actually sold to the local consumer. A product may be sold overtly as a global brand (like Coke or Pepsi) but it may also be sold under a more local label and packaging, even if the product itself is the same everywhere.

While some food companies do market their products as global brands, others are less inclined to do so. Nestlé, for example, dismisses the idea of 'global brands':

> There is a trade-off between efficiency and effectiveness in global brands … Operational efficiency comes from our strategic umbrella brands. But we believe there is no such thing as a global consumer, especially in a sector as psychologically and culturally loaded as food. As a result, Nestlé retains its brand strength by using … very strong local brands.[49]

The increased consumer interest in food health and safety has important implications for food producers' strategies. Capitalizing on the enhanced interest in local and organic foods becomes increasingly important. All the big food companies have to deal with these market changes. They are doing so in various ways: for example, by acquiring local companies and by retaining their brand identities rather than rebranding them with the new corporate identity. Nestlé, for example, announced its intention to 'accelerate the evolution of Nestlé from a respected, trustworthy Food and Beverage Company to a respected, trustworthy *Food, Nutrition, Health and Wellness* Company'.[50] Note the very significant change of emphasis. This shift in priority towards 'healthy' products has become virtually universal among the large food companies. Unilever boasts about how it is 'bringing Vitality to life' and has launched the 'Unilever Health Institute – a centre of excellence in nutrition, health and vitality'.[51] Likewise, Kraft Foods has a 'health and wellness strategy'.[52]

Changes in organizational and geographical architectures

Traditionally, the major food manufacturers expanded overseas by setting up (or acquiring) operations in each of their major geographical markets. The existence of highly protected domestic food markets, together with the idiosyncrasies of local consumer tastes, made each national market distinctive. As a result, the leading transnational food producers established organizational structures that were strongly *multi*national, with all the characteristics shown in Figure 5.9.[53] The agro-food industries, therefore, are the clearest example of the 'global–local tension' discussed in Chapter 5. Because the traditional organizational-geographical structures are less and less effective, all the major food producers are engaged in large-scale reorganization programmes. Two examples help to illustrate these processes.

Nestlé currently has operations in 80 countries and employs 250,000. In announcing its intention to transform itself into a 'Food, Nutrition, Health and Wellness Company', the company recognized that this has implications that go beyond products and brands.

> Nestlé is changing from a decentralized multinational company to a global, and ultimately, a global multifocal company.[54]

In fact, Nestlé has been involved in substantial geographical reorganization for some time, as its actions within South East Asia reveal.[55] With the increasing liberalization of agro-food trade within ASEAN, Nestlé progressively rationalized its multidomestic operations there (in the early 1990s it had more than 40 factories in the region). Under the 'centres of excellence' programme, the company established such centres for production of breakfast cereals in the Philippines, chocolate and confectionery in Malaysia, non-dairy creamer in Thailand, soya sauce in Singapore, and instant coffee in Indonesia.

Such developments formed part of the company's broader reorganization programme at the global scale.

> In the 1990s, the company dramatically expanded its intra-firm trade of final products ... Because many Nestlé products sell under globally recognised brand names and are manufactured according to globally consistent recipes, there is a certain footlooseness in the intra-firm trade patterns of the company.[56]

Unilever, like Nestlé, has long operated a decentralized multinational strategy but it, too, has made strenuous efforts to create a more efficient and responsive global structure. In the late 1990s Unilever operated around 300 food factories, with a presence in virtually every country in the world. The acquisition of Bestfoods brought in a further 70 factories in 60 countries. In its 'Path to Growth' strategy of the late 1990s and in the subsequent 'One Unilever' programme, Unilever has drastically rationalized and reorganized its entire production and supply chain activities. Its two major divisions, Food and Home and Personal Care Products, have been combined into one category. The focus on a much smaller number of brands (see above) has involved closing a large number of plants in favour of concentrating production on around 150 key sites, together with a further 200 sites for manufacturing local market-leading or nationally profitable products.

These kinds of organizational and geographical restructuring are typical of all the major multibrand food producers, although with variations in detail from one company to another. They involve a very strong macro-regional dimension to the organization of the production network (as in Figure 5.14c). Recent research on European food production networks indicates that

> global firms had launched a restructuring process aimed at developing large macro-regional factories specialized by product lines and serving the entire region, with the objective of generating scale economies and productivity increases. These macro-regional factories had been progressively replacing traditional national factories through continuous restructuring and cost cutting programmes, involving plant closures and lay-offs at the national level ... [for example] in the early 2000s, Nestlé launched its own version of a macro-regional production system in ice cream, distinguishing between 'global factories' that would perform initial production stages for global or macro-regional markets, and 'finishing factories' in which products would be adapted to local markets ... The adoption of global strategies in marketing and production entailed a centralization of support functions such as sourcing, aimed at controlling and coordinating the activity of local buyers.[57]

'Big Food' and 'Big Retail': two sides of the same coin

These developments in the strategies of the major transnational food producers have to be seen within the context of the retailing systems through which their products are sold. One of the most significant developments in the agro-food industries, in fact, has been the evolving, symbiotic relationship between the big food producers and the big supermarket chains.

> 'Big Food' and 'Big Retail' are really two sides of the same coin. Big global food manufacturers need big supermarket chains to get their products on to the shelves and our big supermarkets need big food processors … Mass-produced food that can be churned out over and over again in vast, uniform quantities, made by a handful of big manufacturers who jump to the big retailers' tune, processed food lends itself to supermarket retailing: it gives them the ability to put a standard, regular product into every store nationwide, a prod-uct that does not require any specialist handling … Industrial food lends itself to the supermarkets' heavily centralised, highly mechanical distribution systems.[58]

This is an arena of continuous power struggles in which power lies increasingly with the big transnational food retailers. And there is no doubt that the biggest food retailers have become increasingly *transnational* after being essentially domestically oriented for most of their histories.[59] However, they vary considerably in the extent of their transnationalization (Figures 9.10, 9.11). The biggest food retailers are not invariably the most transnational, as the case of Wal-Mart shows. The world's biggest food retailer is ranked ninth in terms of international sales as a share of its total sales. Figure 9.11 maps the distribution of stores of three of the leading transnational food retailers. There are some significant differences between them in the specific geography of their overseas activities but all share a common characteristic: a very strong focus on their home region.

Wal-Mart has 54 per cent of its stores in the US and 73 per cent in North America (when Canada and Mexico are included). However, Wal-Mart continues to pursue an aggressive transnationalization strategy. At present, its overseas stores are concentrated in East Asia (China, Japan – although it disposed of its Korean stores), Latin America (Brazil, Chile, Argentina) and Central America, where it acquired a substantial equity stake in the region's largest retailer from Ahold. In contrast, Wal-Mart's only base in Europe at the moment is in the UK. Its attempts to establish a presence in Germany failed, largely because of its inability to under-stand the fundamental differences between the German and US retail food mar-kets. However, Wal-Mart has plans to expand aggressively into Eastern Europe and especially Russia.

The French company *Carrefour* has 54 per cent of its stores in its home market and 91 per cent in Europe. Elsewhere, it has a significant presence in Latin America (primarily in Argentina and Brazil) and in East Asia. However, Carrefour

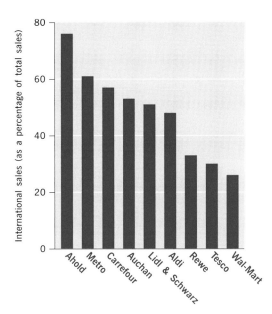

Figure 9.10 Variations in the transnational scope of leading food retailers

Source: based on material supplied by Neil Coe

has a policy of getting out of countries in which it cannot become one of the top three retailers.[60] It withdrew from Japan and Mexico, and sold its stores in the Czech Republic and Slovakia to Tesco. At the same time, it has bought Tesco's Taiwan operations. Significantly, Carrefour has no stores in North America, having failed to transfer its hypermarket model to the US.

The UK retailer *Tesco* has grown extremely rapidly in recent years. It now totally dominates the UK grocery market, where almost 60 per cent of its stores are located. This makes it, like Wal-Mart in the US, a target for strong opposition from different interest groups. Tesco is pursuing a very aggressive – but geographically focused – transnationalization strategy, based on expansion in East Asia (22 per cent of its stores) and Eastern Europe (16 per cent). Interestingly, Tesco has no stores in Western Europe, apart from Ireland. Its recent buying and selling deals with Carrefour are part of this strategy, strengthening Tesco's position in Eastern Europe. In East Asia, Tesco's major store concentrations are in Thailand, Japan, China and Korea (where it initially entered through a joint venture with Samsung[61]). Having stayed out of the US, Tesco has recently set up a chain of convenience stores – known as Fresh and Easy – initially on the West Coast. It also planned to enter the highly protected Indian market through collaboration with a local enterprise, but this has stalled.

Overall, therefore, there has been very considerable growth in the transnational operations of some of the leading retail chains. But such expansion has

Figure 9.11   The global geographies of leading transnational food retailers

Source: company reports

not been problem-free, as the sell-offs listed above demonstrate. The use of local partners within a joint venture often helps to avoid the problems of misunderstanding local market conditions. But even joint ventures are not without their difficulties, especially if the foreign partner fails to learn from the knowledge embedded in the local partner. It is also the case that, while the strength of most of the leading retailers is based on their high levels of profitability in their home market, their returns on international operations are often far lower.

So, the transnationalization of food retailing is far from being a straightforward or unproblematic process. Competing head-to-head with local firms is particularly difficult in this sector. A major problem is that of identity. Because food retailing has traditionally been very much a domestic activity, there is little knowledge of foreign retail store brands (as opposed to product brands). For many customers outside the US, for example, Wal-Mart is a totally unknown quantity. The same applies to non-French residents' knowledge of Carrefour, or non-UK residents' awareness of Tesco. Yet building up a respected and trusted brand identity takes a long time. Meanwhile, local competition remains, in most cases, a very serious problem for transnational food retailers.

Geographical expansion of the store network is one dimension of food retailers' strategies. A second dimension is from whom, and from where, its products are sourced. The big retail chains have vastly increased the geographical extensiveness of their sourcing systems as well as exerting increasing power and influence over their suppliers. As in the case of clothing (Chapter 10), the major retailers have come to dominate their supply networks, forcing suppliers to meet their increasingly stringent demands on price, delivery and quality. There is a great deal of criticism of the treatment of suppliers by the big supermarkets, although suppliers are often afraid to object out of fear of losing their contracts. An investigation of the accounts of transnational food retailers claimed that they gain huge financial benefits simply by delaying payments to their suppliers:

> stock is turned into cash at the check-out counters long before suppliers have to be paid … In effect, suppliers have acted as surrogate bankers … [however] the burden is not shared equally … the most powerful manufacturers are able to shunt the burden of increased trade debt down the supply chain … life is very much tougher for smaller suppliers who do not have the luxury of their burden down the line.[62]

It is also increasingly common practice for the big supermarket chains to ask the major food producers to pay for 'preferred status'.[63]

As the big food retailers have increased their direct presence in foreign countries (especially in the emerging market economies) they have also drastically changed the geography and organization of the sourcing networks, both for their local stores and for their entire network.[64] Typically, the degree of centralization of procurement has greatly increased. When a transnational retailer establishes operations in a specific country, one of its first actions is to replace 'a per store procurement system with the distribution centre (DC) model used in established markets. Each DC may have responsibility for a particular range of products or a particular territory.'[65]

The second aspect of the changing procurement practices of transnational retailers is the changing balance between global and local sourcing.

> On the one hand, transnational retailers have increased levels of global sourcing for their home markets ... On the other hand ... there are the supply chain impacts that result from the retailers establishing store operations *within* the various markets ... The foreign subsidiaries of retailers such as Tesco, Ahold, and Carrefour commonly source over 90% of products from within the country ... *contra* accounts of the continuing rise of global sourcing, local sourcing may actually *increase* over time as the supply base develops and retailers therefore import fewer products.[66]

However, the recent strategic shift of Wal-Mart towards a more global sourcing system reflects what may become an increasingly common practice.

> Wal-Mart intends a drive ... to cut billions of dollars from its supply chain by combining its store purchasing across national frontiers in a fresh stage of the globalization of its business ... It is ... shifting to direct purchasing of its fresh fruit and vegetables on a global basis, rather than working through supplier companies.[67]

NOTES

1 Kiple (2007).
2 Bonanno et al. (1994), Roberts (2008), Ward and Almås (1997), Watts and Goodman (1997), Weiss (2007), Wilkinson (2002).
3 McMichael (2007: 218).
4 Page (2000: 245, emphasis added).
5 Blythman (2004: Chapter 11).
6 ETC Group (2008).
7 ETC Group (2008: 5).
8 In addition to the cases discussed here, see Neilson and Pritchard's (2009) analysis of the tea and coffee chains in South India.
9 Raynolds (2004), Whatmore and Thorne (1997), Whatmore et al. (2003).
10 Whatmore et al. (2003: 389).
11 Ponte (2002) examines the conventional coffee production circuit at a global scale.
12 Sonnino and Marsden (2006: 183).
13 Sonnino and Marsden (2006: 183).
14 www.newfarm.org/international/news/120104/121604/br_chicken/html.

15 This section draws heavily on Huang (2004).

16 Huang (2004: 3).

17 Huang (2004: 7–8, 10, 11).

18 Freidberg (2004: 10–11).

19 See Ponte (2002).

20 Munro and Schurman (2009).

21 Quoted in Paul and Steinbrecher (2003: 173).

22 Blythman (2004: 76, 77).

23 See Blowfield (1999), Hughes et al. (2008), Leclair (2002).

24 *The Guardian* (8 March 2006).

25 Friedland (1994: 223).

26 *The Guardian* (10 May 2003).

27 Murray (2007).

28 Huang (2004: 19).

29 Whatmore (2002: 131).

30 Millstone and Lang (2003).

31 Raworth and Kidder (2009).

32 Phillips (2009).

33 Oxfam (2004: 2–3, 7, 8).

34 Grigg (1993: 236).

35 Braithwaite and Drahos (2000: 401).

36 Braithwaite and Drahos (2000: 401).

37 Wilkinson (2002: 338).

38 World Bank (2008b: 97).

39 Sonnino and Marsden (2006: 192).

40 US Institute for Agriculture and Trade Policy, quoted in *The Observer* (3 July 2005).

41 World Bank (2008b: 97).

42 UNCTAD (2009: 128).

43 Vidal (2009: 24).

44 UNCTAD (2008: 105).

45 ETC Group (2008).

46 Palpacuer and Tozanli (2008: 81).

47 Tyson Foods Inc. website: www.tysonfoodsinc.com.

48 *Financial Times* (22 February 2005).

49 Nestlé CEO, quoted in the *Financial Times* (22 February 2005).

50 Nestlé company website: www.nestle.com, emphasis added.

51 Unilever company website: www.unilever.com/aboutus/ourhistory.

52 Kraft Foods company website: www.kraftfoodscompany.com/brands/healthandwellness.

53 For cases in the agro-food industries, see Pritchard (2000a; 2000b; 2000c).

54 Nestlé company website: www.nestle.com.

55 Pritchard (2000a: 252–4).

56 Pritchard (2000a: 253).

57 Palpacuer and Tozanli (2008: 82–3).

58 Blythman (2004: xvii, 73).

59 Coe and Wrigley (2009), Wrigley and Lowe (2007).

60 *The Economist* (16 April 2005).

61   Coe and Lee (2006).

62   *Financial Times* (7 December 2005).

63   *Financial Times* (30 March 2006).

64   Coe and Hess (2005), Durand (2007), Reardon et al. (2007).

65   Coe and Hess (2005: 464).

66   Coe and Hess (2005: 463).

67   *Financial Times* (4 January 2010).

Ten

'FABRIC-ATING FASHION': THE CLOTHING INDUSTRIES

Changing rules

On 1 January 2005, the clothing industries entered a new era. The special international framework which had regulated virtually all trade in the industries for four decades – the Multi-Fibre Arrangement (MFA) – ceased to exist. Trade in clothing (as well as in textiles) was no longer to be subject to import quotas. This represented a massive change in the rules of the game. Cries of anguish emanated from developed country producers, fearing annihilation through competition from developing country producers, especially in Asia, and most of all from China. On the other hand, developed country retailers were more sanguine, viewing with enthusiasm the prospect of being able to buy their garments more cheaply. But it was not only developed country producers that feared the repercussions of the MFA abolition. Many developing countries had been able to survive in these industries only because they had some degree of quota protection. Without that they, too, feared the Chinese dragon.

In fact, the clothing industries exemplify many of the intractable issues facing today's global economy, particularly the trade tensions between developed and developing economies. It is not difficult to see why. Millions of workers are officially employed worldwide in the clothing industries, in addition to countless unregistered workers, employed both in factories and in their own homes. These industries were the first to take on a global dimension because of the low barriers to entry to clothing production; in the 1970s, they epitomized the so-called 'new international division of labour'.[1] These industries continue to be important sources of employment in the developed economies, employing many of the more 'sensitive' segments of the labour force: females and ethnic minorities, often in tightly localized communities. In developing countries the industries employ predominantly young female workers in conditions that sometimes recall those of the sweatshops of nineteenth-century cities in Europe and North America.

The clothing production circuit

The clothing industries form part of a larger production circuit involving textile production, in which each stage has its own specific technological and organizational characteristics and particular geographical configuration (Figure 10.1). The clothing industries are far more fragmented organizationally than textiles and far less sophisticated technologically. They are also industries in which outsourcing is especially prominent. Very often the design and even the cutting processes are performed quite separately from the sewing process, the latter being particularly amenable to outsourcing. The garments industries produce an enormous variety of often rapidly changing products to a very diverse, and often unpredictable, consumer market.

Figure 10.1   The clothing production circuit

Figure 10.2   An idealized sequence of development in the textiles and
clothing industries

Increasingly, it is the distributors of garments – particularly the retailers – which have
come to play the dominant role in shaping the organization and the geography of
the clothing industries. These are strongly *buyer-driven* industries.[2]

Figure 10.2 suggests a generalized sequence of development through which
individual producing countries appear to have passed. Six stages are shown,

beginning with the embryonic stage typical of the least developed countries through to the maturity and decline of the older industrialized countries, together with the type of production likely to be characteristic of each stage. The sequence is a useful summary of what has happened so far but, like all such sequential models, it should not be regarded necessarily as being predictive of what will happen in the future. Although many countries have passed through some or all of these stages, the precise path of development depends upon a number of factors that, together, produce the specific geographical patterns of these industries.

Global shifts in the clothing industries

The low barriers to entry into clothing manufacture make it one of those activities accessible to virtually any country, even at low levels of economic development. Because of its continuing labour intensity, the map of employment (Figure 10.3) provides a useful indicator of global clothing production. Asia dominates the world map. China is now the world's biggest producer, employing some 2.7 million workers, followed a long way behind by Indonesia, India, Japan, Vietnam and Thailand. Outside Asia, clothing production is highest in Mexico, the US and Brazil in the Americas; in Italy in Western Europe; in Romania and Poland in

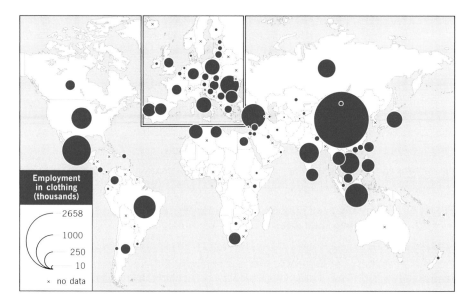

Figure 10.3   Employment in the global clothing industries

Source: calculated from UNIDO *International Yearbook of Industrial Statistics*, 2005; ILO, 2005

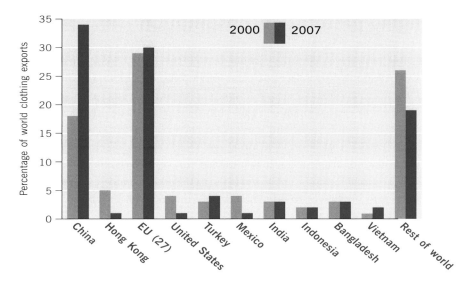

Figure 10.4   Leading clothing exporters, 2000 and 2007

Source: based on WTO, 2009; Chart II.8

Eastern Europe; in the Russian Federation. There has, indeed, been a major global shift in the clothing industries, away from the old-established producers towards newer ones in the developing world.

Such geographical shifts are even more apparent when we look at patterns of trade. Asia dominates exports, generating more than 50 per cent of the world total. Figure 10.4 shows the leading clothing exporters in terms of their share in 2000 and 2007. China's share of world clothing exports almost doubled between 2000 and 2007 (in 1980, China generated a mere 4 per cent of world clothing exports). The EU has maintained its position, but this aggregate figure includes intra-regional exports and also masks significant geographical shifts within the EU (see below).

In terms of clothing imports, the most striking feature is the spectacular increase in the US share. In 1980, 16 per cent of the world total went to the US; in 2007, its share was 24 per cent, about the same as the extra-EU. The net result is that both the US and the EU have huge trade deficits in clothing. The US deficit amounts to $81billion, that of the EU to $60billion. Between 2000 and 2007, imports of Chinese clothing to the US accelerated by 18 per cent per year and to the EU by 21 per cent per year. Growth of clothing imports from smaller East Asian countries grew even more spectacularly. US clothing imports from Vietnam, for example, increased by 35 per cent between 2006 and 2007. In contrast, US clothing imports from Mexico fell by 15 per cent between 2006 and 2007. Such spectacular shifts appear to be related to China's accession to the WTO and to the abolition of the MFA in 2005 (see later section).

Changing patterns of consumption

At the most basic level, clothing satisfies one of the most fundamental human needs. But beyond that basic level, demand for clothing becomes more discretionary and subject to a whole variety of complex social and cultural forces, including people's desires to express themselves through their choice of clothing. Clothing can be a highly symbolic good, suggestive of certain self-perceptions and external self-projections. Such variables as income, age, social status, gender, ethnicity and so on play very important roles. It is a market full of uncertainty and volatility. Much of the business of producing and selling clothing, therefore, depends upon firms' abilities to predict, or to influence, what consumers wish to buy.

Figure 10.5   Composition of demand for different clothing categories in the US

Source: based on Abernathy et al., 1999: Figure 1.1

Clothing can be divided into three major types: basic garments, fashion–basic garments and fashion garments (Figure 10.5). The fastest growth is occurring in the fashion-basic segment.[3] The major general determinant of both the *level* of demand and the *composition* of demand (in terms of these three basic categories) is the level and distribution of personal income. Since personal incomes are so very unevenly distributed geographically at the global scale (see Figure 5.1), it is the affluent parts of the world – including the newly affluent consumers in East Asia – that largely determine the level and the nature of the demand for garments. It is in these markets that demand for fashion-basic clothing is growing most rapidly. Figure 10.5 shows that 45 per cent of the dollar volume of US clothing sales is in the basic product category, while the remaining expenditure is split more or less evenly between fashion and fashion-basic products. On the other hand, the generally low incomes in developing countries clearly restrict the size of their domestic garment markets and produce a consumer focus on the basic segment, although with aspirations among many consumers to move into the fashion-basic segment.

The conventional economic wisdom is that, beyond the level of basic necessities, demand for clothing increases less rapidly than the growth of incomes. This poses a major problem for clothing manufacturers and retailers: they need to stimulate demand through *fashion change*; they need to shift consumer demand away from low-margin basic garments to higher-margin garments. Enormous expenditure goes into promoting fashion products and creating 'designer' labels. Designer labelling is basically a device to *differentiate* what are often relatively similar products, and to cater to – and to encourage – the segmentation of market demand for garments. Such a practice covers a very broad spectrum of consumer income levels from the exceptionally expensive to the relatively cheap.

Consumer behaviour in the clothing industries is not just about fashion choice. It is also about concerns that some producers (and retailers) are utilizing dubious labour practices to reduce costs. Some segments of the clothing industry, and some high-profile retailers, have become the target of large-scale anti-sweatshop campaigns. Consumer resistance has come to be a major feature of these industries.[4] As a result of pressure from groups such as Oxfam, from labour unions, and from other anti-sweatshop groups, the major clothing companies have given undertakings to monitor the operations of their suppliers and subcontractors to remove illegal practices, especially employment of child labour. The major UK retailers have promised to end contracts with firms that contravene their guidelines. Similarly in the US, leading clothing firms (including Nike, Liz Claiborne, Nicole Miller, L. L. Bean and Reebok) subscribe to a voluntary code of conduct to eliminate domestic and overseas sweatshop conditions and to back the Fair Labor Association.

However, new cases of labour exploitation in subcontracting factories continually appear in the media. The process of monitoring and detection is difficult. It is even more difficult to monitor the practice of home-working which, again, tends to be highly exploitative of the most disadvantaged groups who work at home for minimal rates of pay and no benefits. But in an industry as fragmented and organizationally complex as clothing, this is an immense task: 'Codes of conduct are awfully slippery. Unlike laws, they are not enforceable'.[5] Despite such confusion, and continuing evasion of such codes by some companies, there is no doubt that some progress has been made in improving conditions in these industries, although problems certainly remain. A recent initiative known as 'Better Factories Cambodia', for example, linked to the ILO and supported financially by such companies as Nike, Reebok, Levi Strauss, Wal-Mart and H&M, is being heralded as a model initiative in the industry. These issues of company codes of conduct will be discussed in more depth in Chapter 17.

Production costs and technology

In clothing manufacture, capital intensity is generally low, labour intensity is generally high, the average plant size is small, and the technology is relatively unsophisticated. These characteristics contrast markedly with other parts of the textiles–clothing production circuit, as Figure 10.6 shows.

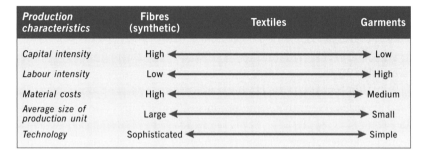

Figure 10.6   Variations in production characteristics between major components of the textiles–clothing production circuit

Labour

Variations in labour costs

Labour costs are the most significant production factor in the clothing industries. Figure 10.7 shows just how wide the labour cost gap can be between different producer countries. The spread is enormous and appears to be getting wider. The highly uneven geography of labour costs, and the increased ability of manufacturers to take advantage of such differences because of improvements in the speed and relative costs of transportation and communications, drives most of the locational shifts in the clothing industries. The major advantage of low-labour-cost producers lies in the production of basic items, which sell largely on the basis of price, rather than in fashion garments in which style is more important. The difference between the two is one of *rate of product turnover*. Fashion garments have a rapid rate of turnover reflecting the idiosyncrasies of particular markets. Geographical proximity to such markets is vital and this helps to explain the survival of many developed country clothing manufacturers. It also partly explains the relative advantage of low-cost countries located close to the major consumer markets of the US (e.g. Mexico, the Caribbean), Europe (e.g. Central and Eastern Europe, the Mediterranean rim) and Japan (the Asian countries). We will return to this regional situation in the final section of this chapter.

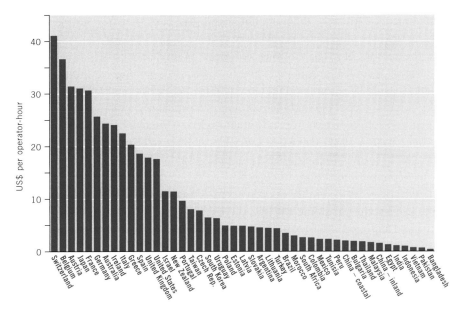

Figure 10.7   Hourly labour costs in the clothing industries, 2008

Source: Werner International

Characteristics of the labour force and conditions of work

Some 80 per cent of the workers in the clothing industries are female.[6] A substantial proportion of the labour force is also relatively unskilled or semi-skilled.
The specific socio-cultural roles of women, in particular their family and domestic responsibilities, also make them relatively immobile geographically. A further
characteristic of the clothing workforce in the older industrialized countries is
that a large number tend to be immigrants or members of ethnic minority
groups. This is a continuation of a very long tradition. The early clothing industries of New York, London, Manchester and Leeds in the late nineteenth and
early twentieth centuries were major foci for poor Jewish immigrants. Subsequent
migrants from other origins have also seen the industry as a key point of entry
into the labour market. The participation of Italians and Eastern Europeans in
both the US and the UK has been followed more recently by the large-scale
employment of blacks, Hispanics and Asians in the US and by non-white
Commonwealth immigrants in the UK.

The history of these industries is one of appalling working conditions in sweatshop premises. At least in the clothing industries of the developed economies such
conditions are now relatively rare; factory and employment legislation have seen
to this. But the sweatshop has certainly not disappeared from the clothing industries of the big cities of North America and Europe. The highly fragmented and
often transitory nature of much of the industry makes the regulation of such

establishments extremely difficult. The result has been a major resurgence of clothing sweatshops in some big Western cities.[7]

In the rapidly growing clothing industries of the developing countries the labour force is similarly distinctive. Employment tends to be geographically concentrated in the large, burgeoning cities and in the export processing zones. The labour force is overwhelmingly female and predominantly young. Many workers are first-generation factory workers employed on extremely low wages and for very long hours: a seven-day week and a 12- to 14-hour day are not uncommon. Employment in the clothing industry in particular tends to fluctuate very markedly in response to variations in demand.

Hence, a very large number of outworkers is used; women working as machinists or hand-sewers at home on low, piecework, rates of pay. Such workers are easily hired and fired and have no protection over their working conditions. Many are employed in contravention of government employment regulations. Yet there is no shortage of candidates for jobs in these fast-growing industries in some developing countries. Factory employment is often regarded as preferable to un- or underemployment in a poverty-stricken rural environment. A factory job does provide otherwise unattainable income and some degree of individual freedom. Often the wages earned are a crucial part of the family's income and there is much family pressure on young daughters to seek work in the city clothing factories or in the EPZs.

Technological change

Both the cost of production and the speed of response to changes in demand are greatly influenced by the technologies used. Technological innovation can reduce the time involved in the manufacturing process and make possible an increased level of output with the same size – or even smaller – labour force. As global competition has intensified in the clothing industries the search for new, labour-saving technologies has increased, especially among developed country producers. Two kinds of technological change are especially important:

- those that increase the speed with which a particular process can be carried out
- those that replace manual with mechanized and automated operation.

The nature of the clothing production process means that the potential for such innovation varies very considerably between the different stages shown in Figure 10.1.[8] In fact, there was relatively little change in clothing technology between the industry's initial emergence in the late nineteenth century and the early 1970s. The manufacture of clothing remains a complex sequence of related *manual* operations, especially in those items in which production runs are short.

> The basic reason is the nature of the production process itself, where two-dimensional materials, i.e. cloth that is rather soft and limp in nature, are subjected to a series of individual labour-intensive handling/assembly steps, culminating in a product which then fits/drapes a three-dimensional human body.[9]

Hence, most of the recent technological developments in the industry, including those based on microelectronic technology, have been in the non-sewing operations: grading, laying out and cutting material in the pre-assembly stage, and in warehouse management and distribution in the post-assembly stage. The application of computer-controlled technology to these operations can achieve enormous savings on materials wastage and greatly increase the speed of the process. For example, the grading process may be reduced from four days to one hour; computer-controlled cutting can reduce the time taken to cut out a suit from one hour to four minutes. But these developments do not reach the core of the problem. The sewing and assembly of garments account for 80 per cent of all labour costs in clothing manufacture. So far only very limited success has been achieved in mechanizing and automating the sewing process.

Current technological developments in the manufacture of clothing are focused on three areas:

- Increasing the *flexibility* of machines, to enable them to recognize oddly shaped pieces of material, pick the pieces up in a systematic manner and align the pieces on the machine correctly, whilst also being able to sense the need to make adjustments during the sewing process.
- Addressing the problem of *sequential operations*, particularly the difficulty of transferring semi-finished garments from one work station to the next while retaining the shape of the limp material.
- Developing the *unit production system* to deliver individual pieces of work to the operator on a conveyor belt system. This greatly reduces the amount of (wasted) production time spent by the operator on unbundling and rebundling work pieces. The handling process has been estimated to take up to 60 per cent of the operator's total time.

The drive to introduce such new technologies has been stimulated by very low-cost competition from developing countries. But cost reduction is not the only benefit derived from the new technologies. At least as important, if not more so, are the *time savings* that result from automated manufacture. This has two major benefits:

- Speeding up the production cycle reduces the cost of working capital by increasing the velocity of its use.
- It becomes possible for the manufacturer to respond more quickly to customer demand.

In addition, electronic-point-of-sale (EPOS) technologies permit a direct, real-time link between sales, reordering and production. As the production circuit has become increasingly buyer driven, these IT-based innovations have become extremely important. They not only permit very rapid response to sales and demand at the point of sale but also enable the buyer firm to pass on the costs of producing and holding inventory to the manufacturer. These technological developments, when combined with the pressures exerted by the big buyers to be faster and more flexible (see below), create enormous stresses on supplier firms and, consequently, on the labour force.[10]

The role of the state and the Multi-Fibre Arrangement

In developing economies, textiles and clothing manufacture have occupied a key position in national industrialization strategies. Hence, the kinds of import-substituting and export-oriented measures outlined in Chapter 6 have been applied extensively. But it is in the older-established producing countries of Europe and North America and, more recently, Japan, faced with increasingly severe competition from low-cost producers, that government intervention has been especially marked. The political sensitivity of these industries has forced governments to intervene in three major ways:

- to encourage *restructuring and rationalization* through the use of subsidies and adjustment programmes
- to *stimulate* offshore assembly (for example, by granting tariff concessions on imports of products assembled abroad using domestic materials) and to secure preferential trading agreements
- to *protect* from competition from low-cost producers in developing countries.

This third strategy is intimately bound up with the Multi-Fibre Arrangement.

An international regulatory framework: the Multi-Fibre Arrangement

For more than 40 years, the textiles and clothing industries were subject to an industry-specific *international regulatory framework*. Initially formulated, in 1962, as the Long-Term Arrangement to cover cotton textiles, the framework was broadened in 1973 as the *Multi-Fibre Arrangement* (MFA).[11] From that time until January 2005, the MFA regulated most world trade in textiles and clothing. Its provisions and their implementation – and avoidance – were major factors in the changing global pattern of production and trade.

The MFA was initially negotiated for a limited period of four years from January 1974. Its principal aim was to create 'orderly' development of trade in textiles and clothing that would benefit *both* developed and developing countries. Access to developed country markets was to increase at an annual average rate of 6 per cent, although this was far below the 15 per cent sought by the developing countries. At the same time, the developed countries were to have safeguards to protect the 'disruption' of their domestic markets. Within the MFA, individual quotas were negotiated setting precise limits on the quantity of textiles and clothing that could be exported from one country to another. For every single product, a quota was specified beyond which no further imports were allowed.

In practice it was the disruptive, rather than the liberalizing, aspect which was at the forefront of trading relationships in these industries. The MFA was renegotiated, or extended, four times (in 1977, 1982, 1986, 1991). Progressively, the MFA became more, rather than less, restrictive. Both the EU and the US negotiated much tighter import quotas on a bilateral basis with most of the leading developing country exporters and, in several cases, also invoked anti-dumping procedures.

The effects of the MFA on world trade in textiles and clothing have been immense. Without doubt, it greatly restricted the rate of growth of exports from developing countries. A major initial beneficiary of this dampening of the relative growth of developing country exports was the US, which increased its penetration of European textiles and clothing markets during the 1970s. During the early 1980s, however, it was the European producers who greatly increased their presence in the US market.

An inevitable consequence of the increased restrictiveness of developing country exports of textiles and garments was a parallel increase in evasive action, which took a variety of forms. For example:

- A producing country which had reached its quota ceiling in one product would switch to another item.
- False labelling was used to change the apparent country of origin (an illegal act).
- Firms relocated some of their production to countries which were not signatories to the MFA or whose quota was not fully used by domestic producers.

As a result, the entire clothing industry of some developing countries was, in effect, created by MFA quotas (Nepal is a case in point).

In 1995, the regulation of trade in textiles and clothing was incorporated into the WTO, with the MFA being phased out over a 10-year period (1995–2004), but in three stages. However, the process was 'heavily back-loaded, putting most of the difficult liberalization off to the future'.[12] In fact, both the US and the EU 'integrated' first those products which already entered their markets freely – hardly a major concession. The US 10-year liberalization schedule, in effect, left the integration of 70 per cent of imports by value to the very end of the transition period. Not surprisingly, developing countries were extremely unhappy with what they regarded as a deliberate dragging of feet by the world's two largest textiles and garments markets. In response, European and US producers argued that developing countries needed to be more positive in increasing access to imports into their own domestic markets. Finally, on 1 January 2005, the MFA was abolished. But, of course, this was not the end of the story. Both the US and the EU set up monitoring procedures and negotiated new import quotas with China which lasted until the end of 2008.

Inevitably, most of the concern voiced by both developed and developing country clothing producers has focused on China, which appears to be the most likely beneficiary of MFA abolition. In a preliminary assessment in mid 2005, the ILO found that 'Bangladesh, Sri Lanka, Cambodia and Indonesia have been able to increase their market shares, while Pakistan and Thailand have been able to maintain theirs'.[13] The more recent experience of Cambodia also suggests that 'with the exception of the EU market, the increasingly competitive environment … [created by the abolition of the MFA] did not undermine expansion of the industry prior to the onset of global recession in 2008'.[14] Indeed, the fact that the final phase-out of quotas in 2008 coincided with the global recession, which severely dampened down clothing exports, has made it even more difficult to assess the long-term impact of the abolition of the MFA on the global clothing industries.[15]

Corporate strategies in the clothing industries

A highly fragmented industry – but increasing retailer dominance

The clothing industries are relatively rare instances of globally significant industries that are important in many developing countries, rather than in just a few. But although vast numbers of, mostly small, developing country firms are involved in clothing production, the industry's globalization has been driven primarily by developed country firms. Indeed, it is paradoxical that a significant proportion of the clothing imports that are the focus of such concern in developed countries are, in fact, organized by the international activities of those very countries' own firms. But the processes and strategies involved are both complex and dynamic. One fundamental point needs to be made: the globalization of the clothing industries cannot be explained simply as a relocation of production in search of low labour costs. Other factors are involved including, in particular, orientation to specific markets.

The manufacture of clothing is heavily fragmented and far less dominated by large firms than textiles. Even in this archetypal small-firm industry, however, large firms are becoming increasingly important. Only they can afford to invest in the new technologies and to build a worldwide brand image based on mass advertising.

Thus, although the clothing industry of most countries is made up of a myriad of very small firms, many of which operate as subcontractors within a multi-tiered system,[16] there is an undoubted trend towards increased concentration.

Several broad categories of clothing company can be identified:

- Producers of basic goods for large markets utilizing economies of scale to lower costs and to be price competitive.
- Operators of small workshops – often in the form of 'sweatshops' in large cities – using immigrant and sometimes undocumented labour. Such firms generally work as short-term subcontractors producing lower-quality garments.
- 'Factoryless' firms that organize entire systems of garments production. Such major international *retail chains* and *buying groups* exert enormous purchasing power and leverage over clothing manufacturers.
- Large-scale integrated firms, particularly in East Asia, producing for a number of leading retailers in the fashion sector.

The most significant structural change in the clothing industry is, without doubt, the fact that the production circuit has become increasingly dominated by the purchasing policies of the major multiple retailing chains.[17] In the US, the five largest retailers (including Wal-Mart, Sears, J. C. Penney, Dayton Hudson) account for a huge proportion of clothing sales, as do Daiei, Mitsukoshi, Daimaru and Ito Yokado in Japan. In Germany, the leading garments retailers include Karstadt, Kaufhof, Schickendanz; in the Netherlands, C&A; in France, Carrefour; in Britain, Marks & Spencer, Primark and Tesco. However, the extent and the nature of multiple retailer dominance over the clothing market vary a good deal from one country to another.

In addition to the growth in influence of the big retailers there has also been a burgeoning of specialist clothing retailers, catering to the higher end of the fashion-basic market. In the US, leading examples include The Gap, Banana Republic, The Limited, Liz Claiborne – serving niche markets. A similar process has occurred in Europe. In the UK, specialist chains, such as Next and New Look have emerged, together with local branches of some of the US firms (notably The Gap). During the 1990s, this trend intensified further with the spread of such firms as Jigsaw, DKNY, Zara, H&M and, more recently, the Japanese company Uniqlo catering to affluent young consumers.

Changing relationships between buyers and suppliers

These kinds of development have profound implications for clothing manufacturers. The highly concentrated purchasing power of the large retail chains gives them enormous leverage over clothing manufacturers. When the market was dominated largely by the mass market retailers, demand was for long production runs of standardized garments at low cost. As the market has become more differentiated, and more frequent fashion changes have become the rule, manufacturers have been forced to respond far more rapidly to retailer demands. Under such circumstances, the *time* involved in meeting orders becomes as important as the cost.

> Two to four fashion 'seasons' each year was once an industry standard for garment retailing; now the norm is six to eight, and the Spanish retailer Zara has led the move toward a model that puts out twelve seasons a year. Quick response means shorter production lead times – that is, the period from when the order is received to when the garments must be shipped off to the market … these lead times are falling significantly, in step with the shorter seasonal cycles … Fashion is fickle … buyers typically demand rapid response flexibility from suppliers … Lead firms are placing orders for smaller initial batches of garments and then following up with rapid reorders for styles that sell well.[18]

This basic shift in the structure of marketing is having repercussions throughout the clothing industries, and influencing both the adoption of new technologies and also corporate strategies (as we shall see in later sections of this chapter). Although relatively few retail chains are themselves manufacturers of garments, they are very heavily involved in subcontracting and outsourcing arrangements. The production circuit in these industries is becoming transformed into a *buyer-driven* circuit. Figure 10.8 shows how the modern 'lean' manufacturer–retailer system differs from the traditional system. In the new system, deliveries of new/replenishment items are very frequent, based on real-time sales information. Rather than large consignments of garments, much smaller quantities are delivered as needed; little, if any, back-up stock is held by the retailer. Shipments are, for the most part, direct from manufacturer to retailer. The boundary between production and retailing, therefore, is becoming increasingly blurred as the power within the production circuit shifts further towards the buyers (including the department stores, mass merchandisers, discount chains and fashion-oriented firms as well as the specialized buyers). Precisely how these organize the sourcing of their garments varies according to the position they occupy within the market.

The demise of the MFA (see above) seems likely to have a considerable impact on the number and location of suppliers being used by the large buyers.

> Industry sources claim that large retailers and manufacturers such as Gap, JC Penney, Liz Claiborne and Wal-Mart that once sourced from 50 or more countries will source from only 10–15 countries when quotas no longer constrain their sourcing decisions.[19]

The 2008 recession has accelerated this trend: the number of suppliers serving the US clothing market fell by 70 per cent in 2008 as buyers focused their purchasing more selectively.[20]

(a) Traditional retailing–apparel supplier relations

(b) 'Lean' retailing–apparel supplier relations

Figure 10.8   Changing relationships between garments manufacturers and retailers

Source: based on Abernathy et al., 1999: Figures 3.1, 4.1

Strategies of US, European and East Asian companies

US firms

The strategies developed by US clothing firms to cope with the intensified competition of the 1970s and 1980s were either to focus on the leading edge of the fashion market or to cut costs and raise productivity. The larger US firms increased their level of offshore processing using suppliers in developing countries. Several strategic mixes have been used by those clothing firms that compete in mass markets, but on the basis of brand names supported by extensive advertising. A good example is the jeans manufacturer Levi Strauss. Even by the late 1970s Levi Strauss was spending $50 million a year on worldwide advertising. But increasingly it faced the problem of how to adapt to the demographic change which was altering the size of its traditional market segment of 15- to 24-year-olds without moving too far from its core product, the denim jean.

   One strand of Levi Strauss's global strategy was to develop its own branch factories in Western and Eastern Europe, Latin America and Asia. At its peak, Levi

Strauss employed directly some 40,000 workers worldwide, of whom 28,000 were in North America, 7000 in Europe and 2000 in Asia. But in the late 1980s, the company began to make massive cuts in its operations in the US and Europe and to shift more of its operations to lower-cost locations. In 1998, the company closed 13 of its plants in the US and four in Europe, shedding 7400 jobs. The following year (1999) Levi Strauss closed half of its remaining 22 US factories and eliminated 30 per cent of its US labour force (almost 6000 jobs). At the same time, the company reduced the proportion of its production manufactured in-house to 30 per cent (in 1980, Levi Strauss had manufactured 90 per cent of its own production).[21] In 2002, a further six manufacturing plants were closed in the US, with the loss of more than 3000 jobs. Finally, in 2003, the company announced the closure of its last four remaining North American manufacturing and finishing plants, with a loss of a further 2000 jobs.[22]

Levi Strauss, therefore, has become an entirely offshore producer. It has, at the same time, entered into licensing agreements with other firms, including Li & Fung (see below), which will sell its own Levi-branded tops directly to US retailers.[23] Levi has also, very reluctantly, had to agree to supply Wal-Mart, something it had resisted for a long time, fearing it would devalue the brand. Retailer power won, once again.

European firms

The adoption of offshore production strategies by European clothing firms has been most pronounced among German and British companies. Already by the 1970s around 70 per cent of all the (then West) German clothing firms, including some quite small ones, were involved in some kind of offshore production. Roughly 45 per cent of the arrangements involved international subcontracting; a further 40 per cent involved varying degrees of equity participation by German firms in local partners.

The German fashion company Hugo Boss provides a good example. Faced with high domestic production costs, Hugo Boss has long used offshore subcontractors. In 1989, Boss acquired an American garments producer, Joseph & Feiss of Cleveland, Ohio. In 1991, Hugo Boss itself was acquired by Marzotto, the Italian textiles and clothing group. In addition to sourcing an increasing proportion of its garments overseas, the company also moved strongly into retailing, through franchising its brand name in around 200 stores worldwide. According to its (German) chairman, 'we are no longer a production-oriented company. Today, we are a company with a strong emphasis on creativity and design, marketing and logistics.'[24] Similarly, the leading British clothing companies have developed a strong focus on offshore production and subcontracting.

Until very recently, Italian firms were the major exception to this strong shift of production to low-cost foreign locations by European producers. Italy is the only major European country whose clothing industries have continued to perform relatively well in the teeth of intensive global competition. In general, Italian producers have pursued a strategy of product specialization and fashion orientation with the aim of avoiding dependence upon those types of garment most strongly affected by low-cost competition. This has involved mainly small firms in a decentralized production system, capitalizing on the traditional reputation of specific towns or regions such as Como, Prato and the like. More recently, however, some Italian firms have established international licensing or production agreements for high-fashion and designer-label products. Armani, for example, is now using some Chinese firms, although the company claims that most of its production remains in Italy. As a result, the localized Italian 'clothing districts' are undergoing major change.[25]

The best-known Italian company to have developed an especially distinctive strategy, of course, is Benetton.[26] Benetton sees itself not as a manufacturer or retailer of garments but as a 'garments services company'. But it very much sells itself as an 'Italian' company, franchising 6000 stores around the world. Whereas most European firms shifted much of their production to Asia, most of Benetton's garments ... :till manufactured in Europe, mostly in Italy – but ... ompany used around 500 subcontractors for its ... ich are located in the Veneto region of north-east ... nsiderable flexibility in responding to changing ... etton itself performed only those functions – ... and packing – considered crucial to maintain

... s the only major European clothing firm in the ... ined its manufacturing operations in a higher- ... an relocating to low-cost Asian locations. It did ... ed range of garments, but differentiating them ... r. Most of the others, including the Swedish ... le Asian route. However, a much newer cloth- ... cular progress by producing 'fast fashion': a ... on-basic garments from its domestic produc-

... pany Inditex, is located in La Coruña in north- ... the Iberian textile industry.

At Inditex's heart is a vertical integration of design, just-in-time production, delivery and sales. Some 300 designers work at the firm's head office ... Fabric is cut in-house and then sent to a cluster of several hundred local co-operatives for sewing ... Production is deliberately carried out in small batches to avoid oversupply. While there is some replenishment of stock, most lines are replaced quickly with yet more new designs rather than more of the same. This helps to create a scarcity value ... The result is that Zara's production cycles are much faster than those of its nearest rival, Sweden's Hennes &

> Mauritz (H&M). An entirely new Zara garment takes about five weeks from design to delivery; a new version of an existing model can be in the shops within two weeks. In a typical year, Zara launches some 11,000 new items, compared with the 2,000 to 4,000 from companies like H&M or America's giant casual-fashion chain, GAP.[28]

In other words, not only has Zara used a manufacturing model long ago jettisoned by the major US and European garments companies (that is, producing most of its garments in-house) but also it operates within a highly volatile part of the fashion-basic sector of the industry. Zara achieved dramatic results by combining highly efficient production and distribution logistics with a continuous monitoring of the fashion scene. In 2008, Zara's parent company Inditex overtook The Gap to become the world's largest clothing retailer.[29]

However, more recently, the geography of Zara's production network has become more diverse.

> According to Inditex, in 2006, 64% of the group's production was carried out in Europe and neighbouring countries while 34% was carried out in Asia. Products with a greater fashion component were manufactured in the group's own factories or by suppliers 'whose processes are significantly integrated with the group's dynamics' ... China seems to account for 12% of Zara's production, less than that of its rivals ... but still considerable for a firm with the reputation of being an anomaly to globalization ... Today, Zara stores are full of garments made in India, Pakistan, Bangladesh, Sri Lanka and Indonesia. And the supply chains of Zara also include Morocco, Bulgaria, Lithuania and Turkey.[30]

A similar situation exists in the case of Benetton, which aimed to produce 80 per cent of its clothing items outside Italy, mostly in Hungary, Croatia and Tunisia, by 2007. This compares with 60 per cent in 2004 and around half that five years earlier.[31]

These shifts towards greater non-domestic sourcing have also occurred in the UK firm Marks & Spencer (M&S), which built its entire reputation on developing extremely close relationships with domestic, rather than foreign, suppliers.[32]

> M&S was involved with these suppliers in every aspect of the manufacturing process from fabric selection to design and finishing ... Because the suppliers tended to be long-established, financially sound, well-equipped and technically developed firms, they were also able to provide strong design input into the M&S lines ... M&S required its suppliers to refrain from bidding for work from other retailers, thus allowing M&S exclusive access to their design and technological competencies.[33]

However, the intensification of competition through the 1990s forced M&S either to abandon some of its established UK suppliers or to put pressure on them to relocate or to outsource production overseas. Firms were given no more than a few months' notice; as a result there were major factory closures throughout the industry.

> By 2004, M&S had 15 core suppliers that accounted for 92 per cent of its business, many of which were UK companies sourcing products from overseas … during 2004–2005, M&S also turned to direct buying, opening regional buying offices in Turkey, India and Hong Kong … By 2006, the number of regional offices had increased to seven, and these buying offices handled around 30 per cent of all clothing purchases by M&S – most of the remaining 70 per cent still being provided by an even smaller number of UK-based full service vendors.[34]

East Asian firms

Japanese clothing firms were among the earliest to make extensive use of offshore subcontracting. During the 1960s and 1970s Japanese companies established outsourcing arrangements in Hong Kong, Taiwan, South Korea and Singapore. Their production was mostly exported to the US and not to Japan's own domestic market. The Japanese general trading companies (*sogo shosha*) were at the leading edge of these international outsourcing developments, often using minority investments in local firms. Probably 90 per cent of the remaining Japanese overseas garments operations are still located in East and South East Asia, most having been set up in the 1970s.

More recently, firms from other East Asian countries have established large and complex clothing production networks. For example, the Chinese trading and logistics company Li & Fung controls and coordinates all stages of the clothing supply chain, from design and production planning, through finding suppliers of materials and manufacturers of products, to the final stages of quality control, testing and the logistics of distribution (see Chapter 13). The company also 'produces' private-label brands for retailers which lack the resources to do this, especially smaller companies. By organizing and managing supply chains over the Internet for such smaller retail chains, Li & Fung can combine many small orders and so achieve economies of scale in production and distribution.[35]

A number of very large East Asian clothing firms have emerged in recent years.[36]

- The Taiwanese company Nien Hsing is the world's largest jeans manufacturer, operating factories in Taiwan, Mexico, Nicaragua and Lesotho. The company sells millions of pairs of jeans annually to the major US retailers and is the sixth largest producer of denim fabric.
- The Hong Kong company TAL Apparel manufactures shirts in East Asian and Mexican factories and sells to major US buyers. It has developed a powerful position in relation to retailers because of the integrated nature of its

operations. For example, 'by relying on TAL as its principal supplier, J. C. Penney is able to virtually eliminate inventory of its private label dress shirts. TAL runs point-of-sale data from Penney's North American stores through its proprietary software to determine the quantity of different styles, colors and sizes of shirts to make … TAL provides similar services to Brooks Brothers and Land's End. This represents a significant shift in power from retailer to contractor since it is now the contractor that manages the supply chain' (73–4).

- The Chinese company Luen Thai Holdings 'has created a "supply-chain city" in Dongguan (Guangdong province in southern China) … including a two-million square foot factory, a 300 room hotel, a dormitory for the factory's 4,000 workers, and product development centers. The factory permits apparel manufacturer Liz Claiborne and other Luen Thai customers to work in a single location, so that designers can meet with technicians from the factory and fabric mills to plan production far more efficiently … Luen Thai is developing a second supply chain city in Qing Yuan (also in Guangdong Province … [and] maintains supply chain centers in the US and the Philippines' (73).

Regionalizing production networks in the clothing industries

Much of the explanation for the recent global shifts in the clothing industries can be explained in terms of the trade-off between labour costs on the one hand and the need for market proximity on the other, set within the regulatory constraints of the MFA. The result is increasing *regionalization* of clothing production networks. Figure 10.9 shows that a significant, though varying, proportion of clothing trade is *intra-regional*. In the light of these developments, let us look briefly at the three major global regions: East Asia, North America and Europe.

East Asia

The key to the internal transformation of the industry in East Asia lies in the changing strategies of the northern tier East Asian NIEs.[37] In the face of increasing competitive pressures from the newer wave of Asian producers (notably China, Malaysia, Thailand, Indonesia and, more recently, Vietnam and Cambodia), as well as restrictions on their trade with North America and Europe through the MFA, firms from Hong Kong, South Korea and Taiwan progressively shifted their production offshore. In fact Hong Kong firms began to shift clothing production to other Asian countries as early as the mid 1960s. With the tightening grip of the MFA in the 1970s, Hong Kong firms set up plants in the Philippines, Thailand,

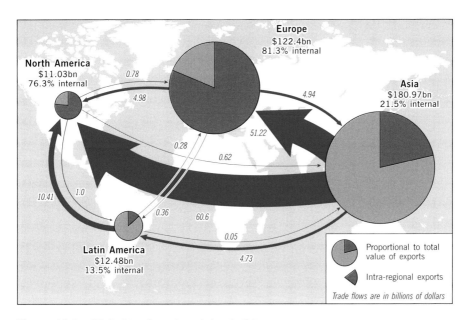

Figure 10.9 Global trade network in clothing

Source: calculated from WTO, 2009; Table A10

Malaysia and Mauritius and, subsequently, in Indonesia and Sri Lanka, to get round quota restrictions.

As the clothing industry in East Asia has matured – and especially in response to shifting market conditions – its organization has acquired a particular 'geometry': that of *triangle manufacturing*.

> The essence of triangle manufacturing … is that US (or other overseas) buyers place their orders with the NIE manufacturers they have sourced from in the past, who in turn shift some or all of the requested production to affiliated offshore factories in low-wage countries (e.g. China, Indonesia, or Guatemala). These offshore factories can be wholly owned subsidiaries of the NIE manufacturers, joint-venture partners, or simply independent overseas contractors. The triangle is completed when the finished goods are shipped directly to the overseas buyer … Triangle manufacturing thus changes the status of NIE manufacturers from established suppliers for US retailers and designers to 'middlemen' in buyer-driven commodity chains that can include as many as 50 to 60 exporting countries.
>
> Triangle manufacturing is socially embedded. Each of the East Asian NIEs has a different set of preferred countries where they set up their new factories … These production networks are explained in part by social and cultural factors (e.g. ethnic or familial ties, common language), as well as by unique features of a country's historical legacy.[38]

Geographical proximity is also an influential factor. For example, Hong Kong and Taiwanese firms are the major investors in China while Singaporean firms are strongly represented in Malaysia and Indonesia.

As Figure 10.9 shows, Asia remains the most globally connected region of clothing production. Only one-fifth of its clothing trade is intra-regional compared with much higher levels in North America and Europe. However, Asia has undoubtedly become a major market in its own right: in 1980 less than 5 per cent of the Asian garments trade was intra-regional.

North America

Traditionally, the US clothing market was served primarily by domestic production. But, in the past few decades, the market has become increasingly dominated by imports from low-cost producing countries, initially in Asia but also from Mexico and the Caribbean.[39] Most of these imports are organized through the buyer–retailer–supplier complex that has become increasingly important.

As we have seen, China has emerged as the leading supplier of garments for the US market. But China – or any other East Asian producer – is unlikely to dominate completely for two reasons:

- The trade-off between minimizing production costs and maximizing speed of access to consumer markets has become more critical. Proximity to markets has become a key factor in determining the geography of clothing production as the dominant buyers/retailers insist on fast product turnover.
- The development of regional economic initiatives by the US, in particular the signing of the NAFTA and the preferential arrangements with the Caribbean countries (the Caribbean Basin Initiative), has reinforced the benefits of geographical proximity driven by changing buyer–supplier relationships.

Initially, apart from the rapid growth in Chinese imports, the other major growth area for imports into the US was the Caribbean Basin, whose share of the total grew from less than 3 per cent in 1981 to 13 per cent in 1995. During the same period, Mexico's share of US clothing imports grew from 3 to 7 per cent. However, by 2000, Mexico had overtaken China to become the leading source of clothing imports into the US – a dramatic turnaround indeed, or so it seemed. But it was ephemeral, even though Mexico continues to be the second most important source of US clothing imports.[40]

Part of the explanation for this increased intra-regional trade lies in Mexico's emergence as a major source of US clothing imports. Under the terms of the NAFTA, tariffs and quotas on clothing imported from Mexico to the US were eliminated. In addition, under the rules of origin for garments in the NAFTA, clothing must be cut and sewn from fabric made from fibre originating in North

America in order to qualify for duty-free access. This provided a stimulus for the development of a more integrated industry within North America. Thus, 'through NAFTA, apparel and textile manufacturers are acquiring the freedom and flexibility to create – duty and quota free – transborder production networks that best suit their individual needs'.[41]

Because Mexico's comparative advantage lies in clothing production while the US comparative advantage lies in textile manufacture, synthetic fibre production and retailing, a clear division of labour has emerged. The combination of the NAFTA and the benefits of geographical proximity, together with low production costs, have stimulated many clothing firms in the US to source more of their garments from Mexico.

The precise form of this geographical division of labour is still evolving. Traditionally, Mexico's clothing industry was dominated by *maquiladora* production: simple sewing of garments made from imported fabrics and using extremely cheap labour (see Figure 2.22). In other words, it was dominated by the very basic operations in a vertically integrated system coordinated and regulated by US manufacturers and retailers. Although this is still the dominant mode of operation, there are signs of rather more sophisticated arrangements in which Mexican firms perform some of the higher-level functions in the production chain. There is some evidence of the development of *full-package production* in which selected local manufacturers are responsible for the entire process of clothing production. Figure 10.10 shows an example of this development in the Torreón district of

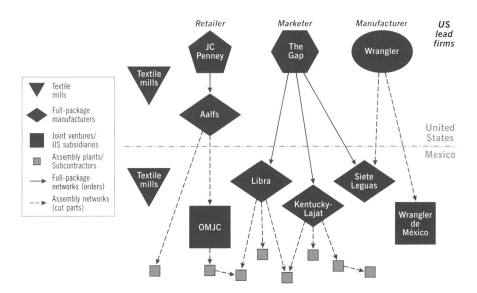

Figure 10.10   Development of 'full-package' garments production in Torreón, Mexico

Source: based on Bair and Gereffi, 2001: Figure 2

Coahuila in northern Mexico. However, even this most developed full-package cluster in Mexico has 'experienced significant declines in both production and employment in recent years'.[42]

At the same time, the geographical pattern of clothing production within Mexico itself is changing.

> There appears to be a significant shift in southern California sourcing from the western border region to central Mexico and, to a lesser extent, the northern states (excluding the border cities) and the Yucatan peninsula. The central states of Guanajuato, Puebla, Tlaxcala and the greater Mexico City area figure prominently as new production sites. Also included is the west coast state of Jalisco, located due west of Mexico City.[43]

Major reasons for the relative shift away from the border are that labour costs in the interior of Mexico tend to be lower than along the border while the quality of production tends to be higher. There is also a much lower rate of labour turnover away from the border zone.

The rapid growth of Mexico as a local source of clothing imports into the US has had significant implications for the Caribbean Basin producers, to whom the level of preferential access to the North American market under NAFTA is denied. In particular, the Caribbean countries must still pay import duty on the value added in the clothing assembly process, a contentious issue for these producers. However, with the abolition of the MFA, the huge shadow of China hangs over the North American clothing industries. China's share of US clothing imports had already once again overtaken those of Mexico by 2003, two years before the end of the MFA, and by 2005 Chinese clothing imports into the US were more than three times greater than Mexico's. Clearly, within the North American clothing market, the battle between low production costs and market proximity is still being waged.

Europe

Europe is the most highly integrated regional market in the world and its clothing industries are no exception.[44] Historically, most European clothing production was located in the leading European economies themselves, notably France, Germany, Italy and the UK. During the past three decades, however, the clothing industries of these countries have experienced massive decline and restructuring. Some of this has been caused, of course, by the rise of the low-cost Asian producers. But much of the restructuring is the result of the geographical reconfiguration of clothing production within what might be called 'greater Europe': the EU27, together with non-member countries in Eastern and Central Europe (ECE), the CIS, and the Mediterranean rim. In Europe, of course, the high level of politico-economic integration embodied in the EU is a critical influence.

Through the 1980s and 1990s, European clothing production networks became geographically more extensive, but within an expanded regional context. This is a situation created by the intersection of the changing sourcing strategies of clothing firms and the changing political agreements with ECE and Mediterranean countries, some of which became – or will become in the future – members of the EU. It is a pattern with some clear geographical consistencies but also with considerable dynamism, as some supplier countries lose their dominance and others emerge.

As in the case of Mexico and the Caribbean countries, the advantages of geographical proximity in the clothing industries of Europe (in terms of their effect on speed of delivery) can offset lower production costs at more distant locations. 'It takes 22 days by water to reach the UK from China, while products from Turkey can take as little as five days to arrive.'[45] Of course, both sets of forces operate. The continued attraction of low-cost sourcing of garments is shown most graphically by China's increased share of the EU clothing market, from 14 per cent in 1995 to 30 per cent in 2005, and rising with the abolition of the MFA, as we have seen. Thus, although a substantial proportion of the EU's sourcing of clothing still takes place in Asia, the countries on the immediate geographical periphery of the EU have become tightly integrated into the production networks of European clothing manufacturers and the purchasing networks of European retailers.

This process of regionalization of European clothing production networks became increasingly common from the early 1980s, when Outward Processing Trade (OPT) provisions were introduced by the EU. These established import quotas between the EU and individual countries in Eastern and Southern Europe. Such provisions facilitated significant patterns of production relationship between EU clothing firms (both producers and retailers) and clothing manufacturers in lower-cost countries nearby. German firms were especially heavily involved in such activities. Overall, more than 80 per cent of all (West) German garment imports manufactured under subcontracting arrangements came from the former East Germany, Poland, Hungary, Romania, Bulgaria and the former Yugoslavia.[46] Conversely, Italian producers, until very recently, continued to keep production at home. However, this has changed, though less drastically, as we saw earlier. Similar trends have occurred among the clothing manufacturers and retailers in the other EU countries, often with distinctive geographical sourcing patterns with preferred supplier countries.

The regional reconfiguration of the clothing industries in Europe, therefore, can be summarized as follows:[47]

- The phasing out of quotas in the final stages of the MFA (from 1994) favoured the Eastern and Central European (ECE) and Mediterranean countries far more than the Asian suppliers. 'Between 1991 and 1995 OPT quotas for the ECE grew at the rate of 36.2%, whereas those for Asia were growing at only 6.9%' (2202).
- A series of preferential trade agreements was signed between the EU and applicant countries in the early 1990s, which facilitated greater integration of the region's clothing industries.
- 'Among the top ten suppliers … ECE and the Mediterranean countries increased their share of EU apparel imports from 26.8% in 1989 to 30.8% in 2000, with Romania, Tunisia, Morocco and Poland being the largest suppliers from the region' (2194). By 2005, their share had risen to 37 per cent.[48]
- 'ECE producers have become … much more important sources for the EU apparel market during the 1990s. Romania, Hungary, and Poland played the leading role in the early part of the 1990s; Bulgaria and, to a lesser extent, Slovakia, have also become increasingly important … albeit from smaller bases' (2194–5).
- Turkey has emerged as the second most important individual clothing supplier to the EU after China, with 14 per cent of EU clothing imports.

The processes of organizational and geographical restructuring of the clothing industries of 'greater Europe' will continue to produce changes in the sourcing map and could well see further inroads by Asian competitors. However,

> to the extent that production costs continue to shape the geographies of export production in conjunction with other demands on buyers and producers, such as proximity to market, time-to-delivery, and garment quality, the 'golden belts' of European clothing production may continue to supply EU markets as alternatives to the relentless pursuit of lower cost production elsewhere in the global economy. Yet the extent to which such cross-border geographies can withstand competitive pressures remains an open question … there is evidence of ECE shares of core EU markets seeing a decline in some product areas. In others, however, where sourcing strategies are different, time to delivery is more critical and quality considerations may be high. The result is that cross-border arrangements have been introduced as one way of tapping lower cost but regionalized production possibilities.[49]

NOTES

1   Fröbel et al. (1980).
2   See Gereffi (1994) and subsequent writings.
3   Abernathy et al. (1999: 9).

4   See, for example, Klein (2000), Ravoli (2005).

5   Klein (2000: 430).

6   See the contributions in Hale and Wills (2005).

7   Ross (2002).

8   Detailed accounts of technology in the clothing industries are provided by Abernathy et al. (1999), OECD (2004: Chapter 4).

9   OECD (2004: 139).

10   Raworth and Kidder (2009).

11   See Hoekman and Kostecki (1995, Chapter 8), ILO (2005), Nordäs (2004), OECD (2004), Ravoli (2005).

12   Hoekman and Kostecki (1995: 209).

13   ILO (2005: 13).

14   Beresford (2009: 366).

15   See Bair (2008) for a discussion of some of the issues involved.

16   Hurley (2005: Figure 5.1).

17   The increasingly significant role of the retailers in the clothing industries is discussed by Abernathy et al. (1999; 2004), Appelbaum (2008), Gereffi (1999), Taplin (1994).

18   Raworth and Kidder (2009: 174).

19   Appelbaum (2008: 71).

20   *Financial Times* (10 December 2008).

21   *Financial Times* (23 February 1999).

22   *Financial Times* (26 September 2003).

23   *Financial Times* (20 August 2003).

24   *Financial Times* (9 January 1996).

25   Dunford (2006).

26   Jarillo (1993), Schary and Skjøtt-Larsen (2001) provide accounts of Benetton's operations.

27   Schary and Skjøtt-Larsen (2001: 103).

28   *The Economist* (18 June 2005).

29   *The Guardian* (12 August 2008).

30   Tokatli (2008: 34).

31   *Financial Times* (23 July 2004).

32   Tokatli et al. (2008).

33   Tokatli et al. (2008: 265).

34   Tokatli et al. (2008: 266, 268).

35   Schary and Skjøtt-Larsen (2001: 383–4).

36   The following examples come from Appelbaum (2008); numbers in parentheses refer to pages in that work.

37   Gereffi (1996; 1999) and Khanna (1993) provide detailed analyses of the changing industry in Asia. Dicken and Hassler (2000) analyse Indonesian clothing networks within East Asia.

38   Gereffi (1996: 97–8).

39   See Abernathy et al. (1999; 2004), Bair (2002; 2006), Bair and Gereffi (2003), Gereffi and Memedovic (2004), Gereffi et al. (2002), Kessler (1999).

40   Bair (2006: Table 2).

41   Kessler (1999: 569).

42   Bair (2006: 2240).

43   Kessler (1999: 584).

44   Bair (2006), Begg et al. (2003), Palpacuer et al. (2005), Smith et al. (2005; 2008)

45   *Financial Times* (30 August 2005).

46   Fröbel et al. (1980).

47   Begg et al. (2003); numbers in parentheses in the following list refer to pages in that work.

48   Smith et al. (2008: Table 1).

49   Smith et al. (2008: 304).

Eleven

'WHEELS OF CHANGE': THE AUTOMOBILE INDUSTRY

All change?

The 2008 global financial crisis hit the automobile industry with cataclysmic force. Other than the financial services sector itself (see Chapter 12), no other major industry attracted such high-profile attention in the turmoil. Former behemoths of the industry faced bankruptcy; extensive corporate restructuring began to occur, especially in North America. Governments injected massive financial assistance into the automobile industries within their territories to try to stem huge job losses and to ride out the crisis. All of this in what Peter Drucker once called 'the industry of industries'.[1] The internal combustion engine was, so to speak, the major engine of growth until the mid 1970s and is still seen as a key contributor to industrial development. The industry's significance lies both in its scale and in its linkages to many other manufacturing industries and services. Around 8 million people are employed directly in automobile production. If we add those involved in selling and servicing vehicles, we reach a total of up to 20 million workers. Not only this.

> Its products are responsible for almost half the world's oil consumption, and their manufacture uses up nearly half the world's output of rubber, 25% of its glass and 15% of its steel.[2]

The global automobile industry is made up of very large corporations, which have increasingly organized their activities on transnationally integrated lines. In so doing, they engage very closely – sometimes collaboratively, sometimes conflictually – with national governments, themselves anxious to establish, nurture or enhance automobile production within their territories. It is not surprising, therefore, to find that competitive bidding for investment is endemic in this industry. It is also an industry in which, after decades of dominance by firms from developed economies, new global players – from India, from China, from South Korea – have arrived on the scene. The 'industry of industries' is beginning to look very different from the apparently stable picture of a few decades ago. Change is, indeed, in the air.

The automobile production circuit

The automobile industry is essentially an *assembly* industry. It brings together an immense number and variety of components. At the centre of the automobile production circuit (Figure 11.1) is the complex set of relationships between the assemblers of vehicles and the suppliers of components, which account for between 50 and 70 per cent of the cost price of the average car.[3] As Figure 11.1 shows, there are three major processes prior to final assembly: the manufacture of bodies, of components, and of engines and transmissions, which may be performed by the assemblers as part of a vertically integrated

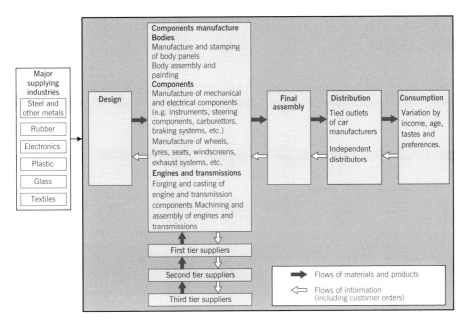

Figure 11.1   The automobile production circuit

sequence. However, there is a strong trend towards the deverticalization of automobile production as assemblers pass more responsibility to the suppliers. Figure 11.1 shows just three tiers of suppliers, although there can be more.[4] The first-tier suppliers supply major components systems direct to the assemblers and have significant research and development and design expertise. Second-tier suppliers generally produce to designs provided by the assemblers or by the first-tier suppliers, while third-tier suppliers provide the more basic components. In essence, the automobile industry is a strongly *producer-driven* industry, as opposed to the predominantly buyer-driven nature of the clothing industries.

The intensely transnational nature of automobile production renders the concept of 'national' automobile industries virtually meaningless, although governments like to believe otherwise. All are connected, to a great or lesser degree and in multifarious ways, to the larger transnational production networks which are in a continuous state of flux. The old idea that a country's automobile industry followed a generalized developmental sequence, starting with local assembly of vehicles from a full 'kit' of component parts and moving through to full-scale manufacture of automobiles, is no longer an accurate picture of reality.

Global shifts in automobile production and trade

For a good many years, the map of automobile production remained fairly stable. But that is changing. Figure 11.2 shows that current production is very strongly concentrated geographically. Not surprisingly, the three major regions – North America, Europe and Asia – contain around 90 per cent of total production. However, the level of concentration is even higher: almost two-thirds of global production is concentrated in just seven countries. Of these, Japan is, by a large margin, the world's leading automobile producer (18.8 per cent), followed by China (12.8 per cent), Germany (10.5 per cent), the US (7.2 per cent), South Korea (6.6 per cent), Brazil (4.9 per cent) and France (4.1 per cent).

Today's global production map is the outcome of some profound developments over the past four decades as new centres of production have emerged and as older centres have declined in importance (Figure 11.3). Initially, by far the most dramatic development was the spectacular growth of the Japanese automobile industry. Most recently, it has been the remarkable growth of the

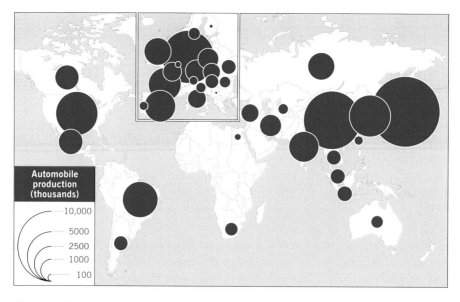

Figure 11.2   Global production of passenger cars

Source: calculated from OICA (International Organization of Motor Vehicles Manufacturers) statistics, 2009

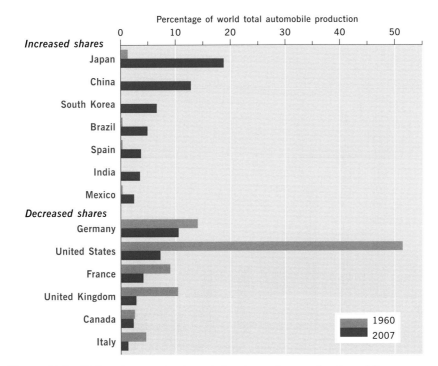

Figure 11.3   Major changes in the relative importance of automobile
producing countries

Source: calculated from MVMA *World Motor Vehicle Data*; OICA statistics, 2009

Chinese automobile industry.[5] There has also been significant growth of automobile production in Spain, Mexico, South Korea, Brazil, India, Russia and the
emerging market economies of Eastern Europe. Conversely, the former dominant producer, the US, has seen its share of world automobile production fall
dramatically.

Between 2007 and 2008, of course, there was a dramatic decline in automobile production as the credit crunch suddenly took hold. US and Canadian
car production fell by almost 20 per cent, Japan's and Italy's by a little over
20 per cent, France's by 15 per cent, South Korea's by 7 per cent and the UK's
by 6 per cent. Conversely, Brazil's output grew by 8 per cent, China's by 5 per
cent and India's by 3 per cent. Such differential growth reflects a deeper shift in
automobile production growth to a number of developing countries.

A high level of geographical concentration is also evident in the pattern of
automobile trade (Figure 11.4). But, in this case, there are also huge differences in
the balance of trade. On the one hand, the US has an automobile trade *deficit* of

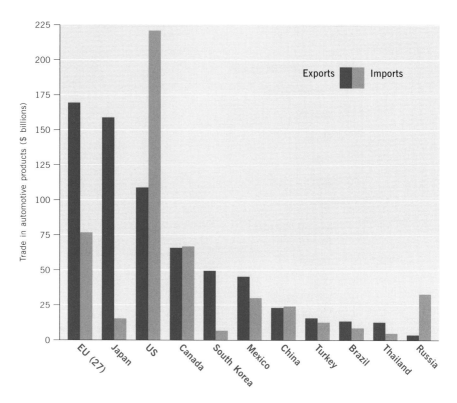

Figure 11.4 **The world's leading exporters and importers of automobiles**

Source: WTO, 2009: Tables II.60, II.61

$112 billion; on the other, Japan has an automobile trade *surplus* of almost $160 billion. In summary, an industry dominated in 1960 by the US and, to a much lesser extent, Europe was transformed initially during the 1970s and 1980s by the spectacular growth of Japan as a leading automobile producer. This was reflected in terms of growth of production in Japan itself, of Japanese exports to the rest of the world, and of the increasing proportion of Japanese automobile production located abroad. The recent emergence of China as a major producer of automobiles may soon be enhanced by its increasing importance as an exporter of cars. In 2005, for the first time, China exported more cars than it imported – its sights set on breaking into the North American market.[6] At the same time, other potentially important new centres of automobile production are emerging, notably in India and Russia. More broadly, the industry has become increasingly concentrated in the three major global regions of North America, Europe and East Asia. Much of this reconfiguration of global automobile production is related to developments at the 'macro-regional level', as we shall see in the final section of this chapter.

Changing patterns of consumption

The intoxicating allure of private transportation makes the automobile one of the most significant of all *aspirational goods*. Car ownership offers (at least in theory) immense personal freedom to travel to places otherwise inaccessible (including travel to work, to shop, to engage in all kinds of recreation). It also – and just as importantly – embodies a complex range of symbolic attributes through which people can project their self-images and their social position, and indulge in the fantasies of driving. Certain kinds of vehicle become emblematic of particular lifestyles. The obvious example in recent years was the sports utility vehicle (SUV), which was rarely used for those purposes for which it was originally designed (how many SUV drivers ever used them off-road, or even knew how to do so?). In one respect, therefore, car ownership is a *discretionary* good. However, in some countries – notably the US and the UK – the failure to continue to invest in high-quality, accessible public transportation systems means that car ownership has actually become an absolute *necessity* for people to be able to go about their daily lives.

Changes in personal income levels and in consumer tastes and preferences over time, as well as the extent to which car ownership has already spread through the population, are key variables in influencing the demand for automobiles. Such demand has always been volatile. However, it has become significantly more volatile – and more complex – in recent years. Three interrelated characteristics of the market for new automobiles are especially important:

- It is highly cyclical.
- There are long-term (secular) changes in demand.
- There are signs of increasing market segmentation and fragmentation.

For several decades, demand has been growing very slowly in the mature markets of Europe and North America. However, the effect of the 2008 crisis produced a virtual overnight collapse. In the US, sales of new cars fell from almost 15 million in 2000 to around 9 million in 2009.[7] In particular, the demand for SUVs in the US has plummeted in response. At one stage, SUVs (known as 'axles of evil' by critics of their environmental damage) accounted for three out of every four vehicles sold in the US. In the mature markets there is huge excess capacity (at least 30 per cent: equivalent to several million automobiles). The major automobile manufacturers, therefore, are pinning their hopes on continuing high levels of growth in demand elsewhere, especially in Asia, Eastern Europe and Latin America.

Of these, it is in Asia that the major growth is expected to occur. Whereas the number of vehicles per 1000 population in the US is almost 800, in India it is only 18 and in China it is around 25. The potential for growth is obvious. This can be seen already, especially in the cities of China where automobile sales have grown at such a phenomenal rate that it is now the largest automobile market in the world. In most developing countries the demand is primarily for small, cheap cars but, among the increasingly affluent segments of the population, demand for large luxury cars is growing at remarkable speed. While SUVs may have gone out of fashion in the US, in China their sales continue to grow apace. They, like such luxury marques as Mercedes or BMW, are significant aspirational goods among the newly rich.

The slow growth in demand for automobiles in the mature markets is more than merely cyclical. There are deeper *secular* or structural characteristics in these markets that limit future growth in car sales. Rapid growth in demand is associated with new demand. But as a market 'matures' and automobile ownership levels approach 'saturation', more and more car purchases become replacement purchases. In the mature automobile markets today some 85 per cent of total demand for automobiles is replacement demand. Such demand is generally slower growing, and also more variable, because it can be postponed.

> Even as consumers in China, India and other emerging economies proudly take delivery of their first vehicle, many Americans, Europeans and Japanese are coming to the conclusion either that they no longer want or need a car or that they can hold on to their existing model for longer. In America, the average age of trade-ins has soared to 75 months at the end of last year from 62 months in the final quarter of 2006 …
>
> Another factor constraining future demand for cars is – paradoxically – their improving quality. Vehicles do not rust or break down as they used to … most can be driven for many years, allowing recession-spooked drivers to delay replacing their current vehicles.[8]

The third characteristic of today's automobile market is its increasing *segmentation and fragmentation*, as affluent consumers demand different types of vehicle for different purposes or want more sophisticated specifications, as the demographic profile of consumer markets changes, and as emerging customers demand basic (low-cost) cars.

> The need to respond to an increasingly diverse set of customers generated a large proliferation of segments and models … the number of different vehicle models offered for sale in the US market alone doubled from 1980

to 1999, reaching 1,050 different models in 2000. In addition to the different models, there is also a myriad of features that can be added to each of the models.[9]

Taken together, the volatile and geographically uneven nature of demand for, and consumption of, automobiles creates huge problems for the manufacturers. In particular, the continuing problems of excess capacity facing many of the companies result in changes in both *how* vehicles are manufactured and also *where* they are manufactured.

Technological change in the automobile industry

From mass production to lean production

The basic method of manufacturing automobiles changed very little between 1913, when Henry Ford introduced the moving assembly line, and the early 1970s. It was the mass production industry *par excellence*. This certainly brought the automobile within the reach of millions of customers. To do so, however, the industry had to produce a limited range of standardized products at huge production volumes – around 2 million vehicles per year – to obtain economies of scale, together with a very high level of worker specialization. It was the antithesis of craft production (Figure 4.13): automobile workers were cogs in the continuously running assembly-line machine.

This situation changed dramatically in the early 1970s. Highly efficient and cost-competitive Japanese automobile firms, led by Toyota, totally transformed the automobile industry. What had appeared to be a stable, technologically mature industry, based on well-established technologies and organization of production, entered a phase of change (not unlike the first transformation in the early twentieth century when a mass production system displaced craft-based production). The basis of this second transformation was the displacement of mass production techniques by a system of *lean production* (see Figure 4.13).

Within the broad framework of lean production systems, two of the most significant technological developments are related to the *architecture* of the vehicle. The first is the increasing use of *shared platforms* between different vehicle models. Hitherto, each model produced by an individual manufacturer aimed at different market segments was distinctive not only on, but also below, the surface. By using a smaller number of common platforms, it is possible to share many components across what are, on the surface, very different vehicles (often in different price segments of the market). So, one of the paradoxes of the modern automobile industry is that, although the number of models has increased, such diversity is based on a much smaller number of platforms. Beauty, it seems, really may only be skin deep as far as automobiles are concerned.

Platform sharing has become the norm among most automobile manufacturers. For example, VW reduced the number of platforms used in its Audi, Seat, Skoda and VW models from 16 to four, although recently VW appeared to be moving away from this practice.[10] GM reduced its number of platforms from 25 to eight, and used the same platform for seven vehicles across four of its brands.[11] Among Japanese producers, Nissan reduced its number of platforms from 24 to five; Toyota from 20 to seven.

The second significant technological development linked to vehicle architecture is the *modularization* of certain components and the development of component *systems* (see Chapter 5). In the case of automobiles, a *module* is a group of components arranged close to each other within a vehicle which constitute a coherent unit. A component *system* is a group of components 'located throughout a vehicle that operates together to provide a specific vehicle function. Braking systems, electrical systems and steering systems are examples.'[12] A modular and system-based architecture has become the norm, although it is not as easy to implement in the automobile industry as in some other industries such as electronics.[13]

Many of the most significant developments in the technology of automobile manufacture, and of the automobiles themselves, are based upon the increasing use of *electronics*.

> The modern car has become completely dependent on electronics for engine management, satellite navigation, suspension controls and a raft of other enhancements from memory seats to rain-activated windscreen wipers. The next big step in the integration of electronics in the vehicle is the connection of all computers on a 'vehicle intranet' which will provide a simple and flexible installation with a minimum of wiring ... it is believed that electronics will continue to grow in all cars, accounting for more than 30% of a vehicle's value in the executive class to around 20% in 3-door hatchbacks.[14]

However, the very rapid introduction of complex electronic systems into vehicles poses problems for an industry whose expertise is in different areas. Not only does this make automobile manufacturers more dependent on electronics and software suppliers but also 'the electronics in the car bring six or seven times more faults than normal mechanical parts'.[15] Problems of reliability, and their impact on brand image, have become important again, as in earlier stages of technological change.

The increased complexity of vehicle production produces huge pressures on materials costs, which have escalated in price in recent years.

> Steel, the price of which has nearly doubled over the last year, is the biggest single component in cars, which typically use 700 kg to 800 kg of the metal per unit. Car makers are also struggling with the surging cost of platinum, which they use in catalytic converters – up 135 per cent since the beginning of 2005 – and plastics, which are rising in tandem with higher oil prices.[16]

As a result, automobile manufacturers are trying to find ways of reducing the amounts of materials used. For example, Toyota is planning 'to reduce the thickness of resins it uses in its cars by more than 30 per cent, and to cut its use of sheet steel by 20 per cent'.[17]

Changing the product: the search for cleaner, more efficient cars

The drive for more efficient production processes is one part of the challenge facing automobile manufacturers. The other (not unrelated) challenge is to produce different kinds of vehicle to meet the pressures of environmental regulation on emissions and to reduce the amount (and type) of fuel used in cars that consumers are prepared to buy. Three major new technologies are being developed by automobile manufacturers:[18]

- *Hybrid cars*: a combination of a conventional internal combustion engine and a battery which recharges from energy produced by the car.
- *Plug-in cars*: hybrid or pure electric cars which can be recharged using a plug.
- *Hydrogen fuel cells*: electric cars powered by hydrogen fuel cells.

Although all the major manufacturers are engaged in each of these areas, so far only hybrids have had a significant impact, led by the success of the Toyota Prius and being followed by others. The widespread use of purely electric-driven cars has been limited so far by the range of the batteries. However, a huge amount of research and investment is going into the development of lithium-ion batteries by automobile and electronics manufacturers, often in collaboration, as in the case of Honda's joint venture with Yuasa and Nissan's collaboration with NEC.

A rather different product focus is the drive to develop small, cheap-to-make and cheap-to-run cars primarily, though not exclusively, for developing country markets. Some, like the Renault Logan and the Suzuki Maruti, are produced by developed country manufacturers. Others, however, reflect the emergence of substantial local firms, especially in China and India. In China the Chery QQ3 sells at less than $5000, but it is in India that the most ambitious project has been developed: the Nano produced by the Indian firm Tata. The Nano is the world's cheapest car, advertised as the 'one-lakh car' – half the cost of the cheapest car in India, although Renault plans to produce an even cheaper car in India.[19] Of course, the production of a cheap, mass market car is far from new: think of the

Ford Model T or the VW Beetle and their many successors. But a combination of stagnating developed country markets and the attractions of tapping into the huge potential first-time-buyer market in developing countries has intensified the pressures to do so.

The role of the state

Protection and stimulation

Throughout the history of the automobile industry the state has always played a key role, notably in two respects:

- determining the *degree of access* to its domestic market, including the terms under which foreign firms are permitted to establish production plants
- establishing the kind of *support provided by the state* to its domestic firms and the extent to which the state *discriminates* against foreign firms.

Use of tariff and non-tariff barriers against automobile imports has been pervasive in virtually all countries at various times, although the level of tariffs has fallen enormously.[20] Today, few developed market economies operate particularly high tariffs against automobiles. Tariffs are substantially higher, though unevenly so, in the developing markets. Far more prevalent has been the continued use of various non-tariff barriers, including import quotas.

The specific geographical configuration of the automobile industry is influenced not just by the *level* of tariffs or quotas but also by frequently used *differential* tariffs and quotas between assembled vehicles and components. States may levy high tariffs on imported vehicles but lower tariffs on imported components in order to stimulate local production, especially where there is an insufficiently well-developed local components sector. *Local content* regulations have become particularly pervasive and have been especially influential in affecting automobile firms' policies towards their suppliers and in influencing the geographical configuration of the automobile components industries. The perceived importance of the automobile industry as a key developmental sector has meant that national governments have invariably been extremely active in offering financial and other stimuli to producers to establish or maintain production within their national territories. Indeed, the automobile industry is the paradigmatic example of the kinds of competitive bidding and TNC–state bargaining discussed in Chapter 7.

However, the sudden onset of the global financial crisis in 2008 dramatically changed the relationship between states and automobile firms. Outside the financial sector itself, the automobile industry became the highest-profile casualty of the drying up of credit and the collapse in consumer demand. The very scale and nature of the industry meant that states were virtually forced into massive intervention.

Every major automobile producing country, but especially the US and European countries, invested massive funds to try to save 'their' industries from extinction as the firms lobbied strenuously for support. The amount of money involved was astronomical – in the billions. Several governments, including the US, Germany, France and the UK, implemented a 'cash for clunkers' scheme, whereby consumers could receive a lump sum to trade in their older cars for new ones.

The auto assistance packages inevitably altered the relationship between governments and producers, at least temporarily. This was especially so in the US where, in order to receive government aid, GM and Chrysler were forced to agree to draconian restructuring measures. As one headline put it, the US auto industry was forced to opt for the 'unthinkable': supervision by the government. But because of the transnationally integrated nature of automobile production, and the fact that the major producers have operations in many countries, action (or inaction) by one government has massive implications for other governments. The most egregious example involved the attempts by GM to restructure its European operations by selling a controlling interest to another firm. Because GM's major European plants were in its Opel division, based in Germany, the German government offered a huge amount of financial assistance. This immediately raised concerns amongst other European governments that GM's German plants (and jobs) would be favoured at the expense of those in the UK, Belgium and Spain.

> Politicians and trade union leaders expressed growing fears over Germany's plan to provide billions of euros in loan guarantees for the restructuring of GM's Opel unit, warning that the planned rescue was protectionist ... The furore threatened member states' commitment to the single market ... [because of] concerns that restructuring at Opel will be driven by political rather than purely commercial considerations.[21]

As it turned out, GM ultimately decided against selling its European operations but still bargained with EU governments for state aid. At the same time, Renault was under pressure from the French government to retain production of the Clio in France instead of moving it to Turkey. Other EU governments argued that such pressure could contravene EU regulations on state aid.[22]

Environmental regulation

The state is also heavily involved through environmental and vehicle safety policies, each of which has profound implications for the design, technology and materials used in cars and, therefore, in their cost. Complying with changes in legislation can be especially problematical where it involves fundamental design changes. Legislation to control noxious emissions from automobile engines has become increasingly stringent. But such measures vary enormously from country to country. The EU has introduced legislation that will cut carbon emissions by

19 per cent by 2012 by insisting on tight controls on engine efficiency. In the US, the Obama administration announced national limits on car exhaust emissions aimed at cutting CO_2 by 30 per cent by 2016. At the same time, the US government will make billions of dollars available in cheap loans to auto manufacturers to build a new generation of fuel efficient (including electric) vehicles.

A more recent development within the EU is policy towards 'end-of-life' vehicles. Here, the EU has issued a directive under which automobile manufacturers would have to cover the cost of recycling the vehicles they have manufactured. It is estimated that the annual cost of this operation in Europe will be around 2.1 billion euros. Manufacturers will have to ensure that recyclable components account for 85 per cent of each vehicle's weight. Also in the EU, significant changes are being implemented to the permitted relationships between manufacturers and distributors in an attempt to increase competition.

Corporate strategies in the automobile industry

Concentration and consolidation

From being an industry in which virtually every major producing country had large numbers of nationally based firms, the automobile industry is now dominated by a small number of transnational producers (Table 11.1). At the same time, the seemingly permanent dominance of the US 'Big Three' has been destroyed by the rise, in particular, of Japanese and European firms.

As Figure 11.5 shows, it has been the spectacular emergence of Japanese firms – notably Toyota, Nissan and Honda – that has created the biggest changes, although an unexpected recent development has been the very rapid emergence of the Korean firm Hyundai. Table 11.1 ranks the leading automobile assemblers by the number of passenger cars produced. The most important single development is that GM has finally been displaced from its long-time number one position to number three.

The consolidation of large numbers of automobile producers into a much smaller number of large TNCs is the result of successive waves of merger and acquisition over many years, as well as the organic growth of some individual producers. During the 1990s, for example, both GM and Ford acquired firms in the luxury market segments: Saab in the case of GM; Jaguar, Land Rover and Volvo in the case of Ford. BMW acquired the British company Rover. In 1999, the French company Renault acquired 44 per cent of the equity in the Japanese firm Nissan and also bought the South Korean firm Samsung. But the biggest acquisition, by far, was of the American firm Chrysler by the German-owned Daimler-Benz in 1998. In 2000, DaimlerChrysler acquired 34 per cent of Mitsubishi

Table 11.1   The world league table of automobile manufacturers, 2008

Rank	Company	Headquarters country	No. of passenger cars produced
1	Toyota	Japan	7,768,633
2	Volkswagen	Germany	6,110,115
3	GM	US	6,015,257
4	Honda	Japan	3,878,940
5	Ford	US	3,346,561
6	Peugeot-Citroën	France	2,840,884
7	Nissan	Japan	2,788,632
8	Hyundai	South Korea	2,435,471
9	Suzuki	Japan	2,306,435
10	Renault	France	2,048,422

Source: based on OICA statistics

Figure 11.5   The rise of Japanese and Korean automobile manufacturers

Motors. In 2002, GM acquired the Korean assets of the bankrupt Korean firm Daewoo.

Similar consolidation and concentration trends have occurred in the components industries as leading companies have tried to develop positions as global suppliers. Both Delphi and Visteon were formerly in-house component divisions of GM and Ford respectively before being hived off. Both have experienced serious problems of surviving as independent companies (Delphi filed for Chapter 11 bankruptcy protection in 2005). As with the assemblers, much of the continuing consolidation among suppliers is being driven by mergers and acquisitions.

Several of these consolidations were relatively short-lived. BMW, for example, quickly divested itself of Rover. More dramatic, though not unexpected, was the break-up of the DaimlerChrysler marriage in 2007. But the 2008 crisis resulted in even bigger changes. GM contemplated selling its entire European operation,

Opel, to a Canadian–Russian consortium led by the Canadian auto parts firm Magna International, but finally pulled back. GM sold its Swedish luxury brand, Saab, and also its Hummer brand. Ford sold its Jaguar–Land Rover business to the Indian company Tata in 2008 and also sold Volvo to the Chinese firm Geely. Chrysler, having gone into Chapter 11 bankruptcy, has been merged into an alliance with the Italian firm Fiat. The significant point about these changes is that they have been dictated by the US government as an essential condition of its huge financial assistance package.

Consolidation continues in the industry, quite apart from these enforced changes. VW, for example, has acquired a 20 per cent equity stake in the Japanese firm Suzuki, primarily to expand its presence in the Asian small-car market. Peugeot-Citroën plans to buy a stake in Mitsubishi Motors.[23] However, not all growth has been through acquisition and merger. The world's most successful automobile company, Toyota, has grown entirely organically. 'Apart from scooping up Daihatsu to get small-car engineering and engines years ago, Toyota has concentrated solely on improving its own offering, with a relentless focus on efficiency, cost-cutting and a flood of new variations of successful models brought to market at an increasingly rapid rate.'[24]

In addition to these changes in ownership and control, all the world's automobile manufacturers are deeply embedded in *collaborative agreements* with other manufacturers:

> In recent years, there have been about 100 new alliances in the automobile industry per year. The majority of these are manufacturing joint ventures … indicating the high degree of globalization in this sector.[25]

In fact, the automobile industry is a veritable spider's web of short- and long-term technical and marketing alliances in a continuous state of flux. One example is the new strategic partnership between Daimler, Renault and Nissan.[26] Technology joint ventures continue to be especially important for all automobile manufacturers because of the huge cost of producing new cars and components.

Changing relationships between automobile assemblers and component manufacturers

The fundamental driving force behind consolidation amongst automobile component manufacturers is the increasing pressure being exerted by assemblers to deliver quickly (just-in-time), to deliver at lower cost on a continuous basis, and to raise the quality of components. Such pressures are manifested in two important ways. One is the pressure on suppliers to take on more of the design, research and risk of developing component modules and systems. The second is the pressure on suppliers to locate geographically close to assembly plants.[27]

Taken together, such pressures have resulted in a massive decline in the number of supplier companies. In 1990 there were some 30,000 suppliers in North America, and 10,000 by the year 2000, and there is a predicted further decline to between 3000 and 4000 by the year 2010. Ford's '2000' strategy envisaged reducing its total number of component suppliers in North America by more than 50 per cent over 10 years – from more than 2000 to less than 1000. Of that 1000, a mere 180 companies would be awarded around two-thirds of the orders. Amongst European firms, Peugeot-Citroën has reduced its suppliers from 900 to less than 500, BMW from 1400 to 600. In turn, the major component suppliers themselves are reducing the number of their suppliers. Visteon, for example, announced that 'it would, in future, do business with only two or three companies in "each segment" of business for the next five years'.[28]

The effects of the 2008 crisis have undoubtedly accelerated this reduction in suppliers. One headline termed this 'the "living dead" among supply chains'.[29] Meanwhile, the incessant pressure on suppliers to reduce their prices to the assemblers continues unabated and seems to be increasing.

> Toyota Motors … expects to pay 30 per cent less for many components by the time it rolls out new models for 2013 … the price cuts demanded of suppliers were the largest in the company's recent history.[30]

But there are risks, as the disastrous experience of Toyota demonstrated when it had to recall several million cars in early 2010 because of faulty components involving a number of its models.

As part of the process of supplier consolidation, the precise roles played by suppliers are changing. The supply system is becoming more *functionally segmented*. In place of the myriad of specialist raw materials and component suppliers, four major strategies seem to be evolving, as Figure 11.6 shows. The raw material and component specialist strategies are, of course, not new. What is new is the emergence of other categories of supplier, notably the standardizers and the integrators, both of which have significantly greater design and manufacturing responsibilities and have a different kind of relationship both with assemblers and also with their own suppliers. This latter characteristic is especially significant in the case of the integrators.

As a consequence the overall supply chain of the automobile industry is being transformed. Figure 11.7 shows one possible trajectory. The relatively simple tiered hierarchy that has developed in recent years is metamorphosing into a structure in which the connection between tier 1 suppliers and the assemblers is being mediated by a new layer of module and system integrators – what some analysts term a 'tier 0.5' to signify its closer relationship with the assemblers. These suppliers are also more powerful because 'carmakers can no longer design certain modules by themselves … There has been a spectacular rise in suppliers' production and research capacities.'[31] At the same time, the major suppliers have been drastically redrawing their own production map.

	Raw material supplier	Component specialist	Standardizer	Integrator
Focus	A company that supplies raw materials to the OEM or their suppliers	A company that designs and manufactures a component tailored to a platform or vehicle	A company that sets the standard on a global basis for a specific component or system	A company that designs and assembles a whole module or system for a car
Market presence	• Local • Regional • Global	• Global for tier 1 • Regional or local for tiers 2 and 3	• Global	• Global
Critical capabilities	• Material science • Process engineering	• Research, design and process engineering • Manufacturing capabilities in varied technologies • Brand image	• Research, design and engineering • Assembly and supply chain management capabilities	• Product design and engineering • Assembly and supply chain management capabilities
Types of components or systems	• Steel blanks • Aluminium ingots • Polymer pellets	• Stampings • Injection moulding • Engine components	• Tyres • ABS • ECU	• Interiors • Doors • Chassis

Figure 11.6   Supplier strategies in the automobile industry

Source: based on Veloso and Kumar, 2002: Table 1

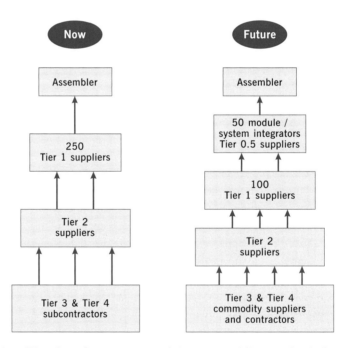

Figure 11.7   The changing structure of the automobile supply chain

Source: based on ABN-AMRO, 2000: 10

> Taking one example, between 2001 and 2006, the French supplier Valeo closed 59 sites, opened 29 new sites, sold 26 locations and acquired 13 units.[32]

In effect, organizationally 'distant' relationships have been replaced by much 'closer' relationships. Much greater degrees of organizational interdependence between automobile manufacturers and components suppliers have developed. Relationships with key suppliers have become longer term. At the same time, the need for suppliers – especially 'first-tier' suppliers of complex modules and systems – to locate geographically close to their customers has intensified. The intensified drive to shorten the time involved in vehicle production means that 'just-in-time' supply has become the norm in the automobile industry. Even so, enormous diversity persists in the geography of supplier–assembler relationships: a mixture of long- and short-distance arrangements, reflecting the path dependency of present patterns on those that evolved in earlier periods. This is especially the case for second- and third-tier component suppliers. Geographical change tends to be incremental rather than radical.

However, in the case of first-tier suppliers, especially modular suppliers, there is no doubt that profound changes are occurring in the geography of their relationships with their customers. The most developed situation involves their co-location in so-called *industrial condominiums*:

> a small group of the automaker's direct suppliers … are physically installed within the walls of the automaker's plant and participate in a share of the plant's infrastructure costs. These suppliers generally supply the automaker with systems (usually more complex systems with difficult logistics or that facilitate postponing diversification of the product and increase its customization potential) on a just-in-time … basis right next to the assembly line, but do not participate in the vehicle's final assembly line. The final assembly is done by the automaker.[33]

Whether or not these 'assembly lines of the future' become accepted practice remains to be seen. Certainly it is much harder to introduce such revolutionary practices in the old-established manufacturing heartlands of the automobile industry. It is significant that most of the existing cases are located well away from traditional automobile manufacturing areas (Brazil has been a favoured location). A diluted version of the industrial condominium, more common in Europe, is the *supplier park*: 'complexes that bring suppliers together in close proximity to one another, contiguous to the assembly site – a contiguity that is sometimes materialized through the overhead tunnels that connect the various plants'.[34]

Clearly, profound changes are occurring in the nature of the assembler–supplier relationship, driven primarily by the time, price and technology/design pressures exerted by the assemblers on suppliers. Suppliers have been driven to consolidate and to take on enhanced roles. That, in turn, changes the balance of power between assemblers and the mega-suppliers upon which the assemblers now depend for a much larger part of their business. So, although in general the assemblers have more bargaining power than the suppliers, there are clear exceptions to this: those mega-suppliers which have developed particularly valuable capabilities and which are able to provide a global supply service to their geographically dispersed customers.

Table 11.2   Transnational profiles of leading automobile producers (foreign as % of total)

Company	TNI[a]	Employment	Assets	Sales
US				
Ford	51.4	54.8	46.2	53.1
GM	48.5	59.8	41.3	44.5
Japanese				
Honda	82.3	88.8	75.2	82.9
Nissan	62.1	51.0	58.9	76.3
Toyota	51.9	38.5	53.9	63.2
European				
Fiat	64.5	59.1	61.4	72.9
Volkswagen	56.9	46.7	48.8	75.3
Renault	53.1	51.5	40.0	67.8
South Korean				
Hyundai	27.9	9.3	29.0	45.3

[a]TNI is the average of three ratios: foreign assets to total assets; foreign sales to total sales; foreign employment to total employment.

Source: calculated from UNCTAD 2009: Table A.1.9

Contrasting transnationalization strategies of the major automobile producers

In view of the kinds of technological and competitive pressures facing all automobile producers, it is not surprising to find that their strategies have some similarities. However, they are far from being identical. The big producers remain creatures of their specific histories: as noted in Chapter 5, firms develop a 'strategic predisposition', built up over time, which leads them to favour some kinds of approaches rather than others. For example, some firms have preferred to grow organically, some have grown mainly by merger and acquisition, whilst others have grown through a varying mixture of the two. They also remain creatures of their particular geographies. Where they come from, where they are still headquartered, matter a lot in terms of the precise ways in which they pursue their objectives (see Chapter 5). In this section, therefore, we look very briefly at the contrasting ways in which the major automobile producers have transnationalized and, especially, at current developments in their strategies. In the final section, we will focus on the *regionalized* patterns of automobile production. Table 11.2 summarizes the transnational profiles of the leading US, Japanese and European producers.

The US big two

GM and Ford dominated the world automobile industry for decades. This was mainly, of course, due to the massive size of the North American market for cars. In addition, however, they were the first automobile firms to transnationalize their production, initially (and logically) in Canada and then in Europe. Ford built its first European manufacturing plant in Manchester in 1911 (subsequently replaced in 1931 by the massive integrated plant at Dagenham, near London), and spread into France and Germany. GM expanded transnationally through acquiring existing companies in both Canada and Europe (Opel in Germany, Vauxhall in the UK).

These early transnational ventures were triggered by the existence of protective barriers around major national markets as well as by the high cost of transporting assembled automobiles from the US. Subsequently, both Ford's and GM's transnational strategies were concerned, initially, with expanding and integrating, and then with rationalizing their operations on a global scale. Figure 11.8 shows the broadly similar geography of Ford's and GM's transnational activities, although they reached their current positions by rather different routes. The biggest single difference between GM's and Ford's global operations is GM's massive involvement in China, where Ford is weak. But, as Table 11.2 shows, overall Ford is more transnationalized than GM. Indeed, GM is the least transnationalized of all the leading producers. In both cases, however, the relative importance of overseas operations has increased as Ford and GM have been forced to close large numbers of plants in the US.

Japanese producers

Whereas both Ford and GM have had international operations for many decades, the spectacular rise of the leading Japanese companies up the world league table (Figure 11.5) was achieved almost entirely without any actual overseas production, apart from small-scale, local assembly operations, using imported kits. Beyond such operations, Toyota had no overseas production facilities for cars before the early 1980s, while less than 3 per cent of Nissan's total production was located outside Japan. The biggest Japanese producer, Toyota, was in fact the slowest to transnationalize. Toyota did not build its first European plant until 1992, six years after Nissan. Paradoxically, it was one of the smaller Japanese automobile manufacturers, Honda, which was the first to build production facilities outside Asia (in Ohio in 1982).

However, the transnationality of the Japanese producers changed dramatically during the 1980s, mainly as a result of a combination of political pressures in the US and Europe and the increased need to be inside major markets. By 1989, 28 per cent of Honda's output was produced outside Japan; today the proportion is 68 per cent. Toyota vastly increased its overseas production share (from 8 to 45 per cent); Nissan now produces 61 per cent of its cars outside Japan compared with 14 per cent in 1989. As Table 11.2 shows, the three leading Japanese producers are now far more transnationalized than either Ford or GM. Figure 11.9 shows the current geographical pattern of Toyota's, Nissan's and Honda's production. The US is the most important single overseas focus for all three Japanese companies.

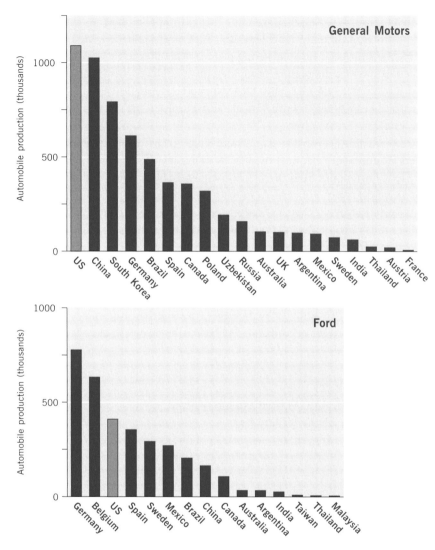

Figure 11.8   The transnational production geography of US producers: GM and Ford, 2008

Source: calculated from OICA statistics

European producers

The major European automobile producers are strongly Eurocentric in their production geographies (Figure 11.10). Indeed, while the Japanese were busy building large manufacturing plants in the US during the 1980s, both VW and Renault pulled out of their earlier involvement there. However, of all the European producers, VW has pursued by far the most extensive and systematic transnational strategy, although two-thirds of its car production is located in Europe, initially in Germany and Spain but with an increasing emphasis on Eastern Europe

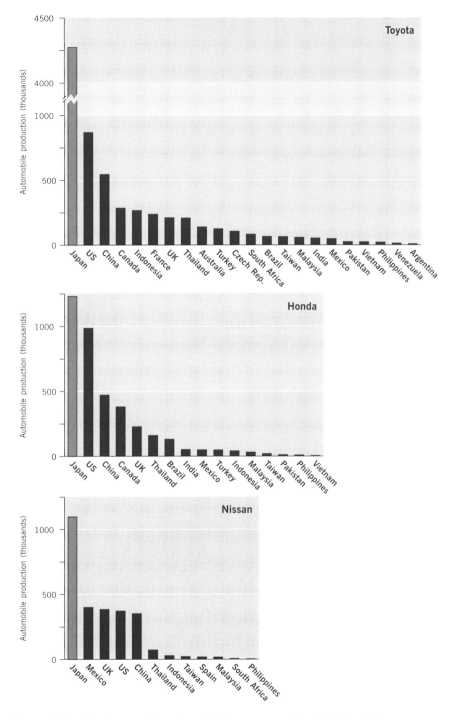

Figure 11.9   The transnational production geography of Japanese
producers: Toyota, Honda and Nissan, 2008

Source: calculated from OICA statistics

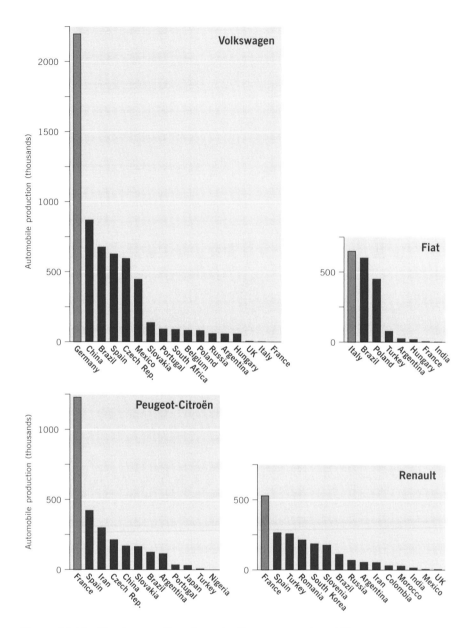

Figure 11.10 The transnational production geography of European producers: VW, Peugeot-Citroën, Renault and Fiat, 2008

Source: calculated from OICA statistics

(especially the Czech Republic and Slovakia). Outside Europe, VW is a major producer in Brazil, Mexico and, especially, China.

While VW was expanding its European production base to incorporate Spain in the 1980s, the Italian automobile firm Fiat initially moved in the opposite direction and reconcentrated production in its home market. But that has changed radically in recent years. Only around one-third of Fiat's production is now in Italy, although two-thirds is in Europe. Brazil is Fiat's major focus outside Europe. In 2008, Fiat made a failed attempt to buy GM's European operations which, together with its acquisition of Chrysler, would have made it a truly major global player.

The two French automobile companies, Renault and Peugeot-Citroën, were both traditionally strongly home country oriented in their production. Renault has been, for more than 40 years, the French government's national champion, supported by massive state aid, which served to constrain its activities. State control has been reduced to 15 per cent and Renault has been involved in major restructuring, including its major coup in acquiring a large equity stake in Nissan. This has become the central pillar of Renault's international strategy. For Renault itself, Europe remains the dominant production location with 75 per cent of its total world production, although it now has a presence in South Korea through its acquisition of Samsung. Peugeot-Citroën was formed by a state-induced merger in 1975. It has recently become far more transnational in its operations. Although 73 per cent of its production is in Europe, it has a growing presence in China.

Korean, Indian and Chinese producers

The US, Japanese and European automobile companies exert such market dominance that there have been virtually no new entrants in the industry during the past 30 years. The major exception is in South Korea and, more recently, India and China. In the case of Korea,

> automobiles were identified as one of the priority industries in the Heavy and Chemical Industry Plan of 1973. In 1974 an industry-specific plan for automobiles was published covering the next ten years. The objectives were to achieve a 90 per cent domestic content for small passenger cars by the end of the 1970s and to turn the industry into a major exporter by the early 1980s.[35]

Although the Korean government effectively made Hyundai the leading producer in the industry, giving it an enormous relative advantage, by 1997 there were still five Korean automobile producers. Today, there is just one – Hyundai – the others being victims, directly or indirectly, of the East Asian financial crisis of 1997.

Hyundai depended for its early development on close technological and marketing relationships with US and Japanese firms. Its strategy was to compete with the Japanese in a very narrow product range and entirely on price. Its initial export success was remarkable. In 1986, 300,000 cars were exported to North America, a level more or less maintained for the following two years. On the strength of this success, Hyundai built a second new plant in Korea. More ambitiously still it built a plant in Canada, with the capacity to produce 120,000 cars and to employ 1200 workers directly, but this plant was closed in 1991 because of quality problems.

As a result of the 1997 crisis, Hyundai was forced to undertake major restructuring and refocusing of its operations. First, it acquired Kia, one of the smaller Korean automobile firms. Second, in 2000, it separated from its parent company, the Hyundai *chaebol*. Third, it began to move away from being merely a low-price regional producer of cars primarily for the Asian market to one with much wider ambitions. Hyundai sees itself as a major global producer of high-quality vehicles (operating a two-brand strategy, with Kia providing the lower-cost cars). It is shedding its cheap-car image and focusing, like Toyota, on superior quality control. It has rapidly expanded geographically to operate plants in China, India, Turkey, the US (a new plant in Alabama opened in 2005) and the Czech Republic. As a result, over 40 per cent of its production is now located outside Korea. It is a remarkable record of rapid growth to become the world's eighth largest automobile producer (see Table 11.1).

The Indian company Tata is in a very different league. But it has huge ambitions to become a global automobile producer. As a result of its acquisition of Jaguar–Land Rover in 2008, Tata now produces more cars outside India than domestically. Its introduction of the Nano small car will undoubtedly help to expand its international operations.

So far, Chinese firms have made little impact outside China. But this will change. The most likely candidate is the Shanghai Automotive Industrial Corporation (SAIC), which acquired the Ssangyong plants in South Korea, the Nanjing Automobile Corporation which had itself acquired the British MG brand, and the Beijing Automotive Industrial Corporation (BAIC) which has bought some of Saab's assets from GM.

Regionalizing production networks in the automobile industry

Although, in one sense, the automobile industry is one of the most globalized of industries, it is also an industry in which the *regionalization* of production and distribution is especially marked.[36] Geographically, rather than attempting to organize (and reorganize) operations on a truly global scale, the tendency of most of the leading automobile producers is towards the creation of distinctive production and marketing networks within each of the three major world regions. Figure 11.11 shows that this is especially the case in both North America and Europe, where more than three-quarters of automobile trade is intra-regional.

Europe

Europe has the most complex automobile production networks in the world, a reflection of the legacy of formerly nationally oriented automobile industries, the

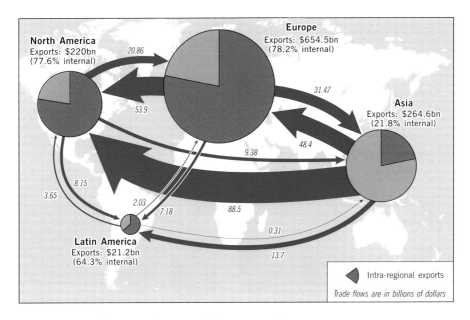

North America
Exports: $220bn
(77.6% internal)

20.86

Europe
Exports: $654.5bn
(78.2% internal)

31.47

Asia
Exports: $264.6bn
(21.8% internal)

53.9

9.38

48.4

8.15

3.65

2.03

7.18

88.5

0.31

Latin America
Exports: $21.2bn
(64.3% internal)

13.7

Intra-regional exports

Trade flows are in billions of dollars

Figure 11.11 Global trade network in automobiles

Source: calculated from WTO, 2009: Table A10

particular ways in which the political environment has evolved in the past four decades, and the responses of automobile firms to these changes in the context of increasingly intensive global competition. Two political-economic transformations during the 1990s dramatically reshaped the region's automobile industry: the completion of the Single Market in 1992 and the opening up – and subsequent political integration – of Eastern Europe (see Chapter 6).

The actual geographical configuration of automobile production within Europe bears the very strong imprint of each firm's national origins and the history of their development within this evolving political framework (Figure 11.12). For example, Ford and GM have been in Europe for almost 100 years, building up multilocational, initially nationally oriented, production networks. Both have rationalized their European operations in recent years, a process accelerated by the 2008 crisis. GM, in particular, aims to cut its European production capacity by one-fifth, which will involve the closure of its plant in Antwerp, Belgium and a loss of more than 8000 jobs within Europe.[37] In contrast, the position of the Japanese producers is very different. With no history of European car production and no inherited structure, the Japanese were able to treat Europe as a 'clean sheet'. Beginning in the early 1980s, Japanese firms established production facilities in Europe. All three leading Japanese firms – Toyota, Nissan, Honda – initially built their plants in the UK. This led to political friction within the EU during the 1980s and 1990s. Significantly, Toyota's second European plant was built in northern France.

Figure 11.12   Automobile production in Europe

Source: calculated from OICA statistics

   The geographical configuration of the indigenous European automobile producers is, of course, much more embedded in their national contexts. Only VW has anything approaching a pan-European production network, focused around the three nodes of Germany, Spain, and its acquired Eastern European plants in the Czech Republic and in Slovakia. Prior to the opening up of Eastern Europe, VW had developed a clear strategy of geographical segmentation. High-value, technologically advanced cars were produced in the former West Germany; low-cost, small cars were produced in Spain. After 1990, VW moved very rapidly to establish production of small cars in Eastern Germany and to take a controlling stake in the Czech firm Skoda. VW now has operations in the Czech Republic, Hungary, Poland and Slovakia.

Indeed, it is Eastern Europe that is now the primary focus of change in European automobile production networks.[38] In addition to joining with (or taking over) existing local automobile firms, automobile producers are building new plants in Eastern Europe. For example, GM established operations in Poland and Russia; Toyota has established a joint venture with Peugeot-Citroën to develop and assemble small cars for the European market at Kolin in the Czech Republic. Peugeot-Citroën itself has established operations plants in Slovakia and the Czech Republic and closed its UK plant; the Hyundai affiliate Kia has established an assembly plant in Slovakia, while Hyundai itself has built a large assembly plant in the Czech Republic; and Renault operates plants in Romania and Slovenia.

At the same time, substantial components production is also shifting towards the East. On the one hand, there are the affiliates of foreign companies set up primarily to follow the assemblers. While some of these investments may be genuinely 'new' (in the sense that they did not formerly exist elsewhere), or are acquisitions of local companies by foreign firms, others are, in effect, locational transfers from elsewhere in Europe. On the other hand, there are the indigenous suppliers, many of them the successors of formerly state-owned enterprises prior to the onset of privatization. In many cases, these have been restricted to the production of low-value components and are rather peripherally connected into transnational production networks. However,

> the specialization of many CEE countries is no longer limited to simple standard and labour intensive products and assembly of small vehicles. A significant value creation takes place due to manufacturing of more complex, high-value-added products and growing local sourcing.[39]

Inevitably, the question arises of the extent to which the shift in focus towards the East has adverse effects on automobile plants (and jobs) in the core European countries and the Iberian region. There is little doubt that it has, as the German case shows:

> What has taken place is not a broad relocation from Germany to low-wage countries but a dramatic shift in the regions of origin for component imports to Germany. The share of CEE in German automotive component imports rose from 9 per cent to 37 per cent between 1995 and 2005. Rather than displacing manufacturing in Germany, component imports from CEE countries seem to have supplanted imports from Western Europe and the Iberian peninsula. In the case of Spain and Portugal, the share of German imports was not only halved: their absolute value was reduced.[40]

North America

Although political-economic integration in North America is much shallower than in the EU, in the case of the automobile industry political agreements have had profound repercussions on its geographical structure. By the early 1970s, the US–Canadian automobile industry was fully integrated as a result of the 1965 Automobile Pact. The 1988 Canada–US Free Trade Agreement (CUSFTA)

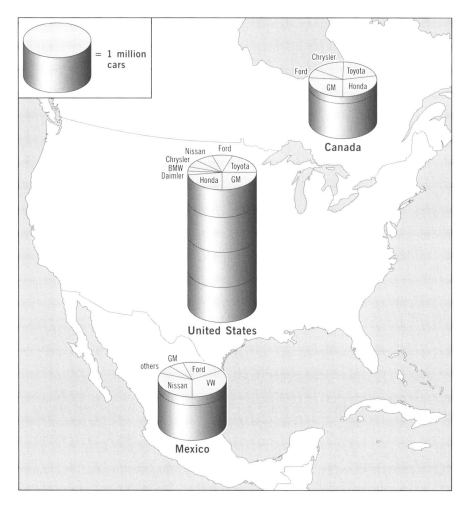

Figure 11.13   Automobile production in North America

Source: calculated from OICA statistics

redefined the level of 'North American content' necessary for a firm to be able to claim duty-free movement within the North American market. The 1994 North American Free Trade Agreement (NAFTA) had even more far-reaching implications for the automobile industry because it incorporated the Mexican auto industry with its vastly lower production costs.

Figure 11.13 shows the broad geographical structure of the North American production system. Prior to the 1980s, it was totally dominated by US producers; attempts by Volkswagen and Renault to produce cars successfully in the US had failed. But from the mid 1980s onwards the position changed dramatically. Three major waves of foreign involvement have occurred.

First, each of the major Japanese firms established large-scale production facilities in the US and Canada during the 1980s. The pioneer was Honda, which established a manufacturing plant at Marysville in Ohio in 1982. This was followed, in 1983, by the Nissan plant at Smyrna, Tennessee. In contrast, Toyota entered North America very cautiously in 1984, through a joint venture (NUMMI) based at GM's Fremont, California, plant. Since then, each of the major Japanese firms has continued to increase its capacity and to make major investments in engine, transmission and components plants. Today, there are 16 Japanese automobile assembly plants, employing around 60,000 workers, in the US and Canada.[41] As the Japanese plants progressively increased their North American content they were followed by a wave of Japanese component manufacturers. In other words, during a period of less than a decade an entirely new Japanese-controlled automobile industry was created in North America in fierce, direct competition with domestic manufacturers. This 'new' automobile industry had a very different geography from that of the traditional one, simply because the Japanese had no existing plants or allegiance to specific areas. With few exceptions, the old-established automobile industry centres were not favoured.

The second, very much smaller, wave of foreign investment in the North American automobile industry began in the mid 1990s in the form of German luxury car manufacturers, Daimler-Benz and BMW. Daimler-Benz built a new plant at Tuscaloosa, Alabama in 1993; BMW built a plant at Spartanburg, South Carolina in 1994. Subsequently, of course, Daimler-Benz created a major shake-up of the North American automobile industry when it acquired Chrysler in the late 1990s (sold to Fiat in 2007). These incursions by the two upmarket German producers were the first major European involvement in North America after the failed ventures of Volkswagen and Renault in the 1970s. In 2005, the Korean firm Hyundai opened a major plant in Montgomery, Alabama, and its subsidiary Kia has built a new plant in Georgia.

The third development has been the large-scale investment by foreign automobile producers in Mexico.[42] Prior to the Mexican economic reforms of the 1980s and later the NAFTA in 1994, most of the automobile investment in Mexico was domestic market oriented. Subsequently, these investments were replaced by 'strategic asset-seeking and cost-reducing FDI'.[43] Most of these newer investments in vehicle assembly and major component plants have rather different locational characteristics from the earlier import-substituting investments. The latter, being oriented to the Mexican domestic market, tended to be concentrated in the central region around Mexico City. The newer investments, oriented to the North American market as a whole, are located nearer the border with the US. The major exception is VW's large integrated facility in Puebla. At the same time, rationalization of some of the former core-region plants has occurred.

By the early 2000s, then, a very different regional production network had evolved in North America compared with that existing before the 1980s, which had been dominated by the US manufacturers.[44] The arrival of Japanese firms in the 1980s created a new geography of production away from the old-established automobile concentration in the US Midwest. The NAFTA, together with earlier reforms within Mexico, transformed that system by incorporating into the North American regional production network a production location with very low costs (and a potentially fast-growing domestic market). The long-term decline of the US Big Three producers became almost a collapse with the 2008 crisis and this will have a massive effect on the geography of North American automobile production. It is the traditional heartland of the US automobile industry – Michigan – which will be hardest hit, but the effects will be widespread, involving Canada in particular.

East Asia

The development of distinctive regional automobile production networks in both Europe and North America reflects the combination of two forces: the size and affluence of the market and the political-economic integration of the market through the EU and the NAFTA respectively. In these circumstances, the development of a high level of intra-regional integration of supply, production and distribution becomes possible. The situation in East Asia is very different: the region remains primarily a series of individual national markets, some of them very heavily protected against automobile imports. On the other hand, the undoubted potential of the East Asian market, set against the saturation of most Western markets, makes it an absolutely necessary focus for the leading automobile manufacturers. It is against this background that the current automobile production network in East Asia needs to be set.

As Figure 11.14 shows, automobile production in East Asia is dominated by Japan and, to a lesser extent, Korea and China. Not surprisingly, therefore, the region's automobile production is dominated by Japanese firms.[45] Through a network of assembly plants and joint ventures with domestic firms, Japanese cars are assembled in Thailand, Malaysia, the Philippines, Indonesia, Taiwan and China. In several of these countries, Japanese manufacturers totally command the automobile market. Most of these are assembled locally in individual countries to serve the local market. This is less out of choice on the part of the Japanese manufacturers than out of the necessity created by high levels of import protection in virtually all the East Asian countries, particularly those in South East Asia (notably Malaysia). Faced with increasingly difficult circumstances in the Japanese market itself, Japanese firms have placed greater emphasis on raising their penetration of the Asian market by developing cars specifically tailored to that market and not just versions of existing models.

In comparison, Korean firms have preferred to serve East Asian markets from their domestic bases, although Hyundai has operations in Indonesia. Western

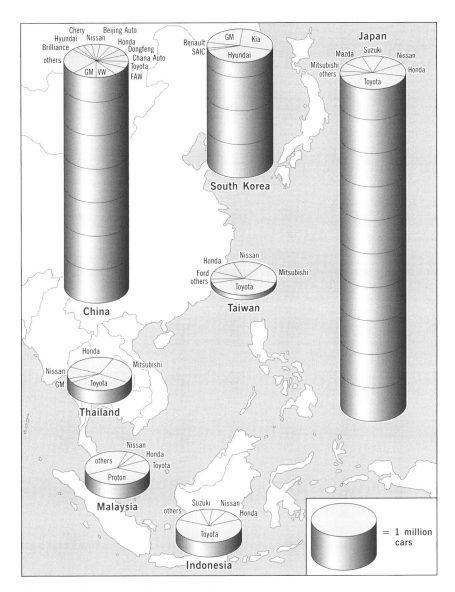

Figure 11.14 Automobile production in Asia

Source: calculated from OICA statistics

automobile companies have only recently taken a really serious interest in East Asia. Of course, several US and European firms have had small complete knock-down (CKD) plants in different parts of the region for many years, while GM and Ford have had significant equity involvement in Japanese firms. Today, virtually all the major Western automobile companies are in the process of establishing operations in the region, particularly in Thailand and in China.

The continued restrictive nature of trade policy within ASEAN makes the development of a genuinely regionally integrated automobile industry difficult to achieve, although significant regulatory changes have been introduced to facilitate cross-border flows of vehicles and components.[46] Within South East Asia, Thailand has become the preferred production focus for many major automobile assemblers and component manufacturers, a deliberate outcome of state policy. Thailand has set out to be the 'car capital' – the Detroit – of South East Asia, and with some considerable success. Virtually all the major foreign producers have a presence there. Not only does it have a major concentration of Japanese automobile and components production but also it is the favoured point of entry of Western car manufacturers, notably GM and Ford through Japanese partners. BMW established an assembly plant for its 3 Series model in Thailand. However, Thailand was hit hard by the 2008 crisis as exports (and therefore production) fell sharply. More than half of Thai automobile production is exported, so it is very vulnerable to the global slowdown.

Whereas Western automobile firms see Thailand as potentially a base for serving the whole of South East Asia, their reasons for wishing to establish operations in China are rather different: access to potentially the world's biggest market. Because all the major automobile manufacturers are extremely anxious to establish themselves in China, the Chinese government has been able to retain the bargaining power to impose specific entry restrictions (see Chapter 7).[47]

The Chinese automobile industry consists of a large number of state corporation groups together with a number of joint ventures between members of these groups and foreign firms.[48] VW was one of the earliest Western automobile firms to establish a joint venture in China, first with the Shanghai Automotive Industry Corporation (SAIC) in 1985, and then with First Auto Works (FAW). For more than 10 years VW was virtually unchallenged in the Chinese market and it still has the biggest market share, although its position has been heavily eroded by new entrants. US firms have found entry to China rather more difficult. GM also established a joint venture with SAIC in Shanghai. Ford took considerably longer and only agreed a joint venture with the CAIC Group in 2001. Japanese firms continue to strengthen their presence in China: Toyota has established a new joint venture with Guangzhou Automotive. Hyundai is also expanding in China through its Kia affiliate, which already had Chinese operations before it was acquired by Hyundai.

The prospect of gaining access to what is seen as the world's largest and fastest-growing consumer market has led to a scramble by automobile producers to enter China. But the Chinese government has exerted virtually complete control over such entry and has adopted a policy of limited access for foreign firms, including the form that their involvement can take. Here, therefore, we have the obverse of the usual situation. Whereas, in many cases, TNCs are able to play off one country against another to achieve the best deal, in the Chinese case it is the state whose unique bargaining position has enabled it to play off one TNC against another.[49]

NOTES

1   Drucker (1946: 149).
2   *The Economist* (4 September 2004).
3   ABN-AMRO (2000: 11); Freyssenet and Lung (2000: 83).
4   UNIDO (2003: 22).
5   Liu and Yeung (2008).
6   *Financial Times* (6 December 2005).
7   *Financial Times* (3 February 2009).
8   *Financial Times* (3 February 2009).
9   Veloso and Kumar (2002: 3).
10 *Financial Times* (15 April 2003).
11 Veloso and Kumar (2002: 6).
12 Delphi Automotive Systems, quoted in EIU (2000: 1).
13 Berger (2005: 86).
14 EIU (2000: 7).
15 *Financial Times* (16 June 2004).
16 *Financial Times* (9 May 2008).
17 *Financial Times* (9 May 2008).
18 *Financial Times* (7 August 2008).
19 *Financial Times* (11 November 2009).
20 Humphrey and Oeter (2000: 42).
21 *Financial Times* (17 September 2009).
22 *Financial Times* (18 January 2010).
23 *Financial Times* (10 December 2009).
24 *The Economist* (10 September 2005: 73).
25 Kang and Sakai (2000: 4–5). See also Mockler (2000: Figure 1.5).
26 *Financial Times* (6 May 2010).
27 Frigant and Layan (2009), Frigant and Lung (2002).
28 *Financial Times* (4 March 2003).
29 *Financial Times* (25 February 2009).
30 *Financial Times* (23 December 2009).
31 Frigant and Layan (2009: 13).
32 Frigant and Layan (2009: 13).
33 Pires and Neto (2008: 329).
34 Frigant and Lung (2002: 746).
35 Wade (1990: 310).
36 See Dicken (2003a), Freyssenet and Lung (2000), Rugman and Collinson (2004), Sturgeon et al. (2008), UNIDO (2003: 9–16).
37 *Financial Times* (22 January 2010).

38 See Domanski and Lung (2009), Frigant and Layan (2009), Jürgens and Krzywdzinski (2009), Pavlinek et al. (2009).

39 Domanski and Lung (2009: 9).

40 Jürgens and Krzywdzinski (2009: 32).

41 Sturgeon et al. (2008: Table 2).

42 Carillo (2004), Mortimore (1998: 411–17), UNCTAD (2000: 130–1).

43 Mortimore (1998: 417).

44 Rutherford and Holmes (2008), Sturgeon and Florida (2004), Sturgeon et al. (2008).

45 Horaguchi and Shimokawa (2002).

46 Guiher and Lecler (2000).

47 Liu and Dicken (2006).

48 Liu and Dicken (2006), Liu and Yeung (2008).

49 Liu and Dicken (2006).

Twelve

'MAKING THE WORLD GO ROUND': ADVANCED BUSINESS SERVICES – ESPECIALLY FINANCE

The centrality of advanced business services

As we saw in Chapter 3, services, especially advanced business services (ABS) – banking, accountancy, insurance, logistics, law, advertising, business consultancy, high-level personnel recruitment – are central to the operation of the economy. Not only are they the 'lubricants' to all production circuits but also they have become increasingly dominant. For example, financial services are both *circulation* services, fundamental to the operation of every aspect of the economic system, and also *commodities* or *products* in their own right, produced and traded in the same way as more tangible manufactured goods are traded.

Money counts

Every economic activity (whether a material product or a service) has to be financed at all stages of its production. Without the parallel development of systems of money- and credit-based exchange there could have been no development of economies beyond the most primitive organizational forms and the most geographically restricted scales.

> The geographical circuits of money and finance are the 'wiring' of the socio-economy … along which the 'currents' of wealth creation, consumption and economic power are transmitted … money allows for the deferment of payment over time–space that is the essence of credit. Equally, money allows propinquity without the need for proximity in conducting transactions over space. These complex time–space webs of monetary flows and obligations underpin our daily social existence.[1]

Finance is also one of the most controversial of economic activities because of its historical relationship with state 'sovereignty'. Ever since the earliest states emerged on the scene, the creation and control of money have been regarded as central to their legitimacy and survival.[2] Today, in the context of a globalizing world economy, this tension has become especially acute. The periodic financial crises that are endemic to the system intensify these tensions and also create legitimate fears over the accountability and responsibility of financial institutions.

A global casino

In 1986, Susan Strange coined the graphic term 'casino capitalism' to describe the international financial system:

> every day games are played in this casino that involve sums of money so large that they cannot be imagined. At night the games go on at the other side of the world … [the players] are just like the gamblers in casinos watching the clicking spin of a silver ball on a roulette wheel and putting their chips on red or black, odd numbers or even ones.[3]

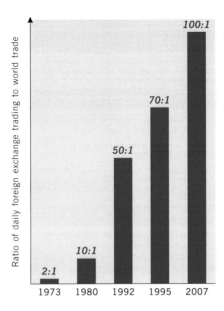

Figure 12.1   The growing disparity between foreign exchange trading
and world trade, 1973–2007

Source: based on Dore, 2008: 3; Eatwell and Taylor, 2000: 3–4

Twelve years later, she used the term 'mad money' to reflect the increased volatility of the financial system and the uncertainty it generates throughout the world economy. These terms are even more appropriate in the light of the 2008 global financial crisis.

International financial flows and foreign currency transactions have reached unprecedented levels. They totally dwarf the value of international trade in manufactured goods and in other services and have done so at an increasing rate over the past three decades, as Figure 12.1 shows. In 1973, daily foreign exchange transactions were roughly twice that of world trade; in 2007, they were 100 times greater! Of course, some of those financial transactions are directly related to international trade (and production) and are essential for that purpose. But only a very small percentage of international financial transactions are of this kind. The remainder take the form of what are, essentially, *speculative* dealings – aimed at making short- or long-term profits as ends in themselves – through a bewildering variety of financial instruments. Of course, it is often difficult to draw a clear line between speculative and productively essential financial transactions.[4]

The structure of advanced business services

Advanced business services encompass a very broad range of activities. Figure 12.2 identifies the major categories of ABS firm, distinguishing between financial and

Financial services

Type	Primary functions
Commercial bank	Administers financial transactions for clients (e.g. making payments, clearing cheques). Takes in deposits and makes commercial loans, acting as intermediary between lender and borrower.
Investment bank/ securities house	Buys and sells securities (i.e. stocks, bonds) on behalf of corporate or individual investors. Arranges flotation of new securities issues.
Credit card company	Operates international network of credit card facilities in conjunction with banks and other financial institutions.
Insurance company	Indemnifies a whole range of risks, on payment of a premium, in association with other insurers/reinsurers.
Accountancy firm	Certifies the accuracy of financial accounts, particularly via the corporate audit.

Professional business services

Type	Primary functions
Legal firm	Provides legal advice on regulatory requirements in specific territorial and international jurisdictions.
Business consultancy firm	Provides advice in diverse aspects of business organization, including strategic issues, corporate reorganization, etc.
Advertising agency	Designs and implements commercial campaigns across the media to promote branded products and/or corporate identity.
Executive recruitment ('headhunting') firm	Searches for and recruits high-level executive personnel.

Figure 12.2   Major types of advanced business services

professional business service firms. They are all basically providers of highly specialized knowledge which facilitates the increasingly complex configuration and operation of global production networks. All are, in some sense, *intermediaries* in the processes of production, distribution and consumption. In the case of banking, the key function is

> the pooling of financial resources among those with surplus funds to be lent out to those who choose to be in deficit, that is to borrow … With financial intermediation, investors in new productive activities do not themselves have to generate a surplus to finance their projects; instead the projects can be financed by surpluses generated elsewhere within the economy.[5]

The process of intermediation has constituted the basic function of banks from the very beginning. Figure 12.3 shows the sequence of development of the banking system. The first two stages of credit provision to borrowers depend greatly upon the nature of geographically specific knowledge to legitimize lend–ing and borrowing. The geographical scope of knowledge and trust grows through such developments as inter–bank lending (that is, lending outside the local area) in stage 3 and, eventually, of a central bank that ultimately acts as the lender of last resort to the banking system as a whole (stage 4). Subsequent developments, especially in securitization, create a totally different scale and complexity of financial activity.

The stages of banking development	Banks and space	Credit and space
Stage 1: Pure financial intermediation Banks lend out savings. Payment in commodity money. No bank multiplier. Saving precedes investment.	Serving local communities. Wealth-based, providing foundation for future financial centres.	Intermediation only.
Stage 2: Bank deposits used as money Convenient to use paper money as means of payment. Reduced drain on bank reserves. Multiplier process possible. Bank credit creation with fractional reserves. Investment can now precede saving.	Market dependent on extent of confidence held in banker.	Credit creation focused on local community because total credit constrained by redeposit ratio.
Stage 3: Inter-bank lending Credit creation still constrained by reserves. Risk of reserves loss offset by development of inter-bank lending. Multiplier process works more quickly. Multiplier larger because banks can hold lower reserves.	Banking system develops at national level.	Redeposit constraint relaxed somewhat, so can lend wider afield.
Stage 4: Lender-of-last-resort facility Central bank perceives need to promote confidence in banking system. Lender-of-last-resort facility provided if inter-bank lending inadequate. Reserves now respond to demand. Credit creation freed from reserves constraint.	Central bank oversees national system, but limited power to constrain credit.	Banks freer to respond to credit demand as reserves constraint not binding and they can determine volume and distribution of credit within national economy.
Stage 5: Liability management Competition from non-bank financial intermediaries drives struggle for market share. Banks actively supply credit and seek deposits. Credit expansion diverges from real economic activity.	Banks compete at national level with non-bank financial institutions.	Credit creation determined by struggle over market share and opportunities in speculative markets. Total credit uncontrolled.
Stage 6: Securitization Capital adequacy ratios introduced to curtail credit. Banks have an increasing proportion of bad loans because of over-lending in Stage 5. Securitization of bank assets. Increase in off-balance sheet activity. Drive to liquidity.	Deregulation opens up international competition, eventually causing concentration in financial centres.	Shift to liquidity by emphasis being put on services rather than credit; credit decisions concentrated in financial centres; total credit determined by availability of capital, i.e. by central capital markets.
?	?	?
Stage 7: Response to 2008 crisis Potential for redrawing of boundaries between different banking functions.	Possible reregulation at national and/or international scales.	Possible refocus on lending to domestic borrowers.

Figure 12.3 The sequence of development of the banking system

Source: based in part on Dow, 1999: Tables 1 and 2

Such increased complexity of the financial system has resulted in the development of a huge variety of different types of financial institution, each of which has
a specific set of core functions (Figure 12.2). In fact, the boundaries between these
individual activities and institutions have become increasingly blurred. The first
three types of financial institution shown in Figure 12.2 are concerned with the
creation and distribution of credit in various forms. The two remaining categories
are concerned with different forms of risk indemnification (insurance companies)
and with certifying the accuracy of financial accounts (accountancy firms).

Dynamics of the markets for advanced business services

Demand for advanced business services is primarily driven by the increasing complexity and specialization of functions within economies in general and in production networks in particular. ABS providers are both the beneficiaries of such developments and also, in turn, contributors to that increased complexity, thus helping to create their own growing markets. This is especially the case as production networks have become increasingly global, creating more and more market opportunities for firms to follow their clients abroad. Very often the relationships established between ABS firms and their customers in a domestic context are transferred to an international context because of the build-up of trust. Alternatively, the geographical differentiation of rules and regulations between different national territories creates opportunities for ABS firms to construct more complex and geographically diverse operations and to build extensive networks.

The increased diversity (and volatility) of the market for financial services

From being fairly simple and predictable, the markets for financial services have become increasingly diverse and far less predictable. The intensity of competition for consumers (whether corporate or individual) has increased enormously. Four processes have been especially important:

- *Market saturation*: by the late 1970s, traditional financial services markets were reaching saturation. There were fewer and fewer new clients to add to the list; most were already being served, particularly in the commercial banking sector but also in the retail sector in the more affluent economies.
- *Disintermediation*: this is the process whereby corporate borrowers make their investments or raise their needed capital without going through the 'intermediary' channels of the traditional financial institutions, particularly the bank. Instead, they have increasingly sought capital from non-bank institutions, for example through securities, investment trusts and mutual funds. However, the process is extremely dynamic. Disintermediation may well be challenged by reintermediation, as new forms of supplier–customer relationship emerge (as, for example, through the Internet).[6]
- *Deregulation of financial markets*: financial services markets have traditionally been extremely closely regulated by national governments. One of the most important developments of the past 30 years was the increasing deregulation or liberalization of financial markets. Deregulation has facilitated:

○ the opening of new geographical markets

○ the provision of new financial products

○ changes in the way in which prices of financial services are set.

- *Internationalization of financial markets*: demand for financial services is no longer restricted to the domestic context: financial markets have become increasingly global. Three trends have been especially significant:

  ○ the massive growth in international trade

  ○ the global spread of transnational corporations

  ○ the vastly increased institutionalization of savings.

Each of these forces for change in the demand for financial services is inter-related; together they created a *new competitive environment*. But, of course, such developments do not always run smoothly. Indeed, the inherent volatility of financial markets creates periodic large-scale upheavals. The history of the twentieth century provides clear evidence of such a succession of 'financial disasters':[7] the bankers' panic in the US in 1907; the Wall Street Crash in 1929; 'Black Monday' in 1987; the Asian financial crisis in 1997; and most recently the financial crisis of 2008, triggered by the collapse of the US subprime mort-gage market. Such market volatility has profound implications for the ABS sector in general. Some ABS firms prosper – notably those concerned with corporate bankruptcies and restructuring – whilst others experience difficulties as demand for their services contracts. Advertising, for example, tends to be hard hit.

Technological innovation and advanced business services

Centrality of information and communication technology

Information and communication technology (ICT) is absolutely central to all advanced business services because they are all, essentially, providers of special-ist information and knowledge. Information is both the process and the prod-uct of ABS. Consequently, the innovations in communication and in the storing and processing of information, discussed in Chapter 4, helped to shape ABS. This is overwhelmingly so in the case of financial services, whose raw materials are information: about markets, risks, exchange rates, returns on investment, creditworthiness. Their products are also information: the result of adding value to these informational inputs. In the words of one financial services executive:

> We don't have warehouses full of cash. We have *information* about cash – *that* is our product.[8]

Indeed, money itself

> is primarily an item of information governed by rules. Money is therefore shaped by the development and adoption of information and communication technologies ... (how the information is managed, and to a degree the very nature of the information) and regulation (how information is ruled).[9]

Not surprisingly, therefore, all the major financial services firms invest phenomenal sums in information technologies.

It is, of course, the *speed* with which financial services firms can perform transactions and the *global extent* over which they can be made that are especially important.

> Travelling at the speed of light, as nothing but assemblages of zeros and ones, global money dances through the world's fiber-optic networks in astonishing volumes ... National boundaries mean little in this context: it is much easier to move $41 billion from London to New York than a truckload of grapes from California to Nevada.[10]

From a technological viewpoint, global 24-hours-a-day trading or 'following the sun' – whether this be in securities, foreign exchange, financial and commodities futures or any other financial service – is perfectly feasible.[11] As Figure 12.4 shows, the trading hours of the world's major financial centres overlap. In fact, genuine 24-hour trading is currently limited to certain kinds of transaction partly because, although the technology is available, either the organizational structure or the national regulatory environment creates an obstacle (see next section).

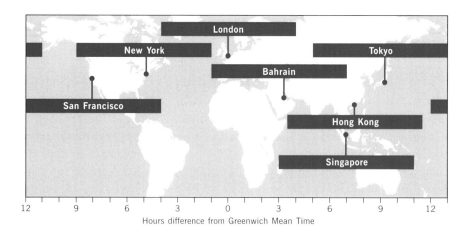

Figure 12.4   The potential for 24-hour financial trading

Source: based on Warf, 1989: Figure 5

To the extent that electronic transactions do not require direct physical proximity between seller and buyer, they are a form of 'invisible' international trade. In that sense, therefore, financial services are one form of ABS that is *tradable*. The global integration of financial markets brings many benefits to its participants in the speed and accuracy of information flows and the rapidity and directness of transactions, even though the participants may be separated by many thousands of miles and by several time zones. But such global integration and instantaneous financial trading also create costs. 'Shocks' occurring in one geographical market now spread instantaneously around the globe, creating the potential for global financial instability. Financial 'contagion' is endemic in the structure and operation of the contemporary financial system. It is nothing new – just more extreme.

An epidemic of new financial products

Innovations in telecommunications and in process technologies, therefore, have helped to transform the operations of financial services firms. They have also helped to create new financial products. Electronic communications have contributed greatly to the bypassing of the commercial banks and the trend towards the greater *securitization* of financial transactions: the conversion of all kinds of loans and borrowings into 'paper' securities which can be bought and sold on the market. Such transactions may be performed directly by buyers and sellers without necessarily going through the intermediary channels of the commercial banks.

As a consequence, a whole new array – a virtual epidemic – of financial instruments (product innovations) appeared on the scene with increasing frequency, notably:

- those providing new methods of lending and borrowing
- those facilitating greater spreading of risk.

The most important product innovation since the mid 1980s has been the phenomenal growth of the *derivatives* markets. Derivatives are

> financial tools derived from other financial products, such as equities and currencies. The most common of these are futures, swaps, and options ... The derivatives market aims to enable participants to manage their exposure to the risk of movements in interest rates, equities, and currencies.[12]

Figure 12.5 gives examples of what some have called the 'alphabet soup' of such 'structured financial products'. The underlying logic of these instruments is the spreading of risk. However, the 2008 crisis showed, with great force, that the nature and extent of such risks was simply not understood: 'risk has become

Type of financial instrument	Basic characteristics
Asset-backed Securities (ABS)	Debt parcelled up and sold as securities backed by the repayment from those loans.
e.g. Mortgage-backed Securities (MBS)	Securities based on the selling-on of mortgages in packages.
Credit Default Swaps (CDS)	Insurance against corporate default.
Collateralized Debt Obligations (CDOs)	Structured financial products that pool different kinds of loans and bonds, funding themselves by issuing new bonds whose price depends upon the risk level.
Constant Proportion Debt Obligations (CPDOs)	Leveraged bets on a group of high-quality US and European companies. These vehicles issued securities to generate to pay out by selling protection on credit default swaps.

Figure 12.5   Examples of recent product innovations in financial markets

Source: based on the *Financial Times,* 13 October 2009: 33

delocalized and outsourced'.[13] It was the packaging, repackaging and selling on (and on and on) of mortgage-based securities (MBS) based on loans in the US sub-prime mortgage market (loans to individuals without the means to repay them) that triggered the crisis when borrowers began to default. Nobody, not even the financial institutions themselves, quite knew where the risks lay. When it is realized that 'the notional value of the derivatives market was almost eleven times the value of the world's financial assets'[14] then the riskiness of such risk-taking becomes apparent. No wonder the US investor Warren Buffett called derivatives 'time bombs' or 'financial weapons of mass destruction', or that Gillian Tett talked about 'destructive creation' – a neat reversal of Schumpeter's notion of 'creative destruction' (see Chapter 4).

In effect:

> The modern financial services industry is a casino attached to a utility. The utility is the payments system, which enables individuals and companies to manage their daily affairs. It allows them to borrow and lend in line with the fundamental value of business activities. In the casino, traders make profits from arbitrage – differences in the prices of related assets – and from short-term price movements. The users of the utility look to fundamental values. The players in the casino are preoccupied with the mind of the market.[15]

Without question, therefore, developments in information and communication technology, as well as in product innovations, have transformed the financial services industries. The global integration of financial markets has become possible, collapsing space and time and creating the potential for virtually instantaneous financial transactions in loans, securities and a whole variety of financial instruments. However, completely borderless financial trading does not actually exist, for the simple reason that most financial services remain very heavily supervised and regulated by individual national governments. Let us now see how the regulatory system works – or doesn't – and how it has changed.

The role of the state: regulation, deregulation, reregulation

Although some ABS are 'tradable', most depend fundamentally on having a direct presence within their markets. This is especially true of legal and accounting services because both are subject to tight regulation at the national scale. Even within the EU, national regulatory structures still operate. But it is in the financial sphere that regulatory systems are especially significant. The history of the past six decades is one of a dramatic shift from tight regulation to looser – even to deregulation – until the 2008 crisis hit the world with such force that the whole regulatory system is again in question. Reregulation is back on the agenda.

A tightly regulated financial system

Before the 1960s a 'world' financial market did not exist. The IMF, together with the leading industrialized nations, operated a broadly efficient global mechanism for monetary management based, initially, on the post-war Bretton Woods agreement (see Chapter 17). At the national level, financial markets and institutions were very closely supervised, primarily because of concerns over the vulnerability of the financial system to periodic crisis and because of the centrality of finance to the operation of a country's economy.

Financial services, therefore, have been the most tightly regulated of all economic activities, certainly more so than manufacturing industries. Such regulation can be divided into two major types:

- Those governing the *relationships* between different financial activities. National financial services markets have generally been *segmented* by regulation: banks performed specified activities; securities houses performed other activities. Neither was allowed to perform the functions of the other.
- Those governing the *entry* of firms (whether domestic or foreign) into the financial sector. Restricted entry into the different financial services markets has been virtually universal, although the precise regulations differ from country to country. Governments have been especially wary of a too-ready expansion of the *branches* of foreign banks and insurance companies. This is because, unlike separately incorporated subsidiaries, branches are far more difficult to supervise: they form an integral part of a foreign company's activities. In almost every case, there are limits on the degree of foreign ownership permitted in financial services.

'The crumbling of the walls'

Although many of these restrictions continued to exist, the regulatory walls crumbled – even collapsed altogether in some cases. The process was relatively slow at first but accelerated rapidly after the late 1980s. Deregulatory pressures came from several sources, most notably the increasing abilities of transnational firms to take advantage of 'gaps' in the regulatory system and to operate outside national regulatory boundaries.

> Money has a habit of seeking out geographical discontinuities and gaps in these regulatory spaces, escaping to places where the movement of financial assets is less constrained, where official scrutiny into financial dealing and affairs is minimal, where taxes are lower and potential profits higher.[16]

The starting point was the emergence of the Eurodollar (that is, offshore) markets in the 1960s. Initially, Eurodollars were simply dollars held outside the US banking system largely by countries anxious to prevent their dollar holdings being subject to US political control. The rapid growth of this new currency market outside national regulatory control was reinforced by pressure from banks and other financial services firms to operate in a less constrained and segmented manner, both domestically and internationally. The internationalization of financial services and the deregulation of national financial services markets, therefore, are virtually two sides of the same coin. Forces of internationalization were one of the pressures stimulating deregulation; deregulation is a necessary process to facilitate further internationalization.

Major deregulation occurred in all the major developed economies. In the US, a series of changes since the 1970s both eased the entry of foreign banks into the domestic market and facilitated the expansion of US banks overseas, as well as allowing banks to become involved in a whole variety of financial services and to operate nationwide branching networks. In 1999 the Glass–Steagall Act, which prohibited the joint ownership of commercial and investment banking, was abolished. In the UK, the so-called 'Big Bang' of October 1986 removed the existing barriers between banks and securities houses and allowed the entry of foreign firms into the Stock Exchange. In France, the 'Little Bang' of 1987 gradually opened up the French Stock Exchange to outsiders and to foreign and domestic banks. In Germany, foreign-owned banks were allowed to lead-manage foreign issues, subject to reciprocity agreements.

Financial deregulation also occurred in East Asia. In Japan the restrictions on the entry of foreign securities houses were relaxed (though not removed) and Japanese banks could open international banking facilities. But the Japanese financial system remained more tightly regulated than elsewhere. In 1996, the Japanese government announced its intention to undertake a wide-ranging deregulation of the country's financial system, a process made more difficult by Japan's attempt to recover from its deep financial crisis of the 1990s. Even the Singaporean government has progressively loosened the restrictions on the financial sector in order to maintain the country's position as a major Asian financial centre. Most recently, China has allowed foreign participation in big state-owned banks and has listed them on overseas stock exchanges.

Increasing deregulation of financial services has been an important component of the major regional economic blocs. A financial services agreement was part of the Canada–US Free Trade Agreement whilst, under the NAFTA, Mexico had to open up its financial sector to North American firms by 2007. EU reforms aim at removing the individual national financial regulatory structures inhibiting the creation of an EU-wide financial system so that financial services flow freely throughout the EU and financial services firms could establish a presence anywhere within the Single Market. The creation of a single European currency transformed wholesale financial markets in the EU but retail financial markets remained fragmented on national lines.

Reintervention of the state

The unexpected financial crisis of 2008 stopped this apparently inexorable trend towards the deregulation of financial services in its tracks. The collapse of major banks and investment firms, initially in the US and the UK, was a shock of unprecedented magnitude, at least since the Wall Street Crash of 1929. As a result of the virtual collapse of the financial system in 2008, the IMF estimated that financial institutions faced losses of $4.1 trillion.[17] Governments have ploughed billions of dollars, pounds, euros, yen and other currencies into propping up their collapsing banking systems. Some institutions – like Lehman Brothers in the US – have been allowed to fail. But, for the most part, governments have stepped in with massive financial support. In effect, a number of leading US and British banks have been nationalized. Rescuing their banks became the preoccupation of national governments, simply because credit is essential for an economy to operate. The banks were regarded as being too big to fail. But the cost to the taxpayer has been immense and poses major problems for future public expenditure and for people's economic well-being.

In the short run the need is to stabilize the financial system, but in the longer run the need, clearly, is for a new financial architecture for the global economy. This is an issue we will explore in Chapter 17. Suffice it at this stage to note that the accepted wisdom of the past 20 years of the efficiency of free, unregulated financial markets and the benefits of derivatives and other exotic financial products has been destroyed.

The state as capitalist investor: sovereign wealth funds

A rather different state financial phenomenon has emerged in recent years: the state as a large and active investor in international financial markets. The mechanism is the government-owned *sovereign wealth fund* (SWF). Figure 12.6 shows the geographical origins and magnitude of the major SWFs in 2007. Their combined

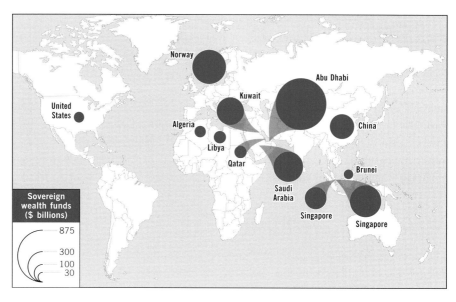

Figure 12.6   The geography of sovereign wealth funds

Source: press reports

value was $2.9 trillion, equal to around 2 per cent of the world's total financial assets (bank deposits, bonds, shares). The leading SWFs are virtually all from emerging economies, notably those that are oil-rich. In effect, SWFs

> are a way to help recycle emerging-market surpluses. And yet suspicion about their motives could make their money much less welcome: rather than accepting investment from sovereign-wealth funds, countries could turn to financial protectionism … For some, the rub is that governments are less interested in money than in power … Others are worried for precisely the opposite reason: that the funds are interested chiefly in making money. This would not matter much but for the sheer size that some funds have now attained. They are big enough to shift markets.[18]

The virtual collapse of Dubai World, a state-owned holding company, in late 2009 raised some critical questions about such funds.

Corporate strategies in advanced business services

Concentration and consolidation

The history of most advanced business services is a more or less continuous trend towards greater concentration into a smaller number of companies.

Top 10 banks		Tier 1 capital ($m)
1. JPMorgan Chase	US	136,104
2. Bank of America	US	120,814
3. Citigroup	US	118,758
4. Royal Bank of Scotland	UK	101,818
5. HSBC	UK	95,336
6. Wells Fargo	US	86,397
7. Mitsubishi UFJ	Japan	77,218
8. ICBC	China	74,701
9. Crédit Agricole	France	71,681
10. Santander	Spain	65,267

Top 10 law companies		Turnover ($m)
1. Clifford Chance	UK	1,030
2. Linklaters	UK	935
3. Skadden ARPS	US	885
4. Freshfields Bruckhaus Deringer	UK	882
5. Latham & Watkins	US	776
6. Baker & Mckenzie	US	743
7. Allen & Overy	UK	736
8. Jones Day	US	706
9. Sidley Austin	US	618
10. White & Case	US	575

Top 10 accountancy networks	Fee income ($m)
1. PricewaterhouseCoopers	83,600
2. Deloitte	39,474
3. Ernst & Young	37,241
4. KPMG	28,857
5. BDO	26,985
6. Grant Thornton	26,900
7. Geneva Group	26,500
8. RSM	25,000
9. Praxity	24,219
10. Crowe Horwath	19,975

Top 10 global headhunting firms		Revenue ($m)
1. Korn/Ferry	US	402
2. Heidrick & Struggles	US	375
3. Spencer Stuart	US	362
4. Egon Zehnder	Switzerland	336
5. Russell Reynolds	US	268
6. Ray & Berndtson	US	147
7. Amrop Hever	Belgium	135
8. TransSearch	France	79
9. Globe	UK	76
10. IIC Partners	Canada	75

Figure 12.7   Dominant firms in advanced business services

Source: based on data in *The Banker*, July 2009; *The Lawyer*, October 2009; *Accountancy Magazine*, June 2009; Faulconbridge et al., 2008: Table 3

Much of this consolidation has occurred through the conventional route of organic growth and of merger and acquisition. However, in some ABS, like accounting, law and executive recruitment, for example, the development of alliances and networks has become especially apparent. As a result, virtually all ABS sectors are dominated by a small number of very large firms or networks of firms (Figure 12.7).

The changes in banking have been especially marked. In 1989, no fewer than seven of the top 10 banks were Japanese, a reflection of Japan's spectacular economic growth during the 1980s. However, Japanese banks suffered very badly in the collapse of the Japanese 'bubble economy' in the early 1990s. In 2009, only one of the top 10 banks was Japanese. Western banks, especially US and UK banks, still dominate, although it is highly significant that one of the top 10 banks in 2009 was Chinese. Mergers have been endemic in the banking sector for the past 20 years at least. For example, the Mitsubishi UFJ Financial Group has evolved from a whole series of mergers. First, the Bank of Tokyo, Mitsubishi Bank and Mitsubishi Trust merged to form MTFG. Then, Sanwa Bank and Tokai Bank merged in 2002 to form the UFJ Bank. Finally, MTFG merged with UFJ in 2005. In the US, Chase Manhattan Bank merged with JP Morgan to form JP Morgan Chase. Citigroup grew aggressively through acquiring a whole series of banks and financial services firms, including Travelers Group. In the UK, the major banks have all grown through merger and acquisition: for example, Bank of Scotland and Halifax combined to form HBOS.

In the aftermath of the 2008 financial crisis, however, many of these deals involving commercial and investment banks unravelled. For example, Bank of America acquired Merrill Lynch; in the UK, HBOS was acquired by Lloyds which, in turn, had to be rescued by the British government, as did the largest bank of all, RBS. Both are currently largely owned by the UK government. Not part of their corporate plan! In the investment banking sector, JP Morgan Chase acquired Bear Stearns; and the Japanese firm Nomura acquired the Asian and European operations of Lehman Brothers, which had been allowed to collapse in September 2008 by the US government. The collapse of Lehman was, without doubt, one of the biggest shocks of all. The UK company Barclays acquired some of Lehman's core US assets. A great deal of financial blood was spilled.

Product diversification

It is a short, and supposedly logical, step from this kind of growth orientation to the notion that ABS firms should not only operate in their own core area of expertise but also supply a *complete package of related services*. The services conglomerate or the services supermarket arrived, greatly stimulated, in the case of financial services, by increasing deregulation. As we saw earlier, it became increasingly possible for banks to act as securities houses, for securities houses to act as banks, and for both to offer a bewildering array of financial services way beyond their original operations. A typical leading bank's portfolio of offerings came to include: clearing banking, corporate finance, insurance broking, commercial lending, life assurance, mortgages, unit trusts, travellers' cheques, treasury services, credit cards, stockbroking, fund management, development capital, personal pensions and merchant banking. At the same time, entirely new non-bank financial services companies emerged. In non-financial ABS sectors a similar trend developed. For example, companies offering accountancy, consulting and other services under a single umbrella became common.

The rationale for product diversification was the familiar one of economies of scale and scope. The argument for a strategy of diversified service operations was that it offered a complete package of services – a 'one-stop shop' – to customers. Their supply by a large, globally recognized, brand-name firm was supposed to give reassurance to potential customers that they would receive the highest-quality service. However, there is little evidence that such diversifying mergers lead to significant improvements in efficiency. One potential problem is the nature of financial services products themselves:

> Mergers between car manufacturers or consumer goods companies allow production to be centralized because the products are essentially the same ... The same is not true for many financial services ... 'A bottle of beer is a real thing but financial products are intangible constructs of regulation, culture and behaviour. A current account is a different product in every country, while life insurance policies are tax-driven products and tax systems are not harmonised. Where will the synergies come from?'[19]

Nevertheless, the merger waves in the financial sector showed no sign of disappearing until the 2008 crisis intervened and threw such ideas into question.

Transnationalization

The provision of advanced business services to customers depends, more than in any other sector, on *geographical proximity*. Although it is certainly true that some services can be supplied at a distance – including, of course, many financial services – the need for face-to-face contact is hugely important. As their major customers have expanded their overseas operations, the pressure on ABS firms to follow has intensified. Not surprisingly, then, all the leading ABS firms have become increasingly *transnational* in their operations.[20] In this section, we look at three examples: banking, legal services and executive recruitment (headhunting).

Financial services

Although banks have long engaged in international business – for example, through foreign exchange dealing or providing credit for trade – historically this kind of business was carried out from their domestic locations. Any business that could not be carried out by mail or using telecommunications was handled by local correspondent banks; there was no need for a direct physical presence abroad. A small number of banks certainly set up a few overseas operations towards the end of the nineteenth century. But even in the early part of the twentieth century, the international banking network was very limited indeed. Almost all international banking operations were 'colonial' – part of the imperial spread of British, Dutch, French and German business activities. In 1913 the four major US banks had only six overseas branches between them. By 1920 the number of branches had grown to roughly 100 but there was little further change until the 1960s.

As with TNCs in manufacturing industries, the most spectacular expansion of transnational banking occurred in the 1960s and 1970s. In both cases US firms led the initial surge, a reflection of both the focal role of the US in the post-war international financial and trading system and also the rapid proliferation of US manufacturing TNCs. The number of foreign affiliates of banks increased from 202 in 1960 to 1928 in 1985. At the same time, the *geographical composition* of the international banking network changed. US banks became less dominant, whilst European and Japanese banks increased the size of their international branch network. Today, the extent of transnationalization among financial services firms is considerable but also variable, as Table 12.1 shows. Although size and transnationality are related, it is not necessarily the biggest firms that are the most transnationalized. It is notable that only two US firms are among the most transnational financial services firms: Citigroup and AIG. However, JP Morgan Chase plans to launch 'a global business aimed at selling loans and commercial banking services to multinational corporations, pitting the US bank against Citigroup and HSBC'.[21]

Table 12.1   The transnational scope of leading financial services firms, 2008

Rank by geographical spread	Company	Headquarters	No. of foreign affiliates	No. of host countries
1	Citigroup	US	723	75
2	Allianz	Germany	612	52
3	ABN Amro	Netherlands	703	48
4	General Spa	Italy	342	41
5	HSBC	UK	683	54
6	Société Générale	France	345	53
7	Zurich Financial Services	Switzerland	383	34
8	UBS	Switzerland	432	35
9	Unicredito Italiano Spa	Italy	1052	34
10	Axa	France	464	39
11	BNP Paribas	France	425	48
12	Deutsche Bank	Germany	713	36
13	AIG	US	356	45
14	Credit Suisse	Switzerland	252	31
15	Swiss Re	Switzerland	173	26
16	Dexia	Belgium	231	26
17	Crédit Agricole	France	234	39
18	Natixis	France	182	38
19	ING	Netherlands	555	38
20	Banco Santander	Spain	267	30

Source: based on material in UNCTAD, 2009: Annex Table A.I.12

Although the turmoil of the 2008 crisis undoubtedly clipped the wings of many financial institutions and brought their transnational expansion to a halt, some actually increased their transnational presence. The Nomura takeover of the Asian and European operations of Lehman, for example, 'turned Nomura from a bank serving Japanese clients globally to a bank serving local clients in global markets'.[22] Chinese banks are also beginning to pursue active transnationalization strategies.

The specific reasons for, and the pace of, the transnationalization of financial services firms may well vary from one case to another, but there is an overall general pattern.

• In the immediate post-1945 period, the major overseas function of the small number of US transnational banks was to provide finance for trade. But as the overseas operations of US TNCs in manufacturing and other activities accelerated in the early 1960s, the functions of the US transnational banks evolved to meet their particular demands. Thus, the staple business of US banks in London became that of servicing the financial needs of their major industrial clients who were rapidly extending their operations outside the US.

- In the second half of the 1960s, transnational banking functions took on a significant additional dimension with the growth of the Eurodollar market. As a consequence, US banks could raise money there for relending domestically as well as overseas.
- The attractions of transnational banking widened progressively both as the global capital market evolved and as local capital markets overseas developed. As banks from the other industrialized economies also transnationalized, the process became *self-reinforcing*. All large banks had to operate transnationally; they had to have a presence in all the leading markets.
- The transnationalization of financial markets received fresh impetus in the 1970s from two sources: first, the 'windfall' capital acquired by the OPEC oil-exporting countries which they sought to lend abroad; and second, the progressive dismantling of exchange controls on capital movements by the Federal Republic of Germany, the US, Japan and the UK.
- The major trend towards greater deregulation of national financial markets from the late 1980s and through the 1990s gave a fresh impetus to transnationalization, especially to transnational mergers and acquisitions in the banking and financial services sector in general.

Figure 12.8 summarizes the major phases of development of transnational banking.

Such broad developments also pulled more and more securities firms into international operations.

> Up to 1979/80, the US multinational investment bank had little more than a large office in London and perhaps some much smaller ones in other European countries, perhaps an Arab country and possibly (though less likely) Japan. From 1980 onward, the development of the US investment bank as a multinational changed qualitatively.[23]

	Phase I National banking	Phase II Transnational banking	Phase III Transnational full- service banking	Phase IV World full- service banking
Transnationalization of customer companies	Export – import.	Active direct overseas investment.	Transnational corporation.	
Transnational operations in banking	Mainly foreign exchange operations connected with foreign trade. Capital transactions are mainly short-term ones.	Overseas loans and investments become important, as do medium- and longer-run capital transactions.	Non-banking fringe activities such as merchant banking, leasing, consulting and others are conducted.	Retail banking.
Methods of transnationalization	Correspondence contracts with foreign bank.	To strengthen own overseas branches and offices.	By strengthening own branches and offices, capital participation, affiliation in business, establishing non-bank fringe business firms, the most profitable ways of fund-raising and lending are sought on a global basis.	
Customers of transnational operations	Mainly domestic customers.	Mainly domestic customers.	Customers are of various nationalities.	

Figure 12.8 Major phases in the development of international banking

Source: based on Fujita and Ishigaki, 1986: Table 7.6

As a result, all of the transnational financial services firms have been basing their strategy on a direct presence in each of the major geographical markets and on providing a local service based on global resources. They are, in fact, selling a *global brand image*, with the clear message that a global company can cope most easily and effectively with every possible financial problem that can possibly face any customer wherever they are located. This may, or may not, be what actually happens.

Legal services

The provision of legal services to companies requires a direct contact with clients in each of the territories in which they operate for two main reasons:

- Legal regulations differ from country to country, so a lawyer qualified and registered in one country may not be able to operate in another country. It is impossible to offer legal services at a distance.
- The nature of the information being transmitted and the high level of trust involved necessitates a high level of face-to-face interaction (see Chapters 3 and 4).

The leading law firms have, as a result, developed increasingly extensive and complex transnational operations.[24]

> Because of the high degree of trust required, and the interpretative complexities of law, legal services work can thus only be acquired through repeated copresence. Acquiring and retaining legal services business is embroiled in close relations with clients which places extensive face-to-face interaction at the centre of lawyers' work. Thus, the operational practices by which firms acquire new business are dominated by face-to-face meetings and discussions … as firms seek to globalize, *transnational operations* remain inextricably reliant on *knowledge practices* constituted through face-to-face interactions.[25]

The jurisdictional constraints within which legal firms have to work have a major effect on the kind of organizational structures that transnational legal firms employ. These are very different from the conventional structures of TNCs discussed in Chapter 5. Legal firms are primarily organized as *partnerships*, in which the top individuals/partners own the company. A direct presence in individual markets is achieved by establishing an office staffed by local and/or expatriate lawyer staff. An indirect presence is usually organized through membership of a 'legal network, such as Interlex or through the establishment of a "best friends" arrangement with "local" law firms in overseas jurisdictions'.[26] An increasingly common way of operating transnationally is through

> 'temporary teams' that are formed to fulfil a client's requirements and then disbanded … The main strategy transnational law firms have used to manage this need for team-work is the practice group. As worldwide groupings practice groups act as an umbrella under which all lawyers with the same

legal speciality sit … the aim of firms is to make practice groups cohesive and based on a common set of values.[27]

However, perhaps more than many other kinds of TNC, legal firms face an especially strong tension between creating a global way of working and local integration.[28]

Table 12.2 lists the leading legal services firms, all of which are from either the US or the UK. These leading firms tend to use their own direct operations rather than work within a network.[29]

The nature of transnationalization in the sector has marked regional patterns … UK and European firms have extended their operations primarily into Asian markets not North America, and conversely North American firms have shown little interest in expanding into Europe. In that sense, the pattern of sector transnationalization in legal services is a more complex and fragmented one than in the investment banking sector.[30]

Table 12.2   The transnational scope of leading legal services firms, 2006

Company	Headquarters	No. of lawyers	No. of offices
Clifford Chance	UK	2432	28
Linklaters	UK	2072	30
Skadden Arps Slate Meagher & Flom	US	1699	22
Freshfields Bruckhaus Deringer	UK	2013	28
DLA Piper Rudnick Grey Cary	UK	2900	59
Latham & Watkins	US	1669	22
Baker & Mckenzie	US	2975	70
Allen & Overy	UK	1760	25
Jones Day	US	2178	29
Sidley Austin Brown & Wood	US	1495	16
White & Case	US	1783	38
Weil Gotshal & Manges	US	1129	20
Mayer Brown Rowe & Maw	US	1331	14
Kirkland & Ellis	US	1056	8
Sullivan & Cromwell	US	589	44
Shearman Sterling	US	910	19
Wilmer Cutler Pickering Hale & Dorr	US	976	15
McDermott Will & Emery	US	1018	14
Lovells	UK	1353	26
Dechert	US	831	18

Source: based on Faulconbridge, 2008: Table 2

Executive recruitment

The global executive search (headhunting) industry has a rather brief history, originating in the US in the 1950s, but growing very rapidly from the 1970s. It developed primarily out of the management consultancy sector.[31] Headhunting exemplifies one of the key attributes of contemporary global business: the perceived importance of business leaders with transnational experience. Headhunters are firms which search out suitable senior managerial or board executives on behalf of corporate clients. It is an elite labour market function. As a rule, the target individuals are already employed in another firm, so the term 'headhunting' is rather appropriate.

Table 12.3   The transnational scope of leading headhunting firms, 2008

Company	Headquarters	Organizational form	No. of consutants	No. of worldwide offices
MRI Worldwide	n.a.	Network	4500	65
Korn/Ferry International	US	Owned	426	73
Heidrick & Struggles International	US	Owned	297	58
Spencer Stuart	US	Owned	292	49
Egon Zehnder International	Switzerland	Owned	290	59
Russell Reynolds Associates	US	Owned	133	33
Ray & Berndtson	US	Hybrid	300	48
Amrop-Hever	Belgium	Hybrid	264	78
Globe	UK	Network	n.a.	15
EMA Partners	n.a.	Hybrid	130	42

Source: based on Faulconbridge et al., 2009: Table 1

It is estimated that the top 10 firms listed in Table 12.3 account for around one-third of the global executive search market. These firms are hired by clients for a fee (based upon a candidate's salary) to fill a vacant senior position (either actual or potential).

> Whilst they are fundamentally offering the same service ... different firms have their own unique executive search cultures and styles ... Distinctions can be made between specialist boutiques that concentrate on headhunting in a limited number of sectors ... and integrated 'complete service' corporations that offer executive search in any major industry ... As with other producer services, a long 'tail' exists with firms that have some form of 'international operation' – circa 5000 firms.[32]

It is the very largest headhunting firms that have expanded the most rapidly and aggressively.

By 2005 the leading fifteen global headhunters had increased their number of offices by 48% since 1992, from 461 to 684, with substantial absolute growth in Europe, North America and the Asia–Pacific ... Five of the consistently ranked global top-six headhunters had increased their regional office networks by 173%, from 100 offices to 273, between 1987 and 2005.[33]

As in other service sectors, headhunters use a variety of organizational forms to operate transnationally (see Table 12.3, third column):[34]

- *The wholly owned firm.* A firm that operates a tightly organized set of offices across the world, all of which work within the parent firm's brand identity, control and work practices.

  The fact that all offices use the same brand name and corporate culture allows clients to trust that they will receive the same level and type of service wherever their executive search is in demand ... In addition, the owned firm is able to share successful practices and strategies in the form of 'know-how' management. These are then used to improve services and create demand in each market. Offices also share lists of 'headhunted ' executives between offices such that they maximize the number of people they can offer to their clients in the shortlist, colloquially known as the 'beauty parade'. (227)

- *The networked firm.* A strategic alliance between several independent firms:

  Networks are not businesses in themselves but architectures linking single country firms together into a global network of 'best friends' that can perform labour searches across many nations when needed ... Headhunting networks are *temporary* and *dynamic* interfirm collaborations that grow through repetitive use. There is no long-term lock-in to these collaborations, thus allowing the member firms the flexibility to draw on the resources and knowledge base of the most suitable firm in the network. (227)

- *The hybrid firm.*

  Part of a formalized global alliance bringing initially independent firms together to trade under one corporate name but operate as independent businesses ... Hybrids involve tighter integration than in a network which has only one office in each country and shared standards and approaches existing across the alliance. However, it is not as culturally, socially, or economically integrated as the wholly owned firm. Hybridity eliminates the potential for competition between different member firms operating in the same country as might be the case in the network. (227)

- *Combined structures.* In reality, some of the biggest headhunting firms may adopt different approaches at the same time to meet specific circumstances, as Korn/Ferry demonstrates.

  Predominantly, Korn/Ferry operates as a wholly owned firm ... however ... in certain markets it adopts three other organizational structures – what it terms the 'alliance', the 'satellite', and the 'affiliate office' ... It shows ... how ... a blurred typology is a valuable way of engaging in internationalization that responds to locally variegated opportunities. (230)

Geographies of advanced business services

Cities as the 'natural habitat' for advanced business services

At first sight, ICT developments would appear to release business services, especially financial services, from geographical constraints. Such firms might seem to be especially footloose: they are not tied to specific raw material locations, whilst at least some of their transactions can be carried out over vast geographical distances, using telecommunications facilities. Their business, as we have seen, is *information*. Such considerations have led many to write geography and distance out of the script as far as financial services, in particular, are concerned.[35]

There is no doubt that the revolutionary developments in ICT permit information (including financial transactions) to whizz around the world electronically, and that deregulation has reduced the resistance of national boundaries to financial flows. But, far from heralding the 'end of geography', this has in fact made geography *more* – not less – important. Indeed, we find that, at global, national and local scales, advanced business services continue to be extremely *strongly concentrated geographically*. They are, in fact, more highly concentrated than virtually any other kind of economic activity, except those based on highly localized raw materials. However, there are some subtle variations according to the particular function involved: there is a division of labour within ABS firms, parts of which may show a greater degree of geographical decentralization.

The geographies of ABS are enmeshed and embedded in cities: cities of all kinds but, especially, the biggest cities whose top tier consists of the so-called global or world cities.[36] The reason is the primary importance of face-to-face contact for all ABS. That has been the recurring theme throughout this chapter. Such services need geographical proximity to their clients. They also create, and benefit from, the kinds of traded and untraded interdependencies discussed in Chapters 3 and 4 – the 'buzz' that comes from localized clustering. The geographies of ABS, then, are synonymous with the geographies of big cities. These cities are their 'natural habitat'. In this section we will focus on global financial centres but we should bear in mind that such centres are also the primary locations of the leading legal, accounting, consultancy, headhunting, advertising and other ABS. Indeed, they tend to form an ecology of ABS, in which each feeds upon the others.

The global network of financial centres

The network of global financial centres shown in Figure 12.9 has three major levels, with London and New York forming the top level. The widespread deregulation of

Figure 12.9   The global network of financial centres

Source: based on Reid, 1989: Figure 1; data in Taylor, 2004

financial services during the 1980s and 1990s had an especially significant impact on the structure of this network. Such developments

> made it possible for footloose financial firms to set up directly in the world's leading metropolitan centres rather than serving them from a distance … International firms want to locate in these different metropolitan financial centres because each has a different financial specialization, and each is the hub of a different (although of course overlapping and inter-connected) continental global region. Foreign banks and related institutions have moved into these centres precisely because of geography, that is to expand their presence or gain access to specific markets, to capitalize on the economies of specialization, agglomeration and localization (skilled labour, expertise, contact, business networks, etc.) available in these centres, or to specialize their own operations and activities geographically.[37]

The locational attractions of international financial centres consist of four interlocking processes:[38]

- The characteristics of the *business organizations* involved in international financial centres: (a) much of the production of financial products and services occurs at the boundaries of firms and there is a strong reliance on repeat business; (b) the firms tend to be 'flattened and non-hierarchical' and based around 'small teams of relationship and product specialists'; (c) firms need to cooperate as well as to compete, as in the case of syndicated lending; (d) firms need to compare themselves with one another to judge their performance; (e) there is a need for a constant search for new business and for rapid response.

These shared characteristics point to two important correlates. First, in general, these firms must be sociable. Contacts are crucially important in generating and maintaining a flow of business and information about business. 'Who you know' is, in this sense, part of what you know … 'relationship management' is a vital task for both employees and firms. Second, this hunger for contacts is easier to satisfy if contacts are concentrated, are proximate. When contacts are bunched together they are easier to gain access to, and swift access at that.[39]

- The *diversity of markets* in international financial centres: (a) their large size which makes them both flexible in terms of entry and exit and also socially differentiated: 'more likely to consist of social "micro-networks" of buyers and sellers, whose effect on price-setting can sometimes be marked'; (b) their basis in rapid dissemination of information which may lead to major market movements; (c) their speculative and highly volatile nature'. Again, as with the case of organizations, there are the two obvious corollaries to these characteristics: the twin needs for sociability and proximity.'[40]
- The *culture* of international financial centres: (a) such centres receive, send and interpret increasing amounts of information; (b) they are the focus of increasing amounts of expertise which arise from a complex division of labour involving workforce skills and machinery; (c) they depend on contacts and such contacts have become increasingly reflexive because of their basis in trust founded on relationships. Such cultural aspects of international financial centres are actually increasing in importance.
- The *dynamic external economies of scale* which arise from the sheer size and concentration of financial and related services firms in such centres. Such economies include: (a) the sharing of the fixed costs of operating financial markets (for example, settlement systems, document transport systems) between a large number of firms; (b) the attraction of greater information turnover and liquidity; (c) the enhanced probability of product innovations in such clusters (the 'sparking of mind against mind'); (d) the increased probability of making contacts which rises with the number of possible contacts; (e) the attraction of linked services such as accounting, legal and computer services, which reduces the cost to the firm of acquiring such services; (f) the development of a pool of skilled labour; (g) the enhanced reputation of a centre which, in a cumulative way, increases that reputation and attracts new firms. In other words, the constellation of traded and untraded interdependencies, described in Chapter 3, tend to be especially strongly developed in international financial centres.

In effect, therefore, a small number of cities controls almost all the world's financial transactions. It is a remarkable level of geographical concentration. But such cities are more than just financial centres. There is clearly a close relationship with the distribution of the corporate and regional headquarters of transnational corporations (see Chapter 5). These global cities are, indeed, the geographical *control points of the global economic system*. They are what Cassis calls 'the capitals of capital'.[41]

But this does not mean that all global financial centres – even those at the top of the hierarchy – are identical. Far from it. Each has distinctive characteristics reflecting its specific history and geography. On criteria measuring both the breadth and depth of global financial activity, New York and London stand at the apex of the global financial hierarchy. London is the more broadly based international financial centre, particularly in terms of its strengths in foreign exchange, international equities and derivatives. The daily turnover on the London foreign exchange market is almost as large as the turnover in New York and Tokyo put together.

London's significance as a global financial centre can be attributed to the following factors:[42]

- The historical evolution of the City as a world centre has created both a large pool of relevant skills and also an almost unparalleled concentration of linked institutions within a very small geographical area.
- Its geographical position locates it in a time zone between Asia and New York.
- The regulatory environment has encouraged the growth of transnational banking. Foreign banks in London can operate as 'universal' banks.
- It has a key role as a 'capital switching centre': 'the London market brings together in one place great diversity of market participants and, consequently, great diversity of risk preferences and profiles'.[43]

London has the largest concentration of foreign banks in the world, with more than 470 foreign branches, subsidiaries or representative offices located there in 2001. In comparison, Paris had 214 and Frankfurt 320. In 2001,

> London had 20 per cent of all cross-border bank lending worldwide, 52 per cent of foreign equity trading, and 31 per cent of all foreign exchange dealing: as much as its three closest rivals (New York, Tokyo, and Singapore) put together.[44]

London's strength as a financial centre, therefore, rests on the scale of its foreign exchange business and its deregulated securities markets. New York, in comparison, is the world's largest securities market in addition to having a huge concentration of transnational banks and other financial activities. London and New York stand apart from Tokyo as truly global financial centres. The international significance of Tokyo has rested primarily on the strength of the Japanese economy itself. Tokyo's financial community has been far more domestically oriented although, as we have seen, Japanese banks have regained some of their international strength. London also maintains its lead over such key European cities as Frankfurt and Paris, even though both of these cities have strengthened their financial centres. In addition, London has made strong efforts to become a global centre of Islamic finance.

Although this global financial network has certain stable features, it is by no means static. Financial centres may change their status in the network in response to changing conditions; new centres may emerge. But these are long-term processes.

It takes a long time for real change to become apparent, which is why it is impossible to predict, with any certainty, the effect of the 2008 crisis on London's or New York's standing. On the one hand, there are anecdotal stories of financial firms planning to move out of London because of the fear of increased regulation or higher taxation. On the other hand, a 2009 Global Financial Centres Index report[45] showed London improving its standing among the world's leading financial centres (as did New York). But especially interesting was the increasing status of East Asian financial centres, particularly Singapore, Hong Kong and Shanghai. The two latter cities are locked in competition as the leading financial centres of China.[46]

Geographical decentralization and offshoring of business services

All of the discussion of global financial centres suggests that the potential for other cities, outside the favoured few shown in Figure 12.9, to develop as significant centres of finance and related activities is very limited. In the UK, for example, the sheer overwhelming dominance of London makes it extremely difficult for provincial cities to develop more than a very restricted financial and ABS function.

It is, of course, the 'higher-order' financial and ABS functions which are especially heavily concentrated in the major global financial centres. However, as we have seen, the essence of ABS activities is the transformation of massive volumes of *information*. Much of that activity is routine data processing performed by clerical workers. Such 'back-office' activity can be separated from the front-office functions and performed in different locations. The early adoption of large-scale computing by banks, insurance companies and the like from the late 1950s initially led many of them to set up huge *centralized* data processing units. To escape the high costs (of both land and labour) in the major financial centres, such units were often relocated to less expensive centres or in the suburbs. Access to large pools of appropriate (often female) labour was a key requirement.

The introduction of dispersed computer networks made such centralized processing units unnecessary and the trend changed to *decentralize* back-office functions more widely. At the same time, the distinction between back-office and front-office functions became less clear. In fact, it is not only routine back-office activities that have been decentralized. It has become increasingly common for some of the higher-skilled functions to be relocated away from head office into dispersed locations, both nationally and, in some case, transnationally. However, centralization of back-office functions is by no means obsolete. For example, Citicorp gathered all its back offices from around the world and recentralized them in large and more efficient centres to achieve economies of scale. Even in the case of back offices, therefore, geographical centralization is far from dead.

Beyond the continued tendency to retain their major presence in key centres, the major ABS firms have become increasingly involved in *offshoring* some of their

	Vendor direct	Captive direct	Vendor indirect
	Place contract with specialist firm in specific country	Set up own directly-owned operation(s) overseas	Place contract with specialist firm with operations in several countries
Potential benefits	Cost reduction Use of specialist expertise Speed	Increased control Reduced risk Greater security	Lower costs Use of specialist expertise Vendor reputation
Potential costs	Loss of control Security risks	High cost of establishment and control	Control issues Security risks

Figure 12.10   Alternative modes of offshoring

Source: based in part on material in the *Financial Times*, 18 February 2004

functions. (Note that the term 'offshoring' in this context does not have the same meaning as the 'offshore financial centres' discussed in the next section.)

> In 2006, over 75 per cent of major financial institutions had offshore activities, compared with less than 10 per cent in 2001 ... The main activities offshored are those involving the use of IT, lower value-added activities (such as payroll) and lower value-added contact with customers (such as scripted outbound sales calls). But offshoring has spread across nearly all business functions, with significant growth in transaction processing, finance and various aspects of human resources activity. Even activities requiring specific skills, such as financial research and modelling, have the potential to be ultimately offshored as well.[47]

As the extent of offshoring has increased, its particular organizational form has become more varied, as Figure 12.10 shows. Initially, most offshoring by financial services firms was *vendor direct outsourcing* to a foreign firm located overseas. As major financial services firms became increasingly involved in offshoring they began to establish systems of *captive direct offshoring*: setting up their own subsidiary operations in other countries. The third and most recent arrangement, *vendor indirect offshoring*, reflects the tendency for specialist outsourcing companies to establish their own transnational networks to serve more diverse customers. So, for example, one of the leading Indian IT outsourcing companies, Tata Consultancy Services (TCS), has recently established its own operations in Hungary as part of its increasingly global network.

> TCS first opened a software centre in Hungary in 2001 ... it is now building a *global delivery network* so that projects can be completed closer to the customer where necessary ... TCS chose Hungary because, as well as English, many Hungarians can speak other European languages, including German, French, and Italian. 'We want to provide a European front and [point of contact] for our European customers' ... TCS preferred eastern Europe over western Europe because it was much cheaper ... Eastern Europe is where India was a decade ago.[48]

However, India itself remains by far the most popular offshoring location with around two-thirds of global offshored staff employed in the sub-continent. A number of other countries have also attracted offshoring activity. These include South Africa, Malaysia and the Philippines, where financial institutions can find the necessary skill and work quality. These countries have large pools of young, educated, technologically competent and English-speaking workers. There are a large number of graduates with finance, accounting or management and information technology backgrounds, who are ideally suited to offshore work in the financial sector.[49]

Offshore financial centres

Scattered across the globe, a series of little places – islands and micro-states – have been transformed by exploiting niches in the circuits of fictitious capital. These places have set themselves up as offshore financial centres; as places where the circuits of fictitious capital meet the circuits of 'furtive money' in a murky concoction of risk and opportunity. Furtive money is 'hot' money that seeks to avoid regulatory attention and taxes.[50]

The speculative nature of financial transactions and the desire to evade regulatory systems have led to the development of a number of offshore financial centres (OFCs).[51] With few exceptions, the sole rationale for such centres is to operate outside the regulatory reach of national jurisdictions. They attract investors through their low tax levels and 'light' regulatory regimes.[52] For example, although more than 500 banks are 'located' in the Cayman Islands – with more than $500 billion in their accounts – only around 70 of these actually have a physical presence there. The vast majority are no more than 'a brass or plastic name plate in the lobby of another bank, as a folder in a filing cabinet or an entry in a computer system'.[53] Similarly, there are roughly 300,000 companies registered in the Virgin Islands, although 'only 9,000 of them show any signs of activity locally'.[54]

Figure 12.11 shows the geographical distribution of offshore financial centres. Each tends to fill a specific niche which it exploits in competition with other centres in the same geographical cluster and with similar niche centres elsewhere in the world. Much of their growth occurred in the 1970s, in places that were already operating as tax havens, to act as banks' 'booking centres' for their Eurocurrency transactions.

By operating offshore booking centres international banks could act free of reserve requirements and other regulations. Offshore branches could also be used as profit centres (from which profits may be repatriated at the most suitable moment for tax minimization) and as bases from which to serve the needs of multinational corporate clients.[55]

The location of these offshore centres, and especially their geographical clustering, is partly determined by time zones and the need for 24-hour financial trading.

There is now a concerted international drive to crack down on these offshore tax havens. Such action was initiated by the OECD but has been followed by

Figure 12.11 Offshore financial centres

Source: based on Roberts, 1994: Figure 5.1

specific actions by the US, UK and other European governments. These initiatives reflect the fact that huge tax losses are being incurred as firms and individuals hide their profits offshore. A notable breakthrough was the 'raid' on German accounts held in Liechtenstein. It is not only developed countries that are affected by off-shore tax havens. Oxfam estimated that developing countries are losing out on annual income of up to $124 billion because more than $6 trillion of developing country wealth is held in offshore accounts.[56]

NOTES

1 Martin (1999: 6, 11).
2 See Braithwaite and Drahos (2000) for a discussion of the history of money and its regulation.
3 Strange (1986: 1).
4 Pauly (2000: 120).
5 Dow (1999: 33).
6 French and Leyshon (2004).
7 *Financial Times* (18 March 2008).
8 *Financial Times* (16 March 1994).
9 O'Brien and Keith (2009: 245–6).
10 Warf and Purcell (2001: 227).
11 See Langdale (2000).
12 Kelly (1995: 229). See also Crotty (2009), Dore (2008), Mügge (2009), Tett (2009).
13 O'Brien and Keith (2009: 249).
14 O'Brien and Keith (2009: 249).
15 Kay (2009: 57).

16   Martin (1999: 8, 9).

17   *Financial Times* (22 April 2009).

18   *The Economist* (19 January 2008: 70, 71).

19   *Financial Times* (26 May 2000).

20   Jones (2005).

21   *Financial Times* (29 January 2010).

22   *Financial Times* (9 September 2009).

23   Scott-Quinn (1990: 281).

24   This section is based primarily on Faulconbridge (2008) and Jones (2007). See also Beaverstock (2004).

25   Jones (2007: 234, original emphasis).

26   Faulconbridge (2008: 502).

27   Faulconbridge (2008: 504).

28   Faulconbridge (2008: 504).

29   Faulconbridge (2008: 502).

30   Jones (2007: 233).

31   This section is based upon Faulconbridge et al. (2008; 2009).

32   Faulconbridge et al. (2008: 214).

33   Faulconbridge et al. (2008: 222).

34   Faulconbridge et al. (2008: 226–7, 230). Numbers in parentheses refer to pages in this work.

35   O'Brien (1992). See also O'Brien and Keith (2009).

36   There is a large literature on world cities, notably Sassen (2001), Taylor (2004). See also the Globalization and World Cities Research Network (GaWC) based at Loughborough University, UK: www.lboro.ac.uk/gawc.

37   Martin (1999: 19–20).

38   Thrift (1994). Quotations are from that work.

39   Thrift (1994: 333).

40   Thrift (1994: 334).

41   Cassis (2006).

42   Lewis and Davis (1987).

43   Clark (2002: 448).

44   *Financial Times* (8 February 2002).

45   *Financial Times* (22 September 2009).

46   Karreman and van der Knaap (2009).

47   WTO (2008: 114).

48   *Financial Times* (3 August 2005, emphasis added).

49   WTO (2008: 114).

50   Roberts (1994: 92).

51   See Hudson (2000), Palan (2003), Roberts (1994).

52   Eatwell and Taylor (2000: 189).

53   Roberts (1994: 92).

54   *Financial Times* (7 December 2001).

55   Roberts (1994: 99).

56   *The Guardian* (14 March 2009).

Thirteen

'MAKING THE CONNECTIONS, MOVING THE GOODS': LOGISTICS AND DISTRIBUTION SERVICES

Taking distribution for granted

Whereas there is a huge literature and a continuous, often frenzied, debate on the role of financial services in the processes of globalization, distribution rarely makes an appearance on the stage.[1] It remains hidden, mainly confined to the specialist fields of supply chain management and transportation. The logistics and distribution processes get taken for granted. It is more or less assumed that, as transportation and communication systems have allegedly shrunk geographical distance, the problems of getting products from points of production to points of consumption have been solved.

This is far from being the case. Indeed, the *circulation processes* that *connect* together all the different components of the production network are absolutely fundamental. The logistics industries themselves are huge, worth around $4 billion per year. They have become especially significant in the light of the broader forces of change discussed in earlier chapters, notably:

- new production methods, involving increased flexibility
- changing relationships between customers and suppliers
- increasing use of just-in-time procurement and delivery systems
- increasing geographical complexity and extent of production networks
- changing consumer preferences.

In particular, *time* has come to be seen as the essential basis of successful competition.[2] In such a context, the nature and efficiency of distribution systems become central.

> Time- and quality-based competition depends on eliminating waste in the form of time, effort, defective units, and inventory in manufacturing-distribution systems … [requiring] firms to practice such logistical strategies as just-in-time management, lean logistics, vendor-managed inventory, direct delivery, and outsourcing of logistics services so that they become more flexible and fast, to better satisfy customer requirements.[3]

The structure of logistics and distribution services

The essential function of the logistics and distribution services is to *intermediate* between buyers and sellers at all stages of the production circuit (Figure 13.1). This involves not only the *physical movement* of materials and goods but also the transmission and manipulation of *information* relating to such movements. They involve, above all, the organization and coordination of complex flows across increasingly extended geographical distances. In that respect, these services have been revolutionized by the kinds of technological developments in transportation and communication discussed in Chapter 4. They have also been transformed by the increased outsourcing of logistics and distribution services by manufacturing firms, by the intensifying pressures from the big retailers, and by the emergence of new forms of logistics service providers.

Flows of materials and products
Flows of information (including customer orders)

Figure 13.1 Logistics and distribution in the production circuit

Source: based in part on Schary and Skjøtt-Larsen, 2001: Figure 1.6

In Figure 13.1 there are no political or other obstacles to complicate the basic system. In reality, of course, such phenomena greatly affect the structure and operation of logistics and distribution processes. Two kinds of 'barrier' to movement are especially significant:

- Physical conditions that necessitate the transfer from one transportation mode to another – for example, land/water interfaces.
- Political boundaries that create complications of customs clearance, tariffs, duties, administration and the like. Such barriers have become increasingly significant as economic activity has become more globalized.

Hence, as Figure 13.2 shows, there are many stages in the process of getting products to their final market.

> A typical door-to-door journey for containerised international shipments involves the interaction of approximately 25 different stakeholders, generates 30–40 documents, uses two to three different transport modes and is handled in 12–15 physical locations.[4]

However, the more extended the production circuit becomes – both organizationally and geographically – the greater the potential problems.

> Companies deciding to source in China rather than producing in-house may think they are adding a single link to their supply chain … In fact, they are probably adding at least five: the production agent in China, a logistics company in China, China customs, the freight shipper, customs and transport in the domestic market.[5]

Figure 13.2   Logistics processes in a transnational context

Source: adapted from Schary and Skjott-Larsen, 2001: Figure 11.7

The logistics and distribution processes shown in Figures 13.1 and 13.2 can be performed in a variety of ways and by a variety of organizational forms. At one extreme, each individual transaction may be performed by a separate firm; at the other extreme, the entire process may be carried out by a single integrated firm or related group of firms. The major types of organization involved in logistics and distribution include:

- transportation companies
- logistics service providers
- wholesalers
- trading companies
- retailers
- e-tailers.

Transportation companies (rail, road, shipping, airlines), wholesalers and retailers perform fairly clearly defined and restricted roles in the production circuit. On the other hand, trading companies and the more recent logistics service providers perform a far broader range of activities. Of course, the categories are not clear-cut. Not only are the boundaries between them often blurred but also one form of organization may mutate into another, as in the case of some transportation and trading companies that have evolved into more comprehensive logistics service providers (see later in this chapter). At the same time, the significance of some types of intermediary has changed.

   For example, traditionally the wholesaler played a major role in collecting materials or products from a range of individual producers and then distributing them to the next stage of the production process, or to the retailer in the case of final demand. However, the importance of the wholesaler as the key intermediary has changed substantially as the major retailers have bypassed the wholesaler to

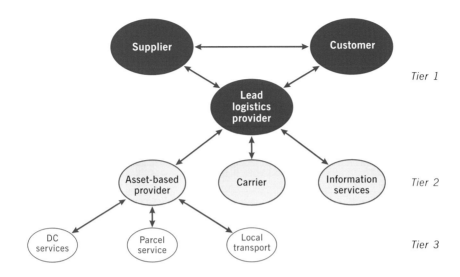

Figure 13.3   A potential way of organizing logistics services

Source: adapted from Schary and Skjøtt-Larsen, 2001: Figure 7.4

deal directly with the manufacturer, or as other forms of logistics and distribution services have developed. In a similar way, the development of e-commerce makes it possible to bypass the traditional retailer as the key intermediary between producer and final consumer and to create a new type of retailer: the *e-tailer*. Figure 13.3 shows just one possible way in which the production/supply circuit may be organized internationally, although great diversity remains.

The dynamics of the market for logistics services

In aggregate terms, the growth of the market for logistics and distribution services is closely related to growth in the economy as a whole. Hence, the 2008 economic recession had a huge impact, reducing demand for transportation and logistics services and putting on hold some major infrastructural projects in ports and other transportation and communications hubs and routes. But beyond this cyclical variation in demand, the market for logistics and distribution services is highly heterogeneous and we would not expect all parts to grow at similar rates. Demand for certain kinds of distribution services has been growing more rapidly than others, driven by the different characteristics of individual services.

Ultimately, as Figure 13.1 shows, the system is driven by the demands of the final consumer, although this influence becomes increasingly indirect the further back up the production circuit we go. Although the primary driver of final consumer demand is the level of disposable income, consumption, as we have discussed at various points in this book, is an immensely complex socio-cultural process. The intensely competitive retail markets have major repercussions on the demand for distribution and logistics services further up the production circuit. As we saw in the case of the clothing and agro-food industries, the major retailers and buyers exert very heavy pressure on their suppliers to deliver more rapidly, more cheaply, and in greater variety. This in turn creates opportunities (and challenges) for the suppliers of logistics and distribution services to provide a faster and more integrated supply system between the different components of the production circuit.

The enhanced power of the major retailers greatly affects the logistics firms responsible for getting the products to the retail stores.

> A shifting power structure in the retail trade not only changes market shares but also the structure of the distribution network. The major international retail customers ask for customized logistics solutions across borders. Apart from negotiating frame orders with significant price advantages with suppliers, the most powerful retailers also require information sharing services, such as electronic data interchange, advance shipping notices via the Internet and track and trace capabilities. They typically prefer delivery to their own distribution centers where goods are consolidated with other products for delivery to their retail stores.[6]

Such demands intensify the search for new logistical systems, in terms of both their technology and their organization. In such a context, the role of electronic systems has become increasingly important. Hence, there is a link between the changing demand pressures on the suppliers of logistics and distribution services and changing technologies. Let's now look at these technologies.

Technological innovation and logistics and distribution services

Three criteria dominate the logistics and distribution services:

- speed
- flexibility
- reliability.

Technological innovations have transformed all three. At a general level, technological developments in transportation and communication have been immensely important in transforming the basic time–space infrastructure of the logistics and distribution industries. Likewise, these industries have also been revolutionized by the shift in process technologies from mass production to more flexible and customized production systems. The mass production systems of the late nineteenth century and first two-thirds of the twentieth century were facilitated by mass distribution systems, based on the rapidly developing rail, road and ocean shipping networks (see Chapter 4).

Such mass distribution systems depended heavily on the use of large warehouses to store components and products and from which deliveries were made to customers on an infrequent basis. This was an immensely expensive system in terms of the capital tied up in large inventories. It was also, very often, a source of waste in terms of faulty products that were not discovered until they were actually used. Together with a major shift towards lean, just–in–time, systems of production there has also been a parallel shift towards *lean systems of distribution*, whose purpose is to minimize the time and cost involved in moving products between suppliers and customers, including the holding of inventory.

Three key elements form the core of such lean distribution systems:[7]

- *Electronic data interchange (EDI).* This enables the rapid transmission of large quantities of data electronically (rather than using paper documents). Such data can encompass all aspects of the logistics and distribution system throughout the production circuit, including the retailer. Information on product specifications, purchase orders, invoices, status of the transaction, location of the shipments, delivery schedules and so on can be exchanged instantly. EDI requires a common software platform to enable data to be read by all participants in the chain. For example, P & G, the consumer products firm, and Wal-Mart have piloted a system in the US

  > using live store sales data … to schedule replenishment deliveries on a store-by-store basis … Rather than shipping the required volume to a distributions centre, where it is then broken up for each store, the shipments are instead tailored at the factory for the right store. When the goods arrive at the Wal-Mart distribution centre they are moved directly from P & G's truck to the appropriate Wal-Mart truck, with no time in storage. 'It is assembled for a store, and it is just flowing through the system' … [it is estimated] that the process will speed the progress from P & G's factory to Wal-Mart's store by about 10 days, with further inventory savings possible from the store back room to the shelf for Wal-Mart.[8]

- *Bar code systems and radio frequency identification technology.* Bar codes were first developed in the 1970s by grocery manufacturers and food chain stores to enable each item to be given a unique, electronically readable identity. They have now become ubiquitous throughout the production circuit. 'Bar codes permit organizations to handle effectively the kind of vast product differentiation that would have been prohibitively expensive in an earlier era. They also facilitate instantaneous information at the point of sale, with significant effects on inventory management and logistics.'[9] Now, radio frequency identification technology (RFID) is beginning to be applied to increase the sophistication and flexibility of the bar code principle. Bar codes can be difficult to read (they require a clear line of sight). RFID gets around this by using small radio tags that allow goods to be instantaneously tracked throughout their journey through a production circuit. By combining the tag with a unique electronic product code (EPC) it becomes possible to incorporate a large quantity of information about each object. One observer (admittedly with a vested interest in RFID) described it as 'a bar code on steroids'.[10]

- *Distribution centres.* Modern distribution centres hold inventory for much shorter periods of time and turn it over very frequently. 'Four technologies have made the modern distribution centre possible: (1) bar codes and associated software systems; (2) high-speed conveyors with advanced routing and switching controls; (3) increased reliability and accuracy of laser scanning of incoming containers; and (4) increased computing capacities.'[11] In the most advanced distribution centres – such as the system used by the US retailer Wal-Mart – a method known as 'cross-docking' is used. This is a 'largely invisible logistics technique … [in which] goods are continuously delivered to Wal-Mart's warehouses, where they are selected, repacked, and then dispatched to stores, often without ever sitting in inventory. Instead of spending valuable time in the warehouse, goods just cross from one loading dock to another in 48 hours or less. Cross-docking enables Wal-Mart to achieve economies that come with purchasing full truckloads of goods while avoiding the usual inventory and handling costs. Wal-Mart runs a full 85% of goods through its warehouse system – as opposed to only 50% for Kmart.'[12] Of course, few firms can afford the scale of investment required to implement such a sophisticated system.

E-commerce: a logistics revolution

Computer-based electronic information systems are at the heart of all three of these technological developments in logistics and distribution systems. They have evolved over a period of 30 years, often incrementally rather than as a spectacular 'revolution'. However, the later 1990s brought into existence a new set of distribution methods based upon the Internet: *e-commerce*. In essence, e-commerce has developed out of the convergence of several technological strands: electronic data interchange, the Internet, e-mail, and the medium of the World Wide Web (WWW).[13] Few developments in recent years have been so heavily hyped as the e-commerce revolution. In fact, after a stuttering start, it has developed with incredible speed, with huge implications for logistics and distribution systems. It has, indeed, changed the world of distribution and the main reason, once again, is *speed*.

Figure 13.4 Types of e-commerce

Source: based in part on Gereffi, 2001: Figure 2

Although four types of e-commerce are shown in Figure 13.4, two dominate: B2B and B2C.

- *B2B (business-to-business)*. This encompasses potentially the whole range of transactions between businesses, notably procurement of products and services and logistics. B2B websites are electronic 'marketplaces' where firms come together to buy or sell products and services. They may be 'vertical', that is industry specific (for example, the B2B procurement system Covisint established in 2000 by GM and Ford, together with some other automobile manufacturers, to increase the efficiency of component purchasing), or they may be 'horizontal', organized around the products and services provided rather than the industry. Connecting together large numbers of buyers and sellers through electronically automated transactions has a number of potential benefits, notably vastly increasing choice to both sellers and buyers, saving costs on transactions, and increasing the transparency of the entire supply chain.
- *B2C (business-to-consumer)*. B2C business is simply the selling of consumer products and services directly over the Internet by a web-based firm. The pioneers included Amazon, eBay and Dell but, of course, the dotcom revolution created millions of 'etailers', some with a very brief life. E-tailing has also been adopted by the traditional retailers. Indeed, contrary to predictions that traditional retailers would be adversely affected by Internet shopping, the opposite has occurred, especially with the development of comparison sites which allow customers to compare products and prices and read reviews. As in the case of B2B, the potential benefits of B2C transactions are, to the consumer, greater choice, ease of comparison of prices, and instant (or very fast) delivery to the

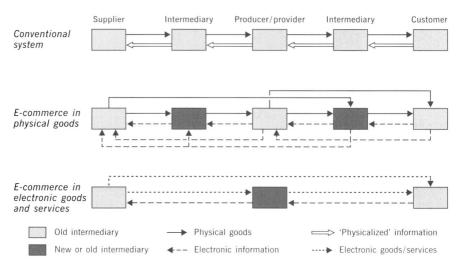

**Figure 13.5   The continuing role of intermediaries in an e-commerce
world**

Source: based on Kenney and Curry, 2001: Figure 3.2

home; and, to the seller, direct access to a massive potential market without the
need for physical space in the form of retail outlets and the associated inventory
and staffing costs. As a result, online shopping has grown extremely rapidly.

E-commerce (both B2B and B2C) has enormous potential implications for the
traditional intermediaries of business and retail transactions (for example,
wholesalers, shippers, travel agents and the like). The early predictions were that
many would disappear as their functions were displaced by direct online transactions. In fact, this has not happened to the extent predicted. On the contrary,
e-commerce has actually enhanced opportunities for such roles and created
entirely new Internet-based service companies. Some traditional intermediaries
have adapted and found new ways of adding value as providers of logistics,
information and financial services; new intermediaries have emerged.[14] Some of
these are what are sometimes termed *infomediaries*, notably the Internet service
and content providers shown in Figure 13.4. To some extent, these new infomediaries are increasing their relative bargaining power *vis-à-vis* producers and buyers. More generally, Figure 13.5 shows that in the case of both physical goods and
electronic goods and services, either old intermediaries transform themselves or
new ones appear.

Related to the perception that e-commerce spells the end for the traditional
intermediary organization is the idea that the traditional physical infrastructures
will also be displaced by the new technological forms. Again, this is an illusion.
As Figure 13.6 shows, there are several ways of fulfilling e-commerce orders.[15]
Inherent in each of these is the question of physical space which, paradoxically,

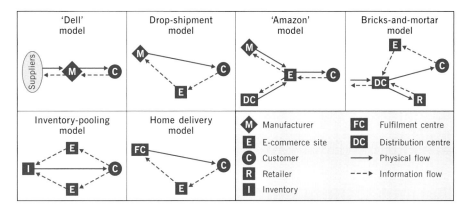

Figure 13.6   Methods of fulfilling e-commerce orders

Source: based in part on Schary and Skjott-Larsen, 2001: Figure 4.5

becomes more, not less, important. In addition to warehousing space the Internet-based system also requires another kind of dedicated physical space: the so-called *web 'hotels'* described in Chapter 4.

- *'Dell' model*: the supplier receives orders for specific products, which are then integrated directly into production. 'The customer order activates the supply chain. Customers can "design" their products from a list of options to be incorporated into a production schedule. The order then initiates a flow of component parts from suppliers to be assembled into a final product, turned over to a logistics service provider, merged with a monitor from another source and delivered to a final customer. The system avoids holding finished product inventory, providing both lower cost and more product variety.'[16]
- *Drop-shipment model*: the e-commerce firm receives an order and passes the order on to a manufacturer for production and delivery direct to the customer from the manufacturer.
- *'Amazon' model*: this is the electronic version of an old mode of direct retailing where a 'catalogue' of products is held electronically and accessed via the Internet. Customer orders are either fulfilled by the seller from its own distribution centre or 'drop-shipped' direct from the manufacturer.
- *Bricks-and-mortar model*: combines both conventional retail stores, fed by distribution centres, with an Internet website that channels orders to the same distribution centres. A problem with this system is that whereas retail orders generally require large orders, individual Internet-based orders require individual units.
- *Inventory pooling model*: enables customers in a specific industry to acquire common components from an inventory pool controlled by a web-based provider.
- *Home delivery model:* customers requiring regular deliveries of, say, groceries can place their order with a web-based service which will deliver on a routine basis to the customer's home address.

Thus, a whole variety of technological developments has helped to transform the nature and operations of the logistics and distribution industries. Initially, in the early twentieth century, they were the technologies that enabled mass distribution systems to facilitate the output of the mass production systems of the day. By the last two decades of the twentieth century, the technologies had become predominantly electronic. Such technologies facilitate the operations of more flexible production systems through their ability to transmit and process vast quantities of information on all aspects of the supply circuit.

The role of the state: regulation and deregulation of logistics and distribution services

There is a significant obstacle to the smooth, seamless operation of the kinds of logistics and distribution systems made possible by these technological innovations: state *regulatory* regimes. By definition, transnational production and distribution involve crossing political boundaries. All national governments regulate, in various ways, the cross-border movement of goods and services. We have discussed one aspect of this in Chapter 6 and in the other case study chapters: the variety of trade measures (both tariff and non-tariff barriers) that states use. The existence of such regulations, for example customs requirements and procedures, creates a major discontinuity in the geographical surface over which distribution services operate (see Figure 13.2).

In this section, we are concerned with the regulatory structures affecting the basic functions of the logistics and distribution services themselves, especially transportation and communication systems. Such regulations are devised and implemented at various political–geographical scales: international, regional and national. They are also in a continuous state of flux. In the past three decades, in particular, there have been major waves of deregulation.

Regulation and deregulation of transportation and communications systems

Regulation of transportation and of communications has a very long history.[17] It has involved a varying mix of national and international level systems in the public sphere, as well as private organizations in the form of the operators themselves. Much of the regulatory system in air and sea transportation relates to issues of safety and security, whilst in communications a key issue is harmonization of standards to enable communications originating in one place to be received and understood in other places. Such international bodies as the IMO (International

Maritime Organization), the ICAO (International Civil Aviation Organization) and the ITU (International Telecommunication Union) constitute the primary elements of such an international regulatory framework.

Within such an international framework, individual national states have also regulated telecommunications and air transportation. They are both sectors in which states believe (or have believed until recently) that 'natural monopolies' exist. For example,

> telecommunications' regulation contains one of the earliest examples of international regulatory cooperation between states, with the creation of the International Telegraphic Union (ITgU) in 1865. But in other respects the regulation of telecommunications is a story of territorial containment. Much of the early regulatory development in the first half of the twentieth century was influenced by the economic view that telecommunications is a 'natural monopoly'. But no state thinks that there should be one world monopolist. Instead, the contours of this natural monopoly correspond with state boundaries.[18]

In most cases this involved state ownership, although in the US it was a private monopoly, AT&T.

Similarly in the air transportation industry,

> just as almost every nation has its telecommunications carrier (and rarely more than one), almost every nation has a flagship airline (and rarely more than one). The state controls landing rights (just as it tends to control the telecommunications infrastructure) and rations those rights, usually in ways that favour the national flag-carrier.[19]

In both cases, the operation of the regulatory framework has involved a tension between

- the desire on the part of most states for control over their own national spaces
- the drive (primarily by business organizations) for the least possible regulation consistent with safety and efficiency.

As globalizing processes have intensified, however, the balance has shifted decisively towards greater deregulation of the nationally based systems and the privatization of state-owned companies. In the case of telecommunications, the initial impetus came in the US, with the enforced break-up of the AT&T monopoly in the early 1980s, when the company was obliged to divest itself of its local Bell Telephone operating companies. The US example stimulated a wave of European deregulation in telecommunications during the 1980s, led by the UK's Thatcher government.

The air transportation industry has experienced a similar wave of deregulation. Again, the early moves began in the US. In the late 1970s, a bilateral agreement was signed between the US and the UK, which helped to undermine the cartelization of the airline industry within IATA. In 1978, the US domestic airline industry was deregulated. Subsequently,

> both the US and the UK then set about reshaping their bilateral agreements towards more liberal policies. For example, France has been the most vigorous opponent of liberalization, so the US worked at isolating France by negotiating open-skies agreements with Belgium and other countries around France ... In short, the process in the 1990s is US-led liberalization that is seeing the world become gradually and chaotically more competitive. The process is chaotic because even the most liberal states, such as the US and UK ... are 'liberal mercantilists' ... Another chaotic element is that many European, African, and South American states support liberalization within their continents but want protection from competition outside the continent (especially from the US).[20]

The continuing tensions between states in terms of their own air spaces (and often their 'national' airlines) have important implications for logistics and distribution services. Two examples illustrate this. First, the continuing disagreement between the US and the UK over mutual access over the North Atlantic route means that, on the one hand, US airlines have restricted access to London Heathrow whilst, on the other, British airlines are not allowed to fly routes onwards within the US beyond their initial point of entry. This also means that the US company FedEx cannot operate a fully fledged operation from its UK base at Stansted; it is allowed to fly from the US to Stansted but only to a small number of destinations from there. Instead, it has to charter planes to fly from Britain to Paris to connect with its European hub.[21]

A second example is the recently resolved dispute between the US and Hong Kong, which was especially important for the large express couriers (FedEx, DHL and UPS). FedEx was allowed only five flights a week from Hong Kong to destinations outside the US. This was because Hong Kong wanted its airline, Cathay Pacific, to be able to fly within, as well as to, the US – which the US refused to allow. The agreement signed in 2002 increased the daily flights for all-cargo carriers from eight to 64, phased in over three years, although Cathay Pacific insisted that the agreement over-benefited US carriers.[22]

Some of the biggest changes in the regulatory environment have resulted from the emergence of regional economic blocs, such as the EU and the NAFTA. The completion of the Single European Market in 1992 removed virtually all obstacles to internal movement of goods and services within the EU. Liberalization of trucking within and between the US, Canada and Mexico was also a part of the NAFTA. Under this agreement, the US and Mexican border states were to be opened to international trucking by the end of 1995. By January 1997, Mexican trucking companies would be allowed to operate as domestic carriers in the border states and for international cargo in the rest of the US and, by January 2000, they would be able to file to operate in the entire US. In fact this did not happen. Not until 2004 did the US Supreme Court overthrow the opposition of the House of

Representatives to Mexican and US truckers operating in each other's domestic markets. In fact, it still hasn't happened. In 2009, Mexico retaliated with tariffs against US products because of the continued failure to implement the NAFTA agreement. The Obama administration promised to work out a new agreement.

Regulating transportation and communication systems is not easy, given the number of conflicting interests involved. But it is far easier than regulating the Internet. As a medium that 'knows no boundaries' and that is allegedly (although, as we have seen, not actually) 'placeless' it involves some intractable issues as to who regulates it. The answer is far from clear, not least because of the very newness of the Internet and e-commerce and their phenomenally rapid growth. The key issue is 'whose laws apply?' when e-commerce transactions transcend different national jurisdictions.

Regulation of transnational retailing

Retail markets tend to be a sensitive national and local issue. Many countries have protected their domestic retail sector either by keeping out or by constraining the entry and operations of foreign retailers. Restrictions on ownership (for example, by insisting on local partners or minority foreign ownership) have been very common and continue to exist, especially in emerging economies where there is a great fear of the domestic retailing sector (primarily a small-firm sector) being swamped by foreign incursion. Despite the considerable relaxation of such restrictions on foreign retailers, the sector remains one in which regulatory considerations are important.

The rules of operation in national retail markets continue to be very diverse. This is the case even within the EU where, despite the Single Market, considerable differences still exist in the regulatory structures of individual member states. 'Each country continues to make and enforce its own rules about hours of operation, the building of large-scale retail stores, the doing of part-time and overtime work, and Sunday trading practices'.[23] In the case of store opening hours, for example, the UK is the most liberalized EU state, whereas in Germany, Austria and most parts of Italy, most stores are closed on Sundays. This is changing, especially in the big cities, but not rapidly. The US has probably the most lenient regulatory system towards retailing whereas Japan has been very restrictive, although it has begun to liberalize.

Corporate strategies in logistics and distribution services

Logistics and distribution services cover an immensely wide range of activities and consist of a mix of traditional shipping and carriage of goods through to the highly complex and sophisticated *logistics service providers* (LSPs), from trading companies to large transnational retail chains. In this section we outline the major trends in corporate strategies as firms respond to market, technological and regulatory forces. Although there are many niche areas within the distribution sector there is a broad tendency in most activities for the size of firms to be increasing and for higher degrees of concentration in a smaller number of large firms. Growth through merger and acquisition, and through network alliances, has been especially prominent in this sector as firms strive to provide *global* logistics services. This has meant that the names and identities of many firms are continuously changing. Table 13.1 lists the world's 10 largest logistics firms.

Table 13.1   Leading global logistics firms (ranked by revenue)

Company	Country	Revenue 2007 ($m)	Employment	Number of offices	Number of countries
DHL International	Germany	30,015	300,000	18,000	>220
Kuehne & Nagel	Switzerland	14,919	>55,000	–	100
Schenker/BAX	Germany	14,000	59,000	1,500	–
UPS Supply Chain Solutions	US	7,706	–	–	175
Panalpina	Switzerland	7,200	>15,000	–	90
C H Robinson Worldwide	US	6,556	>7,500	230	–
Geodis	France	5,016	26,465	–	120
Agility	US	4,900	>37,000	–	120
Expeditors International	US	4,626	–	258	–
CEVA Logistics	US	4,600	54,000	–	>150

Source: based on company and press reports

Global logistics: from transportation companies to integrated logistics service providers

As customer demands have become more complex (and more global), the providers of logistics and distribution services have responded in a number of ways.[24] Some have diversified into complete 'one-stop shops'; others have remained more narrowly focused on providing a limited range of functions. In both cases, the trend has been towards greater consolidation and concentration through acquisition and merger. Some examples illustrate the trend.

In the shipping sector, Maersk acquired Nedlloyd in 2005 to become the largest container operator in the world. In the logistics field, acquisitions and mergers have accelerated since 2000, when Exel was formed from a merger of a shipping company, Ocean, and a contract logistics supplier, NFC. In 2004,

Figure 13.7 Types of logistics service providers

Source: based in part on Schary and Skjott-Larsen, 2001: Figure 7.3

Exel purchased the second largest UK logistics company, Tibbett and Britton, to become the sector leader with 111,000 employees in more than 135 countries. In turn, in 2005, Deutsche Post World Net (owner of DHL, which it had acquired in 2003) acquired Exel. This created by far the world's largest logistics service company, providing air freight, ocean freight and contract logistics services. The new group, DHL International, employs around 300,000 people worldwide.

As a result of such developments, together with the movement of other service companies into logistics provision, we can identify four major types of logistics service firm, classified according to the kinds of physical and management services provided (Figure 13.7). The simplest functions are provided by the *traditional transportation and forwarding companies*. The *asset-based logistics providers* first emerged during the 1980s, developing primarily from the diversification of some traditional transportation companies into more complex logistics service providers. Several of the world's leading container shipping companies, such as Maersk–Sealand and Nedlloyd/P&O, moved in this direction. For example, in 1992 Nedlloyd took on responsibility for all of IBM's distribution activities as part of its strategy to become a worldwide logistics provider.

During the early 1990s, a number of *network-based logistics providers* appeared on the international scene, notably DHL, FedEx, UPS and TNT.

These third-party logistics providers started as couriers and express parcel companies and built up global transportation and communication networks to be able to expedite express shipments fast and reliably. Supplemental information services typically include electronic proof-of-delivery and track-and-trace options from sender to receiver ... Recently, these players have moved into the time-sensitive and high-value-density third-party logistics market, such as electronics, spare parts, fashion goods and pharmaceuticals, and are competing with the traditional asset-based logistics providers in these high margin markets.[25]

The nature of these services necessitates creating geographically extensive, and tightly integrated, networks of operations. All the leading firms, therefore, have a global presence; Figure 13.8 shows just one such network, DHL. Each of these companies operates on the basis of global hub-and-spoke transportation networks, owned either by themselves or with partners.

   The fourth type of logistics service firm shown in Figure 13.7 – the *skill-based logistics providers* – became increasingly significant in the later 1990s. These are firms that do not own any major physical logistics assets but provide a range of primarily information-based logistics services. These encompass consultancy services (including supply chain configuration), financial services, information technology services, and a range of management expertise. Examples of such skill-based logistics service providers include GeoLogistics, a firm created in 1996 through the merger of three existing logistics companies (Bekins, LEP, Matrix) and recently rebranded as Agility, now the eighth largest logistics company in the world (Table 13.1).

Figure 13.8   DHL's global network

Source: DHL

Global trading companies

Trading companies have a history going back many hundreds of years. From the earliest days of long-distance trade they played an especially important role in facilitating trade in materials and products. Here we look at two important contemporary examples, both taken from East Asia.

The first example is the Japanese *sogo shosha*. The common translation of the term *sogo shosha* is 'general trading company'; but they are very much more than this, having been central to the development of the Japanese economy since the late nineteenth century.[26] The six leading *sogo shosha* – Mitsubishi, Mitsui, Itochu, Marubeni, Sumitomo and Nissho-Iwai – are gargantuan commercial, financial and industrial conglomerates. They operate a massive network of subsidiaries and thousands of related companies across the globe (Figure 13.9) and handle tens of thousands of different products. In the early 1990s, they were responsible for roughly 70 per cent of total Japanese imports and for 40 per cent of Japanese exports. This is the true Japanese general trading oligopoly, each member of which has a major coordinating role within one of the Japanese *keiretsu* (see Figure 5.7).

Historically, the *sogo shosha* developed to organize exchange and distribution within the Japanese domestic market. Subsequently, they became the first Japanese companies to invest on a large scale outside Japan. These foreign investments were primarily designed to organize the flow of imports of much-needed primary materials for the resource-poor Japanese economy and to channel Japanese

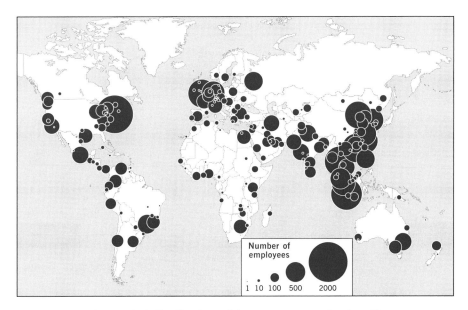

Figure 13.9   The global distribution of Japanese *sogo shosha* **offices**

Source: company reports

exports of manufactures to overseas markets. It was the particular demands of these Japanese-focused trading activities that necessitated the development of the globally extensive networks of *sogo shosha* offices around the world. In other words, they were to set up a global marketing and economic intelligence network. Once in place, this network, with all its supporting facilities, not only facilitated the growth of Japanese trade but also enabled a whole range of Japanese firms to venture overseas. Indeed, a good deal of the early overseas investment by Japanese manufacturing firms was organized by the *sogo shosha*.

They perform four specific functions:

- *trading and transactional intermediation*: matching buyers and sellers in a long-term contractual relationship
- *financial intermediation*: serving as a risk buffer between suppliers and purchasers
- *information gathering*: collecting and collating information on market conditions throughout the world
- *organization and coordination of complex business systems*: for example, major infrastructural projects.

As the position of the Japanese economy in the global system has changed, the role of the *sogo shosha* has also had to change. Figure 13.10 shows one example: the changing strategies of the Mitsubishi Corporation.

(a) Past business model

Major function: to act as intermediary in commercial transactions

(b) Present business model

Major function: to participate in entire value chain

Figure 13.10   Mitsubishi Corporation's strategic shift

Source: Mitsubishi Corporation

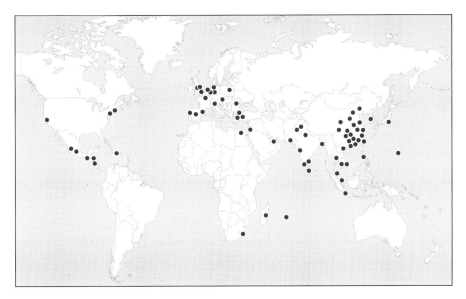

Figure 13.11   The global spread of the offices of Li & Fung

Source: Li & Fung

The second example of a trading company, also taken from East Asia, is the Hong Kong-based firm Li & Fung.[27] This firm is not only the biggest export trading company in Hong Kong but also – and more importantly – a highly innovative logistics company, with offices spread across 40 countries (see Figure 13.11), employing more than 14,000. Established in Canton in 1906, Li & Fung was originally a simple commodity broker, connecting together buyers and sellers for a fee. Today, although still a Chinese family firm, it has been transformed from the simple brokerage to an immensely sophisticated organizer of geographically dispersed manufacturing and distribution operations in a whole variety of consumer goods, but with a strong specialization in garments (see Chapter 10). Li & Fung controls and coordinates the entire process. In the company's own words:

> We act as extension of your own business to manage all aspects of your global supply chain … Dedicated teams of product specialists focus on each customer segment to professionally manage the entire supply chain – from product design and development, through raw material and factory sourcing, production planning and management, quality assurance and export documentation, to shipping control.[28]

These two examples show that traditional trading companies have carved out new roles for themselves, both responding to, and creating, new demands for distribution and logistics services.

Globalizing retailers

Retailing is the final link in the production circuit. As such, it is extremely sensitive to the specific characteristics of the consumer markets it serves. Such markets
continue to have a high degree of individuality, despite the apparent universalization
of some types of consumer preference. Consequently, retailing has always had – and
continues to have – a strong domestic orientation, although retailers invariably
source their products from a much broader spectrum of geographical locations. A
few retailers moved into foreign markets at a relatively early stage in their development. One of the best examples was the US company F. W. Woolworth, which
opened stores in Canada in 1897, in the UK in 1909, and in Germany in 1926.
Indeed, so familiar did Woolworths become in most big cities in the UK that few
of its customers realized it was a foreign firm. But this was an exceptional case. For
the most part, retailers were very reluctant entrants into foreign markets. Where they
did so, it was usually into geographically and/or culturally proximate locations.

But there has been a marked acceleration in the transnational activities of major
retailers in recent years.[29] Table 13.2 lists the world's leading transnational retailers
ranked by their international sales volume. The list includes the big food retailers

Table 13.2   The world's leading transnational retailers, 2008 (ranked by international
sales volume)

Company	Headquarters	International sales (US$m)	% of total sales	No. of countries
Wal-Mart	US	113,020	26	16
Carrefour	France	91,763	57	33
Metro	Germany	70,724	61	32
Ahold	Netherlands	49,440	76	9
Lidl & Schwartz	Germany	43,931	51	24
Auchan	France	38,924	53	11
Aldi	Germany	35,269	48	15
Tesco	UK	32,717	30	13
IKEA	Sweden	29,763	94	37
Rewe	Germany	25,955	33	14
Seven & I	Japan	25,490	30	4
Delhaize	Belgium	21,545	77	6
Costco	US	18,900	24	8
PPR	France	17,365	61	48
Tengelmann	Germany	13,036	47	15
Casino	France	9,287	23	11
Amazon	US	9,777	51	7
Kingfisher	UK	9,055	55	9
Best Buy	US	8,103	18	4
Home Depot	US	7,843	11	7

Source: data supplied by Neil Coe

discussed in Chapter 9 (see Figures 9.9 and 9.11). It is significant that only five of the top 20 transnational retailers are from the US; many very large US retailers remain entirely domestically oriented. Although the firms shown in Table 13.2 have extensive transnational operations, only three of them (Wal-Mart, Metro, Carrefour) figure in the world's top 100 non-financial TNCs and none of these are in the top 25.[30]

Figure 13.12 Two dimensions of transnational retailing

Transnational retailing has two main dimensions: selling products and sourcing products (Figure 13.12). Let's take each of these in turn.

Selling products in transnational markets involves either setting up a new store, merging with or acquiring an existing retailer in a target market, or setting up a joint venture with a local firm. The latter two modes have been by far the most prevalent. In some cases, this was because local regulations restricted direct entry (see above). The major retail chains have shown a particular propensity to invest heavily in the emerging markets of East and South Asia, Latin America and Eastern Europe.

The core of this dimension of the retail transnationalization process involves four major types of transfer into a new market:[31]

- *Transfer of the total culture and business model of the firm.* 'All aspects of the culture and business model of the retailer are transferred to the host retail economy when retailers decide that they are international firms with internationalization integrated into their strategy. Within Tesco, for example, this has become known as "Tesco in a Box"' (389).
- *Transfer of the capability to adapt to the market.* 'Retailing is a response to culture. An international retailer, in order to be successful, has to adapt to the consumer culture in the market … Adaptation involves not only the understanding of the difference between home and host country but also the differences in consumer culture within the host country … The absence of this capability either in the firm generally (Boots, Marks and Spencer) or in the transfers to

a particular country (Ahold in China, Carrefour in Japan and in the USA, IKEA's original entry to Japan, Wal-Mart in Germany) is one of the reasons for "failed" international retailing' (390).

- *Transfer of operational techniques of retailing.* 'The operations of an international retailer (the formula of the retailer) interact with and become part of the structure of the total retail system … A firm may use different entry and growth mechanisms with acquisitions, joint ventures, agents and merchandising agreements with consequential different types of transfer of operations in each case' (391).
- *Transfer of consumer values and expectations.* 'Retailers create consumption in addition to responding to consumer needs. In a foreign market international retailing often brings to a country new consumer values and expectations. These in turn change the ways that consumers behave … The retailer helps to create the consumer culture and in doing this delivers changes in lifestyle … In countries where consumption cultures have been weak for an extended period, for example in Central and Eastern Europe, and in cultures where there is rapid change in consumption culture, for example, East Asia, then the foreign retailer, with a clearly defined formula, generates a substantial impact on consumer values and expectations' (391, 392).

The second dimension of transnational retailing shown in Figure 13.12 is the sourcing of products. We referred to this process briefly in the case of food retailing and clothing in Chapters 9 and 10. But there has been a general trend across virtually all retail sectors for firms to increase the geographical extent of their sourcing systems as well as to extend their power and influence over their suppliers. As a result, retail supply and logistics networks have been transformed in the following ways:[32]

- *Centralization*: the establishment of centralized distribution centres, distribution systems and buying activities.
- *Upgrading of logistics systems*: adoption of sophisticated logistics technologies and management systems (see above), including electronic data exchange, vendor management inventory etc.
- *A shift from traditional to specialized/dedicated procurement agents*: switch away from use of wholesalers to specialized procurement agents, often involving contractual-type relationships with suppliers.
- *A shift towards preferred supplier systems*: the use of a smaller number of suppliers willing/able to meet the stringent standards of quality, price and speed and flexibility of delivery.
- *Increased use of quasi-formal and formal contracts*: to increase control and ensure on-time delivery.
- *Imposition of private standards*: adoption of private rather than public standards of quality and/or safety.

Logistics 'places': key geographical nodes on the global logistics map

These developments in the global logistics industries have a highly distinctive geography, which both helps to shape their activities and is also shaped by them. Amongst the thousands of seaports and airports across the world, a few key nodes have become increasingly important. They reflect three sets of forces:

- Their position in the twenty-first-century global economy, especially in the light of the global shifts in economic activities we have been discussing throughout this book.
- The strategies of states in investing in port, airport and IT facilities. An example is the highly focused investment strategies of the Singaporean government to create a 'globally integrated logistics hub':

> an integrated IT platform that manages the flow of trade-related information … will enable exchange of information between shippers, freight forwarders, carriers and financial institutions to facilitate the flow of goods within, through and out of Singapore … The government will invest up to S$50 million over five years to develop the platform.[33]

Other states are pursuing broadly similar strategies to develop their logistics capabilities.[34]
- The strategies of the major logistics firms in creating their own globally dispersed operations and choosing certain key places as their 'hubs'.

Figures 13.13 and 13.14 show two examples of these trends. The emergence of East Asia as the most dynamic economic region in the world is clearly reflected in Figure 13.13. No fewer than 14 of the 20 leading container ports are located in East Asia, eight of them in China (excluding Hong Kong). None of them was in the top 10 in 1995; now six of them are. Conversely, the leading European container ports – Rotterdam and Hamburg, as well as some US ports – have slipped down the rankings.

The global map of leading cargo airports (Figure 13.14) has some features in common with the container ports map. Certain key cities, notably Hong Kong, Singapore, Shanghai, Tokyo, Los Angeles, New York and Dubai, have developed as leading air cargo hubs as well as major container ports. They are, indeed, key geographical nodes on the global logistics map. But there are other leading cargo airports that are quite different. They are the strategic hubs of the leading specialist freight and logistics firms. The place of Memphis, Tennessee as the world's biggest cargo airport is entirely due to its role as FedEx's main hub. In similar vein, Louisville, Kentucky is the main hub of UPS. The importance of Anchorage airport in Alaska, likewise, is attributable to its role as a key hub for FedEx and

Figure 13.13   The leading world container hubs, 2009

Source: based on Baird Maritime data

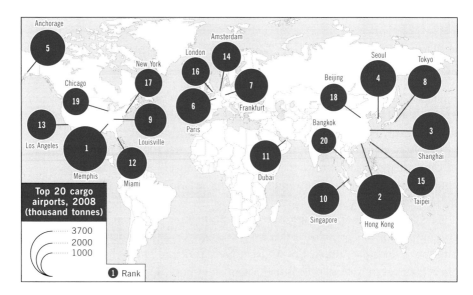

Figure 13.14   The leading world cargo airports, 2008

Source: based on Airports Council International data

UPS in their links with China. Leipzig, in Germany, is likely to join this group in the future: DHL opened its principal European hub there in 2008, replacing its former hub in Brussels.

NOTES

1   See Wrigley (2000: 292).
2   Schoenberger (2000).
3   Min and Keebler (2001: 265).
4   OECD (2004: 178).
5   *Financial Times* (25 August 2005).
6   Schary and Skjott-Larsen (2001: 129).
7   Abernathy et al. (1999: Chapter 4).
8   *Financial Times* (22 August 2008).
9   Abernathy et al (1999: 61).
10 Quoted in the *Financial Times* (20 April 2005).
11 Abernathy et al. (1999: 66).
12 Stalk et al. (1998: 58).
13 Leinbach (2001: 15).
14 US Department of Commerce (2000: 18).
15 Schary and Skjøtt-Larsen (2001: 132–6).
16 Schary and Skjøtt-Larsen (2001: 132). See also Fields (2004).
17 See Braithwaite and Drahos (2000).
18 Braithwaite and Drahos (2000: 322).
19 Braithwaite and Drahos (2000: 454).
20 Braithwaite and Drahos (2000: 456–7).
21 *The Sunday Times* (23 January 2005).
22 *Commercial Aviation Today* (21 October 2002).
23 Sternquist (1998: 151).
24 This section is based primarily on Schary and Skjott-Larsen (2001: 230–41).
25 Schary and Skjøtt-Larsen (2001: 231).
26 See Dicken and Miyamachi (1998).
27 See *The Economist* (2 June 2001), Schary and Skjott-Larsen (2001: 383–5).
28 www.lifung.com/eng/business/service_chain.php.
29 Coe and Wrigley (2009), Dawson (2007).
30 UNCTAD (2009: Annex Table A.I.9).
31 Dawson (2007: 388–92). Numbers in parentheses refer to pages in this work.
32 Coe and Wrigley (2009).
33 Singapore Economic Development Board, June 2004.
34 Wang and Cheng (2010) provide a detailed analysis of the transition of the port of Hong Kong from a hub port city to a 'global supply chain management centre'.

PART FOUR

WINNING AND LOSING IN THE GLOBAL ECONOMY

Fourteen

'CAPTURING VALUE' WITHIN GLOBAL PRODUCTION NETWORKS

Placing places in GPNs

Our focus so far has been on the *patterns* and *processes* of global shift: on the *forms* being produced by the globalizing of economic activities and on the *forces* producing those forms. These transformations of the geoeconomy are the outcome of extraordinarily complex processes, involving major changes in the nature of production, distribution and consumption. My central argument in this book is that the reshaping of the global economic map has been driven increasingly by the emergence of extremely complex organizational and geographical networks of production, distribution and consumption: what we have called global production networks (GPNs). The precise form of such networks – how they are controlled and coordinated, as well as the shape and extent of their specific geographies – varies enormously, as the case studies of Part Three revealed. As we have seen, TNCs operate through a complex mix of intra-organizational and inter-organizational networks: the internalized networks of TNCs themselves, varying from centrally controlled hierarchies to flatter 'heterarchies'; and the externalized captive, relational and modular networks created through strategic alliances and various kinds of subcontracting and supplier relationships within GPNs.

These complex production networks are grounded in specific places: *organizational networks connect into geographical networks*. GPNs, therefore, not only integrate *firms* (and parts of firms) into structures which blur traditional organizational boundaries (for example, through the development of diverse forms of equity and non-equity relationships) but also integrate *places* (national and local economies) in ways that have enormous implications for their economic development. It is this *place dimension* that provides the focus of this chapter. The questions posed are those relating to the ways in which a place's insertion (or non-insertion) into GPNs affects its developmental prospects.

We can think of places, at whatever geographical scale, as having an *organizational ecology* (Figure 14.1): a mix of firms and parts of firms, large and small, old and new, foreign and domestically owned, connected together through geographically extensive production circuits and networks. The branches and affiliates of TNCs are obviously part of a specific corporate structure and are constrained in their autonomy by parent company policy. The extent to which they are functionally connected into the local economy is enormously variable. But even the 'independent' firms in a local economy may, in fact, be rather less independent than they appear at first sight. Many are integrated into the supply networks of larger firms, whose decision-making functions are very distant. Other local firms may be linked together through strategic alliances or they may be a part of the flexible business networks coordinated by key 'broker' firms.

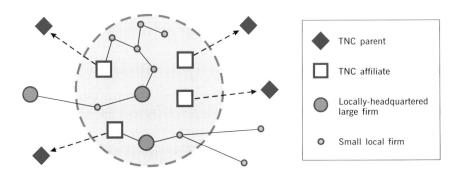

Figure 14.1   A place's 'organizational ecology'

In this context, four highly interconnected sets of relationships are especially important:

- *intra-firm relationships*: between different parts of a corporate network, as each part strives to maintain or to enhance its position *vis-à-vis* other parts of the organization
- *inter-firm relationships*: between firms belonging to separate, but overlapping, networks as part of customer–supplier transactions and other inter-firm interactions
- *firm–place relationships*: as firms attempt to extract the maximum benefits from the communities in which they are embedded and as communities attempt to derive the maximum benefits from the firms' local operations
- *place–place relationships*: between places, as each community attempts to capture and retain the investments (and especially the jobs) of the component parts of GPNs.

Each of these sets of relationships is embedded within and across *national/state* political and regulatory systems that help to determine the parameters within which firms and places interact.

The key issue addressed in this chapter, therefore, is the extent to which a place's involvement in GPNs creates net benefits (or net costs) for its inhabitants. There is a good deal of disagreement about this, as there is about the more specific issue of the impact of TNCs on local and national economies. In that respect, virtually every aspect of TNC operations – economic, political and cultural – has been judged in diametrically opposed ways, depending upon the ideological viewpoint adopted. Thus, TNCs are seen to

- either expand national and local economies or exploit them
- either act as a dynamic force in economic development or have a distorting influence
- either create jobs or destroy them
- either spread new technology or pre-empt its wider use.

Similar polarization of opinion applies to the impact of GPNs. From the viewpoint of particular places, then, are GPNs a 'good' thing or a 'bad' thing?

> [Global production networks] can be seen as opportunity structures for organizational learning on the part of developing countries. Not only can local firms access international markets via such [networks], but the implication is that firms can actively seek to *change* the way that they are linked to global [networks] in order to increase the benefits they derive from participating in them – a process of repositioning that is called upgrading ... [On the other hand] particular strategies to increase the competitiveness of suppliers in global [networks] may look like upgrading from the vantage point of the firm but in fact constitute a form of downgrading for the workers involved.[1]

Creating, enhancing and capturing value in GPNs

Each stage in a production circuit (Figure 3.3), each node in a global production network, *creates value* through the combined application of labour skills, process and product technologies, and the organizational expertise involved in coordinating complex production and logistical processes and in marketing and distribution. In this sense, value is a *surplus* over and above the costs involved in performing the transformations and transactions at that particular stage or node. In the economists' terminology, it would be called *economic rent*.[2] By definition, the process is dynamic: the aim is continuously to *enhance* value – to increase profits and/or to reduce competition – through a whole variety of means: product and process innovation, improved labour productivity, more efficient logistical systems, and so on.

When we turn to *value capture* the situation is far more complicated. A detailed analysis of the value chain for the production of the Apple iPod shows just how complicated the capture of value can be and also the extent to which the highest-value capture tends to be at the high end of the value chain (design, brand ownership and control) whilst assembly is far less significant in the total value added.[3] Geographically in the case of the iPod, this means that the US captures most of the value even though all iPods are actually manufactured in China (in Taiwanese-controlled factories) and the hard disk drive (the most expensive component) is manufactured by the Japanese firm Toshiba but mostly in factories located in China and the Philippines.

So, the key questions addressed in this chapter are: Who captures the value created within production networks? Who benefits from value creation and enhancement? This raises issues way beyond the narrow confines of firm competitiveness and profitability to encompass all the different *stakeholders* involved in global production networks in different geographical locations. The key issue is the configuration of *power* within GPNs which, as we have seen already, tends to be highly asymmetrical and subject to complex bargaining processes. One dimension of this is the relationship between capital and labour. In general over the past few decades, there has been a pronounced shift in which capital has gained massively at the expense of labour, not least because of the increased *financialization* of all parts of the economy (see Chapter 3). This is shown, for example, in the increased unevenness in the distribution of incomes in many developed economies (Chapter 16). Another dimension is the relationship between lead firms and their multilayered tiers of suppliers: the extent to which lead firms are able to squeeze their first-tier suppliers who, in turn, try to squeeze their suppliers and so on through the entire production network. This is apparent in several of the cases discussed in Part Three.

In this chapter, however, we are concerned with how value within GPNs is created, enhanced and captured in the *places* – the national and local economies – in which the component parts are located. In other words, the focus is developmental at the 'community' level. To what extent is the value created within GPNs captured for the benefit of the places in which the activities occur? To what extent does participation in global production networks offer the potential to *upgrade* a place's economic well-being?

Upgrading (or downgrading) of local economies within GPNs

The potential effects of GPNs on local economies involve a whole range of complex direct and indirect interactions, as Figures 14.2 and 14.3 show. They are contingent upon the relationships between the nature of the GPN operations themselves and the nature and characteristics of the local economy. In the following sections we focus on four especially important dimensions of a place's involvement in a GPN: capital injection, local firm stimulus, knowledge diffusion, and local employment creation.

Injecting capital?

The inflow of capital is the most obvious impact of foreign investment, especially for those countries suffering from capital shortage. TNCs have certainly been responsible for injecting capital into host economies, both developed and developing. But not all new overseas ventures undertaken by TNCs involve the actual transfer of capital into the host economy. One estimate for the 1990s was that around 50 per cent of US foreign direct 'investment' was actually raised on host-country capital markets and not imported.[4] Thus, local firms may be bought with local money. Local firms may even be squeezed out of local capital markets by the perceived greater attractiveness of TNCs as an outlet for local savings.

Even where capital inflow does occur there will, eventually, be a reverse flow as the local operation remits earnings and profits back to its parent company. This outflow may, in time, exceed the inflow. A recent analysis of the impact of FDI on the Mexican economy concluded that

> when profit remittances are deducted from gross FDI flows, the economic impact of the resulting 'net' FDI capital per worker variable is reduced in magnitude and statistical significance.[5]

Any net financial gain to the host country also depends on the trading practices of the TNC. A host economy's balance of payments will be improved to the extent that the local plant exports its output and reduced by its propensity to import. A vital issue, therefore, is the extent to which financial 'leakage' occurs from host

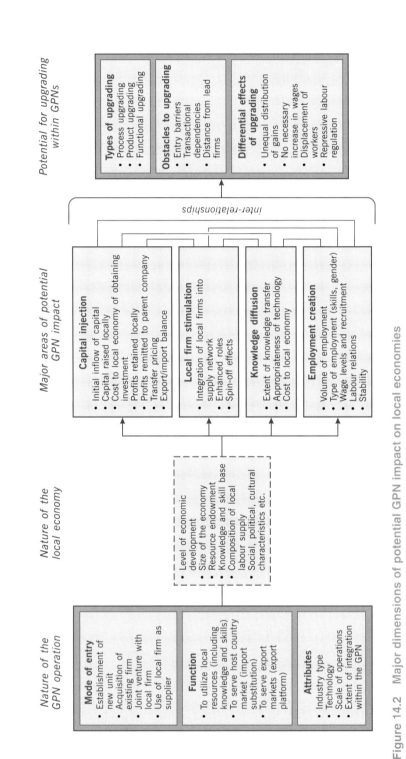

Figure 14.2   Major dimensions of potential GPN impact on local economies

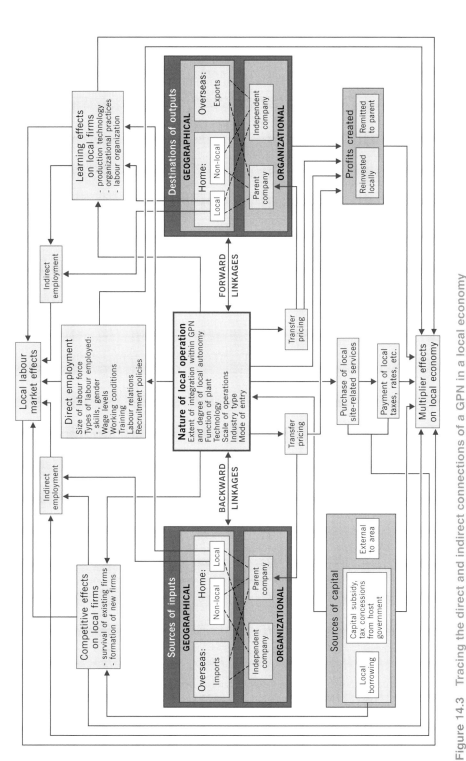

Figure 14.3 Tracing the direct and indirect connections of a GPN in a local economy

economies through the channel of the TNC. This raises the question of the ability of host-country governments to obtain a 'fair' tax yield from foreign-controlled operations whose parent companies are capable of manipulating the terms of their intra-corporate transactions through transfer pricing and tax avoidance (see Chapter 7).

Stimulating local firms?

The extent to which local firms may be stimulated by involvement in a GPN depends upon the roles such firms perform and upon whether or not the direct affiliates of TNCs create positive linkages within the local economy. Which level in the supply network do local firms occupy? Are they first-, second- or lower-tier suppliers? What kinds of operations do they perform? What is the skill and technology level involved? If the local operation is a subsidiary of a TNC, what kinds of subsidiary responsibilities does it have?

Inter-firm linkages are the most important channels through which technological change is transmitted. When TNCs place orders with local suppliers for materials or components that must meet stringent specifications, technical expertise is raised. The experience gained in new technologies by local firms enables them to compete more effectively in broader markets, provided, of course, that they are not tied exclusively to a specific customer. The sourcing of materials locally may lead to the emergence of new domestic firms to meet the demand created, thus increasing the pool of local entrepreneurs. The expanded activities of supplying firms, and of ancillary firms involved in such activities as transportation and distribution, will result in the creation of additional employment. But such beneficial spin-off effects will occur only *if* the foreign affiliates of TNCs *do* become linked to local firms. Where TNCs do not create such linkages they remain essentially foreign enclaves within a host economy, contributing little other than some direct employment.

As far as local linkages are concerned, the most significant are *backward* or *supply* linkages (Figure 14.3). Here, the crucial issue is the extent to which TNCs either import materials and components or procure them from local suppliers. The actual incidence of local linkage formation by foreign-controlled plants depends upon three major influences:

- *The particular strategy followed by the TNC and the role played by the local operation in that strategy*. TNCs that are strongly vertically integrated at a global scale are less likely to develop local supply linkages than firms with a lower degree of corporate integration. But even where vertical integration is low, the existence of strong links with independent suppliers in the TNC's home country or elsewhere in the firm's GPN may inhibit the development of local linkages in the host economy. Familiarity with existing supply relationships may well discourage the development of new ones, particularly where the latter are perceived to be potentially less reliable or of lower quality. Foreign plants that serve the host market are more likely to develop local supply linkages than export platform plants.

- *The characteristics of the local economy.* In general, we would expect to find denser and more extensive networks of linkages between TNCs and domestic enterprises in developed, compared with developing, economies. Within developing countries such linkages are likely to be greatest in the larger and more industrialized countries than in others. In many developing countries, the existing supplier base is simply not sufficiently developed to meet TNC criteria, that is, the *absorptive capacity* is too low. However, host-country governments may well play a very important role in stimulating local linkages, both by implementing policies to upgrade local suppliers and through local content policies. But much depends on the relative strength of the host country's bargaining power *vis-à-vis* the TNC. Again, it tends to be in the larger and the more industrialized developing countries that such local content policies have the greatest impact, and also in those TNC activities serving the local market. Indeed, it could be that the export-oriented industrialization strategies of developing countries actually inhibit the development of local supply linkages.

- *Time.* Local supply capabilities do not develop overnight. Particularly in view of the closer relationships between firms and their suppliers (see Chapter 5) it should not be expected that a foreign plant, newly established in a particular host economy, would immediately develop local supplier linkages. Not only do appropriate suppliers have to be identified but also it takes time for supplier firms to 'tune in' to a new customer's needs.

The linkage question is not only a quantitative one. More important than the number of local linkages is their *quality* and the degree to which they involve a beneficial transfer of technology (either production or organizational) to supplier firms. A common criticism is that many TNCs tend to procure only 'low-level' inputs from local sources, for example cleaning and maintenance services and the like. This may be because of deliberate company policy to keep to established suppliers of higher-level inputs or because such inputs are simply not available locally (or are perceived not to be so). Where development of higher-level supply linkages occurs there does seem to be a positive effect on supplier firms. Figure 14.4 summarizes the differences between 'dependent' and 'developmental' linkages. Clearly, from a local economy's perspective, the aim must be to achieve a linkage structure that is developmental. In this respect, much will depend upon its bargaining power (see Chapter 7).

Empirical evidence of local linkage formation by TNCs presents a very uneven picture.[6] Studies within smaller developing countries, particularly those with a short history of industrial development, tell a fairly uniform story of shallow and

Attribute	Dependent structure	Developmental structure
Form of local linkages	Unequal trading relationships. Conventional subcontracting. Emphasis on cost-saving.	Collaborative, mutual learning. Basis in technology and trust. Emphasis on added value.
Duration and nature of local linkages	Short-term contracts.	Long-term partnerships.
Degree of local embeddedness of inward investors	Weakly embedded. Branch plants restricted to final assembly operations.	Deeply embedded. High level of investment in decentralized, multi-functional operations.
Benefits to local firms	Markets for local firms to make standard, low-technology components. Subcontracting restricts independent growth.	Markets for local firms to develop and produce their own products. Transfer of technology and expertise from inward investor strengthens local firms.
Prospects for the local economy	Vulnerable to external forces and 'distant' corporate decision-making.	Self-sustaining growth through cumulative expansion of linked firms.
Quality of jobs created	Predominantly low-skilled, low-paid. May be high level of temporary and casual employment.	Diverse, including high-skilled, high-income employment.

Figure 14.4   Dependent and developmental linkage structures

Source: based on Turok, 1993: Table 1

poorly developed supply linkages between local firms and foreign-controlled plants. A common observation is that foreign plants located in export processing zones (EPZs) are particularly unlikely to develop supplier linkages with the wider economy. In the case of the Mexican *maquiladora* plants, for example, less than 5 per cent of the inputs used are sourced from within Mexico. Additionally, most of those inputs are low-value and low-technology products whose production does little to upgrade the local technological and skill base.

In some cases, there may be a considerable amount of local sourcing but with relatively little involvement of genuinely local firms. For example, although the new foreign manufacturing plants established in the Johor region of southern Malaysia 'are sourcing a large part of their inputs in Johor … the regional effect is confined to foreign, mainly Japanese and Singaporean, suppliers. As a result, the linkages of the new manufacturing plants are only in part beneficial to the local economy.'[7] Overall, Japanese firms in the Malaysian electronics industry tend 'to rely more heavily on relocated suppliers from their home country, supporting the general belief about the effect of Japanese business ties'.[8]

> In the electronics industry, sourcing patterns appear to differ significantly by host country. For example, in 2001, foreign affiliates in the colour TV industry in Tijuana, Mexico, sourced about 28 per cent of their inputs locally, of which only a very small proportion (3 per cent) was supplied by Mexican-owned firms … in Malaysia, locally-procured components by foreign affiliates in the electronics and electrical industries comprised 62 per cent of exports in 1994; the corresponding figure for Thailand was 40 per cent. However, in both countries, *the most strategic parts and components were supplied mainly by foreign-owned companies rather than domestic ones.*[9]

This latter point is confirmed by a study of 227 Japanese electronics companies operating in 24 countries,[10] which found that although local procurement was widespread, such increase in local content did not necessarily involve local suppliers.

Nevertheless, involvement in a GPN may well create opportunities for the enhancement of local businesses. Existing firms may receive a boost to their fortunes or new firms may be created in response to the stimulus of demand for materials or components. The formation of new enterprises may be stimulated through the 'spin-off' of managerial staff setting up their own businesses on the basis of experience and skills gained in participation in a GPN.

Diffusing knowledge?

> GPNs in their operations … disseminate important knowledge to local suppliers in low-cost locations, which could catalyze local capability formation.[11]

Simply by locating some of its operations outside its home country, a TNC engages in the geographical transfer of knowledge. In so far as a foreign affiliate employs local labour there will be a degree of knowledge transfer to elements of the local population through training in specific skills and techniques. But the mere existence of a particular technology within a foreign-controlled operation does not guarantee that its benefits will be widely diffused through a host economy. The critical factor here is the extent to which the technology is made available to potential users outside the firm either directly, through linkages with indigenous firms, or indirectly via 'demonstration effects'.

In fact, the very nature of the TNC inhibits the spread of its proprietary technologies beyond its own organizational boundaries. Such technologies are not lightly handed over to other firms. Control over their use is jealously guarded: the terms under which technologies are transferred are dictated primarily by the TNC itself in the light of its own overall interests. They tend to transfer the results of innovation but not the innovative capabilities – the 'know-how' rather than the 'know-why'. A major tendency, as we saw in Chapter 5, is for TNCs to locate most of their technology-creating activities either in their home country or in the more advanced industrialized, and some of the more advanced newly industrializing, countries. So far, relatively little R&D, other than lower-level support laboratories, has been relocated to developing countries. In some cases this is a direct result of host government pressure on TNCs to establish R&D facilities in return for entry. Such leverage is greatest where the TNC wishes to establish a branch plant to serve the host–country market itself.

The evidence for TNCs transferring technologies beyond a fairly basic level to developing countries is very mixed. A study of the electronics industry in Malaysia, the Philippines and Thailand was fairly positive:

> Their [TNCs'] participation has at least produced latent technological capabilities for absorption by local firms ... foreign firms' participation and the high levels of ... [human resource and process technology] capabilities generated have at least transformed the local environment to facilitate export manufacturing in these countries involving a high-tech industry.[12]

On the other hand, the conclusions of a study of two Caribbean countries (Trinidad and Tobago and Costa Rica) were more pessimistic:

> Despite the attractiveness of both countries to foreign investors, foreign investment has made only a minimal contribution to strengthening local innovation systems in these countries.[13]

A critical issue, however, is the ability of local firms to actually *absorb* new knowledge and technologies.

> Knowledge transfer ... is not automatic. It requires a significant level of absorptive capacity on the part of local suppliers and a complex process to internalize disseminated knowledge ... Of course, knowledge transfer is not a sufficient condition for effective knowledge diffusion. Diffusion is completed only when transferred knowledge is internalized and translated into the capability of the local suppliers. Much depends on the types of knowledge involved and the mechanisms that [lead firms] use to disseminate different types of knowledge.[14]

In Chapter 4 we distinguished between two types of knowledge: *codified (or explicit) knowledge*, the kinds of knowledge that can be expressed formally in documents, blueprints, software, hardware etc.; and *tacit knowledge*, the deeply personalized knowledge possessed by individuals that is virtually impossible to make explicit and to communicate to others. Codified knowledge can be transmitted relatively easily across distance. Tacit knowledge, on the other hand, has a very steep 'distance–decay' curve. It is much more 'sticky'. Both types of knowledge are essential ingredients in the knowledge diffusion process within GPNs, whether that occurs within the organizational boundaries of a TNC's internal network or across organizational boundaries to other firms within the GPN. However,

> local suppliers can only effectively absorb knowledge disseminated by global network flagships if they have developed their own capabilities. Knowledge internalization and capability building require individual and organizational learning.[15]

Creating good jobs?

For most ordinary people, as well as for many governments, the most important issue is the effect of GPNs on local jobs:

- Do they create new jobs?
- What kinds of jobs are they?

- Do local firms embedded within GPNs pay higher or lower wages than other, non-GPN firms?
- Do GPN firms operate an acceptable system of labour relations?

In other words, do GPNs create a 'high-road' job scenario, in which the emphasis is on quality, skill and good labour conditions, or a 'low-road' scenario, characterized by low wages, low skills, job insecurity and poor labour conditions?[16]

Number of jobs

The number of jobs created (or displaced) by a GPN operation in a local economy consists of both those created in the operation itself and those created/displaced elsewhere in the local economy (Figure 14.3).

The number of *direct jobs* created in a particular operation depends upon two factors:

- the *scale* of its activities
- the *technological* nature of the operation, particularly on whether it is capital intensive or labour intensive.

The number of *indirect* jobs created also depends upon two major factors:

- the extent of *local linkages* forged with local firms
- the *amount of income generated* by the TNC and *retained* within the local economy. In particular, the wages and salaries of employees and of those in linked firms will, if spent on locally produced goods and services, increase employment elsewhere in the domestic economy (Figure 14.3).

Against the number of local jobs *created* in GPNs we need to set the number of jobs *displaced* by any possible adverse effects on other local enterprises. Hence, the overall employment effect depends upon the balance between job-creating and job-displacing forces. The *net* employment contribution of a GPN to a local economy, or the net jobs (NJ), can therefore be expressed as:

$$NJ = DJ + IJ - JD$$

where DJ is the number of direct jobs created locally in the GPN, IJ is the number of indirect local jobs in firms linked to the GPN, and JD is the number of jobs displaced in other local firms.

Quality of jobs

The number of jobs created by GPNs in local economies is only part of the story. What kind of jobs are they? Do they provide employment opportunities that are appropriate for the skills and needs of the local labour force? The answer to these questions depends very much on the attributes of the GPN operation (see Figure 14.3).

In particular, where the operation 'fits' into the GPN's overall structure and how much decision-making autonomy it has are key factors. In general, the fact that TNCs tend to concentrate their higher-order decision-making functions and their R&D facilities in the developed economies produces a major geographical bias in the pattern of types of employment at the global scale.

In developing countries, the overwhelming majority of jobs in GPN plants are *production* jobs. In export processing zones, of course, low-level production jobs, especially for young females, are the rule, although this partly reflects the types of industry that dominate in EPZs. Overall, the proportion of higher-skilled workers employed within GPNs in developing countries has tended to increase over time, as has the proportion of local professional and managerial staff. Such changes have progressed furthest in the more advanced industrializing countries of Asia. For example, the shift of IT activities to India involves more than low-level call centre jobs:

> Anyone who assumes J. P. Morgan will simply be doing low-level 'back office' tasks in the country – a bit of data entry and paper-shuffling – would be flat wrong. One task for the new recruits is to settle complex structured-finance and derivative deals, what one insider calls 'some of the most sophisticated transactions in the world'.[17]

Even so, the GPN labour force in developing countries remains concentrated in low-skill production and assembly occupations. The experience of individual developing countries varies in the extent of TNC-induced labour upgrading, as a study of the TV industry in East Asia shows.[18] In each case, the extent of human capital formation in the industry was very limited prior to the mid 1990s:

- In Malaysia, specialized staff were still foreign but there was significant training by leading firms and for their partners in their regional production networks. There was evidence of rising skill levels and increasing numbers of specialized technical and managerial staff.
- In Mexico, the first signs of upgrading were apparent as a result of significant training efforts and linking with local education institutions, rising labour skill levels, and increasing numbers of specialized technical and managerial staff.
- In Thailand, the skill levels of the labour force were low but rising with increased emphasis on labour training. But there was not much evidence of an increasing involvement of more highly educated specialist staff.

Wages and salaries

In so far as TNCs take advantage of geographical differences in prevailing wage rates between countries they do, in fact, 'exploit' certain groups of workers. The exploitation of cheap labour in developing countries at the expense of workers in developed countries is one of the major charges levelled at the TNC by labour

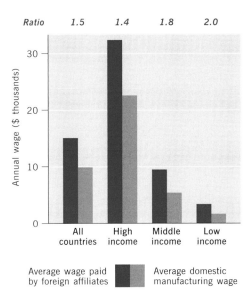

Figure 14.5   Differences in average wages paid by foreign affiliates of TNCs and domestic firms

Source: based on Crook, 2001: 15

unions in Western countries. The general response of TNCs to such allegations is that they do not have complete control over what goes on in independent factories although, in the face of these criticisms, many TNCs are now implementing codes of practice to which their suppliers must conform (see Chapter 17).

However, as far as their *directly owned affiliates* are concerned, the general consensus seems to be that TNCs generally pay either at or above the 'going rate' in the host economy. Figure 14.5 shows two aspects of the wage comparison. First, the relative height of the columns shows that TNCs pay very much more to workers in high-income countries than to those in middle- and low-income countries. This differential reflects a number of factors, including the composition of economic activity, educational and skill levels, cost of living, and so on. Second, although TNCs certainly pay higher wages overall than domestic firms in the same country group (a ratio of 1.5), the pattern varies between country groups: 1.4 in high-income countries, 1.8 in middle-income countries and 2.0 in low-income countries.

TNCs that do pay above the local rate may well 'cream off' workers from local firms and possibly threaten their survival. This point relates to the kinds of *recruitment policies* used by TNCs, which may well mean that employees for a newly established local plant are drawn from existing firms, rather than from the ranks of the unemployed. Another aspect of recruitment, at least in some industries, is the extent to which TNCs recruit particular types of workers to keep labour costs low. In the textiles, garments and electronics industries, for example, there is a very strong tendency to prefer females to males in assembly processes and, in some cases, to employ members of minority groups as a means of holding down wage costs and for ease of dismissal. But such practices appear to be specific to particular industries and should not necessarily be regarded as universally applicable to all TNCs in all industries.

Labour relations

In many developing countries, either labour is weakly organized or labour unions are strictly controlled (or even banned) by the state. Even in developed economies some major TNCs simply do not recognize labour unions in their operations while deregulation of labour markets has become widespread. But most TNCs, however reluctantly, do accept labour unions where national or local circumstances make this difficult to avoid. Whether labour unions are involved or not, the question of the nature of labour relations within TNCs focuses on whether they are 'good' or 'bad', that is, harmonious or discordant. Some studies suggest that TNCs tend to have better labour relations in their plants than domestic firms; others point to a higher incidence of strikes and internal disputes in TNCs. But it is often difficult to separate out the 'transnational' element. In the case of strikes, for example, it may be plant or firm size that is the most important influence rather than nationality of ownership.

One of the most acute concerns of organized labour is that decision-making within TNCs is too remote: that decisions affecting work practices and work conditions, pay and other labour issues are made in some far-distant corporate headquarters which has little understanding or even awareness of local circumstances. Some labour relations decisions are far more centralized than others, either being made at corporate headquarters or requiring its approval. These areas tend to relate to the parent company's concern to control financial and labour costs. However, there is considerable variation between TNCs in their degree of headquarters' involvement in labour relations.

The dispersed nature of TNC operations and the tendency towards remoteness in decision-making have made it very difficult for labour unions to organize effectively to counter such issues as plant closure or retrenchment. Two developments, although relatively limited so far, are significant.[19] One is the initiation by global union federations (such the International Confederation of Free Trade Unions – ICFTU) of networks of workers within specific TNCs in an attempt to move industrial relations issues to the global level. The second development has occurred within the European Union:

> As part of the social protocol of the 1993 Maastricht Treaty, at least 15 million employees in some 1500 [TNCs] operating in Europe now have rights to information and consultation on all matters that affect more than one member state ... Each company that employs more than 1000 people, of whom at least

150 are located in two (or more) member states, has to meet the representation, transportation, accommodation, and translation costs of bringing employee representatives from across the European Union on an annual basis … they provide a new opportunity for workplace representatives to meet their counterparts from every division of their companies' operations in Europe.[20]

Despite such developments, labour unions remain primarily contained within national state boundaries while TNCs are not. This structural difference creates inevitable tensions.

A key issue is the kind of employment contract involved. It is common for firms to differentiate between *core workers* (employed on secure contracts and with good conditions of employment) and *non-core workers* (with less secure contracts and fewer fringe benefits and who can be more easily dismissed if the firm wishes to scale down its labour force). Labour force flexibility is a key element in GPNs. Non-core workers are frequently hired through employment and temporary staffing agencies.[21] This kind of problem was graphically illustrated in early 2009 when the German auto company BMW terminated the contracts of 850 agency workers at its UK plant. The workers were given just one week's notice and no redundancy payments. In contrast, permanent staff would be entitled to receive redundancy payments.[22]

The other side of the coin: exporting jobs from 'headquarters countries'

As TNCs have increasingly established global production networks they have, inevitably, engaged in significant reconfiguration of their home/overseas balance. What are the implications? Does overseas investment adversely affect the home country's economic welfare by, for example, drawing away investment capital, displacing exports or destroying jobs? Does it represent a 'hollowing out' of a local or national economy? Is it an inevitable feature of today's highly competitive global economy that forces firms to expand overseas in order to remain competitive?

- *Proponents* of overseas investment argue that the overall effects on the domestic economy will be positive, raising the level of exports and of domestic activity to a level above that which would prevail if overseas investment did not occur. Profits from overseas operations will flow back to the home economy, enhancing the firm's competitive position and making funds available for investment in appropriate activities in the home economy, as well as overseas.
- *Opponents* of overseas investment argue that the major effect will be to divert capital that could have been invested at home and to displace domestic exports. Profits earned overseas will be reinvested in other overseas ventures, rather than in creating new job opportunities at home.

A critical issue is the extent to which domestic investment could realistically be *substituted* for overseas investment. This raises a whole series of questions:

- What would have happened if the investment had not been made abroad?
- Would that investment have been made at home?
- Would the resources that went into the foreign investment have been used in higher levels of consumption and/or public services?
- What would have been the effect of foreign investment on domestic exports?
- Would the foreign sales of the product of the investment have been filled by exports from the home economy in the absence of the investment?
- Or would they have been taken over by foreign competitors?

It is impossible to say, with any certainty, that overseas investment could equally as well have been made in the firm's home country. We can make various assumptions about what might have happened, but that is all. Ultimately, the key lies with the *motivations* that underlie specific investment decisions. As we have seen, firms invest abroad for a whole variety of reasons, for example:

- to gain access to new markets
- to defend positions in existing markets
- to circumvent trade barriers
- to diversify the firm's production base
- to reduce production costs
- to gain access to specific assets and resources.

It might be argued that foreign investment undertaken for *defensive* reasons – to protect a firm's existing markets, for example – is less open to criticism than *aggressive* overseas investment. The argument in the case of defensive investment would be that, in its absence, the firm would lose its markets and that domestic jobs would be lost anyway. Such investment might be made necessary by the erection of trade barriers by national governments, by their insistence on local production, or by the appearance of competitors in the firm's international markets. But, presumably, defensive investment might also include the relocation of production to low-wage countries in order to remain competitive. Here, the alternative might be the introduction of automated technology in the domestic plant that would lead to a loss of jobs anyway without any outward investment. Although there may well be some clear-cut cases – particularly where access to markets is obviously threatened or where proximity to a localized material is mandatory – there will inevitably be many instances where there is substantial disagreement over the need to locate overseas rather than at home.

The possible direct employment effects of such overseas investment fall into four categories:[23]

- *Export stimulus effect* (XE): employment gains from the production of goods for export created by the foreign investment which would not have occurred in the absence of such investment.
- *Home office effect* (HE): employment gains in non-production categories at the company's headquarters made necessary by the expansion of overseas activities.
- *Supporting firm effect* (SE): employment gains in other domestic firms supplying goods and services to the investing firm in connection with its overseas activities.
- *Production displacement effect* (DE): employment losses arising from the diversion of production to overseas locations and the serving of foreign markets by these overseas plants rather than by home-country plants, that is, the displacement of exports.

Thus, the *net employment effect* (NE) of overseas investment on the home economy is:

$$NE = XE + HE + SE - DE$$

Unfortunately, the data needed to disaggregate employment change into these components are rarely available so that, once again, large assumptions have to be made. That is why the estimates of the numbers of jobs either created or destroyed vary so widely – often by hundreds of thousands.

Area of impact	DIRECT		INDIRECT	
	Positive	**Negative**	**Positive**	**Negative**
Quantity	Creates or preserves jobs in home location, e.g. those serving the needs of affiliates abroad.	Relocation or 'job export' if foreign affiliates substitute for production at home.	Creates or preserves jobs in supplier/service industries at home that cater to foreign affiliates.	Loss of jobs in firms/ industries linked to production/activities that are relocated.
Quality	Skills are upgraded with higher-value production as industry restructures.	'Give backs' or lower wages to keep jobs at home.	Boosts sophisticated industries.	Downward pressure on wages and standards flows on to suppliers.
Location	Some jobs may depart from the community, but may be replaced by higher-skilled positions, upgrading local labour market conditions.	The 'export' of jobs can aggravate regional/local labour market conditions.	The loss of 'blue-collar' jobs can be offset by greater demand in local labour markets for high-value-added jobs relating to exports or international production.	Demand spiral in local labour market triggered by layoffs can lead to employment reduction in home-country plant locations.

Figure 14.6   The potential effects of outward investment on home country employment

Source: based on UNCTAD *World Investment Report*, 1994: Table IV

Figure 14.6 summarizes the potential positive and negative aspects of both direct and indirect employment effects of outward investment in terms of three attributes: quantity of jobs, quality of jobs and location of jobs. We need to bear in mind that the precise effects of outward investment on home-country employment are highly contingent on the specific circumstances involved. But even though we cannot put precise numbers on jobs gained or lost through FDI, one thing is clear: *the winners and the losers are rarely the same.* At one time, it could be said with some accuracy that the dominant losers were production workers while the major gainers were white-collar managerial workers. But such a simple distinction no longer holds, as the recent rapid increase in the outsourcing/offshoring of white-collar jobs has shown. Also, given the complex geography of TNC networks (Chapter 5), it is almost inevitable that jobs created in the home country through outward investment effects (XE, HE, SE in the above formula) will be in *different places* from those where jobs are lost.

The importance of being there

> One main challenge is to use globalization as a lever for local development, by helping local firms and workers take advantage of the opportunities opened up by the global economy. This derives from an awareness that the development of transnational networks of economic activities generates unprecedented possibilities for accessing new markets and resources, acquiring new skills and capabilities and developing international competitive advantage.[24]

Indeed, the fact that GPNs have become the predominant mode within which production is organized means that it is very difficult indeed for local firms/economies to prosper outside them. Being there – as an insider – is virtually a prerequisite for development. Whether or not a local firm is able to gain entry into a particular GPN depends on the extent to which a GPN is actually accessible.

> The openness of a production network can be defined as the ease of entry for both new firms and new locations … The degree of network openness varies according to industry-specific characteristics and the features of the business systems within which network firms are embedded. Buyer-driven networks in garments and footwear tend to be more open than producer-driven networks in, say, automobiles, mainly as a result of lower entry barriers in the low-skilled, labour-intensive production activities … [In addition] lead firms in the same industry might exhibit different networking behaviours depending on the idiosyncrasies of their national environments. For example, Japanese electronics companies have been slower than their American coun-terparts to diversify their supply base and extend the geographical scope of their production networks in East Asia … Japanese networks also tend to be more socially embedded and less market-oriented than American networks … The most successful production networks, however, are neither closed nor open but 'permeable' … They are characterized by an evolving tiered structure in which a first-tier of selected, stable partners is surrounded by a more mobile row of second-tier suppliers.[25]

But just being there is not enough

Gaining access to a GPN may be a necessary step in the short run but in the long run it is not enough. For sustainable developmental benefits to occur it is necessary for a local firm to *upgrade* its performance – to achieve a 'better' position within its GPN. Economic upgrading can take a number of forms (Figure 14.2):[26]

- *Process upgrading*: the more efficient transformation of inputs into outputs through improved technology and/or better organization of the production process.
- *Product upgrading*: diversification into more sophisticated, higher-value product lines. This might also involve movement into new sectors using knowledge acquired in one sector (for example, from TV manufacture to computer monitors and related equipment).
- *Functional upgrading*: taking on new functions, that is, moving up the skill ladder.
- *Inter-sectoral upgrading*: 'using the knowledge gained in particular chain functions to move into different sectors'.[27]

To these economic forms of upgrading we need to add a fifth:

- *Social upgrading*: which 'promotes employment based on decent work and respect for labour standards … whilst economic upgrading can enhance international trade performance, it does not automatically lead to social upgrading'.[28]

One example of an ideal-typical sequence of upgrading has already been mentioned in the case of East Asian clothing firms (see Chapter 10). This involved moving progressively from the simple assembly of imported inputs, through increased local production and sourcing, to the design of products sold under a buyer firm's label and, finally, to own-brand production.[29] However, such a progression is by no means inevitable (Figure 14.2). There are a number of *obstacles* to local industrial upgrading within GPNs:[30]

- 'Local firms are likely to face substantial entry barriers into the most profitable parts of value chains, nowadays increasingly associated with strategic services such as marketing and R&D. As global networks evolve towards greater functional integration, entry barriers also rise in network positions that previously provided a port of entry into more profitable activities, such as first-tier supplying.'
- 'Local supply firms face the difficulty of overcoming transactional dependency *vis-à-vis* lead firms … the learning process by which suppliers can evolve towards more complex and remunerative activities involves a phase of high concentration in which lead firms might account for as much as 80 per cent

of suppliers' revenues. Serving one major customer facilitates the development of trust and the acquisition of specific competences … but also increases suppliers' vulnerability. The next step for suppliers is thus to diversify their clientele, a phase that requires some degree of standardization of products and production.'

- 'The advantages provided by geographical proximity in strengthening network relations might impede industrial upgrading in distant locations … Global transactions might thus remain limited to standard arm's-length exchanges involving few interdependencies between lead firms and their remote suppliers … [however] remoteness from lead firms' core locations is not an insurmountable obstacle to local industrial upgrading.'

Even if upgrading does occur, there are likely to be *differential effects*:[31]

- 'The gains derived from industrial upgrading may be unequally spread among different groups of workers. Vulnerable groups include "guest workers" imported in response to local labour shortages, as well as workers employed by smaller suppliers and subcontractors that perform lower value-added activities within global networks … Accordingly, upgrading *per se* does not correct the inequalities in employment conditions that are inherent to outsourcing practices. On the contrary, such practices might contribute towards explaining the rising wage inequalities observed in developed and developing countries over the last decades.'
- 'The value created through industrial upgrading does not seem to be shared with workers under the form of higher wages … higher wage levels appear to depend more on tight local labour market conditions and/or demanding collective agreements and labour laws, than on individual firms' upgrading strategies. These results underline the role of local institutions in improving employment conditions, in the face of global downward pressures on workers' wages.'
- 'Industrial upgrading typically involves some forms of workers' displacement, either directly, through declining numbers of production workers, or indirectly, through the emergence of new job profiles that make workers' skills obsolete or less valuable in the local labour market.'
- 'In a number of countries such as the Republic of Korea, Singapore and Malaysia, the "high road" has been combined with elements of a "low road" including union repression and/or restrictive labour laws.'

In other words, what 'may look like upgrading from the vantage point of the firm … [may] in fact constitute a form of downgrading for the workers involved'.[32]

Both the ability of local firms to participate in GPNs and the ability of a local economy to capture value created in those parts of a GPN located there depend, therefore, on far more than just what happens in a firm. The *local context* itself

Figure 14.7   Relationships between local economic development and
                  global production networks

Source: based on Coe et al., 2004: Figure 1

matters enormously. Figure 14.7 summarizes the kinds of relationships involved in what has been called a 'strategic coupling' process.[33] In effect, this means that to participate in a GPN successfully a local economy needs to develop institutions and practices (including training and education, support for local entrepreneurial activities, development of high-quality physical infrastructure etc.) which meet the needs of GPNs.

Of course, this will not guarantee success in capturing GPN value. As we have seen, TNCs have enormous potential flexibility in deciding where to locate their operations or source their inputs. The relative bargaining power of firms versus local economies is critical (see Chapter 7). This poses a huge dilemma for local economic development in a GPN-dominated world. Not to try to create the 'right' conditions to attract GPN activities will, undoubtedly, close off a major avenue for economic development. On the other hand, to try to couple local assets too closely to specific GPNs also has its dangers, not least that of being left stranded if the local operation is relocated elsewhere, or of becoming too tightly locked in.

The dangers of external dominance

Whereas the involvement of some foreign activities in a local/national economy will generally have beneficial effects – not only in creating employment but also in introducing new technologies and business practices – overall dominance by foreign firms is almost certainly undesirable. There are real dangers in acquiring the status of a branch plant economy or of being totally at the mercy of shifting configurations within GPNs. But precisely what constitutes an undesirable level of foreign penetration is open to debate. A high level of dependence on foreign enterprises *potentially* reduces the host economy's sovereignty and autonomy – its ability to make its own decisions and to implement them. At the heart of this issue are the different – often conflictual – goals pursued by nation-states on the one hand and TNCs on the other (see Chapter 7). Each is concerned to maximize its own 'welfare' (in the broadest sense). Where much of a host country's economic activity is effectively controlled by foreign firms, non-domestic goals may well become dominant. It may be extremely difficult for the host government to pursue a particular economic policy if it has insufficient leverage over the dominant firms.

The tighter the degree of control exercised by TNCs within their own production networks, and the lower the degree of autonomy of individual plants, the greater this loss of host-country sovereignty is likely to be. In the *individual* case this may not matter greatly, but where such firms *collectively* dominate a host economy or a key economic sector it most certainly does matter. The most significant aspect of dependence upon a high level of foreign direct investment is *technological*: the inability to generate the knowledge, inventions and innovations necessary to generate self-sustaining growth. As we have seen, TNCs have a strong propensity to keep their higher-level R&D, design and decision-making functions close to home. When a domestic firm is taken over by a foreign firm there is, almost inevitably, a loss or downgrading of such functions in the acquired firm. However, this is not to argue that foreign investment should be avoided completely. On the contrary. What should be avoided by host economies is an *excessive* degree of foreign domination. In other words, *ownership still matters*. This is an especially vital message for those economies – like the UK – which take a totally laid-back view of the indiscriminate acquisition of domestic firms by foreign firms. Seller beware!

NOTES

1   Bair (2009: 29, 30).
2   Kaplinsky (2004) discusses economic rent in the context of global value chains. See also Henderson et al. (2002), Coe et al. (2004), Palpacuer (2008).
3   Dedrick et al. (2009).
4   UNCTAD (1995: 142–3).
5   Ramirez (2006: 812).
6   Girourd and Mirza (2006), Tavares and Young (2006), UNCTAD (2000; 2001).
7   Van Grunsven et al. (1995: 3).
8   Linden (2000: 210).
9   UNCTAD (2001: 135, emphasis added).
10 Belderbos and Capannelli (2001).
11 Ernst and Kim (2002: 2).
12 Rasiah (2004: 619).

13 Mytelka and Barclay (2004: 553).
14 Ernst and Kim (2002: 2, 6).
15 Ernst and Kim (2002: 8).
16 See Palpacuer and Parisotto (2003: 109–11), Jürgens and Krzywdzinski (2009: 29).
17 *The Economist* (17 December 2005).
18 UNCTAD (2001).
19 Wills (1998).
20 Wills (1998: 122).
21 See, for example, Coe et al. (2008b).
22 *Financial Times* (17 February 2009).
23 Hawkins (1972).
24 Palpacuer and Parisotto (2003: 97).
25 Palpacuer and Parisotto (2003: 105–6).
26 Humphrey and Schmitz (2002).
27 Neilson and Pritchard (2009: Chapter 8).
28 Barrientos and Gereffi (2009).
29 Gereffi (1999: 38).
30 Palpacuer and Parisotto (2003: 107–8).
31 Palpacuer and Parisotto (2003: 110–11).
32 Bair (2009: 30).
33 Coe et al. (2004).

Fifteen

'DESTROYING VALUE': ENVIRONMENTAL IMPACTS OF GLOBAL PRODUCTION NETWORKS

> [We should think] about production not as value creation but as a process of materials transformation in which environmental change and the organization/disorganization of matter and energy are *integral* rather than incidental to economic activity.[1]

Production–distribution–consumption as a system of materials flows and balances

Throughout all of our discussion of global production networks, we have focused on the *creation of value* at various points in a network. Such value, as we saw in

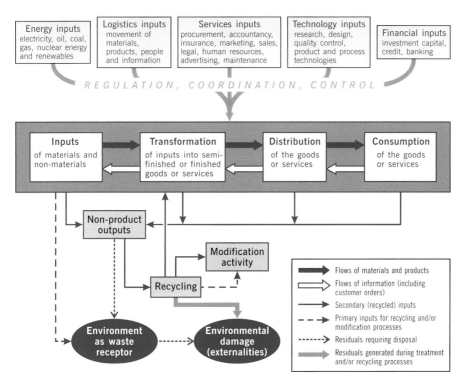

Figure 15.1   Production circuits and the environment

Source: based in part on Turner et al., 1994: Box 1.2

Chapter 14, takes on different forms for different actors within a network. Firms make profits, shareholders receive dividends, workers are paid wages or salaries. In a developmental context, what matters is how much – and what kinds of – value are 'captured' for the benefit of the local community. However, there is another – darker – side to the picture. We can see this more clearly using Figures 15.1 and 15.2. In Figure 15.1, the basic production circuit, shown originally in Chapter 3 as Figure 3.3, has been set within a much broader framework which presents the production–distribution–consumption circuit as a *system of materials flows and balances*. Figure 15.2 provides a more detailed picture of the ways in which materials flows involved in the processing, residual recycling and residual discharging are configured within a production system.

Negative spillovers: unintentional effects of production

What Figures 15.1 and 15.2 demonstrate is that there are unintentional external effects (*negative externalities* or *spillovers*) involved in all economic activities. In other words, just as production creates value it also has the capacity – albeit

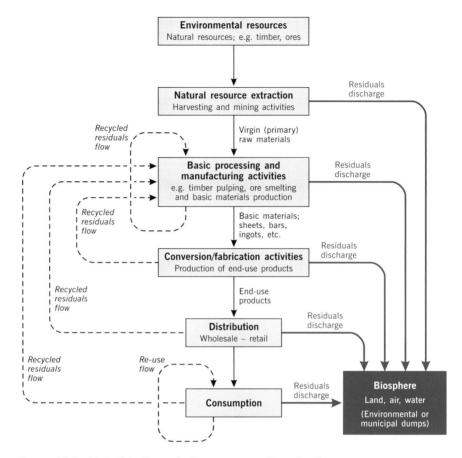

Figure 15.2   Materials flows in the process of production

Source: based on Turner et al., 1994: Box 1.3

unintentionally – to *destroy* value. Three aspects of such environmental damage are especially important:[2]

* over-use of non-renewable and renewable resources (including exploitation of fossil fuels, water resources, clearance of forests)
* over-burdening of natural environmental 'sinks' (for example, the increasing concentration of greenhouse gases in the earth's atmosphere and of heavy materials in the soil)
* destruction of increasing numbers of ecosystems to create space for urban and industrial development.

The key point of all production processes is that what goes in has to come out again, albeit transformed, but without being reduced. In Figures 15.1 and 15.2 the materials used in the production process are dispersed and chemically transformed. In particular, they enter in a state of low entropy (as 'useful' materials) and leave in a state of high entropy (as 'useless' materials, such as low temperature heat emissions, mixed municipal wastes, etc.) … No material recycling processes can therefore ever be 100 per cent efficient.[3]

Thus, even after all efforts are made to recycle the unused energy and materials involved in production, there will still be 'things' left over in the form of residual waste and environmental damage. This is simply because the fundamental laws of thermodynamics cannot be overruled:

the total mass of inputs to a transformation process is equal to the total mass of outputs. If inputs do not emerge as desired products, they must therefore appear as unwanted by-products or wastes.[4]

Such negative externalities are of various kinds and of varying geographical extent. For example, the negative externalities from a factory or from an airport are, at one level, geographically localized. The impact is greatest at the location of the facility itself and its immediate neighbourhood but then declines with increasing distance away from that location. On the other hand, the smoke pollution from the factory or the effect of aircraft fuel combustion may have much more extensive geographical effects, particularly on the atmosphere. The problem is that many adverse environmental effects cannot be contained within geographical boundaries. Some are, indeed, global.

The environmental problems that are inherent in all aspects of production, distribution and consumption raise serious questions about the future sustainability of economy and society as we know them. They raise big issues relating to the future of the world's economic and trading system and, indeed, to most aspects of contemporary economic life. In this chapter, we will focus on two aspects of negative environmental impacts of production: atmospheric damage (including climate change, atmospheric pollution) and waste. The question of environmental regulation will be addressed in Chapter 17.

Disturbing the delicate balance of life on earth: damaging the earth's atmosphere

Human life is only made possible by a complex, and extremely delicate, balance of processes: atmospheric, hydrological and biological. As the history of the earth clearly shows, such a critical balance may be disturbed by natural forces. Periods of widespread freezing and glaciation, drought and high temperatures, rises and falls in sea level, are all evident in the earth's geological record. Until relatively recently, it was generally assumed that human activity would have little effect on natural processes; it was simply too small in relative terms to influence such enormous natural forces. It is now widely accepted that this is not the case. Indeed, the evidence of not only large-scale, but potentially irreversible, damage to the natural environment by human activity is accumulating day by day. By far the most contentious aspect of negative environmental externalities relates to potential *atmospheric damage*, that is, damage to the gaseous membrane that sustains all life on earth.

The processes of material transformation involve the use of massive quantities of energy, especially of fossil fuels whose combustion products are the major source of damage to the earth's atmosphere. The problems arise because some of the key gaseous components of the earth's atmosphere – notably carbon dioxide, methane and ozone – are becoming excessively concentrated in the atmosphere. The issue is one of balance. Without these and other gases, the earth would have a surface temperature like that of the planet Mars; it would be uninhabitable. The earth's surface remains habitable precisely because of the presence of such gases in the atmosphere. In combination, they act like a 'greenhouse', preventing both excessive solar heating and excessive cooling. But it is a very delicate balance.

CO_2 emissions and climate change

It is now abundantly clear that this balance is dangerously disturbed by human action.

> The causes of contemporary and future changes in climate, their rate and their potential significance for the human species … are all notably different from anything that has occurred previously in history or prehistory. The *causes* are now dominated by human perturbation of the atmosphere, the *rate* of warming already exceeds anything experienced in the last 10 000 years and is set to be more rapid, probably, than anything experienced in human history, and the *significance* for humanity is qualitatively different from the previously given ecological imprint made by our current and growing population of 6 billion and more.[5]

The overwhelming scientific consensus is that human-induced climate change has become dominant. In the view of the Intergovernmental Panel on Climate Change (IPCC),

> Warming of the climate system is unequivocal, as is now evident from observations of increases in global average air and ocean temperatures, widespread melting of snow and ice, and rising global mean sea level … The updated 100-year linear trend (1906–2005) of 0.74 [0.56 to 0.92] °C is … larger than the corresponding trend for 1901–2000 … of 0.6 [0.4 to 0.8] °C. The linear warming trend over the last 50 years … is nearly twice that for the last 100 years. The total temperature increase from 1850–1899 to 2001–2005 is 0.76 [0.57 to 0.95] °C.[6]

Figure 15.3   Changes in global land and sea temperatures, 1850–2008

Source: based on www.cru.uea.ac.uk/cru/info/warming

Figure 15.3 plots these rising trends in global temperature compared with the mean temperature for the 1961–1990 period. As the graph shows, although the overall trend is clearly upwards there are always annual variations in temperature change. The acceleration in rising average temperatures is due to the fact that

> global atmospheric concentrations of carbon dioxide, methane and nitrous oxide have increased markedly as a result of human activities since 1750 and now far exceed pre-industrial values determined from ice cores spanning many thousands of years. The global increases in carbon dioxide concentration are due primarily to fossil fuel use and land use change, while those of methane and nitrous oxide are primarily due to agriculture.[7]

Because carbon dioxide is the main 'greenhouse gas' its increasing concentration in the atmosphere is *the* major cause of global climate change. The association between rising CO_2 levels and the growth of economic activity is abundantly clear. There was a significant acceleration after around 1800.[8] Before that time, carbon dioxide levels in the atmosphere remained fairly stable at between 270 and 290 parts per million (ppm). Since then, the following escalation in levels has occurred:

- 1900: 295 ppm
- 1950: between 310 and 315 ppm
- 1995: 360 ppm
- 2008: 387 ppm

As we might expect, there is a clear geography to CO_2 emissions, as Figure 15.4 shows. These emissions map primarily on to the usage of fossil fuels (mainly coal

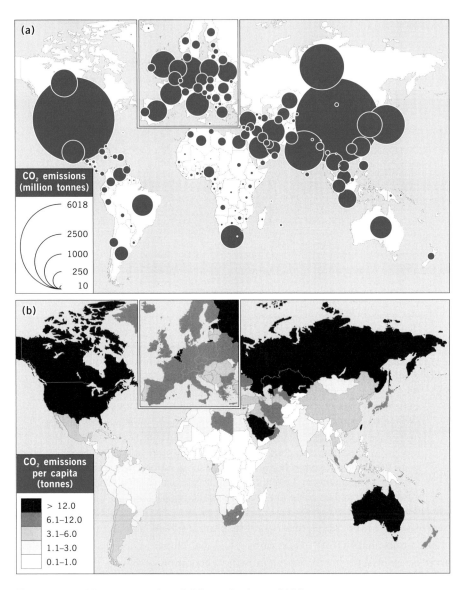

Figure 15.4 The geography of CO$_2$ emissions, 2008

Source: based on data in www.ela.doe.gov/environment

and oil for industrial production, transportation and domestic use), which accounts for almost two-thirds of total CO$_2$ emissions. Within that figure, emissions from power plants account for 27 per cent, industry for 14 per cent, road transport for 12 per cent, refineries for 6 per cent, and international transport for 2 per cent.[9] A further one-third is created by emissions from global biomass (mainly forest fires). In absolute terms, the world's biggest emitters of CO$_2$ were

China and the US. Together, these two countries produced no less than 42 per cent of the world's total emissions. Europe contributed around 15 per cent. But the picture is rather different when we look at the volume of emissions per head of population. From such a per capita perspective, China contributes less than 79 other countries.

But there is a further complication in interpreting the geography – and, therefore, the politics – of CO_2 emissions. The emissions data shown in Figure 15.4 are *production* data. What happens if we take a different perspective: that of *consumption*? The CO_2 emission figures, especially for countries like China, India and other developing countries, particularly in East Asia, are greatly influenced by the fact that much of those countries' industrial production is for export to the developed markets of the US and Europe. For example, Chinese CO_2 emissions grew by 45 per cent between 2002 and 2005. One estimate is that half of that increase was associated with production for export and 60 per cent of that export production was for Western economies.[10] In effect,

> Quite a lot of carbon production was simply outsourced abroad. We then imported the carbon intensive goods back to Britain and then consumed that carbon … It is not the Chinese who are consuming the outputs from its coastal economic boom. The extra two large coal stations per week in China are being built for export manufacturers. And since it is likely that the efficiency of coal-fired generation is lower in China than in developed countries, outsourcing carbon intensive industries may be more polluting – before adding in the pollution from shipping and other transport back to developed countries.[11]

Predicting the precise effects of global warming is, like all predictions of the outcome of highly complex processes, far from easy. However, it is abundantly clear that the current upward trend in temperatures is potentially catastrophic for many parts of the world, as the IPCC reports show. But the effects will be far from geographically evenly spread. Shifting climatic zones will create intensified drought in some areas but higher rainfall and increased frequency of flooding in others. The geography of food production will be very different from that of today. Rising sea levels produced by the melting of polar ice will drastically change the shape of coastlines, with especially serious effects on those cities located on low-lying land. The global economic map will be drastically reshaped.

Atmospheric pollution

Industrial processes (including transportation) create other forms of atmospheric damage in addition to the effect of CO_2 emissions on climate change. Some of these types of atmospheric pollution are invisible to the naked eye; others are very visible indeed, most notably the dense clouds of yellow polluted air found in major cities and industrial clusters. One of the most important types of atmospheric damage occurs in the earth's *ozone layer*. Ozone is formed in the stratosphere through the chemical reaction of oxygen and sunlight. At this level, ozone is vital to the sustainability of human life on earth because it absorbs almost all the ultra-violet radiation from the sun, which would otherwise make human life impossible. Equally, an excess of ozone in the atmosphere is inimical to temperature change and to human health. Any damage to this vital protective shield poses a serious problem.

Just such thinning of – or even holes in – the ozone layer (beyond natural occurrences) began to be identified in certain parts of the world in the early 1970s. One of the major effects of ozone depletion is an increase in the incidence of skin cancer. A primary cause was believed to be the chlorofluorocarbons (CFCs), which had become extensively used in refrigeration and aerosols. Although CFCs are now heavily restricted, the fact that these chemicals are immensely stable means that the amount already in the stratosphere will still be affecting the ozone layer until about 2087.[12] In fact, there is no guarantee that holes in the ozone layer will not continue to appear and even to grow.

The most significant types of atmospheric pollution induced by the processes of production, distribution and consumption result from the emission of a whole range of tiny particles of sulphur dioxide, nitrogen oxides, lead, copper, zinc and other products of combustion. Such particles may remain in the atmosphere as solid particulate matter (SPM) or in a dissolved state in rainfall or in rivers and lakes. In each case, the result is a serious environmental and health problem. Although such pollution may have localized sources it frequently spreads very widely, depending on the nature of the pollutant and the prevailing atmospheric conditions, notably air mass and wind directions and intensities. What is usually called *acid rain*, for example, is generated at specific locations (coal-fired power stations, metallic ore smelters) but can travel across considerable distances to affect places far from the point of generation. It causes acidification of rivers and lakes, damages vegetation, degrades soils and corrodes buildings. Such acidic pollutants are classic cases of global – or at least, trans-boundary – environmental damage.

Figures 15.5 and 15.6 provide two examples of pollution through the concentration of particulate matter that are closely linked to the operation of global production networks. Figure 15.5 maps the particulate matter emitted by ocean-going ships, a key element in the movement of materials, commodities, products and wastes within GPNs. This is a much bigger source of environmental pollution than air transport. It is estimated that merchant shipping emits 1.2 billion tonnes of CO_2 per year. For example,

> When the world's largest merchant ship ferries its monthly cargo of 13,000 containers between China and Europe it burns nearly 350 tonnes of fuel a day … its giant diesel engine can emit more than 300,000 tonnes of CO_2 a year – equivalent to a medium-sized coal power station.[13]

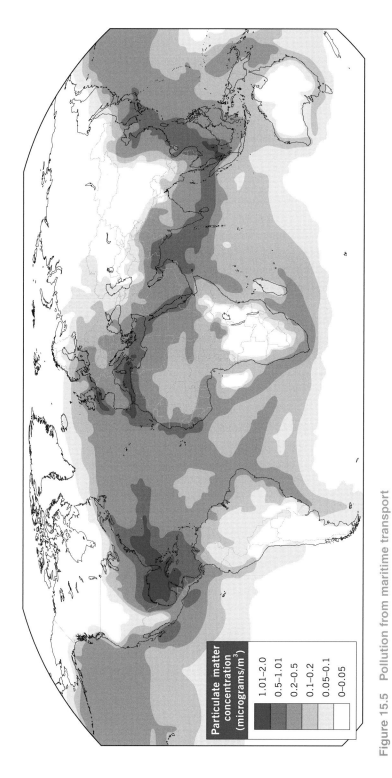

Figure 15.5 Pollution from maritime transport

Source: based on Corbett et al., 2007: Figure 1; *The Guardian*, 13 February 2008

Particulate matter
concentration
(micrograms/m³)

1.01–2.0
0.5–1.01
0.2–0.5
0.1–0.2
0.05–0.1
0–0.05

Most significant is the fact that ships use the most polluting type of oil – what is known as 'bunker fuel' – which is the residue from crude oil refining after all the cleaner elements have been removed. It is an extremely potent source of pollution-induced health problems.

> Our results indicate that shipping-related emissions from maritime shipping contribute approximately 60,000 deaths annually at a global scale, with impacts concentrated in coastal regions on major trade routes. Most mortality effects are seen in Asia and Europe where high populations and high shipping-related PM concentrations coincide.[14]

Apart from such concentrated sources of atmospheric pollution as power stations, metal smelters and oceanic shipping routes, among the most significant locations of health-threatening pollution are the world's major cities. Figure 15.6 shows the variation in concentrations of particulate matter across major world cities. Virtually all cities have levels of concentration above the World Health Organization guidelines of 20 micrograms per cubic metre. However, the biggest problems are clearly in big cities in developing countries, where there has been rapid industrialization, inefficient power generation and an accelerated increase in car ownership (often of old polluting vehicles). One extremely serious by-product of such high levels of atmospheric pollution is the high number of premature deaths (Figure 15.7).

The 'double exposure' problem

> Climate change is an emerging threat to global public health. It is also highly inequitable, as the greatest risks are to the poorest populations, who have contributed least to greenhouse gas (GHG) emissions. The rapid economic development and the concurrent urbanization of poorer countries mean that developing-country cities will be both vulnerable to health hazards from climate change and, simultaneously, an increasing contributor to the problem.[15]

> Climate change is claiming 300,000 lives a year and costing the global economy $125bn annually, with the damage set to escalate rapidly … A further 300m people around the world are seriously affected by climate change through, for instance, malnutrition or disease and by being displaced from their homes.[16]

The highly uneven incidence and impact of climate change and atmospheric pollution, in conjunction with the immense variations in global economic well-being discussed in Chapter 16, create what has been called a 'double exposure' problem.

> Both climate change and economic globalization are ongoing processes with uneven impacts, and both include implicit winners and losers … Double exposure refers to cases where a particular region, sector, ecosystem or social group is confronted by the impacts of both climate change and economic

Figure 15.6   Air pollution in world cities

Source: based on data from World Bank, 2008a: Table 3.14

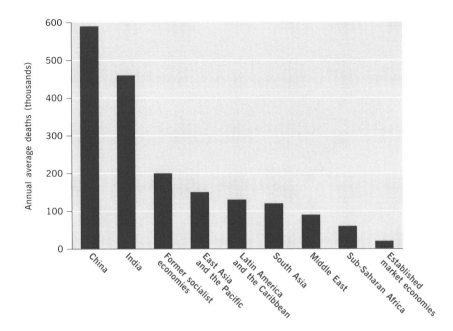

Figure 15.7   Premature deaths due to urban air pollution

Source: data from World Bank; WorldWatch Institute, cited in the *Financial Times*, 27 January 2006

globalization. It recognises that climate impacts are influenced not only by current socioeconomic trends, but also by structural economic changes that are reorganizing economic activities at the global scale ... different outcomes emerge when the two processes are considered together.[17]

It is the world's poorest countries that are most seriously threatened. Although Africa is a 'double loser' overall, the situation is more varied than this generalization suggests. There are sectoral effects, as in the case of Mexican agriculture: 'farmers who are trying to compete in ... international markets as well as agricultural wage labourers in Mexico are ... likely to be double losers in terms of climate change and globalization'.[18] Among the most vulnerable social groups affected by double exposure are the poor residents of cities in both the developed and developing worlds:

At the same time that globalization is contributing to the economic vulnerability of disadvantaged residents of US cities, climate change may increase the physical vulnerability of these groups to weather-related events. Climate change may increase mean summer temperatures in Northern cities, and may also increase the frequency and magnitude of summer heat waves, consequently increasing heat-related illnesses and deaths ... Residents of poor, inner-city communities are among the most vulnerable to heat waves due to lack of resources to pay for air conditioning or to leave stifling central city areas … Globalization and climate change thus represent a dual threat to these groups.

For poor residents of cities in the developing world, the double impacts of globalization and climate change may be even more severe … In conjunction with increased financial vulnerability as the result of globalization, poor residents of developing world cities are also among the groups that are most vulnerable to climatic change. Many of the urban poor live in shantytowns and squatter settlements located in precarious areas such as on hillsides … Such areas are especially vulnerable to mudslides or flooding as the result of severe storms, events that may increase in both frequency and magnitude as the result of climate change. In addition to direct physical hazards, the urban poor are also vulnerable to climate change related health-hazards, particularly outbreaks of diseases such as cholera and malaria, both of which increase with warm spells and heavy rains.[19]

The argument, therefore, is that different sets of winners and losers from globalization may emerge when the effects of the two sets of global processes – economic globalization and environmental change – are superimposed both on those who are vulnerable and on those who may benefit.

Fouling the nest: creating and disposing of waste

Distinguishing between 'valueless waste' and 'valuable materials'

Wastes are materials that are not prime products (that is, products produced for the market) for which the generator has no further use in terms of his/her own purposes of production, transformation or consumption, and which he/she wants to dispose.[20]

However, distinguishing between 'waste' (valueless or useless materials) and valuable/useful materials is far from straightforward. A glance back to Figures 15.1 and 15.2 show why this is so.

Conventionally 'waste' is seen as the end-of-pipe/end-of-process unwanted and valueless product of a linear process. In contrast, given a conceptualization of the economy as complex, marked by recursive flows and feedback loops, 'waste' is more appropriately seen as an unintended consequence of every stage in the economy, every material transformation. Equally, however, such 'waste' has the potential once again to become a valued and valuable material. *Whether a material is seen as valueless waste or valuable resource is therefore a contingent and context dependent matter, depending on specific combinations of material, technological, economic and regulatory influences in time/space.*[21]

An inexorable avalanche of waste

It is almost impossible to calculate the exact amount of waste generated at a global scale by producers and consumers. According to UNEP, many countries do not report waste levels at all or, where such reporting does exist, there are large inconsistencies in reporting practices.[22] The Basel Convention supposedly monitors the situation but only for those states that are signatories, and these exclude the US. However, some specific examples can give us an idea of the size of the waste avalanche:

- 4 billion tonnes of waste generated by the OECD countries in 2001
- 254 million tonnes of municipal solid waste (MSW) generated by the US in 2007
- 155 million tonnes of MSW generated by China in 2005, growing at an annual rate of 8 to 10 per cent
- 1.3 billion tonnes of industrial waste generated by China
- 108 million tonnes of hazardous waste produced by the countries covered by the Basel Convention in 2001.

Hazardous wastes, which may come in liquid, gaseous or solid form, are especially problematical. They have four distinctive characteristics:[23]

- *ignitability*: wastes that may be spontaneously combustible or create fires under certain conditions
- *corrosivity*: acids or bases that corrode metals
- *reactivity*: wastes that are unstable under normal conditions and can cause explosions when mixed with water
- *toxicity*: wastes that are harmful, even fatal, if ingested or absorbed; may pollute ground water through the leaching of toxins from the waste.

Radioactive waste – from nuclear power plants and military installations, as well as from research and medical facilities – poses especially difficult problems.

Not surprisingly, some activities produce more – and nastier – waste than others. Mineral extraction (Chapter 8) is an especially potent creator of waste as earth is stripped away to gain access to the desired material. It has been estimated that

> at a typical copper mine around 125 tonnes of ore are excavated to produce just one tonne of copper. The amount of earth moved is mind-boggling and mining now strips more of the Earth's surface each year than does natural erosion.[24]

In addition, the waste rock and the 'tailings' (waste products created during mineral recovery) include toxic chemicals.

Different industries obviously generate different kinds of hazardous wastes. The industries shown in Figure 15.8 are 'traditional' industries. Newer industries create

Food and beverages		Chemicals	
Animal waste Cleaning wastes Refrigerants		Strong acids and bases Reactive wastes Ignitable wastes Discarded commercial chemical products	
Metals		**Paper and printing**	
Paint wastes containing heavy metals Strong acids and bases Cyanide wastes Sludges containing heavy metals		Ink wastes including solvents and metals Photography waste with heavy metals Ignitable and corrosive wastes Heavy metal solutions	
Construction		**Furniture and wood**	
Ignitable wastes Paint wastes Spent solvents Strong acids and bases		Ignitable wastes Spent solvents Paint wastes	
Vehicle maintenance shops		**Cleaning and cosmetics**	
Paint wastes Ignitable wastes Spent solvents Acids and bases		Heavy metal dust and sludges Ignitable wastes Solvents Strong acids and bases	

Figure 15.8   Typical hazardous wastes generated by selected manufacturing industries

Source: based on UNEP, 2004: 20

different problems. What has come to be called 'e-waste' is now the biggest and fastest-growing source. Such waste is highly problematic.

> On average a computer is 23% plastic, 32% ferrous metals, 18% non-ferrous metals (lead, cadmium, antimony, beryllium, chromium and mercury), 12% electronic boards (gold, palladium, silver and platinum) and 15% glass. Only about 50% of the computer is recycled, the rest is dumped. The toxicity of the waste is mostly due to the lead, mercury and cadmium – non-recyclable components of a single computer may contain almost 2 kilograms of lead. Much of the plastic used contains flame retardants, which make it difficult to recycle.[25]

The above examples of waste are producer generated. But, as consumers, we also generate huge volumes of what is usually classified as municipal solid waste (MSW):

> Our trash, or municipal solid waste (MSW), is made up of the things we commonly use and then throw away. These materials range from packaging, food scraps, and grass clippings, to old sofas, computers, tires, and refrigerators.[26]

As the figures above show, the volume of MSW is astronomical and poses huge disposal problems. Figure 15.9 shows the broad breakdown of MSW for the US. Although the largest share of the total materials is organic in nature – paper,

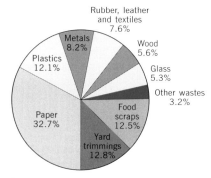

(a) MSW generation (by category) 2007
    254 million tons (before recycling)

(b) MSW generation (by material) 2007
    254 million tons (before recycling)

**Figure 15.9   The composition of municipal solid waste in the United
States**

Source: based on USEPA, 2008: Figures 5, 6

paperboard, yard (garden) trimmings and food scraps – the biggest single category is containers and packaging, followed by non-durable goods. The throwaway consumer society is the major source of MSW, at least in developed countries. Indeed, the trend is clear: 'as countries get richer, the organic share decreases whereas the paper and plastic ones increase'.[27]

Re-creating value from waste

As we saw earlier, waste almost always has the *potential* once again to become a valued and valuable material. Each stage in the materials flow and transformation cycle presents opportunities to recycle at least some of the waste created (see Figure 15.2). The problems inherent in dumping waste in landfill sites, or the burning of waste in incinerators (other than to generate energy), are so great that the recovery and recycling of waste at all stages of the production–distribution–consumption circuit has become a major priority. All countries now operate some kind of waste recycling strategy, although its scale and effectiveness vary widely. Indeed, such activity is now on such a large scale that it forms the basis of entirely new businesses and industries. In that respect, it could be said that value is being re-created. However, the economics of recycling are quite volatile. At times of very high commodity prices in, say, steel or paper, the market for scrap steel or recycled paper will be very buoyant. When such commodity prices weaken, the obverse applies. Recycling may be seen as too expensive, although national regulations will invariably insist that it is carried out.

On the other hand, there is little doubt that recycling has significant environmental benefits.

> The most valuable benefit of recycling is the saving in energy and the reduction in greenhouse gases and pollution that result when scrap materials are substituted for virgin feedstock ... Recycling aluminium, for example, can reduce energy consumption by as much as 95%. Savings for other materials are lower but still substantial: about 70% for plastics, 60% for steel, 40% for paper and 30% for glass. Recycling also reduces emissions of pollutants that can cause smog, acid rain and the contamination of waterways.[28]

A global shift *in waste*

In many cases, wastes are dealt with locally at, or close to, the point of generation. However, one of the most significant developments of recent years is the *relocation* of waste on an international or global scale. In other words, there is a *global shift in waste*. In large part, this arises from the existence of wide geographical differentials in the nature and stringency of environmental regulations. Just as firms may seek out tax havens or union-free labour havens so, too, some may seek out *pollution havens*. The notorious environmental problems within the US–Mexico border zone are often cited as evidence, as are examples of serious environmental damage in the newly industrialized economies of East and South Asia.[29]

> This differential capacity to pollute and produce dangerously in part reflects the increasing involvement of national states with environmental regulation, which creates opportunities and constraints for companies in their locational strategies. As a result of this, and changes in production and transportation technologies, 'dirty' industries and the production of pollutants can *to a degree* be shifted to spaces where their localized impacts are more tolerated ... [With the tightening of] environmental regulation ... companies began to relocate 'dirty', hazardous and polluting production activities, initially to peripheral regions within their home national territories but increasingly to parts of the global periphery ... Companies were often encouraged to do this by financial inducements and low (or no) levels of environmental regulation as national governments eagerly encouraged the perceived benefits of modernization via industrial growth, regardless of environmental or social cost.[30]

A specific aspect of this issue concerns safety and environmental management. Industrial disasters, such as the oft-quoted one at the Union Carbide plant at Bhopal, India, in 1984, have focused attention on the safety practices of TNCs. A frequent claim was that TNCs tend to adopt less stringent safety practices in their developing country plants than in their home plants. The more recent conflict in Nigeria involving Shell's environmental practices in Ogoniland raised both environmental and political issues. The now collapsed – and infamous – US company, Enron, clearly rode roughshod over environmental regulations in many parts of the world with some devastating effects.

These cases, and others, are serious in the extreme. But it is dangerous to generalize from them to produce universal statements. 'The significance of lower environmental standards in relocation should not be overestimated.'[31] A study of US companies in the late 1980s, at a time when environmental regulatory differentials were steeper than today, did not show such firms engaging in industrial flight to pollution havens on a large scale. The period following the introduction of stringent environmental regulations in the US was not characterized by the widespread relocation of pollution-intensive industries to countries with lower regulatory standards.[32]

The tendency for TNCs to relocate their environmentally noxious production has almost certainly been exaggerated, especially as regulatory pressures have intensified. However, there is another dimension to the global shift in waste that is most certainly on the increase: *international trade*.[33] According to UNEP:

> Between 1993 and 2001 the amount of waste crisscrossing the globe increased from 2 million tonnes to more than 8.5 million tonnes … Unfortunately data on waste movements are incomplete – not all countries report waste movements to the Basel Convention. However, we do know that the movement of waste is big business.[34]

It is also highly contentious business, not least because of the argument that developed countries are, in effect, dumping their waste – especially their hazardous waste – on to poor countries. Although there is certainly some truth in this, it is not the whole story.[35]

Only 2 per cent of the waste generated worldwide in 2000 was actually traded. However, the vast majority of the waste that was traded (around 90 per cent) was hazardous waste, consisting of radioactive materials, toxic heavy metals and printed circuit boards. The biggest single waste component by volume was lead and lead compounds. The most contentious material, however, is that of radioactive waste.

> Over 50 countries currently have spent fuel stored in temporary locations, awaiting reprocessing or disposal. Major commercial reprocessing plants operate in France, the UK and the Russian Federation with a capacity of some 5000 tonnes per year. Countries like Japan have sent 140 shipments of spent fuel for reprocessing to Europe since 1979.[36]

The idea of container ships moving such hazardous materials round the world is not a very comforting one. But it is going on all the time and is likely to increase.

Where does this traded waste end up? Although most of the publicity focuses on China, in fact the majority of the world's waste (around 75 per cent in 2000) is actually traded between developed countries. During the late 1990s, Germany was the biggest exporter and France the biggest importer of waste. Nevertheless, there is no doubt that China plays a huge role in international trade in waste. In large part this is because of China's recent insatiable appetite for industrial materials (see Chapter 8). For example, in 2004 the US exported $3.1 billion in scrap to China, making scrap the US's biggest dollar value export to China, outstripping airplane parts and electronics.[37] Some 70 per cent of the UK's exports of plastic waste go to

Hong Kong and, thence, to the mainland; 50 per cent of the UK's exports of paper waste go to China.[38] A similar situation applies to most other developed countries: China is the magnet for waste.

One repercussion is that it has become more difficult for domestic recycling firms to compete with Chinese recyclers, who may offer prices for plastic waste some two-and-a-half times higher than UK companies.

> [The result is that] China drives the waste trade … But the trade is being driven equally by tough EU legislation forcing local authorities and businesses to recycle more. Landfill charges are rising steeply, making it relatively cheaper to send the waste abroad. Meanwhile, major companies have moved in, offering to collect and dispose of large quantities. The trade is made possible by the vast numbers of shipping containers arriving in Britain with Chinese exports … the return waste trade to China is accelerating rapidly.[39]

This, in effect, takes us back full circle. Not only are waste materials reused in further manufacturing processes but also the huge imbalance in trade between China and the West creates yet another form of reverse trade. Not least, some of the packaging materials used in the consumer goods exported from China go back to their origin.

Global production networks are, indeed, powerful shapers of our world, both positively and negatively. Environmental degradation is, therefore, a major social problem throughout the world. It is especially problematic in many of the newly industrialized, and emerging market, economies where the

> single-minded pursuit of rapid economic growth has caused particularly severe environmental degradation … Rising environmental costs in both urban and rural areas are materializing in poor health, physical damage, loss of amenities, and other problems that demand extensive remedial spending … In order to stimulate rapid growth, the NIEs have used up significant environmental capital that can only be restored, if at all, at considerable cost to future generations.[40]

The thorny question of what can, or should, be done to ameliorate such negative effects of production, distribution and consumption will be addressed in Chapter 17.

NOTES

1   Bridge (2008a: 77, emphasis added). Hudson (2009) discusses the 'neglect of materiality' in the social sciences.
2   Simonis and Brühl (2002: 98).
3   Turner et al. (1994: 17).

  4   Hudson (2001: 288).
  5   Hulme (2004:48).
  6   IPCC (2007: 4).
  7   IPCC (2007: 2).
  8   McNeill (2000: 109).
  9   *Financial Times* (9 July 2008).
 10   Guan et al. (2009).
 11   Helm (2009: 7–8).
 12   McNeill (2000: 114).
 13   *The Guardian* (13 February 2008).
 14   Corbett et al. (2007: 8517).
 15   Campbell-Lendrum and Corvalán (2007: 109).
 16   Global Humanitarian Forum, cited in *The Guardian* (30 May 2009).
 17   O'Brien and Leichenko (2000: 227).
 18   O'Brien and Leichenko (2000: 229).
 19   O'Brien and Leichenko (2000: 229).
 20   UNEP (2004: 1). See also Taylor and Morrissey (2004), USEPA (2008).
 21   Hudson (2009: emphasis added).
 22   The following section draws extensively on UNEP (2004).
 23   UNEP (2004: 34).
 24   UNEP (2004: 16).
 25   UNEP (2004: 36).
 26   USEPA (2008: 2).
 27   UNEP (2004: 22).
 28   *The Economist Technology Quarterly* (9 June 2007: 22).
 29   Bello and Rosenfeld (1990).
 30   Hudson (2005: 194).
 31   Hudson (2005: 195). See also Smarzynska and Wei (2001).
 32   Leonard (1988).
 33   See, for example, Beukering (2001), Beukering and Bouman (2001), UNEP (2004).
 34   UNEP (2004: 30).
 35   UNEP (2004: 30).
 36   UNEP (2004: 31).
 37   Goldstein (2007).
 38   UK Department for Environment, Food and Rural Affairs (Defra) figures.
 39   *The Guardian* (20 September 2004).
 40   Brohman (1996: 126, 127).

Sixteen

WINNING AND LOSING:
WHERE YOU LIVE REALLY MATTERS

> *'Old' and 'young' populations*
> *An urban explosion*
> People on the move: migration
> *Global migration trends*
> *Home-country implications of out-migration*
> *Host-country implications of in-migration*

Location matters

There is no such thing as being born equal. It depends upon whether the address is good or bad.[1]

The real *effects* of globalizing processes are felt not at the global or the national level but at the *local* scale: the communities within which people struggle to meet the needs of their daily lives. It is at this scale that physical investments in economic activities are actually put in place, restructured or closed down. It is at this scale that most people make their living and create their own family, household and social communities. Despite the undoubtedly large volumes of migration that have occurred throughout human history, most people live out their lives within the country – often even the locality – of their birth. A person's place of birth or residence, therefore, is a key determinant of the range of 'life chances' that are available. These are highly unevenly distributed across the earth's surface at all geographical scales: between countries, within countries, even within individual cities.

The contours of the well-being map show a landscape of staggeringly high peaks of affluence and deep troughs of deprivation interspersed with plains of greater or lesser degrees of prosperity. Writing before the onset of the 2008 global economic crisis, the UN *Human Development Report* observed:

The era of globalization has been marked by dramatic increases in technology, trade and investment – and an impressive increase in prosperity. Gains in human development have been less impressive. Large parts of the developing world are being left behind. Human development gaps between rich and poor countries, already large, are widening … The scale of the human development gains registered over the past decade should not be underestimated – nor should it be exaggerated. Part of the problem of global snapshots is that they obscure large variations across and within regions … Progress towards human development has been uneven across and within regions and across different dimensions.[2]

Today, this statement is even more valid.

Looking at the world through the lens of global production networks leads us to think of the map of economic activities as a set of variably interconnected

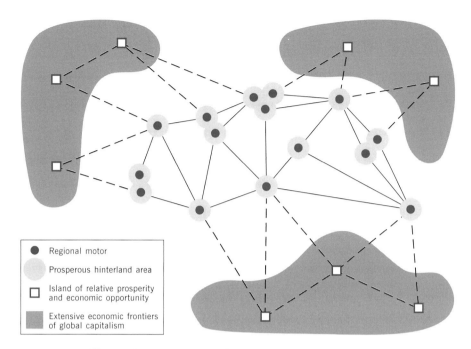

Legend:

- ● Regional motor
- ⬤ Prosperous hinterland area
- ☐ Island of relative prosperity and economic opportunity
- ▮ Extensive economic frontiers of global capitalism

Figure 16.1 The global economy as interconnected 'islands'

Source: based on Scott, 1998: Figure 4.2

'islands', rather than as a continuous surface. Figure 16.1 is one such representation by Allen Scott, in which

> the developed areas of the world are represented as a system of polarized regional economies each consisting of a central metropolitan area and a surrounding hinterland (of indefinite extent) occupied by ancillary communities, prosperous agricultural zones, smaller tributary centers, and the like ... Each metropolitan nucleus is the site of intricate networks of specialized but complementary forms of economic activity, together with large, multi-faceted labour markets, and each is a locus of powerful agglomeration economies and increasing returns effects ... These entities can be thought of as *the regional motors of the new global economy* ... Equally, there are large expanses of the modern world that lie at the extensive economic margins of capitalism ... Even so, underdeveloped areas are occasionally punctuated by islands of relative prosperity.[3]

This notion of 'islands of relative prosperity' resonates with the more general metaphor of the global economy as an *archipelago* (literally, a sea studded with many islands).[4]

The processes of winning and losing in the global economy are highly interconnected. Development and underdevelopment are, in a very real sense, two sides of the same coin, although the relationships are more complex than is often suggested. In particular,

> establishing a link between globalization and inequality is fraught with difficulty, not only because of how globalization is defined and how inequality is measured, but also because the entanglements between globalization forces and 'domestic' trends are not that easy to separate out ... However, there is sufficient evidence to conclude that contemporary processes of globalization have been accompanied by a rise in global inequality and vulnerability.[5]

At the global scale, the development gap is stunningly wide. The developed countries are clearly 'winners'. They continue to contain a disproportionate share of the world's wealth, trade, investment and access to modern technologies (especially information technologies). The 20 per cent of the world's population living in the highest-income countries have well over 80 per cent of world income, trade, investment and communications technology. The 20 per cent of the world's population living in the poorest countries have around 1 per cent.

In the developed countries of the world, the trajectory has been of generally increasing affluence, although not everybody has been a winner. The picture in the developing countries of the world is very different. Although there are some undoubted winners, there are also many losers. In large part, though by no means entirely, the economic progress and material well-being of developing countries are linked to what happens in the developed economies. A continuation of buoyant economic conditions in those economies, stimulating a general expansion of demand for both primary and manufactured products, would undoubtedly help developing countries. But the notion that 'a rising tide will lift all boats', while containing a kernel of truth, ignores the enormous variations that exist between countries. The shape of the 'economic coastline' is highly irregular; some economies are beached and stranded way above the present water level. Indeed, the global financial and economic crisis that erupted in 2008 may well have redrawn the economic coastline in rather dramatic ways, just as the effects of climate change threaten to redraw the physical coastline. In both cases, we cannot yet see precisely what new forms will emerge.

For the poorest countries, however, there is no automatic guarantee that a rising tide of economic activity would, on its own, do very much to refloat them. The internal conditions of individual countries – their histories, cultures, political institutions, forms of civil society, resource base (both natural and human) – obviously influence their developmental prospects. However, despite the claims of the 'neo-environmental determinists', low levels of development cannot be explained simplistically in terms of the natural environment (for example, climatic conditions).[6] As always, it is a specific combination of external and internal conditions which determines the developmental trajectory of individual countries. For the developing world as a whole, the basic problems are those of extreme poverty, continuing rapid population growth, and a lack of adequate employment opportunities.

Apart from the yawning gap between developed and developing countries as a whole, however, there are enormous disparities within the developing world itself.

In this chapter, we focus on two tightly interconnected dimensions of the problems posed by globalizing processes for both developed and developing countries: incomes and jobs. There is a very good reason for adopting such a perspective. *Income* is the key to an individual's or a family's material well-being. However, income – or the lack of it in the form of *poverty* – is not an end in its own right but, rather, a means towards what Amartya Sen calls 'development as freedom'. In that sense, poverty is an 'unfreedom': 'a deprivation of basic capabilities, rather than merely a low income'.[7]

The major source of income (for all but the exceptionally wealthy) is *employment*, or *self-employment*. Hence, the question '*Where will the jobs come from?*' is a crucial one throughout the world. The major employment changes that have been occurring in both developed and developing countries are the result of an intricate interaction of processes. Job losses in the developed market economies, for example, cannot be attributed simply to the relocation of production to low-cost developing countries. There is far more to it than this. What is clear, however, is that the industrialized economies face major problems of adjusting to the decline in manufacturing jobs in particular but also, increasingly, in some service jobs, especially in the current global crisis. However, the problems facing developing countries are infinitely more acute, despite the spectacular success of a small number of newly industrialized economies.

Incomes and poverty

The contours of world poverty

Before the beginning of the nineteenth century, the differences in levels of income between different parts of the world were relatively small:

> At the dawn of the first industrial revolution, the gap in per capita income between Western Europe and India, Africa, or China was probably no more than 30 per cent. All this changed abruptly with the industrial revolution.[8]

Figure 16.2 shows the huge unevenness in the map of incomes. Although it is conventional to draw a distinction between developed and developing countries, the latter category is highly problematic. It implies a degree of homogeneity which simply does not exist within this group of countries. In this respect, the World Bank makes a useful distinction between three groups of developing countries based on per capita income level: upper-middle-income, lower-middle-income, and low-income countries.

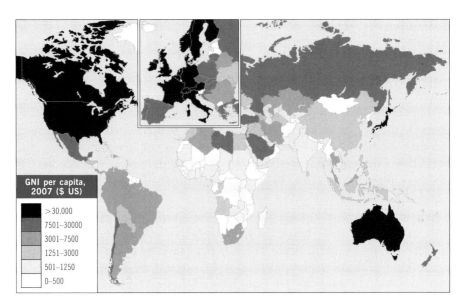

Figure 16.2   The huge global unevenness in per capita income

Source: based on World Bank, 2009b: Table 1

There is a striking geography to these categories. The whole of the Indian subcontinent falls into the lower-middle- or low-income categories. In contrast, most East Asian countries are in the middle-income categories. Despite its recent spectacular economic growth, China is still in the lower-middle-income category, although Malaysia is in the upper-middle-income group, while Singapore, Taiwan and Korea now have sufficiently high per capita incomes to fall into the high-income category, along with the world's developed countries. Singapore, in particular, now has a per capita income level higher than several European countries. All countries in Latin America and the Caribbean are in the middle-income group, apart from low-income Haiti. No fewer than 33 of the world's poorest countries (two-thirds of the total) are in Africa. Their average per capita income is $578 compared with the average for the high-income countries of $37,566 (a ratio of 1:65!). But within the low-income group, 26 of the 33 countries have a per capita income less than the group's average. Indeed, the very poorest have per capita incomes of less than $200. These are the world's most deeply impoverished countries, many of which face mass starvation, and again the vast majority are located in Africa.

Figure 16.3 provides an especially graphic perspective on gross national income (GNI) distribution.

> The height of the bars is the level of GNI per head by decile of the population in the 140 countries … Each country has a number of bars equivalent to its population. The graph, therefore, gives a general simultaneous impression of two distributions – between countries (the longer axis ascending from left to right) and between income groups (the shorter axis from left to right).[9]

Annual income (international $), 2008

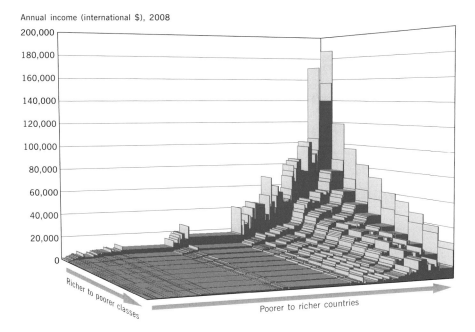

Figure 16.3   Global distribution of income per capita

Source: graph compiled by Bob Sutcliffe (December 2009)

Poverty brings with it a whole host of other problems. For example:

- The life expectancy at birth of males in the low-income countries averages 56 years, compared with 76 years in high-income countries. But the range within the poor countries is very wide: from 41 to 68 years.
- The life expectancy at birth of females in the low-income countries averages 58 years (82 years in high-income countries). The range is from 43 to 73 years.
- The average adult literacy rate (as a percentage of the population over 15 years) in low-income countries is 61 per cent (99 per cent in high-income countries). The range in low-income countries is 24 to 74 per cent.

The income patterns shown in Figures 16.2 and 16.3 are snapshots of a single point in time. But what are the trends in global income distribution over time? Is the poverty gap getting bigger? Are the numbers living in poverty increasing or falling? Unfortunately, there is no simple and straightforward answer to these questions. The extent to which the income gap is widening, narrowing or staying about the same is controversial and depends on how it is measured.[10] Not only this, but also the statistical data are incomplete and often out of date. Figure 16.4 provides one perspective over a lengthy historical period (from 1820 to 2007). It is a striking picture which shows how dramatically the gap between the richest and the poorest countries progressively widened as industrialization (and globalization)

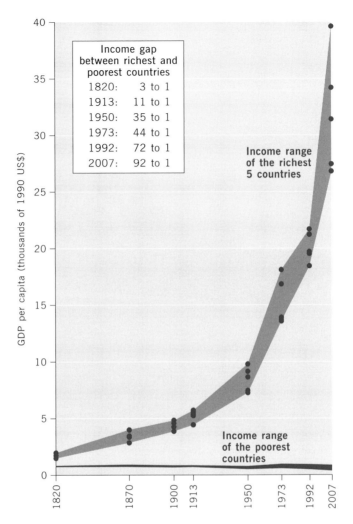

Figure 16.4   The widening income gap between countries

Source: based on UNDP *Human Development Report*, 1999: Figure 1.6; World Bank, 2009b: Table 1

proceeded. In 1820, the ratio between the richest and the poorest countries was 3 to 1; by 2007 it had grown to a staggering 92 to 1.

A rather different way of measuring global poverty is to calculate the number of people living on less than $1 per day. Despite very considerable advances in some parts of the world, one in five people (around 1.1 billion) live on less than this minuscule sum. Nearly 70 per cent of these utterly impoverished people live in South Asia and sub-Saharan Africa (Figure 16.5). There have been changes, but such improvement has been extremely uneven, as Figure 16.5 shows. The biggest improvement was in East Asia and the Pacific. But this is almost entirely accounted

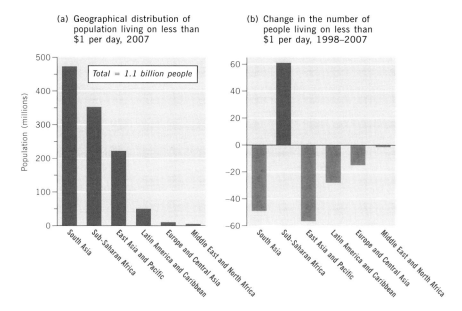

Figure 16.5 Distribution of the world's poorest population

Source: based on data in World Bank *World Development Report*, 2001; 2009

for by China. Take out China, where there has been very substantial progress in reducing poverty, and the position looks very different. In a number of African countries, for example, well over half the population has to survive on less than $1 a day and more than four-fifths on less than $2.[11]

As we have seen in earlier chapters, the spectacular economic growth of a relatively small number of developing countries – especially in East Asia – has been one of the most significant developments in the global economy in the past 50 years. In particular, the four East Asian tigers – Korea, Singapore, Taiwan and Hong Kong (although now incorporated into China) – have industrialized at a rate 'unmatched in the nineteenth and twentieth centuries by Western countries and, for that matter, by Latin American economies'.[12] The spread of the growth processes to encompass some other East Asian countries during the 1980s and 1990s – Malaysia, Thailand, the Philippines, Indonesia and, most of all China – means that

> in little more than a generation, hundreds of millions of people have been lifted out of abject poverty, and many of these are now well on their way to enjoying the sort of prosperity that has been known in North America and Western Europe for some time.[13]

In general, however, the winners – and the losers – have been the usual suspects. The already affluent developed countries have sustained – even increased – their affluence, and some developing countries have made very significant progress, but there is a hard core of exceptionally poor countries that remains stranded. Despite the generally rising tide associated with overall world economic growth, it has not lifted all boats. These data are somewhat historic, especially in the light of the 2008 crisis. But there is little doubt that poor countries will be hit especially hard.

> The World Bank … estimates that lower growth in poor countries will trap an additional 53m people on less than $2 a day this year [2009], a rise in absolute poverty that is additional to the 130m–155m increase in 2008 caused by soaring food and fuel prices.[14]

> The Asian Development Bank has warned that the global economic malaise is creating a social crisis in Asia, with slower growth leaving millions more people than expected mired in poverty and malnutrition.[15]

Inequalities within countries

Focusing the analytical lens at the country level provides a useful first cut at mapping the contours of poverty and income. But, of course, such a focus obscures the detail of the economic landscape both at smaller geographical scales and in terms of non-geographical criteria (gender, social class and so on). For example, even though most people in developed countries are significantly better off than in the past,

> it is remarkable that the extent of deprivation for particular groups in very rich countries can be comparable to that in the so-called third world. For example, in the US, African Americans as a group have no higher – indeed have a lower – chance of reaching advanced ages than do people born in the immensely poorer economies of China or the Indian state of Kerala (or in Sri Lanka, Jamaica or Costa Rica).[16]

In other words, the distribution of income *within* an individual country's population can be extremely variable.

Income inequalities within developed countries

One measure of such variation is the Gini coefficient, a summary statistic whose value ranges theoretically from zero (complete income equality) to one (complete income inequality). Although neither of these extremes is likely in reality, the extent to which individual countries tend towards one or the other extreme is a useful, if crude, indicator. A striking feature of Figure 16.6 is the relative income equality within the Nordic countries, as well as in Japan and Germany; and, in contrast, the fact that the US has a much poorer income distribution than any other leading developed economy and this has worsened since the 1960s. In 1967, the Gini coefficient for the US was 0.39; by 2007 it was 0.46.[17]

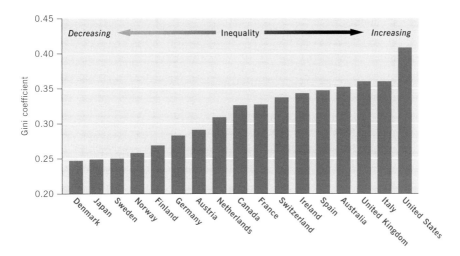

Figure 16.6 Variations in income inequality within developed countries

Source: calculated from data in UNDP, 2008

The Gini coefficient is a highly aggregative measure of income distribution. Another approach is to examine the share that each quintile (fifth) of the population has of national income and how that changes over time. Figure 16.7 shows this for the US and the UK between 1977 and 2007. In both cases, the only group that increased its share of total household income was the highest-income group. Figure 16.8 shows the trends in the ratio of the 10 per cent highest paid to the 10 per cent lowest paid workers in leading industrialized countries between the mid 1980s and mid 1990s, the latest years for which comparable data are available. Most striking is the extent to which the US and the UK stand out from the rest. In those two countries, the gap between the highest and lowest paid increased by more than one-third. The pattern is more varied across the other industrialized countries shown in Figure 16.8. For example, the same degree of increasing income dispersion within the labour force did not occur in many of the continental European countries. In the case of Germany the gap actually narrowed slightly.

These differences of detail between individual countries reflect specific social policies, most notably the contrast between the neo-liberal market capitalist systems of the US and the UK and the social market systems of continental Europe. But it is generally the case – as with employment – that it is the less skilled workers who have been most adversely affected.

> [A]s compensation has fallen for the unskilled worker, it has increased mightily for highly educated workers ... in 1979 male workers with a college degree earned on average about 50 per cent more than unskilled workers; by 1993

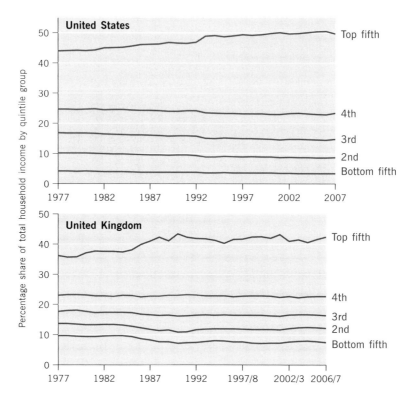

Figure 16.7   The top end wins: changing income distribution within the
US and the UK

Source: calculated from US Census Bureau *Historical Income Inequality Tables*, 2008:
Table A.3; Jones et al., 2008: Figure 3

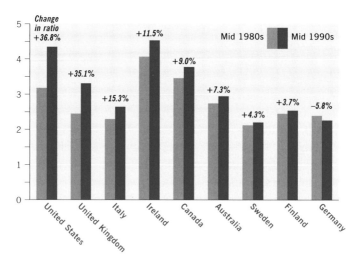

Figure 16.8   The widening gap between the highest-paid and lowest-
paid workers in developed economies

Source: based on ILO, 2004b: Figure 16

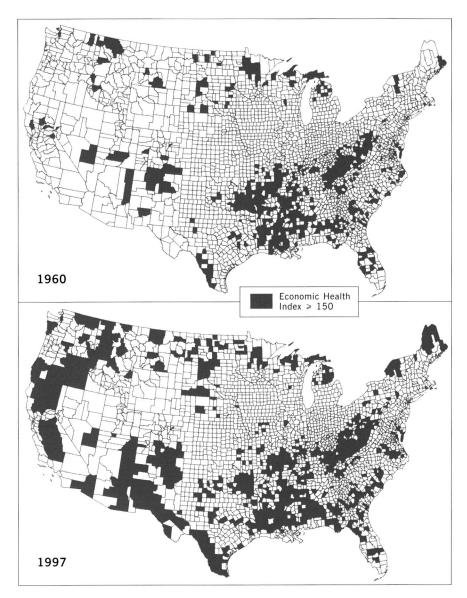

Figure 16.9   Counties within the US with high levels of economic distress

Source: based on Glasmeier, 2002: Figure 1

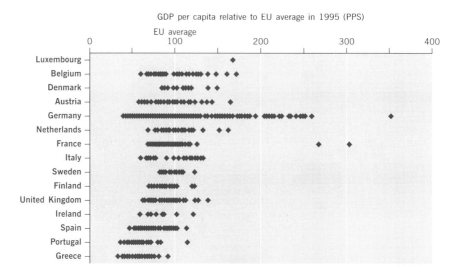

Figure 16.10   Regional income inequalities in Europe

Source: based on Dunford and Smith, 2000: Figure 2

> that difference was nearly 90 per cent. To put the inequality problem in its
> starkest terms, between 1979 and 1994 the upper 5 per cent of American
> families captured *99 per cent* of the nation's per capita gains in gross domes-
> tic product! That is, with a mean family gain over this period of $4,419, $4,365
> went to the upper 5 per cent.[18]

Such uneven income distributions also have a distinctive *geographical* manifestation.
As this chapter's title suggests, 'where you live *really* matters'. Figures 16.9 and 16.10
illustrate the enormous geographical unevenness in well-being within the US and
Western Europe. And even within the so-called 'global cities', like New York and
London, where wealth tends to be highly concentrated, there is huge income
inequality. Because of their particular functions in the global economy as the 'control points' of global financial markets and of transnational corporate activity, cities
like New York and London contain both highly sophisticated economic activities,
with their highly paid, cosmopolitan workforces, and also large supporting workforces in low- and medium-level services. The result is a high degree of social and
spatial *polarization* within these cities.[19] During the 1990s, for example, income
inequality in New York City grew much more sharply than in the US as a whole.
'New York has the worst income inequality in the U.S.'[20] Similarly, earnings differentials within London have increased substantially since the mid 1980s.

Income inequalities within developing countries

A widely voiced criticism of industrialization in developing countries is that its
material benefits have not been widely diffused to the majority of the population.

There is indeed evidence of highly uneven *income distribution* within many developing countries, as Figure 16.11 shows. Although some developing countries actually have a more equal income distribution than the US (see Figure 16.6), the situation is significantly worse in others, notably in Latin America.

Table 16.1 shows this in a different way. In countries such as Brazil, Chile and Mexico, for example, the share of total household income received by the top 20 per cent of households is very much higher than in the industrial market economies. However, this pattern does not apply in all cases. For example, Korea has a household income distribution very similar to that of the industrial market economies. Of course, the question of income distribution is very much more complex than these simple figures suggest and is the subject of much disagreement among analysts. The fact remains, however, that in general the East Asian countries have a more equitable income distribution than the Latin American countries, where there is a 'hugely unequal distribution of income and wealth. A disproportionately large number of Latin Americans are poor – some 222m or 43% of the total population.'[21]

Such differences reflect specific historical experiences and social policies, in particular the different patterns of land ownership and reform. In Korea and in Taiwan, for example, post-war reform of land ownership had a massive effect, increasing individual incomes through greater agricultural productivity, expanding domestic demand, and contributing to political stability.[22] This has not happened in most Latin American countries.

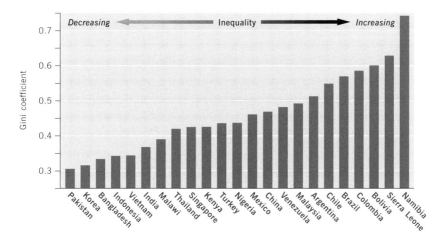

Figure 16.11 Variations in income inequality within developing countries

Source: calculated from data in UNDP, 2008

Table 16.1   Distribution of income within selected developing countries

Country (year)	Lowest 10%	Lowest 20%	Highest 20%	Highest 10%
Brazil (2001)	0.7	2.4	63.2	46.9
Chile (2000)	1.2	3.3	62.2	47.0
Mexico (2000)	1.0	3.1	59.1	43.1
Malaysia (1997)	1.7	4.4	54.3	38.4
Philippines (2000)	2.2	5.4	52.3	36.3
Korea (1998)	2.9	7.9	37.5	22.5
Singapore (1998)	1.9	5.0	49.0	32.8
China (2001)	1.8	4.7	50.0	33.1
India (1999–2000)	3.9	8.9	43.3	28.5

Source: based on World Bank, *World Development Indicators* 2005: Table 2.7

> In 1953, while Taiwan was still recovering from World War II, the island had a level of income inequality that was about the level found in *present-day* Latin America. Ten years later it had dropped to the level *now found* in France. At the same time, growth rates in this period were of the order of 9 per cent per annum … this outcome was due primarily to improved income distribution in Taiwan's agriculture sector. This improvement, in turn, rested on a specific set of governmental policies, that focused in the first instance on agricultural reforms – especially land reform, infrastructure investment, and price reform – coupled with a rapid proliferation of educational opportunities for Taiwanese students at all levels. In terms of distributive measures, land reform was of greatest significance.[23]

However, especially in geographically extensive countries, like Brazil, China or India, such aggregative income distribution data are misleading. As always, there are vast differences in income levels (and in other measures of well-being) between different parts of the same country. China, for example, faces massive internal problems. Its spectacular economic growth since its opening up in the early 1980s has created vast inequalities between different parts of the country (Figure 16.12), especially between inland and rural areas on the one hand and coastal and urban areas on the other.

> Currently, rural incomes are less equally distributed than urban incomes. However, urban inequality is increasing faster than rural inequality. At its current rate, urban inequality will eventually overtake rural inequality. Moreover, this trend would further accelerate the increase in inequality as people move to urban areas. On the other hand, the Chinese government restricts free migration from rural to urban areas. Even if such migration were permitted, it probably is not possible for the urban economy to accommodate the majority of the gigantic rural population. Thus … gaps between rural and urban incomes may persist and cause overall inequality to rise for an extended period.[24]

Winners and losers

How we identify the winners and losers in terms of incomes depends very much on the scale of analysis we adopt. As we have seen, there are huge income differentials

Figure 16.12   Income inequalities within China

Source: based on data in *Statistical Yearbook of China*, 2009

both between and within countries. However, there are two broad groups of winners and losers that merit our brief attention at this stage. These two groups cut right across the broad development divide.

The clear winners are the elite *transnational capitalist class* (TCC)[25] whose members are predominantly, although no longer exclusively, drawn from developed countries. Indeed, the emergence of a substantial class of extremely wealthy and influential individuals within most developing countries, who see themselves as global players, has become a major feature of the global economy. The dominant group within the TCC consists of the owners and controllers of the major corporations and leading financiers – the globe-trotting, jet-setting TNC executives. To these we can add globalizing bureaucrats and politicians, globalizing professionals (with particular technical expertise – even including some academics), merchants and media people. Without question, these are winners in the global economy and are highly influential in global policy discourses.[26]

This transnational capitalist class displays a number of significant characteristics:[27]

- Economic interests increasingly globally linked rather than exclusively local and national in origin.
- Behaviour based on specific forms of global competitive and consumerist rhetoric and practice.
- Outward-oriented global, rather than inward-oriented local, perspectives on most economic, political and culture ideology issues.
- Similar lifestyles, especially patterns of higher education (for example, in business schools) and consumption of luxury goods and services. 'Integral to this process are exclusive clubs and restaurants, ultra-expensive resorts in all continents, private as opposed to mass forms of travel and entertainment and, ominously, increasing residential segregation of the very rich secured by armed guards and electronic surveillance.'
- Self-projection as citizens of the world as well as place of birth.

While transnational elites are clear winners, *women* – at least in many parts of the world – tend to be losers in the global economy. A staggering two-thirds of the world's population living on less than $1 per day are women, surviving 'on the margins of existence without adequate food, clean water, sanitation or health care, and without education'.[28] In Sen's terms of 'development as freedom', women are significantly more disadvantaged than men. At the same time, because of their key role in nurturing children, women hold the key to development, especially in the poorest countries of the world. The problem is that in many developing countries (as opposed to developed countries), women have a much higher mortality rate and lower survival rate than men. As a result, the female/male ratio is lower than in developed countries, implying a phenomenon of 'missing women'. Where this occurs – as in China and India, for example – the main explanation would seem to be 'the comparative neglect of female health and nutrition, especially, but not exclusively, during childhood'.[29]

Where will the jobs come from?

People strive to make a living in a whole variety of ways: for example, exchanging self-grown crops or basic handcrafted products; providing personal services in the big cities; working on the land, in factories, or in offices as paid employees; running their own businesses as self-employed entrepreneurs; and so on. For the overwhelming majority of people, *employment* (full-time or part-time or as self-employment) is the most important source of income and, therefore, one of the keys to 'development as freedom'. However, there are simply not enough jobs to meet the growing demand.

Between 1980 and 2005, the effective global labour supply quadrupled. Half of that increase was in East Asia, primarily the result of China entering the world

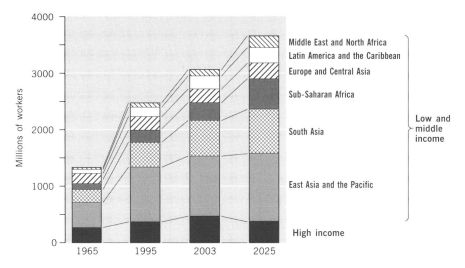

Figure 16.13 Distribution of the global labour force

Source: calculated from World Bank *World Development Report* 1995: Table 1; 2005: Table 2

market economy. In 2005, approximately 192 million people were unemployed in the world economy, 'an increase of 2.2 million since 2004 and 34.4 million since 1995' (and this figure refers only to 'open' unemployment; it does not include the millions of people suffering from 'hidden' unemployment who are not measured in the official figures).[30] And, as always, the pattern of unemployment is extremely uneven between different parts of the world, between different parts of the same country, and between different population groups.

Serious as the unemployment position is in the industrialized nations, it pales into insignificance compared with the problems of most developing countries, particularly the least industrialized countries. At least in older industrialized countries the growth of the labour force is now easing. Only 1 per cent of the projected growth of the global labour force between 1995 and 2025 will be in the high-income countries, while more than two-thirds of the projected growth will occur in developing countries. As Figure 16.13 shows, the low- and middle-income countries already account for 85 per cent of the global labour force. In many of these countries, extremely high rates of population growth mean that the number of young people seeking jobs will continue to accelerate for the foreseeable future.

> Some 46 million new workers will be joining the world's labour force every year in the future, the bulk of them in developing countries. While the world's labour force is concentrated in developing countries, its capital and skills are concentrated in advanced industrial countries. The global employment situation reflects this huge asymmetry in the distribution of the world's productive resources.[31]

Writing in 2006, the Director-General of the ILO warned:

> We are facing a global jobs crisis of mammoth proportions, and a deficit in decent work that isn't going to go away by itself.[32]

This statement was made well before the onset of the current global crisis. In 2009, the ILO set up its 'Global Jobs Crisis Observatory' producing weekly online reports of employment and unemployment trends across the world:

> What began as a crisis in financial markets has rapidly become a global jobs crisis. Unemployment is rising. The number of working poor is increasing. Businesses are going under.[33]

So, as we examine employment and unemployment trends in the following sections, we need to bear in mind that the current situation is extremely volatile and unpredictable.

Employment and unemployment in developed countries

Changing employment structures

During the past 50 years, two particularly important developments have occurred in the employment structures of developed economies:

- the displacement of jobs in manufacturing industries by jobs in services
- the increasing participation of women in the labour market.

One of the most striking trends, since at least the 1960s but especially since the 1970s, has been the disappearance of manufacturing jobs (Figure 16.14), leading to the view that developed economies have become *deindustrialized*[34] and that they are now effectively service economies. Today, between three-quarters and four-fifths of their labour forces are employed in service occupations – even higher in the UK and North America. In recent years, virtually all the net employment growth in the developed economies has been in services, although manufacturing remains relatively strong in such countries as Germany, Italy and Japan.

Within the older industrialized countries, three broad geographical trends in these processes of manufacturing decline are apparent:

- *Broad interregional shifts* in employment opportunities, as exemplified by the relative shift of investment from 'Snowbelt' to 'Sunbelt' in the US, from north to south within the UK.
- *Relative decline of the large urban-metropolitan areas* as centres of manufacturing activity and the growth of new manufacturing investment in non-metropolitan and rural areas.

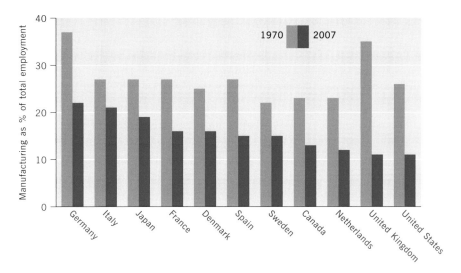

Figure 16.14 The declining share of manufacturing in total employment

Source: calculated from ILO data

- *Hollowing out of the inner cities of the older industrialized countries*: in virtually every case, the inner urban cores have experienced massive employment loss as the focus of economic activity shifted first from central city to suburb and subsequently to less urbanized areas.

Thus, deindustrialization has been experienced most dramatically in the older industrial cities as well as in those broad regions in which the decline of specific industries (including agriculture) has been especially heavy. In many cases, the vacuum left by the decline of traditional manufacturing remains unfilled. The physical expression of these processes is the mile upon mile of industrial wasteland; the human expression is the despair of whole communities, families and individuals whose means of livelihood have disappeared. One outcome of these cataclysmic changes has been the growth of an *informal* or *hidden economy*, a world of interpersonal cash transactions or payments in kind for services rendered, a world much of which borders on the illegal and some of which is transparently criminal (see below for a more detailed discussion of informal labour markets).

Some of the sharpest contrasts in the nature of employment occur in the major cities, especially in the so-called 'global cities':[35]

- In both London and New York, the proportion of the labour force employed in manufacturing declined from over 20 per cent in 1977 to well under 10 per cent in the mid 1990s.
- 'There has been a pronounced increase in casual employment and in the informalization of work in both New York and London … In addition, jobs that

were once full-time ones are now being made into part-time or temporary jobs … A majority are low-wage jobs.'[36] The precise forms of casualization vary between individual cities: in New York the emphasis has been on informal work, whereas in London most growth has been in part-time work.[37]

- In New York, 'Blacks and Hispanics increased their share of jobs, while whites lost share. Half of all resident workers in New York are now minority … Blacks and Hispanics are far less likely than whites to hold the new high-income jobs and far more likely than whites to hold the new low-wage jobs.'[38] London is the major focus of Asian and Afro-Caribbean populations in the UK. 'In inner and outer London, 29 per cent and 22 per cent respectively of residents are from ethnic minorities in 2000.'[39]

A common general criticism levelled at the new service jobs is that they are essentially poorly paid, low skilled, part-time and insecure – at least compared with the kinds of jobs in manufacturing that were characteristic of the developed countries until the 1960s. There is certainly some truth in this. Many of the new service jobs are, indeed, 'McJobs'. But that isn't the entire story. An OECD report suggested that

> most of the growth in new private services jobs in western industrialized countries is well-paid and skilled … the expansion in service employment brought faster growth in the 1990s in high-paid than low-paid work … 'There does not appear to be any simple trade-off between job quality and employment.' While the US has a higher proportion of its working-age population employed in low-paying jobs than most other OECD countries, it also has a higher proportion in higher-paying jobs.[40]

The shift in the balance of employment towards services has been closely associated with the increasing participation of women in the labour force.[41] In all developed economies, the changing roles of women, away from an automatically assumed domestic role, has gone hand-in-hand with the growth of service jobs. Although women are certainly employed in manufacturing industries, their relative importance is far higher in service industries. This is especially so where there are greater opportunities for part-time work, which allows women with families a degree of flexibility to combine a paid job with their traditional gender roles.

Female participation in the labour market has increased in virtually all countries. In the US, for example, it was around 38 per cent in 1960; today it is 60 per cent. In the UK, a similar trend is evident: from 40 per cent in 1971 to 55 per cent today. But, as Figure 16.15 shows, there is considerable variation between countries. The highest female participation rates are found in the Scandinavian countries and the Netherlands; significantly lower rates are found in Germany, France, Spain, Belgium and Italy.

There are large differences between individual developed economies in their rates of job creation. In terms of *total* jobs created, there is no doubt that, in recent years, the US has been in a different league from most of the other industrialized

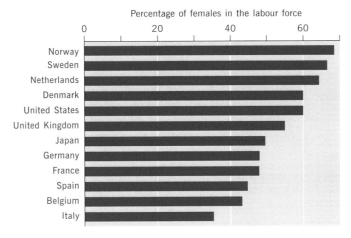

Percentage of females in the labour force

Figure 16.15 Variations in female participation in the labour markets of developed countries

Source: based on ILO, 2001: Table 2

countries. Between the mid 1980s and mid 1990s, total employment in the US grew almost four times faster than in the European Union and 50 per cent faster than in Japan. But this differential is now far less pronounced. Rates of employment growth overall have been modest – and variable – for all the developed economies. Between 1996 and 2005, US employment grew by 1.5 per cent, EU employment grew by 1.3 per cent. Within the EU, the UK has had significantly higher employment growth rates in recent years.

Resurging unemployment

The obverse of employment growth is, of course, *unemployment*. Figure 16.16 demonstrates just how volatile unemployment rates have become since the so-called 'golden age of growth' of the 1960s and early 1970s. Since then, unemployment rates in the industrialized countries have increased dramatically, though very unevenly. The overall pattern of change in unemployment rates is clearly related to the 'roller-coaster' of production and trade shown in Figure 2.3. Over the entire period, the trend has been one of significantly higher levels of unemployment in the major European economies, excluding the UK, compared with both the US and especially Japan. However, the unemployment situation in Japan has undergone a particularly significant change. Historically, unemployment rates in Japan were extremely low (well below 2 per cent throughout the 1960s and most of the 1970s). A combination of a rapidly growing economy and a very strong orientation towards job security in the large-company sector of the economy sustained lower rates of unemployment than in any other industrialized country for almost 30 years. But the burst of the bubble economy at the end of the 1980s and persistent

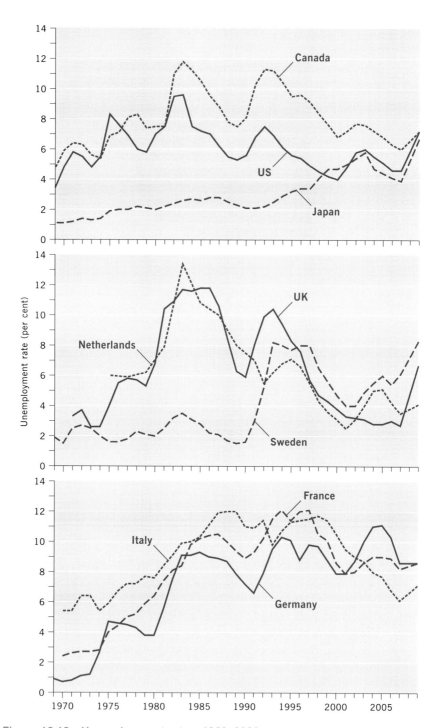

Figure 16.16   Unemployment rates, 1969–2009

Source: ILO data

domestic recession throughout the 1990s changed all that. The lifetime job system has crumbled – the days of the 'salaryman' are numbered.

The current financially induced economic crisis has drastically altered the situation once again, although it is too soon to tell how long its employment effects will last, how deep they will be and which countries will be worst affected. Estimates for 2009 show that unemployment rates rose sharply again in several countries. Reports from virtually all the developed economies suggest huge job losses, either actual or in the pipeline. For example, the OECD predicted that 'one in ten workers in advanced economies' would be unemployed by 2010.[42] Increases in unemployment rates were highest in Spain and Ireland, followed by the US, but significantly lower in the UK and France, while Germany's unemployment rate improved slightly.[43]

Whatever its precise level at any point in time, unemployment is always a *selective* process. The drastic collapse of financial services employment in 2008 clearly affected particular groups of workers and particular places where such activities are concentrated. Some manufacturing industries (automobiles being a prime example) have also been very hard hit. More generally, however, males aged between 25 and 54 years, with a good education and training, are far less likely to be unemployed, on average, than women, younger people, older workers and minorities. Most of these latter categories tend to be unskilled or semi-skilled workers.

The vulnerability of women and young people to unemployment reflects two major features of the labour markets of the older industrialized countries. First, as we have seen, the increased participation of women in the labour force – particularly married women – has increased dramatically. A large proportion of these are employed as part-time workers in both manufacturing and services, especially the latter. Second, youth unemployment during the 1980s partly arose from the entry on to the labour market of vast numbers of 1960s 'baby boom' teenagers. In most industrialized countries, therefore, unemployment rates among the young (under 25 years) have been roughly twice as high as that for the over-25s. In some cases youth unemployment is three times higher than adult unemployment. Unemployment tends to be especially high among *minority groups* within a population. In the US, for example, unemployment among black youths can be 150 per cent higher than among white youths. Similarly, unemployment rates among Hispanic youths are at least 50 per cent higher than among white youths. In Europe the problem of minority group unemployment reflects the large-scale immigration of labour in the boom years of the 1960s.

Why is it happening?

Put this question to most politicians, journalists, quite a lot of academics, and many ordinary people and you are likely to get a simple answer: 'It's globalization, stupid.' In fact, it isn't as simple as that. These highly uneven trends in employment, unemployment and incomes in the industrialized economies cannot be explained simplistically in terms of a single set of causes. In so far as globalization contributes to these trends it does so precisely because globalizing processes are themselves highly complex and intrinsically uneven. It's a matter of searching for explanatory needles in very messy haystacks.

For example, the most general explanation of an overall high level of unemployment in the older industrialized countries between the early 1970s and mid 1980s, in the 1990s and again in the 2010s is the effect of world recession. Recession, whatever its causes, drastically reduces levels of demand for goods and services. By this explanation, the bulk of unemployment in the older industrialized countries as a whole is cyclical: it is *demand-deficient* unemployment. But the general force of recession does not explain the *geographical variation* in unemployment between and within countries. In fact, a whole set of interconnected processes operates simultaneously to produce the changing map of employment, its reverse image, unemployment, and the increasingly uneven map of income.

Technological change?

Technological developments in products and processes are widely regarded as being a major factor in changing both the number and the type of jobs available. In general, *product innovations* tend to increase employment opportunities overall as they create new demands. On the other hand, *process innovations* are generally introduced to reduce production costs and increase productive efficiency. They tend to be labour saving rather than job creating. Such process innovations are characteristic of the mature phase of product cycles (see Figure 4.11) and became a dominant phenomenon from the late 1960s onwards.

The general effect of process innovations, therefore, is to increase labour productivity: an increased volume of output from the same, or even a smaller, number of workers. But, again, the impact of such technological change on jobs tends to be uneven. In most cases, it has been the semi-skilled and unskilled workers who have been displaced in the largest numbers. Initially, it was manual workers rather than professional, technical and supervisory workers whose numbers were reduced most of all, although this is no longer the case.

There is no doubt that changes in process technology have adversely affected the employment opportunities of less skilled members of the population. However, there is much disagreement about the overall contribution of technological change to unemployment. Some argue that the 'end of work' is nigh, and that much of this is due to the job-displacing effects of technological change. The explosive spread of new information and communications technologies (ICT) would seem to confirm such apocalyptic views. But do they? Not in the opinion of the ILO, which argues that:[44]

- ICT does not destroy jobs.
- In the 'core' ICT sector, the jobs being lost in manufacturing are more than compensated for by rapid growth in the services segment of these industries (software, computer and data processing services).
- There is huge potential for high-cost economies to move up the value chain and to create higher-skill jobs.
- For most workers, employment stability remains the norm.
- However, these changes in employment tend to reinforce gender inequalities.

Although technological change may continue to create, in net terms, more jobs than it destroys, the problem is the actual *distribution* of such new jobs in relation to those destroyed. Certainly, the ever-increasing pervasiveness of computerization in all areas of the economy is dramatically transforming existing divisions of labour and contributing towards a 'hollowing out' of labour market structures.[45] New technologies redefine the nature of the jobs performed, the skills required and the training and qualifications needed. They alter the balance of the labour force between different types of worker, involving processes of deskilling and reskilling. The geography of the employment effects of technological change is also extremely uneven. The 'anatomy of job creation' is rather different from the 'anatomy of job loss'; the terms 'sunrise' and 'sunset' industries imply (probably unconsciously) a geographical distinction (the sun does not rise and set in the same place).

Globalization of production?

In Chapter 14 we explored the impact of global production networks on local economies. The development of complex GPNs in virtually all sectors of the economy has a major impact on the geographical distribution of employment and incomes. In an increasingly volatile competitive environment, and driven by the imperatives of profit, TNCs continuously reconfigure their operations across, and within, national boundaries. As a result, *which* jobs are created (or destroyed) *where* is contingent upon the specific strategic behaviour of TNCs headquartered in different countries. The strong tendency to locate certain functions in particular kinds of place creates an internal geographical division of labour which, inevitably, is highly uneven by type of employment (and by income). As we have seen, TNCs are also increasingly connected into external networks of suppliers and collaborators and this creates indirect effects on employment patterns and more complex implications for local communities.

One way in which these externalized relationships impact on employment and incomes is through the currently highly controversial processes of outsourcing/ offshoring of white-collar activities, especially in financial services (Chapter 12) but also in other sectors. Estimates of the scale and likely future trajectory of such offshoring vary enormously; scare stories abound. In fact, the numbers involved are minuscule compared with the number of job changes that occur within individual countries all the time. For example, "'an average of 4.6m Americans started work with a new employer every month" in the year to March 2005'.[46] However, as always, the effects are experienced differentially, by different groups of people in different places. It is not so much the aggregate numbers affected by the reconfiguration of global production networks that counts but, rather, their distribution.

Trade competition from developing countries?

One of the most widely accepted explanations for the employment and income problems facing workers in the older industrialized countries is the competition from imports of cheaper manufactured goods from developing countries. The rapid development of manufacturing production in a small number of NIEs, and their accelerating involvement in world trade, has been a major theme of this book. It is one of the most striking manifestations of global shifts in the world economy.

The basic question is: how far has the industrialization of these fast-growing economies – as expressed through *trade* – contributed towards the *de*industrialization of the older industrialized countries, to the increased levels of unemployment, and to the pauperization of workers at the bottom end of the labour market? This has become an even more contentious issue with the recent emergence of China (and, to a lesser extent, India) as a major global economic force.

> China is no longer a marginal supplier … China's low production costs arise from and are coupled with growing industrial competence … developments in these labour forces, when these economies are integrated into the global labour force, have the capacity to significantly affect global wage levels.
> It is not just the wages of unskilled labour in the global economy which are being and will increasingly be undermined by the size of the labour reservoir in China (and India). One of the most striking features of the Chinese labour market is its growing level of education and skilling.[47]

There is a wide range of views on the relationship between developing country trade and employment and income changes in industrialized countries.[48] Wood, for example, argues that trade with developing countries has had a considerable impact, especially in widening the gap between skilled and unskilled workers:

> Countries in the South have increased their production of labour-intensive goods (both for export and domestic use) and their imports of skill-intensive goods, raising the demand for unskilled but literate labour, relative to more skilled workers. In the North, the skill composition of labour demand has been twisted the other way. Production of skill-intensive goods for export has increased, while production of labour-intensive goods has been replaced by imports, reducing the demand for unskilled relative to skilled workers … up to 1990 the changes in trade with the South had reduced the demand for

unskilled relative to skilled labour in the North as a whole by something like 20 per cent … Thus expansion of trade with the South was an important cause of the de-industrialization of employment in the North over the past few decades. However, it does not appear to have been the sole cause.[49]

The general conclusion of the ILO is that the results of the many economic studies of the relationship between trade and wage and income inequality in the older industrialized countries are 'inconclusive':

Although international trade has contributed to income inequality trends to some extent, it has not played a major role in pushing down the relative wage of less-skilled workers … [in the case of the US] employment patterns in industries least affected by trade moved in the same direction as those in trade-affected manufacturing industry, increasing the share of high-wage employment. This pattern of change in the employment structure is not well explained by the argument relying on the trade effect.[50]

Again, however, the focus tends to be on the aggregate geographical picture. Given the *particular* ways in which the internal geographies of national economies have evolved, there will inevitably be a correspondingly uneven impact of trade on different parts of the same country. But such effects are very complex, as a study of US regions shows.[51]

Many regions benefited from cheaper imports. The Southeast and South Central regions, however, both of which are dominated by low-wage, import-sensitive manufacturing industries, were made worse off by both cheaper imports and by greater orientation toward the production of import-competing goods. By contrast, the Great Lakes, a region with industries that are highly reliant on imported intermediate inputs, was helped by cheaper imports and a greater orientation toward the production of goods in import-competing sectors. On the export side, cheaper exports hurt most regions, but helped states on the West Coast, a highly export-oriented region.[52]

Recent detailed empirical research into the Los Angeles labour market suggests that

An increase in foreign competition significantly reduces the wages of less-skilled workers in the Los Angeles CMSA. The wages of more highly educated workers are unaffected by imports and appear to rise with exports. Between 1990 and 2000, the negative impact of import competition moves up the skills ladder, suggesting that higher education may not insulate all workers from the pressures of the global economy over the long-run … the impact of trade on wage inequality eclipses the influence of technological change through the 1990s, at least in our study region.[53]

Searching for explanatory needles in messy haystacks

Which of these forces are responsible for changing employment and income levels and distribution in developed economies? Is one more important than the

Positive effects	Negative effects
Cheaper imports of relatively labour-intensive manufactures promote greater economic efficiency through the demand side while releasing labour for higher productivity sectors.	Particularly in relatively labour-intensive industries, the rising imports from developing countries, together with competition-driven changes in technology and other factors, lead to inevitable losses in employment and/or quality of jobs, including real wages. This increases inequality between skilled and unskilled workers, and causes extreme redeployment difficulties.
Growth in developing countries through industry relocation and export-generated income leads to (a) increased demand for industrialized country exports and (b) shifts in production in industrialized countries from lower- to higher-valued consumer goods, to more capital- and/or skill-intensive manufacturing and services.	Employment gains from rising industrialized country exports are unlikely to compensate fully for the job losses, especially if (a) industrialized country wages remain well above those of the NIEs and other emerging developing countries and (b) the rates of world economic growth are relatively low, and/or excessively concentrated in East and South East Asia.
Employment growth and job quality improvement for skilled workers are likely to be significant in the short and medium term, even though in the long run the effects are unclear.	The employment growth and job quality improvement for skilled workers will dwindle in the long run, as a result of relatively cheaper and more productive skilled labour in the NIEs.
Relocation of production and/or imports causes negative short-term effects on workers but promotes labour market flexibility and efficiency through greater mobility of workers within countries (and, to a lesser extent, within regional economic spaces) to economic activities and areas with relative scarcity of labour.	Increased trade will further reduce demand for unskilled labour. This exacerbates unemployment because, in a world of mobile capital, the industrialized countries no longer retain a capital-based comparative advantage.

Figure 16.17   A balance sheet of effects of globalizing processes on employment in developed economies

Source: based on ILO, 1996: Table Int. 1

others? In fact, efforts to separate out individual influences, and to calculate their precise effects, have not been very successful. The basic problem in all of the individual factor explanations is that each of the factors is treated *independently* of the others. It is as though changes in one of the variables are unrelated to the others. But this is clearly not the case.

For example, although the *direct* effects of trade may be relatively small, the *indirect* effects may be larger because of the ways in which firms respond to the threat of increased global competition. They may, for instance, invest in labour-saving technologies to raise labour productivity and to reduce costs. This would appear as a 'technology effect' whereas the underlying reason for such technological change may be quite different: a response to low-cost external competition. How do we separate out 'trade' effects from 'TNC' effects when so much of global trade either is intra-firm trade or is controlled and coordinated by TNCs? In some cases, a major driving force in import penetration has actually been the direct – or indirect – involvement of domestically owned TNCs. Is this a trade effect or a TNC effect?

In fact, the decline in overall manufacturing (and increasingly some service) employment in the older industrialized countries is primarily the result of increased productivity. But this has affected the labour force differentially with the greatest relative losses of jobs and of income falling on the least skilled, least educated workers. The geographies of such effects are highly uneven, depending on the particular circumstances of individual regional and local economies.

In summary, Figure 16.17 sets out a rough balance sheet of the positive and negative effects of the globalizing processes on employment in developed economies.

Employment and unemployment in developing countries

Changing employment structures

As in the case of developed countries, the employment structures of developing countries have undergone considerable transformation over the past few decades. Some, as we saw in Chapter 2, have become highly significant manufacturing centres; others have begun to develop important higher-level service sectors. Nevertheless, allowing for such cases, most developing countries remain predominantly agricultural economies. More than 50 per cent of the labour force in the lowest-income countries is employed in agriculture (compared with 4 per cent in the high-income developed economies). Even in the upper-middle-income group (in which most industrial development has occurred) agriculture employs almost 20 per cent of the labour force. In each category the relative importance of agriculture has declined even though, in absolute terms, the numbers employed in agriculture continue to grow. The balance of employment has shifted towards the other sectors in the economy: industry and services. However, as Figure 16.18 shows, there is a clear geography to these developing country employment structures.

Some of the biggest changes are taking place within Asia which contains, as we have seen, some of the most rapidly growing economies in the world. According to a recent ILO report:

> The rapid transition from predominantly rural and agricultural employment to urban-based manufacturing and service-oriented activities in developing Asian countries will continue, and the trend is expected to even accelerate in some countries. Between 2006 and 2015, total employment in agriculture is expected to contract by nearly 160 million, with employment in industry and services expanding by 172 million and 198 million respectively ... Not only will the services sector be the main source of job creation but, by 2015, will also become the largest sector, representing about 40.7 per cent of the region's total employment ... Yet, given its size and importance for poverty alleviation, agriculture will remain an important sector, even though the main engines of the region's growth will be elsewhere ... The stage and speed of the structural change will vary across the region.[54]

As in the case of developed countries, there has also been a trend towards increased participation by women in the labour force (quite apart from their

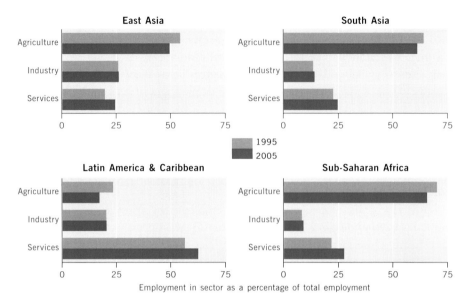

Figure 16.18   Geographical variations in employment structures in developing countries

Source: ILO, 2006a: Table 5

huge role in the informal sector – see below). But its extent varies enormously between different developing countries, ranging from East Asia and sub-Saharan Africa, where around two-thirds of women of working age are in the labour force, to one-quarter in North Africa and the Middle East. Within Asia itself, female participation rates are lowest in South Asia (around one-third). These broad structural changes in employment in developing countries have to be seen within the broader context of growth in the overall size of the labour force.

The contrast with the experience of the industrialized countries in the nineteenth century is especially sharp. During that earlier period, the European labour force increased by less than 1 per cent per year on average; in today's developing countries the labour force is growing at more than 2 per cent every year. Thus, the labour force in the developing world has doubled roughly every 30 years compared with the 90 years taken in the nineteenth century for the European labour force to double. Hence, it is very much more difficult for developing countries to absorb the exceptionally rapid growth of the labour force into the economy. The problem is not likely to ease in the near future because labour force growth is determined mainly by past population growth with a lag of about 15 years. As we will see later in this chapter, virtually all of the world's population growth since around 1950 – more than 90 per cent of it – has occurred in the developing countries.

There is, therefore, an enormous difference in labour force growth between the older industrialized countries on the one hand and the developing countries on the other. But the scale of the problem also differs markedly between different parts of the developing world itself. The situation is especially acute in low-income Asian countries like Bangladesh, India and some in South East Asia. It is also a major problem even for fast-growing East Asian economies, which are not creating sufficient numbers of jobs for their burgeoning labour forces. In the case of China, for example, it is estimated that 15 million jobs need to be created every year.[55] The basic dilemma facing most developing countries, therefore, is that the growth of the labour force vastly exceeds the growth in the number of employment opportunities available.

Formal and informal labour markets

It is extremely difficult to quantify the actual size of the unemployment problem in many developing countries. Published figures often show a very low level of unemployment, in some cases lower than those recorded in the industrialized countries. However, the two sets of figures are not comparable. One reason is the paucity of accurate statistics. But the major reason is that unemployment in many developing countries is not the same as unemployment in industrial economies. To understand this we need to appreciate the strongly segmented nature of the labour market in developing countries, in particular its division into two distinctive, though closely linked, sectors: *formal* and *informal*.

- In the *formal sector*, employment is in the form of wage labour, where jobs are (relatively) secure and hours and conditions of work clearly established. It is the kind of employment characteristic of the majority of the workforce in the developed market economies. But in most developing countries the formal sector is not the dominant employer, even though it is the sector in which the modern forms of economic activity are found.
- The *informal sector* encompasses both legal and illegal activities, but it is not totally separate from the formal sector: the two are interrelated in a variety of complex ways. The informal sector is especially important in urban areas; some estimates suggest that between 40 and 70 per cent of the urban labour force may work in this sector. It is especially important for women, who depend on the informal sector to a much greater extent than men. But measuring its size accurately is virtually impossible. By its very nature, the informal sector is a floating, kaleidoscopic phenomenon, continually changing in response to shifting circumstances and opportunities.

In a situation where only a minority of the population of working age are 'employed' in the sense of working for wages or salaries, defining unemployment is, thus, a very different issue from that in the developed economies, although even there an increasing informalization of the economy is apparent. The major problem in developing countries is *underemployment*, whereby people may be able to find work of varying kinds on a transitory basis, for example, in seasonal agriculture, as casual labour in workshops or in services, but not permanent employment.

Positive and negative effects of globalizing processes on developing country employment

There is no question that the magnitude of the employment and unemployment problem in developing countries is infinitely greater than that facing the older industrialized countries. The high rate of labour force growth in many developing countries continues to exert enormous pressures on the labour markets of both rural and urban areas. Such pressures are unlikely to be alleviated very much by the development of manufacturing industry alone. Despite its considerable development in at least some developing countries, manufacturing industry has made barely a dent in the unemployment and underemployment problems of most developing countries.

Only in small, essentially urban, NIEs (like Hong Kong and Singapore) has manufacturing growth absorbed large numbers of people. Indeed, Singapore has a labour shortage and has had to resort to controlled in-migration while Hong Kong firms have had to relocate most of their manufacturing production to southern China. In most other cases, the problem is not so much that large numbers of people have not been absorbed into employment – they have – but that the *rate of absorption* cannot keep pace with the growth of the labour force. Globalizing processes, whilst offering some considerable employment benefits to some developing countries, are again a double-edged sword, as Figure 16.19 shows.

Over-dependence on a narrow economic base

There is no single explanation for the deep poverty of low-income countries (and of some of the lower-middle-income countries too). There is no doubt, for example, that problems of inadequate internal governance (including corruption) play a major role in some cases. But in the context of the global economy, one factor is especially significant: an over-dependence on a very narrow economic base, together with the nature of the conditions of trade. We saw earlier (Figure 16.18) that the overwhelming majority of the labour force in low-income countries is employed in agriculture. This, together with the extraction of other primary products, forms the basis of these countries' involvement in the world economy. Two-thirds of developing countries have more than a 50 per cent dependence on commodity exports (including agricultural food and non-food products, ferrous metals, industrial raw materials and energy). In most sub-Saharan African countries, the level of dependence is around 80 per cent. Apart from the more successful of the East Asian NIEs, therefore,

> the exports of developing countries are still concentrated on the exploitation of natural resources or unskilled labour; these products generally lack dynamism in world markets.[56]

Positive effects	Negative effects
Higher export-generated income promotes investment in productive capacity with a potentially positive local development impact, depending on intersectoral and inter-firm linkages, the ability to maintain competitiveness, etc. Employment growth in relatively labour-intensive manufacturing of tradeable goods causes (a) an increase in overall employment and/or (b) a reduction of employment in lower-wage sectors. Either of these outcomes tends to drive up wages, to a point which depends on the relative international mobility of each particular industry, labour supply-demand pressure and national wage-setting/bargaining practices. These increases in employment and/or wages – if substantial and widespread – have the potential effect of reducing social inequality if the social structure, political institutions and social policies play a favourable role. Exposure to new technology and, in some industries, a considerable absorption of technological capacity leads to improvements in skills and labour productivity, which facilitate the upgrading of industry into more value-added output, while either enabling further wage growth or relaxing the downward pressure.	The increases in employment and/or earnings are (in contradiction to the supposed positive effects) unlikely to be sufficiently large and widespread to reduce inequality. On the contrary, in most countries, inequality is likely to grow because unequal controls over profits and earnings will cause profits to grow faster. Relocations of relatively mobile, labour-intensive manufacturing from industrialized to developing countries, in some conditions, can have disruptive social effects if – in the absence of effective planning and negotiations between international companies and the government and/or companies of the host country – the relocated activity promotes urban-bound migration and its length of stay is short. Especially in cases of export assembly operations with very limited participation and development of local industry and limited improvement of skills, the short-term benefits of employment creation may not offset those negative social effects. Pressures to create local employment, and international competition in bidding for it, often put international firms in a powerful position to impose or negotiate labour standards and labour management practices that are inferior to those of industrialized countries and, as in the case of some EPZs, even inferior to the prevailing ones in the host country.

Figure 16.19   A balance sheet of effects of globalizing processes on developing country employment

Source: ILO, 1996: Table Int. 1

In the classical theories of international trade, based upon the comparative advantage of different factor endowments, it is totally logical for countries to specialize in the production of those goods for which they are well endowed by nature. Thus, it is argued, countries with an abundance of particular primary resources should concentrate on producing and exporting these and import those goods in which they have a comparative disadvantage. This was the rationale underlying the 'old' international division of labour in which the core countries produced and exported manufactured goods and the countries of the global periphery supplied the basic materials (Figure 2.1). According to traditional trade theory, *all* countries benefit from such an arrangement. But such a neat sharing of the benefits of trade presupposes:

- some degree of equality between trading partners
- some stability in the relative prices of traded goods
- an efficient mechanism – the market – which ensures that, over time, the benefits are indeed shared equitably.

In the real world – and especially in the trading relationships between the industrialized countries and the low-income, primary-producing countries – these conditions do not hold. In the first place, there is a long-term tendency for the composition of demand to change as incomes rise. Thus, the growth in demand for manufactured goods and services tends to be greater than the growth in demand for primary products. This immediately builds a bias into trade relationships between the two groups of countries, favouring the industrialized countries at the expense of the primary producers.

Over time, these inequalities tend to be reinforced through the operation of the *cumulative* processes of economic growth. The prices of manufactured goods tend to increase more rapidly than those of primary products and, therefore, the *terms of trade* for manufactured and primary products tend to diverge. (The terms of trade are simply the ratio of export prices to import prices for any particular country or group of countries.) As the price of manufactured goods increases relative to the price of primary products, the terms of trade move against the primary producers and in favour of the industrial producers. For the primary producers it becomes necessary to export a larger quantity of goods in order to buy the same, or even a smaller, quantity of manufactured goods. In other words, they have to run faster just to stand still or to avoid going backwards. Although the terms of trade do indeed fluctuate over time (as the recent commodities boom demonstrated: see Chapter 8), there is no doubt that they have generally, and systematically, deteriorated for the non-oil primary producing countries over many years.[57]

Table 16.2 illustrates the seriousness of this problem for some African countries, each of which is heavily dependent on a single commodity for export earnings. There was a dramatic deterioration of the terms of trade for these countries at the end of the 1990s (although, as suggested above, this was nothing especially new). The figures show how the effects of the deepening slowdown in Western economies at the end of the 1990s and in the early 2000s were transmitted to these commodity producers.

In other words, one of the major problems facing these economies, especially those rich in extractive resources, is that of the so-called *resource curse*.[58] This is the apparent paradox that an abundant endowment of resources does not necessarily create rapid economic growth and development.

Table 16.2   Deteriorating terms of trade for primary producing countries

Country	1998	1999	2000	Main commodity	Exports (%)
Uganda	−5	−17	−34	Coffee	56
Zambia	−20	−26	−25	Copper	56
Mali	−11	−23	−28	Cotton	46
Rwanda	6	−11	−25	Coffee	45
Chad	−6	−15	−20	Cotton	42
Burkina Faso	−4	−16	−25	Cotton	39
Guyana	0	7	−14	Gold	16
Tanzania	1	−7	−13	Coffee	11

Source: based on material in the *Financial Times*, 30 January 2002

> In a ... study covering a sample of 95 developing countries, a negative relationship was found between natural-resource-based exports (including agricultural products, metallic minerals and energy minerals) and economic growth during the period 1970–1990 ... relatively poor per capita growth performance has generally characterized resource-rich developing countries, especially mineral-exporting countries ... Oil exporters have not been immune either to the 'resource curse' in terms of low growth ... Many studies also emphasize that countries rich in oil and solid minerals have performed worse in terms of alleviating poverty compared with countries with little or no such mineral wealth.[59]

The reason seems to be that the apparent ease of exploitation of natural resources makes it a 'soft option' and that such low-growth commodities tend to 'crowd out' potentially more profitable activities.[60]

Populations on the move

The contours of world population

Geographical variations in population growth rates, in the age composition of the population, and in migration, exert an extremely important influence on how globalizing processes are worked out in different places. They also relate, very clearly, to issues of poverty, to the ability of people in different places to make a living through employment, and to issues of environmental impact.

Population growth

At the beginning of the twenty-first century the world's population reached a total of 6.1 billion. One hundred years earlier, it was less than 2 billion. Not unreasonably, then, was the twentieth century called 'the century of population' and the 'explosion of population ... [cited as] one of its defining characteristics'.[61]

> This is an absolute increase that far exceeds that which has occurred in any other period of human experience. It took until 1825 to reach one billion humans *in toto*; it took only the next 100 years to double; and the next 50 years to double again, to 4 billion in 1975. A quarter of a century later, as we were celebrating the millennium, the total jumped to six billion. True, the pace of increase has been slowing in the last decade or so but, like a large oil tanker decelerating at sea, that slowdown is a protracted process.[62]

The UN's latest medium projection is that world population in 2050 will be around 9.2 billion, although it could be as high as 10.5 billion or as low as 8 billion, depending on what happens to fertility rates.[63]

The most striking feature of world population growth is that it now occurs overwhelmingly in developing countries. In 2005, 81 per cent of the world's

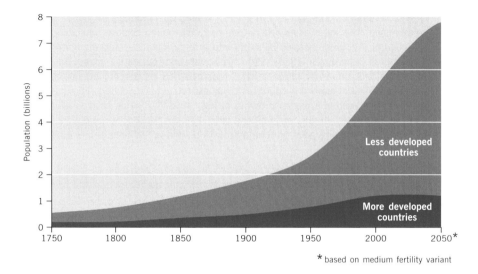

* based on medium fertility variant

Figure 16.20   World population growth

Source: based on data in UN Population Division, *World Population Prospects,* 2009

6.5 billion population was in the developing countries. Figure 16.20 shows this massive – and accelerating – divergence in population growth between developed and developing countries. The year 1950 was an especially significant turning point. That year marked the beginnings of the 'population explosion' brought about by the rapid fall in death rates in Africa, Asia and Latin America coupled with continuing high fertility rates in those areas. Since then, the contrast between the very low population growth rates of the developed countries and the very high rates in many developing countries has become even more marked.

Just to replace an existing population requires a fertility rate of 2.1 children per woman. In most developed countries, fertility rates are now well below the replacement level – at 1.56 and declining – although with an expected rise in the mid twenty-first century to just below replacement levels. In contrast, fertility rates in the developing world as a whole are currently at 2.9, although the UN estimates a possible decline to 2.57 by 2045–50. In one or two cases, they are now a little lower; for example, China is now actually below replacement level. But fertility rates remain exceptionally high in the very poorest countries: 5.02 in 2000–5. Despite high mortality rates through HIV/AIDS in many of these poorest countries, their population is expected to grow from 762 million to 1.67 billion by 2050. For developing countries as a whole, the 2050 population is predicted to be about 7.9 billion (that compares with a *total* world population in 2005 of 6.5 billion).

'Old' and 'young' populations

Persistent unevenness in fertility rates between developed and developing countries creates significant differentials in the *age composition* of the population. Put in

Table 16.3   Geographical variations in the age composition of the population
              (% in region)

Region	Under 15 years		15–64 years		Over 65 years	
	2005	2050	2005	2050	2005	2050
World	28.2	20.2	64.5	63.7	7.4	16.1
Africa	41.5	28.7	55.1	64.7	3.4	6.7
Asia	27.8	18.3	65.8	64.3	6.4	17.5
Japan	13.8	11.2	66.3	50.9	19.9	37.8
Europe	15.9	15.0	68.3	57.4	15.9	27.6
Latin America & Caribbean	30.0	18.1	63.9	63.6	6.1	18.4
North America	20.5	17.1	67.1	61.8	12.4	21.1
Oceania	24.8	18.0	65.1	62.7	10.0	19.3

Source: based on data in UN Population Division *World Population Prospects,* 2009

a nutshell, developed countries are ageing while most developing countries continue to be youthful in population terms. Table 16.3 shows the marked geographical variations in the relative importance of different age groups. Europe, North America and Japan all have relatively old populations; 'young' countries (in population terms) are overwhelmingly in the developing world, particularly in Africa, which is the youngest region in the world. Over the next few decades, both the Japanese and European populations will age very significantly. Such wide variations in age structure are enormously important for economic and social development, especially in terms of the dependency of an ageing population on support from the working population.

An urban explosion

> The urban population of the world is estimated to increase from 2.86 billion in 2000 to 4.98 billion by 2030 … By comparison, the size of the rural population is expected to grow only very marginally, going from 3.19 billion in 2000 to 2.29 billion in 2030.[64]

In 2007, a major threshold was passed: more than half of the world's total population lived in cities. The extent to which populations are urbanized, however, varies significantly from one part of the world to another. Not only is most of the world's population, and population growth, located in developing countries but also that population is increasingly concentrated in cities. In complete contrast to the older industrialized countries, therefore, where a growing *counter-urbanization* trend has been evident for some years, urban growth in most developing countries has continued to accelerate. The highest rates of urban growth are now in developing countries, where the number of very large cities has increased enormously. Figure 16.21 shows that three-quarters of the world's 'megacities' (populations of more than 10 million) are in developing countries and this is projected to increase to four-fifths by 2025.

Rank 2007	Urban agglomeration	Population (thousands)
1.	Tokyo	35,676
2.	New York–Newark	19,040
3.	Mexico	19,028
4.	Mumbai	18,978
5.	São Paulo	18,845
6.	Delhi	15,926
7.	Shanghai	14,987
8.	Kolkata	14,787
9.	Dhaka	13,485
10.	Buenos Aires	12,795
11.	Los Angeles	12,500
12.	Karachi	12,130
13.	Cairo	11,893
14.	Rio de Janeiro	11,748
15.	Osaka–Kobe	11,294
16.	Beijing	11,106
17.	Manila	11,100
18.	Moscow	10,452
19.	Istanbul	10,061

Rank 2025	Urban agglomeration	Population (thousands)
1.	Tokyo	36,400
2.	Mumbai	26,385
3.	Delhi	22,498
4.	Dhaka	22,015
5.	São Paulo	21,428
6.	Mexico City	21,009
7.	New York–Newark	20,628
8.	Kolkata	20,560
9.	Shanghai	19,412
10.	Karachi	19,095
11.	Kinshasa	16,762
12.	Lagos	15,796
13.	Cairo	15,561
14.	Manila	14,808
15.	Beijing	14,545
16.	Buenos Aires	13,768
17.	Los Angeles	13,672
18.	Rio de Janeiro	13,413
19.	Jakarta	12,363
20.	Istanbul	12,102
21.	Guangzhou	11,835
22.	Osaka–Kobe	11,368
23.	Moscow	10,526
24.	Lahore	10,512
25.	Shenzhen	10,196
26.	Chennai	10,129

Figure 16.21   The world's megacities, 2007 and 2025

Source: based on data in UN-HABITAT, 2008

In some cases, notably the cities within the newly industrializing economies of East Asia, urban growth is driven, and sustained, by the forces of economic dynamism. But, in most cases, the link between economic growth and urban growth is less clear, and owes more to high rates of population fertility coupled with rural poverty, which drive millions of people towards what are seen to be the economic honeypots of the city. In these latter cases, therefore, what we have is a process of *over-urbanization*: circumstances where the basic physical, social and economic infrastructures are not commensurate with the sheer size and rate of growth. The sprawling shanty-towns endemic throughout the developing world are the physical expression of this explosive growth.

In the developing countries, virtually all industrial growth is in the big cities. Stark polarization between rich and poor is one of the most striking features of developing country cities. United Nations data show that 80 per cent of the urban population of the 30 least developed countries live in slums.[65] Increasingly, very high levels of poverty tend to be concentrated in urban areas. Whereas rural dwellers may be able to feed themselves and their families from the land, such an option is not available in the cities. In addition, there is a whole syndrome of urban pathologies to contend with:

About 220 million urban dwellers, 13 per cent of the world's urban population, do not have access to safe drinking water, and about twice this number lack even the simplest of latrines. Women suffer the most from these deficiencies ... poverty also includes exposure to contaminated environments and being at risk of criminal victimization ... Poverty is closely linked to the wide spread of preventable diseases and health risks in urban areas.[66]

People on the move: migration

Global migration trends

The subtitle of this chapter is: 'where you live really matters'. It reflects the fact that most people stay close to where they are born. According to the International Organization for Migration,[67] the number of international migrants in the world represents only around 3 per cent of the total global population. This is significantly lower than in the nineteenth century, when international migrants accounted for 10 per cent of the world population.[68]

On the other hand, in absolute terms, international migration is higher today than it has ever been. There are more than 200 million international migrants, to which must be added a further 20–30 million unauthorized migrants. Some international migrants – asylum seekers – are fleeing various kinds of persecution, and these tend to reflect very specific political, social and religious conditions in their home countries. But the majority of international migrants are *migrant workers*.

The geographical distances over which international migration occurs are enormously varied. A large proportion of migrant flows are to countries close to the place of origin – for fairly obvious reasons, including cost, greater knowledge of closer opportunities, possibly greater cultural compatibility. But over and above such short-distance migrations are the long-distance, often intercontinental, flows. Certain migration paths are especially important, as Figure 16.22 indicates for the world's major regions. In the case of large countries, like China, there is also a vast amount of internal migration whose geographical scale is greater than much cross-border migration. The Chinese government estimates that there are 130 million internal migrant workers in China, of whom around 80 million have moved from poorer interior regions to the coastal cities.[69] Table 16.4 shows the major migrant destinations.

One of the most important results of international migration is the creation of geographically dispersed *transnational migrant communities*, particularly in cities in developed countries.[70] These complex networks created by migrants – especially labour migrants – between their places of origin and their places of settlement constitute particular kinds of transnational social spaces held together by financial remittances and social networks derived from ethnic ties. Such transnational communities play an extremely significant role not only in channelling subsequent migrant flows but also in investment patterns and in the creation of distinctive forms of entrepreneurship.

Region	Migrants (millions)	% of region's population	Migration characteristics
Europe	64.1	8.8	Substantial migration from outside, but most is internal migration within the EU. Large flows from east following enlargement of EU.
Asia	53.3	1.4	Huge intra-regional flows of migrant workers, both between Asian countries and within large countries. China has 130 million internal migrant workers, Asia is world's largest source of temporary contractual migrant workers.
North America	44.5	13.5	Dominated by very strong south–north migrant flows from Latin America/Caribbean to US and Canada. Increasing flows to Europe from Latin America.
Latin America	6.7	1.2	
Africa	6.7	1.2	Most migration is to other African countries. Most important migration foci are Southern Africa, the Maghreb and West Africa.
Oceania	5	15.2	Australia and New Zealand are the large destination countries, with increasing migration from Asian countries.

Figure 16.22   International migration trends by region

Source: based on data in www.iom.int/jahia/Jahia/about-migration/facts-and-figures; press reports

Table 16.4   Major migrant destinations, 2005

Host country	Migrants (millions)	% of world migrant stock
US	38.4	20.1
Russian Federation	12.1	6.3
Germany	10.1	5.3
Ukraine	6.8	3.6
France	6.5	3.4
Saudi Arabia	6.4	3.4
Canada	6.1	3.2
India	5.7	3.0
UK	5.4	2.8
Spain	4.8	2.5
Australia	4.1	2.2

Source: based on www.iom.int/jahia/Jahia/about-migration/facts-and-figures

Home-country implications of out-migration

At one level, the decision to migrate abroad in search of work is an individual decision, made in the context of social and family circumstances. When it is successful – that is, when the migrant succeeds in obtaining work and building a life in a new environment – the benefits to the individual and his/her family are clear (although there may be problems of dislocation and emotional stress). There is invariably, as well, discrimination against migrant workers in host countries. In many cases, migrants are employed in very low-grade occupations, they may have few, if any, rights, and their employment security is often non-existent. They may also be subject to abuse and maltreatment.

But what are the effects of out-migration on the exporting country? From a *positive* perspective, out-migration helps to reduce pressures in local labour markets. In addition, the remittances sent back home by migrant workers make a huge contribution, not only to the individual recipients and their local communities but also to the home country's balance of payments position and to its foreign exchange situation. Indeed, migrants' remittances have reached epic proportions: almost $300 billion in 2006. Annual remittances to Latin America and the Caribbean ($54 billion in 2005) are greater than the combined flows of foreign direct investment and development aid.[71] In many cases, the value of foreign remittances is equivalent to a large share of the country's export earnings (Figure 16.23). In a few cases, remittances are worth between one and three times *more* than their total exports. More commonly, remittances can account for between one-fifth and one-half of exports. However, migrant remittances are highly susceptible to downturns in the host economy. For example, the annual growth of remittances from the US to Latin America fell from 25 per cent in early 2006 to zero in early 2008.[72]

Paradoxically, such remittances do not always help the poorest people back home, as recent Mexican research indicates.

> 'For some people, remittances allow them to buy a basic basket of essential goods,' says Rodolfo Tuiran, of Sedesol, Mexico's social development ministry. 'But overall, in terms of poverty, remittances do not have a significant impact. They do, however, have an important impact on inequality – they increase it. Of every $100 received, $75 goes to homes that aren't poor.' Anecdotal evidence supports this. In areas of high migration, the houses in good repair, with a satellite dish, are the ones that receive remittances.[73]

On the other hand, again in Mexico, there are schemes which capitalize on the fact that migrants from the same home town often tend to cluster together in their host country. As a result, there is now a network of Mexican 'home town associations' across the US. Collective remittances to a home-town in several Mexican states are organized in a '"three-for-one" programme, where each dollar from the home town association for a development project is matched by a dollar each from the municipal, state, and federal governments'.[74] However, the 2008 financial crisis has had a disastrous effect on remittances, as labour migrants lose their jobs and incomes.

The other side of the out-migration coin is less attractive for the labour exporting countries: there are important *negative* consequences. The migrants are often the young and most active members of the population. Further,

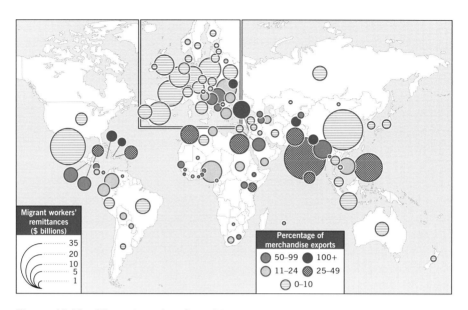

Figure 16.23   Migrant workers' remittances

Source: based on World Bank, 2009a: Tables 4.4, 6.17

returning migrants are rarely bearers of initiative and generators of employment. Only a small number acquire appropriate vocational training – most are trapped in dead-end jobs – and their prime interest on return is to enhance their social status. This they attempt to achieve by disdaining manual employment, by early retirement, by the construction of a new house, by the purchase of land, a car and other consumer durables, or by taking over a small service establishment like a bar or taxi business; there is also a tendency for formerly rural dwellers to settle in urban centres. There is thus a reinforcement of the very conditions that promoted emigration in the first place. It is ironic that those migrants who are potentially most valuable for stimulating development in their home area – the minority who have acquired valuable skills abroad – are the very ones who, because of successful adaptation abroad, are least likely to return. There are also problems of demographic imbalance stemming from the selective nature of emigration.[75]

Of course, there are important exceptions to this pattern. One is the large number of ethnic Chinese, part of the Chinese diaspora after 1949, who have returned to their homeland as the Chinese economy has opened up. Another is what Saxenian calls 'the new Argonauts' of Silicon Valley.

A small but meaningful proportion of individuals who left their home countries for greater opportunities abroad have now reversed course, transforming a brain drain into a 'brain circulation'. They are returning home to establish business relationships or to start new companies, while maintaining their professional and social ties to the US … In the early 1980s, emigrants returning from Silicon Valley began to transfer the model of early-stage high-risk investing to Taiwan and Israel. These native born investors brought cultural and linguistic know-how as well as the capital needed to operate profitably in these markets. They also brought technical and operating experience, knowledge of new business models, and networks of contacts in the US. Today, Israel and Taiwan boast the largest venture capital industries outside of North America, and both support high rates of new firm formation.[76]

Host-country implications of in-migration

Without migration, the population of more developed regions as a whole would start declining in 2003 rather than in 2025, and by 2050 it would be 126 million less than the 1.18 billion projected under the assumption of continued migration.[77]

It may seem paradoxical to think of migration as helping to solve the adjustment problems of the older industrialized countries. After all – especially in Europe – we have been talking about not enough jobs to meet the demands of the existing populations. To add further to what appears to be an over-supplied labour market seems perverse to say the least. It is such considerations, together with fears of social unrest between indigenous and immigrant populations, that have made current immigration policies in most developed countries so rigid. But, as ever, things are not as simple as aggregate figures suggest. In addition to humanitarian concerns for refugees, asylum seekers, or people simply trying to improve their lives, there are two reasons why developed countries need to create a sensible policy towards in-migration. One is immediate, the other is longer term.

The immediate reason for asserting the need for more enlightened immigration policies is the fact that, in most developed countries, there is a *severe shortage of labour*. This applies as much in high-skill sectors such as IT and healthcare as in some low-skill service sectors. The longer-term reason is that the populations of such countries are *getting older* (see Table 16.2). Their active populations are shrinking. There will not be enough people of working age to support future dependent populations. For both short- and longer-term reasons, then, there is a pressing need to rethink immigration policies. But, of course, there are major political obstacles to doing so.

Fears (sometimes justified, often not) of being squeezed out of jobs by incomers, or of local cultures and practices being diluted by 'foreign ways', generate powerful forces of opposition. Such fears are easily exploited by political groups of the extreme right, as can be seen today in many European countries, as well as in the US. Labour force displacement does, indeed, happen. But not invariably so – and not on the scale so often imagined. One of the biggest obstacles to popular support for more liberal migration policies is that the size of the host country's immigrant population tends to be greatly over estimated.[78] As Figure 16.24 shows, foreign workers make up a very small percentage of the working population in EU states. Of course, the distribution of immigrants tends to be highly uneven within individual countries and this is an important factor in people's perceptions. Specific transnational

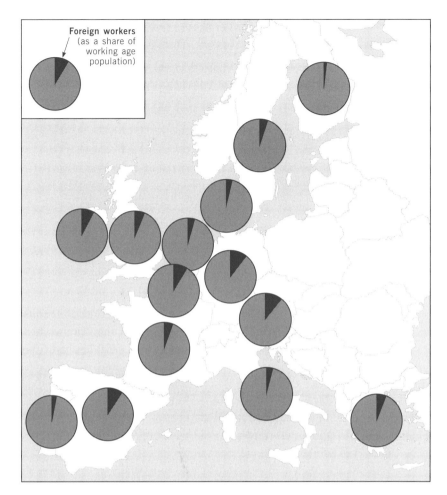

Figure 16.24   Foreign workers as a percentage of working age population in Europe

Source: based on European Commission data, cited in the *Financial Times*, 3 February 2006

communities tend to develop specific geographies, some of which are more apparent than others, and that is where the greatest tension tends to develop.

Controls on immigration are now much tighter than in the past. Despite the fact that labour migration is an integral part of the European Union, the enlargement of 2005 to incorporate a further 10 countries, mostly from the former Soviet bloc, led to 12 of the existing 15 EU member states imposing 'transitional' restrictions on migration from Eastern Europe (the exceptions are the UK, Sweden and Ireland). This is despite pleas from the European Commission for an open door policy for new members and the fact that 'in most EU15 countries, workers from the new members make up less than 1% of the workforce'.[79] Similar problems exist in the case of Mexican migration into the US. Indeed, proposals to build a more robust physical barrier along the border to reduce the roughly 400,000 Mexicans who cross the border into the US illegally every year appear to be supported by a majority of the US population.

Yet, many parts of the European and US economies – as well as many public services – simply could not operate without the employment of migrant workers. The need for an influx of new workers will not go away. On the contrary, given the demographic trends in all the developed countries, the need will increase. It can also be argued that not only does in-migration fill important needs – often performing tasks that, otherwise, will go unperformed – but also it need not have the negative effects claimed by opponents. A recent study of Europe claims that increased immigration leads to economic expansion rather than to job losses.[80] Indeed, the sharp decline in the value of the UK pound against the Euro in 2008 led to large numbers of Eastern European nationals returning home.[81] Migration is, indeed, a highly volatile process.

NOTES

1   Higbee (1970: 109–10).
2   UNDP (2005: 19, 21).
3   Scott (1998: 68, 70).
4   Veltz (1996). For an elaboration of this concept within a GPN framework, see Hess (2009).
5   Amin (2004: 218).
6   One of the surprising developments of recent years has been the return to the old – and totally discredited – 'environmental' explanations of differences in economic development by the historian Landes (1998) and the economist Sachs (1997).
7   Sen (1999: 20).
8   Bairoch quoted in Cohen (1998: 17).
9   Sutcliffe (2009: 764).
10 See, for example, Basu (2006), Crow et al. (2009), Edward (2006), Kaplinsky (2001), Wade (2004b), Wolf (2004: Chapter 9).
11 UNDP (2008: Table 3).
12 Ito (2001: 77).
13 Henderson (1998: 356–7).
14 *Financial Times* (19 February 2009).
15 Cited in the *Financial Times* (29 June 2009).
16 Sen (1999: 21).
17 US Census Bureau *Historical Income Inequality Tables*. www.census.gov/hhes/www/income/historic/ineqtoc.html.
18 Kapstein (1999: 101).
19 See Friedmann (1986), Sassen (2001).
20 Sassen (2001: 270).

21   *The Economist* (17 September 2005).

22   Kapstein (1999: 118).

23   Kapstein (1999: 119).

24   Wu and Perloff (2005: 23).

25   Sklair (2001).

26   Carroll and Carson (2003), Carroll (2007).

27   Sklair (2001: 18–23); quotation is from that work.

28   Department of International Development (2000: 12).

29   Sen (1999: 106).

30   ILO (2006a: 2).

31   Ghose et al. (2009: 1).

32   ILO Press Release (24 January 2006).

33   www.ilo.org/jobcrisis.

34   See Rowthorn and Ramaswamy (1997), Treganna (2009).

35   Sassen (2001: Chapters 8 and 9) provides much detailed empirical data on London, New York and Tokyo.

36   Sassen (2001: 289, 290).

37   Sassen (2001: 294).

38   Sassen (2001: 306).

39   Sassen (2001: 309).

40   *Financial Times* (22 June 2001).

41   See ILO (2004b).

42   *Financial Times* (31 March 2009).

43   *Financial Times* (22 January 2010).

44   ILO (2001: 140–1).

45   Levy and Murname (2004).

46   *The Economist* (2 July 2005).

47   Kaplinsky (2001: 56–7).

48   See, for example, Cline (1997), ILO (1997), Kaplinsky (2001), Kapstein (1999; 2000), Rigby and Breau (2006), Silva and Leichenko (2004), Wood (1994).

49   Wood (1994: 8, 11, 13).

50   ILO (1997: 71, 73).

51   Silva and Leichenko (2004).

52   Silva and Leichenko (2004: 283).

53   Rigby and Breau (2006: 18).

54   ILO (2007b: 10).

55   *The Economist* (14 January 2006), *Financial Times* (7 October 2005).

56   UNCTAD (2002: 53).

57   Kaplinsky (2004: 78–9).

58   See Bridge (2008b), Sachs and Warner (2001), UNCTAD (2007: 93–4)

59   UNCTAD (2007: Box III.3, p. 94).

60   Sachs and Warner (2001: 833).

61   Population Reference Bureau (1999: 1).

62   Kennedy (2002: 3).

63   UN Population Division (2009).

64   Cohen (2004: 27).

65   UN Centre for Human Settlements (2003).

66   UN Centre for Human Settlements (2001: 14).

67   International Organization for Migration (2009) *Facts and Figures*. www.iom.int/
      jahia/Jahia/about-migration/facts-and-figures.

68   Castles and Miller (2009) provide a comprehensive review of migration. See also
      UNDP (2009).

69   *Financial Times* (8 January 2009).

70   Coe et al. (2003).

71   *Financial Times* (30 March 2006).

72   *Financial Times* (4 June 2008).

73   *Financial Times* (13 December 2005).

74   *Financial Times* (13 December 2005).

75   Jones (1990: 250).

76   Saxenian (2006: 7–8).

77   UN Population Division (2001: vii).

78   Dustmann and Glitz (2005).

79   *The Economist (*11 February 2006).

80   Dustmann and Glitz (2005).

81   Pollard et al. (2008).

Seventeen
MAKING THE WORLD A BETTER PLACE

Global shifts: pasts and futures

During the past 60 years, the world economy has experienced enormous cyclical variation in economic activity. The unparalleled growth of the long boom lasting from the early 1950s to the mid 1970s has been followed by periods of rapid growth interspersed with recession, stagnation and some deep and unanticipated traumas, most notably and most recently the 2008 financial crisis. Cyclical volatility is, indeed, the norm; 'boom and bust' have certainly not been eradicated. Underlying these global cyclical trends, however, are deeper, longer-term structural changes – *global shifts* – creating the *geographical rescaling* (local, national, regional, global) of economic activities. Geographically, the global economy has become increasingly *multipolar*. New centres of production – new geographical divisions of labour – have emerged in parts of what had been, historically, the periphery and semi-periphery of the world economy. There have been big changes in the relative growth rates of different parts of the world. At the same time, many parts of the world remain, to a greater or lesser degree, disarticulated from the engines of economic growth. The geography of the world economy is, indeed, a 'mosaic of unevenness in a continual state of flux'.

Without doubt, the biggest single global shift reshaping the contours of the global economic map is the resurgence of East Asia to a position of global significance, commensurate with its importance before 'the West' overtook it in the nineteenth century. But this has not been a sudden event. Like the tectonic processes that reshape the earth's crust, the build-up takes time before we become aware of the true magnitude of the change. As we saw in Chapter 2, the resurgence of East Asia since the 1960s was manifested initially in the rise of Japan, whose spectacular growth across a whole range of manufacturing sectors transformed competitive relationships in the global economy. The relative decline of the Japanese economy in the 1990s was, however, counterbalanced by the spectacular (re-)emergence of China. At the same time, the original four 'tiger' economies continued to consolidate their strengths. The result is an undoubted shift in the centre of gravity of the world economy, a shift that seems now to be on solid foundations and not a mere passing phase. But what of the future?

It is always tempting to look at recent trends and to extrapolate them into the future. There is, of course, some logic in this. After all, there is a strong element of *path dependency* in human affairs. But it isn't as simple as that. Path dependency does not mean *determinacy*. All paths have branching points: some go off in unexpected directions, others into dead-ends. This means that we need both a good map and a clear sense of the direction we wish to travel. The first requires a better understanding of how the world actually works (that's what this book has been about). The second requires an ethical and moral vision. It is about values.[1] It is about where we want to be.

Unfortunately, we are not very good at making predictions. Every year (at least), new books or articles appear claiming to set out what the world will be like in X years' time. Most are soon forgotten – usually for the very good reason that what was predicted hasn't actually happened. It is very difficult indeed to identify which contemporary events and circumstances are likely to have long-lasting effects. For example, when the East Asian financial crisis broke with such suddenness in 1997, the literature was full of prophecies of doom: the end of the East Asian 'miracle' had arrived. The future of the region was dire. Few would make those same predictions today. But what of the outcome of the 2008 financial crisis? Because we are still in the thick of it we cannot really see how the world will look in a few years' time. Will it be 'back to the future' or will there really be a 'new world', based on more than the (im)morality of the free market?

Similarly, looking a little further back in time, who, from the standpoint of 1960, would have predicted that Japan would soon challenge the US as an economic power and, in some respects, overtake it to the extent that, in the 1980s, doomsayers in the US were lamenting the demise of the US as the world's leading economy? Japan bashing became a national pastime (and not only in the US: there were outbreaks in Europe, too, especially in France). Who would have predicted that the Japanese economy itself would suddenly find itself deep in economic recession lasting for more than a decade and a half?

Who would have predicted that South Korea would become one of the world's most dynamic economies within the space of 20 years or so? After all, in 1960, South Korea was one of the poorest countries in the world, with a per capita income comparable with that of Ghana. Which observer in the early 1970s would have predicted that China would open up its economy and become, in a very short time, the most dynamic economy in the world? Or that the command economies of the Soviet Union and Eastern Europe would, by the end of the 1980s, begin to be transformed into capitalist market economies, or that Germany would be reunited? Such examples should make us wary of prediction. But we don't learn. Today's big bets are on Chinese world economic dominance within the next few decades.

We are seduced, far too easily, by big numbers. We focus too eagerly on the quantitative, rather than the qualitative, dimensions and processes of change. This raises a much bigger question: will the tendency towards an increasingly highly interconnected and interdependent global economy intensify? Is 'globalization' an inexorable and unstoppable force? Not inevitably, as the period between 1919 and 1939 shows. During that time, the unprecedented openness of the world economy that had come into being in the period between 1870 and 1913 was largely reversed through the actions of states responding to recession through increased protectionism. It took several decades to return to a similar degree of openness, by which time the world was a very different place.

Of course, the interconnections within the global economy are now much deeper – and faster – than in the past because of the ways in which the processes of production and distribution have been transformed. Development of the highly complex, geographically extensive, global production networks, which have figured so prominently throughout this book, epitomizes this. But such increased interdependence may, itself, be a source of vulnerability.[2] Unforeseen damage to one part of the system will inevitably have implications for the other parts. The sources of such potential damage are many and varied, ranging from natural phenomena like volcanoes and earthquakes to the human-made phenomena of geopolitical and religious conflicts.

But there are wider geopolitical issues, both directly and indirectly related to the economy. In the former case, there is undoubtedly a threat of renewed trade wars (not least between the US and China). The Doha Round of trade negotiations is in serious trouble and it is unlikely that anything other than a second-best agreement will be achieved. Not least, this is because of deep tensions that cut across the developed/developing country divide. In particular, there is continuing friction between the world's biggest trading areas, the US and the EU. Within parts of the EU, notably in France and Italy, as well as in some of the new Eastern European member states, there are renewed calls to protect national companies from foreign takeover (even from other EU firms). In the US, the bid by the Dubai Port Authority to purchase P&O and its port facilities in the United States in 2006 was withdrawn in the face of intense US opposition, partly fuelled by security fears in a post-9/ll world. And simmering away beneath the surface are the huge, and ultimately unsustainable, trade imbalances between, in particular, China and the US.

These cases draw attention to the impossibility of separating out the geoeconomic from the geopolitical. Three big geopolitical issues are especially relevant here. The first, and most obvious, is the set of issues that includes the post-9/11 US shift towards pre-emptive action and regime change, the Iraq War, the nuclear stand-off with Iran, the continuing impasse over an Israel–Palestine settlement, and the disturbing rise in religious fundamentalism (of all kinds) associated with these intractable problems. The implications are far-reaching and go beyond the human tragedies of those most closely affected by these conflicts.

From a global economic perspective, the most obvious is the effect on the continued supply (and price) of oil, the energy source which has underpinned the global economy for almost a century. Of course, this makes the need for energy efficiency, and for the development of alternative, renewable energy resources even more urgent. In the short run, however, the effects could be serious. As we have seen, not the least of the implications of the spectacular economic growth of China is its vastly increased need for energy and other natural resources.

The second major geopolitical issue is, again, not unconnected to the rise of China and, more broadly, to political developments in East Asia as whole. Ever since the end of the Second World War in 1945, the US has been deeply involved in the Asia–Pacific for both security and economic reasons. Until recently, this was very much in the context of the Cold War. Indeed, the post-1945 economic revitalization of Japan, Korea, Taiwan and other parts of East Asia was strongly facilitated by US activities and financial aid. With the collapse of the Soviet empire, and the opening up of China economically, the position changed.

Significant geopolitical problems therefore remain in what is now the world's most dynamic economic region. The US still sees China as a potential military threat (as well as an economic rival). The question of Taiwan is always there as a source of potential conflict, even though economic relations between China and Taiwan have improved markedly and there is huge Taiwanese investment in China. Relations between Japan and China remain extremely sensitive, not least because of Japan's reluctance to recognize some of the atrocities it perpetrated when it occupied China in the Second World War and during its longer period of involvement in China. More broadly, Japan's own future geopolitical intentions within East Asia are far from clear. Lastly, there is the intractable question of relationships between North Korea and South Korea, especially the nuclear issue.

The third big geopolitical issue is that of failed, dysfunctional or inadequate states.[3] Although many of the problems facing developing countries – especially the poorest – arise from their position in the global economy and their very weak power base in international negotiations, other problems are undoubtedly 'home grown'. There are substantial internal problems of governance, corruption and inhuman treatment of minority populations in some developing countries which cannot be ignored.

'The best of all possible worlds'?

The world has, indeed, changed and will continue to change in far from predictable ways. But is it a 'better' world? Voltaire, the eighteenth-century French writer, wrote a wonderful satirical novel, *Candide*, in which the eponymous hero lives in a world of immense suffering and hardship yet whose tutor, Dr Pangloss, insists that Candide's world is 'the best of all possible worlds, where everything is connected and arranged for the best'.[4] This Panglossian view of the world is not far removed from those to whom an unfettered capitalist market system – based on the unhindered flow of commodities, goods, services and investment capital – constitutes the 'best of all possible worlds'. Although its proponents agree that globalization is a savage process they also argue that it is a beneficial one, in which, they claim, the winners far outnumber the losers.[5]

Without doubt, large numbers of people in the developed economies, and also in the rapidly growing economies of East Asia, have benefited from much-increased material affluence. There has been immense growth in the production and consumption of goods and services and, through international trade, a huge increase in the variety of goods available. But the evidence discussed in Chapters 14 to 16 suggests a very different reality for a substantial proportion of the world's population, particularly in the poorest countries and regions but also among certain sectors of the population in affluent countries, who have not benefited – or benefited very little – from the overall rise in material well-being. There remains vast inequality between the haves and the have-nots. And that gap has been widening, despite the operation of precisely those globalizing processes that are supposed to create benefits for everybody. The 2008 financial crisis greatly exacerbated this problem.

What can or should be done about such large and pressing issues? How can the world be made a better place for all, including those at the bottom of the heap? There is, of course, no simple answer. Much depends on one's political and ideological point of view. In terms of 'making the world a better place', one person's 'utopia' is another person's 'dystopia'. Of course, choices are rarely – if ever – unconstrained. We are all deeply embedded in specific contexts, structures and places and constrained by our knowledge and resources. As we have seen, the map of such constraints is immensely uneven; for many people, in many parts of the world, the exercise of choice is extremely limited.

Globalization and its 'discontents': emergence of a global civil society?

Such divergences of position and viewpoint are encapsulated in the huge diversity of stances taken by the various GCSOs (see Chapter 3).[6] Within these groups' general focus on the costs of globalization there is huge variation both in their agendas and in how those agendas are pursued, from vociferous, often violent, confrontation through to more reformist movements. The anti-capitalist groups advocate nothing less than the replacement of the capitalist system, although precisely what the alternative should be varies between groups. For some, it would be a democratically elected world government; for some, a structure in which the means of production were controlled by a nationally elected government. For others, it would be a system of locally self-sufficient communities in which long-distance trade would be minimized. This is the position, for example, of the 'deep green' environmental groups. For some, the focus is on 'fair' rather than 'free' trade – although who decides what is 'fair' is a crucial issue. For the more nationalist-populist groups, and for some of the labour unions, the agenda is one of protecting domestic industries and jobs from external competition (especially from developing countries) and restricting immigration. For some, the objective is removing the burden of debt from the world's poorest countries or improving labour standards in the developing world (especially of child labour). The problem is that, very often, these agendas are contradictory. There are some very unholy alliances involved.

Not surprisingly, GCSOs have themselves attracted considerable criticism from some quarters, questioning their legitimacy and, in some cases, their abilities to further economic and social development goals for the poor.[7] Although the proliferation of GCSOs has 'unquestionably projected the globalization debate into the popular political consciousness in important ways … the movements themselves have a severe democratic deficit: representing humanity ultimately requires legitimation through some sort of peoples' mandate.'[8] Despite the phenomenal recent growth of GCSOs (see Figure 3.7), we certainly do not have a truly – or even a partial – global civil society.

Nevertheless, GCSOs undoubtedly force people – including politicians and business leaders – to recognize, and to engage with, the uncomfortable reality that both the benefits and the costs of globalization are very unevenly distributed and that there are severe and pressing problems that need resolution.

> The advocatory movements of global civil society are the originators, advocates and judges of global values and norms. The way they create and hone this everyday, local and global awareness of values is by sparking public outrage and generating global public indignation over spectacular norm violations. This they do by focusing on individual cases.[9]

TNCs and states bear the major responsibility

'Globalization' is a multidimensional syndrome of processes grounded in, and helping to create, specific geographies, involving *multiple actors* engaged in processes of both conflict and collaboration, and connected through asymmetrical *power relationships* (see Figure 3.1). The central argument of this book is that, among the multiplicity of actors involved in the global economy, two in particular – TNCs and states – are responsible for much of the shaping and reshaping of the global economic map. As such, they bear the primary responsibility for improving the lives and livelihoods of people throughout the world. For that reason they form the focus of the next two sections of this chapter. First, we will look at the role of TNCs in terms of their corporate social responsibility (CSR). Second, we will focus on states in the context of global governance issues relating to finance, trade and the environment.

TNCs and corporate social responsibility

'The business of business is business'

This statement, generally attributed to Milton Friedman, the free market economist, implies that the primary purpose of firms is to maximize *shareholder* value. In other words, the only actors who matter are the shareholders (stockholders) – the ultimate owners of the company. Everybody and everything else – employees, customers, suppliers, members of the communities in which the company's facilities are located, the environment – are not the company's direct concern. This is the ideology of business that dominates the US and the UK economies in particular: the neo-liberal model of free market capitalism. It is demonstrated most clearly in the context of company takeovers, where the views of the workers are usually ignored, even though they are much more directly engaged in the company than many of the shareholders (which are predominantly huge financial institutions for whom a firm is simply part of a broader portfolio), and have more at stake (their incomes and livelihoods).

In fact, such a narrow view of business responsibilities is far from universal. In many European countries, for example, a broader concept of *stakeholder* capitalism exists in which other actors ('stakeholders' such as labour, consumers and suppliers) are explicitly recognized as having legitimate interests in business decisions. In fact, issues of corporate responsibility impinge on virtually all aspects of modern life and span the entire spectrum of relationships between firms, states and civil society. We cannot explore all of these. Instead we will concentrate on those aspects of CSR that have an explicitly *international* dimension.[10]

Approaches to corporate social responsibility

Rob van Tulder and his colleagues identify four approaches to CSR (Figure 17.1). Each of these approaches reflects different degrees of relationship to the social environment and to external stakeholders:[11]

- *Inactive* CSR is essentially that embodied in the 'business of business is business' philosophy: 'the only responsibility companies (can) have is to generate profits … no fundamental ethical questions are raised about what they are doing' (143).
- *Reactive* CSR is slightly different: it 'shares the focus on efficiency but with particular attention to not making any mistakes … entrepreneurs monitor their environment and manage their primary stakeholders so as to keep mounting issues in check … Entrepreneurs … respond specifically to actions of external actors that could damage their reputation' (143).
- *Active* CSR 'represents the most ethical entrepreneurial orientation. Entrepreneurs … are explicitly inspired by ethical values … on the basis of which company objectives are formulated. These objectives are subsequently realised in a socially responsible manner regardless of actual or potential social pressures by stakeholders' (145).
- *Proactive* CSR occurs where an entrepreneur involves 'external stakeholders right at the beginning of an issue's life cycle' (145). It implies active and ongoing discussion with stakeholders: a 'discourse ethics' approach.

	Inactive	Reactive	Active	Pro/interactive
	Corporate self-responsibility	Corporate social responsiveness	Corporate social responsibility	Corporate societal responsibility
	'Utilitarian' legal compliance	'Negative duty'	'Positive duty' or virtue based	'Interactive duty'
	Profit maximization	Quarterly profits and market capitalization	Long-term profitability	Medium-term profitability and sustainability
	Inside–in	Outside–in	Inside–out	In/outside–in/out
	'Doing things right'	'Don't do things wrong'	'Doing the right things'	'Doing the right things right'
	'Doing well'	'Doing well and doing good'	'Doing good'	'Doing well by doing good'

Narrow (internal) CSR ◄──── **Scope** ────► Broad (external) CSR

Economic (wealth-oriented) ◄──── **Nature of responsibility** ────► Social (welfare-oriented)

Figure 17.1   Differing approaches to corporate social responsibility

Source: based on van Tulder with Van der Zwart, 2006: Table 8.1; van Tulder et al., 2009: Table I

International corporate social responsibility and GPNs

As we have seen throughout this book, the production, distribution and consumption of goods and services is primarily organized within global production networks, usually controlled and coordinated by TNCs. Such networks raise important questions, particularly those regarding the relationships between lead firms and suppliers and the treatment of labour throughout the network. In Chapter 14, we discussed the developmental implications of involvement (or non-involvement) in GPNs for people and businesses in local economies using the criterion of various types of *upgrading*. Of these, *social upgrading* relates specifically to work and labour standards. This includes a whole spectrum of social, economic and ethical issues, including pay, work conditions, occupational health and safety, and human rights. Questions of corporate social responsibility, therefore, are *intrinsically* involved in the operation of GPNs.[12] We looked briefly at some examples in the cases of agro-food (Chapter 9) and clothing (Chapter 10) in the context of consumer resistances to unethical corporate practices. Here we take a rather more detailed examination.

The primary mechanism for attempting to ensure social upgrading in GPNs is the *code of conduct*. Such codes have proliferated to the extent that they often overlap in highly confusing ways. In 2006, for example, it was estimated that there were around 10,000 different codes of labour practice.[13] Two-thirds of the 100 largest firms in the world operated a code of conduct by the early 2000s.[14] Without doubt, a major reason for such proliferation is the increased geographical extent and organizational complexity of GPNs.

	Inactive	Reactive	Active	Pro/interactive
	Corporate self-responsibility	**Corporate social responsiveness**	**Corporate social responsibility**	**Corporate societal responsibility**
Supply chain relationships				
	Price only. Strong competition for customers. Active use of power position in chain. Suppliers responsible for labour conditions.	Price and quality. Suppliers responsible for labour conditions.	Fair prices and high quality. Suppliers selected on basis of approach to e.g. labour conditions.	Joint responsibilities. Prices and quality set together. Definition of fair wages and labour conditions based on consultation and strategic dialogues.
	Cost, control, risk aversion.	Cost, control, quality.	Control and quality.	Co-development and quality.
	CSR only if not too costly and does not mean higher purchasing prices.	CSR only if needed and/or available and does not mean higher purchasing prices.	Upgrading according to own standards.	Upgrading according to joint and/or open standards.
	Below 5% CSR of purchases.	Below 25% CSR of purchases.	Target of 25–60% CSR of purchases.	Target of 60–100% CSR of purchases.
	Buy	Make or buy	Make	Cooperate
	Global	Global	Regional	Local
Codes of conduct strategy				
Type of code	Internal	Specific supplier	General supplier	Joint/dialogues
Specificity	Low	Medium/high	Medium/low	High
Compliance	Low	Medium/low	Medium/high	High
Implementation	Low	Medium/low	Medium/high	High

Chain liability ←————————————→ Chain responsibility

Figure 17.2 Types of CSR strategy towards suppliers

Source: based on van Tulder et al., 2009: Table II; van Tulder, 2009: Table 4

Codifications are triggered by *intrinsic* motivations ... [including] the greater strategic need to coordinate and control the firm's activities spread over a large number of countries and constituencies ... This is often the area of 'internal codes of conduct' or 'codes of ethics'. The strategic need for the formulation and implementation of external codes of conduct as a coordination mechanism becomes bigger when firms engage in sourcing out activities to dependent affiliates (off-shoring) or to independent suppliers (outsourcing) in developing countries, where the governance quality is often relatively low and the cultural and institutional distance ... is relatively high. A large number of (procurement) codes thus addresses supply chain issues such as human rights, labour standards or the right to association ... In this case firms have an incentive not only to formulate codes of conduct, but also to implement them. *Extrinsic* motivations for [TNCs] are gaining in importance as well: the risk of reputation damage triggered by critical NGOs precipitates [TNCs] to formulate international codes of conduct or principles of 'corporate citizenship'.[15]

Figure 17.2 sets out the different kinds of CSR supplier strategy associated with the four types of CSR discussed above (see Figure 17.1). The upper part of Figure 17.2 sets out the variations in supply chain relationships between different

CSR positions; the lower part shows how codes of conduct strategy may vary. The codes are classified along two dimensions:[16]

- *Specificity* includes 'how many issues it covers, how focused it is, the extent to which it refers to international standards and guidelines, and to what extent aspects of the code are measured' (402).
- *Compliance* 'is generally enhanced by clear monitoring systems in place, combined with a more independent position of the monitoring agency and the possibility of these organizations to formulate and implement sanctions' (402).

Firms positioned at the left-hand side of Figure 17.2 tend to opt (if they do so at all) for internal corporate codes or for codes drawn up in collaboration with other firms without prior dialogue with non-firm stakeholders. On the other hand, firms positioned towards the right-hand side of Figure 17.2 tend to participate in more open agreements with non-firm stakeholders. The pressure, of course, from GCSOs is to move as many firms as possible to that more open, cooperative position. Much will clearly depend upon the relative bargaining power of the participants as well as the 'social conscience' of firms. There has certainly been some movement. Even among the hard-line business-is-business community there is now a considerable (albeit often reluctant) recognition that companies do have broader social responsibilities. Hence, there has been a rush to formulate *corporate responsibility* statements. Some of this may well be altruistic, in other cases mere self-interest. However, it is difficult to avoid the conclusion that a major catalyst for CSR has been the increasing pressure on TNCs to recognize their social responsibilities and to conform to acceptable ethical standards.[17] For example, there is no doubt that such pressures led to Nike's publishing a list of all its global suppliers in its CSR reports. This was an unprecedented step for a company which had always been highly secretive about its supply network.

Types of code of conduct

There are four major types of code of conduct:

- Codes devised by individual TNCs, or groups of TNCs, with no involvement of other stakeholders. Example: the Global Social Compliance Programme established by Wal-Mart, Tesco, Carrefour and Metro.
- Codes drawn up by coalitions of interest groups in specific industries, such as clothing. Example: the Global Alliance for Workers and Communities involving Nike and Gap, together with the World Bank and the International Youth Foundation.
- Codes formulated by TNCs in association with some of their stakeholders. Examples: global framework agreements (GFAs) between a TNC and a global labour union federation;[18] the UK Ethical Trading Initiative (ETI), an alliance of companies, NGOs and labour unions.[19]

Human rights
Principle 1: Support and respect the protection of international human rights within their sphere of influence.
Principle 2: Make sure their own corporations are not complicit in human rights abuses.

Labour standards
Principle 3: The freedom of association and the effective recognition of the right to collective bargaining.
Principle 4: The elimination of all forms of forced and compulsory labour.
Principle 5: The effective abolition of child labour.
Principle 6: The elimination of discrimination in respect of employment and occupation.

Environment
Principle 7: Support a precautionary approach to environmental challenges.
Principle 8: Undertake initiatives to promote greater environmental responsibility.
Principle 9: Encourage the development and diffusion of environmentally friendly technologies.

Anti-corruption
Principle 10: Work against all forms of corruption, including extortion and bribery.

Figure 17.3 Principles of the UN Global Compact

- Codes established by international NGOs. Example: the UN Global Compact,[20] which is based upon the ILO Declaration of Fundamental Principles and Rights to Work. Figure 17.3 sets out its 10 principles.

All such codes are, of course, the outcome of complex bargaining processes.

> They need to be understood as part of a contradictory process, involving collaboration and conflict between commercial and civil society actors, in which inherent tensions play out.[21]

TNCs clearly have an interest in being seen as having a positive relationship with GCSOs, not least because it can be seen as providing a 'seal of approval'. GCSOs need to find ways of increasing their influence on TNC decision-making. But there are problems for both of them in too cosy a relationship. In the final analysis, they have very different aims and objectives. But that need not mean that such collaboration is not worth pursuing.

How effective are codes of conduct?

How effective are such codes? Are they mainly a cosmetic exercise? How fully are they implemented? How are they monitored? These are the questions commonly posed by critics, and to which there are no unambiguous answers. Inevitably, there is a good deal of scepticism about voluntary codes, whether at the individual firm or collective level. This is not only because they are 'voluntary' but also because they are rather marginal in their scope and effect. Without some degree of compulsion – and the monitoring of compliance – there is always the danger that such codes will amount to little more than a gesture or that companies will be able to influence how the process works.

In one sense, of course, anything that contributes to better conditions for people and communities should be welcomed.

> Whilst in themselves codes of labour practice are limited, they do have a role in wider strategies to promote economic and social rights of vulnerable workers. But they are not sufficient (nor have they aimed) to achieve more sustainable systems of global production that address inherent inequalities and poverty … The issue, therefore, is whether and how codes contribute to a wider process that promotes the rights of the most vulnerable workers.[22]

Very often, the impacts are mixed. For example, a study of the effects of the Ethical Trading Initiative reached the following conclusions:

> ETI company codes had had a positive impact in relation to certain code principles, particularly health and safety, documented minimum (not living) wages and employment benefits. Company codes were found to have had little or no impact on other code principles, particularly freedom to join an independent trade union, collective bargaining and discrimination … In general, permanent and regular workers were found to have fared better from company codes of labour practice … [However] whilst there had been positive impacts on regular workers, codes of labour practice were failing to reach more vulnerable casual, migrant and contract workers, many of whom were women.[23]

Two important factors in the implementation of codes of conduct seem to be, first, the extent to which the various stakeholders participate in the formulation of the codes and, second, the firm's country of origin. Both of these were evident in a detailed analysis of global framework agreements involving firms from the US, Europe and Japan.[24]

> First, the involvement of stakeholders in the codification clearly results in different levels of implementation likelihood and, hence, different types of codes … [it] leads to a sort of 'compromise' in terms of the issues addressed, but on the other hand increases the compliance likelihood considerably.
> Second, implemented … codes reveal a country of origin effect. All Japanese firms scored low on both specificity and compliance, indicating inactive codes, whereas the only examples of high specificity and compliance, i.e. active codes, could be found with European firms … The US companies fall somewhere in between and generally represent the re-active CSR strategy. The difference in approach between US and European companies is particularly remarkable, but could be largely explained by the bigger involvement of stakeholders. The implementation likelihood of almost all European codes is higher than that of their American or Japanese counterparts.[25]

Codes of conduct, therefore, are useful mechanisms in the progress to greater corporate social responsibility. They are clearly better than nothing. But they are insufficient, not least because they are partial in terms of both their coverage and their essentially voluntary nature.

States and issues of global governance

Global–national tensions

> The world's economy is global; its politics are national. This, in a nutshell, is the dilemma of global governance.[26]

> While the world has become much more highly integrated economically, the mechanisms for managing the system in a stable, sustainable way have lagged behind.[27]

Virtually the entire world economy is now a *global capitalist market economy* although, as we saw in Chapter 6, there are several variants on this theme. The collapse of the state socialist systems at the end of the 1980s and the headlong rush to embrace the market, together with the more controlled opening up of the Chinese economy after 1979, created a very different global system from the one which emerged after the Second World War. The massive flows of goods, services and especially finance, in its increasingly bewildering variety, created a world whose rules of governance have not kept pace with such changes.

In Chapter 3 (see Figure 3.2) we noted the 'thickening web' of public and private institutions that make up the institutional macro-structures of the global economy. In Figure 17.4 we focus on the *core* institutions. The fundamental problem is that these institutions are a mixture of bodies established in different circumstances, and at different times, in the seven decades since the end of the Second World War. They consist of widely differing memberships, with widely different

Figure 17.4 The core of global governance institutions

methods of reaching agreement. Many of them – especially those set up in the immediate aftermath of the war, like the IMF and the World Bank – have power structures that were put in place in a very different world. Essentially, they reflect the power at that time of the Western nations, most notably the United States and the bigger European nations. Since then, of course, the world has changed but the global institutions have lagged behind the new reality. The G7 group is confined to an even smaller group of such countries. Only very recently has the voice of some of the growing developing countries been accommodated through the G20.

These global governance institutions reflect intricate bargaining relationships based upon asymmetrical power configurations within and between institutions, in which the exercise of 'soft' power predominates.[28] Such bargaining involves very much more than just states. It is a

> multi-actor process among NGOs, states, firms, and international organiza-
> tions. Indeed, even states may be represented by multiple authorities, such as
> departments of environment and state, with conflicting interests ... Organizations
> representing labor, environmentalists, scientists and other elements of civil
> society have been particularly active in negotiations over environmental
> regimes ... Even when not seated directly at the negotiating table, activist
> groups have exerted considerable influence through street demonstrations
> and through the disseminations of information ... Thus firms and governments
> exert less control over the bargaining process, and bargain outcomes are
> more uncertain.[29]

In what follows, we focus specifically on the *global* scale of governance in the three most contentious areas:

- finance
- trade
- the environment.

Regulating the global financial system

The established 'architecture' of the global financial system
The regulatory 'architecture' of the modern global financial system came into being formally at an international conference at Bretton Woods, New Hampshire, in 1944. Two international financial institutions were created: the *International Monetary Fund* (IMF) and the *International Bank for Reconstruction and Development* (later renamed the *World Bank*). The IMF's primary purpose was to encourage international monetary cooperation among nations through a set of rules for world payments and currencies. Each member nation contributes to the fund (a quota) and voting rights are proportional to the size of a nation's quota. A major function of the IMF has been to aid member states in temporary balance of payments difficulties. A country can obtain foreign exchange from the IMF in return

for its own currency, which is deposited with the IMF. A condition of such aid is IMF supervision or advice on the necessary corrective policies – the *conditionality* requirement. The World Bank's role is to facilitate development through capital investment. Its initial focus was Europe in the immediate post-war period. Subsequently, its attention shifted to the developing economies.

The primary objective of the Bretton Woods system was to stabilize and regulate international financial transactions *between nations* on the basis of fixed currency exchange rates, in which the US dollar played the central role. In this way it was hoped to provide the necessary financial 'lubricant' for a reconstructed world economy. However, through a whole series of developments (discussed in Chapter 12) the relatively stable basis of the Bretton Woods system was progressively undermined, particularly after the early 1970s. In effect, a state-led system was transformed into a market-led system.[30]

What we do not have, therefore, is a comprehensive and integrated global system of governance of the financial system. Instead, there are various areas of regulation performed by different bodies, each of which is *nationally*, rather than globally, based. For example:

- The 'G' groups (e.g. G7, G8 – and, recently, G20) take an overall view of the monetary, fiscal and exchange rate relationships between themselves. The 'G' groups have no real institutional base; they are informal arrangements structured around periodic summits of national leaders.
- The international payments system is operated through the national central banks rather than through an international central bank.
- The supervision of financial institutions is carried out through the Bank for International Settlements (BIS), established in 1975. The Basel II Accord sets out standards of banking supervision but their implementation is down to national governments, and not all governments follow these standards (including the US).

Within such a lightly regulated financial system, developing countries are particularly vulnerable to the volatilities of global capital flows. Indeed, one of the major weaknesses of the various reforms to the global financial architecture following the breakdown of the Bretton Woods system was that they maintained a separation between the problems facing developed countries and those facing developing countries, instead of seeing them as inextricably linked together.

> Efforts ... focused on measures designed to discipline debtors and provide costly self-defence mechanisms. Countries have been urged to better manage risk by adopting strict financial standards, improving transparency, adopting appropriate rate regimes, carrying large amounts of reserves, and making voluntary arrangements with private creditors to involve them in crisis resolution. While some of these reforms undoubtedly have their merits, they presume that the cause of crises rests primarily with policy and institutional

weaknesses in the debtor countries and accordingly place the onus of responsibility for reform firmly on their shoulders. By contrast, little attention is given to the role played by institutions and policies in creditor countries in triggering international financial crises.[31]

In fact, the IMF's and World Bank's conditionality 'medicine' often made the patient worse rather than better. By imposing massive financial stringency on countries in difficulty – including raising domestic interest rates, insisting on increased openness of the domestic economy, reducing social spending and the like – it became extremely difficult for countries to help themselves out of difficulty.

Conditionality, at least in the manner and extent to which it has been used by the IMF, is a bad idea; there is little evidence that it leads to improved economic policy, but it does have adverse political effects because countries resent having conditions imposed on them … In some cases it even *reduced* the likelihood of repayment.[32]

In the absence of a more coordinated and institutionalized system, the global financial system could easily spiral out of control. Indeed, this is what appeared to be happening following the East Asian financial crisis of 1997, with its subsequent spillover effects on countries like Russia and Brazil. There was particular concern over the volatile nature of global capital flows in terms of their impact on both the financial system itself and also on the individual countries and their populations most seriously affected by volatile flows of 'hot money'. To many observers, especially in the West, the causes of the 1997 East Asian crisis lay in structures and practices inside the affected countries (including so-called 'crony capitalism'). The remedy was obvious: apply the usual 'Washington Consensus' formula in which all answers lie in the unfettered operation of markets and in the conditionality applied to financial assistance. In fact, the major (though not the only) cause of the East Asian crisis was to be found in flows of speculative capital into (and then out of) the region. It also transpired that corrupt financial practices were by no means unique to East Asia. The collapse of two massive US companies, LTCM and Enron, demonstrated this in graphic terms.

Not surprisingly, there were calls for a new, or reformed, *financial architecture* to ensure that a similar crisis could not recur. In fact, very little happened. It was back to business as usual and the further headlong growth and diversification of financial markets and esoteric financial products discussed in Chapter 12. From a broad developmental viewpoint, the problem still remained that

the global financial market is heavily dominated by financial interests in the industrialized countries. The governments of these countries, especially the economically strongest, determine the rules governing the market through their influence on the IFIs [international financial institutions]. These latter institutions in turn exercise great leverage over the macroeconomic and financial policies of developing countries. At the same time, the banks and financial houses from these same countries enjoy tremendous market power within the global financial system. The system is also characterized by severe market failures and is unstable. The upshot of all this is that most of the risks and the negative consequences of financial instability have been borne by the middle-income countries, currently the weakest players in the system.[33]

Ten years after the East Asian crisis, the much bigger – and potentially catastrophic – financial crisis of 2008 erupted. This time it could not be argued that the causes lay in 'inefficient' or 'corrupt' markets in developing countries. As we have seen in earlier chapters, the origins of the much larger 2008 financial crisis lay in the very heart of the 'Washington Consensus'. The much lauded, solely market-driven, financial system did not work. This time, it has to be fixed or, rather, replaced. The discrediting of the existing, very lightly regulated, financial system means that, this time, new solutions have to be found.

Towards a new global financial architecture?

It is far too early to say what kind of new financial architecture will emerge or how stable it will be. What we can say is that the immediate response of national governments to the 2008 crisis was quite impressive, in the sense that total financial meltdown was avoided. Among the measures proposed by individual governments (in addition to the short-term rescue packages discussed in Chapter 12) were:

- A restriction on the overall size of banks.
- A tax on large-scale financial institutions (in effect, an insurance levy) to force banks to repay the costs of rescuing the financial system. Such a tax could take various forms. The IMF suggested it should be a tax on financial institutions' liabilities.
- Separating the 'utility' and 'casino' functions of banks to prevent cross-contamination from the risky speculative activities (like hedge and private equity funds) to those activities needed to finance the 'real' economy. This harks back, at least in spirit, to the US Glass–Steagall Act of 1933 (see Chapter 12).
- Imposing a tax on every financial transaction. This is the so-called 'Tobin tax', first proposed by James Tobin in the 1970s with the aim of 'throwing some sand in the wheels of cross-border financial transactions'. The idea was to discourage excessive flows of 'hot' money – short-term capital flows which can so easily destabilize financial systems, especially of weaker countries. In its present form it is being seen as a way of raising capital for broader developmental purposes.
- Limiting the size of bonuses paid to bankers. There has been universal condemnation of the obscene sums derived from those financial activities described as 'socially useless' by the chair of the UK's Financial Services Authority.[34]

At the time of writing (2010) these measures are all somewhat in the air. Some are more likely to be implemented than others. Some are more feasible than others.

Each of them is politically contentious and, naturally, mostly opposed by bankers. The cry of 'unworkability' is widely heard. However, there is strong popular support in most countries for measures to limit the excesses of the financial sector.

Perhaps the most important development, however, has been the emergence of the G20 as the central focus of attempts to build a reformed global financial system. The significance of the G20 lies in its much wider membership (the 19 countries shown in Figure 17.4 plus the EU) and especially the involvement of developing countries which, hitherto, were not part of groups like the G7 and G8. The G20 was created in 1999 in the aftermath of the East Asian crisis but it was not until 2007 that it came to real prominence when the G20 finance ministers agreed to pump liquidity into financial markets at the beginning of the global financial crisis. In subsequent meetings in 2008 and 2009, the G20 was at the centre of initiatives to deal with the crisis. At its London summit in April 2009, $500 billion was committed to refinance the IMF; at the Pittsburgh summit in September 2009, the national leaders agreed to expand the G20's role, placing it at the centre of international economic policy-making. Figure 17.5 outlines the major aspects of global financial governance being examined by the G20. Again, it will take time before we know what actually happens, but at least the G20's

Area	Purpose
Financial regulation	Implement higher global standards consistently to ensure a level playing field and avoid fragmentation of markets, protectionism and regulatory arbitrage.
Establish Financial Stability Board (FSB)	Includes all G20 countries, plus Spain and the EC with strengthened mandate to promote financial stability, enhance openness and transparency of the financial sector, implement international financial standards.
International cooperation	Collaborate with IMF to conduct early warning exercises of potential macroeconomic and financial risks. Home authorities of each major financial institution should ensure that the group of authorities with a common interest in that financial institution meets at least annually. Systemically important financial firms should develop internationally-consistent firm-specific contingency and resolution plans. Establish supervisory colleges for significant cross-border firms. Advanced economies, the IMF and other international organizations should provide capacity-building programmes for emerging market economies and developing countries on the formulation and implementation of new major regulations, consistent with international standards.
Prudential regulation	Raise the quality, consistency and transparency of the Tier 1 capital base. Require banks to build buffers of resources in good times that they can draw on when conditions deteriorate. Level of capital in the banking system to be raised relative to pre-crisis levels. All major G20 countries to adopt the Basel II capital framework. Financial institutions should provide enhanced risk disclosures in all their reporting.
Compensation	Align compensation with long-term value-creation, not excessive risk-taking by (i) avoiding multi-year guaranteed bonuses; (ii) requiring a significant portion of variable compensation to be deferred, tied to performance and subject to appropriate clawback; (iii) making firms' compensation policies transparent through disclosure requirements; (iv) ensure compensation committees can act independently.

Figure 17.5   Examples of measures proposed by the G20 to reform the global financial system

Source: based on *Progress Report on the Actions to Promote Financial Regulatory Reform*, www.g20.org

Framework for Strong, Sustainable and Balanced Growth represents a really significant *global* attempt to create a new financial structure for the global economy with an explicit developmental basis.

Regulating international trade

The evolution of world trade regulations

Compared with the international financial system, the governance of international trade is much clearer (though just as controversial).[35] In 1947, the General Agreement on Tariffs and Trade (GATT) was established as the third international institution formed in the aftermath of the Second World War, along with the IMF and the World Bank – completing what some have called the 'unholy trinity'.[36] Establishment of the GATT reflected the view that the 'beggar-my-neighbour' protectionist policies of the 1930s should not be allowed to recur. The objective was to be 'free' trade based upon the *principle of comparative advantage*, first introduced by David Ricardo in 1817. This states that a country (or any geographical area) should specialize in producing and exporting those products in which it has a comparative or relative cost advantage compared with other countries and should import those goods in which it has a comparative disadvantage. Out of such specialization, it is argued, will accrue greater benefit for all.

Whether or not there is such a thing as 'free' trade is highly debatable. In order to work it needs some degree of equality between trading partners and this, as we have seen, at the global scale simply does not exist. The purpose of the GATT was to create a set of *multilateral rules* to facilitate free trade through the reduction of tariff barriers and other types of trade discrimination. The GATT was eventually replaced by the World Trade Organization (WTO) in 1995, an institutional change which greatly broadened the remit of the trade regulator. Today, there are 153 member states in the WTO and around 97 per cent of world trade is covered by the WTO framework. Figure 17.6 traces its evolution.

Since 1947 there have been nine 'rounds' of multilateral trade negotiations, including the current Doha Round, initiated in 2001 and still not completed (see below). Prior to the mid 1960s, the GATT was mostly concerned with trade of manufactures between developed nations. As a result, widespread dissatisfaction emerged among developing countries. A particularly sensitive issue was the lack of access of developing country exports to developed country markets. Pressure led, in 1965, to the adoption within the GATT of a generalized system of preferences (GSP) under which exports of manufactured and semi-manufactured goods from developing countries were granted preferential access to developed country markets. In fact, there were a number of exclusions from the GSP, of which one of the most important was textiles and clothing (separately regulated under the MFA: see Chapter 10).

As Figure 17.6 shows, the first seven GATT rounds were both quite brief and also very limited in scope, although the Kennedy and Tokyo rounds had slightly more

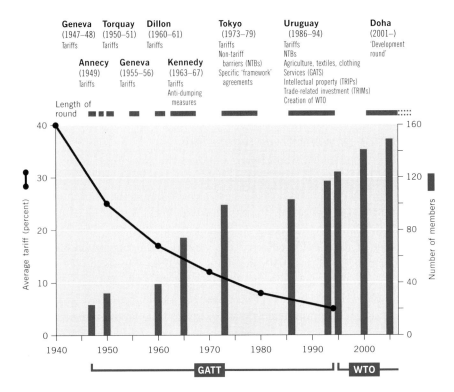

Figure 17.6   Evolution of the international trade regulatory framework: from the GATT to the WTO

extensive agendas. However, it was the Uruguay Round, started in 1986 and eventually concluded in 1994, which constituted the most ambitious and wide-ranging of all the GATT rounds to that point. For the first time, a number of additional trade issues was addressed. Notably, agriculture, textiles and clothing were brought into the GATT, and special agreements were concluded in services (GATS – the General Agreement on Trade in Services), intellectual property (TRIPS – Trade-Related Aspects of Intellectual Property Rights) and investment (TRIMS – Trade-Related Investment Measures). There was a further large reduction in overall tariff levels. The major organizational change was the creation of a new World Trade Organization.

The WTO, like the GATT, constitutes a *rule-oriented* approach to multilateral trade cooperation.

> Rule-oriented approaches focus not on outcomes, but on the rules of the game, and involve agreements on the level of trade barriers that are permitted as well as attempts to establish the general conditions of competition facing foreign producers in export markets.[37]

The fundamental basis is that of *non-discrimination*, based upon two components:

- The *most-favoured nation principle* (MFN) states that a trade concession negotiated between two countries must also apply to all other countries; that is, all must be treated in the same way. The MFN is 'one of the pillars of the GATT' and 'applies unconditionally, the only major exception being if a subset of Members form a free-trade area or a customs union or grant preferential access to developing countries'.[38]
- The *national treatment rule* requires that imported foreign goods are treated in the same way as domestic goods.

Battles within the WTO

The WTO continues to be subject to widespread criticism from many directions and from interest groups in both developed and developing countries.[39] For example, unilateralist groups within the United States regard the WTO as a basic infringement of the country's national sovereignty. Among developing countries there is resentment over what is regarded as the bullying and unfair behaviour of the powerful industrialized countries. To the anti-globalization protestors, the WTO is regarded as an undemocratic, self-interested body acting primarily in the interests of global corporations.

In one sense, in fact, the WTO is a far more democratic organization than the IMF. Whereas in the IMF the voting system is 'weighted', so that the more powerful states have a greater share of the vote, in the WTO each of the 153 member states has an equal vote. However, the position is not as straightforward as it seems. Decisions in the WTO are arrived at through negotiation in formal and informal meetings and through consensus, rather than by vote. Such processes depend heavily on the resources available to countries to lobby and exert influence and most poor countries simply do not have the resources or expertise to have an effective voice.

> [T]here is certainly a problem relating to the systematic absence of many developing countries (particularly those that are small) from both informal and formal meetings in the WTO. Most small delegations from developing countries do not have the appropriate resources either in Geneva or at home to service the increasingly frequent, complex, and resource-intensive negotiation process at the WTO …
>
> However, knowledge and resources are not enough for all countries to be effective in WTO negotiations. *An important reality is that the WTO rules do not entirely remove the inequality in the power of nations. It remains the case that countries with big markets have a greater ability than countries with small markets to secure market access and to deter actions against their exporters.*[40]

Two important sources of tension within the WTO relate to labour standards and the environment. How far do international differences in labour standards and regulations (such as the use of child labour, poor health and safety conditions, repression of labour unions and workers' rights) and in environmental standards and regulations (such as industrial pollution, the unsafe use of toxic materials in production processes) distort the trading system and create unfair advantages?

Several countries, led primarily by the US but also including some European countries, have attempted to incorporate the issue of *labour standards* into the WTO. The attempt has failed, partly because not all industrialized countries support it but also because developing countries are vehemently opposed. The argument of those opposed to its inclusion within the WTO's remit is that labour standards are the responsibility of the International Labour Organization (ILO). Indeed, all members of the ILO have agreed to a set of core principles. The counter-argument is that the ILO lacks any powers of enforcement. It is also notable that the United States, despite its current position on including labour standards in trade agreements, has not signed up to many of the ILO's core labour conventions, arguing that they do not comply with US law.

Similar questions apply to the relationship between trade regulations and the *environment*. To what extent should variations in environmental standards be incorporated into international trade regulations? At one level, the problem is exactly the same as that of labour standards. If a country allows lax environmental standards, it is argued, then it should not be able to use what is, in effect, a subsidy on firms located there to be able to sell its products more cheaply on the international market. The question then becomes one of whether the solution lies in using international trade regulations or in some other forms of regulation.

These labour and environmental questions posed by some developed countries arose in the aftermath of the Uruguay Round in the mid 1990s. But three-quarters of the WTO's membership consists of developing countries. They face, as we have seen in previous chapters, immense economic and social problems. The Uruguay Round helped them in some respects but created major difficulties in others. In particular,

> of the three big agreements coming out of the Uruguay Round – on investment measures (TRIMS), trade in services (GATS), and intellectual property rights (TRIPS) – the first two limit the authority of developing country governments to constrain the choices of companies operating in their territory, while the third requires the governments to enforce rigorous property rights of foreign (generally Western) firms. Together, the agreements make comprehensively illegal many of the industrial policy instruments used in the successful East Asian developers to nurture their own industrial and technological capacities.[41]

In November 1999, a WTO meeting was held in Seattle to try to initiate a new round of trade negotiations. The meeting failed, not so much because of the now notorious anti-WTO and anti-globalization protests but, as the UN Secretary-General Kofi Annan argued, because it failed to initiate a 'development round' that would at last deliver to the developing countries the benefits they have so often been promised from free trade, instead … [we] saw governments – particularly those of the world's leading economic powers – unable to agree on their priorities. As a result, no round was launched at all … The … [developed country] governments all favour free trade in principle, but too often they lack the political strength to confront those within their own countries who have come to rely on protectionist arrangements. They have not yet succeeded in putting across to their peoples the wider interest that we all share in having a global market from which everyone, not just the lucky few, can benefit.[42]

It was not until the end of 2001 that a new global trade round was announced at Doha in Qatar, with the official title of the 'Doha Development Agenda', to be concluded by 2004. However, such good intentions have not been fulfilled. The Doha Round has been possibly even more acrimonious than the Uruguay Round.[43] Deadlines have been missed with (un)impressive regularity. The 'make or break' Ministerial Meeting at Cancun in 2003 collapsed without producing any significant results. Subsequent meetings in Hong Kong (2005) and Geneva (2006, 2008) made very little progress. Although negotiations rumble on in a low-key manner, in fact,

for all the talk of development, the development aspects of the round have been increasingly boiled down to a focus on agriculture (with a few additional sweeteners such as Aid for Trade thrown in along the way). While it is clear that a conclusion to the round will not occur unless movement on agricultural liberalisation is forthcoming, the *quid pro quo* (more than likely greater [non-agricultural market access] to developing country markets) will ensure that the deal struck remains of relatively greater value to the industrial countries. The result is thus likely to be of little benefit to the WTO's poorest and most vulnerable members.[44]

In its communiqué from the London Summit in 2009, the G20 stated its commitment 'to reaching an ambitious and balanced conclusion to the Doha Development Round', noting that it is 'urgently needed'. But whether such rhetoric will make a difference is far from clear. The G20 also reaffirmed its commitment not to raise new barriers to trade. However, 17 of the 20 G20 members introduced some kind of trade protectionist measure in 2008–9.[45]

Global environmental regulation: climate change

As we saw in some detail in Chapter 15, the processes of production, distribution and consumption, articulated within and through global production networks, have the potential to create enormous and long-lasting environmental damage. And yet, compared with finance and trade regulation, there were few systematic attempts to build an appropriate global regulatory structure for the environment until the late 1980s.[46] Today, of course, environmental issues are paramount, and climate change has become one of the (literally) hottest and most contentious policy issues of all – a veritable minefield, politically, economically and scientifically.

The evolution of climate change initiatives

From the outset, the United Nations has been at the centre of global climate change initiatives, beginning with its decision in 1968 to convene the 1972 Stockholm Conference on the Human Environment. This stimulated the setting up of national environmental agencies in most developed, and some developing, countries.[47]

In 1988, the UN established what was to become the scientific core of its environmental programme: the Intergovernmental Panel on Climate Change (IPCC).

> The IPCC ... does not conduct any research ... Its role is to assess on a comprehensive, objective, open and transparent basis the latest scientific, technical and socio-economic literature produced worldwide relevant to the understanding of the risk of human-induced climate change, its observed and projected impacts and options for adaptation and mitigation. *IPCC reports should be neutral with respect to policy*, although they need to deal objectively with policy relevant scientific, technical and socio-economic factors.[48]

The first IPCC Assessment Report was published in 1990 and this formed the basis of the first comprehensive policy framework on climate change: the 1992 *Framework Convention on Climate Change* (FCCC). A key objective of the FCCC was to achieve

> the stabilization of greenhouse gas [GHG] concentrations in the atmosphere at a level that would prevent dangerous anthropogenic interference with the climate system.[49]

The FCCC was based upon *voluntary* reduction of carbon dioxide levels: it merely 'encouraged industrialized countries to stabilize GHG emissions'.

Its (not surprising) lack of success led, in 1997, to the drafting of the *Kyoto Protocol*. In contrast to the FCCC, Kyoto incorporated *binding* emissions targets over the period 2008–12 for 37 developed countries, based on 1990 levels. The Protocol came into force in 2005. A total of 184 countries (excluding, most significantly, the US) were signatories. After the Kyoto Protocol was finally ratified, there was much argument among the signatories, and with the US, over the details of climate change regulation. In December 2005, the UN Conference in Montreal agreed the following measures:

- To strengthen the 'clean development mechanism', which allows developed countries to invest in sustainable development projects in developing countries whilst earning emission allowances.

- To launch the 'Joint Implementation' mechanism, which allows developed countries to invest in other developed countries, especially the transition economies of Eastern Europe. In doing so they can earn carbon allowances, which can be used to meet their emission reduction commitments.
- To implement the 'compliance regime' which ensures that countries have clear accountability for meeting their emission reduction targets.

The Kyoto commitments were time limited (2012). By then,

> a new international framework needs to have been negotiated and ratified that can deliver the stringent emission reductions the Intergovernmental Panel on Climate Change (IPCC) has clearly indicated are needed.[50]

This new agreement was to be negotiated and signed at the UN Conference on Climate Change at Copenhagen in December 2009. Ahead of this meeting the UN Secretary-General Ban Ki-Moon issued this apocalyptic exhortation:

> Failure to reach broad agreement in Copenhagen would be morally inexcusable, economically short-sighted and politically unwise … Now is the moment to act in common cause … There is little time left. The opportunity and responsibility to avoid catastrophic climate change is in your hands.[51]

Burning issues

Climate scientists believe that if global temperatures rise by more than $2°C$ above pre-industrial levels then climate change would become irreversible. To meet such a criterion, a number of specific, but highly variable, targets have been proposed, including:

- Developed countries to halve global CO_2 emissions, compared with 1990 levels, by 2050. This has the support of developed countries in general, while the G8 promised to cut their own emissions by 80 per cent.
- The EU has promised to cut its emissions by 20 per cent by 2020 compared with 1990 levels and to increase this to 30 per cent if other countries also commit.
- The US has promised to reduce its emissions by 17 per cent by 2020, compared with 2005 levels, but this depends upon Congressional approval.
- Japan has promised to reduce its emissions by 25 per cent by 2020.
- China has promised to reduce the growth in its CO_2 output by 40–45 per cent by 2020.

The most intractable problem is the extent to which developing countries should be expected to adopt measures that could prevent their future economic development. Since most of the 'stock' of CO_2 in the atmosphere was produced historically by developed countries, it is argued that developing countries should be given preferential treatment. On the other hand, the developed country argument is that most of the growth in emissions in the future will be in developing countries, especially China, India and Brazil.

Given the 2°C 'bottom line', the major goals of the *Copenhagen* meeting were to reach agreement on the following issues and to embed them into a binding UN treaty with precise numbers and a timescale: developed countries to cut their CO_2 emissions; developing countries to curb their emissions; and provision by developed countries of financial and technological assistance to developing countries to enable them to achieve their emission targets. On every issue, of course, views differed widely between different interest groups: developed and developing countries, environmental groups and other GCSOs, and business firms.

Despite all the pre-meeting hype – and all the dire warnings – no binding agreement was reached on a new climate treaty. At the last minute, and after highly acrimonious negotiations, an 'Accord' was reached, based primarily on a deal put together by a small group of countries: the US, Brazil, China, India and South Africa. Figure 17.7 summarizes the major elements of the Copenhagen Accord. Its most striking aspect is its vagueness. The only numbers relate to the commitment of financial assistance to developing countries. The FCCC tried to put a brave face on the outcome:

> Three key things that Copenhagen produced are: (1) It raised climate change to the highest level of government; (2) The Copenhagen Accord reflects a political consensus on the long-term, global response to climate change; (3) The negotiations brought an almost full set of decisions to implement rapid climate action near to completion … we're now in a cooling off [*sic*] period that gives countries useful and needed time to resume their discussion with each other. 'If countries follow up the outcomes of Copenhagen calmly, with eyes firmly on the advantage of collective action, they have every chance of completing the job.'[52]

The negotiating process continues, but is made more difficult by the prevailing state of the global economy and its effects on individual countries' willingness and/or ability to reach firm and meaningful agreement on such uncertain and contentious issues.

A better world

The future map of the global economy is far from clear. Although the chances are that globalizing processes will continue to operate and that the world will become increasingly interconnected, there is a huge amount of uncertainty. We should certainly not simply extrapolate from past trends. Most of all, however, we need to think about the *kind* of world we, and our children, would want to live in. The key question is not so much what the world *might* be like in the future but what it *should* be like. There are choices to be made. What might these be? After all, globalization is not a force of nature; it is a social process.[53] What are the choices? In theory they are infinite; in practice they are not.

The Copenhagen Accord
● We underline that climate change is one of the greatest challenges of our time. We emphasize our strong political will to urgently combat climate change in accordance with the principle of common but differentiated responsibilities and respective capabilities. To achieve the ultimate objective of the Convention to stabilize greenhouse gas concentration in the atmosphere at a level that would prevent dangerous anthropogenic interference with the climate system, we shall, recognizing the scientific view that the increase in global temperature should be below 2 degrees Celsius, on the basis of equity and in the context of sustainable development, enhance our long-term cooperative action to combat climate change. We recognize the critical impacts of climate change and the potential impacts of response measures on countries particularly vulnerable to its adverse effects and stress the need to establish a comprehensive adaptation programme including international support.
● We agree that deep cuts in global emissions are required according to science … with a view to reduce global emissions so as to hold the increase in global temperature below 2 degrees Celsius, and take action to meet this objective consistent with science and on the basis of equity. We should cooperate in achieving the peaking of global and national emissions as soon as possible, recognizing that the time frame for peaking will be longer in developing countries and bearing in mind that social and economic development and poverty eradication are the first and overriding priorities of developing countries and that a low-emission development strategy is indispensable to sustainable development.
● Adaptation to the adverse effects of climate change and the potential impacts of response measures is a challenge faced by all countries. Enhanced action and international cooperation on adaptation is urgently required to ensure the implementation of the Convention by enabling and supporting the implementation of adaptation actions aimed at reducing vulnerability and building resilience in developing countries, especially in those that are particularly vulnerable, especially least developed countries, small island developing States and Africa. We agree that developed countries shall provide adequate, predictable and sustainable financial resources, technology and capacity-building to support the implementation of adaptation action in developing countries.
● We recognize the crucial role of reducing emission from deforestation and forest degradation and the need to enhance removals of greenhouse gas emission by forests and agree on the need to provide positive incentives to such actions through the immediate establishment of a mechanism including REDD-plus*, to enable the mobilization of financial resources from developed countries.
● We decide to pursue various approaches, including opportunities to use markets, to enhance the cost-effectiveness of, and to promote mitigation actions. Developing countries, especially those with low emitting economies should be provided incentives to continue to develop on a low emission pathway.
● Scaled up, new and additional, predictable and adequate funding as well as improved access shall be provided to developing countries. The collective commitment by developed countries is to provide new and additional resources, including forestry and investments through international institutions, approaching USD 30 billion for the period 2010–2012 with balanced allocation between adaptation and mitigation. Funding for adaptation will be prioritized for the most vulnerable developing countries, such as the least developed countries, small island developing States and Africa. In the context of meaningful mitigation actions and transparency on implementation, developed countries commit to a goal of mobilizing jointly USD 100 billion dollars a year by 2020 to address the needs of developing countries. This funding will come from a wide variety of sources, public and private, bilateral and multilateral, including alternative sources of finance.
● We decide that the Copenhagen Green Climate Fund shall be established as an operating entity of the financial mechanism of the Convention to support projects, programme, policies and other activities in developing countries related to mitigation including REDD-plus, adaptation, capacity-building, technology development and transfer.
● In order to enhance action on development and transfer of technology we decide to establish a Technology Mechanism to accelerate technology development and transfer in support of action on adaptation and mitigation that will be guided by a country-driven approach and be based on national circumstances and priorities.
● We call for an assessment of the implementation of this Accord to be completed by 2015, including in light of the Convention's ultimate objective.

* REDD-plus: Reduced Emissions from Deforestation and Forest Degradation.

Figure 17.7   Major elements of the Copenhagen Accord, 2009

Source: www.denmark.dk/en/menu/Climate-Energy/COP15-Copenhagen-2009/cop15.html

Alternative economies?

In thinking about alternative futures in the context of globalization debates, there is a depressing tendency towards polarization of positions of the kind we identi-fied in Chapter 1. The gung-ho, neo-liberal hyper-globalizers see the solution in yet more openness of markets, in unfettered flows of goods, services and capital. In other words, much, much more of the same. The anti-globalizers argue for exactly the opposite. Whereas the first strategy would almost certainly create a world of even greater inequality (as well as environmental damage), the second embodies the dangers of reverting to a set of medieval subsistence economies.

The diametrical opposition of these two positions can be illustrated by their polarized attitudes towards trade. To the hyper-globalizers, it is a central tenet that trade should be allowed to flourish without hindrance. The anti-globalizers' position is that the pursuit of ever-increasing international trade – which is clearly encouraged by a free trade regime like the WTO – should be totally abandoned, not merely regulated. The argument here is basically that sustainable development is incompatible with the pursuit of further economic growth. An economic system based upon very high levels of geographical specialization inevitably depends upon, and generates, ever-increasing trade in materials and products.

A central criticism is that the energy costs of transporting materials and goods across the world are not taken into account in setting the prices of traded goods and that, in effect, trade is being massively subsidized at a huge short-term and long-term environmental cost.

> More than half of all international trade involves the simultaneous import and export of essentially the same goods. For example, Americans import Danish sugar cookies, and Danes import American sugar cookies. Exchanging recipes would surely be more efficient.[54]

But by no means all environmentalists agree with this kind of viewpoint. As David Pearce argues,

> Unquestionably, there are environmental problems inherent in the existing trading system. But there is also extensive confusion in the environmentalist critique of free trade ... Given the potentially large gains to be obtained from free trade, adopting restrictions on trade for environmental purposes is a policy that needs to be approached with caution. Most importantly, all other approaches to reducing environmental damage should be exhausted before trade policy measures are contemplated ... the policy implication of a negative association between freer trade and environmental degradation is not that freer trade should be halted. What matters is the adoption of the most cost-effective policies to optimize the externality. Restricting trade is unlikely to be the most efficient way of controlling the problem ... The losses can best be minimized by firm *domestic* environmental policy design to uncouple the environmental impacts from economic activity ... The 'first' best approach to correcting externalities is to tackle them directly through implementation of the polluter pays principle (PPP), not through restrictions on the level of trade. Where the PPP is not feasible (e.g. if the exporter is a poor developing country), it is likely to be preferable to engage in cooperative policies, e.g. making clean technology transfers, assisting with clean-up policies etc., rather than adopting import restrictions.[55]

There is, thus, intense disagreement both over the impact of globalization processes and trade on the environment and also over what should (or can) be done.[56] There are, in other words, very different 'shades of green', ranging from the position that human ingenuity and new technologies will find the solutions without necessitating a change in lifestyles (the Panglossian view) through to the 'deep green' arguments that only a return to a totally different, small-scale, highly localized mode of existence will suffice. But such a path, rather than improving the position for the poor in the world economy, 'would condemn the vast majority of people to a miserable future, at best on the margins of the bare minimum of physical existence'.[57] It is not a socially acceptable policy:

> The alternative to an economic system that involves trade is not bucolic simplicity and hardy self-sufficiency, but extreme poverty. South Korea has plenty of problems, but not nearly so many as its neighbour to the north.[58]

But this emphatically does not mean that 'local' economies are irrelevant. On the contrary. There is, in fact, a wide diversity of economies[59] offering different kinds of possibilities and which may occupy different positions in relation to the larger global economy. Many of these are, essentially, 'community economies'. Figure 17.8 summarizes the main ways in which such economies differ from the 'mainstream' economy. 'In some cases, these communities are geographically confined to the "local", while in others they span the "global".'[60] The fair trade networks discussed in Chapter 19 are examples of the latter. The Mondragón Cooperative Corporation is an example of a complex of cooperatives spread across 14 countries but grounded in the Basque region of Spain and organized on worker-owned principles. The LETS (Local Exchange Trading Systems) uses local 'currencies' to facilitate the exchange of services and self-produced or self-earned goods within a network of members in a local community.[61] A micro-finance scheme, which began as a local initiative in Bangladesh in the 1970s, subsequently spread across many other countries and has been a huge contributor to poverty reduction.[62]

The diversity of economies that exists in the world offers significant possibilities for creating fulfilling and fair communities and, more generally, for reconsidering globalization as a transformable social process and not a force of nature. But they are, by definition, mostly small in scale and often highly local in scope. They raise important issues of how such economies connect into the bigger picture (unless they decide to opt out). And it is the 'bigger picture' that still demands our primary attention.

To be 'globalized' or not to be 'globalized': that is the question

> The main losers in today's very unequal world are not those who are too much exposed to globalization. They are those who have been left out.[63]

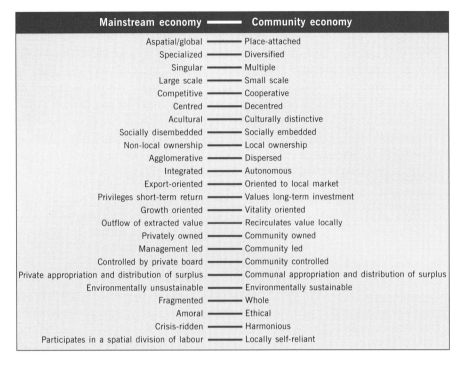

Mainstream economy	━━━━	Community economy
Aspatial/global	━━━	Place-attached
Specialized	━━━	Diversified
Singular	━━━	Multiple
Large scale	━━━	Small scale
Competitive	━━━	Cooperative
Centred	━━━	Decentred
Acultural	━━━	Culturally distinctive
Socially disembedded	━━━	Socially embedded
Non-local ownership	━━━	Local ownership
Agglomerative	━━━	Dispersed
Integrated	━━━	Autonomous
Export-oriented	━━━	Oriented to local market
Privileges short-term return	━━━	Values long-term investment
Growth oriented	━━━	Vitality oriented
Outflow of extracted value	━━━	Recirculates value locally
Privately owned	━━━	Community owned
Management led	━━━	Community led
Controlled by private board	━━━	Community controlled
Private appropriation and distribution of surplus	━━━	Communal appropriation and distribution of surplus
Environmentally unsustainable	━━━	Environmentally sustainable
Fragmented	━━━	Whole
Amoral	━━━	Ethical
Crisis-ridden	━━━	Harmonious
Participates in a spatial division of labour	━━━	Locally self-reliant

Figure 17.8   Contrasting characteristics of mainstream and community economies

Source: based on Gibson-Graham, 2006: Figure 23

> Is the problem actually globalization or not-globalization? Is the difficulty being part of the system or not being part of it? How can globalization be the source of problems for those excluded from it?[64]

It is abundantly clear that the position of many of the world's poorest countries is highly marginal in terms of the global economy. The usual prescription of the IMF and World Bank 'doctors' is that they should open their economies more, for example by positively encouraging exports and by liberalizing their regulatory structures.

> For policymakers around the world, the appeal of opening up to global markets is based on a simple but powerful promise: international economic integration will improve economic performance … *The trouble is … that there is no convincing evidence that openness, in the sense of low barriers to trade and capital flows, systematically produces these consequences. In practice, the links between openness and economic growth tend to be weak and contingent on the presence of complementary policies and institutions.*[65]

'Openness', then, is the name of the game. But this will only work if the playing field is relatively level – which it clearly is not. And it also has to work both ways – which clearly it does not. Tariffs imposed by the developed countries on imports of many developing country products remain very high. It is common for tariffs to increase with the degree of processing (so-called tariff escalation), so that higher-value products from developing countries are discriminated against. At the same time, agricultural subsidies make imports from developing countries uncompetitive. In other words, the odds are stacked against them.[66]

> The human costs of unfair trade are immense. If Africa, South Asia, and Latin America were each to increase their share of world exports by one per cent, the resulting gains in income could lift 128 million people out of poverty … When developing countries export to rich-country markets, they face tariff barriers that are four times higher than those encountered by rich countries. Those barriers cost them $100bn a year – twice as much as they receive in aid.[67]

Simply opening up a developing economy on its own, however, will almost certainly lead to further disaster. There is the danger of local businesses being wiped out by more efficient foreign competition before they can get a toehold in the wider world. Hence a prerequisite for positive and beneficial engagement with the global economy is the development of robust internal structures: 'the development of a national economy is more about internal integration than about external integration'.[68]

Eradicating extreme poverty: the UN Millennium Development Project

Poverty, as we discussed in Chapter 16, is the major problem in many parts of the world. For many years, aid programmes have been devised to help alleviate its major manifestations but such aid has generally fallen far below needs. In 2006, for example, for the group of low-income countries aid amounted to only $35 per head.[69] In 2002, a meeting of heads of state in New York adopted the *UN Millennium Declaration*, whose aim is nothing less than the eradication of extreme poverty as part of a broad and comprehensive development programme.

> Ending this scourge will require the combined efforts of all, governments, civil society organizations and the private sector, in the context of a stronger and more effective global partnership for development. The Millennium Development Goals set timebound targets, by which progress in reducing income poverty, hunger, disease, lack of adequate shelter and exclusion – while promoting gender equality, health, education and environmental sustainability – can be measured. They also embody basic human rights – the rights of each person on the planet to health, education, shelter and security. The Goals are ambitious but feasible and, together with the comprehensive United Nations development agenda, set the course for the world's efforts to alleviate extreme poverty by 2015.[70]

GOAL	TARGET
1: Eradicate extreme poverty and hunger	1: Halve, between 1990 and 2015, the proportion of people whose income is less than $1 a day 2: Achieve full and productive employment and decent work for all, including women and young people 3: Halve, between 1990 and 2015, the proportion of people who suffer from hunger
2: Achieve universal primary education	1: Ensure that, by 2015, children everywhere, boys and girls alike, will be able to complete a full course of primary schooling
3: Promote gender equality and empower women	1: Eliminate gender disparity in primary and secondary education, preferably by 2005, and in all levels of education no later than 2015
4: Reduce child mortality	1: Reduce by two thirds, between 1990 and 2015, the under-five mortality rate
5: Improve maternal health	1: Reduce by three quarters the maternal mortality ratio 2: Achieve universal access to reproductive health
6: Combat HIV/AIDS, malaria and other diseases	1: Have halted by 2015 and begun to reverse the spread of HIV/AIDS 2: Achieve, by 2010, universal access to treatment for HIV/AIDS for all those who need it 3: Have halted by 2015 and begun to reverse the incidence of malaria and other major diseases
7: Ensure environmental sustainability	1: Integrate the principles of sustainable development into country policies and programmes and reverse the loss of environmental resources 2: Reduce biodiversity loss, achieving, by 2010, a significant reduction in the rate of loss 3: Halve, by 2015, the proportion of the population without sustainable access to safe drinking water and basic sanitation 4: By 2020, to have achieved a significant improvement in the lives of at least 100 million slum dwellers
8: Develop a global partnership for development	1: Address the special needs of least developed countries, landlocked countries and small island developing states 2: Develop further an open, rule-based, predictable, non-discriminatory trading and financial system 3: Deal comprehensively with developing countries' debt 4: In cooperation with pharmaceutical companies, provide access to affordable essential drugs in developing countries 5: In cooperation with the private sector, make available benefits of new technologies, especially information and communications

Figure 17.9   The UN Millennium Development Goals

Source: www.un.org/millenniumgoals.html

The precise goals and targets of the UN project are set out in Figure 17.9. They are, indeed, extremely ambitious – especially in the light of the implications of the 2008 global financial crisis.

Goals, aspirations and collective will

> Society is faced with a profound dilemma. To resist growth is to risk economic and social collapse. To pursue it relentlessly is to endanger the ecosystems on which we depend for long-term survival.[71]

The major global challenge is to meet the material needs of the world community as a whole in ways that reduce, rather than increase, inequality and which do so without destroying the environment. That, of course, is far easier said than done. It requires the involvement of all major actors – business firms, states, international institutions, civil society organizations – in establishing mechanisms to capture the gains of globalization for the majority and not just for the powerful minority.

Such a system has to be built on world trading and financial systems that are *equitable*. This must involve reform of such institutions as the WTO, the World Bank and the IMF or, alternatively, their replacement by more effective and more widely accountable institutions. It must involve an equitable and accountable global environmental organization. The emergence of the G20 is a small step in the right direction, but it is little more than that. Much more needs to be done. As we have seen, the exercise of developed country power through the various kinds of conditionality and trade-opening requirements imposed on poorer countries has seriously negative results. Without doubt, trade is one of the most effective ways of enhancing material well-being, but it has to be based upon a genuinely fairer footing than at present. The poorer countries must be allowed to open up their markets in a manner, and at a pace, appropriate to their needs and conditions. After all, that is precisely what the US and European countries did during their phases of industrialization, as did Japan and the East Asian NIEs at a later date. At the same time, developed countries must operate a fairer system of access to their own markets for poor countries.

Of course, this will cause problems for some people and communities in the developed countries and these should not be underestimated. As we saw in Chapter 16, there are, indeed, many losers in the otherwise affluent economies.

> Globalization increases objective and subjective insecurities among a great many workers and producers … different faces of economic globalization can be expected to have different implications for risk. For instance, some faces of globalization more than others are visible, direct, and palpable with respect to job risks – for instance, via threats of outsourcing by companies rather than via trade competition.[72]

Surveys of US workers have shown that 'less-educated, lower-income workers are much more likely to oppose policies aimed at freer trade and immigration'[73] although this is changing as more higher-educated workers are increasingly affected. People who feel threatened by 'globalization' must be assisted effectively, whether this involves financial assistance or education and retraining. Governments must design and implement appropriate adjustment policies for such groups if trade policies helpful to developing countries are to be acceptable politically. Equally, governments of developing countries must engage in their own internal reforms: to strengthen domestic institutions, enhance civil society, increase political participation, remove corruption, raise the quality of education, and reduce internal social polarization. Although difficult, such policies are not impossible if the social and political will is there.

Will the populations of the rich countries be prepared to make some sacrifices for the greater global good? The signs are not very promising. Even at the best of times, it is difficult to persuade people to look beyond their own needs and wants. And these are emphatically not the best of times. The chaos wrought by the near collapse of the financial system, and the debt burdens piling up to deal with its aftermath, have increased general feelings of insecurity. However, even increased material affluence has not necessarily made people 'happier' in proportion to their increased wealth.[74] A number of reasons have been suggested to explain this apparent paradox. Research by the ILO[75] suggests that it is 'economic security', rather than wealth, that 'promotes happiness'.

> The global distribution of economic security does not correspond to the global distribution of income … South and South East Asia have greater shares of economic security than their share of the world's income … By contrast, Latin American countries provide their citizens with much less economic security than could be expected from their relative income levels … income security is a major determinant of other forms of labour-related security … [and] income inequality worsens economic security in several ways … *highly unequal societies are unlikely to achieve much by way of economic security or decent work.*[76]

As we saw in Chapter 16, the trend in many countries has been for inequality to be widening, rather than narrowing.

However, there is a more general argument that 'prosperity' needs to be defined in broader terms than just 'gross domestic product'; that 'well-being' is about more than just material affluence. A number of proposals to measure well-being have emerged, beginning with the rather exotic case of the Kingdom of Bhutan, which introduced the concept of GNH (Gross National Happiness) in the 1970s. Recently, there has been a renewed upsurge of interest. For example, a commission appointed by the French government proposed that the components that go into the measurement of GDP need to be broadened to incorporate a whole range of other measures, such as health, education, security, social connectedness and environmental sustainability.[77] A rather more subjective set of measures proposed for national accounts focuses on two dimensions: personal well-being and social well-being.[78] Whether or not such well-being measures will replace or supplement the conventional measures like GDP is hard to say. But the fact that we must define growth, prosperity and well-being in more meaningful terms is incontrovertible if we are to build a better world.

★★★

The imperatives facing us are both practical and moral. In practical terms, the continued existence across the world of vast numbers of people who are impoverished – but who can see the manifestations of immense wealth elsewhere through the electronic media – poses a serious threat to social and political stability. But the moral argument is, I believe, more powerful. It is utterly repellent that so many people live in such abject poverty and deprivation whilst, at the same time, others live in immense luxury. This is not an argument for levelling down but for raising up. The means for doing this are there. What matters is the *will* to do it – the real acceptance of, to use David Smith's words,

> the imperative of developing more caring relations with others, especially those most vulnerable, whoever and wherever they are, within a more egalitarian and environmentally sustainable way of life in which some of the traditional strengths of community can be realised and spatially extended.[79]

We all have a responsibility to ensure that the contours of the global economic map in the twenty-first century are not as steep as those of the twentieth century. We all have a responsibility to treat others as equals. In a global context, this means being sensitive to the immense diversity that exists, to the world as a mosaic of people equally deserving of 'the good life'.

Paradoxically, the 2008 global financial crisis could offer a real opportunity. For the first time in several decades, both the economic inefficiencies and the social limitations of free, unregulated markets have been exposed for all to see. In particular, an economic system based so heavily on financial speculation is, in any social and moral sense, dysfunctional. It has failed. The opportunity *must* be taken to build a new system to redress the imbalance that has developed between states and markets. Such a project is global in both scale and scope; hence the need for coordinated international policy initiatives rather than individual national measures that would lead to destructive competition rather than collaboration. At the height of the crisis in 2008–9, it seemed that such a rebuilding might, indeed, be on the agenda. But as the worst seemed to be over (or is it?) there is a real danger of going 'back to the future'. It would be a tragedy if that were to happen. *Carpe diem!*

NOTES

1   See Lee (2007), Lee and Smith (2004), Smith (2000).
2   For a US-centric analysis of this problem, see Lynn (2005).
3   Wolf (2004).
4   Voltaire (1947: 8).
5   Micklethwait and Wooldridge (2000: ix).
6   The term 'globalization and its discontents' has been used by several authors, notably Sassen (1998) and Stiglitz (2002).
7   See Williamson (2005) for a review of this issue.
8   Taylor et al. (2002: 15–16).
9   Beck (2005: 238).
10 Van Tulder with van der Zwart (2006: Parts II and III) provide a comprehensive analysis of ICSR.
11 Van Tulder with van der Zwart (2006: 143–5). Numbers in parentheses refer to pages in that study.

12   Van Tulder (2009), van Tulder et al. (2009), Barrientos (2008), Hughes et al. (2008).

13   Barrientos (2008: 979).

14   Van Tulder et al. (2009: 399).

15   Van Tulder (2009: 10).

16   Van Tulder et al. (2009: 402). Numbers in parentheses refer to pages in that study.

17   Gereffi et al. (2001).

18   Van Tulder et al. (2009), Cumbers et al. (2008: 380–4).

19   Barrientos (2008), Hughes et al. (2008).

20   See Rasche (2009).

21   Barrientos (2008: 978).

22   Barrientos (2008: 978).

23   Barrientos (2008: 980).

24   Van Tulder et al. (2009).

25   Van Tulder et al. (2009: 408). See also Maignan and Ralston (2002).

26   Wolf (2007).

27   Commission on Global Governance (1995: 135–6).

28   Gritsch (2005).

29   Levy and Prakash (2003: 143, 144).

30   Hirst et al. (2009).

31   UNCTAD (2001: vi–vii, emphasis added).

32   Stiglitz (2002: 44).

33   ILO (2004b: 88, 89).

34   See the debate in *Prospect* (September 2009: 34–41).

35   See Deese (2008), Hoekman and Kostecki (1995), Peet et al. (2003: Chapter 5), Sampson (2001).

36   Peet et al. (2003).

37   Hoekman and Kostecki (1995: 24).

38   Hoekman and Kostecki (1995: 26).

39   See, for example, Deese (2008), Peet et al. (2003: Chapter 5), Singer (2004: Chapter 3).

40   Sampson (2001: 7–8, emphasis added).

41   Wade (2003: 621).

42   Quoted in Sampson (2001: 19).

43   Stiglitz and Charlton (2005) present a detailed critique of the Doha Round and show how 'fair' trade and development can go together.

44   Wilkinson (2009).

45   Gamberoni and Newfarmer (2009).

46   See Braithwaite and Drahos (2000: Chapter 12), Pearce (1995).

47   Braithwaite and Drahos (2000: 257).

48   IPCC website (www.1.ipcc.ch/about/index.html), emphasis added.

49   Quoted in Pearce (1995: 149).

50   http://unfccc.int/kyoto_protocol/items/2830.php.

51   Address to UN Summit on Climate Change, New York, September 2009 (www.un.org/wcm/content/site/climatechange/lang/eng/p..).

52   UNFCCC Press Briefing (www.unfccc.int/2860.php).

53   Massey (2000: 24).

54   Daly (1993: 25).

55 Pearce (1995: 74, 77, 78).
56 See Hudson (2001: 315–21), Turner et al. (1994: Chapter 2).
57 Hudson (2001: 315).
58 Elliott (2002). See also Elliott (2000).
59 Gibson-Graham (2006).
60 Gibson-Graham (2006: 80).
61 Lee (1996).
62 Hulme and Arun (2009).
63 Kofi Annan, UN Secretary-General, Speech to UNCTAD Meeting in Bangkok, 2000.
64 Mittelman (2000: 241).
65 Rodrik (1999: 136–7, emphasis added).
66 See UNCTAD (2002).
67 Oxfam (2002: 1).
68 Wade (2003: 635).
69 World Bank (2009b: Table 4).
70 Statement by UN Secretary-General, Ban Ki-moon (www.un.org/millenniumgoals/bkgd.shtml).
71 Jackson (2009: 187).
72 Burgoon (2009: 148).
73 Scheve and Slaughter (2001: 87).
74 Jackson (2009), James (2007), Layard (2005), Oswald (1997), Wilkinson and Pickett (2009).
75 ILO (2004a). See also Scheve and Slaughter (2004).
76 ILO press release, www.ilo.org.
77 Stiglitz and Fitoussi (2009).
78 New Economics Foundation (2009).
79 Smith (2000: 208).

BIBLIOGRAPHY

Abernathy, F., Dunlop, J., Hammond, J.H. and Weil, D. (1999) *A Stitch in Time: Lean Retailing and the Transformation of Manufacturing: Lessons from the Apparel and Textile Industry*. New York: Oxford University Press.

Abernathy, F.H., Dunlop, J.T., Hammond, J.H. and Weil, D. (2004) Globalization in the apparel and textile industries: what is new and what is not? In M. Kenney and R. Florida (eds) *Locating Global Advantage: Industry Dynamics in the International Economy*. Stanford: Stanford University Press. Chapter 2.

ABN-AMRO (2000) *European Auto Components: Driven by Technology*. London: ABN-AMRO.

Abo, T. (ed.) (1994) *Hybrid Factory: The Japanese Production System in the United States*. New York: Oxford University Press.

Abo, T. (1996) The Japanese production system: the process of adaptation to national settings. In R. Boyer and D. Drache (eds) *States Against Markets: The Limits of Globalization*. London: Routledge. Chapter 5.

Abo, T. (2000) Spontaneous integration in Japan and East Asia: development, crisis, and beyond. In G.L. Clark, M.P. Feldman and M.S. Gertler (eds) *The Oxford Handbook of Economic Geography*. Oxford: Oxford University Press. Chapter 31.

Agnew, J. and Corbridge, S. (1995) *Mastering Space*. London: Routledge.

Alderson, A.S. and Beckfield, J. (2004) Power and position in the world city system. *American Journal of Sociology*, 109: 811–51.

Amin, A. (2000) The European Union as more than a triad market for national economic spaces. In G.L. Clark, M.P. Feldman and M.S. Gertler (eds) *The Oxford Handbook of Economic Geography*. Oxford: Oxford University Press. Chapter 33.

Amin, A. (2002) Spatialities of globalization. *Environment and Planning A*, 34: 385–99.

Amin, A. (2004) Regulating economic globalization. *Transactions of the Institute of British Geographers*, 29: 217–33.

Amin, A. and Thrift, N.J. (1992) Neo-Marshallian nodes in global networks. *International Journal of Urban and Regional Research*, 16: 571–87.

Amsden, A. (1989) *Asia's Next Giant: South Korea and Late Industrialization*. Oxford: Oxford University Press.

Andersen, P.H. and Christensen, P.R. (2004) Bridges over troubled water: suppliers as connective nodes in global supply networks. *Journal of Business Research*, 58: 1261–73.

Anderson, M. (1995) The role of collaborative integration in industrial organization: observations from the Canadian aerospace industry. *Economic Geography*, 71: 55–78.

Anderson, S. and Cavanagh, J. (2000) *Top 200: The Rise of Corporate Global Power.* Washington, DC: Institute for Policy Studies.

Appelbaum, R.P. (2008) Giant transnational contractors in East Asia: emergent trends in global supply chains. *Competition & Change*, 12: 69–87.

Archibugi, D. and Michie, J. (eds) (1997) *Technology, Globalization, and Economic Performance.* Cambridge: Cambridge University Press.

Archibugi, D., Howells, J. and Michie, J. (eds) (1999) *Innovation Policy in a Global Economy.* Cambridge: Cambridge University Press.

Baaij, M., van den Bosch, F. and Volberda, H. (2004) The international relocation of corporate centres: are corporate centres sticky? *European Management Journal*, 22: 141–9.

Badaracco, J.L. Jr (1991) The boundaries of the firm. In A. Etzioni and P.R. Lawrence (eds) *Socio-Economics: Towards a New Synthesis.* Armonk, NY: Sharpe. pp. 293–327.

Bair, J. (2002) Beyond the maquila model: NAFTA and the Mexican apparel industry. *Industry and Innovation*, 9: 203–25.

Bair, J. (2006) Regional trade and production blocs in a global industry: towards a comparative framework for research. *Environment and Planning A*, 38: 2233–52.

Bair, J. (2008) Surveying the post-MFA landscape: what prospects for the Global South post-quota? *Competition & Change*, 12: 3–10.

Bair, J. (ed.) (2009) *Frontiers of Commodity Chain Research.* Stanford: Stanford University Press.

Bair, J. and Gereffi, G. (2001) Local clusters in global chains: the causes and consequences of export dynamism in Torreón's blue jeans industry. *World Development*, 29: 1885–1903.

Bair, J. and Gereffi, G. (2003) Upgrading, uneven development, and jobs in the North American apparel industry. *Global Networks*, 3: 143–96.

Barham, B.L. and Coomes, O.T. (2005) Sunk costs, resource extractive industries, and development outcomes. In P.S. Ciccantell, D.A. Smith and G. Seidman (eds) *Nature, Raw Materials, and Political Economy.* Amsterdam: Elsevier. pp. 159–86.

Barrientos, S. (2008) Contract labour: the 'Achilles Heel' of corporate codes in commercial value chains. *Development and Change*, 39: 977–90.

Barrientos, S. and Gereffi, G. (2009) Capturing the gains: economic and social upgrading in global production networks. *University of Manchester International Research Network.*

Bartlett, C.A. and Ghoshal, S. (1998) *Managing across Borders: The Transnational Solution*, 2nd edn. New York: Random House.

Bartlett, D. and Seleny, A. (1998) The political enforcement of liberalism: bargaining, institutions, and auto multinationals in Hungary. *International Studies Quarterly*, 42: 319–38.

Basu, K. (2006) Globalization, poverty, and inequality: what is the relationship, what can be done? *World Development*, 34: 1361–73.

Bathelt, H. and Gertler, M.S. (2005) The German variety of capitalism: forces and dynamics of evolutionary change. *Economic Geography*, 81: 1–9.

Bathelt, H., Malmberg, A. and Maskell, P. (2004) Clusters and knowledge: local buzz, global pipelines and the process of knowledge creation. *Progress in Human Geography*, 28: 31–56.

Bayly, C.A. (2004) *The Birth of the Modern World, 1780–1914.* Oxford: Blackwell.

BBC World Service (2008) Widespread unease about economy and globalization – global poll. www.bbc.co.uk/pressoffice/pressreleases/stories/2008/02_february/07/poll.shtml.

Beattie, A. (2005) Top of the crops: Brazil's huge heartland is yielding farms that can feed the world. *Financial Times*, 23 June: 17.

Beaverstock, J.V. (2004) 'Managing across borders': knowledge management and expatriation in professional service legal firms. *Journal of Economic Geography*, 4: 157–79.

Beck, U. (2005) *Power in the Global Age: A New Global Political Economy*. Cambridge: Polity.

Beechler, S.L. and Bird, A. (eds) (1999) *Japanese Multinationals Abroad: Individual and Organizational Learning*. New York: Oxford University Press.

Begg, B., Pickles, J. and Smith, A. (2003) Cutting it: European integration, trade regimes, and the configuration of East-Central European apparel production. *Environment and Planning A*, 35: 2191–207.

Belderbos, R. and Capannelli, G. (2001) Backward vertical linkages of foreign manufacturing affiliates: evidence from Japanese multinationals. *World Development*, 29: 189–208.

Bello, W. and Rosenfeld, S. (1990) *Dragons in Distress: Asian Miracle Economies in Crisis*. San Francisco: Institute for Food and Development Policy.

Benewick, R. and Wingrove, P. (eds) (1995) *China in the 1990s*. London: Macmillan.

Beresford, M. (2009) The Cambodian clothing industry in the post-MFA environment: a review of developments. *Journal of the Asia Pacific Economy*, 14: 366–88.

Berger, S. (2005) *How We Compete: What Companies around the World Are Doing to Make It in Today's Global Economy*. New York: Doubleday.

Berger, S. and Dore, R. (eds) (1996) *National Diversity and Global Capitalism*. Ithaca, NY: Cornell University Press.

Berggren, C. and Bengtsson, L. (2004) Rethinking outsourcing in manufacturing: a tale of two telecom firms. *European Management Journal*, 22: 211–23.

Berndt, C. and Boeckler, M. (2009) Geographies of circulation and exchange: construction of markets. *Progress in Human Geography*, 33: 535–51.

Beukering, P.J.H. van (2001) *Recycling, International Trade and Environment: An Empirical Analysis*. Amsterdam: Kluwer.

Beukering, P.J.H. van and Bouman, M.N. (2001) Empirical evidence on recycling and trade of paper and lead in developed and developing countries. *World Development*, 29: 1717–37.

Bhagwati, J. (2004) *In Defense of Globalization*. New York: Oxford University Press.

Birkinshaw, J. (2001) Strategy and management in MNE subsidiaries. In A.M. Rugman and T.L. Brewer (eds) *The Oxford Handbook of International Business*. Oxford: Oxford University Press. pp. 380–401.

Birkinshaw, J. and Morrison, A.J. (1995) Configurations of strategy and structure in subsidiaries of multinational corporations. *Journal of International Business Studies*, 26: 729–55.

Blanc, H. and Sierra, C. (1999) The internationalisation of R&D by multinationals: a trade-off between external and internal proximity. *Cambridge Journal of Economics*, 23: 187–206.

Blois, K. (2006) The boundaries of the firm: a question of interpretation? *Industry and Innovation*, 13: 135–49.

Blonigen, B.A. (2006) Foreign direct investment behavior of multinational corporations. *NBER Reporter: Research Summary*, Winter 2006.

Blowfield, M. (1999) Ethical trade: a review of developments and issues. *Third World Quarterly*, 20: 753–70.

Blythman, J. (2004) *Shopped: The Shocking Power of British Supermarkets*. London: HarperCollins.

Bonanno, A., Busch, L., Friedland, W. and Mingione, E. (eds) (1994) *From Columbus to ConAgra: The Globalization of Agriculture and Food*. Lawrence, KA: University Press of Kansas.

Borrus, M., Ernst, D. and Haggard, S. (eds) (2000) *International Production Networks in Asia: Rivalry or Riches?* London: Routledge.

Bowles, P. (2002) Asia's post-crisis regionalism: bringing the state back in, keeping the (United) States out. *Review of International Political Economy*, 9: 230–56.

Boyd, W. and Watts, M.J. (1997) Agro-industrial just-in-time: the chicken industry and postwar American capitalism. In D. Goodman and M.J. Watts (eds) *Globalizing Food: Agrarian Questions and Global Restructuring*. London: Routledge. Chapter 8.

Braithwaite, J. and Drahos, P. (2000) *Global Business Regulation*. Cambridge: Cambridge University Press.

Brenner, N., Peck, J.A. and Theodore, N. (2010) Variegated neoliberalization: geographies, modalities, pathways. *Global Networks*, 10.

Bridge, G. (2004) Mapping the bonanza: geographies of mining investment in an era of neoliberal reform. *The Professional Geographer*, 56: 406–21.

Bridge, G. (2008a) Environmental economic geography: a sympathetic critique. *Geoforum*, 39: 76–81.

Bridge, G. (2008b) Global production networks and the extractive sector: governing resource-based development. *Journal of Economic Geography*, 8: 389–419.

Bridge, G. (2009) Material worlds: natural resources, resource geography and the material economy. *Geography Compass*, 3. www.geography-compass.com.

Brohman, J. (1996) Postwar development in the Asian NICs: does the neoliberal model fit reality? *Economic Geography*, 72: 107–31.

Brown, T.J., Hetherington, L.E., Hannis, S.D., Bide, T., Benham, A.J., Idoine, N.E. and Lusty, P.A. (2009) *World Mineral Production 2003–2007*. Nottingham: British Geological Survey.

Brunn, S.D. and Leinbach, T.R. (1991) *Collapsing Space and Time: Geographic Aspects of Communication and Information*. New York: HarperCollins.

Buck, T. and Shahrim, A. (2005) The translation of corporate governance changes across national cultures: the case of Germany. *Journal of International Business Studies*, 36: 42–61.

Buckley, P.J. and Casson, M. (1976) *The Future of the Multinational Enterprise*. London: Macmillan.

Bunker, S. and Ciccantell, P. (2005) *Globalization and the Race for Resources*. Baltimore: Johns Hopkins University Press.

Bunnell, T.G. and Coe, N.M. (2001) Spaces and scales of innovation. *Progress in Human Geography*, 25: 569–89.

Burgoon, B. (2009) Globalization and backlash: Polanyi's revenge? *Review of International Political Economy*, 16: 145–77.

Cable, V. (1999) *Globalization and Global Governance*. London: Royal Institute of International Affairs.

Cable, V. and Henderson, D. (eds) (1994) *Trade Blocs? The Future of Regional Integration*. London: Royal Institute of International Affairs.

Cameron, A. and Palan, R. (2004) *The Imagined Economies of Globalization*. London: Sage.

Campbell-Lendrum, D. and Corvalán, C. (2007) Climate change and developing-country cities: implications for environmental health and equity. *Journal of Urban Health*, 84 (Suppl. 1): 109–17.

Cantwell, J. (1997) The globalization of technology: what remains of the product cycle model? In D. Archibugi and J. Michie (eds) *Technology, Globalization, and Economic Performance*. Cambridge: Cambridge University Press. Chapter 8.

Cantwell, J. and Iammarino, S. (2000) Multinational corporations and the location of technological innovation in the UK regions. *Regional Studies*, 34: 317–32.

Carillo, J. (2004) Transnational strategies and regional development: the case of GM and Delphi in Mexico. *Industry and Innovation*, 11: 127–53.

Carr, N. (2008a) A revolution is taking shape. *Financial Times*, 30 January.

Carr, N. (2008b) *The Big Switch: Rewiring the World, from Edison to Google*. New York: Norton.

Carroll, W.K. (2007) Global cities in the global corporate network. *Environment and Planning A*, 39: 2297–323.

Carroll, W.K. and Carson, C. (2003) Forging a new hegemony? The role of transnational policy groups in the network and discourses of global corporate governance. *Journal of World-Systems Research*, IX: 67–102.

Cassis, Y. (2006) *Capitals of Capital: A History of International Financial Centres, 1780–2005*. Cambridge: Cambridge University Press.

Castells, M. (1996) *The Information Age: Economy, Society and Culture*, 3 vols. Oxford: Blackwell.

Castells, M., Fernández-Ardèvol, M., Qiu, J.L. and Sey, A. (2007) *Mobile Communication and Society: A Global Perspective*. Cambridge, MA: MIT Press.

Castles, S. and Miller, M.J. (2009) *The Age of Migration: International Population Movements in the Modern World*, 4th edn. New York: Guilford.

Castree, N., Coe, N.M., Ward, K. and Samers, M. (2004) *Spaces of Work: Global Capitalism and Geographies of Labour*. London: Sage.

Cerny, P.G. (1991) The limits of deregulation: transnational interpenetrations and policy change. *European Journal of Political Research*, 19: 173–96.

Cerny, P.G. (1997) Paradoxes of the competition state: the dynamics of political globalization. *Government and Opposition*, 32: 251–74.

Cerrato, D. (2006) The multinational enterprise as an internal market system. *International Business Review*, 15: 253–77.

Chang, H.-J. (1998a) South Korea: the misunderstood crisis. In K.S. Jomo (ed.) *Tigers in Trouble: Financial Governance, Liberalization and Crises in East Asia*. London: Zed. Chapter 10.

Chang, H.-J. (1998b) Transnational corporations and strategic industrial policy. In R. Kozul-Wright and R. Rowthorn (eds) *Transnational Corporations and the Global Economy*. London: Macmillan. Chapter 7.

Chang, H.-J. (2007) *Bad Samaritans: Rich Nations, Poor Policies, and the Threat to the Developing World*. London: Random House.

Chase-Dunn, C., Kawano, Y. and Brewer, B.D. (2000) Trade globalization since 1795: waves of integration in the world-system. *American Sociological Review*, 65: 77–95.

Chorev, N. (2007) A fluid divide: domestic and international factors in US trade policy formation. *Review of International Political Economy*, 14: 653–89.

Clark, G.L. (2002) London in the European financial services industry: locational advantages and product complementarities. *Journal of Economic Geography*, 2: 433–53.

Clarke, D. (2007) *The Battle for Barrels: Peak Oil Myths and World Oil Futures*. London: Profile Business.

Cline, W.R. (1997) *Trade and Income Distribution*. Washington, DC: Institute for International Economics.

Coe, N.M. (2003a) Globalization, regionalization and 'scales of integration': US IT industry investment in South East Asia. In M. Miozzo and I. Miles (eds) *Internationalization, Technology and Services*. Cheltenham: Elgar. pp. 117–36.

Coe, N.M. (2003b) Information highways and digital divides: the evolving ICT landscapes of Southeast Asia. In L.S. Chia (ed.) *SouthEast Asia Transformed: A Geography of Change*. Singapore: ISEAS. Chapter 9.

Coe, N.M. and Hess, M. (2005) The internationalization of retailing: implications for supply network restructuring in East Asia and Eastern Europe. *Journal of Economic Geography*, 5: 449–73.

Coe, N.M. and Lee, Y.-S. (2006) The strategic localization of transnational retailers: the case of Samsung-Tesco in South Korea. *Economic Geography*, 82: 61–88.

Coe, N.M. and Wrigley, N. (eds) (2009) *The Globalization of Retailing*, 2 vols. Cheltenham: Elgar.

Coe, N.M., Kelly, P.F. and Olds, K. (2003) Globalization, transnationalism and the Asia-Pacific. In J. Peck and H.W.-c. Yeung (eds) *Remaking the Global Economy: Economic-Geographical Perspectives*. London: Sage. Chapter 3.

Coe, N.M., Hess, M., Yeung, H.W.-c., Dicken, P. and Henderson, J. (2004) 'Globalizing' regional development: a global production networks perspective. *Transactions of the Institute of British Geographers*, 29: 468–84.

Coe, N.M., Dicken, P. and Hess, M. (2008a) Global production networks: realizing the potential. *Journal of Economic Geography*, 8: 271–95.

Coe, N.M., Johns, J. and Ward, K. (2008b) Flexibility in action: the temporary staffing industry in the Czech Republic and Poland. *Environment and Planning A*, 40: 1391–415.

Cohen, B. (2004) Urban growth in developing countries: a review of current trends and a caution regarding existing forecasts. *World Development*, 32: 23–51.

Cohen, D. (1998) *The Wealth of the World and the Poverty of Nations*. Cambridge, MA: MIT Press.

Cohen, S.S. and Zysman, J. (1987) *Manufacturing Matters: The Myth of the Post-Industrial Economy*. New York: Basic.

Collis, D., Young, D. and Goold, M. (2007) The size, structure, and performance of corporate headquarters. *Strategic Management Journal*, 28: 383–405.

Comer, J.C. and Wikle, T.A. (2008) Worldwide diffusion of the cellular telephone, 1995–2005. *Professional Geographer*, 60: 252–69.

Commission on Global Governance (1995) *Our Global Neighbourhood*. New York: Oxford University Press.

Corbett, J., Winebrake, J.J., Green, E.H., Kasibhatla, P., Eyring, V. and Lauer, A. (2007) Mortality from ship emissions: a global assessment. *Environmental Science & Technology*, 41: 8512–18.

Crane, G.T. (1990) *The Political Economy of China's Special Economic Zones*. Armonk, NY: Sharpe.

Crook, C. (2001) Globalization and its critics: a survey of globalization. *The Economist*, 29 September.

Crotty, J. (2009) Structural causes of the global financial crisis: a critical assessment of the 'new financial architecture'. *Cambridge Journal of Economics*, 33: 563–80.

Crow, B., Zlatunich, N. and Fulfrost, B. (2009) Mapping global inequalities: beyond income inequality to multi-dimensional inequalities. *Journal of International Development*, 21: 1051–65.

Cumbers, A., Nativel, C. and Routledge, P. (2008) Labour agency and union positionalities in global production networks. *Journal of Economic Geography*, 8: 369–87.

Daly, H.E. (1993) The perils of free trade. *Scientific American*, November: 24–9.

Daniels, P.W. and Bryson, J.R. (2002) Manufacturing services and servicing manufacturing: knowledge-based cities and changing forms of production. *Urban Studies*, 39: 977–91.

D'Aveni, R.A. (1994) *Hypercompetition: Managing the Dynamics of Strategic Manoeuvring*. New York: Free.

Dawson, J.A. (2007) Scoping and conceptualizing retailer transnationalization. *Journal of Economic Geography*, 7: 373–97.

Dean, M. and Sebastia-Barriel, M. (2004) Why has world trade grown faster than world output? *Bank of England Quarterly Review*, Autumn: 310–20.

Dedrick, J., Kraemer, K.L. and Linden, G. (2009) Who profits from innovation in global value chains? A study of the iPod and notebook PCs. *Industrial and Corporate Change*, 18.

Deese, D.A. (2008) *World Trade Politics: Power, Principles and Leadership*. Abingdon: Routledge.

Department of International Development (2000) *Eliminating World Poverty: Making Globalization Work for the Poor*. London: DoID.

Dicken, P. (2000) Places and flows: situating international investment. In G.L. Clark, M.P. Feldman and M.S. Gertler (eds) *The Oxford Handbook of Economic Geography*. Oxford: Oxford University Press. Chapter 14.

Dicken, P. (2003a) Global production networks in Europe and East Asia: the automobile components industries. *University of Manchester GPN Working Paper 7*. www.sed.manchester. ac.uk/geography/research/gpn/gpnwp.htm.

Dicken, P. (2003b) 'Placing' firms: grounding the debate on the 'global' corporation. In J. Peck and H.W.-c. Yeung (eds) *Remaking the Global Economy: Economic-Geographical Perspectives*. London: Sage. Chapter 2.

Dicken, P. (2004) Geographers and 'globalization': (yet) another missed boat? *Transactions of the Institute of British Geographers*, 29: 5–26.

Dicken, P. and Hassler, M. (2000) Organizing the Indonesian clothing industry in the global economy: the role of business networks. *Environment and Planning A*, 32: 263–80.

Dicken, P. and Lloyd, P.E. (1990) *Location in Space: Theoretical Perspectives in Economic Geography*, 3rd edn. New York: Harper & Row.

Dicken, P. and Malmberg, A. (2001) Firms in territories: a relational perspective. *Economic Geography*, 77: 345–63.

Dicken, P. and Miyamachi, Y. (1998) 'From noodles to satellites': the changing geography of the Japanese *sogo shosha*. *Transactions of the Institute of British Geographers*, 23: 55–78.

Dicken, P. and Yeung, H.W.-c. (1999) Investing in the future: East and Southeast Asian firms in the global economy. In K. Olds, P. Dicken, P.F. Kelly, L. Kong and H.W.-c. Yeung (eds) *Globalization and the Asia–Pacific: Contested Territories*. London: Routledge. Chapter 7.

Dieter, H. and Higgott, R. (2003) Exploring alternative theories of economic regionalism: from trade to finance in Asian cooperation. *Review of International Political Economy*, 10: 430–54.

Dodge, M. and Kitchin, R. (2001) *Atlas of Cyberspace*. Reading, MA: Addison-Wesley.

Dolan, C. and Humphrey, J. (2002) Changing governance patterns in the trade in fresh vegetables between Africa and the United Kingdom. *Environment and Planning A*, 36: 491–509.

Domanski, B. and Lung, Y. (2009) The changing face of the European periphery in the automotive industry. *European Urban and Regional Studies*, 16: 5–10.

Donaghu, M.T. and Barff, R. (1990) Nike just did it: international subcontracting and flexibility in athletic footwear production. *Regional Studies*, 24: 537–552.

Dore, R. (1986) *Flexible Rigidities: Industrial Policy and Structural Adjustment in the Japanese Economy, 1970–1980*. Stanford, CA: Stanford University Press.

Dore, R. (2008) Financialization of the global economy. *Industrial and Corporate Change*, 17: 1097–113.

Doremus, P.N., Keller, W.W., Pauly, L.W. and Reich, S. (1998) *The Myth of the Global Corporation*. Princeton, NJ: Princeton University Press.

Dosi, G., Freeman, C., Nelson, R., Silverberg, G. and Soete, L. (eds) (1988) *Technical Change and Economic Theory*. London: Pinter.

Douglass, M. (1994) The 'developmental state' and the newly industrialized economies of Asia. *Environment and Planning A*, 26: 543–66.

Dow, S.C. (1999) The stages of banking development and the spatial evolution of financial systems. In R. Martin (ed.) *Money and the Space-Economy*. Chichester: Wiley. Chapter 2.

Doz, Y. (1986a) Government polices and global industries. In M.E. Porter (ed.) *Competition in Global Industries*. Boston, MA: Harvard Business School. Chapter 7.

Doz, Y. (1986b) *Strategic Management in Multinational Companies*. Oxford: Pergamon.

Drogendijk, R. and Slangen, A. (2006) Hofstede, Schwartz, or managerial perceptions? The effects of different cultural distance measures on establishment mode choices by multinational enterprises. *International Business Review*, 15: 361–80.

Drucker, P. (1946) *The Concept of the Corporation*. New York: Day.

Dunford, M. (2006) Industrial districts, magic circles, and the restructuring of the Italian textiles and clothing chain. *Economic Geography*, 82: 27–59.

Dunford, M. (2007) Le développement économique en Europe depuis 1950. *L'Information Géographique*, 71: 68–99.

Dunford, M. and Kafkalas, G. (1992) The global–local interplay, corporate geographies and spatial development strategies in Europe. In M. Dunford and G. Kafkalas (eds) *Cities and Regions in the New Europe: The Global–Local Interplay and Spatial Development Strategies*. London: Belhaven. Chapter 1.

Dunford, M. and Smith, A. (2000) Catching up or falling behind? Economic performance and regional trajectories in the 'new Europe'. *Economic Geography*, 76: 169–95.

Dunning, J.H. (1992) The competitive advantages of countries and the activities of transnational corporations. *Transnational Corporations*, 1: 135–68.

Dunning, J.H. (2000) The eclectic paradigm as an envelope for economic and business theories of MNE activity. *International Business Review*, 9: 163–90.

Dunning, J.H. and Lundan, S.M. (2008) *Multinational Enterprises and the Global Economy*. 2nd edn. Reading, MA: Addison-Wesley.

Durand, C. (2007) Externalities from foreign direct investment in the Mexican retailing sector. *Cambridge Journal of Economics*, 31: 393–411.

Dustmann, C. and Glitz, A. (2005) *Immigration, Jobs and Wages: Theory, Evidence and Opinion*. London: CEPR.

Eatwell, J. and Taylor, L. (2000) *Global Finance at Risk: The Case for International Regulation*. Cambridge: Polity.

Eden, L. and Monteils, A. (2002) Regional integration: NAFTA and the reconfiguration of North American industry. In J.H. Dunning (ed.) *Regions, Globalization and the Knowledge-Based Economy*. Oxford: Oxford University Press. Chapter 7.

Edgerton, D. (2007) *The Shock of the Old*. London: Profile.

Edward, P. (2006) Examining inequality: who really benefits from global growth? *World Development*, 34: 1667–95.

EIU (2000) *World Automotive Components: Market Prospects to 2005*. London: The Economist Intelligence Unit.

Elango, B. (2004) Geographic scope of operations by multinational companies: an exploratory study of regional and global strategies. *European Management Journal*, 22: 431–41.

Elliott, L. (2000) Free trade, no choice. In B. Gunnell and D. Timms (eds) *After Seattle: Globalization and its Discontents*. London: Catalyst. Chapter 2.

Elliott, L. (2002) Morals of the brothel. *The Guardian*, 15 April.

Emel, J., Bridge, G. and Krueger, R. (2002) The earth as input: resources. In R.J. Johnston, P.J. Taylor and M.J. Watts (eds) *Geographies of Global Change: Remapping the World*. Oxford: Blackwell. Chapter 24.

Epstein, G.A. (ed.) (2005) *Financialization and the World Economy*. Cheltenham: Elgar.

Ericsson, M. (2008) Global mining: new actors! *Nordic Steel and Mining Review*, 2008/03: 112–18.

Ernst, D. and Kim, L. (2002) Global production networks, knowledge diffusion, and local capability formation. *Research Policy*, 1419: 1–13.

ETC Group (2008) *Who Owns Nature? Corporate Power and the Final Frontier in the Commodification of Life*. Toronto: ETC Group.

Faulconbridge, J.R. (2008) Negotiating cultures of work in transnational law firms. *Journal of Economic Geography*, 8: 497–517.

Faulconbridge, J.R., Hall, S.J.E. and Beaverstock, J.V. (2008) New insights into the internationalization of producer services: organizational strategies and spatial economies for global headhunting firms. *Environment and Planning A*, 40: 210–34.

Faulconbridge, J.R., Beaverstock, J.V., Hall, S. and Hewitson, A. (2009) The 'war for talent': the gatekeeper role of executive search firms in elite labour markets. *Geoforum*, 40: 800–8.

Faux, J. and Mishel, L. (2000) Inequality and the global economy. In W. Hutton and A. Giddens (eds) *On the Edge: Living with Global Capitalism*. London: Cape. pp. 93–111.

Feenstra, R.C. (1998) Integration of trade and disintegration of production in the global economy. *Journal of Economic Perspectives*, 12: 31–50.

Fields, G. (2004) *Territories of Profit: Communications, Capitalist Development, and the Innovative Enterprises of G.F. Swift and Dell Computers*. Stanford: Stanford Business Books.

Florida, R. (2005) The world is spiky. *The Atlantic Monthly*, October: 48–51.

Forsgren, M., Holm, U. and Johanson, J. (2005) *Managing the Embedded Multinational: A Business Network View*. Cheltenham: Elgar.

Frank, A.G. (1998) *ReORIENT: Global Economy in the Asian Age*. Berkeley: University of California Press.

Freeman, C. (1982) *The Economics of Industrial Innovation*. London: Pinter.

Freeman, C. (1987) The challenge of new technologies. In OECD (ed.) *Interdependence and Cooperation in Tomorrow's World*. Paris: OECD. pp. 123–56.

Freeman, C. (1988) Introduction. In G. Dosi, C. Freeman, R. Nelson, G. Silverberg and L. Soete (eds) *Technical Change and Economic Theory*. London: Pinter. Chapter 1.

Freeman, C. (1997) The 'national system of innovation' in historical perspective. In D. Archibugi and J. Michie (eds) *Technology, Globalization and Economic Performance*. Cambridge: Cambridge University Press. Chapter 2.

Freeman, C. and Perez, C. (1988) Structural crises of adjustment, business cycles and investment behaviour. In G. Dosi, C. Freeman, R. Nelson, G. Silverberg and L. Soete (eds) *Technical Change and Economic Theory*. London: Pinter. Chapter 3.

Freeman, C., Clark, J. and Soete, L. (1982) *Unemployment and Technical Change*. London: Pinter.

Freidberg, S. (2004) *French Beans and Food Scares: Culture and Commerce in an Anxious Age*. Oxford: Oxford University Press.

French, S. and Leyshon, A. (2004) The new, new financial system? Towards a reconceptualization of financial reintermediation. *Review of International Political Economy*, 11: 263–88.

Freyssenet, M. and Lung, Y. (2000) 'Between globalisation and regionalisation: what is the future of the motor industry?' In J. Humphrey, Y. Lecler and M.S. Salerno (eds) *Global Strategies and Local Realities: The Auto Industry in Emerging Markets*. London: Macmillan. Chapter 4.

Friedland, W. (1994) The new globalization: the case of fresh produce. In A. Bonanno, L. Busch, W. Friedland and E. Mingione (eds) *From Columbus to ConAgra: The Globalization of Agriculture and Food*. Lawrence, KA: University Press of Kansas. Chapter 10.

Friedman, T.L. (1999) *The Lexus and the Olive Tree*. New York: HarperCollins.

Friedman, T.L. (2005) *The World Is Flat: The Globalized World in the Twenty-First Century*. London: Penguin.

Friedmann, J. (1986) The world city hypothesis. *Development and Change*, 17: 69–83.

Frigant, V. and Layan, J.-B. (2009) Modular production and the new division of labour within Europe. *European Urban and Regional Studies*, 16: 11–25.

Frigant, V. and Lung, Y. (2002) Geographical proximity and supplying relationships in modular production. *International Journal of Urban and Regional Research*, 26: 742–55.

Fröbel, F., Heinrichs, J. and Kreye, O. (1980) *The New International Division of Labour*. Cambridge: Cambridge University Press.

Fruin, W.M. (1992) *The Japanese Enterprise System*. Oxford: Clarendon.

Frynas, J.G. and Paulo, M. (2006) A new scramble for African oil? Historical, political, and business perspectives. *African Affairs*, 106: 229–51.

Fujita, M. and Ishigaki, K. (1986) The internationalisation of commercial banking. In M.J. Taylor and N.J. Thrift (eds) *Multinationals and the Restructuring of the World Economy*. London: Croom Helm. Chapter 7.

Fukuyama, F. (1992) *The End of History and the Last Man*. London: Hamish Hamilton.

Gabrielsson, M. and Kirpalani, V.H.M. (2004) Born globals: how to reach new business space rapidly. *International Business Review*, 13: 555–71.

Gallagher, K.P., Moreno-Brid, J.C. and Porzecanski, R. (2008) The dynamism of Mexican exports: lost in (Chinese) translation? *World Development*, 36: 1365–80.

Gamberoni, E. and Newfarmer, R. (2009) Trade protection: incipient but worrisome trends. *Trade Notes*, International Trade Department, World Bank.

Gamble, A. and Payne, A. (eds) (1996) *Regionalism and World Order*. London: Macmillan.

Gereffi, G. (1990) Paths of industrialization: an overview. In G. Gereffi and D.L. Wyman (eds) *Manufacturing Miracles: Paths of Industrialization in Latin America and East Asia*. Princeton, NJ: Princeton University Press. Chapter 1.

Gereffi, G. (1994) The organization of buyer-driven global commodity chains: how US retailers shape overseas production networks. In G. Gereffi and M. Korzeniewicz (eds) *Commodity Chains and Global Capitalism*. Westport, CT: Praeger. Chapter 5.

Gereffi, G. (1996) Commodity chains and regional divisions of labor in East Asia. *Journal of Asian Business*, 12: 75–112.

Gereffi, G. (1999) International trade and industrial upgrading in the apparel commodity chain. *Journal of International Economics*, 48: 37–70.

Gereffi, G. (2001) Shifting governance structures in global commodity chains, with special reference to the Internet. *American Behavioral Scientist*, 44: 1616–37.

Gereffi, G. (2005) The global economy: organization, governance and development. In N. Smelser and R. Swedberg (eds) *The Handbook of Economic Sociology*, 2nd edn. Princeton: Princeton University Press. Chapter 8.

Gereffi, G. and Memedovic, O. (2004) The global apparel value chain: what prospects for upgrading by developing countries? In J. O'Loughlin, L. Staeheli and E. Greenberg (eds) *Globalization and its Outcomes*. New York: Guilford. Chapter 4.

Gereffi, G., Garcia-Johnson, R. and Sasser, E. (2001) The NGO–industrial complex. *Foreign Policy*, July–August: 56–65.

Gereffi, G., Spener, D. and Bair, J. (eds) (2002) *Free Trade and Uneven Development: The North American Apparel Industry after NAFTA*. Philadelphia: Temple University Press.

Gereffi, G., Humphrey, J. and Sturgeon, T. (2005) The governance of global value chains. *Review of International Political Economy*, 12: 78–104.

Gerlach, M. (1992) *Alliance Capitalism: The Social Organization of Japanese Business*. Berkeley, CA: University of California Press.

Gertler, M.S. (1995) 'Being there': proximity, organization and culture in the development and adoption of advanced manufacturing technologies. *Economic Geography*, 71: 1–26.

Gertler, M.S. (2003) Tacit knowledge and the economic geography of context, or the undefinable tacitness of being there. *Journal of Economic Geography*, 3: 75–99.

Gertler, M.S., Wolfe, D.A. and Garkut, D. (2000) No place like home? The embeddedness of innovation in a regional economy. *Review of International Political Economy*, 7: 688–718.

Ghose, A.K., Majid, N. and Ernst, C. (2009) *The Global Employment Challenge*. Geneva: ILO.

Gibb, R. and Michalak, W. (eds) (1994) *Continental Trading Blocs: The Growth of Regionalism in the World Economy*. Chichester: Wiley.

Gibson-Graham, J.K. (2006) *Post-Capitalist Politics*. Minneapolis: Minnesota University Press.

Gilpin, R. (1987) *The Political Economy of International Relations*. Princeton, NJ: Princeton University Press.

Gilpin, R. (2000) *The Challenge of Global Capitalism: The World Economy in the 21st Century*. Princeton, NJ: Princeton University Press.

Gilpin, R. (2001) *Global Political Economy: Understanding the International Economic Order*. Princeton, NJ: Princeton University Press.

Girourd, A. and Mirza, H. (2006) Factors determining supply linkages between transnational corporations and local suppliers in ASEAN. *Transnational Corporations*, 15: 1–32.

Glasius, M., Kaldor, M. and Anheier, H. (eds) (2002) *Global Civil Society, 2002*. Oxford: Oxford University Press.

Glasmeier, A. (2002) One nation pulling apart: the basis of persistent poverty in the United States. *Progress in Human Geography*, 26: 155–74.

Glassner, M.I. (1993) *Political Geography*. New York: Wiley.

Goldstein, J. (2007) China's international recycling trade. *USC-China Institute* (http:/ China.usc.edu).

Gomes-Casseres, B. (1996) *The Alliance Revolution: The New Shape of Business Rivalry*. Cambridge, MA: Harvard University Press.

Gordon, D.M. (1988) The global economy: new edifice or crumbling foundations? *New Left Review*, 168: 24–64.

Graham, M. (2009) Known unknowns. *Technology Guardian*, 3 December: 3.

Graham, S. and Marvin, S. (1996) *Telecommunications and the City: Electronic Spaces, Urban Places*. London: Routledge.

Granovetter, M. (1985) Economic action and social structure: the problem of embeddedness. *American Journal of Sociology*, 91: 481–510.

Granovetter, M. and Swedberg, R. (eds) (1992) *The Sociology of Economic Life*. Boulder, CO: Westview.

Greider, W. (1997) *One World, Ready or Not: The Manic Logic of Global Capitalism*. London: Penguin.

Gretschmann, K. (1994) Germany in the global economy of the 1990s: from player to pawn? In R. Stubbs and G.R.D. Underhill (eds) *Political Economy and the Changing Global Order*. London: Macmillan. Chapter 29.

Grigg, D. (1993) *The World Food Problem*, 2nd edn. Oxford: Blackwell.

Gritsch, M. (2005) The nation-state and economic globalization: soft geo-politics and increased state autonomy? *Review of International Political Economy*, 12: 1–25.

Grugel, J. (1996) Latin America and the remaking of the Americas. In A. Gamble and A. Payne (eds) (1996) *Regionalism and World Order*. London: Macmillan. Chapter 5.

Guan, D., Peters, G.P., Weber, C.L. and Hubacek, K. (2009) Journey to world top emitter: an analysis of the driving forces of China's recent CO_2 emissions surge. *Geophysical Research Letters*, 36.

Guiher, G. and Lecler, Y. (2000) Japanese car manufacturers' component makers in the ASEAN region: a case of expatriation under duress – or a strategy of regionally integrated production? In J. Humphrey, Y. Lecler and M.S. Salerno (eds) *Global Strategies and Local Realities: The Auto Industry in Emerging Markets*. London: Macmillan. Chapter 9.

Gwynne, R. (1994) Regional integration in Latin America: the revival of a concept? In R. Gibb and W. Michalak (eds) *Continental Trading Blocs: The Growth of Regionalism in the World Economy*. Chichester: Wiley. Chapter 7.

Haggard, S. (1995) *Developing Nations and the Politics of Global Integration*. Washington, DC: Brookings Institution.

Haig, R.M. (1926) Toward an understanding of the metropolis. *Quarterly Journal of Economics*, 40: 421–33.

Hale, A. and Wills, J. (eds) (2005) *Threads of Labour: Garment Industry Supply Chains from the Workers' Perspective*. Oxford: Blackwell.

Hall, P. and Preston, P. (1988) *The Carrier Wave: New Information Technology and the Geography of Innovation, 1846–2003*. London: Unwin Hyman.

Hall, P.A. and Soskice, D. (2001) *Varieties of Capitalism: The Institutional Foundations of Comparative Advantage*. Oxford: Oxford University Press.

Hamilton, G.G. and Feenstra, R.C. (1998) Varieties of hierarchies and markets: an introduction. In G. Dosi, D.J. Teece and J. Chytry (eds) *Technology, Organization and Competitiveness*. Oxford: Oxford University Press. pp. 105–46.

Hamilton-Hart, N. (2003) Asia's new regionalism: government capacity and cooperation in the Western Pacific. *Review of International Political Economy*, 10: 222–45.

Harzing, A.-W. (2000) An empirical analysis and extension of the Bartlett and Ghoshal typology of multinational companies. *Journal of International Business Studies*, 31: 101–20.

Hawkins, R.G. (1972) Job displacement and the multinational firm: a methodological review. *Center for Multinational Studies Occasional Paper 3*, Washington, DC.

Hedlund, G. (1986) The hypermodern MNC: a heterarchy. *Human Resource Management*, 25: 9–35.

Heenan, D.A. and Perlmutter, H. (1979) *Multinational Organizational Development: A Social Architecture Perspective*. Reading, MA: Addison-Wesley.

Held, D. and McGrew, A. (2007) *Globalization/Anti-Globalization: Beyond the Great Divide*, 2nd edn. Cambridge: Polity.

Helm, D. (2009) Environmental challenges in a warming world: consumption, costs and responsibilities. *Tanner Lecture, New College Oxford*. www.dieterhelm.co.uk.

Henderson, J. (1998) Danger and opportunity in the Asia–Pacific. In G. Thompson (ed.) *Economic Dynamism in the Asia–Pacific*. London: Routledge. Chapter 14.

Henderson, J. and Castells, M. (eds) (1987) *Global Restructuring and Territorial Development*. London: Sage.

Henderson, J., Dicken, P., Hess, M., Coe, N. and Yeung, H.W.-c. (2002) Global production networks and the analysis of economic development. *Review of International Political Economy*, 9: 436–64.

Herod, A. (1997) From a geography of labor to a labor geography: rethinking conceptions of labor in economic geography. *Antipode*, 29: 1–31.

Herod, A. (2001) *Labor Geographies: Workers and the Landscape of Capitalism*. New York: Guilford.

Hess, M. (2004) 'Spatial' relationships? Towards a re-conceptualization of embeddedness. *Progress in Human Geography*, 28: 165–86.

Hess, M. (2009) Investigating the archipelago economy: chains, networks and the study of uneven development. *Journal für Entwicklungspolitik*, 2009/2: 20–37.

Higbee, E. (1970) *A Question of Priorities: New Strategies for our Urbanized World*. New York: Morrow.

Higgott, R. (1999) The political economy of globalization in East Asia: the salience of 'region building'. In K. Olds, P. Dicken, P.F. Kelly, L. Kong and H.W.-c. Yeung (eds) *Globalization and the Asia–Pacific: Contested Territories*. London: Routledge. Chapter 6.

Hirsch, F. (1977) *Social Limits to Growth*. London: Routledge and Kegan Paul.

Hirst, P. and Thompson, G. (1992) The problem of 'globalization': international economic relations, national economic management and the formation of trading blocs. *Economy and Society*, 21: 357–96.

Hirst, P., Thompson, G. and Bromley, S. (2009) *Globalization in Question*, 3rd edn. Cambridge: Polity.

Hoekman, B. and Kostecki, M. (1995) *The Political Economy of the World Trading System: From GATT to WTO.* Oxford: Oxford University Press.

Hofstede, G. (1980) *Culture's Consequences.* London: Sage.

Hollingsworth, J.R. (1997) Continuities and changes in social systems of production: the cases of Japan, Germany, and the United States. In J.R. Hollingsworth and R. Boyer (eds) *Contemporary Capitalism: The Embeddedness of Institutions.* Cambridge: Cambridge University Press. Chapter 9.

Hollingsworth, J.R. and Boyer, R. (eds) (1997) *Contemporary Capitalism: The Embeddedness of Institutions.* Cambridge: Cambridge University Press.

Holmes, J. (2000) Regional economic integration in North America. In G.L. Clark, M.P. Feldman and M.S. Gertler (eds) *The Oxford Handbook of Economic Geography.* Oxford: Oxford University Press. Chapter 32.

Hood, N. and Young, S. (2000) Globalization, corporate strategies, and business services. In N. Hood and S. Young (eds) *The Globalization of Multinational Enterprise Activity and Economic Development.* London: Macmillan. Chapter 4.

Horaguchi, H. and Shimokawa, K. (eds) (2002) *Japanese Foreign Direct Investment and the East Asia Industrial System.* Berlin: Springer.

Hosman, L. (2009) Dynamic bargaining and the prospects for learning in the petroleum industry: the case of Kazakhstan. *Perspectives on Global Development & Technology,* 8: 1–25.

Hotz-Hart, B. (2000) Innovation networks, regions and globalization. In G.L. Clark, M.P. Feldman and M.S. Gertler (eds) *The Oxford Handbook of Economic Geography.* Oxford: Oxford University Press. Chapter 22.

Howells, J. (2000) Knowledge, innovation and location. In J.R. Bryson, P.W. Daniels, N. Henry and J. Pollard (eds) *Knowledge, Space, Economy.* London: Routledge. Chapter 4.

Huang, S.W. (2004) Global trade patterns in fruits and vegetables. *US Department of Agriculture, Agriculture and Trade Report WRS–04–06.*

Hudson, A. (2000) Offshoreness, globalization and sovereignty: a postmodern geo-political economy? *Transactions of the Institute of British Geographers,* 25: 269–83.

Hudson, R. (2001) *Producing Places.* New York: Guilford.

Hudson, R. (2002) Changing industrial production systems and regional development in the New Europe. *Transactions of the Institute of British Geographers,* 27: 262–81.

Hudson, R. (2005) *Economic Geographies: Circuits, Flows and Spaces.* London: Sage.

Hudson, R. (2009) The neglect of materiality in the social sciences: filling the theoretical void. *Environment and Planning A.*

Hughes, A., Wrigley, N. and Buttle, M. (2008) Global production networks, ethical campaigning and the embeddedness of responsible governance. *Journal of Economic Geography,* 8: 345–67.

Hulme, D. and Arun, T. (eds) (2009) *Microfinance: A Reader.* Abingdon: Routledge.

Hulme, M. (2004) A change in the weather? Coming to terms with climate change. In F. Harris (ed.) *Global Environmental Issues.* Chichester: Wiley. Chapter 2.

Humbert, M. (1994) Strategic industrial policies in a global industrial system. *Review of International Political Economy,* 1: 445–64.

Humphrey, J. and Oeter, A. (2000) Motor industry policies in emerging markets: globalization and promotion of domestic industry. In J. Humphrey, Y. Lecler and M.S. Salerno (eds) *Global Strategies and Local Realities: The Auto Industry in Emerging Markets.* London: Macmillan. Chapter 3.

Humphrey, J. and Schmitz, H. (2002) How does insertion in global value chains affect upgrading in industrial clusters? *Regional Studies*, 36: 1017–27.

Hurley, J. (2005) Unravelling the web: supply chains and workers' lives in the garment industry. In A. Hale and J. Wills (eds) *Threads of Labour: Garment Industry Supply Chains from the Workers' Perspective*. Oxford: Blackwell. Chapter 5.

Hutton, W. (2007) *The Writing on the Wall: China and the West in the 21st Century*. London: Little, Brown.

Hymer, S.H. (1976) *The International Operations of National Firms: A Study of Direct Foreign Investment*. Cambridge, MA: MIT Press.

ILO (1996) *Globalization of the Footwear, Textiles, and Clothing Industries*. Geneva: ILO.

ILO (1997) *World Employment, 1996/97: National Policies in a Global Context*. Geneva: ILO.

ILO (2001) *World Employment Report 2001: Life at Work in the Information Economy*. Geneva: ILO.

ILO (2003) *Employment and Social Policy in Respect of Export-Processing Zones (EPZs)*. Geneva: ILO.

ILO (2004a) *Economic Security for a Better World*. Geneva: ILO.

ILO (2004b) *A Fair Globalization: Creating Opportunities for All*. Geneva: ILO.

ILO (2005) *Promoting Fair Globalization in Textiles and Clothing in a Post-MFA Environment*. Geneva: ILO.

ILO (2006a) *Global Employment Trends Brief, January 2006*. Geneva: ILO.

ILO (2007a) ILO database on export processing zones. *ILO Sectoral Activities Working Paper 251*.

ILO (2007b) *Visions for Asia's Decent Work Decade: Sustainable Growth and Jobs to 2015*. Geneva: ILO.

International Energy Agency (2009) *World Energy Outlook, 2008*. Paris: OECD/IEA.

International Telecommunication Union (2009) *Measuring the Information Society: The ICT Development Index*. Geneva: ITU.

IPCC (2007) *Climate Change 2007: The Physical Science Basis*. Paris: Intergovernmental Panel on Climate Change.

Ito, T. (2001) Growth, crisis, and the future of economic recovery in East Asia. In J.E. Stiglitz and S. Yusuf (eds) *Rethinking the East Asia Miracle*. New York: Oxford University Press. Chapter 2.

Jackson, T. (2009) *Prosperity without Growth: Economics for a Finite Planet*. London: Earthscan.

James, O. (2007) *Affluenza*. London: Vermillion.

Jarillo, J.C. (1993) *Strategic Networks: Creating the Borderless Organization*. London: Butterworth-Heinemann.

Jessop, B. (1994) Post-Fordism and the State. In A. Amin (ed.) *Post-Fordism: A Reader*. Oxford: Blackwell. Chapter 8.

Jessop, R. (2002) *The Future of the Capitalist State*. Cambridge: Polity.

Johnson, C. (1985) The institutional foundations of Japanese industrial policy. *California Management Review*, XXVII: 59–69.

Jones, A. (2005) Truly global corporations? Theorizing 'organizational globalization' in advanced business service. *Journal of Economic Geography*, 5: 177–200.

Jones, A. (2007) More than 'managing across borders'? The complex role of face-to-face interaction in globalizing law firms. *Journal of Economic Geography*, 7: 223–46.

Jones, A. (2008) The rise of global work. *Transactions of the Institute of British Geographers*, 33: 12–26.

Jones, F., Annan, D. and Shah, S. (2008) The distribution of household income 1977 to 2006/07. *Economic and Labour Market Review*, 2 (12): 18–31.

Jones, H.R. (1990) *A Population Geography*, 2nd edn. London: Chapman.

Jürgens, U. and Krzywdzinski, M. (2009) Changing east–west division of labour in the European automotive industry. *European Urban and Regional Studies*, 16: 27–42.

Kaldor, M. (2003) *Global Civil Society: An Answer to War*. Cambridge: Polity.

Kaltenthaler, K. and Mora, F.O. (2002) Explaining Latin American economic integration: the case of Mercosur. *Review of International Political Economy*, 9: 72–97.

Kang, N.-H. and Sakai, K. (2000) International strategic alliances: their role in industrial globalization, *OECD STI Working Paper 2000/5*.

Kaplinsky, R. (2001) Is globalization all it is cracked up to be? *Review of International Political Economy*, 8: 45–65.

Kaplinsky, R. (2004) Spreading the gains from globalization: what can be learned from value chain analysis? *Problems of Economic Transition*, 47: 74–115.

Kapstein, E.B. (1999) *Sharing the Wealth: Workers and the World Economy*. New York: Norton.

Kapstein, E.B. (2000) Winners and losers in the global economy. *International Organization*, 54: 359–84.

Karreman, B. and van der Knaap, B. (2009) The financial centres of Shanghai and Hong Kong: competition or complementarity? *Environment and Planning A*, 41: 563–80.

Kay, J. (2009) Making banks boring again. *Prospect*, January: 54–8.

Kelly, P.F. (1999) The geographies and politics of globalization. *Progress in Human Geography*, 23: 379–400.

Kelly, R. (1995) Derivatives: a growing threat to the international financial system. In J. Michie and J. Grieve-Smith (eds) *Managing the Global Economy*. Oxford: Oxford University Press. Chapter 9.

Kennedy, P. (2002) Global challenges at the beginning of the twenty-first century. In P. Kennedy, D. Messner and F. Nuscheler (eds) *Global Trends and Global Governance*. London: Pluto. Chapter 1.

Kenney, M. and Curry, J. (2001) Beyond transaction costs: e-commerce and the power of the Internet dataspace. In T.R. Leinbach and S.D. Brunn (eds) *Worlds of e-Commerce: Economic, Geographical, and Social Dimensions*. Chichester: Wiley. Chapter 3.

Kessler, J.A. (1999) The North American Free Trade Agreement, emerging apparel production networks and industrial upgrading: the southern California/Mexico connection. *Review of International Political Economy*, 6: 565–608.

Keynes, J.M. (2007) *The General Theory of Employment, Interest and Money*. Basingstoke: Palgrave Macmillan.

Khanna, S.R. (1993) Structural changes in Asian textiles and clothing industries: the second migration of production. *Textile Outlook International*, September: 11–32.

Kindleberger, C.P. (1969) *American Business Abroad*. New Haven, CT: Yale University Press.

King, A.D. (1983) The world economy is everywhere: urban history and the world-system. *Urban History Yearbook*: 7–18.

Kiple, K.F. (2007) *A Movable Feast: Ten Millennia of Food Globalization*. New York: Cambridge University Press.

Klein, N. (2000) *No Logo*. London: Flamingo.

Kobrin, S.J. (1987) Testing the bargaining hypothesis in the manufacturing sector in developing countries. *International Organization*, 41: 609–38.

Koh, T. (1993) 10 values that help East Asia's economic progress and prosperity. *Singapore Straits Times*, 14 December.

Kolk, A. and van Tulder, R. (2005) Setting new global rules? TNCs and codes of conduct. *Transnational Corporations*, 14: 1–27.

Koo, H. and Kim, E.M. (1992) The developmental state and capital accumulation in South Korea. In R.P. Appelbaum and J. Henderson (eds) *States and Development in the Asian Pacific Rim*. London: Sage. Chapter 5.

Korten, D.C. (1995) *When Corporations Rule the World*. West Hartford, CT: Kumarian.

Kozul-Wright, R. (1995) Transnational corporations and the nation-state. In J. Michie and J. Grieve-Smith (eds) *Managing the Global Economy*. Oxford: Oxford University Press. Chapter 6.

Kozul-Wright, R. and Rowthorn, R. (1998) Spoilt for choice? Multinational corporations and the geography of international production. *Oxford Review of Economic Policy*, 14: 74–92.

Krugman, P. (1994) Competitiveness: a dangerous obsession. *Foreign Affairs*, March–April: 28–44.

Krugman, P. (1998) What's new about the new economic geography? *Oxford Review of Economic Policy*, 14: 7–17.

Lall, S. (1994) Industrial policy: the role of government in promoting industrial and technological development. *UNCTAD Review*: 65–90.

Landes, D.S. (1998) *The Wealth and Poverty of Nations*. New York: Norton.

Langdale, J.V. (2000) Telecommunications and 24-hour trading in the international securities industry. In M.I. Wilson and K.E. Corey (eds) *Information Tectonics: Space, Place, and Technology in an Electronic Age*. Chichester: Wiley. Chapter 6.

Lasserre, P. (1996) Regional headquarters: the spearhead for Asia–Pacific markets. *Long Range Planning*, 29: 30–7.

Law, J. (1986) On the methods of long-distance control: vessels, navigation and the Portuguese route to India. *Sociological Review Monograph*, 32: 234–63.

Lawrence, R.Z. (1996) *Regionalism, Multilateralism, and Deeper Integration*. Washington, DC: Brookings Institution.

Layard, R. (2005) *Happiness: Lessons from a New Science*. London: Penguin Allen Lane.

League of Nations (1945) *Industrialization and Foreign Trade*. New York: League of Nations.

Leclair, M.S. (2002) Fighting the tide: alternative trade organizations in the era of global free trade. *World Development*, 30: 949–58.

Lee, R. (1996) Moral money? LETS and the social construction of local economic geographies in southeast England. *Environment and Planning A*, 28: 1377–94.

Lee, R. (2007) The ordinary economy: tangled up in values and geography. *Transactions of the Institute of British Geographers*, 31: 413–32.

Lee, R. (2009) Economic society/social geography. In Smith, S.J., Pain, R., Marston, S.A. and Jones, J.P. III (eds) *The Sage Handbook of Social Geographies*. London: Sage. Chapter 8.

Lee, R. and Smith, D.M. (eds) (2004) *Geographies and Moralities: International Perspectives on Development, Justice and Place*. Oxford: Blackwell.

Lee, R., Clark, G.L., Pollard, J. and Leyshon, L. (2009) The remit of financial geography: before and after the crisis. *Journal of Economic Geography*, 9: 723–47.

Leinbach, T.R. (2001) Emergence of the digital economy and e-commerce. In T.R. Leinbach and S.D. Brunn (eds) *Worlds of e-Commerce: Economic Geographical and Social Dimensions*. Chichester: Wiley. Chapter 1.

Leonard, H.J. (1988) *Pollution and the Struggle for World Product: Multinational Corporations, Environment and International Comparative Advantage*. Cambridge: Cambridge University Press.

Levinson, M. (2006) *The Box: How the Shipping Container Made the World Smaller and the World Economy Bigger*. Princeton, NJ: Princeton University Press.

Levitt, T. (1983) The globalization of markets. *Harvard Business Review*, May–June: 92–102.

Levy, D.L. (2008) Political contestation in global production networks. *Academy of Management Review*, 33: 943–63.

Levy, D.L. and Prakash, A. (2003) Bargains old and new: multinational corporations in global governance. *Business and Politics*, 5: 131–50.

Levy, F. and Murname, R. (2004) *The New Division of Labour: How Computers Are Creating the Next Job Market*. Princeton, NJ: Princeton University Press.

Lewis, M.K. and Davis, J.T. (1987) *Domestic and International Banking*. Oxford: Allan.

Liao, S. (1997) ASEAN model in international economic cooperation. In H. Soesastro (ed.) *One South East Asia in a New Regional and International Setting*. Jakarta: Centre for Strategic and International Studies.

Linden, G. (2000) Japan and the United States in the Malaysian electronics sector. In M. Borrus, D. Ernst and S. Haggard (eds) *International Production Networks in Asia: Rivalry or Riches?* London: Routledge. Chapter 8.

List, F. (1928) *The National System of Political Economy*. New York: Longman.

Liu, W. and Dicken, P. (2006) Transnational corporations and 'obligated embeddedness': foreign direct investment in China's automobile industry. *Environment and Planning A*, 38: 1229–47.

Liu, W. and Yeung, H.W.-c. (2008) China's dynamic industrial sector: the automobile industry. *Eurasian Geography and Economics*, 49: 523–48.

Luhmann, N. (1998) *Observations on Modernity*. Stanford: Stanford University Press.

Lundvall, B.-Å. (2007) National innovations systems: analytical concept and development tool. *Industry and Innovation*, 14: 95–119.

Lundvall, B.-Å. and Maskell, P. (2000) Nation-states and economic development: from national systems of production to national systems of knowledge creation and learning. In G.L. Clark, M.P. Feldman and M.S. Gertler (eds) *The Oxford Handbook of Economic Geography*. Oxford: Oxford University Press. Chapter 18.

Lüthje, B.-Å. (2002) Electronics contract manufacturing: global production and the international division of labor in the age of the Internet. *Industry and Innovation*, 9: 227–47.

Lynn, B.C. (2005) *End of the Line: The Rise and Coming Fall of the Global Corporation*. New York: Doubleday.

Maddison, A. (2001) *The World Economy: A Millennial Perspective*. Paris: OECD.

Maignan, I. and Ralston, D.D. (2002) Corporate social responsibility in Europe and the US: insights from businesses' self-presentations. *Journal of International Business Studies*, 33: 497–514.

Malecki, E.J. (2002) The economic geography of the Internet's infrastructure. *Economic Geography*, 78: 399–424.

Malecki, E.J. and Hu, W. (2006) A wired world: the evolving geography of submarine cables and the shift to Asia. Presented at the Association of American Geographers Annual Conference, Chicago.

Malmberg, A. (1999) The elusive concept of agglomeration economies: theoretical principles and empirical paradoxes. *SCASSS Seminar Paper*.

Malnight, T.W. (1996) The transition from decentralized to network-based MNC structures: an evolutionary perspective. *Journal of International Business Studies*, 27: 43–63.

Mansfield, E. and Milner, H.V. (1999) The new wave of regionalism. *International Organization*, 53: 589–627.

Markusen, A. (1996) Sticky places in slippery space: a typology of industrial districts. *Economic Geography*, 72: 293–313.

Markusen, A. (1999) Fuzzy concepts, scanty evidence, policy distance: the case for rigor and policy relevance in critical regional studies. *Regional Studies*, 33: 869–94.

Martin, R. (1999) The new economic geography of money. In R. Martin (ed.) *Money and the Space-Economy*. Chichester: Wiley. Chapter 1.

Martin, R. (2000) Institutional approaches in economic geography. In E. Sheppard and T. Barnes (eds) *A Companion to Economic Geography*. Oxford: Blackwell. Chapter 6.

Martin, R. and Sunley, P. (2003) Deconstructing clusters: chaotic concept or policy panacea? *Journal of Economic Geography*, 3: 5–36.

Mason, M. (1994) Historical perspectives on Japanese direct investment in Europe. In M. Mason and D. Encarnation (eds) *Does Ownership Matter? Japanese Multinationals in Europe*. Oxford: Clarendon. Chapter 1.

Massey, D. (2000) The geography of power. In B. Gunnell and D. Timms (eds) *After Seattle: Globalization and Its Discontents*. London: Catalyst.

Mathews, J.A. and Zander, I. (2007) The international entrepreneurial dynamics of accelerated internationalization. *Journal of International Business Studies*, 38: 387–403.

Mattsson, H. (2007) *Locating Biotech Innovation: Places, Flows and Unruly Processes*. Uppsala: Uppsala University.

McConnell, J. and MacPherson, A. (1994) The North American Free Trade Agreement: an overview of issues and prospects. In R. Gibb and W. Michalak (eds) *Continental Trading Blocs: The Growth of Regionalism in the World Economy*. Chichester: Wiley. Chapter 6.

McHale, J. (1969) *The Future of the Future*. New York: Braziller.

McMichael, P. (2007) Globalization and the agrarian world. In G. Ritzer (ed.) *The Blackwell Companion to Globalization*. Malden, MA: Blackwell. Chapter 10.

McNeill, J. (2000) *Something New Under the Sun: An Environmental History of the Twentieth Century*. London: Allen Lane.

Melén, S. and Nordman, E.R. (2009) The internationalization modes of Born Globals: a longitudinal study. *European Management Journal*, 27: 243–54.

Merino, F. and Rodriguez, D.R. (2007) Business services outsourcing by manufacturing firms. *Industrial and Corporate Change*, 16: 1147–73.

Metcalfe, J.S. and Dilisio, N. (1996) Innovation, capabilities and knowledge: the epistemic connection. In J. de la Mothe and G. Paquet (eds) *Evolutionary Economics and the New International Political Economy*. London: Pinter. Chapter 3.

Micklethwait, J. and Wooldridge, A. (2000) *A Future Perfect: The Challenge and Hidden Promise of Globalization*. New York: Crown Business.

Milberg, W. (2008) Shifting sources and uses of profits: sustaining US financialization with global value chains. *Economy and Society*, 37: 420–51.

Miles, R. and Snow, C.C. (1986) Organizations: new concepts for new forms. *California Management Review*, XXVIII: 62–73.

Miles, R., Snow, C.C., Mathews, J.A. and Miles, G. (1999) Cellular-network organizations. In W.E. Halal and K.B. Taylor (eds) *Twenty-First Century Economics: Perspectives of Socioeconomics for a Changing World*. New York: St Martin's Press. Chapter 7.

Miller, D. (1995) Consumption as the vanguard of history. In D. Miller (ed.) *Acknowledging Consumption: A Review of New Studies*. London: Routledge. Chapter 1.

Millstone, E. and Lang, T. (2003) *The Atlas of Food*. London: Earthscan.

Min, S. and Keebler, J.S. (2001) The role of logistics in the supply chain. In J.T. Mentzer (ed.) *Supply Chain Management*. Thousand Oaks, CA: Sage. Chapter 10.

Mitchell, K. (2000) Networks of ethnicity. In E. Sheppard and T. Barnes (eds) *A Companion to Economic Geography*. Oxford: Blackwell. Chapter 24.

Mittelman, J.H. (2000) *The Globalization Syndrome: Transformation and Resistance*. Princeton: Princeton University Press.

Mockler, R.J. (2000) *Multinational Strategic Alliances*. Chichester: Wiley.

Mol, M.J., van Tulder, R.J.M. and Beije, P.R. (2005) Antecedents and performance consequences of international outsourcing. *International Business Review*, 14: 599–617.

Morgan, G., Kristensen, P.H. and Whitley, R. (eds) (2004) *The Multinational Firm: Organizing across Institutional and National Divides*. Oxford: Oxford University Press.

Morgan, K. (2004) The exaggerated death of geography: learning, proximity and territorial innovation systems. *Journal of Economic Geography*, 4: 3–21.

Morrison, A.J. and Roth, K. (1992) The regional solution: an alternative to globalization. *Transnational Corporations*, 1: 37–55.

Mortimore, M. (1998) Mexico's TNC-centric industrialization process. In R. Kozul-Wright and R. Rowthorn (eds) *Transnational Corporations and the Global Economy*. London: Macmillan. Chapter 13.

Mortimore, M. and Vergara, S. (2004) Targeting winners: can foreign direct investment policy help developing countries industrialise? *The European Journal of Development Research*, 16: 499–530.

Mügge, D. (2009) Tales of tails and dogs: derivatives and financialization in contemporary capitalism. *Review of International Political Economy*, 16: 514–26.

Muller, A.R. (2004) *The Rise of Regionalism: Core Company Strategies under the Second Wave of Integration*. Rotterdam: Erasmus University.

Munro, W.A. and Schurman, R.A. (2009) Chain (re)actions: comparing activist mobilization against biotechnology in Britain and the United States. In J. Bair (ed.) *Frontiers of Commodity Chain Research*. Stanford: Stanford University Press. pp. 207–27.

Murray, S. (2007) *Moveable Feasts: The Incredible Journeys of the Things We Eat*. London: Autumn.

Myrdal, G. (1958) *Rich Lands and Poor*. New York: Harper & Row.

Mytelka, L.K. and Barclay, L.A. (2004) Using foreign investment strategically for innovation. *The European Journal of Development Research*, 16: 531–60.

Narine, S. (2008) Forty years of ASEAN: a historical review. *The Pacific Review*, 21: 411–29.

Neilson, J. and Pritchard, B. (2009) *Value Chain Struggles: Institutions and Governance in the Plantation Districts of South India*. Chichester: Wiley.

New Economics Foundation (2009) *National Accounts of Well-Being: Bringing Real Wealth onto the Balance Sheet*. London: NEF.

Nixson, F. (1988) The political economy of bargaining with transnational corporations: some preliminary observations. *Manchester Papers in Development*, IV: 377–90.

Nolan, P. (2001) *China and the Global Business Revolution*. London: Palgrave.

Nordàs, H.K. (2004) The global textile and clothing industry post the Agreement on Textiles and Clothing. *WTO Discussion Paper* 5.

Nye, J.S. Jr (2002) *The Paradox of American Power: Why the World's Only Superpower Can't Go It Alone*. Oxford: Oxford University Press.

O'Brien, K.L. and Leichenko, R.M. (2000) Double exposure: assessing the impacts of climate change within the context of economic globalization. *Global Environmental Change*, 10: 221–32.

O'Brien, R. (1992) *Global Financial Integration: The End of Geography*. London: Royal Institute of International Affairs.

O'Brien, R. and Keith, A. (2009) The geography of finance: after the storm. *Cambridge Journal of Regions, Economy and Society*, 2: 245–65.

Odell, P.R. (1997) The global oil industry: the location of production – Middle East domination or regionalization? *Regional Studies*, 31: 311–22.

OECD (2004) *A New World Map in Textiles and Clothing: Adjusting to Change*. Paris: OECD.

Ohmae, K. (1990) *The Borderless World*. London: Collins.

O'Rourke, K.H. and Williamson, J.G. (1999) *Globalization and History: The Evolution of a Nineteenth-Century Atlantic Economy*. Cambridge, MA: MIT Press.

O'Shaughnessy, J. (1995) *Competitive Marketing: A Strategic Approach*, 3rd edn. London: Routledge.

Oswald, A.J. (1997) Happiness and economic performance. *Economic Journal*, 107: 1815–31.

Oviatt, B.M. and McDougall, P.P. (2005) Toward a theory of international new ventures. *Journal of International Business Studies*, 36: 29–41.

Oxfam (2002) *Rigged Rules and Double Standards: Trade, Globalization, and the Fight against Poverty*. London: Oxfam.

Oxfam (2004) *Like Machines in the Fields: Workers without Rights in American Agriculture*. Boston: Oxfam America.

Page, B. (2000) Agriculture. In E. Sheppard and T.J. Barnes (eds) *A Companion to Economic Geography*. Oxford: Blackwell. Chapter 15.

Palan, R. (2003) *The Offshore World: Sovereign Markets, Virtual Places, and Nomad Millionaires*. Ithaca, NY: Cornell University Press.

Palloix, C. (1975) The internationalization of capital and the circuit of social capital. In G. Radice (ed.) *International Firms and Modern Imperialism*. Harmondsworth: Penguin. Chapter 3.

Palloix, C. (1977) The self-expansion of capital on a world scale. *Review of Radical Political Economics*, 9: 1–28.

Palpacuer, F. (2008) Bringing the social context back in: governance and wealth distribution in global commodity chains. *Economy and Society*, 37: 393–419.

Palpacuer, F. and Parisotto, A. (2003) Global production and local jobs: can global enterprise networks be used as levers for local development? *Global Networks*, 3: 97–120.

Palpacuer, F. and Tozanli, S. (2008) Changing governance patterns in European food chains: the rise of a new divide between global players and regional producers. *Transnational Corporations*, 17: 69–97.

Palpacuer, F., Gibbon, P. and Thomsen, L. (2005) New challenges for developing country suppliers in global clothing chains: a comparative European perspective. *World Development*, 33: 409–30.

Patel, P. (1995) Localized production of technology for global markets. *Cambridge Journal of Economics*, 19: 141–53.

Patel, P. and Pavitt, K. (1998) Uneven (and divergent) technological accumulation among advanced countries: evidence and a framework of explanation. In G. Dosi, D.J. Teece and J. Chytry (eds) *Technology, Organization and Competitiveness*. Oxford: Oxford University Press: 289–317.

Paul, H. and Steinbrecher, R. (2003) *Hungry Corporations: Transnational Biotech Companies Colonise the Food Chain*. London: Zed.

Pauly, L.W. (2000) Capital mobility and the new global order. In R. Stubbs and G.R.D. Underhill (eds) *Political Economy and the Changing Global Order*. Oxford: Oxford University Press. pp. 119–29.

Pauly, L.W. and Reich, S. (1997) National structures and multinational corporate behavior: enduring differences in the age of globalization. *International Organization*, 51: 1–30.

Pavlinek, P., Domanski, B. and Guzik, R. (2009) Industrial upgrading through foreign direct investment in central European automotive manufacturing. *European Urban and Regional Studies*, 16: 43–63.

Pearce, D.E. (1995) *Capturing Environmental Value*. London: Earthscan.

Peck, J.A. (1996) *Work–Place: The Social Regulation of Labour Markets*. New York: Guilford.

Peck, J.A. (2000) Places of work. In E. Sheppard and T. Barnes (eds) *A Companion to Economic Geography*. Oxford: Blackwell. Chapter 9.

Peck, J.A. (2001) *Workfare States*. New York: Guilford.

Peck, J.A. and Theodore, N. (2007) Variegated capitalism. *Progress in Human Geography*, 31: 731–72.

Peet, R. et al. (2003) *Unholy Trinity: The IMF, World Bank and WTO*. New York: Zed.

Perez, C. (1985) Microelectronics, long waves and world structural change. *World Development*, 13: 441–63.

Perez, C. (2010) Technological revolutions and techno-economic paradigms. *Cambridge Journal of Economics*, 34: 185–202.

Phelps, N. and Fuller, C. (2000) Multinationals, intra-corporate competition and regional development. *Economic Geography*, 76: 224–43.

Phillips, N. (2009) Migration as development strategy? The new political economy of dispossession and inequality in the Americas. *Review of International Political Economy*, 16: 231–59.

Picciotto, S. (1991) The internationalisation of the state. *Capital & Class*, 43: 43–63.

Pires, S.R.I. and Neto, M.S. (2008) New configurations in supply chains: the case of a condominium in Brazil's automotive industry. *Supply Chain Management*, 13: 328–34.

Pitelis, C. (1991) Beyond the nation-state? The transnational firm and the nation-state. *Capital and Class*, 43: 131–52.

Pollard, N., Latorre, M. and Sriskandarajah, D. (2008) *Floodgates or Turnstiles? Post-EU Enlargement Migration to (and from) the UK*. London: IPPR.

Ponte, S. (2002) The 'latte revolution'? Regulation, markets and consumption in the global coffee chain. *World Development*, 30: 1099–122.

Poon, J.P.H. and Thompson, E.R. (2004) Convergence or differentiation? American and Japanese corporations in the Asia–Pacific. *Geoforum*, 35: 111–25.

Population Reference Bureau (1999) *World Population Data Sheet*. Washington, DC: Population Reference Bureau.

Porter, M.E. (1990) *The Competitive Advantage of Nations*. London: Macmillan.

Porter, M.E. (1998) Clusters and the new economics of competition. *Harvard Business Review*, November–December: 77–90.

Porter, M.E. (2000) Locations, clusters and company strategy. In G.L. Clark, M.P. Feldman and M.S. Gertler (eds) *The Oxford Handbook of Economic Geography*. Oxford: Oxford University Press. Chapter 13.

Porter, M.E., Takeuchi, H. and Sakakibara, M. (2000) *Can Japan Compete?* London: Macmillan.

Prahalad, C.K. and Doz, Y. (1987) *The Multinational Mission*. New York: Free.

Pritchard, B. (2000a) Geographies of the firm and transnational agro-food corporations in East Asia. *Singapore Journal of Tropical Geography*, 21: 246–62.

Pritchard, B. (2000b) The tangible and intangible spaces of agro-food capital. Paper presented at the International Rural Sociology Association World Congress, Rio de Janeiro.

Pritchard, B. (2000c) The transnational corporate networks of breakfast cereals in Asia. *Environment and Planning A*, 32: 789–804.

Rabach, E. and Kim, E.M. (1994) Where is the chain in commodity chains? The service sector nexus. In G. Gereffi and M. Korzeniewicz (eds) *Commodity Chains and Global Capitalism*. Westport: Praeger. Chapter 6.

Ramesh, M. (1995) Economic globalization and policy choices: Singapore. *Governance: An International Journal of Policy and Administration*, 8: 243–60.

Ramesh, R. (2005) Chindia, where the world's workshop meets its office. *The Guardian*, 30 September.

Ramirez, M.D. (2006) Is foreign direct investment beneficial for Mexico? An empirical analysis, 1960–2001. *World Development*, 34: 802–17.

Rasche, A. (2009) 'A necessary supplement': what the United Nations Global Compact is and is not. *Business & Society*, 48: 511–37.

Rasiah, R. (2004) Exports and technological capabilities: a study of foreign and local firms in the electronics industry in Malaysia, the Philippines and Thailand. *The European Journal of Development Research*, 16: 587–623.

Ravoli, P. (2005) *The Travels of a T-Shirt in the Global Economy*. New York: Wiley.

Raworth, K. and Kidder, T. (2009) Mimicking 'lean' in global value chains; it's the workers who get leaned on. In J. Bair (ed.) *Frontiers of Commodity Chain Research*. Stanford: Stanford University Press. pp. 165–89.

Raynolds, L.T. (2004) The globalization of organic agro-food networks. *World Development*, 32: 725–43.

Reardon, T., Henson, S. and Berdegué, J. (2007) 'Proactive fast-tracking' diffusion of supermarkets in developing countries: implications for market institutions and trade. *Journal of Economic Geography*, 7: 399–431.

Reich, S. (1989) Roads to follow: regulating direct foreign investment. *International Organization*, 43: 543–84.

Reid, H.C. (1989) Financial centre hegemony, interest rates, and the global political economy. In Y.S. Park and N. Essayyad (eds) *International Banking and Financial Centres*. Boston, MA: Kluwer. Chapter 16.

Rennstich, J. (2002) The new economy, the leadership long cycle and the nineteenth K-wave. *Review of International Political Economy*, 9: 150–82.

Rigby, D.L. and Breau, S. (2006) Impacts of trade on wage inequality in Los Angeles: analysis using matched employer–employee data. UCLA *Center for Economic Studies Discussion Paper*.

Roberts, P. (2008) *The End of Food: The Coming Crisis in the World Food Industry*. London: Bloomsbury.

Roberts, S. (1994) Fictitious capital, fictitious spaces: the geography of offshore financial flows. In S. Corbridge, R. Martin and N.J. Thrift (eds) *Money, Power and Space*. Oxford: Blackwell. Chapter 5.

Roche, E.M. and Blaine, M.J. (2000) Telecommunications and governance in multinational enterprises. In M.I. Wilson and K.E. Corey (eds) *Information Tectonics: Space, Place, and Technology in an Electronic Age*. Chichester: Wiley. Chapter 5.

Rodan, G. (1991) *The Political Economy of Singapore's Industrialization*. Petalang Jaya: Forum.

Rodrik, D. (1999) *The New Global Economy and Developing Countries: Making Openness Work*. Washington, DC: Overseas Development Council.

Ross, R.J.S. (2002) The new sweatshops in the United States: how new, how real, how many and how why? In G. Gereffi, D. Spener and J. Bair (eds) *Free Trade and Uneven Development: The North American Apparel Industry after NAFTA*. Philadelphia: Temple University Press. Chapter 5.

Rowthorn, R. and Ramaswamy, R. (1997) De-industrialization: causes and implications. *IMF Working Paper*.

Rugman, A.M. and Brain, C. (2003) Multinational enterprises are regional, not global. *Multinational Business Review*, 11: 3–12.

Rugman, A.M. and Collinson, S. (2004) The regional nature of the world's automotive industry. *European Management Journal*, 22: 471–82.

Rugman, A.M. and Verbeke, A. (2004) Regional transnationals and triad strategy. *Transnational Corporations*, 13: 1–20.

Rugman, A.M. and Verbeke, A. (2008) A regional solution to the strategy and structure of multinationals. *European Management Journal*, 26: 305–13.

Rutherford, T. and Holmes, J. (2008) 'The flea on the tail of the dog': power in global production networks and the restructuring of Canadian automotive clusters. *Journal of Economic Geography*, 8: 519–44.

Sachs, J. (1997) Nature, nurture, and growth. *The Economist*, 14 June: 19–22.

Sachs, J.D. and Warner, A.M. (2001) The curse of natural resources. *European Economic Review*, 45: 827–38.

Saith, A. (2008) China and India: the institutional roots of differential performance. *Development and Change*, 39: 723–57.

Sampson, G.P. (ed.) (2001) *The Role of the World Trade Organization in Global Governance*. Tokyo: United Nations University Press.

Sasi, V. and Arenius, P. (2008) International new ventures and social networks: advantage or liability? *European Management Journal*, 26: 400–11.

Sassen, S. (1998) *Globalization and its Discontents*. New York: New Press.

Sassen, S. (2001) *The Global City: New York, London, Tokyo*, 2nd edn. Princeton, NJ: Princeton University Press.

Saxenian, A. (2002) Transnational communities and the evolution of global production networks: the cases of Taiwan, China and India. *Industry and Innovation*, 9: 183–202.

Saxenian, A. (2006) *The New Argonauts: Regional Advantage in a Global Economy*. Cambridge: Harvard University Press.

Sayer, A. (1986) New developments in manufacturing: the just-in-time system. *Capital & Class*, 30: 43–72.

Schary, P.B. and Skjott-Larsen, T. (2001) *Managing the Global Supply Chain*, 2nd edn. Copenhagen: Copenhagen Business School Press.

Scheve, K. and Slaughter, M.J. (2001) *Globalization and the Perceptions of American Workers*. Washington, DC: Institute for International Economics.

Scheve, K. and Slaughter, M.J. (2004) Economic insecurity and the globalization of production. *American Journal of Political Science*, 48: 662–74.

Schiff, M. and Winters, L.A. (2003) *Regional Integration and Development*. Washington, DC: World Bank.

Schoenberger, E. (1997) *The Cultural Crisis of the Firm*. Oxford: Blackwell.

Schoenberger, E. (1999) The firm in the region and the region in the firm. In T. Barnes and M. Gertler (eds) *The New Industrial Geography: Regions, Regulation and Institutions*. London: Routledge. Chapter 9.

Schoenberger, E. (2000) The management of time and space. In G.L. Clark, M.P. Feldman and M. Gertler (eds) *The Oxford Handbook of Economic Geography*. Oxford: Oxford University Press. Chapter 16.

Schumpeter, J. (1943) *Capitalism, Socialism and Democracy*. London: Allen & Unwin.

Schwartz, S.H. (1994) Beyond individualism/collectivism: new cultural dimensions of values. In U. Kim, H.C. Triandis, C. Kagitcibasi, S.C. Choi and G. Yoon (eds) *Individualism and Collectivism: Theory, Methods and Applications*. Thousand Oaks, CA: Sage. pp. 85–119.

Scott, A.J. (1998) *Regions and the World Economy: The Coming Shape of Global Production, Competition and Political Order*. Oxford: Oxford University Press.

Scott, A.J. (2008) Resurgent metropolis: economy, society and urbanization in an interconnected world. *International Journal of Urban and Regional Research*, 32: 548–64.

Scott-Quinn, B. (1990) US investment banks as multinationals. In G. Jones (ed.) *Banks as Multinationals*. London: Routledge. Chapter 5.

Seidler, E. (1976) *Let's Call it Fiesta*. London: Stephens.

Sen, A. (1999) *Development as Freedom*. Oxford: Oxford University Press.

Silva, J.A. and Leichenko, R.M. (2004) Regional income inequality and international trade, *Economic Geography* 80: 261–86.

Simonis, U.D. and Brühl, T. (2002) World ecology: structures and trends. In P. Kennedy, D. Messner and F. Nuscheler (eds) *Global Trends and Global Governance*. London: Pluto. Chapter 4.

Singer, P. (2004) *One World: The Ethics of Globalization*, 2nd edn. New Haven: Yale University Press.

Sklair, L. (2001) *The Transnational Capitalist Class*. Oxford: Blackwell.

Smarzynska, B.K. and Wei, S.-J. (2001) Pollution havens and foreign direct investment: dirty secret or popular myth? *NBER Working Paper* 8465.

Smelser, N. and Swedberg, R. (eds) (2005) *The Handbook of Economic Sociology*, 2nd edn. Princeton: Princeton University Press.

Smith, A., Pickles, J., Begg, B., Roukova, P. and Bucek, M. (2005) Outward processing, EU enlargement and regional relocation in the European textiles and clothing industry. *European Urban and Regional Studies*, 12: 83–91.

Smith, A., Pickles, J., Bucek, M., Begg, R. and Roukova, P. (2008) Reconfiguring 'post-socialist' regions: cross-border networks and regional competition in the Slovak and Ukrainian clothing industry. *Global Networks*, 8: 281–307.

Smith, D.A. (2005) Starting at the beginning: extractive economies as the unexamined origins of global commodity chains. In P.S. Ciccantell, D.A. Smith and G. Seidman (eds) *Nature, Raw Materials, and Political Economy*. Amsterdam: Elsevier. pp. 141–57.

Smith, D.M. (2000) *Moral Geographies: Ethics in a World of Difference*. Edinburgh: Edinburgh University Press.

Sonn, J.W. and Storper, M. (2008) The increasing importance of geographical proximity in knowledge production: an analysis of US patent citations, 1975–1997. *Environment and Planning A*, 40: 1020–39.

Sonnino, R. and Marsden, T. (2006) Beyond the divide: rethinking relationships between alternative and conventional food networks in Europe. *Journal of Economic Geography*, 6: 181–99.

Stalk, G., Evans, P. and Shulman, L.E. (1998) Competing on capabilities: the new rules of corporate strategy. *Harvard Business Review*, March–April: 57–69.

Stephens, P. (2005) Why nostalgia is futile at the beginning of history. *Financial Times*, 27 May: 26.

Stephens, P. (2008) Broken banks put the state back in the driving seat. *Financial Times*, 28 November: 24.

Sternquist, B. (1998) *International Retailing*. New York: Fairchild.

Stiglitz, J.E. (2002) *Globalization and Its Discontents*. London: Allen Lane.

Stiglitz, J.E. and Charlton, A. (2005) *Fair Trade for All: How Trade Can Promote Development*. Oxford: Oxford University Press.

Stiglitz, J.E. and Fitoussi, J.P. (2009) *Report of the Commission on the Measurement of Economic Performance and Social Progress*. Report submitted to the President of the French Republic.

Stopford, J.M. and Strange, S. (1991) *Rival States, Rival Firms: Competition for World Market Shares*. Cambridge: Cambridge University Press.

Storper, M. (1995) The resurgence of regional economies, ten years later: the region as a nexus of untraded interdependencies. *European Urban and Regional Studies*, 2: 191–221.

Storper, M. (1997) *The Regional World: Territorial Development in a Global Economy*. New York: Guilford.

Storper, M. and Venables, A.J. (2004) Buzz: face-to-face contact and the urban economy. *Journal of Economic Geography*, 4: 351–70.

Storper, M. and Walker, R. (1984) The spatial division of labour: labour and the location of industries. In L. Sawers and W.K. Tabb (eds) *Sunbelt/Snowbelt: Urban Development and Regional Restructuring*. New York: Oxford University Press. Chapter 2.

Strahan, D. (2007) *The Last Oil Shock: A Survival Guide to the Imminent Extinction of Petroleum Man*. London: Murray.

Strange, S. (1986) *Casino Capitalism*. Oxford: Blackwell.

Strange, S. (1995) The limits of politics. *Government and Opposition*, 30: 291–311.

Stross, R. (2008) *Planet Google: How One Company Is Transforming Our Lives*. London: Atlantic.

Sturgeon, T.J. (2002) Modular production networks: a new American model of industrial organization. *Industrial and Corporate Change*, 11: 451–96.

Sturgeon, T.J. (2003) What really goes on in Silicon Valley? Spatial clustering and dispersal in modular production networks. *Journal of Economic Geography*, 3: 199–225.

Sturgeon, T.J. and Florida, R. (2004) Globalization, deverticalization, and employment in the motor vehicle industry. In M. Kenney and R. Florida (eds) *Locating Global Advantage: Industry Dynamics in the International Economy*. Stanford: Stanford University Press. Chapter 3

Sturgeon, T.J., van Biesebroeck, J. and Gereffi, G. (2008) Value chains, networks and clusters: reframing the global automotive industry. *Journal of Economic Geography*, 8: 297–321.

Sutcliffe, B. (2009) The world distribution of gross national income, 2007. *Environment and Planning A*, 41: 764.

Swyngedouw, E. (2000) Elite power, global forces, and the political economy of 'glocal' development. In G.L. Clark, M.P. Feldman and M.S. Gertler (eds) *The Oxford Handbook of Economic Geography*. Oxford: Oxford University Press. Chapter 27.

Taplin, I.M. (1994) Strategic reorientations of US apparel firms. In G. Gereffi and M. Korzeniewicz (eds) *Commodity Chains and Global Capitalism*. Westport, CT: Praeger. Chapter 10.

Tavares, A.T. and Young, S. (2006) Sourcing patterns of foreign-owned multinational subsidiaries in Europe. *Regional Studies*, 40: 583–99.

Taylor, P.J. (1994) The state as container: territoriality in the modern world-system. *Progress in Human Geography*, 18: 151–62.

Taylor, P.J. (2001) Commentary: being economical with the geography. *Environment and Planning A*, 33: 949–54.

Taylor, P.J. (2004) *World City Network: A Global Urban Analysis*. London: Routledge.

Taylor, P.J., Watts, M.J. and Johnston, R.J. (2002) Geography/globalization. In R.J. Johnston, P.J. Taylor and M.J. Watts (eds) *Geographies of Global Change: Remapping the World*. Oxford: Blackwell. Chapter 1.

Taylor, R. and Morrissey, K. (2004) Coping with pollution: dealing with waste. In F. Harris (ed.) *Global Environmental Issues*. Chichester: Wiley. Chapter 9.

Terpstra, V. and David, K. (1991) *The Cultural Environment of International Business*. Cincinnati: South-Western.

Tett, G. (2009) *Fool's Gold: How Unrestrained Greed Corrupted a Dream, Shattered Global Markets and Unleashed a Catastrophe*. London: Little, Brown.

Thornhill, J. (2008) The nature of the beast. *Financial Times*, 28 June: 17.

Thrift, N.J. (1990) Doing regional geography in a global system: the new international financial system, the City of London and the South East of England, 1984–1987. In R.J. Johnston, J. Hauer and G.A. Hoekveld (eds) *Regional Geography: Current Developments and Future Prospects*. London: Routledge. pp. 180–207.

Thrift, N.J. (1994) On the social and cultural determinants of international financial centres: the case of the City of London. In S. Corbridge, R. Martin and N.J. Thrift (eds) *Money, Power and Space*. Oxford: Blackwell. Chapter 14.

Thrift, N.J. (1996) *Spatial Formations*. London: Sage.

Tokatli, N. (2008) Global sourcing: insights from the global clothing industry – the case of Zara, a fast fashion retailer. *Journal of Economic Geography*, 8: 21–38.

Tokatli, N., Wrigley, N. and Kizilgön, Ö. (2008) Shifting global supply networks and fast fashion: made in Turkey for Marks and Spencer. *Global Networks*, 8: 261–80.

Tregenna, F. (2009) Characterising deindustrialization: an analysis of changes in manufacturing employment and output internationally. *Cambridge Journal of Economics*, 33: 433–66.

Turner, R.K., Pearce, D. and Bateman, I. (1994) *Environmental Economics: An Elementary Introduction*. Hemel Hempstead: Harvester Wheatsheaf.

Turok, I. (1993) Inward investment and local linkages: how deeply embedded is 'Silicon Glen'? *Regional Studies*, 27: 401–17.

Ulset, S. (2008) The rise and fall of global network alliances. *Industrial and Corporate Change*, 17: 267–300.

UN Centre for Human Settlements (Habitat) (2001) *Global Report on Human Settlements, 2001*. New York: United Nations.

UN Centre for Human Settlements (Habitat) (2003) *Global Report on Human Settlements, 2003*. New York: United Nations.

UNCTAD (1995) *World Investment Report 1995: Transnational Corporations and Competitiveness*. New York: United Nations.

UNCTAD (2000) *The Competitiveness Challenge: Transnational Corporations and Industrial Restructuring in Developing Countries*. New York: United Nations.

UNCTAD (2001) *World Investment Report 2001: Promoting Linkages*. New York: United Nations.

UNCTAD (2002) *Trade and Development Report 2002: Developing Countries in World Trade*. New York: United Nations.

UNCTAD (2005) *World Investment Report 2005: Transnational Corporations and the Internationalization of R&D*. New York: United Nations.

UNCTAD (2007) *World Investment Report 2007: Transnational Corporations, Extractive Industries and Development*. New York: United Nations.

UNCTAD (2008) *World Investment Report, 2008*. New York: United Nations.

UNCTAD (2009) *World Investment Report 2009: Transnational Corporations, Agricultural Production and Development*. New York: United Nations.

UNDP (2005) *Human Development Report 2005*. New York: United Nations.

UNDP (2008) *Human Development Report 2007/8*. New York: United Nations.

UNDP (2009) *Human Development Report 2009*. New York: United Nations.

UNEP (2004) *Vital Waste Graphics*. Nairobi: United Nations.

UN-HABITAT (2008) *State of the World's Cities, 2008/2009*. Nairobi: United Nations.

UNIDO (2003) *The Global Automotive Industry Value Chain: What Prospects for Upgrading by Developing Countries?* Vienna: UNIDO.

UN Population Division (2001) *World Population Prospects: The 2000 Revision*. New York: United Nations.

UN Population Division (2009) *World Population Prospects: The 2008 Revision*. New York: United Nations.

US Department of Commerce (2000) *Digital Economy 2000*. Washington DC: US Department of Commerce.

USEPA (2008) *Municipal Solid Waste Generation, Recycling, and Disposal in the United States: Facts and Figures for 2007*. Washington, DC: USEPA.

USGS (2009) *Copper: Statistics and Information*. Washington, DC: US Geological Survey.

Van Grunsven, L., van Egeraat, C. and Meijsen, S. (1995) New manufacturing establishments and regional economy in Johor: production linkages, employment and labour fields. *Department of Geography of Developing Countries, University of Utrecht Report Series*.

Van Tulder, R. (2009) Chains for change. *Max Havelaar Lecture*.

Van Tulder, R. with van der Zwart, A. (2006) *International Business–Society Management: Linking Corporate Responsibility and Globalization*. London: Routledge.

Van Tulder, R., van Wijk, J. and Kolk, A. (2009) From chain liability to chain responsibility. *Journal of Business Ethics*, 85: 399–412.

Van Veen, K. and Marsman, I. (2008) How international are executive boards of European MNCs? National diversity in 15 European countries. *European Management Journal*, 26: 188–98.

Veloso, F. and Kumar (2002) The automotive supply chain: global trends and Asian perspectives. *Asian Development Bank ERD Working Paper 3*.

Veltz, P. (1996) *Mondialisation, Villes et Territoires: L'Économie d'Archipel*. Paris: Universitaires de France.

Vernon, R. (1966) International investment and international trade in the product cycle. *Quarterly Journal of Economics*, 80: 190–207.

Vernon, R. (1979) The product cycle hypothesis in a new international environment. *Oxford Bulletin of Economics and Statistics*, 41: 255–68.

Vernon, R. (1998) *In the Hurricane's Eye: The Troubled Prospects of Multinational Enterprises*. Cambridge, MA: Harvard University Press.

Vidal, J. (2009) Fears for the world's poor countries as the rich grab land to grow food. *The Guardian*, 4 July: 24.

Vitols, S. (ed.) (2004) The transformation of the German model? *Special Issue of Competition and Change*, 8 (4).

Voltaire (Arouet, F.-M.) (1947) *Candide*, trans. J. Butt. London: Penguin.

Wade, R. (1990) Industrial policy in East Asia: does it lead or follow the market? In G. Gereffi and D.L. Wyman (eds) *Manufacturing Miracles: Paths of Industrialization in Latin America and East Asia*. Princeton, NJ: Princeton University Press. Chapter 9.

Wade, R.H. (1996) Globalization and its limits: reports of the death of the national economy are greatly exaggerated. In S. Berger and R. Dore (eds) *National Diversity and Global Capitalism*. Ithaca, NY: Cornell University Press. Chapter 2.

Wade, R.H. (2003) What strategies are viable for developing countries today? The World Trade Organization and the shrinking of 'development space'. *Review of International Political Economy*, 10: 621–44.

Wade, R.H. (2004a) *Governing the Market: Economic Theory and the Role of Government in East Asian Industrialization*, 2nd edn. Princeton, NJ: Princeton University Press.

Wade, R.H. (2004b) Is globalization reducing poverty and inequality? *World Development*, 32: 567–89.

Wallerstein, I. (1979) *The Capitalist World-Economy*. Cambridge: Cambridge University Press.

Wang, J.J. and Cheng, M.C. (2010) From a hub port city to a global supply chain management centre: a case study of Hong Kong. *Journal of Transport Geography*, 18: 104–15.

Ward, N. and Almås, R. (1997) Explaining change in the international agro-food system. *Review of International Political Economy*, 4: 611–29.

Warf, B. (1989) Telecommunications and the globalization of financial services. *Professional Geographer*, 41: 257–71.

Warf, B. (2006) International competition between satellite and fiber optic carriers: a geographic perspective. *Professional Geographer*, 58: 1–11.

Warf, B. (2007) Geopolitics of the satellite industry. *Tijdschrift voor Economische en Sociale Geografie*, 98: 385–97.

Warf, B. and Purcell, D. (2001) The currency of currency: speed, sovereignty, and electronic finance. In T.R. Leinbach and S.D. Brunn (eds) *Worlds of e-Commerce: Economic Geographical and Social Dimensions*. Chichester: Wiley. Chapter 12.

Watts, M.J. and Goodman, D. (1997) Agrarian questions: global appetite, local metabolism: nature, culture and industry in *fin-de-siècle* agro-food systems. In D. Goodman and M.J. Watts (eds) *Globalizing Food: Agrarian Questions and Global Restructuring*. London: Routledge. Chapter 1.

Webber, M.J. and Rigby, D.L. (1996) *The Golden Age Illusion: Rethinking Postwar Capitalism*. New York: Guilford.

Weiss, A. (2007) *The Global Food Economy: The Battle for the Future of Farming*. London: Zed.

Weiss, L. (1998) *The Myth of the Powerless State: Governing the Economy in a Global Era*. Cambridge: Polity.

Weiss, L. (ed.) (2003) *States in the Global Economy: Bringing Domestic Institutions Back In*. Cambridge: Cambridge University Press.

Wells, L.T. Jr (ed.) (1972) *The Product Life Cycle and International Trade*. Boston, MA: Harvard Business School.

Whatmore, S. (2002) *Hybrid Geographies: Natures, Cultures, Spaces*. London: Sage.

Whatmore, S. and Thorne, L. (1997) Nourishing networks: alternative geographies of food. In D. Goodman and M.J. Watts (eds) *Globalizing Food: Agrarian Questions and Global Restructuring*. London: Routledge. Chapter 11.

Whatmore, S., Stassart, P. and Renting, H. (2003) What's alternative about alternative food networks? *Environment and Planning A*, 35: 389–91.

Whitley, R. (1999) *Divergent Capitalisms: The Social Structuring and Change of Business Systems*. Oxford: Oxford University Press.

Whitley, R. (2004) How and why are international firms different? The consequences of cross-border managerial coordination for firm characteristics and behaviour. In G. Morgan, P.H. Kristensen and R. Whitley (eds) *The Multinational Firm: Organizing across Institutional and National Divides*. Oxford: Oxford University Press. Chapter 2.

Wilkinson, J. (2002) The final foods industry and the changing face of the global agro-food system. *Sociologia Ruralis*, 42: 329–46.

Wilkinson, R. (2009) Concluding the Doha Round. *Development at Manchester*, 2.

Wilkinson, R. and Pickett, K. (2009) *The Spirit Level: Why More Equal Societies Almost Always Do Better*. London: Allen Lane.

Williamson, H. (2005) Under attack. *Development and Cooperation*, April.

Wills, J. (1998) Taking on the CosmoCorps? Experiments in transnational labour organization. *Economic Geography*, 74: 111–30.

Wills, J. (2002) Bargaining for the space to organize in the global economy: a review of the Accor–IUF trade union rights agreement. *Review of International Political Economy*, 9: 675–700.

WIPO (2008) *World Patent Report: A Statistical Review, 2008*. Geneva: WIPO.

Wolf, M. (2002) Countries still rule the world. *Financial Times*, 6 February.

Wolf, M. (2004) *Why Globalization Works*. New Haven: Yale University Press.

Wolf, M. (2007) The dilemma of global governance. *Financial Times*, 24 January.

Wolf, M. (2008a) China changes the whole world. *Financial Times*, 23 January 2008.

Wolf, M. (2008b) Big questions in a fast-changing world. *Financial Times*, 7 November. Special Report, Global Agenda: 2.

Womack, J.R., Jones, D.T. and Roos, D. (1990) *The Machine that Changed the World*. New York: Rawson.

Wood, A. (1994) *North–South Trade, Employment, and Inequality*. Oxford: Oxford University Press.

World Bank (2008a) *World Development Indicators 2008*. Washington, DC: World Bank.

World Bank (2008b) *World Development Report 2008: Agriculture for Development*. Washington, DC: World Bank.

World Bank (2009a) *World Development Indicators, 2009*. Washington, DC: World Bank.

World Bank (2009b) *World Development Report 2009: Reshaping Economic Geography*. Washington, DC: World Bank.

Wrigley, N. (2000) The globalization of retail capital: themes for economic geography. In G.L. Clark, M.P. Feldman and M.S. Gertler (eds) *The Oxford Handbook of Economic Geography*. Oxford: Oxford University Press. Chapter 15.

Wrigley, N. and Lowe, M. (eds) (2007) Transnational retail, supply networks, and the global economy. *Journal of Economic Geography*, 7, Special Issue.

WTO (2008) *World Trade Report, 2008*. Geneva: WTO.

WTO (2009) *International Trade Statistics, 2009*. Geneva: WTO.

Wu, X. and Perloff, J.M. (2005) China's income distribution, 1985–2001. Institute for Research on Labor and Employment Working Paper Series, University of California, Berkeley.

Yao, S. (1997) The romance of Asian capitalism: geography, desire and Chinese business. In M.T. Berger and D.A. Borer (eds) *The Rise of East Asia: Critical Visions of the Pacific Century*. London: Routledge. Chapter 9.

Yergin, D. (1991) *The Prize: The Epic Quest for Oil, Money, and Power*. New York: Simon & Schuster.

Yeung, H.W.-c. (1998) The political economy of transnational corporations: a study of the regionalization of Singaporean firms. *Political Geography*, 17: 389–416.

Yeung, H.W.-c. (1999) Regulating investment abroad: the political economy of the regionalization of Singaporean firms. *Antipode*, 31: 245–73.

Yeung, H.W.-c. (2000) The dynamics of Asian business systems in a globalizing era. *Review of International Political Economy*, 7: 399–433.

Yeung, H.W.-c. (2001) Organising regional production networks in South East Asia: implications for production fragmentation, trade, and rules of origin. *Journal of Economic Geography*, 1: 299–321.

Yeung, H.W.-c. (2004) *Chinese Capitalism in a Global Era: Towards Hybrid Capitalism*. London: Routledge.

Yeung, H.W.-c., Poon, J. and Perry, M. (2001) Towards a regional strategy: the role of regional headquarters of foreign firms in Singapore. *Urban Studies*, 38: 157–83.

Yoffie, D.B. and Milner, H.V. (1989) An alternative to free trade or protectionism: why corporations seek strategic trade policy. *California Management Review*, 31: 111–31.

Young, D., Goold, M. et al., (2000) *Corporate Headquarters: An International Analysis of their Roles and Staffing*. London: Pearson.

Zanfei, A. (2000) Transnational firms and the changing organization of innovative activities. *Cambridge Journal of Economics*, 24: 515–42.

Zheng, Y. (2004) *Globalization and State Transformation in China*. Cambridge: Cambridge University Press.

Ziltener, P. (2004) The economic effects of the European Single Market Project: projections, simulations – and the reality. *Review of International Political Economy*, 11: 953–79.

Zook, M.A. (2001) Old hierarchies or new networks of centrality: the global geography of the internet content market. *American Behavioral Scientist*, 44: 1679–96.

Zook, M.A. (2005) *The Geography of the Internet Industry*. Oxford: Blackwell.

INDEX

Key words and terms are in **bold**